Biomental Child Development

Biomental Child Development

*Perspectives on Psychology
and Parenting*

Frank John Ninivaggi, M.D.

*To Sandip Mukherjee my, April 3- 2013
your skill and compassion
as a physician and healer
has made a profound impact
on my life. For that I am grateful.
I look forward to an enduring
relationship both professionally
and in friendship. Sincerely
Frank*

ROWMAN & LITTLEFIELD PUBLISHERS, INC.
Lanham • Boulder • New York • Toronto • Plymouth, UK

Published by Rowman & Littlefield Publishers, Inc.
A wholly owned subsidiary of The Rowman & Littlefield Publishing Group, Inc.
4501 Forbes Boulevard, Suite 200, Lanham, Maryland 20706
www.rowman.com

10 Thornbury Road, Plymouth PL6 7PP, United Kingdom

British Library Cataloguing in Publication Information Available

Library of Congress Cataloging-in-Publication Data

Ninivaggi, Frank John.
Biomental child development : perspectives on psychology and parenting / Frank John Ninivaggi.
p. cm.
Includes bibliographical references.
ISBN 978-1-4422-1904-5 (cloth : alk. paper)—ISBN 978-1-4422-1906-9 (electronic)
1. Developmental psychobiology. 2. Child development. 3. Mind and body. I. Title.
BF723.M48.N56 2013
155.4—dc23
2012020480

♾™ The paper used in this publication meets the minimum requirements of American National Standard for Information Sciences Permanence of Paper for Printed Library Materials, ANSI/NISO Z39.48-1992.

Printed in the United States of America

With deep and lasting gratitude,
to my mother and father.

Medical Disclaimer

This book is intended to serve as an informational, educational resource and reference guide about normal child development, psychology, and parenting. Its primary descriptive aim for all readers also provides strategic behavioral considerations rather than treatment interventions. Care has been taken with regard to the accuracy of the information presented. However, the authors, editors, and publisher are not responsible for errors or omissions or for any consequences from application of the information in this book and make no warranty, expressed or implied, with respect to the currency, completeness, or accuracy of the contents of the publication. Since knowledge and best practices in these fields are constantly evolving and changing, applicable changes in practices may become necessary or appropriate.

This book is not intended to create a physician-patient relationship or to supplant clinical testing, assessment, consultation, examination, evaluation, or treatment. The information in this book is not intended to diagnose, treat, or cure. It does not intend to replace—and cannot replace—proper patient-provider medical care administered in the setting of a patient-provider relationship wherein appropriate safety precautions must be routine and individualized. It is not a substitute for examination, diagnosis, or medical care provided by a licensed and qualified health professional.

Contents

List of Tables

Foreword

Fred R. Volkmar, M.D.

Over the last several decades there have been explosions of knowledge in many areas. These have included our understanding of basic aspects of child, adolescent, and adult development as well in the various neurobiological processes that underlie development and developmental change. Unfortunately this literature has not always been well integrated, so that while the influence of parents on children is well appreciated, the converse has been less well studied. In addition, the many potential clinical applications of advances in the basic sciences of child development have not always been well or deeply appreciated. Finally, an integration of current knowledge with perspectives from clinical work is missing. This book aims to address these issues.

Adopting a more integrated systems approach in this volume, Frank John Ninivaggi provides a clinically oriented but user-friendly textbook. Although well referenced and relying on the scientific literature, he has produced a "user-friendly" introduction to the topic, highlighting the important role parents and children play in each other's development. Beginning with a succinct overview of relevant concepts, the volume moves quickly to a discussion of parenting, the psychology of the child, and the context of infant and child development before returning to issues of parental psychology and parenting style.

This volume brings a unique and integrated perspective to a set of topics often viewed in isolation from each other. In enriches the literature and will be of great interest to those of us who work with children and parents alike.

Fred R. Volkmar, M.D., is the Irving B. Harris Professor of Child Psychiatry, Psychology, and Pediatrics and director of the Yale Child Study Center, Yale University School of Medicine, in New Haven, Connecticut.

Introduction

Biomental Child Development provides the reader with a basic understanding of child, adolescent, and adult psychology. In addition, it presents a clear and succinct overview of fundamental ideas and strategies that may contribute to thoughtful parenting. Central to this presentation is a perspective for which the focus is relevance and one that remains "in proportion" to both everyday experience and clinical facts. Being a single-authored text, its perspective reflects an integrative coherence. Time-tested theories are integrated with the realities of modern life, making the principles and strategies presented cutting edge, pragmatic, and relevant. An aim is to provide assistance for professionals seeking to help parents (and also grandparents) achieve effective, positive parenting skills. Effective denotes that which works and produces intended results. These skills do not have to be extraordinary; instead, they simply entail genuine, engaged, committed, and nurturing day-to-day care. *Biomental Child Development* aims to dignify the individual child who is transitioning into a social adult.

This work focuses on a particular subset of important facts—child development, both its tangibles and the constructs inferred from them with an emphasis on their psychological underpinnings. Examples of significant constructs include *emotions, transactional sensitivity, the epistemophilia within the self,* and *projective internalization,* to name a few. *Constructs* are technically and academically understood to be subsurface propositions viewed as implicit source foundations for their empirical and measurable expressions. Constructs denote conceptual underpinnings characterized by focus, simplicity, and resilience that influence key research and its application in a designated field.

1

Biomental Child Development intentionally introduces a select group of novel terminology to sharpen attention toward recognizing innovative integrations of biomental processes. While this strategy may at first appear cumbersome or superfluous, I believe it may be unproductive to discount the value of such an approach. Put simply, the biomental perspective is designed to provide multiple opportunities for releasing cognitive *in*flexibility. New and unfamiliar terminology may act to force a breakage of strictured thinking. Metaphorically speaking, such innovations can open the "lock box" of thought patterns that automatically regard themselves as "the way it is." Thus, it is hoped that the proposed new terminology and its conceptualizations may create conditions for the emergence of creative insight-oriented patterns of thinking.

Although the consciously identified derivatives of an unconscious construct may appear unrelated, they instantiate and concretely manifest their source. Emphasis on the details of development offers a unique theoretical and practical advantage. Copious, concrete examples of applicable parenting techniques are given throughout the text. Tables and key points that highlight my emphases are dispersed throughout the text. These illustrate an integration of theories and everyday events in childcare.

Written by a practicing child, adolescent, and adult psychiatrist, this book outlines a developmental roadmap from infancy through childhood to support healthy growth and maturation. In addition, this text suggests concrete strategies about optimizing development and addressing undesirable behaviors. By combining knowledge of development with suggestions for practical application, the mission of *Biomental Child Development* lays a foundation for making raising a child manageable and fulfilling. Since this text has been written by a child psychiatrist, some important logistical and pediatric infant and child rearing matters have not been addressed, as, for example, bathing and vaccinations. These very practical day-to-day situations, important as they are, are best left to parental discretion in collaboration with other childcare specialists such as pediatricians and recommendations from the websites and publications of the American Academy of Pediatrics.

The developmental roadmap contained herein provides necessary perspectives for contextualizing behavior. In this manner, *the emergence of each individual behavior is seen in the context of the whole child.* This observational approach implies appreciating future potentials and continuing reconfigurations as unique. As will be reiterated throughout, each child has an individual tempo of growth and development. Children need ample time to grasp, understand, assimilate, and then master each milestone along this progression. To this end, development must be allowed to unfold at its own pace with the support and encouragement of those around. The immense significance of recognizing the heterogeneity of individual development is an overarching theme.

A great deal of developmental data from extensive interdisciplinary literature has been assembled in this one volume. It is intended to be read by those who have some training or are in training in child development or psychology. This group includes—but is not limited to—psychiatrists, psychologists, social workers, nurse practitioners, psychotherapists, educators, and any professionals with childcare responsibilities. One aspect of the book's mission is to provide a translational neuroscience that is "experience-near" to the reader.

Integrated, collaborative, patient-centered care is modern medicine's "systems" approach to best practices. In this view, psychological hypotheses are integrated systematically with biological and social variables. In addition to providing professionals with such a compendium of care, parents interested in gaining a more profound understanding of their role will find this book useful. Furthermore, *understanding* the knowledge behind the skills may help to defuse "parenting anxiety" that can interfere with self-confidence and thus good parenting.

The basic orientation of this text references Western perspectives. The burgeoning relevance of other cultures, for example, China and India, is a modern reality. It is important to recognize that cross-cultural studies demonstrate the contextual validity of many of the basic constructs presented here. One such example reproduced across cultures is the body of objective findings about the long-term benefits of paternal warmth. Such results are discussed in detail in a variety of child and adult psychology textbooks, some of which are cited in this book's references.

While the aim is to provide a clinically oriented yet user-friendly text, this contribution is not formally academic. My sparing use of the personal pronoun "I" at selected points in the text attests to this more clinically cordial approach. In fact, informal colloquial terminology such as "baggage," "heads up," and "on the spot" are terms and phrases used to illustrate some of the principles discussed. This book lies somewhere between being a textbook and a parenting primer. As such, it attempts to impart an experientially intimate feel for understanding the life of a child. All sections of this book are interrelated and best understood in their entirety as a child development and a parenting "learning program." Practical action plans aimed at specific parenting goals and styles are suggested.

The ingredients of positive parenting are vast and varied. They include continuing *transactional sensitivity* and responsiveness, as discussed in detail in chapter 1. In that section, the book helps parents learn not only how to listen but also to hear and appropriately respond to children's explicit and implicit needs. The construct *transactional sensitivity* implies interactional observation between a caregiver and child. The physical body, cognition, and emotion are each used as a mode of interaction, and ways to do so are discussed.

To speak of *positive parenting* does not exclude human variance. Parenting, like all other human activities, is not always consistent. People—parents and children—have good days as well as "off" days. Positive parenting is not always faultless, but makes best efforts to be engaged and attentive despite inevitable obstacles. Positive parenting encompasses a supportive attitude, positive physical contact, helpful verbal feedback, and beneficial encouragement. Although parenting is a serious endeavor, maintaining an appropriate sense of humor, playfulness, joy, and amusement is also vital. Together with intentionality, understanding, and dedication, they make parenting as wonderful and extraordinary as it can become.

Such parenting also encourages the development of children's life skills. These include adaptive behaviors that enable individuals to deal effectively with the challenges of everyday life. Childhood and adolescence are the developmental periods during which one acquires these skills, initially through the caregiving of parents and then additionally through schooling. Important life skills rooted in childhood that continue to develop in adulthood include critical thinking, creativity, decision making, problem solving, communication skills, stress management, self-awareness, self-reflection, and empathy.

Biomental Child Development targets the optimization of these life skills in a unique manner. Many parenting books outline strategies for helping children grow and develop in healthy ways, and some perspectives emphasize "discipline" as the essential ingredient. Often, these approaches focus on troubleshooting "bad" behaviors. Others speak to a limited audience of mothers. What may be missing on the bookshelves is a more focused and positive emphasis on child development, *an understanding of the changing conditions of childhood over time.* These transitions are viewed as occurring in a life cycle process never fully realized. Not only how fathers as men, but also all male caregivers, may benefit from this view is made clear in this book.

Put differently, the developmental stream is continuously unfolding, and is both open to and influenced by a number of inner and outer factors. In fact, the biomental perspective attributes unique salience to the concept of transitions—change and the psychological responses to it. Since "objects" both animate and inanimate are defined primarily by their contours, namely their edges or borders, the notion of movement across space and in time also denotes the concept of transition. The developmental nexus of human psychology is inextricably tied to transitions—outer change and inner experience.

The spirit and emphases in *Biomental Child Development* derive from my extensive clinical work with children and from theoretical considerations about human psychological development. These perspectives have been enriched by seminal insights from the many diligent transdisciplinary contributors in a number of fields, on whose conceptual models I have gratefully relied. For example, psychological, social, and developmental neuroscience perspectives are joined in describing emerging human development. Deemphasizing insular distinctions aims at building greater communicational bridges to ensure better patient care. Specific citations are not integrated into the prose of the text so that the narrative flows more smoothly and sounds less academic. Selected references, however, are found at the end of each chapter, and a comprehensive reference section is located at the end of the book.

Biomental Child Development attempts to fill the gap between developmental fact and its application in real life. The practical significance of such integration offers inestimable possibilities.

The book recognizes that *children are not miniature adults that merely grow up. The newborn does not come into the world with fully developed and realized abilities; rather, a maturation and development of resources through learning and experience is essential. This fact means that recognizing and supporting the developmental transitions that span a child's biomental development from birth onward are crucial.* These dynamic conversions organize the *biomental self* and are enhanced by the features of positive parenting.

I have coined the innovative phrase *biomental child development,* in which the word *biomental* indicates a specific child development perspective. This term refers to the *integrity—nonduality and emergent integration— of the whole individual at all ages in processes that are both psychological and physical.* It connotes simultaneity, a responsiveness of the total organism, and the dynamic relatedness among its aspects. In states of health, this relatedness reflects a synergy that promotes emerging dynamic integration. The construct and phenomenon of *integration*—apparently split-off parts understood to be aspects of a primary whole—is axiomatic in the biomental perspective, and remains a golden thread running throughout this text.

Scientific fields as well as conventional descriptions typically approach a focus of attention from a definite perspective. In using "viewpoints," the inescapable fact that human perception has strong linear processing biases— emphasis on perception of distinct parts—must be recognized and needs to be underscored here. While accepting this as true, the biomental perspective emphasizes the underlying unity, a basic though not absolute monism, among these apparent parts and understands this unity to be primary. The central nervous system and biology exist in an interpersonal context where change and transitions create functioning and identities that are both dynamic and multifaceted. The essence of the concept *biomental,* therefore, encompasses both simultaneity and nonduality as foundational while deemphasizing reductionist approaches.

Conceptual terms related to but distinct from the biomental idea proposed here fall into two broad categories: (1) psychophysiological and (2) neuropsychological. While traditional conceptions of child and adolescent psychiatry have defined it as addressing disorders that affect cognitive and emotional development, it has always grounded this on developmental principles addressing normative trends characterized by heterogeneity. All these domains—psychophysiology, neuropsychology, and psychiatry—refer to biological and psychological perspectives and a relationship that exists therein. Without an exhaustive delineation, the following characteristics may help clarify further distinctions and nuanced differences.

Psychophysiology deals with the study of the physiological responses to psychological stimuli. These responses include those of the autonomic nervous system such as measured by skin conductance, galvanic skin response, and cardiovascular parameters but may also involve measuring central nervous system or brain changes such as using electroencephalography and event-related potentials (ERPs), to name just a few. Emphasis is on the interface between body and mind, and also on typically normal, nonpathological functioning. This may include the way the body responds to stressors. Such studies of the physiological processes that accompany emotions and cognitive processes are also encompassed in the closely allied fields of psychobiology, biopsychology, physiological psychology, cognitive neuroscience, and behavioral neuroscience. Each of these fields has its own nuanced emphasis.

Neuropsychology deals with the study of the relationship between central nervous system anatomy and function and mental functions such as perception, memory, language, and so forth. The sensorium (vision, hearing, and so forth) and motor function also play a role in such assessments. When disordered psychological and behavioral states are recognized or suspected, as, for example, traumatic brain injuries or learning disabilities, neuropsychological test batteries are used to discern the neural basis underlying cognitive impairments.

The subspecialty of neuropsychiatry, for example, recognizes the intimate relationship of brain function and behavior. This field and related fields that study behavior and development use a variety of brain imaging technologies. Two broad imaging techniques are (1) structural and (2) functional.

Structural imaging provides information about physical appearance of the brain. Two of these noninvasive procedure categories are computed tomography (CT) that measures tissue density, and magnetic resonance imaging (MRI) that measures the magnetic properties of brain structures such as white matter and grey matter, blood vessels, fluid, and bone to produce three-dimensional images that reveal surface and deep structures in great anatomical detail.

Functional imaging of the brain measures changes related to neuronal activity with indirect measures such as blood flow and glucose metabolism. In this functional category are included the following: positron emission tomography (PET) using radioactive tracers in blood or tissues, single-photon emission computed tomography (SPECT) using radioactive tracers in tissue, xenon-enhanced computed tomography (Xe/CT) using xenon concentrations in blood, functional magnetic resonance imaging (fMRI), which noninvasively measures deoxyhemoglobin levels in blood, magnetoencephalography (MEG) measuring magnetic fields induced by neuronal discharges, and magnetic resonance spectroscopy (MRS) measuring metabolic concentrations in tissues. A number of disorders such as delirium, dementias, and cerebrovascular accidents ("strokes") are examined so that evidence-based interventions may offer some remediation and rehabilitation.

In addition, the complex structural organization of the white matter of the brain (and myelination trajectories) can be depicted in vivo in great detail with advanced diffusion magnetic resonance (MR) imaging schemes. Diffusion MR imaging techniques are increasingly varied, from the simplest and most commonly used technique—the mapping of apparent diffusion coefficient values—to the more complex, such as diffusion tensor imaging (DTI), q-ball imaging, diffusion spectrum imaging, and tractography. The type of structural information obtained differs according to the technique used. Diffusion MR, for example, has provided valuable evidence of the prolonged neurodevelopment of white matter tracts and hence how this biomental reality affects significant behavioral faculties such as impulse control, a concept essential in child development.

And lastly, clinical diagnosis is being buttressed with evidence-based data. For example, atypical development and insight into children on the autistic spectrum, as discussed clinically in chapter 1 in the important section "The Enduring Biomental Significance of Early Infant Motion Detection, Reaching, Grasping, and Letting Go" and in chapter 3 in the section on "Typical versus Atypical Development in the First Year," has only recently been supported by exciting evidential findings provided by diffusion tensor imaging techniques. Infants as young as six months have been followed through twenty-four months with DTI suggesting that aberrant development of white matter pathways may precede the manifestations of autistic symptoms in the first year of life.

An important social feature of the "biomental" concept is that all bodily processes are, in fact, part of a person's emotional expression toward another person. This, in a noteworthy manner, is true for children. For example, in the preverbal period, roughly up to two years of age, parents have to rely on nonverbal appearance, gestures, and behaviors to decipher the state and needs of their children. For example, awareness of self and self as distinguished from others is the net result of the interactions among multiple brain systems experienced subjectively.

In addition, the idea of *biomentalism* acknowledges that the typical labels attributed to diverse phenomena such as happiness, anger, anxiety, depression, good behavior, and bad behavior are strongly associated with complex biological processes. Even though thoughts and feelings are biologically driven, psychodynamic meanings are always attached to them. Although to some extent these somatic processes remain largely nonconscious, they also exist psychologically in forms that are partially accessible to conscious awareness.

Although metaphorical, the phrase "We are lived by the flesh" echoes a profound consideration. Mind may be thought of as existing in a fleshy platform with a visceral core of passions. The biomental perspective understands mind as the interior body, and body as the exterior mind. Most of these associations remain difficult to identify and definitively measure in valid and reliable ways, though progress is being made. The findings in cognitive neuroscience over the last ten years, for example, have provided intriguing insights into early infant cognitive sophistication. The biomental perspective reiterates that no neuron or group of neurons is an island unto itself. All have some level of substantial interconnectivity and mutual influence. Moreover, though the specific distinctions—if truly diverse—between mind and body have not been elucidated, their associations are undeniable. This fact is respected throughout the book.

"Biomental," in addition, suggests the interactions and transactions between self and environment. In other contexts, I have termed this embeddedness *eco-corporeality*—the individual as an integral aspect of the extended environment. The physical body and its psychological experiences arise from the matrix of the real world around. Children naturally appreciate this closeness. Their play both reflects and can be encouraged to retain these pleasurable and restorative ties.

The National Institute of Mental Health (NIMH) has designated the present decade as the "Decade of Discovery." The Institute's vision of preventing and curing mental illness and its mission of research to that end include explicit strategic planning. The plan's four objectives are: (1) research in the brain and behavioral sciences, (2) charting mental illness trajectories over the lifespan, (3) refining individualized interventions, and (4) clinically implementing research-tested interventions. A similar trajectory from the perspective of primary well-child development is implied in this text. Moreover, this text may provide conceptualizations that can enhance the advancement of contemporary *neuromental therapies*—integrated treatments that incorporate diet, nutraceuticals, medications, instrumental technologies, exercise, lifestyle elements, and psychosocial interventions.

Professionalism denotes integrated caregiving that is comprehensive and coordinated among specialists trained in discrete areas, each attending to a specific aspect of the whole person. Contemporary civilization is beginning to mandate the participation of diverse groups—professionals and varied patient populations—in diverse settings. The goal is to increase the capacity to predict those at risk for harm in order to develop new health-promoting strategies to preempt the development of disease, especially by using personalized interventions.

Biomental Child Development is an attempt to further enhance this vision by providing primary principles to both professionals and other caregivers. Its hope is to expand an integral, organic understanding of child and adult psychology and so foster healthy child development and enhance successful parenting.

Overview

1. WHAT ARE EMOTIONS?

An understanding of the significance of emotions is important to undertake here since it adds to an appreciation of the biomental perspective. Throughout this book, I underscore the positive correlation of valuing this biomental viewpoint—emotional literacy—with effective parenting and its underlying *transactional sensitivity*. In fact, since identifying emotions is a central, if not paramount, theme throughout, the at-times bold propositions advanced may arouse a plethora of feelings in the reader. Reactions may be interesting, ambivalent, even reactively avoidant. A rational response, however, is best in identifying and powering through these in order to examine whatever value may lie within.

Emotions, affects, and feelings are the excitation of biomental responses to changing stimuli inside and outside the individual. Processes of sensation—the registration of sensory input and its elementary correlates—and perception—the more complex organization of sensory information and its preliminary interpretation—are mechanisms bringing emotion into biomental experience. How one grasps a situation or person in either a positive or negative evaluative manner has a strong base in one's emotional orientation.

Emotions have two fundamental components: (1) feeling state and (2) object of that feeling; in academic psychology, the technical term "object" denotes person, thing, or event. The biomental perspective, however, places dedicated emphasis on defining "object" as emotionally salient other person.

Emotions as states of feelings can be characterized on two dimensions: (1) valence: positive or pleasurable, and negative or distressing, and (2) level of arousal: a range from low to high intensity.

When environmental stimuli are perceived, they travel two brain pathways: (1) "fast path," from point of sensory entry to amygdala where their threat salience is *felt*, and (2) "slow path," from perception to cortex to thalamus where their threat detection is modified and thoughtfully considered in realistic ways according to perceived context.

The special and, to some extent overriding, significance of the amygdala is crucial to note. The amygdala is understood to be the brain's core of a complex set of neural circuitry that processes emotion. It is a major part of the limbic system center of sensing threat detection—salient stimuli with high emotional significance—necessary for basic survival. While this is true for individuals on average, salience is also personality dependent. The amygdala's dual pathways provide both immediate survival and long-term safety consequent to the cerebral cortex's dampening the fear response as a result of prefrontal cortex deliberation, planning, and action. A crucial point for consideration in child development is that while sensory areas of the brain's cortex are essential for conscious perception of stimuli, they are not necessary for unconscious emotional responses to them. Subcortical pathways to the amygdala, notably operative in preverbal infancy, can and do generate emotionally salient responses.

Human emotions, affected by both nonconscious processes and conscious ideas, are positioning elements in one's attitude, grasp, orientation, and response. The term "nonconscious" implies that significant biomental processes are occurring although they appear disconnected from conscious sensory faculties.

When emotions are highlighted within the context of attentional occlusion—nonconscious information processing, their affective tone is emphasized in contrast to their conscious cognitive informational value. *In fact, the construct "emotion" is typically understood as an unconscious reaction and perception originating in a physiological matrix that reverberates psychologically as it organizes itself in infancy and childhood.* In this sense, biomental child development brings this nonconscious material into explicit focus with the book's implicit assumption, namely, discovering the emotions in the child, the child in the adult, and the infant in both.

All emotions, moreover, have an underlying foundation in unconscious processes—amorphous experiential mixtures of organic impressions, sensory imprint, imagination, and fantasy. These processes are present in the newborn whose consciousness during states of wakefulness may be characterized as ones of "phenomenal awareness"—the immediacy of sensory awareness without substantively enduring attention. For example, the well-recognized neurological condition "blindsight" has called into question what was once believed to be true, that perceptions must enter consciousness to affect behavior. Blindsight proves that experience and behavior can be guided by information of which one is completely unaware. In early infancy, such an awareness of environmental phenomena is more of a "noticing" rather than a definitive "attention to." It is predominantly nonconscious information acquisition and processing. Attentional occlusion or nonconscious information processing generally prevails. From birth through approximately six months, however, this noticing, especially of mother, is more than merely salient sensory capture although the latter is also evident.

The science of psychophysics—the study of the relationships between the physical characteristics of stimuli and the sensory experiences that result—is approximately 150 years old. The nuances of biomental signal detection and discrimination continue to be discovered. Sensory systems at all ages are predisposed to respond to change rather than steady states, both externally and internally.

Although admittedly speculative if not controversial, the hypothesis "cellular memory" or experience stored in somatic cells outside the brain has not been assessed by scientific studies yielding unambiguous support or definitive conclusions. This conjecture may be used, however, to metaphorically suggest one aspect of the biological side of internalizing experience, particularly the widespread transactional relations with salient others in infancy. While sensory input preserves patterns of neural activity in the brain, their nonconscious, implicit experiential ingredients (for example, subtle gesture, tone of voice, kinesthetic and proprioceptive aspects of physical handling) may be encoded largely nonconceptually and nonlinguistically in the body as a whole. This acquisition in a child's experiential "being" may then be sensed in some way as memories within feelings. By contrast, cellular memories as biological brain phenomena have been scientifically demonstrated to be regulated by cellular protein modification, morphometric changes in brain structure (seen in brain mapping techniques), and the epigenetic gene-environment influences unique to brain function.

All these diverse biomental processes and events may contribute in multiple ways—predetermined, probabilistic, and as yet unidentified—to laying down the ultimate imprints of experience. Perhaps, some species of somatic cellular memory vitrifies to create biomental "petroglyphs" that embed impressions in diffusely spread unconscious memory systems. Access may be through "recognition memory," which is noticing when a stimulus is similar to one previously experienced even though there may not be nor have been a cognitional thought representing that stimulus. Such gestalt-like imagery may be more allied to right hemisphere functioning and correlate with the sense of imagination, the experience of fantasy, and subliminal preferences.

The nonconscious, fantasy content behind emotions gives them their characteristic intensity. This content may be based on innate temperament or previous experience. Whereas sensory registration and "cellular memory" do not require conscious attention and functional working memory, a more mature form of memory activated by attention and working memory, especially when labeled with words, is termed "recall memory." It involves remember-ing something in the absence of direct perceptual support. In the latter part of the first year and in the second year of life, to some degree, conscious attention enables working memory to encode or transform data into long-term memory. Of note, attention, working memory, and mental processing speed only reach adult typical levels at approximately age fifteen years. Whereas "recognition memory" requires some cue to match the memory, "recall memory" is more spontaneously elicited.

Portions of all experience, especially noteworthy from the preverbal peri-od of infancy and in the second year, are retained in forms that cannot be precisely delineated. Recall memory is evident as early as six months and develops more robustly when language can be used to label internalized experience. No experience becomes irrevocably deleted. Instead, it becomes part of the fabric of the individual, enmeshing itself in the narrative of his or her development. Because of this fact, it is important to realize the signifi-cance of infancy and very early childhood in understanding the life path of a person.

The exact nature of nonconscious fantasies will not be addressed in detail in this book since it has been discussed at length in my work, *Envy Theory* (2010). In that text, they are referred to as "unconscious phantasy" to signify their unique structure and position in nonconscious processes. Chapter 6 briefly addresses these ideas.

Emotional arousal, to a large extent, indicates an organism's awareness and expectation of encountering new information. It orients one to appreciate the significance of such information. In infancy, emotional processing con-sists of a child signaling and sharing his or her "questions" and needs and then receiving "answers" from the primary caregiver. In earliest infancy, nonconscious processes predominate, only to be later enhanced by the more conscious and intentional communication facilitated by language. The term *nonconscious* describes processes that may appear silent in conscious aware-ness and disconnected from sight, hearing, taste, touch, and smell.

The foundational theme of the primacy of nonconscious or unconscious biomental processes is a golden thread running throughout this entire book. Although these two terms describe experience that is outside of awareness, they denote technically different constructs, in different psychological mod-els. The term "nonconscious" is principally used in cognitive science to denote information that is not at the moment available to conscious aware-ness. Put differently, "nonconscious" is used as a descriptive term. By contrast, the term "unconscious," which is principally used in psychoanalytic psychology, denotes a topographical dimension of mind—*the unconscious as a system.* This system of the unconscious, comprising approximately 95 per-cent of mental processing, contains and manages information that typically remains substantively outside of conscious awareness; a *primary process* that is utterly unconscious governs it. Only through complex random (such as "slip of the lip," "dreams," or "ah-ha" insights) or intentional processes (such as concerted introspection, self-analysis, or works of art) can derivatives of the unconscious come closer to awareness, typically in the form of preconscious (subliminal) attitudes that may become more conscious ideas (called "secondary processes" of conscious awareness). From a metaphorical perspective, the secondary processes of conscious thinking are akin to the surface of an ocean, the majority of which is just below the surface; the ocean of information processing is largely a primary nonconscious phenomenon. Biomental child development considers this a foundational proposition of paramount importance. In this book, the two terms—nonconscious and unconscious—are used interchangeably unless qualified to emphasize their distinctive meanings.

Although nuances of theoretical interpretation of the aforementioned abound, most agree that below surface behavior, a substrata of desires, beliefs, and intentions exists. This level of information is predominantly occluded from awareness but is instrumental in formulating meaning, explanations, and predictions both conscious and nonconscious.

The primary processing storehouse and reservoir of all human life resides in the unconscious nodal wellspring at the core of the self. Unconscious psychological processes, at every point in life, fuel what is felt, thought, and done. Becoming aware of this linkage serves to foster a judicious sense of pause. Acknowledging that emotions, preferences, desires, and motivations are biomentally active, though not experienced with full awareness, can empower one to appreciate the infinite layers of meaning behind every word, thought, and deed. Communication and decision making, from this perspective, become ever-changing and ever-challenging adventures.

Emotions, therefore, are principles that organize mental functioning from birth through adulthood. They are alerting signals, notably mediated by eye contact, that inform—consciously and unconsciously—parents and children of a perception, idea, or object requiring attention and appropriate response. Emotions help regulate biomental homeostasis and ensure survival. In addition, emotions act as signals of expression and reception for all social communication. They are noteworthy nonverbal messages that communicate unconscious attitudes.

Positive emotions and attitudes such as love and affection, happiness, enjoyment, surprise, acceptance, and cooperativeness, for example, act as linchpins to secure relationships and support a sense of emotional integrity and self-containment. These contribute to enhancing self-concept and self-esteem. Happiness and its variants such as love and affection appear to be universally recognized by people across cultures.

Negative emotions such as hostility, anger, fear, disgust, and disappointment are disruptors and can act as repellants toward affectionate engagements. They also act to modulate positive emotions producing, for example,
states of ambivalence or confusion. If identified and tempered, negative emotions can be used constructively to help reconfigure feelings and stabilize
mood. Negative emotions, therefore, behave to disrupt the status quo and
offer the potential to reconfigure constructive personality formation. When
modified, the influence of negative emotions can thus add to both personal
and interpersonal emotional integrity. Simply put, negative emotions must
exist with positive emotions; their interactive dependency modulates all experience—both of self and with others.

Subjectively experienced feeling states are communicated through words
and facial expressions. The perception of a person's nonconscious and often
subtle emotion by an outside observer is derived from seeing or hearing the
emotional signals called "feelings." These external manifestations—"feelings"—are both brain-based and culturally determined. They have both innate and universally shared genetic substrates shaped by culture and conven-
tion.

Emotional processing, therefore, is a multilayered activity. It involves
stimuli that elicit nonconscious physiological arousal termed "emotion." In
turn, emotions *mentalize* into psychological units called "affects." These affects are the unconsciously experienced platform out of which arise consciously experienced "feelings." In this technical sense, emotions are always
nonconscious biomental states that operate as subliminal affects, while feelings are conscious states such as love, hate, guilt, depression, and so forth. In
common parlance, however, the terms "emotions," "feelings," and "affects"
are used interchangeably.

Biomental child development defines *mentalization* (as proposed in my
book, *Envy Theory*) as the way the biological human organism develops into
an experiencing psychological self over the life span. In other words, the
term suggests corporeal experience morphing into mental experience.

Emotions exist at birth. Infants and children, however, do not cognitively
understand and label their emotions as conscious feelings until later childhood. From birth, however, they are able to sense the emotional communications of others and to respond adaptively as a survival mechanism. This
nonconscious foundation of emotion and affect persists throughout life, but is
complemented by a more conscious focus (named "feelings" and thoughts
about feelings) toward the end of childhood. One's emotional stability and
successful social interactions have their base in healthy emotional development starting in infancy.

Typically, primary emotions include happiness, sadness, anger, fear, surprise, and disgust. These are basic and diffuse states of mind understood to
have the same meaning for all people across cultures. Secondary emotions

are more complex composites of primary emotions that become more defined as conscious feeling states. These develop between eighteen and twenty-four months of age. They include guilt, shame, embarrassment, pride, and envy. These secondary emotions are understood as *self-conscious emotions* because they entail an emerging sense of self-reflection and consideration of the self in relation to others. For example, shame entails feelings of being "bad," while guilt is the distress about having done something "bad." The special denotations of envy as used by the author are delineated in chapter 6.

Mainstream psychology, in addition to naturalistic, observational studies, uses scientific methodology that includes neuroimaging and electrographic studies to outline a timeline for the development and expression of emotional states. Newborns' emotional tone is unformed and can be classified as states of attraction that are felt in positive ways (as tranquil) and states of withdrawal and avoidance (felt as distressful). Positive states, for example, are expressed as the "social smile"—the clear-cut, responsive, affectionate facial gesture—at about six weeks, and the "belly laugh"—the first laugh of the still nonverbal infant—at about four months. Between three and four months, infants are clearly able to synchronize their own emotional states to those observed in others. By four to five months, infants can distinguish positive from negative emotional tones in others. Between seven and twelve months, electroencephalograph tests measuring the electrical activity of the brain show clear distinctions in infants' emotional processing; typical infants are able to discriminate among different emotional expressions of others. Feelings such as happiness, sadness, anger, and fear can be differentiated as distinct and also evaluatively distinguished. Between four and six months, infants show signs of anger and fear. At about seven months, "stranger anxiety"—an infant's fear response when a stranger appears—is apparent. The phenomenon of "social referencing"—when infants look to parents for emotional cues correlating with safety or danger—is apparent at ten months and confirms infant's basic understanding of the emotions of others.

The aforementioned discussion of the significance of emotions and their measurable timetable from birth into the second year of life demonstrates both the biomental construct and the human interdependency underlying child development and parenting.

Techniques to manage emotions run throughout this book. The psychological attitude of *love* is held as a fundamental biomental experience whose positive nature encompasses an array of emotional manifestations: affection, pleasure, happiness, joy, warmth, attachment, and closeness. These features go beyond mere sentimentality, a romanticized view of interpersonal life, and evolutionary adaptedness. They have both survival and quality-of-life implications. In contrast, negative emotional states such as anger, depression, and inordinate anxiety, for example, are inevitable counterpoints of human experience. Recognizing and managing these negative factors is both necessary and useful.

While the tone of this book is decidedly positive, the disconcerting, perplexing, and oftentimes distressing aspects of parenting are presumed inevitable, yet manageable. This book offers a useful blueprint to that end.

As a matter of fact, appreciating and respecting the developmental transitions that are an inextricable part of maturation acts to safeguard the very nature of childhood itself. This idea argues against dismissing the natural importance of these formative years. In this sense, it may be advisable not to attempt to prematurely accelerate features of development such as cognition, reading, or physical prowess in isolation. The natural rhythms unique to childhood and how each child expresses these stages must be acknowledged and their innate timetables respected.

Biomental child development aims toward balance and harmony, not lopsidedness. This understanding-based perspective trumps other strategies that may attempt to accelerate emotional, intellectual, and overall child development by artificial means. Put simply, fads and approaches that do not have an adequate track record of safety are best avoided. Facilitating healthy child development occurs by understanding it and providing suitable opportunities for its inevitable flow forward.

Understanding emotions is closely allied to and requires an appreciation of motivation. Motivation denotes a level of biomental activation and interest toward self-expansion achieved through goal attainment and resource acquisition—both of which yield pleasurable satisfaction. The construct of *motivation* encompasses innate drives pushing one toward a goal, and environmental incentives pulling one toward rewards. Motivation includes two main components: (1) wanting or desire and (2) effort exerted toward a desired goal. Whereas emotion creates an orienting arousal toward or away from a goal, motivation energizes the intensity of these pursuits. It is the force inherent in seeing past immediate challenges and striving toward a path of continued forward movement. Motivated performance is enhanced when caregivers present desired behaviors in an almost glaringly exceptional light so that it becomes preferred over another behavior (such as lethargy or procrastination) thus making it possible for the child to clearly see that it will more suitably meet his or her expected needs in a specific context.

From a cognitive perspective, both emotions and motivation enhance executive functions—attention, working memory, organization, planning, inhibiting distractors, error correction, and successfully attaining a goal. Emotion, motivation, and executive functions, therefore, power volition. The biological circuitry of motivation is complex but some important elements include neurotransmitters such as dopamine, and possibly glutamate, and brain structures such as the nucleus accumbens of the basal ganglia. The significance of appreciating the value of motivation in parenting is discussed at length in sections on motivational messaging throughout this book.

Although focusing on child development and parenting, *parenthood, itself, is an adult developmental phase*. Since parenting does not come with a ready-made instruction guide, it is an experience that must be lived through, created, and recreated day to day. Parenthood itself is a generative phase of adult development and an opportunity for parents to experience a revival of their own childhood and upbringing. Forgotten emotions resurface and affect current emotional attitudes. Having a working grasp of this empowers informed parental responsiveness and the provision of encouraging motivational messages to children. The shadow of an adult's past—his or her own childhood—truly affects how adults see and parent their own children. Some aspects of this are addressed in chapter 1.

2. THE FAMILY AS A TRANSACTIONAL SYSTEM

The family is a transactional system in which each member significantly influences the others. Consensual validation along with conscious and nonconscious collaboration, in part, drives this vital system. Two levels of bidirectional transactions are: (1) person-to-person and (2) overarching effects in which each member influences the family as a whole. Each level is influenced by the other and can promote the development of all who comprise the family. Thus, not only do parents guide their children, but children also elicit from parents, at times subtly, their own needs and so influence the overall trajectory of the family system. Biomental child development terms this phenomenon *transactional sensitivity*.

The biomental perspective introduced here speaks not only to mothers but also to fathers. Traditional perspectives, on the other hand, have placed great emphasis on the involvement of mothers with their children. Mothering has been synonymous with the day-to-day caregiving of families. The last several decades, however, have brought the crucial role of fathers into sharper and more significant focus. It offers fathers opportunities for greater involvement than were hitherto recognized. Participation rather than detachment is not only the trend but now the norm. Even in divorce or separation, the basic principles of mothering and fathering remain intact regardless of how specific circumstances change. Certainly, these ideas can be cross-applied in nontraditional family structures.

Indeed, any type of caregiver can provide the nurturance, directive guidance, and living example that are the three pillars of good parenting. Each approach counters the negative effects of both isolation and aggression. Human beings are more than just mammals; they are complex integrations of head, heart, and hands into feeling, thinking, and socially responsive persons.

Humans have a psychology and a spirit that require "the milk of human kindness" manifested by nurturance, discipline, and living example. These methods awaken each child's inner capacities and rhythms. Helping infants and children to establish and become sensitive to their own innate rhythms, the rhythms of the day, and extended rhythms of the seasons as well as those of the interpersonal and cultural environment are continuing parental tasks. Natural rhythms, moreover, are flexible and variable. This imparts a carbonated, rather than flat, quality to their daily expression.

Each dimension of parenting has a major role and no individual part is sufficient. When heartfelt, genuine, and informed by a basic developmental understanding, parenting skills may be implemented by a diversified range of individual styles.

3. DEVELOPMENTAL CHILD PSYCHOLOGY

In contrast to texts solely about discipline and behavior, this book's emphasis is on fundamental tenets of evidenced-based developmental child psychology. Material, observable achievements or milestones, rooted biologically, described at each age illustrate this. The term "achievement" denotes attaining or accomplishing a goal; it is task completion. As a dynamic process, development is organic and continuous, but not strictly linear. This process of change is dynamic in that its form, function, and meaning do not remain constant; their significances differ over time. The vacillating equilibriums and disequilibriums achieved are crucial to health and continuing well-being.

In addition, a psychodynamically oriented framework attempts to illuminate the mental side of development. Integrating psychodynamic constructs with evidence-based findings is essential for a biomental understanding that leads to saliently sensitive skill effectiveness in child guidance. In an earlier period (roughly 1930s to 1970s), psychodynamic psychology formulated sets of conceptual models that were concise, often appearing to simplify highly complex phenomena such as emotion and its impact on interpersonal relationships. This was done for heuristic purposes. Grasping psychology in this way facilitated psychotherapists' treatment of patients. Many nonclinicians were either unaware of or chose to trivialize this strategy. Others were critical of speculations that appeared to reach too far beyond empirical findings.

In a noteworthy development over the course of the last two decades, neuroscientific and highly sophisticated infant cognitive development research has introduced a new era in illuminating the previously "under-understood" dark continent of infancy. Modern research is now lending credible support to many psychodynamically inferred ideas. This support is articulated in highly scientific and carefully bounded terminology, but nonetheless acts to unocclude many of the infant's complex mental operations. Some of these include the construct of the unconscious and the nuances of memory and concept formation in the first year of life. While no consensus has been reached (an indication of good science), substantial findings are constantly emerging to support the reality of a complex infant mind. This text incorporates a psychodynamic approach since this book is not purely academic but rather offers a more practical "experience-near" perspective that is materially applicable.

The fields of infant and pediatric neuropsychiatry, developmental child psychology, and pediatric developmental diagnosis provide empirical and quantifiable data about the emergence and relative timing of developmental milestones. Many milestones are sequential dependencies—achievements required as stepping stones upon which later developmental accomplishments may build and organize. For example, infant crawling ordinarily precedes creeping, which, in turn, precedes walking, which then progresses to running. While these sequences are typically true, there may be normal variations and exceptions that do not conform to these progressions.

A central premise of utmost significance in regard to the meaning of constructs and terms such as "norm" and "normal" in the biomental perspective is the following.

Developmental norms suggest the typical or median age at which an infant or child displays certain abilities and behaviors. These norms are group averages with sometimes wide yet normal variations. Differences may be found in the timing or even presence of these milestones, as some children may skip certain steps. Norms are usually based on group findings that describe the "average" person; there are always individual differences that may be understood as normal in the context of the individual. Normative here denotes *typically characteristic* for a specific age or developmental stage. Normal individuals reflect behaviors and competencies that span a wide range of what is understood to be expectable for age, stage, and situation. Atypicality or atypical development, by contrast, suggests conditions that may be on the autistic spectrum. As of March 2012, the Centers for Disease Control (CDC) has stated that rates of cases of autism have increased over the last years and reached one in eighty-eight children affected, with predominance in boys. Proposed explanations for this include a wider spectrum of behaviors and developmental criteria used; greater awareness among clinicians, teachers, and parents; and increased services in schools and communities for children with autistic spectrum disorders.

Specific timing, therefore, is approximate. It may represent trends—windows within which emerging abilities express themselves—in from 60 percent to 75 percent of typically developing infants and children. This significant heterogeneity, sometimes wide-ranging, may be understood as normal and not indicative of pathology. This fact is one of the strongest reasons for using multiple assessments over time by interdisciplinary professionals when evaluating infants and children.

In some sense, these innate developmental milestones can be likened to the figurative concept of organic "archetypes," which are original models upon which their concrete examples are patterned. The emphasis on the archetype construct here is on the individual's unique archetype. Such an idea correlates with that of an individual's genetic blueprint. Milestones are points in time that reflect the emergence of the inner archetype's potential endpoint. For example, crawling at nine months is a milestone at that point, creeping at ten months is a milestone, and both are milestone examples of the archetypal endpoint, independent walking, by about fourteen months.

This developmental perspective contrasts with the psychometric perspective typically found in formalized testing protocols. Psychometrics denotes psychological measurements obtained by tangible test instruments and their resulting scores. Some instruments have child (preschool and up) and adult versions and these are normed for age. Psychometric testing, for example, uses tests of cognitive functions (IQ tests such as the Wechsler Intelligence Scales, Kaufman Assessment Battery, and Woodcock-Johnson Tests of Cognitive Ability) aimed at quantifying intelligence or aptitude using specific scores and subscores. IQ tests yield important information on basic functioning. Neuropsychological test batteries and the use of cross batteries (Halstead-Reitan, Luria-Nebraska, and Delis-Kaplan Executive Functioning Scale or D-KEFS) yield patterns of scores rather than summed or average performance. Attention to the processing style reflected in how a child approaches test items and also on matters of ecological validity—relating assessment findings to everyday functioning—characterize quality neuropsychological assessments. The results obtained from these translational neuroscience instruments provide useful information for psychological and academic planning.

In contrast to the psychometric testing described above, developmental testing spans newborns to children approximately five years old. Developmental status uses instruments such as the Bayley Scales of Infant Development and the Mullen Scales of Early Learning. Developmental assessment perspectives include aspects of the aforementioned but also consider the interrelated progression of advancements in the biological, psychological, social, and environmental facets of a child's life. The child's social relationships, especially with parents, are a central focus of attention. Both testing and play interviews with the child and discussions with family are central to developmental assessments. The developmental and psychometric perspectives are valuable though the emphasis and function of each differ.

The childhood developmental perspective shows not merely what an infant and child can do, but also how he or she does it. This "how" reflects neurophysiological maturity and overall biomental competence. A child must first have the physiological capacity and then the environmental opportunities for practicing skills in order to adequately develop. Development is organic change from within; it is occasioned and can be molded by the plastic opportunities available in the environment. As reiterated throughout this text, the outstanding role of the environment in providing opportunities to add, enhance, and constrain development is crucial and cannot be overemphasized. Understanding where a child is positioned developmentally provides insight into the child's most preferred activities at the moment. Recognizing these tasks and supporting them with developmentally appropriate opportunities to exercise and practice them fosters healthy development.

It is also important to clarify some language. The *developmental perspective* is specific to the period from birth to young adulthood during which the rate of novel development is rapid. In contrast, the phrase *life cycle* denotes the entire period of successive developmental transitions—physical and psychological—from birth through death. Further, for example, sitting down voluntarily at about twelve months ordinarily precedes walking that typically occurs between fifty-two weeks and fourteen months. The term *milestones* emphasizes unfolding maturational competencies with a biological emphasis, whereas the phrase *developmental tasks* emphasizes a combination of maturational unfolding, personal effort, and environmental opportunities for milestone tasks to be practiced, thus with a biomental emphasis.

Transitions, by nature, are often stressful. It is important to emphasize that periods of transition are especially sensitive to disruption. The effect of a disturbance may be the unfortunate impairment of development. The anxieties and tensions experienced during transitions increase one's susceptibility to disruption and thus raise the level of vulnerability. The absence of consistent caregiving, for example, may negatively impact a child's development.

Capacities that arise during milestone windows are vulnerable to disruption if inordinate stress or trauma occurs during these times. In fact, there appear to be emotional, biological, and neuromaturational reasons for this sensitivity. The child learning to walk, for example, is influenced by inner excitement in relation to the reactions of caregivers around him. Traumatic environmental influences, such as a child's limb injury or depression in a parent, influence the development of the child's ability; if the child's leg cannot biologically support his weight or the child's family cannot socially encourage his excitement, walking may be impaired. Understanding milestones and developmental tasks, therefore, focuses attention on these periods as times when adult guidance, support, and protection are essential. Intelligently managing trauma and its sequellae builds resilience.

Milestones are conspicuous markers indicating that a capacity has organized itself into a functional faculty. Milestones are phase-appropriate skill demonstrations. They are measured by specific criteria for age-norms that inform where along the anticipated developmental path a child's functioning lies. A milestone is thus an interim deadline that pinpoints a child's position in reference to an anticipated endpoint.

Developmental norms are merely descriptive of typical children. They, in isolation, cannot suggest developmental delays or disorders. For example, screening a child's motor milestones in isolation is no longer thought to be adequate to determine general developmental status. Certified specialists can only ascertain significant conditions and diagnoses. These professions use a range of assessments that encompass the developmental, cognitive, language, social, emotional, academic, behavioral, family, and health statuses of a particular child.

While behavioral performance denotes a momentary accomplishment of a skill, competency is the enduring ability to perform that task over time. For example, walking may be possible at about twelve months. While this locomotion is technically termed "walking," its proficiency continues to refine itself over time. At a point down the developmental line when walking appears thoroughly competent, it may be described as fluent locomotion that reflects great ease in performance. For some children, this level of gross motor facility occurs only after the preschool period at about age six.

Problems in the preschool years typically involve the following: developmental delays, biomental state dysregulation (such as sleep/wake, feeding, and activity level irregularities), behavioral disturbances, social problems (such as atypical interpersonal relatedness), environmental trauma, medical and genetic difficulties, and exposure to significant environmental stressors (such as emotional, physical, and sexual abuse). There are many different formal assessments for these problems. They include the following: psychiatric, when signs and symptoms of intensive, long-standing, and pervasively impairing psychosocial functioning present themselves; psychological, when basic intelligence and personal-social functioning are of concern; and neuropsychological, when a comprehensive assessment of cognitive functioning that includes intelligence, mental processing, attention, memory, language, perception, executive functions, and motor function is sought. Academic achievement that reflects levels of competence in reading, writing, mathematics, and so forth may also be part of a psychological or neuropsychological evaluation.

The fact that milestone indicators of typical development have been established on the group level—by observing many children over decades—reminds us that their applicability to the individual child cannot consist of direct comparison. Each child has particular genetic traits that uniquely interact with the differing family and social contexts in which they are raised. Thus, while developmental criteria for normalcy have some value, their specificity is flexible and covers ranges of time during which developmental achievements such as walking, talking, and toilet training become evident and can be understood as normal for that child. The phrase *typical development* suggests this normative heterogeneity.

A number of brain imaging studies have been done comparing and contrasting infants with typical versus atypical infants as, for example, in studies characterizing brain white matter fiber tract development. In contrast to research on typical development, child developmentalists have studied atypical developmental patterns, notably eye and gaze, associated with the autistic spectrum disorders. This area is new to child psychology and psychiatry. While a great deal of research using a variety of methods (eye tracking, fMRI, and other brain diagnostic technologies) have provided new and useful data, the area of detailed speech, sound, and phoneme assessments, particularly cooing, babbling, jargon, and so forth in infancy and very early childhood, is yet to be explored. Precise *tonal features* of the infant as subject, and also the way the infant registers and *construes the vocal tones of others* may prove informative. Using contemporary, sophisticated instruments, early patterns of articulation, pronunciation, timing, pitch or frequency, loudness or amplitude, intonation, rate, rhythm, inflection, timbre, and prosody, to name just a few, are yet to be delineated. Identifying and understanding early speech and communicational sounds in greater detail may have valuable diagnostic, prognostic, and interventional value.

4. THE EPISTEMOPHILIC IMPULSE

In many ways, each infant comes into the world as an explorer with a profound urge to gather information. Biomental child development regards this pervasive inner "instinct" or organic impulse as a central driving force motivating all human experience and development. Its aim is to understand.

The *epistemophilic impulse* is this book's phrase used to describe a biomental attraction to knowledge that is both cognitive and emotional in nature. Innate primitive attentional biases—however fleeting and unsustained—initially drive this. Learning and the cumulative development of knowledge further propel this foundational *epistemophilia*. Inexact understanding, typical at all stages in life, spurs this epistemophilia. Its linchpin is based on the desire to form relationships, to know others, and to feel the emotions that enliven these relationships. Using a descriptive psychophilosophical framework, the *epistemophilic impulse* denotes the primary motive force for human life activities.

Experience activates attention and helps to organize the multitude of stimuli in order to make sense and derive meaning from the surrounding world. The newborn starts life with the frail ability to look, then scan the environment, and then track moving objects, with particular attention to human faces. Both the characteristic human face and its movements are essential. In many ways, infant information processing operates in a "prepositional" manner—spatial, temporal, and relational meaning is sought. This primitive, foundational grasp of biomental meaning is not the same as a three- or four-year-old's conceptual understanding of prepositions such as "on," "under," and so forth. The early infant's epistemophilia denotes a nonconscious sense of the rhythms characterized by containment such as movements inside and outside of bounded mental space.

At the end of the first quarter of infancy, by three or four months, arms begin to reach out, and soon thereafter hands start to grasp and hold objects. The ability to release objects later develops in the second half of the first year. As crawling occurs, primitive locomotion gives exploration more depth. At about twelve months, hands are more able to manipulate objects and permit closer examination. At this time, walking starts as toddling—crude, unsteady upright locomotion—and advances steadily over the next years. This trajectory portrays the infant as explorer in his or her personal "ship" that is constructed and developed over the course of weeks, months, and years. Although this vehicle reconfigures in identity over time, its basic structure is established early on. Parenting is stewardship of this valuable cargo.

This book attributes special psychological significance to these meaningful developmental configurations, such as the infant's tracking motions, reaching, and grasping. They are counted heavily in significance. In fact, infancy is considered to remain the abiding unconscious core of personality throughout the lifecycle. All growth, maturation, and development carry the indelible imprint that the infant mind imparts both as a historical event and in the immediacy of each life moment. The author's bias (free from any interest, influence, and funding from industry, commercial, or financial institution) is explicitly acknowledged in this regard.

Far from a sense of crystallized certainty, the ideas presented herein are understood as functional working hypotheses rather than overvalued speculations. A fascinating Eastern parallel conceptualization is found in the millennium old adage of a Zen adept: "Not knowing is the most intimate." This correlates with the biomental perspective termed *anticipatory readiness* discussed in chapter 3. Doubt and skepticism, when reasonable and exploratory, are always interesting and stimulating. They are necessary to develop deeper levels of understanding. Rhetorical wrestling over ideological emphases is less constructive. Put simply, the *epistemophilic impulse* seeks knowing as a dynamic, integral process of *experiential understanding*. It does not denote the mere accumulation of "beliefs" as unalterable chunks of knowledge.

In discussions about child development, particularly from a parenting perspective, absolutes are less helpful than are considerations that remain flexible, contextual, and open to expansion and refinement. Certainly, a great deal of child and human development remains unexplained, but further knowledge is consistently building upon these foundations. Human development, therefore, is not entirely unexplainable. The epistemophilic drive to understand powers child development and adults' comprehension of its significance. A simple truth remains, however, in that continuity of affectionate and helping parental care stands as the basis of optimizing a child's developmental strengths and overall resilience.

5. PARENTING

Parenting counts. As nurturing executive leadership, it is the primary and universal way to promote healthy child development. A parent is a child's first teacher—his or her ambassador to a new world. The content communicated between child and caregiver is secondary to the process used to convey the data. This basic yet complex task—parenting—is the foundation of human survival and the framework for establishing and refining human culture. The family acts locally, yet its repercussions are felt globally.

This book is written to convey core ideas in child development and caregiving to professionals. A great deal of the material presented might be particularly useful when transmitted to the new parent. Professional guidance, informed as it might be, is best communicated as a sharing of ideas and a dialogue respectful of a range of opinions.

Interested parents and caregivers themselves may find this volume a welcome resource. Many people may be unfamiliar with the expected trends in child growth, maturation, and development. This guide lays out those pathways and can serve as a map for understanding how infants and children develop and for recognizing the parental tasks that are essential parts of this path. To this end, biomental child development brings together principles of psychology, psychiatry, neuroscience, philosophy, and considered humanism as an interconnected backdrop to intelligent parenting. Such a consilience of perspectives is more than merely linking diverse fields of specialization;

rather, it is an attempt at meaningful integration that has pragmatic value. While not specifically discussing neurobiological factors in great detail, their essential relevance to the presented material is presumed.

This book offers guidelines within an atmosphere of deep respect for parents and families of varying social strata, economic positions, ethnicities, colors, religions, lifestyles, and cultures. No book of suggestions, however considerate of the kinship of family bonds, can substitute for the warmth, enthusiasm, and "correctness" of the helping attitudes and behaviors of human beings engaged in the shared love and mutuality of an actual family. To this end, *Biomental Child Development* has tried to be aware of and avoid any ideas or wording that may appear offensive or insensitive. No book can replace affectionate caregiving in the differing contexts that characterize real-life situations.

6. EVOLUTIONARY PSYCHOLOGY

The broader ecological contexts of evolution, ethology, and ethnology have deepened the emotional and cultural perspectives of this book. Parenting has roots in the ancient evolutionary development of the human race. It is an evolved adaptation rooted in fostering fitness and survival in ancestral populations. Parenting, in other words, is part of human phylogenetic endowment or evolutionary heritage. The new area of research called *evolutionary developmental psychology* examines the biosocial adaptive roots of human behaviors lending support to the genetically endowed roots of such ancestral wisdom.

Modern DNA is a coded description of human adaptation and successful survival over thousands of years; and parenting is part of humanity's enduring genetic program. Although specific behaviors are not absolutely determined by genetic endowments, they are rooted in them, while being capable of immense variation. While emotional and cognitive biases are real, blatant genetic determinism does not occur. Humans have a reasonable capacity for choice—thinking about options and making decisions about behaviors. It is the genetic developmental program that is inherited, not the behaviors themselves, which are instead the phenotypic expressions of traits at a point in time. Variations in genes among members of a species and also across species interact with the varying environments in which they emerge and develop. All components of this interplay as well as the interactions themselves are subject to ineluctable random changes.

Parents having children and providing an environment of safety are a large part of the innate program underlying and motivating family life. Kin-selection theories, namely the disposition to give help preferentially to close relatives who are genetically most similar to oneself, are understood to be one important basis for the urge to cooperate and help others. For human primates, this urge is able to go beyond merely its biological rooting and be capable of extending symbolically and existentially to all members of the human race. The capacity for impulse control, pause, and choice, especially aimed toward greater intentional self-development, underlies this characteristically human aspiration.

Just as an organism's genetic makeup contributes to its manifest expression, phenotype, or structure in a particular environment, structure emerges within families and parenting environments. While dissociated parts launch the process of organization, human perception quickly regards spatial parts as linking into structures that characteristically are grasped as meaningful groupings of component parts.

Structure, for example, is a large part of the parenting environment. It becomes recognizable as the particular operating form that a family develops. Structure reflects the organized stability of parenting patterns and parent-child relationships. It produces the regular and expectable configuration—both material and psychological—of a family. Family structure emerges from thoughtful planning that is both stable and dynamically flexible. In some sense, the infrastructure of the family is composed of communicational avenues through which *transactional sensitivity* among members establishes directions and working rules.

Within this framework, the child takes an active as well as responsive role in development. Rather than espousing a one-sided environmental approach, this book sees all human experience as being *interactional between persons*. Put differently, no individual passively conforms in toto to the active interventions of another. Although one person may intervene in a pointedly active manner, the response of the other reflects his or her unique processing—acceptance, rejection, and idiosyncratic "editing"—of what was introduced. Choice and self-determination, to varying extents, are parts of the psychological repertoire of infants, children, adolescents, and adults. The construct of *development* is the foundation of this viewpoint. Achievements in growth and maturation presume a worldview that sees all life existing in a stream of transitional experience. Biomental child development focuses on this development as a long-term process rather than merely recognizing its intermittent achievements, such as beginning to speak or walk. The whole and its constituent parts, though different, are equally important.

Being a person and having all the experiences between birth and life's end are dynamic processes characterized by beginnings, middles, endings, and new beginnings. This experiential series correlates with attachments, detachments, separations, losses, disappointments, frustrations, and all the emotional, loving, ambivalent, and conflicting feelings animating them. Put simply, it is not merely the environment—but precisely the human environment—that is vitally important to human beings. Successfully going forward denotes letting go of adhesive yesterdays in order to welcome today.

While evolutionary psychology has uncovered many salient processes in human psychology and its socially related group experiences, one cannot equate these findings about what may seem to be natural and innate with what is automatically correct, right, and moral. This naturalistic perspective is a fallacy when the real human capacity for reason, intention, and choice are realized, as is emphasized in this book.

Positive parenting promotes child well-being, encompassing physical, emotional, and cognitive health. Good parenting not only provides opportunities for a child to develop successfully, but also fulfills each parent's needs to nurture and contribute. Caregiving implies seeing the child as both an extension of oneself and also an individual in his or her own right. In this sense, evolutionary adaptations and biological connections are powerful motivating forces driving caregiving. However, caregiving characterized by beneficence can raise any caregiver, whether biologically related or not, to the status of a suitable provider. The biomental perspective, therefore, regards human relationships as nested in their evolutionary matrix.

7. BIOMENTAL CHILD DEVELOPMENT: A CONCISE PRIMER

There are two important underlying premises of *Biomental Child Development*. First, it does not purport to convey an exhaustive account of child development or of parenting in the manner of a formal textbook. Good parenting always has a child's total well-being in mind. For example, the role of nutrition in childhood is not within the scope of this book, though it is undoubtedly important. Second, this concise primer presents ideas in a relatively formal manner yet intentionally avoids an academic austerity. It is written by a psychiatrist whose intent is to underscore practical and relevant aspects of an immense field. At the same time, this book's aim is to engender hands-on experience (dynamic experiential understanding) rather than mere academic understanding (inflexible information bites).

This book attempts to distill core developmental ideas relevant to parenting without undue simplification. Conciseness, therefore, is a shorthand way—a heuristic strategy—to grasp the essentials of a complex subject while acknowledging its inherent complexity.

Parenting guidelines remain virtually ineffective if not understood, felt, and implemented in a genuinely affectionate way. Good care is not mechanical or doled out "by the book." Having the right tools alone is not enough; loving parenting cannot be manualized. Parental caregiving is successful when it expresses itself in a warm and loving manner. Individuals differ in the way in which they display this practice, but the intent behind effective parenting is always strengthened when grounded in understanding, empathy, sharing, and the impulse to help.

The guidelines suggested in this book, therefore, are tools to assist effective decision making. These strategies, however, need to be customized given the range of individual differences in each parent, child, relationship, and family context. In other words, by using explicit knowledge and combining it with intuitive resourcefulness, parents can optimize an effective fit between their attitudes and actions and those of their children. Conscious knowledge coupled with nonconscious resourcefulness translates into adaptive behaviors. This process allows parenting to be vital, real, and effective.

The advent of electronic media has advanced knowledge in all sectors of individual and social life. Major drawbacks, however, are the "mock relationships" between people and inanimate objects that this virtual world provides. Excessive preoccupation with the world of virtual reality—simulations that involve only a subject in isolation from others—may become escapist and reflect a significant detachment from interpersonal reality. The inescapable condition of need and helplessness, noteworthy in childhood and adolescence, may facilitate turning to omnipotent fantasy as a precarious solution to meeting and managing needs realistically. The strategies emphasized in this book aim to counter this risk by fostering a greater appreciation for the child's inner life and how a compassionate, hands-on parental approach can nourish this vitality.

Although the vast majority of mental processes are outside conscious awareness, this nonconscious information processing can be significantly informed by consciously motivated learning. Becoming aware of the range of subliminal processes beneath the mind's surface can enrich informed decision making. This book emphasizes taking the biomental development of children seriously by understanding its details.

8. OBJECT RELATIONS: THE SUBJECT'S IDIOSYNCRATIC CONSTRUAL OF OTHERS

Humans by nature are intrinsically interactive. Empirically, one can observe external signs and indicators of a child's attachment to mother or father through signs such as physical closeness and action-specific behaviors. These observable behaviors are commonly referred to as social interactions. When their emotional quality is emphasized, the phrase "interpersonal relationships" is typically used. Attachments in the inner world, by contrast, are

less obvious yet complement the outer indications. In many ways, these felt
qualities of interpersonal relationships, although oftentimes indefinable, establish themselves at birth and remain "in command" throughout life.

At birth, the infant is exposed to mother's face. This is a real though
partial grasp of the caregiver as the primary object of attention. The face's
human characteristics and its movements complement the infant's *anticipatory readiness* to easily accept mother as the primary caregiver. While this
process is typical, many variations are also at play; for example, the face may
be a nongenetically related caregiver, a male, or display disinterest in the
infant because of depression or mental illness. The infant as well may not
have typical innate characteristics to adequately participate in this experience; these may be physical limitations, illness, avoidant temperament, and
so forth.

A psychodynamic perspective denotes the mind's adaptive flow of structure building and regulatory processes within and between individuals. The
infant is significantly influenced by the presence of other persons. This physical, emotional, and cognitive influence is essential to survival on all these
levels. Psychodynamics focuses on inferred subjective or inner-world *interactional attitudes* shaped by love, hate, ambivalence, conflict, and attempts
to orchestrate these in relationships.

In the language of psychodynamic psychology, this makes up the "object
relation," which largely comprises how the *subject* grasps the *object* in subtle
and more nonconscious ways. This interactional grasping elicits a stimulating sense of possession of the object's parts, the whole object, or, as is
typical, both parts and the whole. This description uses the classical jargon of
a previous era of psychological investigation. The meaning of the term *object*
in this sense is highly personal. It in no way connotes an objectification;
rather, it denotes an intimate subjectification emerging out of a continuing
transactional sensitivity between two people who participate in a loving
relationship.

Here, the term *object* denotes the intense focal point of intimate attention:
the human object as sensed and experienced by means of desire, love, compelling interest, urge to understand, and need to survive. For the infant,
mother is most often the primary caregiving object. *Primary* connotes that
she is the first and lasting point of reference for infants. Of course, this idea
represents a typical situation. *Mother*, in this context, therefore, may refer to
any primary caregiving person consistently available.

The relation to this primary object of attention and interactive affiliation
is one of profound emotional and stimulating interconnectedness. It becomes
the relational template after which all other perceptions are formulated. Over
time, this primary cognitive and emotional template for relationships adapts
contextually yet always retains its signature emotive and perceptual patterning. The term *attachment* used in this book suggests the intimacy and amal-

gamated emotional binding achieved in the *object relation*, as described above. Social and interpersonal relationships are rooted in the mind's *object relations* at every point in the lifecycle. In many ways, while the construct and reality of "object" is primary," the inextricable meaning of "relation" can be understood as the first in importance among equals.

9. IMPLICIT AND EXPLICIT LEARNING AND MEMORY SYSTEMS

Affiliative attachments or "object relations" have both cognitive and emotional components. They transcend mere material, emotional, or intellectual clinging. While thinking and feeling may be differentiated for purposes of discussion, their inextricable connections are undeniable and need to be regarded seriously. In addition to the affective elements noted above, from birth onward, implicit learning occurs. The fields of cognitive science and cognitive neuroscience, particularly related to perceptual and conceptual development—the epistemological questions of how knowledge is formed and acquired—in infancy, are expanding rapidly. While this is true, findings remain hypothetical and, to some extent, speculative. Since learning and memory are vital to child development and child-parent relations, a brief discussion of their significance—clearly acknowledging the aforementioned—is presented here.

Learning implies the registration of information and memory. Understanding the precise structure of memory remains scientifically unclear, notably in infancy. Most researchers agree that different types of information are housed or represented in different ways using different mechanisms and different formatting such as image-schemas, visual imagery, action scenarios, or factual data. Organization of these clusters of information in long-term memory is understood to format itself in a number of ways. These include schemas (mental models), semantic networks (nodes representing concepts joined by pathways linking related concepts), and connectionist networks, also related to "parallel distributed processing" (computational patterns of activation resembling neural networks).

Two broad classes of learning, memory, and knowledge exist: implicit and explicit, which correlate with the concepts "procedural" and "declarative," respectively. Implicit or procedural information processing is always nonconscious in contrast to explicit or declarative information processing that has the potential to be and become part of conscious awareness. In psychodynamic terminology, the "unconscious" is always nonconscious, while the "preconscious" and "conscious" experiential dimensions of ego or self have descriptively nonconscious groundings and also conscious possibilities. The developmental perspective makes clear that at different chronological ages and developmental stages, cognitive faculties differ. They use different mechanisms and strategies to grasp, learn from, and retain experience.

For example, from birth until about eighteen months, most knowledge operates by implicit, namely nonconsciously aware, cognition. Perception and action hallmark this. Attentional processes are frail and may be better described as "noticing," although terms such as "attention to" and "prolonged looking at" are typically used in describing the visual behaviors of the preverbal infant.

For the first six months, implicit memory is most sensitive to grasping actions, movements, and interactions. This suggests acuity to perceiving action relations. Some hypothesize that at birth through approximately six months of age, cognitive capacities also include the ability to sort, group, and categorize objects chiefly by perceptual associations tapping on similarities. During the second half of the first year and thereafter, primitive-level, global concepts emerge, notably demonstrating a recognition of, for example, containing objects with bounded space having insides and outsides, and animal objects characterized by self-propulsion versus nonanimal stationary objects.

By approximately eighteen months and thereafter, greater conscious awareness emerges. Attentional processes become more focused permitting cognitive processes to operate by explicit and more intentional means to reformat previous information into basic-level concepts. At this time, the development of language restructures previous perceptual and global conceptual models by including greater detail and differentiation. Most thought, however, throughout the life cycle remains unconscious. Put differently, nonconscious information processing remains "in command" throughout life.

Explicit learning involves the conscious and intentional acquisition of information. From the end of the second year of life, explicit learning emerges and can be stored as long-term memory. Studies have shown that most people can recall events that occurred as early as three to three and a half years old, and have personal recollections that involve conscious re-experiencing as early as about four and a half years. Earlier in development, possibly from birth onward, implicit learning or the acquisition of information without conscious awareness or intent occurs. Implicit learning is demonstrated when past experiences influence later behavior and performance, even when the subject is not consciously remembering the past. Implicit memory and its antecedent learning, therefore, are implied. Implicit learning may be stored and become long-term memories.

The biomental perspective places special importance on implicit learning and memory. It has distinctive features that contrast with explicit processes. For example, when carrying out implicit tasks, people's performance differs very little in contrast to the greater variations that occur when explicitly learned information is expressed. Implicit learning is unrelated to IQ scores. Implicit learning changes little across the life span and extends well into older age. It declines more slowly than explicit learning.

Each of the two classes has different neural pathways and brain regions. Implicit learning correlates positively with visual processes associated with the occipital lobe, language production associated with Broca's area in the inferior frontal gyrus, Brodmann's areas 44 and 45, and the motor cortex. Explicit learning, by contrast, correlates positively with the hippocampus in the medial temporal lobe, the prefrontal cortex, and the parietal cortex.

Early learning is a covert acquisition of knowledge that takes place independently of conscious attempts to learn. It occurs largely in the absence of explicit knowledge about what is being learned. Instead, it is automatic and unintentional. The nonconscious nature of implicit perception and learning in early childhood may result from the fact that the emotional processes that contribute to them occur too quickly to be perceived. In addition, the as-yet unmatured nature of cognitive abilities early in development constrains the role that conscious awareness can play.

Implicit memory systems, mostly nonconscious, actively absorb, process, and retain experience. This direct yet covert imprinting of experience has been termed *identification*. The psychodynamic denotation of this construct places emphasis on the subject's direct sense of unification or identity with the presenting stimulus. Identification occurs implicitly and largely independent of explicit awareness of both the process and the products of such information acquisition. This is different from the process of conscious or explicit learning that emerges at about eighteen months of age. At that developmental era, concepts, symbols, and memory systems become available, enabling the mind to unite disparate perceptions and ideas. Identification at the base of all types of learning, moreover, underlies all forms of imitation, especially prominent in the first seven years of childhood. Shortly after language becomes manifest at the end of the first year of life, explicit memory systems begin to come online and gradually add a dimension of emerging conscious awareness to both old and new memories.

In psychoanalytic psychology, *identification* denotes the *primary process* operations of the unconscious as a mental system. By contrast, the *secondary process* denotes the developed ability to form abstract concepts and symbols using explicit learning and memory available to conscious awareness. The primary process operates from birth onward; the secondary process develops toward the end of the second year and, together with its base in the primary process, operates to add reason, logic, and constraint to feeling, thinking, and behaving.

Both implicit (nonconscious) and explicit (conscious) information contributes to inner states of mind, attitudes, and behaviors. These learning systems become integrated into the basic neural structures of the brain and are experienced in both nonconscious and conscious awareness. They form the attitudes that structure the developing personality. Studies demonstrate that the active acquisition of information before age three is later reflected in a child's moral conduct and guilt.

Learning involves exposure to outside stimuli that then activates already present but undeveloped neural networks in the central nervous system. Learning is information processing, and occurs uninterruptedly throughout life, though its speed and form may change. In infancy, learning is primarily sensory and receptive, occurring by such modalities as sight, touch, and sound. The senses play a leading role in exploring and learning from the environment. Once crawling and walking develop at about nine and twelve months of age, respectively, an expanded examination of the extended environment is permitted. At about eighteen months brain structures mature to allow for symbol formation and representation of thought to be formed, structured, and accessed. A modest vocabulary of up to twenty words, being able to point to body parts, and the ability to use three-word sentences at twenty-four months reflect this cognitive achievement.

For example, when children are exposed to an event such as an adult assisting another individual, the child's own internal biomental pathways that correspond to this activity are stimulated. The child's developing biomental pathways can later reproduce what was learned. Recent findings in the field of neuroscience demonstrating *mirror neurons* in area 44 of the frontal lobe and area 40 of the parietal lobe correlate with these ideas about observational learning. The mirror neuron phenomenon shows that certain neurons fire both when an organism is perceiving and performing a given action. In this sense, the neurons allow for learning through "mirroring" the behavior of another individual. It is thought that this pathway is important in the development of empathy, intention, self-awareness, and language.

If the whole child is engaged using sensation, perception, emotion, language, gesture, and behavior, optimal learning is maximized. A delicate balance of both predictability and novelty enhances psychological complexity. The real impact of the bidirectional interaction between parent and child, therefore, cannot be overemphasized. Each child contributes in both obvious and subtle ways toward shaping how parents respond. When parents recognize this, they can consciously adapt and refine their styles to achieve desired goals. The ideas presented in this book help caregivers recognize this complexity more easily.

The vital importance of the infant recognizing and identifying mother's face, for example, has become established scientific fact. Recognition occurs in an astonishing 130 milliseconds. Shortly after birth, when the newborn's visual system matures, mother's face takes on primary salience if it is available. This essential association is in addition to the formative biomental connection of infant's lips to mother's nipple in feeding. The infant's life begins at its mouth and gradually radiates outwards. It is not the lips or mouth alone that are important; instead, it is the mouth *in relation* to nipple, breast, and mother as an interactive person that is so crucial. The infant's internalization of mother's face, however, encompasses a hedonic salience— good and pleasurable versus bad and distressing. This significance is an important indicator of the quality of the child-mother relationship.

10. THE CHILD AS AN EMOTIONALLY DEVELOPING PERSON

Parenting significantly contributes to the development of a sense of self in children. This formation of personal identity is a dynamic process. It is characterized by an ability to construct and express a narrative of self that recognizes individuality and strives for consistency, understanding, and in-tentionality. Parents, therefore, must seek to engage themselves in everything from the motoric to intellectual, emotional, linguistic, psychosexual, social, moral, and adaptational aspects of his child's growth.

Each person—adult or child—is multidimensional and has a core of per-sonhood with unique biomental individuality. Biomental child development acknowledges the array of traits transmitted biologically and biomentally. Whole clusters of factors are genetically transmitted and then influenced by the context of one's upbringing. These features coalesce to produce a person-al sense of subjective self. The family is the crucible in which a sense of self is forged.

An important psychodynamic dimension of development, moreover, is reflected in the phenomena of envy, greed, jealousy, and competitiveness. Having biological, emotional, cognitive, interpersonal, and social roots, these attitudes play enormous roles in biomental development. Seeing child rearing from this angle is novel, and it will be discussed throughout this book. Good parenting creates emotional conditions whereby spoiling the goodness of the parent-child relationship is constrained. The inclusion of a chapter on envy management skills elucidates the role of envy in ordinary life and how, when pronounced, it can become a mental health impairment.

Envy management skills discussed in chapter 6 allow one to identify risk factors and build protective factors that enlist biomental plasticity to promote psychological resilience. In fact, one could regard the development of envy management skills as a prerequisite to training in conflict resolution. This group of skills is necessary in maintaining respectful social interactions and good quality of life. A deeper understanding of envy and the healthy matura-tion of envy underlie a positive psychology that is realistic in its enthusiasm for promoting healthy individual and social development.

11. CHILD DEVELOPMENT AND PARENTING: AMAZING BIOMENTAL RHYTHMS

A final consideration highlights the helpfulness of staying fresh and enthusiastic to support making parenting an amazing endeavor. In many ways, each moment may be thought of as a novel happening, an amazing occurrence reflecting an intimate interpersonal encounter. Each day presents a window of opportunity not only for renewed appreciation, but also for improvement and advancement.

Everything needs maintenance—continual inspection and repair—to ensure proper working order. This basic reality follows from another fundamental characteristic of the human condition—rhythmical change. Change is the inevitable process whereby a thing becomes different over time.

Complex, dynamic forces that stimulate active change—in effect, transitions—energize the mind and all human relationships. Often, circumstances put change and transitions into exceedingly sharp focus. The frequently heard expressions, "It's been a crazy day," or "I'm swamped" attest to this, especially its stress-provoking impact.

Continuous change nonetheless drives life and its needs for survival, endurance, and development. Interpersonal relationships are vital within this context of inevitably changing needs, and the need for relationship maintenance emerges as a recognized priority. Thus, personally taking stock of oneself and one's relations with others—a sort of *self-signature updating*—helps refresh and revise toward enhanced effectiveness one's sense of self and one's being with others.

Relationships between mother and father and those between parents and children need continual vigilance. This constant diligence stimulates fresh perspectives and opens opportunities for reassessment, renegotiation, renewal, and improvement. A particularly effective form of attention is admiration. As one recognizes the value and beauty of another, it naturally evokes feelings of gratitude. Periodic demonstrations of respect and appreciation are valuable forms of communicating loving and encouraging feelings over time. Both implicit and explicit manifestations keep relationships vital and minimize entry into false comfort zones, namely, complacency.

In addition, remembering that nothing stays the same for long and that situations regularly change calls for navigating these transitions in adaptive ways. Appreciating these transitions is rewarding. An atmosphere of enthusiasm correlates with successful families that remain positive and continue to generate new dreams.

Parenting is a time when awe and wonder are elicited on many levels. A sense of reverence, whether conscious or implicit, can be engendered. Keeping these attitudes fresh helps maintain motivation and enthusiasm for both parents and children.

An important and often overlooked way to stay eager is to deliberately instill a rhythm into daily activities. Rhythmicity is dynamic movement typically reaching toward opposites and extremes, then returning back. In essence, rhythm is embedded in a tempo of wholeness—parts in fact creating a whole. Within rhythmicity are complementarities—transient opposites coming together in a range of harmonies and disharmonies. Such dynamisms obviate staleness and maintain fresh perceptions.

An awareness of rhythmicity is an essential part of developing a family structure. This procedure entails trying to perform one's chores in a rhythmical manner that incorporates a to-and-fro pace. This process may involve daily hygiene, cooking, laundry, reading at bedtime, and so forth. Rhythm in activities and in one's state of mind diminishes boredom, drudgery, and fatigue. Rhythm imparts a sense of musicality to work, making it more enjoyable and enlivening. Much like playing music, the rhythm of daily activities involves recognizing patterns, anticipating future moves, working collectively, and feeling fulfillment with recognition and subsequent completion of tasks.

Experiencing each moment to the fullest becomes akin to a breath of fresh air. New experiences become revelations. Each instant provides a partial lesson toward a greater appreciation of oneself and shared experiences with significant others.

Parenting can be amazing. The chances for keeping the spark alive are never simply matters of luck. Preparation for unplanned opportunities can benefit success. It acts to set the stage for good fortune. Both individuals and families benefit.

12. FINAL NOTE

It is hoped that the brevity and conciseness of this volume offers a substantial contribution to the skill and art of parenting. I have used my own style of brush strokes to convey these ideas. A painting, for example, is more than merely the registration of paint marks on the surface of a canvas. When viewed by an observer, the previously objective paint marks become a subjectively experienced piece of art.

In similar fashion, this book with its own stylistic touches presents one perspective. When viewed from the reader's own experience, this perspective will become more than what was initially presented. It offers an understanding that in the end allows parents to make their own parenting decisions. Offering a tempered, humane approach with which to understand and effectively influence behavior, the translational benefits of this contribution may provide a useful compendium of caregiving guidelines.

This book aims to further reinforce the fruitful parenting literature available at this moment, with pertinent references at the end of each chapter and further listings at the end of the text. This extensive reference list, accordingly, provides both an indication of important source material and a guide to further learning and study.

My training in child development and child psychiatry at the Yale Child Study Center in New Haven and my continued affiliation as a teacher and supervisor there continue to be sources of deepening knowledge and understanding. Guidance in theoretical knowledge and exemplary clinical work by the Center's esteemed teachers has been inestimable. Special mention is made of Sally Provence, M.D., who was an extraordinary teacher, wise clinician, and friend. In addition, from 1970 through 2011 when she died, Hanna Segal, distinguished physician and child psychoanalyst in London, was a mentor providing generous guidance on a number of subjects, namely infant mental development, insights into unconscious processes, envy, aesthetics, and psychotherapeutics. The clarity of her views on freeing thought from fear and dogma, whether scientific, philosophical, political, or religious, while retaining a reality perspective was compelling. My own brief psychoanalysis with Wilfred Bion in the late 1970s provided significant firsthand encounters with the aforementioned psychological domains. Admiration and gratitude to Drs. Segal and Bion, who were analysands of Melanie Klein, remains lasting and profound. My formal psychoanalysis with Hans Loewald, M.D., in New Haven further expanded insights both personal and also into the undeniable primacy of the meaning of "relations"—particularly self-other demarcation—as denoted in the psychodynamic formulation "object relations."

The psychological, developmental, and creative orientation in this book owes acknowledgment to the contributions of the following men and women. With differing expertise, these persons had a common interest in and deep concern for the life and optimal development of the child. Each in his or her unique way avoided the constraints of "groupthink"—conventional, uncritical social consensus—and devised systems that tapped the potential creativity in child and adult. Their prolific scholarship provided a stimulus for the present work. Emulation of these pioneers, proceeding from healthy maturation of envy, admiration, and gratitude, fueled this work's uncompromising determination and enthusiasm: Heinrich Pestalozzi (1746–1827), Emile Jaques-Dalcroze (1865–1950), Rudolph Steiner (1861–1925), Maria Montessori (1870–1952), Arnold Gesell (1880–1961), Melanie Klein (1882–1960), and Wilfred Ruprecht Bion (1897–1979). The ideas of these eminent leaders in different fields provided both guidelines and inspiration for the present contribution.

REFERENCES

American Academy of Pediatrics (2009). *Caring for your baby and young child* (5th ed.). S. P. Shelov (Ed.). New York: Bantam.

Barrett, K. C. (2005). The origins of social emotions and self-regulation in toddlerhood: New evidence. *Cognition and Emotion, 19*, 953–979.

Berk, L. (2011). *Infants, children, and adolescents* (7th ed.). Boston: Allyn & Bacon.

Bion, W. R. (1977). *Seven servants*. New York: Jason Aronson.

Carter, C. S., Lederhendler, I. I., & Kirkpatrick, B. (Eds.). (1999). *The integrative neurobiology of affiliation*. Cambridge, MA: MIT Press.

Centers for Disease Control and Prevention. (2012). Prevalence of autistic spectrum disorders—Autism and developmental disabilities monitoring network, 14 sites, United States. *MMWR Surveillance Summary, 61*, 1–20.

Dalcroze, E. (2009). *Rhythm, music, and education*. Ithaca, NY: Cornell University Press.

Forman, D. R., Aksan, N., & Kochanska, G. (2004). Toddlers' responsive imitation predicts pre-school age conscience. *Psychological Science, 15*, 699–704.

Geary, D. C. (2006). Evolutionary developmental psychology: Current status and future directions. *Developmental Review, 26*, 113–119.

Gerrig, R. J., & Zimbardo, P. G. (2002). *Psychology and life* (17th ed.). Boston: Allyn & Bacon.

Gesell, A., & Ilg, F. (1946). *The child from five to ten*. New York: Harper & Brothers.

Grossman, T., Striano, T., & Freiderici, A. D. (2007). Developmental changes in infants' processing of happy and angry facial expressions: A neurobehavioral study. *Brain and Cognition, 64*, 30–41.

Insel, T. R. (1997). A neurobiological basis of social attachment. *American Journal of Psychiatry, 154*, 726–735.

Isaacs, S. (1970) [1948]. *Childhood and after*. New York: Agathon Press.

Kagan, J. (2010). *The temperamental thread: How genes, culture, time and luck make us who we are*. New York: Dana Press.

Kail, R. V. (2007). Longitudinal evidence that increases in processing speed and working memory enhance children's reasoning. *Psychological Science, 18*(4), 312–313.

Kaufman A. S., Lichtenberger, E. O., Fletcher-Janzen, E., & Kaufman, N. L. (2005). *Essentials of KABC-II assessment (Essentials of psychological assessment)*. Hoboken, NJ: Wiley.

Kingdom, F. A. A., & Prins, N. (2009). *Psychophysics: A practical introduction*. New York: Academic Press.

Klein, M. (1952). On observing the behaviour of young infants. In M. Klein, P. Heiman, S. Isaacs, & J. Riviere (Eds.), *Developments in psychoanalysis*, pp. 237–270. London: Hogarth Press.

———. (1975). *Envy and gratitude and other works*. London: Hogarth Press.

Lakoff, G., & Johnson, M. (1999). *Philosophy in the flesh: The embodied mind and its challenge to Western thought*. New York: Basic Books.

Lamme, V. A. F. (2004). Separate neural definitions of visual consciousness and visual attention: a case for phenomenal awareness. *Neural Networks, 17*, 861–872.

LeDoux, J. E. (2000). Emotional circuits in the brain. *Annual Review of Neuroscience, 23*, 155–184.

Lepage, J. F., & Theoret, H. (2007). The mirror neuron system: Grasping others' actions from birth? *Developmental Science, 10*, 513–523.

Lichtenberger, E. O., & Kaufman, A. S. (2009). *Essentials of WAIS-IV assessment (Essentials of psychological assessment)*. Hoboken, NJ: Wiley.

Mandler, J. M. (2004). *The foundations of mind: Origins of conceptual thought*. New York: Oxford.

―――. (2008). On the birth and growth of concepts. *Philosophical Psychology, 21*(2), 207–230.

Mandler, J. M., & McDonough, L. (1993). Concept formation in infancy. *Cognitive Development, 8*(3), 291–318.

Marshall, P. J., & Meltzoff, A. N. (2011). Neural mirroring systems: Exploring the EEG mu rhythm in human infancy. *Developmental Cognitive Neuroscience, 1*, 110–123.

Miller, D. C. (2009). *Best practices in school neuropsychology: Guidelines for effective practice, assessment, and evidence-based intervention*. Hoboken, NJ: Wiley.

Mussen, P., & Eisenberg-Berg, N. (1977). *Roots of caring, sharing, and helping*. San Francisco: Freeman.

Nakayama, K., He, Z. J., & Shimojo, S. (1995). Visual surface representation: a critical link between lower-level and higher-level vision. In S. M. Kosslyn & D. N. Osherson (Eds.), *An invitation to cognitive science, Vol. 2* (2nd ed.), pp.1–70. Cambridge, MA: MIT Press.

Nelson, C. A., Bloom, F. E., Cameron, J. L., Amaral, D., Dahl, R. E., & Pine, D. (2002). An integrative, multidisciplinary approach to the study of brain-behavior relations in the context of typical and atypical development. *Development and Psychopathology, 14*, 499–520.

Ninivaggi, F. J. (2010). *Ayurveda: A comprehensive guide to traditional Indian medicine for the West*. Lanham, MD: Rowman & Littlefield.

―――. (2010). *Envy theory: Perspectives on the psychology of envy*. Lanham, MD: Rowman & Littlefield.

Parke, R. D., Coltrane, S., Fabricius, W., Powers, J., & Adams, M. (2004). Assessing father involvement in Mexican-American families. In R. Day & M. E. Lamb (Eds.), *Conceptualizing and measuring paternal involvement*, pp. 17–38. Mahwah, NJ: Erlbaum.

Pestalozzi, H. (1951). *The education of man*. New York: Philosophical Library.

Plutchik, R. (2002). *Emotions and life: Perspectives from psychology, biology, and evolution*. Washington, DC: American Psychological Association.

Reber, A. S. (1996). *Implicit learning and tacit knowledge: An essay on the cognitive unconscious*. New York: Oxford University Press.

Reber, P. J., Gitelman, D. R., Parrish, T. B., & Mesulam, M. M. (2003). Dissociating explicit and implicit category knowledge with fMRI. *Journal of Cognitive Neuroscience, 15*, 574–583.

Rizzolatti, G., & Craighero, L. (2004). The mirror-neuron system. *Annual Review of Neuroscience, 27*, 169–192.

Rohner, R. P., & Veneziano, R. A. (2001). The importance of father love: History and contemporary evidence. *Review of General Psychology, 5*, 382–405.

Rothbaum, F., Weisz, J., Pott, M., Miyake, K., & Morelli, G. (2000). Attachment and culture: Security in the United States and Japan. *American Psychologist, 55*, 1093–1104.

Saarni, C., Campos, J. J., Camras, L. A., & Witherington, D. (2006). Emotional development: Action, communication, and understanding. In N. Eisenberg (Ed.), *Handbook of child psychology, Vol. 3: Social, emotional, and personality development* (6th ed.), pp. 226–299. Hoboken, NJ: Wiley.

Schacter, D. L., Gilbert, D. T., & Wegner, D. M. (2011). *Psychology* (2nd ed.). New York: Worth.

Schrank, F. A., Miller, D. C., Wendling, B. J., & Woodcock, R. W. (2010). *Essentials of WJIII Cognitive Abilities assessment (Essentials of psychological assessment)*. Hoboken, NJ: Wiley.

Schulte-Ruther, M., Markowitsch, J. J., Fink, G. R., & Piefke, M. (2007). Mirror neuron and theory of mind mechanisms involved in face-to-face interactions: A functional magnetic resonance imaging approach to empathy. *Journal of Cognitive Neuroscience, 19*, 1354–1372.

Steiner, R. (2004). *A modern art of education: Foundations of Waldorf education*. Hemdon, MA: Anthroposophic Press.

von Marenholtz-Bulow, B. (2007). *How kindergarten came to America: Friedrich Froebel's radical vision of early childhood education.* (M. Peabody Mann, trans.). New York: New Press.

Wolff, J. J. (2012). Differences in white matter fiber tract development present from 6 to 24 months in infants with autism. *American Journal of Psychiatry,* 2012. doi:10.1176/appi.ajp.2011.11091447

Chapter One

A Philosophy of Parenting

1. THREE FUNDAMENTAL FACTORS IN PARENTING

1.1 Parenting

This chapter narrates a philosophy of parenting. It is a general overview that includes psychology, development, parenting, and child-rearing guidelines that are specifically detailed in later chapters.

The broad propositions laid out here draw on several perspectives to illustrate this aim: a style of reasoning, hypotheses and theories, assignments of value, and a suggested synchrony among these. Realistic strategies demand maintaining perspectives that are "in proportion" to the perception of facts—as seen by subjective eyes. To meet these component ends, reasoned thinking requires contoured emotional sensitivity. Reason derives from empirical and evidence-based child psychology, psychiatry, and neuroscience. Emotional sensitivity emerges out of the self-reflection deriving from both good clinical care and effective factors found in successful family systems. An integration of this binocular vision is counted heavily in imparting a humane core to an intelligent philosophy of human relationships.

The three fundamental factors that make up successful parenting include *nurturance*, *discipline*, and *living example*. These are global and superordinate in that most other details of parenting can be subsumed therein. Nurturance emphasizes caregiving; discipline emphasizes the way parents teach and respond to undesirable behaviors; and living example incorporates both nurturance and discipline as models for children to emulate. Each component is vital and optimized when acting harmoniously with its companions to produce effective outcomes.

Parenting grounded in nurturance, discipline, and living example counters, in appreciable ways, the deleterious effects that negative emotions and aggressive behaviors inevitably instigate. This point underscores that, although parents have a prime role in the upbringing of their children, children themselves bring an immense array of capacities, abilities, and preferences to this relationship. Both parents and children, in different ways, transact to dynamically form and reconfigure one another over time.

Discussions about parenting may present oversimplifications that can be misleading if not expanded upon through further study and exploration. Effective changes in behavior toward more positive outcomes follow from adaptive changes in perspective. It is hoped, therefore, these discussions will stimulate broadened perspectives and further learning.

Additionally, many of the ideas put forward in fact represent ideal guidelines. Realistically implementing them, if only by approximation, for example, is a worthwhile achievement. Parenting has the best chances for success when begun on day one. *Day one* encompasses in preparation for birth, at the point of birth, and every subsequent day.

Parenting—typically, caregiving by mothers and fathers unto children— is a complex amalgam of multifaceted knowledge and skills. Just as there are diverse pathways in typical human development, there are diverse pathways to sound parenting. This chapter on the philosophy of parenting highlights some noteworthy concepts describing the effective upbringing of children.

Here this book introduces a knowledge base comprised of a psychologically oriented philosophy of parenting. In these discussions the overarching themes are fostering, supporting, and managing emotional and psychological mental health. This section emphasizes acquiring understanding as a foundation for successful parental attitudes. Practical implementation enhances skill know-how. The "details of developmental parenting" include parenting skill and style that are informed by an understanding of the basic principles of child development.

Good parenting presumes that parents actively engage their children, are attuned to subtle attitudinal and behavioral cues, remain vigilant and protective, set appropriate boundaries and limits, and facilitate healthy development. This set encompasses a wide range of skills: responding in a suitable manner that is specific to the situation; monitoring children's contacts with people outside the family; preventing risky behaviors and problems before they arise; mentoring, guiding, and modeling positive attitudes and behaviors not only with words but also—and more importantly—by living example. All these actions make up the motivational messages that enrich quality of life. *Motivational messages* are communications that are sensitive to a child's developmental level, needs, "questions," requirements for guidance through transitions, self-regulation, and containment. Such messaging—whether implicit or explicit—becomes sufficiently powered when delivered with enthusiasm, hopefulness, and tempered optimism. This feedback is oriented around supporting stepwise improvement rather than unrealistic perfection.

Having a child, whether first or last, sets in motion transitional processes that require each parent and the parental couple to leave behind old identities and develop new ones. New self-images within father and mother ordinarily emerge subliminally although the external trappings of a changed environment—additional family member to care for, less personal time, and so forth—are obvious and tangible. Much inner psychological realignment must occur in order to manage this transitional process adequately. When a parent becomes consciously aware of this need, the parental transformative task becomes easier.

When multiple caregivers are available, *parenting children is co-parenting*, a team effort encompassing sharing the care. Sharing never means absolutely equal distribution. Rather, it denotes each partner's actively contributing in the best way possible.

Parenting involves *listening, respecting, committing, negotiating, appreciating, acknowledging, and valuing the other parent's contributions*. This overarching theme needs constant reflection, renewal, and reiteration both on a personal basis and from parent to parent.

An important psychological point to underline is that many factors motivate parental responses. The parent as a child with his or her own parents becomes reactivated from memory. This phenomenon is the "ghosts in the nursery" occurrence that is discussed in chapter 3.

People ordinarily view events and reactively behave as they were conditioned to do during childhood. Such responses usually occur without any changes to old behaviors. Put simply, parents do not approach each situation as novel but instead respond to these events as they would have engaged similar occurrences in the past. This repetition from the past lies buried as a template in the nonconscious mind and is used as an inner model guiding behaviors in the immediate moment. Parents, however, are not unremittingly bound to repeat the past. With self-reflection and an interest in learning such as this book offers, parents can become freer to understand themselves and their children more realistically. This allows them to more effectively adapt to needs.

When present, both parents often take the opportunity to learn from their own mothers in raising their children. If informed, however, parents can learn to reflect on how their past has colored their current values, attitudes, and behaviors. This inquiry allows more fluidity in making necessary parenting changes. In two-parent families, each parent is an individual with a unique personality, set of values, and cultural background. It is important for both parents to recognize and address differences in values, emphases, and disciplinary strategies early on, in fact, before the birth of children. This analysis includes parental aspirations and preferences for moral, spiritual, educational, and other lifestyle models. For example, matters of religion and money, often implicitly running through many aspects of daily living in both families and through the media, require conscious thought insofar as they are demonstrated in family life and presented to children by both everyday example and explicit discussion.

Remembering that parenting is a lifetime endeavor of learning, acquiring experience, and continuously refining skills makes the journey an adventure instead of a chore. In some ways, parents participate, so to speak, in coauthoring their child's life script. Each parent offers the child a different perspective for understanding and adapting to the world. The script is thus the personal narrative that reflects the child's sense of identity as an emotional, thinking, and preferred person.

Parenting children successfully requires that parents nurture and discipline themselves first, and uninterruptedly. Proper nutrition, exercise, and healthy lifestyles have to be part of parents' daily routines. As such, parents need expectable, regularly occurring sequences of activities. Each parent certainly needs and also deserves food, love, and understanding. Each must give these to himself and herself, as well as to one another. Such cooperative helpfulness minimizes splitting—psychologically dividing experiences into polar extremes—and fosters overall family integrity. Splitting is "all-or-none" thinking that tends to categorize experiences in terms of black or white, good or bad. This mind-set can be detrimental to family interactions, which require more careful and subtle evaluations and expressions. Cooperative parenting can be a form of self-development that may improve parents as it simultaneously helps children develop themselves physically, psychologically, and socially.

Much learning occurs as parents and children develop with one another. While the vast majority of parents are well-intentioned and reasonable, their educational values and aims may differ from those a school deems best for their child's overall needs. It is also important to acknowledge the overt and formal educational process as well. A vital area relevant to the successful upbringing of children is academic education, though this aspect of parenting will not be discussed in detail in this book. It is important to stress, however, that parents need to take education seriously. Maintaining an active, collaborative, and cooperative relationship with teachers and school is vital to a child's success. Differences of opinion or noncooperative attitudes on the part of families and schools bodes failure for children's successful learning. Any indication of obstructionist trends requires prompt identification and dialogue. Successful learning arises from parent-school-child coalitions. These must remain team efforts aimed toward goals and strategies met with cooperative and agreeable attitudes and efforts.

Regular contact, especially by appointment, promotes effective learning by maintaining continuity of perspective between parents and teachers. By contrast, trying to momentarily speak with a teacher at the end of a class period is generally unproductive. Many teachers say that if a parent stays involved and works collaboratively, chances are greater that children will act similarly. The converse is true as well. Without positive parent-teacher dialogue, a child's intellectual and social development suffers.

The biomental child development perspective takes into consideration both the consciously understood facts of child rearing as well as their unconscious roots. Understanding these unconscious components and their meaningfully salient subrational logic gives richer meaning to the seemingly irrational problems, typically involving personal responsibility, often encountered. For example, parents who have children with physical or mental disabilities often feel illogical pangs of guilt, as if they had deliberately caused the problems. This is an example of irrational personal responsibility. Children may demonstrate self-defeating behaviors such as failure to do homework or attend classes even though this undermines educational advancement. This signifies irrational irresponsibility. These examples of irrational problems are based, to a large extent, on unconscious conflicts. Each case has unique circumstances and only careful assessment can uncover root issues. When the basis for such self-undermining problems that impair adaptive functioning and quality of life is better understood, richer meaning is uncovered. This process permits people to be more successful and move forward more easily. Reason as well as subrational intuition are valuable tools.

Reason, intuition, and insight guide the *transactional sensitivity*—conscious and nonconscious transformative exchange of information—that gives meaning and direction to parenting. This core feature of the biomental child development perspective will be discussed at length in this chapter. Sensitive parenting takes all these factors into consideration. *Transactional sensitivity* is the basis for intuitive cues into infant and child communicational signals—the words, gestures, and behaviors that indicate the reasons and suggest the hidden variables behind surface behaviors.

1.2 Nurturance and Discipline

Nurturance and discipline are among the three basics of good parenting. These two superfactors form the scaffolding of successful parenting. A third superfactor, providing example, supplies the information that children may use as blueprints to emulate. Although example is undoubtedly the most persuasive aspect of parenting, all three domains help families grow, develop, and become resilient in the face of inevitable perturbations and stressors. Finding the right balance is part of the art of successful parenting.

The vital significance of nurturance, discipline, and living example in raising children, particularly in the first six years of life, is beginning to appear in findings from neuroscience research. The impact of early adversity on the brain has shown that unfavorable neurobiological changes may occur in demonstrable ways in children raised in orphanages. Primary prevention or exposure reduction, which occurs before a deleterious event, and secondary interventions, which occur when such an incident is identified, help reduce adversity. This practice translates into using positive parenting approaches to support biomental resilience.

1.2.1 Nurturance

Nurturance denotes experiential acceptance, closeness, sharing, warmth, protection, love, and understanding. Affectionate stroking, hugging, kissing, and language may express love in concrete ways. A certain amount of loving physical contact is vital in good parenting. As is true of reasonable nurturance, love does not exist in an all-or-none condition. There are levels of love characterized by intensity, duration, and comprehensiveness. The level is achieved by the mutuality of participants' intentions and cooperativity.

Kissing behaviors, for example, are ordinarily not explicitly discussed; rather, they occur spontaneously. Kissing combines sensations of touch, smell, and taste. Kissing expresses sentiments of love, passion, affection, respect, devotion, friendship, greeting, beneficence, and wishing good fortune. Whether an innate response, learned through culture, or a combination of both, kissing is understood to be an expression of affectionate closeness across cultures. Human touch suitable to age and developmental level fosters a child's sense of security and being loved. All these components of adult attention and approval are essential for children. Nurturance provides physical resources, emotional attention, and affectionate caregiving in a context of *transactional sensitivity*.

Effective nurturance emphasizes the give and take of heartfelt human affection in attitude, language, and action. Reciprocal human relationships that are mutually beneficial are the optimal crucible within which this nourishment occurs. Biomental child development primarily elaborates upon the "experiential" and "understanding" component of nurturance. The first dimension of nurturance, however, includes meeting a child's basic needs. Food, for example, provides material nourishment yet can also connote the communication of love and understanding. Meals can be special times when they reflect thoughtful planning, effort, and communal participation. Organized meals throughout the week provide ideal occasions for parents and children to interact, learn, and consolidate values and skills.

Warmth and overall protection are nurturing activities that help sustain physical life and well-being. The manner in which an infant or child is handled may be the most obvious way that love and understanding express themselves in everyday life. Younger children are particularly sensitive to these ministrations. Physical management attends to the senses—sight, sound, tastes, hearing, and touch. This explicit and implicit education of the senses occurs by example, rhythm, and an aesthetic style, for example balance, harmony, and synchrony. Parents who grasp the innate sensitivity of infants to rhythms—to-and-fro motions—may use this in implementing more effective care. Sufficient awareness of the rhythmical nature of biomental processes may be one of the most underdeveloped and underutilized areas in psychology and caregiving. It is an essential ingredient in transactional sensitivity in all its dimensions.

Intermodal perception—simultaneous input from more than one sensory modality—is active in infancy. Parental care that uses concurrent sight, tone, touch, aroma, and so forth supports and enhances learning and biomental development. Good physical management goes hand-in-hand with appropriate love and understanding.

A note on love is worthwhile here. The word *love* may be one of the most overused terms in languages. It is used loosely, often in casual and nonspecific ways. The term *affection* is often used to denote love, but may have a less emotionally charged connotation. On an abstract level, love can be understood to be the overarching force of attraction, attachment, affiliation, bonding, and pleasure. Biomental child development understands love to be more than merely a word or concept. Love in this text denotes a living experience whose unbounded nature in human interactions is a graspable reality yet goes beyond mere verbal definition. This uniting trend is fundamental to all biomental life processes and is primarily constructive and expansive. The experience of love in this sense suggests an underlying primary biomental action as the adaptive and life-promoting force that brings things together, as diverse as cells coalescing into tissues, plants gravitating toward the sun, animals seeking food and shelter, and people falling in love to enhance the quality of their lives. Love for humans, therefore, denotes biomental intimacy that is emotional, cognitive, and material—commitment that is enduring and desire that stirs passion.

Biomental child development presumes that the complex processes subsumed by the idea of love have a powerful base in the anatomy and neural functioning of the central nervous system. This human evolutionary and phylogenetic endowment is experienced, variously influences, and is expressed consciously and behaviorally in very different ways by individuals. Rather than considering the feelings and behaviors that are launched by love as incidental or merely sentimental, this book regards them as legitimate and essential to human life, self-development, and adaptive prosocial growth. Love, along with hate and envy, is a fundamental driving force in the human drama.

In the context of human relationships, love activates within individuals— in differing ways—and brings them together. Feelings of affectionate warmth help achieve, foster, and maintain attachment to another. Attitudes of love, in this sense, include caring, warmth, trust, admiration, empathy, gratitude, kindness, mutuality, respect, encouragement, hope, and reciprocal helping. While these attitudes may appear as surface behaviors, they emanate from deeper levels of motivation. To be sure, there are many forms and degrees of loving relationships. Each participant experiences and demonstrates love in varying, often asymmetrical, ways. The love that brings two people together in bonded relations, marriage, and potential parenting is the same love, *mutatis mutandis*, experienced in the parent-child relationship.

When parental nurturance promotes healthy development, children develop a sense of personal containment. Put differently, children gradually and progressively organize a sense of self that is cohesive and bounded. Such containment denotes biomental spatial relations. Hence, the dynamic interpersonal dialogue between the child and others becomes modulated in realistic ways so that, for example, feelings of loneliness resulting from separations, transitions, and losses are not overwhelmingly intense, unbearable, and disorganizing.

The quality of nurturance has a greater impact than that of merely providing a sufficient quantity of care. Nurturance focuses on transactional interactions between *whole persons*—the whole parent and the whole child—rather than merely on behavior. The quality and intent of the caregiver exert greater effectiveness than biological givens in isolation, such as the temperamental traits characteristic of each individual as discussed below.

1.2.2 Discipline

Discipline (Latin for "learning and teaching") means instructing and guiding another to follow a particular code of conduct, behavior, or order. Its dual goals are to promote desirable behaviors and to correct those actions that are disruptive and noncooperative. Discipline helps establish health-promoting attitudes and prevents negative patterns from developing. The most effective disciplinary strategies provide a scaffolding characterized by suggested preferences, techniques to think through negative and positive responses to these preferences, and reinforcing remembering the consequences of such responses.

One who disciplines effectively first must learn "to hear" before implementing corrective responses. This book is intended to sharpen attentive, explorative listening and grasping what another is communicating. This is accomplished by focusing on a developmental perspective that enables one to understand the architecture surrounding children's temperament, personality, and behavior.

Effective discipline fosters learning. Suitable discipline requires that parents take leadership positions on a daily basis. This role involves setting the limits between what is acceptable and not acceptable and allowing children to understand why. Saying "no" is often necessary, but offering options that fulfill children's needs in more suitable directions should complement this response. Limits are best conveyed as reasonably firm guidelines with alternative opportunities rather than as rigid and inflexible demands. How one communicates these statements determines how effectively they will be understood and respected.

When setting limits, parental patience and calm are advantageous. Being in touch with what children are feeling is essential. This idea involves attunement to children's enthusiasm for exploration, activity, and excitement, as well as feelings of frustration, surprise, and confusion, particularly when children perceive parents thwarting their desires.

Another aspect of good parenting is being mindful of interruptions in family life. Some of these disturbances may take the form of repetitive behavioral problems. Rather than automatically reacting to such intrusions as intentional, willful, and manipulative, a broader contextual approach attempts to clarify their meaning. Special attention to antecedents (what comes before the problems) and context (in what circumstances the difficulties seem to emerge) provides clues for problem resolution.

Problems encountered during the course of parenting can be viewed from different perspectives: (1) before the difficulties occur, (2) when they occur, and (3) after they happen. Prevention is the best strategy to employ. When dilemmas arise, however, timely interventions are needed, and after problems subside, reflection is necessary. Contemplating the cause and context of such behaviors can foster prevention for further occurrences. Corrective action consists of effective feedback. This process helps children learn and improve future performance.

Adult attention to and approval of good behaviors is the strongest reinforcement that can be given. Children of all ages value positive feedback to an inestimable degree. Affirmative recognition of desirable behaviors needs to occur daily. This decisive strategy should not be made feeble by excessive positive or negative attention to undesirable behaviors. The importance of this point cannot be overemphasized. It is one of the foundations for normalizing attention-seeking behaviors and remodeling them in positive ways.

Successful parenting always includes reasonable tolerance for a measure of some undesirable, unacceptable, or unusual behaviors. Finding the proper balance between harshness and leniency requires patience, perseverance, and self-reflection over time.

   Disciplinary strategies may include constructive incentives transmitted by clear communication and founded in reason. These approaches may also include aspects of temporarily withdrawing positive attention and affection, such as ignoring a child who is acting out or temporarily using a quiet time out. Additionally, discipline may involve power assertion strategies that include withdrawal of privileges and behavioral rewards or punishments to achieve a desired response. Another option is psychological control, such as statements of disapproval that elicit a constructive emotional climate (for example, empathy, sorrow, or guilt) inducing a child to follow directions. However, it is important to note that none of the above techniques is effective in excess or in an inconsistent manner.

   In its essence, discipline means providing guidance and supervision through the use of encouraging, motivational messages. The ultimate aims of discipline include promotion of self-discipline, self-control, emotional regulation, delay of immediate gratification, and a capacity to foster the motivation to sustain these. These achievements comprise the journey toward attaining self-containment through internalization of these self-modulators in the face of frustration and disappointment.

   One achievement of establishing self-regulation is learning how to experience loss. This is noteworthy because the emotions elicited by loss are typically intense and difficult to manage. How a child reacts to disappointment reveals his or her developing ability to manage loss and letting go, which may be implicated in any transition or change. Among them are routine changes, such as denying a child a treat, and major losses, such as those incurred in grief over the loss of a pet or bereavement over the death of a family member. Helping children to experience the inevitably recurring phenomena of "endings" in positive, rather than traumatic, ways strengthens their sense of self, self-regulation of reactions, and emotional management.

   However, the only way some children are able to experience perceived loss and subsequent letting go is through the use of unconscious spoiling, which is a common reaction to frustration and disappointment. *Spoiling in this sense means marring and devaluing what was once viewed as ideal.* This negative reaction is predicated on unconscious envious processes that idealize what is perceived to be valuable, notably in the face of its threatened loss, and then turn it bad or "sour" it. Envious processes are the antecedents of such spoiling behaviors.

   Children's spoiling reactions are expressed in temper tantrums, angry outbursts, breaking things, and oppositional and defiant behaviors. Loss denotes a need to let go and move on, but some children are only able to let go in a feeble way by using behaviors that spoil the object or event, hence making it unenjoyable to anyone. Often implied in this is the sense that what once was possessed will be had and enjoyed by another. Some may feel a person who has passed is "in heaven" with its celestial enjoyments shared by others—God, angels, dead relatives, and so forth. Some may be distressed because they cannot enjoy the pleasure of the other's company anymore. In both cases, envious processes are activated and may produce either idealizing or spoiling the lost object.

The basic emotions underlying *unconscious envy,* as will be discussed in chapter 6, do not allow one to tolerate this abrogation and relinquishment of personally owned pleasure. Hence, spoiling what was once perceived as good must occur. *Spoiling*—marring and devaluing what was once viewed as virtually ideal—is the inevitable outcome of pronounced envious processes. The entire construct of spoiling in this sense does *not* denote other connotations of the term such as uncritical, excessive fondness or "doting." Pronounced doting or "spoiling a child" typically denotes giving a child all he or she needs plus more in excess. Such overindulgence provides an overabundance that reinforces instant gratification and an expectation of "on demand" satisfaction. This type of parent-child interaction reduces a child's development of patience and impulse control, and is to be avoided. Last, ideas about unconscious envy are addressed in detail in subsequent chapters. Helping children to experience loss in a variety of real-life circumstances is important for parents to understand and tackle.

Helping children to develop self-regulation is supported by example and discussion. Discussion of the reasons for rules and limits is significant and should always be part of this. A great deal of effective discipline is helping children to behave within provided guidelines. With younger children, distraction from the undesired activity may be achieved when a parent couples it with tangible options and examples. When distraction is most effective, it is accompanied by concrete opportunities for alternatives and assisted by parental involvement. For example, when children are told to stay away from the stove or stairs, parents can redirect the child to another activity such as coloring by actually beginning to color with the child.

In general, monitoring and supervision need to range in intensity across the developmental spectrum. As the child matures, less intense supervision may be required. The exact level of monitoring required depends on many factors, such as chronological age, developmental age, physical condition, and so forth. This idea calls for continuing parental discrimination and judgment.

Disciplinary strategies, to be sure, call for frequent discussion, review, and revision by all involved caregivers. Continuing communication about matters of concern needs to happen almost daily. Such exchange fosters parents' own leadership confidence and supports more unified decision-making skills.

It is important for each caregiver to listen thoughtfully and carefully to the other's thoughts about children and family. If this ability does not come naturally, it is a proficiency that can be developed through practice. In fact, wives frequently regard listening as a skill that husbands can enhance. A family climate of listening and taking turns optimizes good relations through teamwork. Any form of significant splitting between parents undermines the health of families. Parents need to be mindful of maintaining mutual support and recognize any attempts, often inadvertent, of children to split parents into opposing camps when conflicts about rules, discipline, and enforcement arise.

In many ways, discipline—like nurturance—is made more effective when it is characterized by symmetry, proportion, and harmony. Symmetry is reflected in a consonance between the transactional sensitivity of parents with children. That is, both caregivers and their offspring are attuned to the same relevant experience at the same moment. Proportion in the expressed interaction reflects an exchange that is required, without excess or deficiency. Harmony is reflected in the smooth emotional contours that surround any exchanges of meaningful information with a potential for future enhancement.

1.2.2.1 What Discipline Is Not

Thoughtful, effective discipline is neither punishment nor aggression. It is not punitive, heavy-handed, or sadistic in reprimand. Healthy discipline is not mindless authoritarian control. Harsh scolding is generally unhelpful and may be traumatic to a child, particularly over time. Nagging, threatening, endless explanations, yelling, and harsh punishments are all ineffective. In fact, adult attention to misbehaviors, if done repetitively and without constructive learning interventions, powerfully reinforces bad and undesirable behaviors. Children crave attention from their caregivers and may learn to act out in order to receive even negative attention.

Findings in neuropsychiatry over the last several decades have clearly shown that both emotional and physical trauma have detrimental effects on important brain structures such as the hippocampus—a center of learning and memory—and the amygdala, which signals anxiety and fear responsivity. Often, when children are hit, they feel pain, fear, and bewilderment. The younger a child is, the more perplexed he or she is about why this aggressive event is occurring. Fear of harm (harsh discipline) triggers both passive and active avoidance. Hence, avoidance blocks habituation; fear reactivity is maintained in a hypersensitive state and, in turn, both fear and avoidance prevent realistically successful, progressive learning from experience. Emotional trauma can damage such brain structures, but the brain's capacity for *neuroplasticity*, which denotes compensatory and healing reconfiguration, can modify this. Both psychological and pharmacological therapeutic strategies have shown benefits for this healthy, adaptive reorganization of the brain after trauma. The crucial significance of neuroplasticity as fact has opened new vistas for both conceptions of and interventions in mental health.

Discipline, moreover, can never be understood to be corporal punishment. Corporal punishment is an aversive stimulus that is sometimes mistaken to be a useful form of discipline. Parents often think that hitting a child will have positive effects on behavior. However, the sometimes brief changes in negative behavior that occur are overwhelmed by detrimental consequences of this form of punishment.

Experts who study child neglect and maltreatment agree that corporal punishment is intergenerational, which means that adults who were subjected to this form of discipline come to believe that it is acceptable. They, in turn, use corporal punishment to discipline their own children, which reflects the learning from modeling that was previously discussed. Although parents have a wide range of beliefs in terms of what is acceptable or not, this particular area of discipline continues to be controversial. Some parents and most experts propose that all forms of aggressive interaction should be omitted while other parents suggest that "milder" forms such as an occasional slap or spanking are sometimes useful. These parents suggest that such discipline is acceptable if the underlying parent-child relationship is typically warm, affectionate, and accompanied by reasonable dialogue. In other words, occasional mild hitting or "pulling on the ear" to give emphasis to paying attention to a corrective direction is believed to be useful. This form of "hitting" is distinct from beating, which is unquestionably prohibited.

Corporal punishment, typically impulsive and enacted in anger, aims to inflict physical and emotional pain. It is best avoided. It has been officially condemned by the American Academy of Pediatrics. The American Medical Association, American Bar Association, and the American Academy of Child and Adolescent Psychiatry advise against corporal punishment in schools.

While such aversive stimuli may suppress behavior temporarily, they do not change it for good and may cause adverse side effects such as trauma and inordinate fear as mentioned earlier. Such distress prevents constructive learning from occurring. Hitting or any violence to a child wrongly teaches, by bad example, that violence is an acceptable way to handle problems.

Some surveys have suggested that about 39 percent of parents never spank their children, while about 61 percent admit to spanking occasionally. These parents refer to this action as "nonabusive" spanking, typically with children ages two to six years. It accompanies milder forms of discipline using reasoning and verbal reprimands.

Many parents regard the "terrible twos" and "trying threes" as chronological eras wherein spanking is often used to control undesirable behaviors, typically aggressive in nature such as biting a sibling, or grabbing a toy away from another child. This strategy is counterproductive since it backfires into even greater unruliness. Yet, parents find it difficult to restrain themselves from this approach. In documented studies, about 66 percent of parents of very young children ages one and two years reported using physical punishment. By the time children reach fifth grade, 80 percent have been physically punished. By high school, 85 percent of adolescents report that they have been physically punished, with 51 percent reporting that they have been hit with a belt or similar object.

Some research suggests that more fathers than mothers think that spanking is an effective form of discipline and behavioral control. Evolutionary psychologists describe a positive correlation between the use physical discipline by stepfathers because of the nonbiological relationship. Professionals who disagree with this conception are keen to recommend parent management skills and effective parenting training classes to both fathers and mothers whether biological or not. Recent surveys have also positively correlated spouse and intimate partner violence with violence to children in the home. The notion of "ghosts in the nursery," or being influenced by how one was treated or saw parents treat one another, is here exemplified. Early life stress, especially caused by abuse and violence, has been demonstrated to have lasting biological and psychological consequences, as well as a transgenerational impact on family members downstream from the original traumatic events.

Although research findings show corporal punishment use across the socioeconomic spectrum, its frequency and intensity appear elevated among less educated and more disadvantaged persons. This association may occur for a number of reasons. Such persons may be less educated as to the adverse effects of corporal punishment, for example, or high levels of stress associated with lower socioeconomic status may encourage hitting. Hitting, while a violent behavior, is distinct from beating, which is physical abuse and always prohibited.

Yelling is one form of aggression. Yelling when a child misbehaves frightens the child and elicits defensiveness. These feelings and attitudes are not conducive to redirection and learning more desirable behaviors. When parents model aggression, children learn to use it, in turn, to deal with parents, siblings, peers, and others. Inordinate exposure to force and violence causes habituation, tolerance, and insensitivity to violence. This tendency often extends into adulthood and perpetuates the use of adolescent and adult aggression. Studies do show that children who are spanked become more aggressive even by age two years. Most research shows that between 60 and 70 percent of child abuse begins as harsh spanking and progresses to even greater violence and maltreatment.

In contemporary times, corporal punishment is best omitted in any childcare context. Children, notably preschoolers, have heightened emotional and fantasy lives. When exposed to physical violence, particularly spanking, it is not unreasonable to infer that they experience this as a physical and psychological attack. Unable to make sense out of these acts and not helped by adults to become engaged in less violent, more meaningful interactions, children can become traumatized or confused, and feel violated. Linking violence with parenting is inappropriately fostered in the minds of children who are hit. However, this process can be buffered by communication that is founded in reasonable, explanatory language.

At times when heated emotions flare and the impulse to discipline aggressively arises, it is best to pause, step back, and take time to think about the situation. Self-reflection helps temper emotions and dampens automatic reactivity. This personal time-out is a sort of self-debriefing that allows a parent to defuse strong emotions, figure out what just happened, and learn from the context so that future responses may become less volatile and more effective.

Exploring reasons why one would want to hit, for example, may provide important insights. Resorting to aggressive behaviors, even in the guise of disciplinary action, always is triggered by multiple provocateurs. As discussed, parents who discipline children in an aggressive manner were often disciplined this way by their own parents. Thinking about this association gives one the opportunity to review the pros and cons of aggressive discipline and consider the range of recommended nonviolent alternatives—positive reinforcement, ignoring the behavior, time-outs, and logical corrective consequences. These are discussed at length in chapter 5.

1.2.2.2 What Discipline Is1.2.2.2 What Discipline Is   Healthy discipline, in contrast to ineffective discipline, is beneficial to wholesome growth, maturation, and development. Healthy discipline involves clearly setting out desired directions, optimal preferences, and the logical and realistic consequences of unacceptable behaviors. This intervention is best accomplished by using explicit language that is developmentally appropriate for a child's level of emotional and intellectual understanding. Calmness, brevity, and specificity characterize effective discussions. Beneficial discipline may be forceful in that it is clear, explicit, firm, and decisive, though never abusive.

Parents need always to monitor their own anxiety responses to children's undesirable behaviors. *Anxiety* typically denotes pervasive emotional uneasiness that is not particularly related to a specific event. Anxiety has an amorphous quality based on nonconscious fears and conflicts. Fear, whether conscious or nonconscious, is particularly constricting because it evokes feelings of vulnerability, being controlled, and being at the mercy of forces beyond one's control. These typically have mental content not easily accessible to conscious awareness. Such anxiety lingers and cannot be easily dismissed. It is accompanied by feelings of powerlessness to change it.

Worry, by contrast, denotes a distressing feeling about a specific event and its potentially undesirable consequences. Often, the terms *worry* and *anxiety* are used interchangeably. Preoccupation with worries applies equally to both mothers and fathers. While mothers may react with uncertainty, fathers may become either anxiously disengaged or angrily overreactive. Of course, each gender may react in other ways, too. At times, when parents perceive negative aspects of themselves in their children, particularly negative moods or behaviors, the natural tendency to feel anxiety may well up. In many instances, anxiety causes an automatic slowing and inhibition of both thinking and effective action. At these points, pause and self-reflection help reorient thinking and feeling and a normalized return to balanced assessment, so that a suitable action plan can occur.

Discipline is often contrasted with nurturance. This distinction, however, may be misleading. Suitable discipline can be regarded as a form of nurturance and an important aspect of caregiving. Keeping this nurturant emphasis on discipline in mind highlights its corrective, refining, and adaptive dimensions.

In line with the aforementioned ideas, discipline is a continuing process of teaching, promoting, and supporting prosocial attitudes and skills. *Prosocial behavior*, often discussed in this text, consists of actions that benefit other people. Although these strategies will be discussed in detail in chapter 5, a brief outline here of their essential components will be helpful.

Prosocial behaviors are transmitted by techniques such as (1) modeling, or setting an example through behavior; (2) cueing, or prompting children to use prosocial skills; (3) coaching, or direct instructions about how to prepare and then use skills; (4) positive reinforcement, or recognizing and verbalizing children's attempts and successes at using prosocial skills; (5) nonjudgmental statements, or avoiding emphasizing negative statements about children and others; (6) role playing, or creating a safe environment in which to learn and practice prosocial skills; and (7) direct feedback, or asking children for their perspective and notably what could have been done better to improve the problematic situation.

The goal of all these approaches is to reduce unacceptable behaviors. Such behaviors are those deemed undesirable, unwarranted, and violating established family rules, social customs, and moral and civil laws. *Rules must be clearly communicated* in language, facial expression, gesture, and tone that are suitable and understandable to the child at his or her developmental level.

In addition, brief explanations make it easier for the value of rules to be understood and accepted. Such explanations are markedly effective when they avoid taking on the attitude of "preaching," which can be characterized as authoritarian, nonnegotiable, unrelenting demands. Tone of voice is crucial when communicating intent. The younger the child, the more nonconsciously sensitive he or she is to parental meaning and intention as expressed in tone of voice. Tone of voice together with facial expression, eye contact, gesture, and posture communicate the emotional meaning of parental communications. Well-chosen words, brief and to the point, deliver effective ideas. When delivering behavioral messages to children, phrasing them as *preferences*—either toward positive behaviors or toward avoiding or stopping misbehaviors is optimal.

Discipline is *flexible, corrective redirection only at significant moments.* This parenting maxim cannot be emphasized enough. The best adult responses and directives are grounded in understanding the dynamic and changing needs of children and families; hence, adult directions flexibly geared rather than rigidly unalterable toward inevitable changes have the best chances of being met with mutual success. Significant moments connote targeting unacceptable and dangerous behaviors that are absolutely unacceptable. In other words, not every single event viewed undesirable is targeted. Only those behaviors that are urgently dangerous or morally unacceptable should be highlighted selectively and dealt with directly.

It is always important to carefully determine the "battles" one chooses to address. Deciding ahead of time what is urgent versus what is of lower priority helps prepare for parenting "on the spot." Once the decision for a limit is set and communicated in a clear and concrete way, it should remain firm. Certainly, this can be difficult at times, but efforts in this direction can have immense long-term payoffs. Involving children in discussions of the reasons for rules and limits is significantly helpful and should always be part of this process.

Many behaviors can be ignored if they are deemed to be safe. Not directly addressing undesirable behaviors avoids reinforcing them. Parents, for example, need to discern impish and overly enthusiastic explorations and silliness from dangerous, willfully oppositional, and malicious behaviors. This differentiation may be hard to do when parents automatically react to undesired behaviors as if it were a reflection that their child is not as "perfect" as hoped. This delineation also may invoke parental guilt at not being as "great" a parent as they or others expect them to be.

Corrective redirection in response to unacceptable behaviors operates to set implicit limits within an atmosphere that minimizes excessive intrusiveness. When parents behave in a nondomineering manner, cooperation rather than opposition is solicited. Selectively targeting undesirable behaviors and informing children why decisions have been made in this way involves setting explicit limits authoritatively.

The parental mood accompanying such "learning moments" is most effective when it is sober, firm, and warm—not caustic, frightening, violent, or aggressive. Such a tone averts fear and unnecessary shame, allowing children to learn more effectively. Effective discipline avoids humiliation, embarrassment, and dehumanization. Using sensitivity and tact is always beneficial. This approach prevents trauma—the feeling of being abused and tortured—to both child and parent. The child's dignity and self-worth are thus preserved. Effective discipline includes a calm, firm, decisive tone of voice. Such a disciplinary style fosters increased motivation for cooperation and enhanced receptivity for improvement.

When a child misbehaves, a parent's immediate reaction might be to yell loudly under the impact of this stressor. For children who are preadolescent, misbehavior can indicate that more acceptable alternatives are not accessible in memory at the moment or have not yet been learned. With this in mind, it is best for parents to remain calm, to identify and articulate in clear, simple language the inferred feelings involved (first in the child, and later on the caregiver's part), then offer redirection to acceptable behaviors. Often, it is useful to say to the child, "I think you must be feeling upset, frustrated, and angry. Rather than hit or throw things, it's better to say how you feel by using words. Tell me how you feel, and we'll figure out what's happening together." The aforementioned demonstrates an example of parents' modeling of problem-solving skills in action.

Staying as calm as possible cannot be overemphasized. This fact is of special note when feelings of anger—in the child and elicited in the adult— are triggered. Anger stimulates reactive anger, which provokes the fight-or-flight reaction. Feelings associated with fighting are "hot" and often uncontrollable. Flight reactions involve denying the unpleasant situation and leaving the field. Both fighting and fleeing increase angry feelings. The payoff for reacting with anger, therefore, is a "no win–no win" situation for everyone involved. At these times parental self-reflection is a must in order to allow for effective parenting to take place. Such methodology also provides children with a model of how to handle such situations in the future.

Helping children to identify feelings within themselves and as they are expressed in others is essential in promoting healthy emotional development, intelligence, and self-management. The ability to reasonably communicate subtle emotional states fosters an enhancement of emotional regulation, which is a significant substructure of consciously experienced feelings. It builds social intelligence, social skills, and social competence. These abilities are often referred to as *sociability*.

This strategy is sometimes called a "validation of feelings." Accepting the verbal expression of feelings and helping children to articulate the feelings behind behaviors are part of a corrective redirection demonstrating warmth and tolerance. Identifying core feelings in words, then describing the behavioral actions as "bad," which means unhelpful, and why they are unhelpful, allows everyone to pause and step back. A direct instruction such as, "When you are mad, don't push. Instead, say in words how you are feeling, then come to me to figure out the next step," offers a child the opportunity for multiple learning moments over time. Validation of feelings thus entails accurately describing both positive and negative presentations, no matter how painful. For example, when anger, rage, or sadness is expressed, silence, blunted responses, or false reassurances are unhelpful and ineffective.

This positive approach to discipline is an engaging inducement reflecting mutual team effort rather than authoritarian, coercive, or adversarial control. Forceful imposition and harsh indoctrination of rules and ideologies is counterproductive, if not traumatic. *Perpetually maintaining attitudes and operating principles whose underlying premise is teamwork cannot be emphasized enough.*

Proper discipline teaches corrective redirection and fosters self-containment. Proper discipline fosters helping children conform to the expectations of parents and society. If parents support decisions and directions with understandable reasons, this demonstrates—in living example—how to make informed choices. In later life, containment is motivated by the inner self rather than needing to be externally imposed, namely self-discipline.

Discipline and nurturance are linked to social and emotional developmental outcomes. Love, in all its manifestations from feeling states to attitudes and behaviors, becomes the underlying energy driving the spark, organization, and modulation of all emotions.

Emotional development is the development of love in the broadest sense. This maturation occurs through the enactment of nurturance in all its permutations, notably those that constrain negative emotions, such as anger and envy. To these ends, this book offers a primer toward intelligent emotional well-being and management.

Relationships and emotional processes support the growth of the mind and intellectual faculties. These influence how learning occurs and what is learned. The fruits that gradually mature in adolescence and adulthood include self-awareness, self-management, social awareness, relationship skills, and responsible decision making. Remembering to focus on good behaviors optimizes success.

1.3 The Third Parenting Superfactor: "Living Example"

Providing example—that is, demonstrating appropriate behaviors—speaks much louder than precept, rule, and verbal instruction. The phrase "*You are the message*" denotes living example. Put differently, parenting is not merely a series of demands; it is a continuous, living, warm, and communicative flow of directive preferences experientially offered to guide a child's development.

The composite "you" is the effective message. Skill development in the face of exposure to human interaction is a powerful learning tool. Successful parenting and effective discipline are powerful and influential when conveyed assertively and decisively in a framework of compassionate sensitivity demonstrated most persuasively by living example. Compassionate sensitivity is antithetical to attitudes that are merely egocentric, brazen, brash, impudent, inordinately assertive, or perceived as boldly "obnoxious." Parents must take great care that such noncooperative and disagreeable models are not exhibited, since children may internalize and then identify with them. The medium of the caregiver in his or her entirety gives adhesiveness to all motivational messages. Current research studies lend overwhelming scientific support to this foundational idea.

Each individual's biomental structure contains what has been called a "social brain." The functional expressions of this innate neural substrate encompass social perception, social cognition, and a plethora of social communication skills. Some of these include the abilities to differentiate between self and other, to perceive others as having emotions and thoughts, and to infer the intentions and motivations of others. Brain areas correlated with these skills for shared understandings are the superior temporal sulcus and the amygdala.

The family is a system with a culture. A culture is both an explicit and implicit set of attitudes, behaviors, values, beliefs, preferences, goals, and customs that guides the flow of the family system. This family culture by its living example, to a large extent, becomes imprinted on infants and children as they grow within and witness their family's everyday life. This influence is especially powerful in the preschool and early elementary school years to about age seven. During this early time and extending into adulthood, children are situated in complex ecological systems. These relationships include not only family, but also the multilayered networks that encompass the people and logistics comprising the extended culture of community, society, nation, and so forth.

Example is bidirectional; it is a dynamic flow between parent as presenter and child as receiver. Children naturally identify with what they perceive and experience in parental attitudes and behaviors. The parental relationship presents to children a set of values, beliefs, and behaviors—intimacy, problem solving, conflict resolution, balancing work and home life—that they adhere to into adulthood when modifications may occur in the course of new experiences. Living example is thus a performance demonstration of continuing transactional sensitivity.

Children learn from the world around in a number of ways over time. One of the earliest examples of children's need and ability to orient to the world is the observable phenomenon of *social referencing*. This behavior can be seen in infants as early as ten months of age. When infants find themselves in novel, ambiguous, or potentially distressing situations, they look back to the faces of mother or father to see the parental emotional expression. It is presumed that they can differentiate positive from negative expressions and then respond to uncertain events accordingly. This ability contributes to learning suitable responses to difficult situations. Toddlers, eager to actively explore in more expanded ways, such as by locomotion, use social referencing to compare their own emotional preferences with those expressed by trusted adults. They may show behaviors that indicate personal preferences rather than those referenced by the adult. Such manifestations imply increasing autonomy and a developing sense of self. Social referencing between child and caregivers is a prominently shared interpersonal behavior throughout the childhood years.

Such observational learning is the process of learning new responses by watching the behavior of another. In many ways, parental modeling provides children with the capacity to develop more keen psychological sight—"eyes to see" and, in addition, the language to formulate questions and articulate inner experiences. This complex activity includes attention, retention of the experience by forming an inner memory, motoric reproducibility, and a child's motivational level. Perceived similarities between observer and model as well as positive perceptions about the model make this type of learning salient.

Children are keen observers. They carefully watch and, in turn, internalize a parent's emotional attitudes, tone of language, expression, gesture, posture, and behaviors. This entire process is the vehicle that is communicated and assimilated. Reciprocal, active participation in promoting desired behaviors reinforces this practice.

The enduring power of example can be seen clearly, for example, in middle-aged adults who suddenly see that they are "acting just like my parents." This oftentimes abrupt realization is startling, at first troubling, but nonetheless revealing. Gradually, one realizes that the early influence and modeling internalized from parental behaviors is, in fact, real and long lasting.

Modeling by example also helps children identify with, imitate, learn, and internalize such personality characteristics as patience, empathy, self-reliance, trust, and respectful interpersonal attitudes. Good manners, civility, and social competence are positive behavioral outcomes of this process. When parents inspire their children in a wholesome manner, children feel a sense of admiration, which counters negative and envious feelings. Rather than sensing themselves as inferior, children who are positive and see parents as positive in attitude and enthusiasm are stimulated to act similarly.

Parents can also model basic interactional patterns that clearly demonstrate that people do not have to be "perfect" to get along, love, and be loved. For example, parents demonstrating joint responsibility and sharing both financial and domestic duties offers children a fair view of different gender styles and gender cooperativeness. Mothers realize that often they need to clearly ask for what is needed from fathers. Fathers typically respond more cooperatively to such direct requests. School-age children, moreover, who do housework with their fathers, for example, have been shown to better get along with peers and perform more competently in team activities outside the home.

Observational learning becomes notably influential in the elementary school years in the context of observing and interacting with peers. The earlier this foundation is established, the easier it will be to navigate the challenges and difficulties that emerge in adolescence. Particularly important is the early creation of a sense of respect and value for interpersonal communication.

In the adolescent years, observational learning is not only fed by peer interactions and pressure, but to a large extent by what is experienced through the media. This fact suggests that the material seen on the Internet and experienced—sometimes in 3-D—in movie theaters has a powerful effect on stimulating emotions, fantasies, and vicarious wishes for power and romance. It is therefore vital that parents closely monitor children's participation in these influential activities since their negative impact may lead to behaviors that are undesirable.

The enduring influence of observational learning transmits itself across generations. What children witness parents do becomes so strongly internalized that later on in life these children, now as adults, reenact scenarios observed in childhood. Children repeat in adulthood what they are exposed to in childhood. This phenomenon, to a large extent, is the mechanism whereby culture is transmitted from generation to generation.

Lastly, a poignant example of this principle can be found in the work of the German academic scholars, Jacob and Wilhelm Grimm (c.1800). Their studies in philology (the development of written language: history, structure, and meanings) produced voluminous folklore. The tale "The grandfather and his grandson" reflects their findings about the transmission of beliefs. The story describes a family of mother, father, four-year-old son, and grandfather. When the grandfather became aged and feeble, he was removed from his seat at the dining table and assigned to have meals in an obscure corner of the kitchen, using only the barest of utensils and a bowl. After a time, parents noticed their young son in his fantasy play pushing some pieces of wood together on the floor. When they questioned him, he said he was making a little trough for mother and father to use for their meals when they got old like grandfather. Parents began to sob, and realized that their example had created conditions that would be reenacted with them in the future. This realization altered their view of the aged grandfather. After sober self-reflection, they returned him to the dining table to restore his dignity and their family's integrity.

2. THE TWO INTERPERSONAL REALMS THAT STRUCTURE PARENTING

The family and parenting have compositional features that include both structure and systems. *Structure* denotes an organization made up of content that exists in a dynamic mental and material space with bounded components that interact. Structure may also contain subsets of components whose arrangement and relations with each other and with the larger structure continuously interact. *System* denotes processes in dynamic interaction; the term "systems" emphasizes the different relationships that form and reconfigure as the flow of change occurs within structures. The elements of empathy, both in *statu nascendi* and in fruition, design these realms.

Dynamic processes are systems in families that transpire in two overarching interpersonal realms and serve to structure parenting. These realms are (1) example, identification, and imitation, and (2) transactional sensitivity. The ways that these domains are configured in varying family arrangements establishes stability and creates a family's identity.

2.1 Example, Imitation, and Identification

Psychodynamic processes between parents and children actively structure both the relationships between them and the individual structure of each one's personality. From the child's vantage point, example, imitation, and identification are processes of learning from adults. The other interpersonal axiom is that of *transactional sensitivity*, which this book defines as the exquisitely sensitive exchange of conscious and nonconscious information between family members, especially parents and children. As previously mentioned, the latest scientific research, notably relating to development in infancy, attests to this.

The vital importance of parental example in raising children runs throughout the entire body of this book. Children, particularly up to age seven years, naturally imitate parents. They also imitate a great deal from the surrounding environment. Children are natural witnesses.

While this idea of the impressionability of children is generally recognized, it is necessary to clarify some of its nuances. For example, *imitation* typically means reproducing what one sees and hears, a sort of concrete mimicry. Imitation follows actual forthright example and demonstration. Imitation suggests a conscious or consciously aware replication.

The term *copying* denotes a more independent and self-directed duplication of what is seen and heard. It does not necessarily require any preliminary demonstration or living example. The term "copying" used here includes reproducing something from printed matter, for example, copying a circle using a picture of a circle. It may also result from something remembered.

The term *identification*, by contrast, encompasses a mostly nonconscious, automatic, implicit, and silent internalization of what is witnessed. This mode of acquisition notably hallmarks infancy. After earliest infancy, this process may also be accompanied by some consciously aware and intentionally guided imitation and self-directed copying. This identification is the premier biomental process characterized by an emotionally charged interactive absorption.

Whereas the terms *imitation* and *copying* refer to external, concrete events, the term *identification* typically refers to the implicit psychological internalization of emotional attitudes and behavioral styles. The covertly internalized imprints of identification are usually integrated into the person and, in turn, automatically reappear in everyday life.

A developmental example of imitation is the ability of the twenty-four-month old to draw a vertical line after observing the explicit demonstration of another. At about thirty-six months, when biomental development becomes more complex and relatively more self-sufficient, not only can the three year old imitate drawing this basic shape, but he or she can also copy a circle, not by a person's example, but merely from a static representation, as from shapes on a page.

In this book, the terms *imitation, copying, identification*, and *internalization* will be used informally and at times interchangeably unless their specific differences are highlighted.

When *imitation* is referred to in this book, however, it is a shorthand term to suggest the more complex notion of *imitative identification*. The term "imitation" simply used may appear to denote mimicry. In this book, the term *imitation* strongly connotes *imitative identification*, which presumes identification to be its underlying psychological process. Imitative identification occurs most intensely during the earliest years. Thus, in early childhood before ages six or seven, the nonconscious incorporation of aspects of another forms the foundation of the child's "learning" from adults. In this process, the imitator or identifier becomes more like the other. During imitative identification, the child first notices some similarity between himself and the other and goes on to see another attribute that is viewed desirable; the child then psychologically "keys in" and acquires this attitude or behavior.

The nonconscious and automatic aspects of imitation are greatest in the earliest years (newborn period to about two to three years). While infants gradually spend increasingly longer periods of the day in conscious wakefulness, the still-unmatured faculties of memory and expressive language limit the ability to imitate. By about eighteen months, more linguistic and conceptual competencies are achieved.

The original work of Piaget described this point in intellectual development as marked by the achievement of *object permanence* at eighteen months. Later researchers found object permanence to be rooted much earlier in the middle of the first year of life. Unlike previously used mental mechanisms—mental schema that depended totally on perceptions and bodily movements—Piaget portrays the toddler as becoming capable of inventing new means of obtaining goals. This occurs not by direct actions on objects, but by mental representations characterized by novel insights.

These steps are also accompanied by the incrementally expanding capacity for greater conscious awareness. By the preschool years, ages three to five, imitative identification is accompanied by even greater degrees of conscious imitation, while maintaining its base in automatic, nonconscious identification. Many parents begin to recognize the need to change aspects of their own long-standing behaviors as children begin to mirror them in obvious ways during this stage of development.

The practical point made here is that from birth to about age seven, children learn principally through identification and imitation, not by intellectually oriented instruction. The pressures resulting from today's inordinate value placed on speed, efficiency, and acceleration can be stress provoking. The sounds of parents telling their children to "hurry up!" are all-too familiar occurrences in contemporary family life. Recognizing the potential outcomes of this mentality requires caregivers to step back and reassess priorities in a mindful way.

Perceptive parenting remains mindful when a parent realizes that modern technology must not replace the nontechnical expression of people's humanity as mothers, fathers, and *humane* beings. For example, when children see how adults speak with one another and negotiate, how they prepare meals, how they do housework, how they tend a garden, drive a car, and treat children, these living examples become impressed mentally and are used as models for future behaviors.

Teaching children younger than seven years old by *didactic discussions* can be part of helping children to learn, but it plays a secondary role in terms of its effectiveness. Learning by imitation and through activities of movement that include the physical body remains primary. It is not useful and may be ineffectual to teach children under seven using solely intellectual methods. In terms of addressing the whole child, such an overemphasis on direct intellectual instruction may produce lopsided results. Put simply, the principal ways that parents can help children learn include *doing with, reading to,* and permitting children time to engage in *free, relatively unstructured play* in the context of observing and imitating responsible adults. This approach enhances epistemophilic literacy—the inner refinement of a love for knowledge. It also lays the groundwork for future elaborated expressions arising from within.

2.2 Transactional Sensitivity

This book coins the phrase *transactional sensitivity* and finds it useful in highlighting a dynamic set of psychological forces in the parent-child relationship that exert a maximal effect on development. The term also underscores the primacy of such forces in transactions among all family members and in the family as a system. In addition, its significance is applicable to all interpersonal relationships. Transactional sensitivity is an essential ingredient of emotionally meaningful communication, information gathering, and responsiveness. It is developmental in that it grows and refines itself in complexity over time.

Transactional sensitivity denotes a focal point of interdependent engagement comprising the conscious and nonconscious exchange of information, notably the communication of expectations and needs. Interactive signal detection occurs on multiple levels, some of which are conscious and many of which are nonconscious. These attentive focusings encompass, to some degree, strong elements of mental pause, perspective taking, and empathy in developing children, adolescents, and adults. The degree of empathy experienced decreases extraneous interactional noise.

Transactional sensitivity denotes the need to be understood and the process of being affected by the quality of this understanding, particularly in infancy. Its intuitive elements add considerably to the level of clarity, fidelity, and detail included in observation and response among family members. Transactional sensitivity is the kinetically sentient experience of people interacting with one another to achieve congruence. These signal detection interactions occur as each person grasps, understands, and is influenced by the emotional, cognitional, and motivational states of mind exchanged between family members. Such feedback helps regulate the quality of each participant's effectance—the impulse to problem solve and demonstrate competence.

The main elements of this resonant exchange include motivational messages and the state of mind of each member of the relationship. The latter entails several steps: remaining receptive, a reflective transformation of information, being influenced by, and in turn influencing the other through a *synchronous responsiveness*. This mutuality is an experiential interdependence that encompasses giving, receiving, and adaptivity. Both the emotional and cognitive dimensions of empathy are present, but, as part of transactional sensitivity, they have a prominent orientation toward action.

The quality of transactional sensitivity depends, in an imperfect way, on how well a parent holistically grasps the child's biomental disposition and matches expectations, responsiveness, and guidance to fit the specific context of this reciprocal interaction at any given time. Transactional sensitivity is effective to the extent that its rational and subrational components are integrated. Its fidelity is never 100 percent, because hidden variables abound that transcend mere computational logic. When successful, it is sufficient to produce a meaningful exchange. This transactional responsivity in adults presumes forethought and reflection instead of blind reactivity. Although children, by definition, are little, they are constantly in the process of developing. To view them solely as small creatures who lack full capacity is to undermine their potential and inevitable biomental expansion.

The family group, in fact, is a transactional system. The term *psychodynamics* denotes the fluctuating system of regulatory psychological processes occurring within and between each member. Each significantly influences other members on a variety of different levels and in a variety of ways, including emotionally and behaviorally. In this bidirectionality between and among individuals and systems, each member is sensitive to the explicit and implicit communications of others. Each individual then responds in characteristic ways, and, in turn, influences the other and the family as a whole.

Thus, not only are parents guides for their children, but children also act as guides to their parents. In this role, children elicit, sometimes subtly, their needs from their parents. When proper feedback from parent to child and from child to parent occurs, each person's sense of effectance is enhanced. In this energetic give-and-take, the overall trajectory of the family moves in ways specific to the dynamics of that unique family. This book highlights this individual and family dynamic in the phrase *transactional sensitivity*.

In fact, at crucial developmental ages, such as the toddler phase, the two-year-old's exuberance, strong headedness, and natural inclination for opposition may act as a mirror allowing parents to reflect on similar qualities perceived within themselves. To the extent that these realizations become obvious and, perhaps, distressing, "learning moments" can offer parents pause for self-reflection, self-exploration from a secure base, and an opportunity for personal change. Parents may particularly notice these insights arising during struggles involving *interpersonal control* as discussed in chapter 3.

The family as a whole—a complex adaptive system—participates in this mutuality on a macroscopic level. On a microscopic level, the infant-mother relationship, in fact, is the primal template that characterizes the genesis of this transactional sensitivity. Components of this interaction include the following: sensitive and reflective maternal receptivity; the infant's ability to recognize the implicit meaning of a parent's emotional expression and response; sensitive parents recognizing the implicit communications of the infant and child; and, at each moment of this dynamic exchange, each person reconfiguring experience so that personal learning and interpersonal adaptation may occur.

The early infant-mother relationship is a *contingent sharing* of both sequential and simultaneous experience in a holistic engagement. This prototypical transactional sensitivity occurs on numerous conscious and nonconscious levels whose parameters are dynamically interrelated rather than linear. Infants participate in transactional sensitivity, notably through their innate acuity to grasping rhythms and biomental containment kinetics. The infant-mother interaction, moreover, is a dialectic that promotes "becoming"—a person.

Parenting, typically mothering during the early years, elicits the infant's active engagement that stimulates development. This relationship has both formative and transformative interdependent relevance in constructing and organizing mental functioning. This particularly pertains to the development of *emotional intelligence*, which is the ability to integrate cognitive processes with feelings to understand emotions in self and others and to support emotional self-management and social interaction. This dynamic and kinetic interactivity along with the construct of the *epistemophilia within the self*—a search for affiliative and meaningfully salient relations—is discussed at length in chapter 3.

2.3 Empathy: Design of Meaningfully Salient Connectedness

The idea and lived expression of empathy are integral features of biomental child development. This theme in all its variations runs throughout this book. At this juncture, a brief discussion will set the tone that characterizes this sensitive transactional activity.

Empathy, in essence, is instrumental activity that encompasses an individual's active, intuitive grasp of another. This presumes some level of self-reflection, however fragile. Empathy's emotional components, predominant in preverbal infancy, suggest a highly charged directed state of interest, appreciation, and lingering. This occurs through transient, participatory cognition mostly subliminal and nonconscious but also intentionally conscious, with the latter organizing toward the end of the first year and thereafter. Empathy has elements of imaginative projection and introjection that operate dynamically, synergistically, and simultaneously.

Empathy, while primarily an emotional grasp and reactivity, has significant cognitive and social components. These nonconscious information-gathering operations—"intuition"—transcend mere reason. *Intuition* encompasses nonconscious information processing, subliminal priming, implicit learning and memory, gestalt detection, and pattern recognition. All these occur in a state of responsive immediacy.

Empathy's cognitive component presumes the ability to pause, anticipate a grasp of another's perspective, and linger in an exploratory manner with the feelings, ideas, and attitudes that arise. These first phases typically are preludes to helping by means of both gesture and suggested action plans.

Empathy is predicated on intuitive listening and the process of emotional and cognitive understanding. Listening and understanding are the motors that drive transactional sensitivity. As empathy expands over time and self-reflection, more consciously developed insights emerge and amplify the understanding that both the subject and object of empathetic interactions experience. Biomental child development places heavy emphasis on empathy's richness in terms of an individual's innate and developed awareness of care and compassion both interpersonally and socially.

3. PARENTING CREATES MEANINGFULNESS

3.1 Meaningfully Salient Parenting

A discussion of creative and meaningfully salient parenting introduces many ideas that are useful for a deeper understanding of the life of a child. The avalanching pace of modern living requires periodic pause, reflection, and a consideration of basic values in order to maintain balance and mental equanimity.

Meaningful parenting helps children explore themselves and enhance their own development. Such an attitude and style sharpens children's notions of relevance for both the larger and smaller aspects that make up life skills and meaningful relatedness. Thoughtful and intelligent parenting enriches both child and parent insofar as meaningful, satisfying, and purposeful living is concerned.

Helpful parenting creates conditions in which children are empowered to develop themselves in the context of the family, and eventually, in society. Families function best when they act as teams in which a range of shared responsibilies are decided, clearly set forth, and expected. Parents in such systems take leadership roles, setting the tone and emotional climate for positive, enthusiastic, and healthy family life.

Positive parenting aims to awaken conscious awareness, gather attention, and enhance participation in real-time life events. Such parenting is attentive and sensitive to the virtually infinite emotional and motivational palette of a child's inner and outer life. Extended family members can also be instrumental in fostering early talents and curiosities that may open exciting new paths of discovery for the child. In fact, enlisting the help of relatives can be an important parenting strategy in this and other ways, such as fostering psychological resilience.

Parents optimize success when they work to recognize and foster strengths in their children. Limitations in ability may also be identified. When challenges are recognized, children should be provided with new and alternative opportunities for modifying these impediments. An individual's substantial biomental plasticity needs to be recognized and enlisted in such endeavors. Both supporting a child's strengths and remediating his or her vulnerabilities increase a child's psychological resilience.

Meaningful parenting intelligently creates conditions that permit children the freedom to "show" themselves, in a sense their "essence," by expressing their individuality, interests, talents, and even "nastiness"—with all its connotations—when in an environment of safety. Supplying nurturance, discipline, and corrective guidance helps a child achieve integration of body, mind, and heart. Such work, rather than being indoctrination, can be viewed as an educational and learning celebration. In this process, the living child within adults also awakens. This stirring of youth, in itself, further encourages the personal development of parents.

Parenting is a creative engagement for the sake of strengthening and enhancing normal development. Parenting skills are not, on the other hand, psychotherapy for treating psychiatrically disturbed children. Although parenting imparts beneficence, support, and repair, it cannot replace professional care in the face of mental illness.

The following may be understood to be first principles of effective parenting: the importance of both parents and children always maintaining a discriminating sense of reality, being aware of false hope, identifying misleading romanticisms, and recognizing and modulating extremes of emotion, overvalued ideas, and behaviors.

In addition, it is important for parents to manage constructively negative states of mind within themselves and their children. Negative states of mind include anxiety, worry, depression, hostility, pessimism, irrational prejudice, a sense of superiority, and so forth. In addition, any state or expression of emotion may also be viewed as negative if it is extremely frequent, intense, or exclusive and unmodulated by a wider range of suitable feelings.

Many parental attitudes come from past experiences and can reflect the many strengths and sometimes limitations of how one was parented during his or her own upbringing. A very subtle phenomenon that is not uncommon—and not abnormal—involves parents' feelings of implicit envy about what they never had and what their children now possess. It is important to reflect on these feelings and other possible unresolved issues and to make adaptive corrections when needed. The task becomes to figure out how adults can experience and guide children and adolescents in nondefensive ways without becoming overwhelmed, distracted, or shutting down.

3.2 The "Everydayness" of Being with Your Children

One of the important components of meaningful parenting is spending quality time with one's children. To be sure, there is no endless supply of time in modern society. The time that is available for children, however, needs to be spent in shared, valued interactions.

Good parenting consists of a certain "everydayness" of time spent together. Noncomplacency and not taking family life for granted characterize the quality of this time. In this sense, parents also need to take time for rest and personal relaxation. Support from spouses, extended family members, and friends are helpful and lend themselves to stress reduction.

Such an "everyday attitude" presumes maintaining a genuine sense of self and an authentic rapport with the child. This process may not be automatic, although it can become meaninglessly routine and ordinary if its specialness is not appreciated. It is a practice that may have to be examined periodically so that it can be renewed—daily, if necessary. Vital factors in parenting include the general attitude of parents and the way in which the ordinary details of living are viewed and managed.

3.3 Meaningful Parenting as Containment: Starting-Stopping

Biomental child development recognizes that parents' roles are complex and diverse. One frequently underestimated central task is that of recognizing and supporting the development of containment. Parents should not overlook the features of containment, first established in infancy and childhood. Perhaps the first instance of containment is that of infant within mother before birth. While this fact may appear to denote the physical aspects of containing, biomental child development understands it as a reality characterized by innumerable biological and mental integrations. All of these support safety and security, and implicitly minimize a sense of vulnerability.

Containment, as a superordinate design, is a proposition that encompasses biomental boundaries, limitations, self-modulation, self-regulation, pause, and the interpersonal and social ramifications of each. These biomental spatial relations are essential to the development of infants, and, by extension, are essential to the personhood of all human beings. In the biomental perspective, containment also strongly connotes the construct of "face"—namely, the actual face along with the body as a whole demonstrating mental restraint, dignity, poise, pleasantness, agreeableness, and cooperativeness.

A sense of boundaries—an implicit sense of starting and stopping—can be understood to exist on several levels. Elements include the skin containing the body, the body in relation to other bodies, and all levels of the psychological sense that one has about him or herself, as well as relationships of closeness and distance with others. This psychological side, in a sense, is the mind's "skin."

The capacity for nonconscious containment—a cohesive sense of self-integrity—transcends mere discipline acquired through conscious learning. Containment here refers to the psychological concept that encompasses how one implicitly experiences himself or herself as a relatively coherent individual. It counters unqualified chaos and unbridled emotion. The enormity and complexity of this subliminal and unwitting psychological function can only be addressed in this section in barest outline here.

Containment includes developing an awareness of and capacity to contain emotions, impulses, and the need to react in automatic and regressive ways. The normative experience of "urgency" on all levels undergoes a homeostatic modulation, and the faculty for "pause" begins its expansion. This emerging sense of coherent self is reflected in the developing ability to wait over extended periods to obtain satisfaction for needs, desires, and wishes.

Emotions are automatic, brief biomental states of arousal that typically alert and attract people to pleasant versus unpleasant situations. Unpleasant situations connote threat, vulnerability, and insecurity. Parents need to identify emotions and be able to maintain an active management strategy when these biomental states arise both in themselves and in their children. This ability helps support a child develop self-containment, including self-concept, self-integrity, and self-esteem. Self-containment connotes reduced anxiety, and a level of self-confidence implying self-efficacy.

An important dimension of this process for adults is becoming aware of the naturally *regressive pull* toward more immature behaviors that may arise when around children. This regressive pull is inevitable. How it is experienced and handled, however, is the result of the mix of integrity, flexibility, adaptability, rigidity, and defensive structure of the adult.

In optimal circumstances, adults who are well integrated have an established set of mental defense mechanisms that are flexible enough to manage anxiety and its underlying, conflicting fantasies. These mechanisms limit the potentially incapacitating effects of intense stressors. Ideally, these adults are also capable of enlisting mature coping skills to adapt to changing contexts successfully. Both defensively overreacting and defensively withdrawing in challenging situations are less effective responses.

Adults ordinarily take a leadership and guidance role with children. At suitable times, these material positions can be performed in less adult-like and more porous ways that match the child's current and fluid capabilities. Such actions may involve speaking in a simpler fashion, becoming animated, and engaging in imaginative, play-like behaviors that have elements of silliness. Of course, this performance is a temporary excursion suitable to the containment needs of the child at select moments. Adults who retain a healthy sense of personal containment or ego integrity remain elastic in their adult position. Their defenses are flexible and adaptive. This ability ensures that parent-child interpersonal boundaries remain intact and distinct. Maintaining a healthy sense of humor is part of this.

People typically experience negative emotions such as sadness and hate as being "bad," while positive emotions such as love and surprise are felt as being "good." This perceived association is strongest in adults and evident in their discomfort with negative emotions. Negative feelings are often accompanied by a sense of vulnerability and anxiety. Being confronted with children's wide range of positive and negative emotions requires parental sensitivity in helping children to recognize and properly contain all emotional states, especially distressing ones, in developmentally appropriate ways.

Attention to issues of containment also addresses the developing capacity of infants and children to regulate their own biomental impulsivity. Impulsivity is the inability to delay thought and action. Chronological age and developmental status directly influence one's ability to regulate impulses. In the toddler and preschool years, parents' interactions with children in the context of the parental need to say "no" provides both a braking function on interrupting undesirable behaviors and a model for children to begin to internalize. "No" indicates a "stop signal," whereas "yes" offers viable alternative behaviors. In essence, impulsivity is intolerance to experiencing delay. Impulsivity in attention, motor activity, and decision making can become significant problems that impair learning and contribute to a variety of behavioral problems in childhood, adolescence, and adulthood. This idea of containment, in fact, has strong biomental underpinnings.

For example, the impulsivity evident in children and adolescents is associated with both environmentally experienced containment as well as brain maturation over time. Flexible goal-directed behaviors may incrementally be attained as certain brain areas mature over time. In particular, impulse control (capacity for restraint) found in the frontal lobes and higher cerebral cortex exerts its influence by modulating the impulsivity of the subcortical brain. This is a gradual maturation from infancy into young adulthood. Of course, all this brain development occurs within the context of parenting, which can influence the neurobiological course; this is the idea of biomental maturation in the context of experience.

The idea of *self-regulation* draws meaning from such diverse concepts as sense of self, ego boundaries, personal space, regulating the intensity of emotion, impulse control, intention, inhibition, suppression, delay of impulse to act, preference, habit, choice, and intentional action that have a sequence with beginnings and endings. These mental operations—some requiring conscious awareness and others being more nonconsciously reactive—begin at the first moment of life and gradually yet steadily develop in complex and intricate ways over a lifetime.

Containment, therefore, refers to self-containment, interpersonal containment, and prosocial behaviors. The substantive capacity for self-containment in adulthood goes beyond the individual's feeling constrained to merely conform to the expectations of others—the group and extended society. Instead, it centers on internalized self-regulatory values in efforts toward attaining and maintaining healthy socialization.

Containment in its social sense includes ideas of sociability and civility. These encompass restraint prompted by being aware of social norms, values, and constraints. Society's and one's own sense of "others looking" at oneself develop early and support sociability. The safety functions attributed to conscience, morality, and ethics derive from the structure and quality of one's sense of containment. The conceptualization of humankind in constructs such as "individual and group," "individual and community," and "individual as part of a civilization" are directly related to these social constructions.

These cultural concepts correlate with the age-old philosophical construct of the "one and the many," namely the conceptual underpinnings that influence crucial research and practices in various field applications. Such constructs are characterized by their simplicity, resilience, and limited scope. These ideas are further elaborated in chapter 6. From this perspective, a developed sense of personal containment facilitates successful integration into society by affording the individual properly modulated and constrained impulsive, antisocial, and destructive impulses and behaviors. In many indirect ways, these cultural and philosophical ideas correlate with the sense of being alone even though affiliated with others, and being lonely in the sense of feeling incomplete and distressed by the sense of absent connectedness.

On a personal level, self-containment refers to how an individual coherently holds together subjectively possessed impulses, ideas, emotions, and bodily awareness, as well as the expression of these subjective pieces into externally modulated behaviors. This containing function of the self connotes how mental contents are experienced, handled, processed, managed, integrated, and maintained. Controlled impulsivity, reasoned volition, and self-efficacy are various expressions of proper self-containment. These contribute to where in both material and mental space a person senses he or she begins and ends. The basic sense of ego- and self-boundaries denotes where the individual psychologically begins and ends in relation to others. This contained sense of self influences the interpersonal process of how to engage and how to disengage in everyday relationships. A crucial element at the core of this developing skill is first knowing how to prepare for the implementation of this skill.

This state of affairs is launched through the primary relationship between infant and parent and takes shape in different ways as social contact with others occurs thereafter. A child's normal emotional grasp of its interpersonal activities provides salient social information that builds the developing capacity for healthy relationships. Experiencing this "social glue" is a pillar of development.

The issue of containment is an underpinning of the framework of this book. It runs through the entire text, both explicitly and implicitly. A central idea is that the mother typically operates as a living, dynamic, and interactive container for the developing infant. Her level of involvement is characterized by an exquisite receptivity and juxtaposition both physical and psychological, reflecting transactional sensitivity.

Sensitive mothering denotes openness to and acceptance of the child's emotional experiences. Mothers not only recognize physical needs for feeding, warmth, affectionate holding, and physical hygiene, but also sense other, less obvious emotional clusters of anguishing experiences. This "grasping" is much more than an intellectual apprehension. It is a profoundly empathetic engulfment, an identification just short of fusion. Grasping here denotes biomental handling.

In this activity, a mother's containing function remodulates these distressing contents and, in the process, the infant assimilates this constrained and less overwhelming experience. This dynamic action is described more fully in chapters 2 and 3 in sections on infancy.

In terms of father-child containment, the father's role typically comes to the foreground after infancy. From the preschool years through adolescence, the father's role is essential in its parental nurturing capacity, though it is usually different from mother's. Father's crucial influence is discussed throughout this text, with attention to his role in understanding emotional development and implementing healthy emotional skills and management by example. This is highlighted in chapter 3 in the section called "Fathering" and again addressed in chapter 6.

3.4 Children Need Parents as Guides to Navigate Transitions

A major role that a parent plays is that of a guide in the face of transitions. Parents are teachers and leaders, especially as perceived by children. Conventionally, children seek mothers for comfort and fathers for physical protection and pleasurable excitement. They experience both parents as executive "compasses," pointing toward directions that parents help navigate. Mothers often use a relationship-based, negotiable socialization style that tends to emphasize persuasion to guide children toward desirable ends. Fathers, by contrast, tend to spend less time reasoning and explaining directives; instead, they set limits by using more imperative, action-oriented instruction. Both mother and father act as mediators whose mediating function is to provide orientation, direction, and modulation during periods where moods, attitudes, self-regulation, and actual material settings are about to or are required to change.

Parental coaching can provide direction and a modulating quality to the passages children experience in the process of development. For children, transitions regularly occur on multiple levels. Two significant areas where change and needed reconfiguration occur are (1) within inner developmental dynamics and (2) in the course of outer environmental shifts. The biomental endowment of every youth drives the developmental process as the inner individual negotiates its organizing "self" with the outer world of culturally expected demands.

The outer, material aspect is obvious and important; the inner, mental facet, however, is the major arena where cognitive and emotional reorientations are needed to produce a new sense of self. When successfully negotiated, children experience a sense of mastery, accomplishment, and competence. This feat is never a singular event but is instead a recurring series of rhythmic expansions, plateaus, and organizational reconfigurations—both positive and negative.

Parental understanding and recognition of typical development is a great aid to children in helping usher them successfully through these biopsychosocial reconfigurations. Parents often expect either too much or too little. While a great deal of development is driven by a child's own powers and capacities, a facilitating environment—rational, loving, and flexible—created by attentive and helpful parents assists these transitions in proceeding more successfully.

A daily example is the group of transitions surrounding sleep. The process of preparing for bed, falling asleep, staying asleep, and then waking up involves gross and subtle complexities on numerous biomental and interpersonal levels. A large component of this nightly transition is the dual experience within separation—from awakeness and from significant adults. Separations are the emotional testing ground reflecting the quality of one's attachments and the intimacies of interpersonal investments. Being aware of this viewpoint helps parents understand and handle bedtime separations with the sensitivity they deserve. The traditional use of the nighttime lullaby in most cultures attests to this awareness and the beneficial aspects of this soothing ritual.

Another example is anticipation of the developmental ability to stand and then walk, occurring at about twelve months of age. Helping the infant navigate this transition by judicious material assistance (for example, holding up and supporting the body), preparing a physical environment of safety (for example, putting gates on stairs, securing cabinets, and removing fragile items from coffee tables), and offering psychological encouragement (for example, congratulating leg movements that approximate steps) minimizes problems and maximizes secure developmental achievements.

Furthermore, three concrete and everyday examples of some of the most difficult transitions that children face are starting kindergarten at age five, entering first grade at age six, and later transitioning into adolescence. Transitioning from one position to another has dual components. One is the actual material advance; the other involves the psychological "letting go" of what had been, and moving forward toward something new. Both require acceptance and a willingness to move on without undue resistance, resentment, or a begrudging attitude. A novel delivery system includes parents' using the verbal directive, "Take no notice," when narrating the less salient and distracting aspects around transitions. This phrase denotes alertness to the value of ignoring while using a less common expression as an alternative or supplement to the often-overused term, "Ignore." Preparing the psychological as well as material environment for these inevitable biomental reorganizations can help the forward thrust of development to proceed with greater success. Mastering transitioning skills allows for satisfaction with accomplishment and, in turn, the firmer establishment of self-esteem.

3.5 The Enduring Biomental Significance of Early Infant Motion Detection, Reaching, Grasping, and Letting Go

More complex examples of the enduring significance of transitions occurring during the first year of life can be gained from understanding and monitoring how reaching, grasping, and releasing capacities develop on the material level. All of these are not only interpersonally motivated but also intimately correlated with increasing myelination of neurons and synaptogenesis such as dendritic arborization in motor areas of the central nervous system. This section advances one of the core foundations of the author's biomental perspective. It illustrates, as will discussions of infant feeding in chapter 3, prototypical examples of the meaning of *biomental*.

In addition to the essential significance of the infant's lips and eyes in the infant's relations with mother, the hand also holds prominence. While lips and eyes activate at birth, the hand comes online slightly later. By about four months, infants regard objects in their hand, look from their hand to an object, and can engage hands in the midline. With greater motor maturity by approximately five months, the onset of a purposeful though precarious ulnar grasp becomes possible. By seven months, the infant's "handling" abilities enable it to adeptly transfer an object from hand to hand.

Grasping denotes taking hold of while releasing denotes letting go. Equally important is realizing what these behaviors may suggest from an emotional development perspective. *Psychological grasping* denotes the apprehension and wish to understand some thing, person, or event. It connotes using one's own emotions to touch those of another. This grasping is fundamentally impressionistic, only later to become nuanced by details. Grasping both reflects and informs attitudes—conscious and nonconscious orientations and responses. Grasping denotes both a sense of more and an experience of possession, and may take many forms: scooping, holding, catching, adhering, or clinging to an object, to name just a few.

The biomental perspective underscores how material milestones reflect the developmental tasks that organize a psychological self. Grasping abilities presume sufficiently developed visual capacities, permitting exploration of the environment. The role of the typical infant's vision that develops over the course of the first year of life is foundational for infant learning and all biomental development.

Sensory, perceptual, and cognitive abilities positively correlate with their developmental myelination rates in the central nervous system. Myelination, the process of surrounding neurons with physical sheaths called *myelin,* allows for improved conduction of neural signals. Myelination has a definite neurodevelopmental spatiotemporal trajectory. Neurons myelinate first in the medulla and pons, then advance to the cerebral cortex. This is followed by myelination of commissural fibers connecting the left and right cerebral hemispheres. After this, association fibers that interconnect cortical regions within the same hemisphere undergo myelination. In addition, myelination occurs from posterior brain regions forward to anterior regions. Brain myelination and interneuronal synaptic connections in the prefrontal cortex, language, auditory, and visual areas start to form at about two months before birth. These myelinating processes continue to develop at different rates.

Auditory and visual synapses begin to form at about one month of age, peak between three and ten months, then level off from five years on. Language synapses peak from about six to twelve months, then decline and level off from about six years on. Synapses in the prefrontal cortex orchestrating executive functioning—goal attainment—dramatically rise at about six months and robustly increase to peak from about ten months through the early and mid-childhood years.

Adaptive synaptic pruning, or dissolution of unneeded neuronal synapses, follows these normative periods of overproduction. New research suggests that this process of reducing white matter may be lacking in autism and so result in brain overconnectivity. Evidence from prospective studies of high-risk infants suggests that early symptoms of autism usually emerge in the first year of life or early in the second year after a period of relatively typical development. Aberrant development of white matter pathways has been detected in very recent research using diffusion tensor imaging while following high risk infants six to twenty-four months who later develop autism. Behavioral assessments of these high-risk infants at twenty-four months showed that they met criteria for autistic spectrum disorders. It is normal for children to gain and then lose neuronal connections. Synaptic anatomy or hardware dynamically changes. It is activity-dependent, and unused portions are eliminated. During later adolescence, the connections of particular neurons are streamlined by pruning, namely, elimination of axonal projections to inappropriate brain targets. The developmental timing of synaptic and axonal elimination appears highly specific across regions of the brain. Adult levels of prefrontal neuronal synapses are achieved by mid-adolescence. This biological base of myelination and synapse connectivity allows for increasing voluntary and purposeful mental control. This fact is observable, for example, in the development of effortful behaviors that become relatively less impulsive, more directed by reasoning, yet still remain crude during childhood and adolescence.

The relevance of a broad biopsychodynamic perspective is again underscored. Here, this biomental integrity viewpoint is illustrated in visual development and dynamic *motion detection*. Vision, one of the primary sensory modalities for exploring the environment, becomes activated when motion is perceived, thus triggering infant attention. By eight to twelve weeks, the infant is awake for several hours per day and so able to sense and perceive environmental inputs. While motor abilities are still frail and unmatured, vision is used to track and follow the trajectory of what is perceived as moving. As development proceeds, infant exploration and scanning coordinate to track moving objects. Conjoint movements of head and eyes become prominent.

Before the attainment of these skills, however, the young infant's mouth and lips are his chief means of contact with the world. Lips grasp and take in milk. They are innately endowed with what has been termed "suckability" for soft objects, and the nipple on the breast is the certain complement to lips, as will be discussed in chapter 3. Only at about the second quarter of the first year do arm and hand "graspability" add to the infant's repertoire of exploratory instruments.

Studies show that by three to four weeks, visual ability detects and tracks objects in motion, which implies a burgeoning sense of depth perception. By two to three months, the development of binocular vision enhances this discernment of depth. By five to seven months, pictorial depth perception is in place and further enhances exploration. From five to eleven months as crawling occurs, dimensional awareness is further strengthened.

In these perceptual realms, attention to animate objects such as people has a privileged status over attention to inanimate objects. This preference underlies the emergence of social cognition. In the second half of the first year, therefore, attention to and the tracking of the movements of both animate and inanimate objects develops. These skills elicit an urge to sense expectations about and impute meaning to such experiences, contributing to developing cognitive and emotional development and the foundations of social cognition.

As visual, postural, and motor capabilities develop, the triad of *reaching*, *grasping*, and *letting go* is used to explore and engage with the environment. Motor skills are expressed in the actions of the hand as a tool of the mind—how inanimate objects are handled, explored, and manipulated.

From birth until about seven weeks, *pre-reaching* can be detected; this is the act of attempting poorly coordinated swipes toward an object. The biomental perspective presumes at this era and thereafter an innate though inchoate awareness of relations, particularly characterized by a sense of container and containment. This may be strongly correlated with the infant's actual awareness of its physical body in relation to the mother's. These also imply an innate awareness of space or spatial relations. As mentioned previously, lips grasping nipple take milk from its containment in mother to its transferred containment into the infant. Such an introjection is and becomes reinforced as a rhythmic trajectory of introjection and projection, the latter connoting both mother's giving and also the infant's experience of projective activities such as spitting up, urinating, and so forth. The infant's skin may also be a foundation for this awareness of container and the motion paths of inside and outside.

After pre-reaching, *reaching* is the first of the triad of skills to develop; it is the outstretching of an arm aimed toward an object. *Grasping*, a related activity, follows shortly thereafter; it is the use of hand and fingers to hold, seize, and grip an object. Both skills are strongly influenced by postural stability, vision, and proprioception, which is the unconscious perception of bodily positions. Reaching and grasping both reflect and reinforce the infant's orientation and location in space. *Releasing*, or *letting go*, develops later. As will be discussed in the book's section on infancy, an infant's capacity to reach, grasp and hold on to, then release and let go of objects, follows a relatively predictable sequence.

From birth until about seven weeks, infants remain uncoordinated. Hand and arm movements at this age are described as "pre-reaching" gestures. *Gesture* is a vitally important part of human communication. It denotes any bodily motion such as turning the head, eye gaze, facial expression, reaching, pointing, and so forth. At about three months, the onset of apparently *purposeful reaching* toward an object can be seen, and this action progressively increases until four months when reaching with either one or two hands becomes more functional. At four months, using both hands—bimanual reaching—is prominent, notably bringing things to the mouth for exploration by "mouthing." By seven months, infants are able to reach for an object with only one arm, particularly when in a stable position such as sitting. Though present, two-handed reaching with unilateral prehension, clearly seen at five months, is not as prominent behaviorally until about twelve months, when bimanual use again appears to be preferred as it coincides with the emergence of walking, all of which are used to enhance postural stability.

Reaching out reflects the infant's developing sense of space, as well as his or her explorations with movement in time. Developmental sequencing manifests itself as reaching develops before *pointing*, an act that can first be observed between about twelve and a half to seventeen months. Pointing then adds to its earlier precursor, reaching. These gestures or paralinguistic communications are significant indicators of social development and typically should be apparent in this time frame.

Grasping in its reflex form is apparent at one month and proceeds through various stages. Grasping is reflected in the way the hand secures objects. The infant's and toddler's typical *actions on objects* encompasses *object exploration* and examination, which become increasingly complex after six months of age, particularly in the second year of life.

From birth to twelve months, grasping is *crude prehension*. At three months, infants may be able to reflexively grasp and shake hand toys such as rattles. At about four months, infants may be able to use two hands to bring objects to the mouth. At about five months, the onset of precarious and clumsy, though perhaps purposeful, grasping termed the *ulnar grasp* can be detected. At six months, crude but developing purposeful and controlled grasping is described as a *palmar grasp*. This is a *power grip*, which is more of a brute squeezing grasp rather than a stable and precise action. At about six to seven months, infants use the whole hand to rake in objects. An infant's transfer of objects from hand to hand at seven to eight months illustrates this emerging and fragile ability to both voluntarily hold objects and manipulatively explore them. By nine months, grasping is neat and relatively successful. Between nine and ten months, a *precision grip*—grasping an object with the finger and thumb pads—is achieved.

Around six to twelve months, infants can be seen *manipulating and exploring objects* in a variety of ways that are primitive, foundational, yet undeveloped: mouthing, banging, shaking, transferring from hand to hand, fingering, rotating, and dropping them. In general, the term "manipulation" used here denotes how the hand grasps, holds, manually examines, and uses something. Infants particularly enjoy objects with moving parts such as wheels that spin, levers that can be moved, and hinges that open and close. While these manipulative actions may include some purposeful intention, some—like mouthing and banging—may be less intentional and more instinctive.

The aforementioned repetitive behaviors are frequent and typical in the first year of life. They tend to decrease considerably by twenty-four months and are almost entirely eclipsed by other behaviors by about six years of age. If such repetitive object manipulations noticeably persist after the second year of life, notably spinning, rotating, and unusual visual exploration (such as persistent peering using a lateral gaze), atypicality in development should be suspected and professionally assessed.

Normally, however, by twelve months, a more adult ability of a *pincer grasp* (thumb touching tip of pointer finger) is attained. Developing prehension, the voluntary act of grasping, seizing, and gripping an object, permits the toddler to examine the object by various forms of more skilled, varied manipulation. From twelve to twenty-four months, grasping of objects is akin to enveloping them with one's hand. This action can be regarded as a crude form of object manipulation. The toddler with greater coordinated and cooperative bimanual skills adds rotation, flipping objects over, turning them upside down, spinning, and close examination to his typical repertoire.

Object manipulation has a developmental sequence characterized, in part, by cognitive abilities. Primitive object manipulation in earliest infancy to about eighteen months entails an examination of objects that can be differentiated from true object manipulation hallmarked by substantive conceptual abilities toward the end of the second year. Actions on and examination of objects in the first twelve months can be understood to be differing forms of more global grasping; from twelve to twenty-four months—the one-year-old—grasping is crude manipulation such as covering and uncovering boxes or other containers, turning knobs and pages, taking simple toys apart and putting them back together, and making shapes from clay; at twenty-four to thirty-six months—the two-year-old—children can turn book pages one at a time, screw and unscrew jar lids, and turn rotating handles; and from thirty-six months to four and a half years, more refined in-hand manipulation is seen. After four and a half years, true in-hand manipulation is seen and is reflected in the ability to dress and undress without help except for tying shoe laces, and being able to make the bed with help.

Before twelve months, object manipulation is very crude and accompanied by developing perceptual schemas and early global concepts with little to no detail. In the second year, object manipulation is influenced by these schemas and global concepts, but becomes reconfigured at about eighteen months by the emergence of basic-level concepts that contain greater physical detail and awareness of differences. At thirty-six months to four and a half years, object manipulation becomes more refined and is termed *in-hand manipulation*. Complementary use of both hands to explore an object or perform a task such as using a scissors or stringing beads typically becomes successful at about thirty-six months. At four and a half years of age, in-hand manipulation becomes more deft, adroit, dexterous, and agile.

The capacity to *release*, or *let go of an object*, is a more mature faculty than grasping; it develops later in the second half of the first year. The onset of *purposeful releasing* of an object appears at about seven months. At nine months, the first volitional and controlled dropping of an object is seen. Only at about ten months does the infant release an object by putting it down and then removing the hand away in an increasingly willful manner. This capacity to actively release an object is often initially accompanied by a flinging away of the object. At eighteen months, release is accomplished in a more coordinated manner with lower limb stability preventing the toddler from falling. This toddler form of releasing continues to develop and stabilize, only to be understood to be a truly controlled release in the early childhood years. As reiterated throughout this book, the abilities to grasp and to release are both major physical and psychological processes whose style and mature development significantly influence daily living. The paramount importance of these biomental proceedings is axiomatic in the biomental perspective.

The psychological side of grasping is attaching; the psychological side of releasing is letting go. Both of these are grounded in the *psychological relation or link* that exists at first developmentally between the infant and mother and later on between any subject and object.

The biomental perspective understands grasping as the expression of biomental realities that are simultaneously biological and psychological. Denotations and connotations of the term *grasping* reflect the idiomatic and metaphorical meanings that people use to suggest psychological, often emotional, salience. A key idea underlying this biomental perspective is that the fruits resulting from grasping arise as *beliefs.* As has been discussed, grasping encompasses levels of holding and releasing—from loose to tight. Belief as well, so central to human motivation, ranges from normative flexibility, overvalued adherence, rigid fixedness, to possible delusional imperviousness. Language is replete with such multitiered levels of meaning. For example, an individual's apprehensional attitude or acquisitive behavior may reflect taking hold of in several ways: deliberately regarding as in grasping, taking hold of quickly as in grabbing, or holding tightly as in gripping. Confluences inherent in the biomental conceptualization take on salience in such illustrations.

How children and adults experience life events as changes requiring pause and inner reorientations are shaped by their individualized capacities to grasp and let go. The experience of life events connotes the motion of taking hold of, taking possession of, and seizing upon something sensed as salient. This "touching" by the subject to an object is how an individual handles, manages, and copes with experiences of all sorts. This ranges from emotionally negotiating interpersonal relationships to cognitive problem-solving tasks.

To the extent that grasping and letting go are successfully mastered, there is less mental distress when change and transitions in other areas are encountered. For example, one does not necessarily have to spoil resentfully and devalue begrudgingly something before being able to give it up and move on. Such reluctance suggests a conflictual hesitancy that if left unchecked may affect the way disappointment and loss are experienced later in life.

Some normative developmental milestones illustrate the aforementioned. Empirically, infants of about nine months of age are able to engage in "peek-a-boo" games, which are accompanied by displays of joy, smiling, and clapping. At about ten months, they are able to wave "bye-bye." Both these milestones are developmental achievements and reflect the infant's inner sense and behavioral display of presence, absence, and return. These imply the developing mental capacities of holding on, letting go, and anticipation of return.

When parents are aware of the significance of such typical and expectable developmental sequences, they are sensitized, to some extent, to what children may be experiencing. Normally, however, skipping some steps does occur, such as foregoing crawling before walking. The American Academy of Pediatrics (AAP) states that a few children never learn to crawl. Instead, they use alternative movements such as "scooting" on their bottoms or "slithering" on their stomachs. Healthy development, the academy says, is reflected in children's showing signs of learning to coordinate both sides of the body and use each arm and leg equally in movements. This AAP consideration of physical development may also suggest that healthy overall development is enhanced by the coordinated integration of biological and psychological—biomental—processes.

3.6 Play as a Developmental Sequence

Play is a fundamental activity for all humans. It is markedly crucial in the life of children. Play denotes intrinsically motivated activity that encompasses exploration characterized by heightened sensory and perceptual absorption along with motoric activity. Play is felt as pleasurable, exciting, and tension relieving. Emotions such as happiness and surprise are hallmarks of play experiences.

Play promotes cognitive, emotional, social, and motor development. A number of factors encompass the value of play. Some of these include learning, persevering, questioning, data gathering, imagining, thinking flexibly, problem solving, listening, risk taking, sharing, and cooperating, to name just a few. Flexibility in these realms is adaptive in that it enhances trial-and-error options that lead to using diverse paths toward desired goals. Such psychological reconfigurations promote creativeness and skill in novel problem-solving agility. Play in childhood is a preparation for often-unexpected challenges that, in turn, offer opportunities for multiple strategies both at the moment and for future use. Since play is an essential part of the human condition, a brief introduction is given here. Play is further discussed in detail in later chapters.

Play as a set of typical developmental sequences begins with the newborn, infant, and toddler's exploration of the environment. These activities can be regarded as *pre-play*. It involves various sensorimotor components such as exploring the properties of objects. Pre-play is prominent until about eighteen months. During the period from birth until about twelve months, explorative activities are termed *sensory exploration*.

Roughly from twelve months to about eighteen or twenty-four months, pre-play is termed *functional play*, which denotes that the toddler understands the functional use of objects. This functional play is demonstrated by using toys in concrete manners that mimic their real-life, observed purposes. This type of play replaces merely exploring an object's sensory qualities. Examples of functional play include putting a phone to the ear, pushing a toy truck over the floor, and feeding a baby doll.

As cognition develops symbolic and abstraction abilities toward the end of the second year, previous pre-play exploration transitions to more imaginative, symbolic *parallel play* activity. This endeavor involves children in small groups. The interactions of each individual child appear more as monologues than dialogues since the awareness and appreciation of the intentionality of peers as separate individuals is just emerging. This crude pretend play does not replace functional exploration, but adds another, more complex cognitive-emotional dimension. Three-year-olds can now symbolize objects in their absence and begin to understand nonliteral states, which at age four brings about a realization that false beliefs exist, namely, ideas false in reality but true in the mind of the believer. In contrast to its precursor, this style of pretend play is object directed, that is, decentered from a primary focus on self to a greater focus on toys. *Parallel play* denotes that children are not wholly interacting with one another, but are instead playing by themselves alongside one another.

At about three and a half years, parallel play transitions to more social, interactive play. At first, this type of play is seen as *associative play* in which children engage in separate activities but exchange toys and comment on one another's behavior. Shortly thereafter, *cooperative play* emerges. Now, early childhood preschoolers sense interpersonal separateness more distinctly and so transact accordingly. By four to four and a half years, cooperative play becomes highly imaginative. It may reflect constructive play activities such as building structures, and elements of dramatic play that reflect interpersonal and social scenes. Relatively more sophisticated imaginary themes and activities predominate. Pretend play and this developing peer sociability with its reciprocal play sequences and shared goals reflect typical, healthy child development.

At about age six on, play becomes characterized by organization. Teams are formed as part of play activities. Elementary school age children now participate in coordinated games that have beginnings, middle phases, and endings. Clear distinctions emerge around themes of competitiveness, winning, and losing. At this time and thereafter, the distinction between play in contrast to work with its greater emphasis on cognitive, intentional goal-oriented task completion becomes clearer and more significant.

4. THE DEVELOPMENTAL PERSPECTIVE

4.1 Infant and Child Development

A valid and reliable context for understanding children is knowledge of the *developmental perspective*. This complex concept may be described in broad terms with reference to children's ages (table 1.1). These are approximations; some developmentalists vary labels and timing. No absolutely neat distinctions, notably about developmental milestones, can be made although typical sequences can be suggested. Biomental diversity and polymorphisms rule the course of development.

Development connotes organic, dynamic, and formative trends toward a variety of roughly expectable end points. Development as a lengthy *psychobiological* or *biomental process* implies starts, middle periods, and endings within the stream of life. This book gives repeated attention to the toggling between the biological and the mental. All human development is biomental as well as gradual, incremental, and progressive.

Table 1.1.   The Developmental Perspective

Infancy: birth–24 months

Toddlerhood: 12–36 months

Early childhood/Pre-school: ages 3, 4, 5

Childhood: 6–12 years. This period is also termed middle childhood, the elementary school years, and latency phase; late childhood or preadolescence covers ages 10, 11, and 12.

Early adolescence: 13–14 years

Mid-adolescence: 15–16 years

Late adolescence: 17–20 years

Emerging adulthood: 18–25 years

Early adulthood: 21 years

The driving forces behind development are manifold. The progression of age over time—chronological thresholds—is only one observable measure of development. This book uses a biomentally targeted approach to understand development. While there may be many as-yet undiscovered and indeterminate factors, other more obvious forces include the following: genetics; interactional experiences both animate and inanimate; biological growth over time (age); maturational unfolding; emotional prompts; cognitive drives to understand; sexual drives to explore, expand, and experience; social learning and directives; and the wish to belong.

Development denotes diverse pathways of change that encompass biopsychosocial dimensions, notably exposure to environmental opportunities. The interdependency among these routes forms the structure of biomental development. The now well-established concept of central nervous system "plasticity" or adaptive brain reconfiguration that both shapes and reshapes brain and behavior in social and psychological contexts supports this premise.

Development, therefore, is not a "planned" construction but rather a manifestation of organic, inner impulses that express themselves in growth, maturational unfolding, and the influence of experiential opportunities. This concept of development includes an appreciation of both short-term achievements and how they will eventually become integrated into the overall person. All dimensions of development are plastic and adaptable, although perception and motor development appear to be strongly influenced by heredity.

Attachment and bonding, detachment and loss—concepts that characterize interpersonal relatedness—form the biomental matrix in which children develop. Embedded in the developmental process, these processes are organic, living changes primarily directed from within. Development is unique. It is unlike the nonliving plasticity of changes that may be imposed from without. Endings in childhood do not signal finality; in fact, they herald new beginnings. Guiding children through the "letting go" process in multiple situations, contexts, and over time is a valuable skill with many emotional benefits, notably that of modulating the intensity of inevitable loss aversion expectancies.

Biomental development is dynamic, individualized, and encompasses the entire life span. From birth, an individual progresses through an orderly sequence of biological and psychological changes in knowledge, complexity of understanding, and skills. These stages include, for example, changes in body size and abilities, thinking, language, emotions, and social relationships.

What had been loosely termed "invariant sequences" in the past may be more precisely termed "typical sequences." These include the following: the infant's palmar grasp at six months before being able to grasp with fingers at twelve months; crawling at nine months before creeping at ten months; using nouns between twelve and eighteen months before using prepositions at three to four years; skipping on one foot only at four years to alternating feet while skipping at five years; parallel play at two years followed by cooperative play by three and a half years.

These orderly sequences—development—are best understood to be encompassing a range of possibilities *with numerous normal subgroups in terms of timing.* Different children may manifest these sequences during different chronological periods. The period of early development is characterized by the regularity of its vacillating characteristics—periods of smooth equilibrium followed by spans of apparent disequilibrium. This to-and-fro pacing, in fact, characterizes all of life's transitions.

Typical, average, or normal development occurs relatively predictably at expected chronological ages. However, development in some children may be described as slow, lagging, uneven, deviant, or even disturbed. This book outlines typical developmental sequences even though they, themselves, are subject to individual variations. Some expectable steps never occur, and these may be normal variants. Development and developmental milestones are variable within a wide range—roughly six months. For example, walking may begin at ten months or at fifteen months; toilet training may be complete at thirty-six months or not until four and a half years.

Phylogenetic inheritance rooted in human evolutionary history is embedded in an individual's genetic endowments. As part of humankind's genetic program, these innate predilections interact with experience and learning to produce a virtually infinite range of individual variations. Science now recognizes this "nature versus nurture" notion as a "gene-times-environment interaction" that indeterminately predisposes individuals to appearing and behaving in specific ways. Hence, gene expression remains open to possibility rather than being absolutely fixed.

This book proposes a third fundamental factor necessary in the concept of development—*random events eliciting change.* This idea of random events—"confounders"—includes random changes in genetic endowments, random changes in environmental regularities, and, especially, random changes in the interaction over time between genes and environment. Put differently, while genes significantly influence behavior, this influence is indirect and not quite deterministic. Genes interact with the environment to establish or modify biological structures that, in turn, interact with the environment and so generate behavior. Random events may intervene at points and alter these trajectories.

The "soft assembly" of gene-environment-random change transactions cannot be overemphasized, and remains a fundamental presumption throughout this text. The inevitability of indeterminate factors influencing development contributes heavily to both adaptations that retain their original forms and focus, and ancestral adaptations that have taken on revised forms and newly targeted functions. The expression of human attitudes and behaviors always contains implicit and explicit aspects of both forms of adaptedness, and may present apparent contradictions. Examples include evolved psychological mechanisms such as the value of jealousy in eliciting protection and long-term stability of relationships when jealousy is moderately expressed, in contrast to the destructiveness of pronounced forms of jealousy. Another example is "kin versus non-kin" awareness that protects the small kin group from potentially dangerous outsiders versus extreme forms of "kin versus non-kin" xenophobia that indiscriminately regards strangers as threats and so either shuns or reactively attacks them.

Change and modification, therefore, are possible on the individual level. This is what "development" means—biomental experiential transitions toward greater functional capability. This progress connotes psychobiological processes (genetic, constitutional, neurodevelopmental, and experiential) of interrelated reorientations. Although change in anatomical and functional parts may be strikingly apparent, their qualitative impact in creating a new overall status is the essence of development. Transformations of the whole, not isolated rearrangements, thus come into being.

Different parts and functions, on the one hand, as well as the whole person, on the other hand, emerge, shift, and transition over time. *At each defined era, there are ranges of age-salient developmental capacities that emerge and become tasks to be negotiated and mastered.* In a sense, development is a continuing process throughout life regardless of the stages that are often described as if they were completed in toto at certain points in the life cycle.

Sensitive periods are those specific times when particular operations or skills, for example, language or walking, are suited to develop in optimal ways. The concept of sensitive periods connotes times of easier acquisition. During these sensitive periods, however, emerging competencies are also vulnerable to becoming delayed or distorted. An individual is not born "ready-made." Using the developmental perspective sharpens awareness of how three developmental pillars enhance forward advances: (1) biological growth, (2) the organic unfolding of innate abilities, and (3) the interactive effects of parenting and the facilitating environment. Hence, diverse and multiple pathways activate and interact to produce human development.

For the infant—the newborn through the eighteen-month-old—a great deal of learning is mediated through implicit capacities for acquiring knowledge. In other words, knowledge remains in a nonconscious state. After the period of infancy, approximately eighteen months, explicit learning and knowledge acquisition can organize thinking processes using emerging symbol formation, concept formation, and logic. This transition correlates with cognitive modifications occurring from the preverbal period of infancy to the incrementally more verbal period, around eighteen months of age, and thereafter. From a descriptive perspective, states of mind are more nonconscious and covert in the preverbal period and more conscious and overt in the period of explicit language development and expression. An important point here is that learning, whether nonconscious or conscious, is always occurring, even in the newborn.

Progression and regression drive each moment of this overall process. Hence, healthy forward development is the result of the synthesis of advances, regressions, and reorganization. New equilibriums are established, become the norm, and serve as platforms for further growth, maturation, and development.

At any age, there is a search for both the familiar and the strange. Novel experiences have an exciting appeal to everyone, particularly children. Helping a child maintain a safe course in exploring the world is always a challenge to parents, who may serve as "the familiar" in guiding the navigation of children.

Growth, maturation, and development span a lifetime from infancy through the decades of adult life. Each period in this continuing interrelated trajectory has special characteristics and tasks sensitive to that particular era. Mixtures of *challenge to* and *cooperation with* parents and other caregivers (such as teachers) drive the motors of emotional, social, and cognitive development.

Adequately recognizing the specific capacities and abilities that typically emerge during each developmental era helps one understand strengths, weaknesses, vulnerabilities, capabilities, aptitudes, potential capabilities, and objective limitations. Individual variations, as stated, largely are the norm. Psychiatric diagnoses in childhood are, at best, precarious and continually changing. The biomental perspective respects the need for identifying psychological disturbances, classifying them, and providing treatment plans. In childhood and adolescence, however, the biomental perspective sees the overarching significance of a developmental perspective characterized by nuance, variability, heterogeneity, and swift momentary changes.

Notably, a flexible understanding of the child "in progress" over the course of years rather than only at isolated points in time obviates nonconstructive labeling. A therapeutically enthusiastic and rational approach highlights abilities and constructive treatment plans. The aforementioned must take account of political, technical, scientific, legal, and administrative requirements for documentation and rational discourse, but this aspect should not overshadow the child as a developing person.

4.2 A Note on the Attention-Deficit/Hyperactivity (ADHD) Presentation

Parents and clinicians, therefore, must have a reasonable sense of what is and is not the normal range of behaviors for a child of a given age. A practical aspect of this understanding is reflected in some highly detailed, recent research, which has shown that a child's age relative to his or her peers in class directly affects the probability of that child's being diagnosed and treated with medication for perceived disorders such as attention-deficit/hyperactivity. This correlation is mediated by differences in behavior that accompany children of different ages being juxtaposed alongside one another. Picture, for example, a four-year-old child and a six-year-old child in the same kindergarten class. The four-year-old will have less behavioral control because of his stage of development and be more inclined to have trouble paying attention, fidget, waiting her turn, and so forth when compared to the six-year-old. These behaviors are diagnostic indicators of attention-deficit/hyperactivity disorder (ADHD), but may only appear troublesome in light of such a comparison. The behaviors viewed from a developmental perspective, however, may be era-appropriate. Children, by nature, are not sedentary. Children as well do not have a sense of time that encompasses clear recognition of past, present, and future; this developmental capacity matures incrementally into late adolescence and young adulthood and should not signal dysfunctional planning skills if found in isolation. In addition, as will be discussed in chapter 3 in sections on brain maturation and impulse control, brain maturation normally undergoes major growth spurts at several ages: three to ten months, two to four years, six to eight years, ten to twelve years, and fourteen to sixteen years. This incremental neuromaturation is the basis for the gradual and often variable maturation of impulse control and executive functions in behavior, emotion, and cognition.

The psychiatric disorder termed ADHD is currently a generally accepted working paradigm in mainstream academia. Since ADHD is among the most common diagnoses often triggering psychostimulant medication regimens given to children, this diagnostic consideration will be briefly reviewed. Hyperactivity, impulsivity, and inattention have been understood to be the three major features of ADHD. Impulsivity or behavioral disinhibition denotes failure to inhibit or stop responses, especially in the presence of interfering distractors. Hyperactivity denotes overactive, disinhibited motoric behavior, and is closely allied with impulsivity. Inattention denotes inability to sustain focus and concentration. When this group of indicators becomes significantly impairing, it causes a hyperarousable state that disrupts self-regulation. The typical state of normal attentional ability is central in influencing the executive functions that make thinking architecture (structure, organization, and function) fluid and flexible.

While the aforementioned triad is recognized by most in psychiatry and psychology, some stress the primary core deficit as one of an inability for behavioral inhibition, while others emphasize primary problems in executive functions—maintaining an appropriate problem-solving set for forward planning to attain a later goal. Etiologies and atypical or pathological mechanisms underlying behavioral disinhibition and executive functions are currently under investigation.

Biomental child development considers "ADHD" to be a *presentation* reflecting atypical self-regulatory processes. To say that the features associated with children diagnosed as having ADHD presentations are real, complex, and legion may be a gross understatement. What is conventionally understood to be "ADHD" probably is a syndrome rather than a discrete disorder. This syndrome is most likely a complex, heterogeneous, and variable amalgamation of signs, symptoms, behaviors, and brain substrates that requires ongoing research, clarification, and further subtyping.

Although ADHD is imperfectly understood at this time, the biomental perspective heuristically views this presentation as having mixtures of two broad dimensions with one cluster typically predominating: (1) overactive behavior ("hyperactive/impulsive") and (2) executive functions dysregulation of attention/working memory, persistent forward planning, and volitional task completion. While those with impairing overactive behaviors may benefit from psychotropic medications as well as a wide range of behavioral and academic remediations, those with primary executive functions dysregulation require intensive educational/academic remediation as well as behavioral and cognitive-behavioral supports; medication may not be needed. In other words, hyperactive/impulsive behaviors can be "slowed down" with medication; in addition, behavior therapies provide learning to help internalize self-regulation over the longer-term. Executive functions impairments by contrast that involve attention, working memory, organizational skills, prioritizing, and forward planning respond best to specific delineation of weaknesses and intensive skills-based remediation using strategies to learn and strengthen the range of executive functions. Executive functions can be taught, notably with regard to the developmental level of the child. Medications cannot address these elements, their synthetic apprehension, and their motivated implementation, especially since a child's anxiety and need for long-term, hands on guidance are required for success. Executive functions training must include experiences in both academic based contexts and naturalistic situations such as home and in public.

The most cited empirical characteristics of children labeled as having ADHD are behavioral hyperactivity, emotional lability, and a range of aggressive behaviors. These highly disruptive and unsafe signs, whatever their cause, always draw attention and a need for rapid remediation. Logistic realities—time, skilled assessors, the need for speedy elimination of these disturbances, and so forth—often yield the diagnosis of ADHD as primary. Many mainstream authorities agree that, in some respects, ADHD appears poorly understood. In fact, the entire diagnostic category of attention-deficit/hyperactivity disorder as currently conceptualized has been questioned as to its validity and specificity. The variability and typology of ADHD as a disorder needs careful scrutiny. Since comorbidity or disorders occurring in combination with one another are not uncommon, prioritizing which disorder is primary is essential. Signs and symptoms that resemble ADHD may indicate a disorder other than ADHD. Hence, caution is advised with regard to treating ADHD symptomatology in aggregate fashion without acknowledging the host of conditions having attentional impairments. Some researchers who emphasize the hyperactive-impulsive dimension of this presentation, for example, have demonstrated that hyperactivity may be a result of two distinct factors: (1) impaired ability to inhibit activity to low levels (a corticostriatal process) and (2) inability to maintain positional, especially head, stability (a corticovestibular process). Medication alters inhibitory but not positional control.

The signs and symptoms suggesting ADHD, moreover, may indicate another more primary psychiatric condition, or they may be interpreted as nonpathological variations. Some have suggested that the ADHD condition may include a dimension of cultural artifact, that is, an erroneous effect produced by how the observable data is measured and defined. For example, the diagnosis and psychostimulant treatment of ADHD is considerably high in the United States whereas, by contrast, it is virtually negligible in France, Germany, and the United Kingdom. It has been speculated that this discrepancy may be due, for example, to differences in cultural expectations and values. A variety of differing opinions, however, abounds.

Recognizing age and developmentally appropriate ranges of behavior, therefore, can minimize misdiagnoses and unneeded medication with potentially adverse side effects. The psychostimulants often prescribed for ADHD over long periods of time may cause behavioral overactivation, mood irritability, diminished appetite, suppressed growth in height, vocal and motor tics, and sleep problems. Petulant hyperirritability is also seen. Of note, irritability denotes a low threshold for experiencing frustration, which may be understood to be negative affect in response to blocked goal attainment. Often understated is the significant negative impact that suppression in height and body size has on preteen and early adolescent boys. Body image that is dissonant with normatively burgeoning emotional expansivity and enthusiasm dampens these emotional milestones and results in states of perplexed dysphoria. Although findings in children are indecisive at this time, meta-analysis studies have demonstrated that in adults treated with psychostimulant medications statistically significant increased resting heart rate and systolic blood pressure occur; both are viewed as presenting a greater risk for developing adverse cardiovascular related outcomes.

From a cognition-enhancing perspective, recent studies suggest that psychostimulant drugs that maximally control behavioral hyperactivity may not improve cognitive processes, notably executive functions—reaching goals successfully—dependent on the prefrontal cortex. Whether doses that appear optimal for controlling classroom behavior impair, or no longer improve, cognitive and behavioral processes for other domains of academic and social functioning are being questioned. Differing doses of psychostimulants across differing tests of prefrontal-dependent cognition may correlate with impaired cognitive flexibility, which has been termed by some "overconstriction" and "overfocusing." Cognitive flexibility and the ability to modulate mental frameworks in a fluid fashion are significant assets to learning and overall adaptation.

Many mainstream authorities emphasize that 75 percent of children with ADHD can be managed with only behavioral interventions. This variety of ADHD suggests effectiveness for those with hyperactive/impulsive *behavioral disinhibition*. These procedures also subsume parent training and social skills training for children. Hence, treatment planning should be flexible yet comprehensive. Intensive behavioral interventions encompass psychoeducation about the complex nature of ADHD, encouraging parents to strongly reinforce all positive child behaviors, use of quiet and "time out" periods to help children downregulate and refocus on any activity, contingency reinforcement of positive and undesirable behaviors such as token economy strategies characterized by individualization and iron clad consistency, managing misbehavior in public settings, and very close collaboration with school staff with regard to both academic and behavioral daily report cards used both as a metric and as data for refining concrete reinforcements in school and at home. Time frames for effective treatment plans are variable although improvement is typically seen in three to six months with reasonable stabilization at about one year. During this time, daily and weekly interventions are needed; after a year, interventions may attenuate in intensity but require frequent reassessment while academic and behavioral difficulties are impairing. If, however, stimulant medication is being considered, it can never replace the range of needed psychotherapies and educational interventions. The range of psychotherapies or "talk therapies" is essential to help parents, families, and children reconfigure understand, learn positive behavioral strategies, and maintain therapeutic enthusiasm. If ADHD profiles suggest a dominance of impairments in executive functioning, attention/working memory, and volitional consummation, then a focus on intensive academic and scholastic remediation remains primary.

A judicious and levelheaded approach to diagnosing a child is best since diagnoses can remain and become cumulative over time, triggering the prescription of multiple psychotropic medications. This discussion does not invalidate the concept of diagnoses such as ADHD. It is imperative, however, not to underestimate the significant and typically occurring side effect profile when psychostimulant medications are used. Far from being minor, they can be major and significantly impairing. An important yet underrecognized reason for underestimating the negative impact of drug side effects is the fact that diagnostic comorbities (co-occurring conditions) are common. A child with an ADHD presentation may have a mood disorder that is exacerbated, hence producing mood irritability and explosivity; anxiety may also be increased. A child with ADHD may have a predisposition to form tics, and stimulant medications may provoke both motor and vocal tics. Compulsive behaviors such as hair pulling and skin picking may also be provoked.

This conversation simply calls for more sensitive tactics towards understanding problem presentations and offering a broader base of supports. These include considering nonstimulant medications such as the alpha-2 adrenergic agonist class (for example, guanfacine) and others, and especially optimizing educational interventions. Recent FDA approval of extended release guanfacine has provided a medication that downregulates hyperarousability and may have cognitive enhancing effects as a result of moderating norepinephrine levels in the prefrontal cortex. Studies show this medication's safety and efficacy in controlling ADHD symptoms while being well tolerated in terms of side effects. Rational assessments required initially and reassessed periodically integrate multiple sources of information and recognize that apparently straightforward presentations, in fact, often represent heterogeneous disorders that defy narrow classification.

When difficulties with attention or behavior in school impair functioning, examining the entire context of the child's life is crucial. This approach allows one to target primary causes of these difficulties, such as actual cognitive limitations or mental disorders, and differentiate them from secondary effects such as problems with attention attributable to transitory difficulties (for example, the death of a pet or a broken leg) or general lack of motivation. Problems involving family members other than the identified child may include mental illness in a parent, marital discord, substance abuse, economic hardship, and so forth, all of which may cause an ADHD-like presentation in a child.

Long-term outcomes of pharmacological and psychological treatments for ADHD, moreover, have been described as "equifinal," which means that many different approaches may have the same results. A recent study assessing psychoeducational interventions over the last thirty years has shown improvement using such methods, noting parent and child satisfaction as well as treatment adherence. Of note, studies show that hostile parental emotional expressivity, which may be a component of all forms of ineffective parenting, is positively correlated with the development of both ADHD and conduct disorders, the latter of which includes aggression, violence, and significant rule violations.

Psychotropic medications for children, in fact, may eventually become déclassé when other interventions—learning, psychological, behavioral, and so forth—are used both intensively and pervasively early on and over the long term. Such interventions are best applied across settings that include both school and home. In fact, evidence-based psychosocial treatments for ADHD are now well established. These interventions include behavioral parent training (BPT) and behavioral classroom management (BCM) as well as intensive, peer-focused behavioral interventions implemented in recreational settings such as summer programs. Adequate recognition of the social contexts of those children with apparent attentional or learning problems is crucial to providing good care and sustainable outcomes.

For example, some children may not be ready to enter kindergarten. Kindergarten readiness is reflected in a child's ability to play cooperatively with peers, understand the rules of a game, focus on a task for at least five minutes, count ten objects correctly, and dress and undress without help (except for tying shoes). Being toilet trained is also included. If these characteristics seem absent or very uneven, then a consideration of delaying kindergarten enrollment for a year might be a judicious option. Some have referred to this postponement as "redshirting." This whole domain of school readiness needs diligent and thoughtful assessment by parents and professionals since premature acceleration might result in academic or behavioral difficulties, misdiagnoses, unneeded medications, and future class retention. These decisions must never be taken lightly, abruptly, or without very careful deliberation. Furthermore, as is true of any problematic circumstance a child might have, any condition causing distress should not be reified or made the defining feature that characterizes the child. A consideration of the whole child, notably in a context of whatever healthy and adaptive trajectory he or she may possess, is primary and must remain "in-proportion" to all else.

4.3 How Parents Can Promote Healthy Development

Parents promote healthy development through their nurturance, balanced discipline, and living example. In many respects, good parenting is neuroprotective and neurorestorative. These terms refer to creating and maintaining an experiential and material environment that optimize biomental resilience. This approach includes minimizing avoidable trauma, managing it intelligently if it occurs, and maximizing positive cognitive and emotional learning and problem-solving. Modeling empathy and containment are the broad substrata of the blueprint toward promoting healthy child development. Cognitive and intellectual development, an important part of this, is understood to reflect one's thinking architecture—the form, structure, arrangement, process, and flexible flow of thought. Executive cognitive functions are embedded in this; these include selective attending, planning, organizing, implementing, and refining mental plans in preparation for their behavioral performance. Living example and narrative descriptions guide children through and also help them learn the decision making process. Parental attention toward putting these guidelines into action beginning in infancy and throughout childhood increase odds that children's attention, forward planning skills, capacity to pause, and self-containment will be enhanced and reach their potential. Some of the features that promote healthy development are discussed in the brief sections that follow (table 1.2).

4.3.1 Empathetic Listening: How to Hear

Knowing how and in what directions to guide a child are essential components of good parenting. Empathetic listening addresses children's almost "desperate" need to be understood. It is grounded in continuing transactional sensitivity. Being exquisitely receptive to both what a child is experiencing and what he is trying to communicate provides a fundamental source of knowledge and understanding. If it is important to the child, it is important to

Table 1.2.   How Parents Can Promote Healthy Development

Empathetic listening: How to hear

Speaking to children

Heads up: Communicating the expectable—inform and prepare

Respect

Developmental awareness

Labeling feelings

Teaching pause

Making the ordinary special

Helping: How to respond

Helping children learn how to ask for help

Frugality and temperance

Praise, positive statements, and encouragement

Sincerity

Keeping promises

"On the spot" responsiveness: Prompt and timely guidance

The dark side of human nature

the parent, too. To correctly know such significances, one must carefully "listen" to what a child is saying and doing. A family climate of listening is always beneficial and should be encouraged, modeled, and made a family norm.

Empathetic listening hears the feelings and meaning in any communication. While the process of *hearing* implies a passive input of information, *listening* connotes active, intentional, and purposeful interest. Both of these denote a parent's sensitive grasp of a child's subliminal emotional state— fear, surprise, enthusiasm, sadness, and so forth—and underlying intent. Empathetic listening—grasping a child's emotionally laden "reasons"—should always precede talking. Hence, the importance of carefully chosen dialogue—short of excessive and unneeded talking—is of great value. This guideline cannot be emphasized enough.

Parsimony of words, therefore, is best when communicating rules, when monitoring behaviors, and especially when enforcing logical and learning consequences. Too often, people talk automatically in mindless, unconsidered ways. Too much talking and not enough listening are perilous to success in any meaningfully salient relationship.

Explicit statements of validation about what a child says should follow empathetic listening. Adult statements and displays of support to children are affirming, endorsing, and confirming of his or her worthwhileness. Taking seriously the value of the child's contribution to the discussion helps validate a child's sense of worth. Validations such as these provide reminders that the very being of the child is valuable. Potentials for achievement and success are implied in this exchange. Along with other displays of nurturance, such validation is perceived as a motivational message and helps consolidate positive self-image and self-esteem. Of course, as with all strategies, excesses in application are best avoided.

Listening and responding in a suitable fashion is an art. Responding intelligently after pause and deliberation is effective. Reacting rashly in emotionally provocative situations leads to spontaneous action that may be short-sighted and ineffective. It is best to avoid setting up power struggles in negotiations with children. One of the best ways to teach is to use the phrases "In our home, we . . ." and "In our home, we do not . . ." because such communication creates an atmosphere of teamwork that facilitates guidance. For example, rather than giving a direction in an overly straightforward manner, such as "Put these toys away," it may be more useful to say "Where do these toys go? Let's put them where they belong."

4.3.2 Speaking to Children

From day one, speaking to—in addition to loving physical contact with—one's child according to his or her developmental age is important. Speaking—language—is most effective when it is responsive, sensitive, modulated, enthusiastic, and reasonably elaborated. Although throughout development there are many important shared silences, these can be punctuated by deliberate language interactions. What is termed *motherese* or *baby talk* is the high-pitched, slow talk used in infancy to verbally communicate and model speaking that will become utilized later on. "Blankie" meaning blanket, "jammies" meaning pajamas, and "potty" meaning toilet are examples of the infant-directed vocabulary.

Using language to verbally narrate what a baby seems interested in maximizes teaching value, notably in emotionally salient interactions. Many parents prefer to use adult terminology and "words" to their children. This may be especially helpful toward the end of the first year when language is beginning to emerge. After the end of the first year, particularly from age two and through the preschool years, it is very useful to listen attentively to children's speech and language, and to rephrase sentences using more advanced wording and construction. This is best done sensitively and in a matter-of-fact-manner. This type of "hands-on" early education and demonstrated learning is developmentally advantageous.

Infant-directed speech is suitable for about the first twenty-four months, after which it should fade and gradually be replaced by more adult forms of language. Child-directed speech is a form of speaking to children that includes slower speed, distinctive intonation, and structural simplifications. Found in many but not all cultures, this form of speech provides children with information that facilitates acquiring phonemes and words from the language of the surrounding culture. As children grow, continued dialogues that are mindful and avoid being superfluous are important and show children that they are recognized, listened to, appreciated, and respected. Speaking should be regular but not excessive. Too much "empty talk" is mindless and creates a dulling atmosphere of noise without meaning.

For example, it may not be necessary to explain everything that one asks a child to do or that a child questions. It is useful to try to distinguish the child's psychological attitude attending each question. Interest may be different from curiosity. *Interest* is a quiet frame of mind, relatively free from anxiety, fear, and apprehensiveness. It is a direct concern with something that the child wishes to understand. *Curiosity*, by contrast, may involve an element of doubt, uneasiness, or underlying apprehensiveness about a topic. Curiosity can, though certainly not always, suggest an underlying anxiety about what is perceived as strange and unknown; consequently, there arises a compelling need to manage this ambiguous allure with questions and further investigation. Parents, therefore, can reflect on these facts and respond in ways that are more specific to a child's actual needs, whether prompted by interest or curiosity.

A measure of parsimony and frugality demonstrates suitable moderation in answering questions. Further verbal expansions can be added eventually and in steps. Speaking should always be emotionally salient on some level and convey a message. The message is not only transmitted by language but also by tone and physical expression. Tone of voice and tone of attitude are concrete signals to which children are especially receptive.

Speaking to a child throughout development, especially asking questions, also demonstrates how the framing of a question permits inclusion rather than restriction of many possible answers. Questions become the frame into which answers may fall. Showing children a wide and flexible frame supports cognitive flexibility, promotes exploration of possibilities, and spurs creativity in patterning thinking.

In addition, it is essential to acquaint children with how to communicate needs. Given the child's developmental status, teaching children to speak about their needs and to ask for help is vital. The child who is shy and avoidant by temperament may require special attention to help exercise this in a way that is reasonably loud, clear, and expressive.

Mindful, interactive dialogue demonstrates a living example of communication skills and enhances positive socialization, empathy, and prosocial behavior. This behavior is part of *inductive discipline*, or using explicit language to help a child identify feelings, particularly by pointing out the effects of the child's misbehavior on others. Teaching literacy, both language and social-emotional, in this way is developmentally enhancing.

A note of caution is required here. Whereas speaking to children is unquestionably an essential facet of good parenting, parental tendencies to "overspeak" or "overintellectualize" can be detrimental. Speaking in too cleverly a manner, introducing cunning or deceptive frames of reference, and mindless chatter simply to "fill space and time" are to be avoided. Information overinvolvement from electronic media is akin to this. All have little developmental value other than to suggest that anxiety may be stirring in one or both partners. Anxiety situations, as such, need to be identified and addressed in as direct a way as possible. To avoid this typical pitfall of nonproductive overintellectualzation, which can be a common parenting experience, empathetic listening, developmental awareness, teaching pause, and a general demeanor of frugality and temperance, all of which will be discussed in later sections, enhance a child's developing sense of personal and interpersonal containment. Having such positive experiences early on minimizes excessive consolidations of the normative excursions into intellectualizations (splitting off and denying emotions by excessive cognitive explanations) that become covered defensively with rationalizations (justifying acknowledged feelings by making plausible what may be irrational) in adolescence and adulthood.

At times, in fact, communication through gentle silences is optimal. Sharing quiet time with children may entail being together without speaking. Such discourse is receptively open, nonverbal, and communicatively engaging.

4.3.3 Heads Up: Communicating the Expectable—Inform and Prepare

A crucial parenting strategy is to prepare children for change. It denotes proactive readiness. Transitions and preparing for them may elicit anxiety and thwart adequate attention to preparation. Realizing this offers parents a mind-set ready to encounter the inevitable anxieties and avoidant behaviors that precede change and transitions.

It is important to ready a child ahead of time by alerting him or her to expected and even probable significant situational changes. The crucial element here emphasizes that this alert must be *given well in advance* of the upcoming change or transition. Last-minute changes, though inevitable at times, produce significant stress for all involved. In addition, preparing a child to meet these challenges by developing adaptive transitional skills, notably for separations, is essential. The younger the child, the more preparation is needed. Rehearsal in all its forms helps children prepare for transitions.

Biomental child development emphasizes the value of demonstrated learning. Demonstrating concrete techniques for putting ideas into action is a best parenting practice. Showing a child how to prepare and how to do something is far more effective than a straightforward verbal direction. Successful learning starts with simple exposure and progresses toward more complexity. Put simply, one first describes a desired behavior, and then proceeds to break it into small steps. Each component step is explained, demonstrated by the adult, and then enacted by the child. Demonstration entails concrete and practical exhibition of "how to" skills. Such concrete techniques for putting ideas into action is engaging and facilitates learning and preparing for transitions. Incremental learning is more meaningful and easily assimilated than learning that is presented in complicated chunks.

Healthy development is enhanced by regular routines and predictable schedules for activities such as eating, sleeping, bathing, and toilet training. From birth on, regularity—though without fixedness, rigidity, or inflexible rote—in routine sequences helps a child establish internal regulation, biomental rhythms, and a normal sense of anticipatory expectancy. These factors assist in establishing a sense of safety and stability. Periodically varying the routine, to some extent, is also helpful. Clearly communicating to children what to expect alerts them that psychological transitioning is needed to facilitate an impending change.

Family outings, hikes in the woods, physical labor, and art projects may be planned beforehand. Creating special experiences, however, may at times require a modicum of spontaneity, intuition, and surprise. Surprise may facilitate a newfound, budding interest and anticipate new opportunities. The greatest learning moments often arise out of recognizing spontaneously occurring opportunities for previously unplanned activities.

With regard to most daily activities, however, time management and priority setting are important. Thinking about needs and obligations in terms of what is urgent versus what is important helps coordinate scheduling. This procedure, however, is not an excuse for unnecessary and unproductive procrastination.

Sleep schedules, for example, illustrate fundamental routine structures. Medical and pediatric specialists have recommended guidelines for total time spent sleeping in a twenty-four-hour cycle that are useful in establishing schedules. The parameters are as follows: for infants, fourteen to eighteen hours; for toddlers and preschoolers, twelve to thirteen hours; for elementary school age children, ten to eleven hours; and for adolescents, eight to nine hours. Teenagers, as a general rule, should be in bed and heading to sleep no later than 10:30 or 11 p.m. This directive can minimize difficulty waking up in the morning.

Healthy development entails forward progression. Before each advance, however, there may be transitory periods of behavioral and emotional disorganization. This apparent distress, itself, may signal that a forward advance is about to occur. Hence, progression and regression in development are normal and to be expected.

Such a dynamic orientation in caregiving provides a reality-based perspective for seeing a child's needs and developmental potentials. The implication is that effective work must seek to develop and integrate the physical, emotional, and intellectual aspects of the whole person to avoid unnecessary failures and lopsidedness. Preparation and guidelines for daily routines fosters beneficial structure and, therefore, offers opportunities for success.

4.3.4 Respect

A parenting mind-set of respect is a prerequisite to effectiveness and meaningfulness. Respect presumes basic courtesy, empathy, and sensitivity. When respect is accompanied by deep affection, it is called *honor*. This idea entails a basic adult sense of self-confidence and humility in the face of many unknowns. On some level, this sense of profound respect is akin to the awe that characterizes the attitude of veneration. An adult's attitude of honor toward others serves as a powerful model of reciprocity and encourages a relationship that is authentic and genuine.

Respect denotes pause and demonstrates that a parent is both recognizing and allowing a child's manifestation of individuality—style, preferences, and suitable independence. Respect, in fact, is the operationalized counterpoint to unconscious impulses of omnipotence and material demonstrations of forceful control and nonconstructive manipulation. At times, it may be necessary to acknowledge respect for children's thoughts and opinions without immediately judging them as "undesirable," if they are not explicitly destructive. Permitting different points of view to coexist allows children time for consideration and further constructive discussion. Clearly communicating that differences of opinion do not negate love and caring is important. Finally, when respect and helping become integrated, mutual feelings of cooperative interdependence are engendered.

Attitudes of respect are amplified when one thinks, speaks, and acts from personal experience. This firsthand base of understanding eschews trite politically correct formulations and sentimental niceties, which children can see are artificial. Respect provides a model for children to observe and with which they can identify in concrete ways. Seeing attitudes of respect in parents toward each other, toward children, and toward others sets standards that a child can emulate and internalize.

4.3.5 Developmental Awareness

Development implies a progression from simpler to more complex organization. It is facilitated by suitable opportunities for the exercise of potential developmental faculties.

The best jobs or tasks for children to engage in involve some degree of coordinated group effort. These activities should take into account children's developmental needs, abilities, individual tempo, and emerging capacities. Age-salient developmental tasks encompass specific sectors of bodily-emotional-intellectual functioning that can benefit from sensitively devised challenges.

The coordinated interplay of cognitively thinking, emotionally feeling, and physically residing within the body is fundamental to all learning. When hands and legs awaken to a piece of work, the heart joins in this excitement. The mind, in turn, enlists its attention in this flow of effort. Experiences such as these may nourish the child on many levels. Parents become more successful when they recognize and facilitate their child's natural developmental shifts over time. This approach also helps to minimize unrealistic expectations and unreasonable demands that can put unnecessary stress on everyone.

4.3.6 Labeling Feelings

Since emotional development is crucial and often underdiscussed in parenting strategies, attention to the area of experiencing and verbalizing feelings is discussed here. An actively engaged caregiving environment can support emotional competence in children. Both mothers and fathers are able to create conditions whereby the verbal identification and communicational pragmatics of emotions and feeling states are made explicit.

The developmental level of a child determines the manner of such emotional learning strategies. The preverbal period of infancy requires that parents use language and communication gestures to label activities and the feelings attached—enthusiasm, surprise, delight, and so forth. At about thirty months, toddlers are typically able to begin to express feeling states. The preschool years are a prime time to engage children in an interactive exploration of feelings. Defining feelings in a concrete way that is developmentally appropriate and personalized such as "I am happy," "You look surprised," and "It's raining, we can't go outside, and we feel disappointed for now" is a basic strategy.

Both positive feelings (happiness, joy, surprise, and so forth) and negative feelings (sadness, disappointment, frustration, anger, and so forth) are optimally reviewed in interpersonal, often peer, contexts. Helping a child identify the distress of another, and figuring out what these feelings are called, what may have caused them, and how they can be managed are strategies promoting emotional competence. Helping children assess what others may need and attempts at supplying these is also valuable in fostering a sense of perspective taking and empathetic concern.

It is important to demonstrate that different people may experience a feeling with a definite label differently, and that this is expectable and typical. Also, it is beneficial to reinforce accomplishment when a child adequately identifies his or her or other's feelings. Both strategies to express and to reinforce feelings employ speech, language, facial expressions, and gestures. This process of labeling feelings continues into the elementary school and adolescent years. It becomes more indirect and sensitive after puberty.

4.3.7 Teaching Pause

Emotional development is undoubtedly essential in healthy personality formation and social intelligence. Labeling feelings in interacting with children, especially in the younger years, supports this development. Equally as crucial is "teaching pause," which is a demonstration of biomental equipoise. This denotes attention to and modulation between stimuli and responses. When a desirable event is introduced, parents can also introduce a mediating pause before that event is further approached and engaged. This pause encompasses a series of phases between goal identification and action toward achieving that goal. Although this capacity entails phases that are typically implicit or should eventually become implicit, helping children internalize "pause" requires explicit teaching about component parts.

A general schematic of this process that can be applied in concrete ways in different contexts follows. First, when parents recognize that an event or object is perceived as appealing to a child, an identification using developmentally appropriate descriptors of the desirability and attractiveness of the item being considered should precede any further approach toward it. Once this preliminary acknowledgement is made, even if for a few seconds, a second phase of lingering pause should intervene. During this time, verbalization of the pros and cons, reasonableness, and uncertainties about going further can be made. Statements to younger children such as "Let's not jump toward this yet" convey this idea. A third and last phase entails a decision to approach and partake or not, or a consideration of an alternative course of action.

Teaching pause, therefore, identifies children's sensitivity and attraction to rewards. It couples this acknowledgment with a lingering discussion that involves values, salience, and consequences. Helping children to recognize outcomes and possible penalties for choices is an important part of this process. Teaching pause, especially by living example, addresses impulse modulation, the capacity to tolerate delay for rewards, inhibiting an already initiated response, and beginning to meaningfully entertain estimations of the passage of time. Teaching pause promotes mental poise and supports both self-containment and emerging self-discipline.

4.3.8 Making the Ordinary Special

Organized family rituals around household chores, meals, bathing, and bedtime can promote sharing, cooperation, and a sense of mutual accomplishment. These activities can be made enjoyable and understood to be an important part of everyday education.

Some examples follow. Children of about three years can help parents sort laundry and put toys into assigned locations. Four-year-olds can pour glasses of water or milk at the dinner table and also help in the garden. Five-year-olds can help parents prepare meals, and six-year-olds can take out trash and help clean the house. All these activities can be undertaken as enjoyable, cooperative family endeavors if approached with the right attitude.

A specific example of a family activity that can have multiple features of learning is "bread making." A parent may approach this seemingly mundane activity by discussing ideas such as the growing, cultivation, and harvesting of the wheat with children. The mutual efforts of preparation that follow— engaging children in measuring ingredients, mixing components, kneading dough, observing the rise of the bread—can become novel and engaging. This process acts as a reality check to the simple, uninformed consumption of ready-made foods. Bread making is just one potential activity for bringing creativity and social interaction into learning, piquing the imagination and bolstering attentiveness. A modern alternative to this family meal experience might be taking children to a breakfast shop and ordering blueberry pancakes with chocolate chips. While this entails less hands-on "prep" work, the approach of the pancakes with their visual and olfactory appeal can be an occasion for paused observation, description of appearance and aromas, and then hearty engagement accompanied by a mutually experienced sense of enjoyment and satisfaction.

Making an activity engaging requires a keen eye, clever mind, and sensitive insight into a child's preconscious or subliminal inclinations and wishes at a particular time and context. The best well-done jobs possess no ready-made formulas. Working with objects and situations as they arise can create unexpected surprises, offer unforeseen challenges, and foster absorptive attention. This idea means always being ready to seize unplanned opportunities.

Another dimension related to family and team efforts is providing children with models of efforts that require planning, step-by-step work, and subsequent, rewarding accomplishment. When people have to work for something or pay for something, that "thing" takes on greater meaning and personal value. This is a general truth that has many concrete applications.

The typical example for adults is employment and earned salary. Choosing and purchasing an item with this earned money produces a sense of satisfaction and achievement. Trying to convey this experience to children in different ways at different developmental stages is good parenting. It builds personal responsibility and character. In the adolescent years, arranging ways for teenagers to earn money and guiding them through saving and spending are important parenting tools in preparing for the responsibilities of adult life.

4.3.9 Helping: How to Respond

The *helping relationship* is perhaps one of the most intimate and meaningfully salient activities in which adults and children can participate. Biomental child development regards this relationship as foundational for mental health and healthy socialization.

Helping presumes trust and continued trust building. The aims of helping are manifold. They include some sort of "doing" encompassing problem solving, fixing, making something easier, and improving a situation. In this two-person endeavor, the helper is most successful when he or she continues to be acutely aware of what in conventional terminology is called "face." Face denotes the other's sense of self-image, self-worth, self-dignity, and self-respect. Helping requires the utmost implementation of respectful, sensitive, and tactful interventions. Thus, effective helping is not accusatory or confrontational, and should never involve forceful control merely for the sake of control. Successful helpers reinforce another's sense of participatory teamwork rather than superior-inferior directedness. Respectful team efforts preserve "save-face" status for all participants.

Participating and encouraging participation in helping activities is salutary for all. Helping may be regarded as the performance of compassion and the implementation of authentic human love. As an unequivocal commitment, it can emerge as a dramatic venture for all participants.

Helping behaviors are the concrete manifestation of emotional and cognitive empathy. Research is beginning to demonstrate the innate, genetic, and learned dimensions of empathy and helping behaviors. Parents who demonstrate helping in implicit and explicit ways increase the odds of eliciting children's active participation. This complements and surely enhances any biological givens. Modeling helping provides children an optimal opportunity to develop a personal sense of empathy that may continue to emerge and develop throughout life.

Intelligent adult guidance harmonizes itself in mutually beneficial ways with a child's ever-dynamic, changing responsivity. Active self-reflection supports intelligent guidance. *Cooperative relationships*, moreover, correlate with children having better attention and concentration. Such relationships also minimize tendencies for opposition and bullying (manifesting issues of power, control, dominance, and intent to make others suffer) so often seen as significant problems in society. Helping is an implemented behavior that teaches, supports, and encourages reciprocal prosocial behaviors.

A brief note on the ubiquitous issue of interpersonal control dynamics is useful to review here. One of the major breeding grounds for strife and conflict is the expression of noncooperative control between people. This often begins with pronounced and forceful manipulation between two people and may also extend to relations between groups. Such attitudes and behaviors that make others feel manipulated, used, and exploited serve only to provoke anger, opposition, and defiance. Good parenting suggests that work with children can yield beneficial results for both the child and his helpers. When adults are duly sensitive to children's needs, it may optimize positive outcomes for involved parties. Rather than a relationship in which someone has to win and the other lose—a "zero-sum game"—good parenting engenders "win-win" opportunities where all can benefit.

In an adult relationship, optimal interaction is typically based on cooperation and agreed-on roles. Such understanding includes clear and explicit responsibilities, exercise of authority, giving direction, and enforcement of the arrangement. Well thought out, conscious, and intentional sharing of power in virtually all matters between spouses is vital to marital and parenting success. Continuing dialogue keeps such mutual agreements fresh and current.

Adult control over a child must always be predicated on guidance that is health promoting and reinforcing of safety. These criteria are based on the adult's best judgment. Parents need to be alert to the possibility of their own reactive fear of losing control, especially about raising children who might not succeed by conventional rubrics. Parental self-confidence needs continuing work, reassessment, and reinforcement. Arming oneself with knowledge through continuous learning and discussions with helpful others is always beneficial. Unwanted unilateral control between any two people is often perceived as aggressive and hostile. Moreover, it evokes almost instant opposition. In other words, deviations from cooperatively understood norms are unproductive and generate conflict.

Helping itself always involves some matters of control whose features include style and degree of involvement. Helping is most effective when it is asked for. In addition, if seen by the potential helper to be indicated, helping may be offered in a sensitive and tactful manner. For example, the regulation of helping may range from frugal or just enough to generous or abundant. While helping behaviors that are prudent and ample are useful, helpful attitudes and actions that are rich and multifaceted are optimal. Austerity in detecting and offering help reflects biomental inertia; this less desirable position does not advance development. Short-term assistance with provision for the longer-term reflects greater generosity and a prescient perspective aware of probable forthcoming needs.

Heartfelt helping, generosity, and good deeds counter emotional stinginess. The helper and the helped, in turn, become actively engaged so that passivity, habit, and defiant obstinacy are minimized. An awareness of the positive feelings associated with helping counters urges toward exploitation. Exploitation encompasses unruly desires to take more than one needs or requires. Exploitation implies an inability to feel grateful for what one has already received. This behavior, in essence, is rooted in impulses of greed. Exploitation and greed are excesses that have negative interpersonal consequences. Exploitation often morphs into contemptuous, impersonalized, and faceless victimization. People exploiting others can escalate from one-to-one "no win" situations to larger-scale group conflicts in which control, domination, and even war result. The mutual effort and prosocial behaviors entailed in helping, however, work to prevent emphasis on "taking" and counter unhealthy greed and exploitation.

It should be noted that parents helping children should not be misconstrued as parents solving all or most of children's problems. It is not "bailing them out" of situations that might offer reasonable learning opportunities for emotional or intellectual growth. Parental judgment and self-reflection at these times is a must.

Engagement in the helping process is best when the helping becomes, to some degree, an end in itself. *Emphasis here is on effort rather than product.* Praise is best directed to effort—creativity, hard work, and persistence—not exclusively on results. Efforts matter most; they require cultivation. Mistakes, failure, and underachievement become great opportunities for family discussion, learning, and helping. These interventions model hope and successful attitudes. Much better than vague or routine praise are specific expressions of encouragement about a particular job well done. This approach reinforces desired behaviors. Even when a task has not been successfully completed, a positive and encouraging response might be, "I see you're working hard on this, very good. Let's see if it comes out better next time."

Although behaviors may be judged in moral ways as "good" or "bad," the effort behind behavior is important to identify. Goodness of effort toward desirable tasks may be assessed by the degree of effort present. *Encouraging genuine and quality efforts is always constructive.* Praising in the sense of validating effort is crucial. Moreover, adults must always be on guard to keep the child's "being" foremost in mind; this essence of goodness is precious and valuable in all of its expressions. It is the almost inapproachable core of every child's enormous primal authenticity. A parent is the steward of this priceless resource.

4.3.10 *Helping Children Learn How to Ask for Help*

Helping children emphasizes the active role parents take when they identify a need and implement an action plan. Parenting must also lay the foundation for a child's own ability to identify difficulties and ask for help.

The development of this process begins in infancy and childhood with mutual dialogues as parents clearly articulate transpiring events. When challenging situations arise, parents can verbally describe different aspects of the difficulty and then proceed to explain implemented solutions. This modeling sets the stage for children to recognize that stumbling blocks are inevitable parts of daily experiences. Such modeling also establishes a template for recognition, identification, and problem-solving strategies. These are continuing skills that develop in complexity as the child encounters an ever-widening variety of experiences.

4.3.11 Frugality and Temperance

Good parenting is characterized by attitudes and behaviors that minimize extremes. An old adage, "Everything in moderation, including moderation, itself," is quite applicable.

The ideas of frugality and temperance are often obscured in our modern age of glamour and excess. *Frugality* means accumulating and using material in a modest way. *Temperance* means moderation and self-restraint in attitude and action. These ideas are not meant to suggest austerity or deprivation, but rather a modulation that is reasonable in quality, quantity, and context.

Can a parent give a child too much love? The answer is probably a qualified "never." Love as an inward attitude can be unbounded, which is perhaps the sole exception to the aforementioned adage of moderation. But outward expression of this emotion may be unhelpful if it becomes excessively demonstrated in material ways, such as in goods given—toys, electronics, excessive food, and so forth. Other potential detrimental excesses of expressions of "love" are misconceived overprotectiveness, jealousy, corporal punishment, and inappropriate physical contact. In these cases, parents may misinterpret their actions as "loving," when in fact the acts are motivated by additional nonconscious foundations not directly in the best interests of the child.

Excesses usually have their roots in strong feelings. These emotions then become ideas that are expressed in actions. Parents need to reflect on strong feelings and modulate them to avoid going to extremes in an automatic and unreflective way.

To a large extent, modern media unrealistically portrays the glamour of the "ideal family"—a beautiful home, expensive cars, the newest electronic equipment, and so forth. "Keeping up with the Joneses," as the saying goes, needs to be examined so that inordinate competitiveness and mindless envy, greed, and jealousy do not motivate unnecessary acquisitions.

4.3.12 Praise, Positive Statements, and Encouragement

The role of praising children merits examination. It has been a parental recommendation for many years. While suitable encouragement reinforces existing desirable behaviors, praise, as such, may tend to emphasize feedback that is overinflated, even bloatedly ideal. The habitual use of praise is akin to the idea of false reassurance. Both reflect an inauthentic gesture based on unsubstantiated wish rather than fact. Such excesses in wording and descriptions of positive accomplishments and cooperative behaviors may thwart the intention of effective reinforcement. Excesses in any endeavor typically produce a lulling habituation eventually sensed as meaningless and perhaps insincere.

Effective *feedback*, by contrast, promotes new learning as will be discussed in chapter 5. Suitable use of constructive approaches characterized by positive statements and encouragement is more effective in promoting a realistic atmosphere of recognition and reinforcement. Such statements are conducive to supporting prosocial attitudes and behaviors by their emphasis on exceptional—good to very good—performance. Put differently, modestly conveyed feedback reflects even-handed and fair appraisals that are believable. This approach is more likely to produce enduring results.

Excessive praise, however, can create a sense of specialness bordering on egocentric narcissism or unhealthy self-centeredness. This outcome is counterproductive to achieving a balanced sense of self-significance. Too many unfounded statements of "specialness" connote underlying feelings of inadequacy that the speaker may have about himself or his children.

The human condition is precarious in its ability to maintain realistic self-esteem, self-worth, and self-identity. All too often, people feel inadequate. Outwardly, people may employ defense mechanisms to create false veneers of apparent superiority. Arrogance, boasting, and misrepresentations mark these inauthentic devices. Some people, moreover, make an art of intellectualizing the superiority of themselves, their children, and those designated as part of their "in group."

Unreasonable praise is likely to set up expectations for special treatment and entitlements that reinforce envious feelings and derail motivation. These trends are always counterproductive since their immodesty limits authentic teamwork and learning from experience. Inordinate and indiscriminate designations of "being special" both reflect and elicit envy, jealousy, and subtle forms of hostility toward and contempt for others. Whenever sharp contrasts are drawn and matters of being superior become foremost, they act as accelerants igniting the envy dynamic as will be discussed in chapter 6. Excessive praise may also stimulate feelings of guilt in children who do not feel they deserve such extraordinary accolades.

Care in modulating, to reasonable levels, praise, support, and positive statements is always useful. It may even be best to substitute the concept of *praise* with ideas and terms such as *support, encouragement,* and *validation.* Such approaches toward achieving one's personal best foster healthy personal development. This positive support, in contrast to excessive praise, fosters courage, perseverance, honesty, and enthusiasm.

Statements that reinforce effort always are beneficial, notably when given immediately and about specific behaviors. Examples of such feedback include the following: "I see that you put away your toys all by yourself"; "It must feel good to be able to draw a picture of a house"; "I noticed that you were able to share your snack with your friend"; "You must feel proud that you were able to take turns with your sister." Helping children practice these behaviors helps to ensure their continuation. The long-term, beneficial effects of exercising good behaviors cannot be emphasized enough.

Espousing the standard of encouragement to achieve one's personal best is a foundation of effective parenting. Children's ability to *see themselves as their own standards against which to measure and compare* is important for parents to encourage. This approach minimizes envy, hostile competitiveness, and a sense of inferiority. Having internalized standards optimizes a sense of honesty with oneself and fosters perseverance toward desired goals. Encouraging modesty and realism in goal setting tempers extremes of emotion and feelings of distress when success is not achieved. Many parents agree with this but struggle to implement it given the competitive nature of school demands, peer comparisons, media influences, and modern culture at large.

4.3.13 Sincerity

Another important consideration is *purposeful honesty and profound sincerity*. Both concepts need to be personally recognized and interpersonally communicated. It may be necessary for an adult to be "brutally" honest with regard to personally confronting his or her own feelings, attitudes, and shortcomings. By contrast, it is necessary to be honest in more sensitively expressed ways when working with a child.

The importance of sincerity is addressed in the above section on praise wherein the negative effects of excessive praise are detailed. Other insincere articulations with potentially undesirable outcomes include false reassurances and superfluous comforting. These tend to produce inertia and complacency. In the end, it is best for a parent to carefully monitor reality in a case-by-case context and to sensitively communicate to children aspects that require improvement.

4.3.14 Keeping Promises

Effective helpers in all walks of life mean what they say and particularly what they *promise*. Such persons try to be on time and are responsive in a timely fashion when help is needed. This approach is particularly important for successful and caring parenting.

Too many excuses for broken promises and inconsistently carried out agreements weaken one's credibility. This behavior becomes a model for children's consequent undependable and unreliable behaviors. It weakens the child's developing ability to realistically appreciate cause and effect. The uncertainties, disappointments, pressures, and frustrations produced are, indeed, quite stress-provoking.

If plans have to be changed, advanced notice should be given. Time management skills, particularly those that include punctuality, play an important role in staying focused and not changing plans unnecessarily. Disappointment to a child feels like the piercing of a sharp sword. This feeling creates a caustic emotional wound and weakens the fragile bonds of trust and hope. By contrast, communicating and enacting genuine empathetic reflection and validation advances enthusiasm and successful work outcomes.

Of course, many of the aforementioned are ideal guidelines. People are not typically consistent in mood, attitude, or behavior. Some days are "good," while others are "off" days. This variation always needs to be remembered so that parents are not inordinately hard on themselves or their children.

Parents are human. If they make mistakes, parents have an opportunity to reflect, take responsibility, and make apologies in a suitable fashion. This approach represents a living example of realism, modesty, and self-correction for children to learn.

4.3.15 "On the Spot" Responsiveness: Prompt and Timely Guidance

Responding to an infant, child, or adolescent at an age-appropriate level is always important. Reacting rashly is usually ineffective. Listening empathetically is the prelude to responding in a timely manner. Whether by eye contact, gesture, tone, or language, such responsiveness reinforces a child's awareness of a parental availability, vigilance, caring, and guidance.

Suitable and effective responses presume forethought. Put simply, planning ahead for the inevitable mealtimes, requests for toys, unplanned accidents, changes of schedules, disappointments, and so forth is a continuing necessity. This preparation strengthens the ability to be flexible when encountering novel problem-solving situations.

Despite parents always being under some degree of "pressure," remaining level-headed when assessing situations that call for a suitable response is best. *Responding* does not mean reacting in an abrupt, unthinking manner. It means behaving in a fitting way that shows concern, forethought, and planning. It may also include a thoughtful explanation of one's reasons and strategy. With this form of active caring, parents can more efficiently set limits and consistently enforce them. It remains important for infant, child, and adolescent to understand that parents are sensitively paying attention and responding with helpful information. This attentiveness communicates a sense of nurturance, respect, and subtle nonintrusiveness.

4.3.16 Fun and Enjoyable Work

Children love to have fun. Fun and focused absorption are not only parts of play but can also be implicated in work such as cleaning, cooking, gardening, trips to the library, and so forth. In other words, modeling enthusiasm and a sense of excitement in work and play activities engenders motivation. Modeling a sense of determination and focus in any activity helps children to emulate these attitudes. All these counter complacency and boredom.

Giving children and adolescents chores and household jobs provides opportunities for demonstrating accomplishment. Toddlers love helping and can be taught to tidy up toys, help in meal preparation, and assist in collecting laundry. It is beneficial to have preschoolers and school-age children make beds, perform daily hygiene, and dress themselves. Even if these jobs are not done "perfectly," one should avoid redoing them. Helping children "see" their own less-than-perfect results is an important learning experience. Allowing the child some independence and expecting age-appropriate success are strategies for success.

Preschoolers, ages three through five, take pride in showing off their developing skills. Rewards can become the display of performing a task and receiving parents' acknowledgement of this accomplishment. Elementary school children can help set the dinner table, rinse off plates, and put clothing away. Preadolescents show some resistance to tasks by whining, complaining, and appearing to forget. Jobs such as walking the dog, helping to wash the car, and assisting in grocery shopping afford them opportunities to have fun if framed in such a manner. Adolescents want to feel in control; hence, chores should be mutually discussed and agreed upon. These negotiations may have to be frequently readdressed since teenagers often forget the priorities and obligations that they helped establish. A reasonable weekly allowance can be given. It is best to give this money for discretionary spending rather than as payment for doing household chores, which are part of every family member's routine obligations. Housecleaning, yard work, and running errands are some examples of age-suitable jobs for teenagers.

As has been emphasized, aspects of work can have playful qualities. Facilitating a child's play fosters both emotional and cognitive development. Incorporating lively and novel experiences deters feelings of drudgery. In fact, the play of children coordinates physical, cognitive, and emotional faculties in directed, attentive fashion. This absorptive integration helps brain structures to function in ways that promote attention and concentration and lessen distractibility, particularly in early and middle childhood. These skills support school readiness and academic success.

Modeling "helping attitudes" in a creative and fun way fosters motivation and cooperativeness. Offering a reasonable range of intelligent choices obviates habit, rote, and mindless conditioning, all of which are breeding grounds for boredom.

Adults must demonstrate a real capacity for *active participation*, especially when faced with the inevitable challenges that typically and unexpectedly rear themselves. Passive stances by parents often are fueled by fear and inhibitions based on a conditioned sense of inadequacy and fear of failure. Vigilance in this area requires a great deal of keen introspection and renewed commitment.

4.3.17 The Dark Side of Human Nature

Effective work with children requires a personal sense of honesty, namely, seeing reality as it is. Polar opposites, seeming contradictions, and inconsistencies initially elicit confusion and distress. Stressors, difficult situations, conflicts, negative emotions, and undesirable behaviors are inevitable. These occurrences are an essential part of "the rule" and not the exception in everyday life. Often, negative feelings and behaviors appear to have a spontaneous reactivity, namely, fight, flight, or freeze that defies reason.

While the tone of the biomental child development perspective remains positive and solution-oriented, its underlying vision is optimized only when *an integrated and balanced view of both the positive and negative aspects of individual psychology and human relations* is recognized. Emphasis is on the dynamic interactions between constructive and destructive forces. To this end, a discussion of the dark side of human nature has profound importance both theoretically and pragmatically. Rather than constrain awareness, considerations of negative and positive experience, notably their synergy, are wellsprings for renewed interest that fosters creativeness.

Negative emotions such as hostility, envy, greed, and jealousy may be experienced from time to time. The emotional and cognitive dissonance that results typically triggers tendencies to suppress such awareness. Even if blatant denial and repression fail to eliminate such feelings from awareness, more precarious attempts by using rationalizations to justify contradictory ideas and intellectualizations to block conflictual feelings are common.

Negative emotions are not necessarily malignant, particularly when relatively transient and managed suitably. Successful parenting reframes apparent negativity in a larger context. This expanded perspective provides an environment of opportunities for learning, which includes learning from apparently negative experiences. Frustration and disappointment typically surround attitudes of negativity—irritability, hostility, and clouded thinking. Biomental child development argues that caregivers must be relentlessly prepared to create conditions that transform ill fortune to opportunities that promote success. Realistically high expectations and uncompromising determination fuel such development-promoting attitudes.

Negative emotions within the range of being normal are feelings and attitudes that are not too intense or long lasting. The attitudes remain benign when they do not pervasively influence thoughts and behavior in impairing ways, notably by turning to fantasy to avoid realistic solutions. In addition, negative emotions become helpful when their vivid contrast to positive emotions (such as love, kindness, or gratitude) is examined by self-reflection. *The almost constant conjunction between positive and negative experience is axiomatic and cannot be overemphasized. Discriminating their symmetry and asymmetry affords a blueprint for improvement.* In this way, negative feelings become opportunities to further self-understanding, emotional development, empathy, and other positive states of mind.

Many individuals have difficulty tolerating negative emotions and attitudes in themselves and others. Being realistic in a personal self-analysis is an essential part of healthy self-awareness. While identifying negativity in oneself may be painfully revealing, it is valuable in any genuine work toward self-improvement and, in turn, caregiving. The essence of a child is his or her basic core of goodness. With this in mind, a large area that often is eclipsed by adults is recognition of the *dark side of human nature*. This domain encompasses the range of hidden states of mind and explicit behaviors characterized by destructive qualities.

Angry outbursts, hateful attitudes, aggression, cruelty, and feelings of hopelessness are real and must be courageously addressed when they seem pronounced. So too do emotions like envy, greed, and jealousy need similar attention. When a child is pouting, whining, or crying, it is best not to view this merely as the child being "spoiled," a colloquial term for undisciplined, or as the child demonstrating an act of manipulation. The intelligent parent tries to understand what may have triggered this behavior and also what the child's goal is. "What is the child's need at the moment?" is an important question to answer. Boredom, hunger, fatigue, or a developing physical ailment may, for example, trigger irritable states.

Psychological health includes one's ability to identify and acknowledge, rather than deny, the aforementioned unpleasant tendencies. In fact, they all offer endless opportunities for new levels of understanding, insight, compassion, and creative personal growth. Helping children handle stress, disappointment, conflict, and frustration rather than trying to eliminate them provides powerful learning for emotional management and growth. Helping here heavily relies on parents' modeling how to manage unpleasant situations in a variety of contexts.

As will be discussed at length in chapter 6, the challenges presented by the management of negative emotions are crucial to mental health. All individuals experience some elements of unresolved grief, loss, disappointment, envy, greed, and jealousy, including parents and children. The intensity and extent of this possession vary. Some issues remain within normative bounds, while others extend into unhealthy realms and require attention. Maintaining mental health is a continuing process and can be experienced as an adventure of self-understanding and self-development.

If circumstances are right, transformative feelings such as healthy admiration, ambition, sharing, and gratitude may emerge from these negative impulses when they are used as learning moments. A wise perspective is one that strives to see the intrinsic dualities—in other words, the good and the bad—at play in human nature. Such a view will embrace these discrepancies and aim for an integration that fosters reconciliation and constructive problem solving.

5. POTENTIAL ENVIRONMENTAL TOXICITIES

5.1 A Note on Environmental Exposure to Screen Media

Contemporary culture is characterized by global information availability. Media literacy and a media-enriched environment are realities that are expanding in unparalleled ways. The introduction of wide screens and hand-held devices as well as the modification of visual imagery by high definition and other advanced technological sophistications add to brain effects as yet uncharted. The phrase "information-saturated society" may not be hyperbole but a valid description of exposure and accessibility to the vast amounts of data provided by electronic media.

The modern discovery of electricity is approximately 200 years old, and the first functional light bulb about 125 years old. These developments have significantly enhanced the speed of learning, notably through the proliferation of information, books, and now electronic screen media. While such electronic sophistication is undoubtedly a major technological advancement, modern civilization's dependency on it exposes users to exquisite vulnerabilities. System or electrical failures can trigger widespread communications disruptions. In addition, unintended biomental consequences also may be underestimated drawbacks, as will be discussed. As is true with all tools, use requires intelligence, discrimination, and judgment. In this regard, adults, to a large extent, hold the position of responsible mediator between children and what they are exposed to.

Screen media is the phrase that encompasses all forms of visual and auditory stimuli on electronic devices such as computers, hand-held game and video viewers, television, cell phones, the cinema, and so forth. Twenty-seven percent of all screen time for children eight years and younger is spent with digital media. These depict simulations and feigned rather than real-life interactions. Such simulations are sham imitations that use representative analogies in ways that are often more entertaining than educational. This entertaining quality is typically overenhanced in unrealistic ways to capture attention, often for commercial reasons. While modern-day consumerism drives the demand to purchase in ever-greater amounts, Western culture's commercialism has monetized objects, ideas, even emotions to exploit them as commodities that people feel are necessary to satisfy their own or their children's needs.

While such media has obvious benefits when wisely used, they also have potentially negative effects on emotional and mental development. Numerous studies using functional magnetic resonance imaging (fMRI) have demonstrated that violent programs, for example, on electronic media have detrimental effects beyond their obviously negative content. Such media activates brain regions, conditions their durability, and correlates with negative affect, emotion, and cognition. Fast-paced programming, whether cartoons, gaming, movies, or any variety of "flick," positively influences attentional and mood instability.

Electronic gaming has become a prominent form of entertainment both for children and adolescents. Video games, to some extent, are more sophisticated versions of their simpler antecedents, cartoons. Often, parents merely focus on the content of such media—whether it is violent or bad—but the very act of watching and listening may have detrimental effects on developing sensory and central nervous system processes. This possibility is particularly true for the child under age seven whose filtering mechanisms are not mature enough to healthily modulate incoming sensory stimuli.

In addition to the conditioning effects of repetitive exposure to screen media, the sheer magnitude of its multiple stimuli bypasses critical awareness. This process allows such media to act as subliminal, covert communications that may be implicitly learned. This subliminal learning is particularly effective when it is congruent with the viewer's dispositions and traits. Hence, electronic and social media act to condition the mind, and so affect behavior.

Studies show that before age two and half, video and mass media exposure is negatively correlated with attention, memory, reading skills, and language development. Researchers attribute this, in part, to what is termed the *video deficit effect*. This idea states that before age two and a half, children clearly demonstrate poorer performance after viewing a video than after engaged in a live performance. It is suggested that the information transferred via media is not experienced as personally or socially relevant; rather, the data is synthetic, artificial, and often feigned to create illusionary simulations. Such atypical mental processing obstructs the information from being applied in real-life situations to solve problems. The crucial factors that are proposed to be missing are the elements of basic human interaction—eye contact, gesture, verbal exchange, and a shared focus of attention. The absence of these aspects obviates learning. All these findings suggest that beneficial learning before about three years old cannot and does not occur through exposure to electronic media.

One study of "gamers" who played video games over twenty hours a week showed brain activity similar to that seen in drug-addicted and dependent persons. In fact, it is believed that up to 9 percent of children and adolescents suffer from pathological gaming that interferes with normal living. Risk factors include greater time spent playing games, lower social competence, and greater impulsivity. Negative outcomes include poor school performance, depression, inordinate anxiety, and social phobias.

Not all exposure to screen media, however, is toxic. The negative or positive outcome of such exposure depends on dose, potency, duration, type of content, and route of exposure of the media. Also implicated in the outcome are the developmental window of vulnerability and genetic, constitutional, and environmental predisposing factors. While screen media negatively affects some children and not others, there probably are significant subgroups that are affected. These children may have predispositions to addiction embedded within the above factors. Such children are typically impulsive and have obvious social impairments. No isolated factor is deleterious, but certain clusters in vulnerable children can be detrimental and should prompt parents to have a high level of suspicion.

Attention must be drawn to the pervasive enactment of violence in today's entertainment. Pervasive and extended exposure can condition a child to regard violence as typical and acceptable. It also produces habituation in which an undesirable indifference toward violence is experienced. The violence then no longer evokes the negative reaction that originally might have been elicited.

Studies demonstrate a "digital divide" and show differences in the activities of various socioeconomic status (SES) groups and genders in computer use. Lower SES children who do not have access to home computers spend less time on the Internet than their higher SES counterparts. By the beginning of early adolescence, boys spend more time on computers than girls. Gender use is different; boys gravitate toward games, music, buying, and selling whereas girls seek information and use more instant messaging.

Modern screen depictions of aggression and destruction—often romanticized and made unrealistically glamorous and exciting—desensitize attitudes and foster passive compliance. A tacit acceptability for destructiveness follows. This correlation also appears to be true with regard to the currently popular fascination with "combat sports" that involve realistic mixtures of competitive boxing, wrestling, and martial arts. This profitable form of entertainment attracts many viewers. Like other aggressive forms of screen media, it may vicariously fulfill aggressive impulses, lacks the concrete personal consequences of injury, and is emotionally desensitizing to actual material violence. Establishing sane human values—kindness, responsibility, and respect—suffers.

When violence is depicted on the screen, children do not experience its real-life aftermath. The fake simulation removes normal, adaptive responses and distressing reactions toward such destruction and bloodshed. The phrase *mean world syndrome* has been proposed to reflect consequences of this. The pervasiveness of destructiveness and the human cost of its denial must be recognized. One wonders to what extent the nuclear age has unleashed the possibility of an almost irreversible movement toward humankind's deep-seated self-destructive urges.

Children, as this book stresses, learn from what they observe, when alone, with others, and in groups. It is best for parents to decide what has value and what may be deleterious for their children. Parents are encouraged to take an active role in directing children toward positive experiences and away from destructiveness and violence.

The American Academy of Pediatrics (AAP) website (www. healthychildren.org) provides an up-to-date summary of recommended guidelines for a variety of physical and mental health issues. This site includes discussions and recommendations about video games, feeding practices, use of safe cribs and car seats, and so forth. It is an important reference and resource.

Conventional pediatric guidelines suggest that the first five years of life are the most sensitive period of vulnerability to damaging central nervous system and developing cognitive pathways. It has been estimated that about 74 percent of all infants and toddlers watch TV before their second birthday. The American Academy of Pediatrics recommends no more than two hours of viewing a day for children, and no TV viewing under age two. Child psychiatrists and pediatricians suggest that the downstream effects of screen media arousal during the elementary school years may negatively oversensitize violence, decrease focused attention, as well as cause sleep, behavior, and academic difficulties, and possibly contribute to unhealthy weight. Consistent findings in adolescents are unclear at this time.

Childhood overweight and obesity have become a significant problem in the last decade. Some experts have estimated that up to 16 percent of children are overweight or obese. Sedentary behaviors such as increased seat and couch time positively correlate with this weight increase. Parental modeling that includes good nutrition and exercise helps motivate and engage children to participate early on. The influence of TV has been correlated with childhood obesity. Eating in front of the TV is common, and there are many food-marketing commercials associated with children's shows. Watching TV can interfere with a child's ability to respond to cues signaling satiety, thus causing overeating. The above are some of the significant reasons for limiting screen time.

Ordinarily, overly sexualized and aggressive content in visual entertainment has been the focus of concern, with ample justification. Modern film making, however, also skillfully elicits envy, greed, and jealousy through portrayals of idealized physical beauty and attractiveness, romanticized lifestyles, power, and exuberant indulgence. The natural tendency to idealize this array of glamour stimulates mental comparisons, usually of the others— "the haves"—and the self, who is believed to be the "have not." This dichotomy, if left unchecked by parental clarifications, develops into misperceptions of the others who "have" as being "the enemy." Another example of dichotomous thinking that promotes envy is parents' use of phrases such as "our own kind" to highlight and promote perceived differences and attribute "specialness" versus "inferiority" to groups. Unfortunately, the values of children are established early on and easily influenced by such exposure. Such perspectives have long-term consequences. They may contribute to the eventual social unrest that emerges when young adults encounter economic hardships when trying to establish occupational sufficiency.

Such virtual simulations inflate often unrealistic and ill-motivated aspirations. If left unmodulated by a proper and modulating reality, vicarious experiences in such excesses can lead to frustration about unrequited interpersonal and personal satisfaction.

Another fundamental concern with the use of screen media is that it is, in fact, "unsocial." Not only is the child interacting with an inanimate object, but even the "relationships" of social media are essentially mock interpersonal relationships. *Children, therefore, become desensitized to the natural dialogue that occurs between real people.* The nuances of facial expression, eye contact, gesture, and tone of voice—all of which are biomentally essential to cognitive understanding, affective comprehension, and social intelligence—are absent in social media. Social media models "robotic" communicational styles to children. This impersonal format does not promote the social skills of developing youngsters. The screen is deficient in actual physical presence between people, thus lacking the unique immediacy, eye contact, and feedback that modulate appropriate physical spacing. *Social media often turns out to become "pseudosocialization," that is, unbounded, poorly regulated, and mindless stimulation.* It is only through interactive face-to-face encounters between multiple speaking and emotionally responsive people that the meaning of words and language are learned. This modeling of social skills and subsequently forming proper socialization is notably true in early and later childhood.

One wonders whether social media used excessively can be classified as another "defense mechanism" used in response to high levels of anxiety—at times, crippling—in order to avoid more socially engaging activities. If so, these defense mechanisms often become hypertrophied and overgrown. Rather than constrain anxiety, these endeavors mask and perpetuate often hidden pockets of conflict, fantasy, and unresolved personal and interpersonal distress. Pediatricians and psychiatrists are just beginning to correlate some clinical depressions and other psychiatric disorders with the use of social media in those predisposed to mental disorders.

Human interaction in infancy and childhood with its immediacy and mutual feedback elicits prosocial responses—awareness and sensitivity to the meaning of human gestures, intonation, and intentions. In addition, early human interactions demonstrate the need for pause in dialogue, instead of impulsive reaction, the importance of which is discussed throughout this text.

In summary, excessive exposure to screen media desensitizes and dulls cognitive and emotional faculties. Emotional self-management is sorely impaired. Screen time may foster inactivity and expectations of passively receiving information without actively working for it. Emotional reactivity may be blunted, but it also may be hypersensitized to desire more intense forms of stimulation, often overly sexualized or aggressive. Attention span also becomes blunted. Pseudosocialization and impersonal dialogues may even facilitate the transfer of inaccurate information, intentional lying, and deceit. This implies fostering an implicit, unhealthy sense of dehumanization in regard to others. Last, screen media minimize real person-to-person dialogue, thereby diminishing opportunities for language skills development.

Parental supervision, especially regulating screen media exposure, is part of good parenting in the current age of media availability, 24/7 all-access Internet, and "external fantasy" overload. Screen media can be educational and stimulate learning if judiciously chosen. This, however, applies to children older than seven. Also, it is easier to begin establishing guidelines when a child is still young. While it may be impossible to avoid this pervasive aspect of modern technology altogether, disciplined use requires forethought and vigilant parameter setting. The increasing availability and use of communicational devices such as cell or mobile phones by children and adolescents have led to a new phenomenon—"sexting" or sending sexually explicit messages to others. The negative ramifications of this are multiple and increase a child's vulnerability to both health related and emotional dangers of promiscuity as well as risks to safety and welfare resulting from predation.

As has been a major theme of this book, living example is one of the best and most impressive teachers. Parents need to somewhat unplug themselves from their own involvement with screen media. "Fire the electronic babysitter" instructs one to avoid using the television and computer as a way of occupying children, especially when other methods can be devised.

As mentioned previously, helping children to develop healthy media habits early on is a very useful strategy. For preschoolers and early elementary school children, parents being present, to some extent, when screen media is used helps to monitor and establish guidelines. For infants up to two years, no screen media exposure has been judged beneficial by child developmentalists. For toddlers and preschoolers, twenty to thirty minutes of screen time once or twice a day is adequate. For elementary school children, no more than two hours has been suggested. Some experts, however, recommend no or minimal screentime exposure until adolescence. While it may be difficult to avoid exposure to screen media in society's current cultural and business environment, the adage that says "everything in moderation, including moderation itself" is wise to remember.

Being selective in choosing media content that leans toward educational and healthy values should be standard. However, it is also important to be skeptical about what purports to be "educational" and suitable for children. Recommendations from sources such as Common Sense Media (commonsensemedia.org) and The Center on Media and Child Health (cmch.tv) as well as the National Association for Media Literacy Education (www.namle.net) are valuable sources of information.

6. INTELLIGENCE AND COGNITIVE DEVELOPMENT

6.1 Family Environment, Cognition, and Intellectual Development

Another integral dimension of child development is understanding the role of cognitive and intellectual development. The term "cognitive" denotes the mental processes of perception, memory, judgment, and reasoning, as contrasted with emotional and volitional processes. Cognitive development is understood to have a relatively independent trajectory that follows age and experience rather than, for example, being qualitatively influenced by the timing of puberty. Newborns, moreover, clearly do not come into the world with fully developed minds—emotions and cognitive abilities. Such an idea of absolute psychological nativism is contrary to empirical and scientific fact. The biomental developmental perspective emphasizes the incremental growth, maturation, and nuanced development of individuals. Aspects of these considerations run through the entire text. A brief discussion of some related highlights follows.

Alfred Binet developed the first formal tests of children's mental age in 1905 in France. Lewis Terman in America revised the Binet scales in 1916 with the Stanford-Binet tests, and the phrase *intelligence quotient* or *IQ* was introduced. In 1939, David Wechsler at New York City's Bellevue Hospital improved these test measurements with his now generally accepted Wechsler intelligence scales of cognitive abilities. Wechsler advanced the idea of translating raw scores into *standardized deviation IQ scores* based on the normal Bell shaped distribution of tests results. The mean or average of the distribution is 100, and the standard deviation was set at 15. Contemporary assessments emphasize patterns of scores rather than isolated findings.

Intelligence as measured by Intelligence Quotient (IQ) tests of cognitive abilities has both heritable and environmental influences. Genetic influences on brain morphology and intelligence levels have been well studied. A variety of sophisticated brain-mapping approaches is consistent with behavioral studies in demonstrating the complex cortical patterns associated with measures of cognitive ability.

While the debate about the significance and distribution of IQ has been controversial, most professionals agree that there may be a roughly equal contribution of genetic and environmental influences in IQ measurements. The interaction of heredity and environment is reflected in psychology's construct of "reaction range" that denotes that genetic makeup places an upper and lower limit on a person's IQ. Where he or she falls within this range is thought to be the result of environmental influences.

Cutting edge genomic studies in 2011, however, have recently demonstrated confirmation that a substantial proportion of individual differences in human intelligence is attributable to highly heritable genetic variations. For example, approximately 51 percent of the variation in fluid intelligence—the ability to efficiently solve problems by using reasoning processes—between individuals is accounted for by measurable genetic linkage. These extraordinary findings are consistent with the proposition that many genes with small individual effects underlie other additive genetic influences on intelligence.

Some theorists specializing in understanding the interaction of heredity and environment support the influence of both but emphasize the importance of their interaction in governing IQ. Environments that are enriched with greater opportunities for a number of types of development—verbal, mathematics, motoric, aesthetic, and so forth—may be used by individuals to optimize their innate potentials. Environments that lack such opportunities may constrain intellectual expansion.

Examining how nature and nurture interact and manifest can be a useful perspective. What is important to highlight, however, is the role of multiple environmental factors that are partly under the intentional control of parents.

For example, providing developmentally suitable educational opportunities is a somewhat controllable environmental factor that can support children's innate intellectual capacities.

Thinking indeed is a faculty that can be nurtured and enhanced by parents. Thinking skills include comprehension, rule application, analysis, synthesis, and evaluation. The use of critical thinking is essential for lifelong problem-solving capacities in all domains of life. Helping children to see different perspectives, avoid automatic "black and white" assessments, appreciate time frames, and realize that change and new solutions are inevitable can all contribute to the sound development of critical thinking and grounding in realistic perspectives.

The capacity for fluid intelligence can be promoted through active parental involvement. This skill set involves exercising reasoning skills including the following: the ability to make sense out of information, the ability to generate nonverbal mental models to understand complexity, processes of reasoning, and the flow of problem-solving strategies. Parents may facilitate these skills through verbally identifying difficult situations, comparing and contrasting concrete details, and collaboratively working out pragmatic solutions. Reading to children offers a wealth of hypothetical situations and solutions that may serve as fodder for such learning moments, whereas management of family dilemmas provides real-life, concrete modeling. The family projects mentioned in this book (such as school projects, meal preparation, gardening, household chores, and home repair) can encourage a sense of team effort and an expectation for developing enduring competencies.

The majority of early learning, which contributes to emotional, social, and cognitive development, results from implicit exposure and indirect training, teaching, and modeling. This theme reflects the premier process of interactive psychological absorption. The presumption that nonconscious processes are powerful influences and educators runs throughout this book. *Parenting on multiple levels, therefore, exerts its most potent effect by living example and implicit intention.*

7. EMOTIONAL AND MORAL GROWTH

7.1 Character

Good parenting fosters good character in children, and character, in fact, does count. Character can be described as the overall goodness of one's personality, personhood, and "moral fiber." Whereas goodness may sometimes be misconstrued as a simplistic "boy scout" frame of mind, Biomental child development regards it as a sign of overall personal competence. Goodness in this sense is a broad-based positive psychological demeanor characterized by the absence of inordinately self-centered attitudes of impudence, coarse boldness, brash assertiveness, and lack of empathy. In the end, "high character" denotes taking reasonable responsibility for the authorship of one's deeds.

Conventionally, character is an evaluation of an individual's personality as described by others. Subjectively, it is part of one's self-concept, the way one defines him- or herself. Character, to a large extent, is comprised of one's *values*—fundamental and preferred *beliefs* about principles viewed true and used to make decisions about what is good, right, and just. Whereas values are oriented around childhood experience and family culture, in adulthood values reshape themselves by what a person chooses to believe. One's character and values orient life goals, choice of personal and social affiliations, occupation, and how one conducts him- or herself in these pursuits.

Morals connote an inner sense of what is understood to be good or bad. One's sense of *ethics* is based on these inner moral valuations and facilitates choosing between competing behavioral alternatives. Morals and ethical behaviors are influenced not only by cognition (such as values and prosocial beliefs), but also by personal and social factors such as empathy, guilt, temperament, family, peers, society, and culture. While values motivate behaviors, one's sense of morals and ethics constrains behavior. Values, morals, and ethics develop gradually from roots in childhood to their fruition in adulthood. Cognitive and emotional insight is needed. Such an internally perceived locus of control is characterized by expectancies that include confidence in the ability to stably determined choices that will result in future desired outcomes. "Outsight," which is assigning an external locus of control to agencies other than the self, such as excessive task difficulty and chance, denotes failure to accept responsibility and accountability for thoughts, words, and deeds.

Values, morals, and ethics underlie character, which typically manifests in relationships with others. "Virtues" denote behaviors that echo moral excellence. Put differently, character is reflected in the rhetorical question, "Am I my brother's keeper?" This idea may be a self-evident dimension of human psychology and social development. The moral dimension, to some extent, likely has innate roots. Good character implies personally held values and resultant choices that are prosocial and support the constructive survival of both the individual and the extended group. Moral maturity reflects the *way one reasons* about competing individual and social dilemmas rather than merely reflecting ultimate choices.

The ancient Greek philosopher, Heraclitus (c. 500 BC) suggested that a person's character is his fate. This notion implies that one's personality with its values, morals and ethics guides, to a significant extent, the way his or her life will unfold.

Strength of character, moreover, correlates with self-confidence and emotional poise. These faculties underpin one's sense of self-containment. This helps moderate biological needs and emotional desires. Such moral restraint—high character—reflects the fair and noble attributes of human dignity, namely, symmetry, proportion, and harmony in both attitude and nonviolent behaviors. These assets support adaptive and effortful self-control.

Character reflects the confluence of moral intelligence and emotional intelligence. How beliefs, values, and morals are integrated leads to emotional intelligence or understanding feelings in oneself and others. Tendencies toward rigidly fixed, inflexible beliefs prevent constructive learning from experience, and may lead to irrational bias and destructive impulses and actions. Reasonable, flexible integration of ideas based on understanding supports emotional self-management and appropriate social interaction. The qualities of a "good person" reflect this and are far from trivial.

Character develops from its base in the various features of temperament and personality that develop over time. While temperament has strong genetic determinants, positive character can be further built upon this, notably by parental guidance and modeling. This practice occurs first from the "imposition" of living example and then by internalization. Demonstrating gratitude and appreciation, for example, to children who can begin to meaningfully internalize these attitudes lays the foundation for their expression, in turn, toward others. These recursive advances in learning and emotional development develop over a lifetime.

Developmental research suggests that typical preschoolers have some degree of moral understanding. Even in diverse cultures, three categories of ideas and behaviors are distinguished as good or right versus bad or wrong. These include (1) a sense of moral imperatives that protect an individual's basic welfare, (2) social conventions (such as the conventions of saying "please" and "thank you"), and (3) matters of personal choice that do not violate others' basic rights. The category of moral imperatives appears to hold greatest importance for most individuals throughout their lives, although this position tends to be rigid and concrete in its cognitive and emotional parameters.

Some research strongly suggests a significant innate endowment for social and moral cognition, but upbringing and parental guidance are powerful influences in shaping actual behaviors. Thus, susceptibility is not inevitability. The intrinsic ability of infants to assign value to the actions and inferred intentions of others—"evaluative discrimination"—presupposes that they are already equipped to be responsive to others' reinforcements. A detailed discussion of this idea is found in chapter 2's section, "Notes on Intelligence," which also describes some of the differences between "inferred intentions" and "theory of mind" constructs.

Neurological, intellectual, emotional, interpersonal, and social pathways of learning are all activated and fed by impressions from the environment. The coordination of these inputs produces character. One's developed character is the matrix for feelings of hope, purpose, volition, and creating the ability to implement goals. Goal-directed intentionality involves the capacity to inhibit instant gratification, to pause, assess, and only then take planned action.

Parental modeling imprints fundamental human values in children. Values embody the parental vision for children's development. Values that become personalized and firmly entrenched are the framework by which decisions are made. These values set standards for concepts of justice and fairness. *Ethical codes* denote conduct based on values of right and wrong while *morals* denote beliefs, an acceptance of the truth about the goodness or badness of ideas and actions. Both ethics and morals guide how people behave.

Values, ethics, and morals confer both personal and social advantages. For example, children at age four typically develop the ability to misrepresent their beliefs to others—lying. As discussed in more detail in chapter 3, this may precariously help them avoid feared punishment or may be normative since such "tall tales" reflect their newly emerging imaginative skills. While this may benefit children individually, it may fail to support the concomitant development of empathy and cooperative social intelligence. Parental guidance is needed to foster positive cultural and humanizing values that are socially relevant. Hence, adaptive advantages become expanded when truthfulness, cooperation, and helping include benefits to both self and others.

Parenting is a powerful guide influencing children's moral development and subsequent ethical decision-making skills. Coaching in moral reasoning is best communicated in positive ways rather than with harsh and strident injunctions. These moral-based discussions may include family and social issues that are culturally relevant as well as including topics such as non-negotiable safety issues. The intent in instilling basic moral values is to suppress aggressive impulses and enhance prosocial cooperativeness. Discussions such as these can begin as early as the preschool years. When presented tactfully and sensitively, adolescents markedly benefit from discussions about moral direction.

Character formation, moral intelligence, and socialization are forged primarily in two places: (1) by example in the family, which is referred to as *vertical relevance*, and (2) from role modeling that teachers provide in school, which is called *horizontal relevance. Cooperative collaboration between parents and teachers* is essential to the intellectual and moral development of children. The character and culture unique to each school also imprints itself on children and becomes integrated in their personality structure. Parental attention and collaboration provide valuable feedback to schools that contributes to the enrichment of the academic milieu.

Although defining character has endless subtleties and overlapping connotations, for our purposes six fundamental features or principles are mentioned. They are the following:

1. Trustworthiness: associated with honesty, truthfulness, integrity, steadfastness of values, promise keeping, punctuality, and loyalty
2. Respect: associated with tolerance, acceptance of differences, manners, honor, and nonviolence
3. Responsibility: associated with accountability, dependability, excellence, competence, self-restraint, and courage for self-dependent action in the face of personal and social need
4. Fairness: associated with honesty, empathy, nonexploitation, sharing, justice, and integrity
5. Caring: associated with kindness, "being nice," compassion, gratitude, forgiveness, good deeds, and helpfulness
6. Citizenship: associated with obedience, social cooperation, respect for authority, and civic contributions

The above account reflects essential attitudes of good character. Most parents place special worth on the values of kindness, compassion, responsibility, respect, and honesty. Parental encouragement and support foster courage, persistence, enthusiasm, and fortitude in the face of adversity. Compassionate discipline instills self-discipline. This also supports the development of cognitive processes such as differentiation and distinction that serve as the basis for more developed evaluative discrimination skills and a grounding in reality with constraint of inordinate fantasy.

All these interventions build children's character and resilience, notably in early and later childhood. They contribute heavily to enhancing the belief in the very desirability of goodness. Such a belief may be positively correlated with a character style hallmarked by "high mindedness." The courage for self-dependent assessment of one's needs and difficulties as well as the social perception of need in others denotes an action-oriented rather than an inactive "by-stander" position. Taking responsibility for one's actions denotes an internalized sense of personal responsibility. This positive sense of responsibility modulates merely external attributions, namely, minimizing the inclination to blame others in the face of problems. It also fosters self-motivation and corrective action rather than self-blame and inertia.

In adolescence, identity formation coalesces around character traits. The principles that underlie one's character intimately influence the direction that behavior takes. Cooperativeness, ease of engaging in teamwork, and an inclination toward helpfulness strongly suggest good character. What one does and chooses to do in specific situations emerges from this base in character.

Signs of good character typically include both a sense of gratitude and the ability to admit mistakes. Thus positive character traits manifest through "please," "thank you," and "I'm sorry" statements. These sentiments are best instilled in childhood.

8. THE JOURNEY IS THE DESTINATION

Successful parenting is a continuing process. Merely achieving goals or waiting for endpoints to occur can obscure the enrichment and vitality of dynamic parenting—for both parents and children. Within this process, each moment is an end in itself; each moment can be satisfying, pleasurable, and joyful. This journey, moreover, changes, grows, transitions, and develops over time. The child grows as does each parent, the parental couple, and the family as a whole. External conditions also change. Life is full of "bumps" for everyone and at every age. The context of parenting, accordingly, remains a dynamic one that requires a great deal of reflection, reassessment, adaptation, coordination, and grace.

Parenting is a magnanimous effort. It can become an intelligent endeavor of consciously living in tune with reality. Good parenting gracefully begs one to realize that living, helping, and developing cannot be simulations—they must be exercised in real-time as tangible, conscious, and meaningfully salient experiences.

9. KEY POINTS

9.1 Parenting

Parenting is caregiving via nurturance, discipline, and living example. The "details of developmental parenting" include parenting skill and style that is informed by an understanding of the basic principles of child development.

9.2 Nurturance

Nurturance is providing physical and emotional attention and loving care in a context of transactional sensitivity. Nurturance entails giving and sharing food, love, and understanding. Appropriate, affectionate physical contact is also required. In addition, verbal dialogues punctuated by periods of reflective silence demonstrate nurturance.

9.3 Discipline

Discipline encompasses teaching, guiding, corrective redirection, and helping children learn to develop self-containment and self-discipline. Toward these ends, parental expectations and demands are best offered in an atmosphere characterized by the consistent elucidation of optimal preferences.

9.4 Living Example

Children are natural witnesses. Everything children see and hear their parents say and do are living examples that adhesively imprint themselves on lasting psychological levels. This incorporation also applies to what children sense as parental attitudes. Living example encompasses exquisitely persuasive processes of nonconscious and conscious imprinting that includes identification, imitation, and copying. Biomental child development encompasses all these ideas in the concept of imitative identification.

9.5 Transactional Sensitivity

The typical infant-mother relationship is a focal point of intimate interrelatedness denoting each party's exquisitely sensitive experiential attunement to the other. This heuristic relationship of signal detection, understanding, and love is the prototype of transactional sensitivity. The infant's awareness and use of spatial relations and sense of kinetic containment biomentally grasps mother's attentiveness and responses. Such interpersonal resonance is the basis of early and preverbal communication and nurturing responsivity in attitude, gesture, and action.

The family as a whole also participates in this mutually interdependent awareness—nonconscious and conscious—of emotions, moods, and attitudes. Each member is sensitive to the other and the whole family and all adapt accordingly. Patterns of exchanges are unique to each person and the particular makeup of the family. These qualitative and quantitative entanglements persuasively influence individual and family behavioral trajectories. Greater fidelity in this attuned entrainment enhances greater success in forward advances. Empathy is the premier design for this meaningfully salient human rapport.

9.6 Developmental Perspective

From birth, the child incrementally and steadily expands in complexity through physical growth, biological maturational unfolding, and interpersonal experience. Developmental milestones and achievements are more than merely situational changes or rearrangements. The tempo of development is unique to each child as his or her body, mind, and spirit changes. Individual tempo reflects organically motivated, intrinsic shifts in the overall biomental reorientation to self, others, and environment. When caregivers recognize this tempo, suitable expectations prevail over "hurried" frustrations.

Biomental diversity and polymorphisms are "the rule" in development. These ideas denote that what may be understood to be a single stimulus or event, such as the ability to develop language or the variety of intellectual abilities, emerges in a number of different forms and may change over time.

It is not unreasonable to consider that biomental development has a characteristic overarching genetic continuity from birth onward. This perspective appreciates the multilayered nature of change—psychosocial and brain maturation—that includes advances that appear qualitatively novel. While growth, maturation, and development over time add complexity and new ways of comprehending, responding, and behaving, each individual's narrative retains a continuity of its unique *self-signature*.

9.7 Parents as Guides to Transitions

Change is a universal and inevitable occurrence. Dynamic processes in individuals, relationships, and contexts call for such recognition and preparation. As a child develops, expectable changes occur on many levels. In this process, change typically heralds multilayered and complex transitions. In other words, recognizing the complexity of biomental transformations—their stimuli and effects—helps parents to guide their children and family in smoother and more effective ways. Preparing children for change and transitions is crucial. At times, rehearsals in both verbal dialogues and graphic imagery are beneficial. In this way, the emotional intensity associated with conflicts typically around change, loss, and loss aversion may be mitigated.

9.8 Keeping Promises

Time management requires determining priorities—what is urgent and what can wait. Thoughtful planning and reasonable follow-through characterize promises.

9.9 Helping Relationships

Parenting is fostering empathy, compassion, sharing, teamwork, and "win-win" cooperative attitudes that promote adaptive behaviors.

9.10 Positive Statements and Encouragement

Positive statements that are modest and even-handed recognize and encourage a child's personal best. As a result, children come to regard themselves and their behaviors as being capable of being "exceptional," that is, good to very good. This sense of being modestly outstanding and above average sharply contrasts with unrealistically overinflated feedback such as may be conveyed by statements that emphasize "praise," which tends to imply an unrealistic specialness.

Positive statements and encouragement optimize motivation and effort. Accentuating a child's "personal best" references the principal criterion against which to measure effort, success, and need for improvement. Positive support and encouragement drive this helping framework.

9.11 The Dark Side of Human Nature

Negative emotions and attitudes are typical and inevitable. Identifying them in the context of their interaction with positive feelings promotes balance and perspective—an awareness of the modulation and reconfiguration that may produce successful outcomes. Emphasis here is on the interaction and dynamisms between constructive and destructive forces. The widened scope of such realistic thinking is transformative. Negativity so managed becomes the matrix for positive, health-promoting attitudes and subsequent action plans. Viewing and then using expressions of the "dark side" as "challenging moments" provide valuable learning opportunities for such reflection and action. This strategy promotes forward development and mental health.

9.12 Character

Character describes the overall goodness of one's personality, notably agreeable and cooperative relationships with others. Parents can foster a child's character by modeling living examples that reflect values of honesty, integrity, respectfulness, empathy, fairness, sharing, kindness, helpfulness, and those promoting prosocial behaviors.

REFERENCES

Baldwin Dancy, R. (2000). *You are your child's first teacher*. Berkeley, CA: Celestial Arts.
Bandura, A. (1977). *Social learning theory*. Englewood Cliffs, NJ: Prentice Hall.
———. (1986). *Social foundations of thought and actions: A social cognitive theory*. Englewood Cliffs, NJ: Prentice Hall.
Barkley, R. A. (1997). Behavioral inhibition, sustained attention, and executive functions: constructing a unifying theory of ADHD. *Psychological Bulletin, 12*(1), 65–94.

Barkley, R.A. (2012). *Executive functions: what they are, how they work, and why they evolved.* NY: Guilford.

Barnard, L., Stevens, T., To, W. M., Lan, W. Y., & Mulsow, M. (2010). The importance of ADHD subtype classification for educational applications of DSM-V. *Journal of Attention Disorders, 13*, 573–583.

Baumrind, D. (1967). Child care practices anteceding three patterns of preschool behavior. *Genetic Psychology Monographs, 75*(1), 43–88.

———. (1971). Current patterns of parental authority. *Developmental Psychology, 4*(1, pt. 2), 1–103.

———. (1978). Parental disciplinary patterns and social competence in children. *Youth and Society, 9*, 238–276.

———. (1991). Parenting styles and adolescent development. In R. Lerner, A.C. Peterson, & J. Brooks Gunn (Eds.), *The encyclopedia of adolescent development*, pp. 746–758. New York: Garland.

Bender, H. L., Allen, J. P., McElhaney, K. B., Antonishak, J., Moore, C. M., Kelly, H. L., & Davis, S. M. (2007). Use of harsh physical discipline and developmental outcomes in adolescence. *Development and Psychopathology, 19*, 227–242.

Berlin, L. J., Ipsa, J. M., Fine, M. A., Malone, P. S., Brooks-Gunn, J., Brady-Smith, C., & Bai, Y. (2009). Correlates and consequences of spanking and verbal punishment for low-income White, African American, and Mexican American toddlers. *Child Development, 80*(5), 1403–1420.

Berridge, C. W., Shumsky, J. S., Andrzejewski, M. E., McGaughy, J. A., Spencer, R. C., Devilbiss, D. M., &Waterhouse, B. D. (2012). Differential sensitivity to psychostimulants across prefrontal cognitive tasks: Differential involvement of noradrenergic α_1- and α_2-receptors. *Biological Psychiatry, 71*(5), 467–473.

Bhat, A., Heathcock, J., & Galloway, J. C. (2005). Toy-oriented changes in hand and joint kinematics during the emergence of purposeful reaching. *Infant Behavior and Development, 28*, 445–465.

Bornstein, M. H. 2002. *Handbook of parenting* (Vols. 1–5). London: Psychology Press Taylor & Francis.

Brown, K. D., & Hamilton-Giachritsis, C. (2005). The influence of violent media on children and adolescents: a public health approach. *Lancet, 365*, 702–710.

Burke, M. G. (2010). The impact of screen media on children: An environmental health perspective. *Psychiatric Times, 27*(10). www.psychiatrictimes.com/child-adolescent-psych/content/article/10168/1696463?CID=rss.

Charney, D. S. (2004). Psychobiological mechanisms of resilience and vulnerability: implications for successful adaptation to extreme stress. *American Journal of Psychiatry, 161*(2), 195–216.

Christakis, D. A., Zimmerman, F. J., DiGiuseppe, D. L., & McCarthy, C. A. (2004). Early television exposure and subsequent attentional problems in children. *Pediatrics, 113*, 708–713.

Cole, R. (1998). *The moral intelligence of children: How to raise a moral child.* New York: Plume Press.

Crawley, S. B., & Sherrod, R. B. (1984). Parent-infant play during the first year of life. *Infant Behavior and Development, 7*, 65–75.

Dalcroze, E. (2009). *Rhythm, music, and education.* Ithaca, NY: Cornell University Press.

Davies, G., Tenesa, A., Payton, A., Yang, J., Harris, S. E., Liewald, D., Ke, X., Le Hellard, S., Christoforou, A., Luciano, M., McGhee, K., Lopez, L., Gow, A. J., Corley, J., Redmond, P., Fox, H. C., Haggarty, P., Whalley, L. J., McNeill, G., Goddard, M. E., Espeseth, T., Lundervold, A. J., Reinvang, I., Pickles, A., Steen, V. M., Ollier, W., Porteous, D. J., Horan, M., Starr, J. M., Pendleton, N., Visscher, P. M., & Deary, I. J. (2011). Genome-wide association studies establish that human intelligence is highly heritable and polygenic. *Molecular Psychiatry, 16*, 996–1005. doi:10.1038/mp.2011.85

Deary, I. J. Yang, J., Davies, G., Harris, S. E., Tenesa, A., Liewald, D., Luciano, M., Lopez, L. M., Gow, A. J., Corley, J., Redmond, P., Fox, H. C., Rowe, S. J., Haggarty, P., McNeill, G., Goddard, M. E., Porteous, D. J., Whalley, L. J., Starr, J. M., & Visscher, P. M. (2012). Genetic contributions to stability and change in intelligence from childhood to old age. *Nature, 482*(7384), 212–215. doi:10.1038/nature10781

Dillon, D. G., & Pizzagalli, D. A. (2007). Inhibition of action, thought, and emotion: A selective neurobiological review. *Applied and Preventive Psychology, 12*, 99–114.

Donate-Bartfield, D., & Passman, R. H. (1985). Attentiveness of mothers and fathers to their babies' cries. *Child Development, 59*, 506–511.

Dunfield, K. A., O'Connell, L., Kuhlmeier, V. A., & Kelley, E. A. (2011). Examining the diversity of prosocial behavior: Helping, sharing, and comforting in infancy. *Infancy, 16*(3), 227–247.

Elsner, B., Hauf, P., & Aschersleben, G. (2007). Imitation step by step: A detailed analysis of 9- to 15-month-olds' reproduction of a three-step action sequence. *Infant Behavior and Development, 30*(2), 325–335.

Fagard, J., Spelke, E., & von Hofsten, C. (2009). Reaching and grasping a moving object in 6- ,8-, and 10-month-old infants: Laterality and performance. *Infant Behavior and Development, 32*, 137–146.

Gentile, D. A., Choo, H., Liau, A., Sim, T., Li, D., Fung, D., & Khoo, A. (2011). Pathological video game use among youths: a two-year longitudinal study. *Pediatrics, 127*(2), 319–329.

Gershoff, E. T. (2008). *Report on physical punishment in the United States: What research tells us about its effects on children.* Columbus, OH: Center for Effective Discipline.

Gottlieb, G. (2003). On making behavioral genetics truly developmental. *Human Development, 46*, 337–355.

Gredebäck, G., Theuring, C., Hauf, P., & Kenward, B. (2008). The microstructure of infants' gaze as they view adult shifts in overt attention. *Infancy, 13*(5), 533–543.

Green, R. (2010). *The explosive child.* New York: Harper.

Greenhill, L. L., & Hechtman, L. I. (2009). Attention-deficit/hyperactivity disorder. In B. J. Sadock, V. A. Sadock, & P. Ruiz (Eds.), *Comprehensive textbook of psychiatry*, pp. 3560–3572. New York: Wolters Kluwer/Lippincott William's & Wilkins.

Harris, M. (1975). *Thinking about infants and young children.* London: Clunie Press.

Hauf, P. (2007). Infant's perception and production of intentional actions. In C. von Hofsten & K. Rosander (Eds.), *Progress in brain research: From action to cognition, Vol. 164*, pp. 285–301. Amsterdam: Elsevier.

Hauf, P. (2009). The interchange of self-performed actions and perceived actions in infants. In T. Striano & V. Reid (Eds.), *Social cognition: Development, neuroscience and autism*, pp. 129–143. Oxford: Wiley-Blackwell.

Hauf, P., & Aschersleben, G. (2008). Action-effect anticipation in infant action control. *Psychological Research, 72*, 203–210.

Hauf, P., & Försterling, F. (Eds.). (2007). *Making minds: The shaping of human minds through social context.* Amsterdam & Philadelphia: John Benjamins.

Hauf, P., & Prinz, W. (2007). The understanding of own and others' actions during infancy: "You-like-me" or "me-like-you"? In P. Hauf & F. Försterling (Eds.), *Making minds: The shaping of human minds through social context*, pp. 211–226. Amsterdam & Philadelphia: John Benjamins. (Reprinted from *Interaction Studies, 6*(3), 429–445)

Hauf, P., Prior, H., & Sarris, V. (2008). Context-dependent generalization gradients and representation modes after absolute and relational discrimination learning in young chickens. *Behavioural Processes, 78*(1), 93–99.

Hauf, P., & Sarris, V. (2008). Two-dimensional psychophysics in chickens and humans: Comparative aspects of perceptual relativity. *Japanese Psychological Research, 50*(4), 167–182.

Hauser, M. (2006). *Moral minds: How nature designed our universal sense of right and wrong.* New York: Harper Collins.

Hayne, H., Herbert, J., & Simcock, G. (2003). Imitation from television by 24- and 30-month-olds. *Developmental Science, 6*, 254–261.

Henderson, A., & Pehoski, C. (2005). *Hand function in children.* New York: Mosby.

Hibbard, R., Barlow, J., MacMillan, H., & the Committee on Child Abuse and Neglect and AMERICAN ACADEMY OF CHILD AND ADOLESCENT PSYCHIATRY (2012). Psychological maltreatment. *Pediatrics, 130* (2), 372–378.

Hofer, T., Hauf, P. & Aschersleben, G. (2007). Infants' perception of goal-directed actions on video. *British Journal of Developmental Psychology, 25*, 485–498.

Hofer, T., Hohenberger, A., Hauf, P., & Aschersleben, G. (2008). Does the maternal interaction style have an impact on infants' early action understanding? *Infant Behavior and Development, 31*, 115–126.

Hoffman, M. L. (2000). *Empathy and moral development.* New York: Cambridge University Press.

Huttenlocher, P. R. (1979). Synaptic density in human frontal cortex: Developmental changes and effects of aging. *Brain Research, 163*, 195–205.

Isaacs, S. (1968) [1948]. *Children and parents.* London: Routledge & Kegan Paul.

Jackson, L. A., Zhao, Y., Kolenic, A., Fitzgerald, H. E., Harold, R., & von Eye, A. (2008). Race, gender, and information technology use: The new digital divide. *CyberPsychology and Behavior, 11*, 437–442.

Knafo, A., & Plomin, R. (2006). Parental discipline and affection and children's prosocial behavior: Genetic and environmental links. *Journal of Personality and Social Psychology, 90*, 147–164.

Krcmar, M., Grela, B., & Linn, K. (2007). Can toddlers learn vocabulary from television? *Media Psychology, 10*, 41–63.

Kuhlmeier, V. A., Wynn, K., & Bloom, P. (2003). Attribution of dispositional states by 12-month-olds. *Psychogical Science,* 14, 402–408.

Kuhlmeier, V. A., Bloom, P., & Wynn, K. (2004). Do 5-month-old infants see humans as material objects? *Cognition, 94*, 95–103.

Landsford, J. E., Criss, M. M., Dodge, K. A., Shaw, D. S., Pettit, G. S., & Bates, J. E. (2009). Trajectories of physical discipline: Early childhood antecedents and developmental outcomes. *Child Development, 80*, 1385–1402.

Lerner, R. M. (2006). Developmental science, developmental systems, and contemporary theories of human development. In R. M. Lerner (Ed.), *Handbook of child psychology, Vol. 1: Theoretical models of human development* (6th ed.), pp.1–17. Hoboken, NJ: Wiley.

Low, B. S. (2000). *Why sex matters: A Darwinian look at human behavior.* Princeton, NJ: Princeton University Press.

Lynch, S. K., Turkheimer, E., D'Onofrio, B. M., Mendle, J., Emery, R. E., Slutske, W. S., & Martin, N. G. (2006). A genetically informed study of the association between harsh punishment and offspring behavioral problems. *Journal of Family Psychology, 20*, 190–198.

Malloch, S. T., & Trevarthen, C. V. (2010). *Communicative musicality: Exploring the basis of human companionship.* New York: Oxford University Press.

Mandler, J. M. (2010). The spatial foundations of the conceptual system. *Language and Cognition, 2*, 21–44.

Mason, L., O'Sullivan, N., Blackburn, M., Bentall, R., & El-Deredy, W. (2012). I want it now! Neural correlates of hypersensitivity to immediate reward in hypomania. *Biological Psychiatry, 71*, 530–537.

Mayes, L. C., & Cohen, D. J. (2002). *The Yale Child Study Center guide to understanding your child.* Boston: Little, Brown & Co.

McDonough, L., Choi, S., & Mandler, J. (2003). Understanding spatial relations: Flexible infants, lexical adults. *Cognitive Psychology, 46*, 229–259.

Meltzer, L. (Ed.). (2010). *Executive function in education: from theory to practice.* New York: Guilford.

Mick, E., McManus, D. D., & Goldberg, R. J. (2012). Meta-analysis of increased heart rate and blood pressure associated with CNS stimulant treatment of ADHD in adults. *European Journal of Neuropsychopharmacology, July 13.* PMID: 22796229 (Epub ahead of print)

Mitrofan, O., Paul, M., & Spenser, N. (2009). Is aggression in children with behavioral and emotional difficulties associated with television viewing and video game playing? A systematic review. *Child Care Health Development, 35*, 5–15.

Montoya, A., Colom, F., & Ferrin, M. (2011). Is psychoeducation for parents and teachers of children and adoléscents with ADHD efficacious? A systematic literature review. *European Psychiatry, 26*(3), 166–175.

Mullen, E. M. (1995). *Mullen Scales of Early Learning.* Sydney, Australia: Pearson/Psych-Corp.

Murray, J. P., Liotti, M., Ingmundson, P. T., Mayberg, H. S., Pu, Y., Zamarripa, F., Liu, Y., Woldorff, M. G., Gao, J. H., & Fox, P. T. (2006). Children's brain activations while viewing televised violence revealed by fMRI. *Media Psychology, 8*(1), 25–37.

Nicholson, J. S., Howard, K. S., & Borowski, J. G. (2008). Mental models for parenting: correlates of metaparenting among fathers of young children. *Fathering: A Journal of Theory, Research, and Practice, 6*, 39–61.

Ohashi, K., Vitaliano, G., Polcari, A., & Teicher, M. H. (2010). Unravelling the nature of hyperactivity in children with attention-deficit/hyperactivity disorder. *Archives of General Psychiatry, 67*(4), 388–396.

Ostrov, J. M., Gentile, D. A., & Crick, N. R. (2006). Media exposure, aggression, and prosocial behavior during early childhood: A longitudinal study. *Social Development, 15*, 612–627.

Ozonoff, S., Macari, S., Young, G. S., Goldring, S., Thompson, M. N., & Rogers, S. J. (2008). Atypical object exploration at 12 months of age is associated with autism in a prospective sample. *Autism, 12*, 457–472.

Piaget, J. (1952). *The origins of intelligence in children.* New York: International Universities Press. (Original work published 1936)

Prinz, W., Försterling, F. & Hauf, P. (2007). From minds and mirrors: an introduction to the social making of minds. In P. Hauf & F. Försterling (Eds.), *Making minds: The shaping of human minds through social context*, pp. 1–16. Amsterdam & Philadelphia: John Benjamins.

Ross, R. (2010). *Adventures in parenting.* Spring Valley, NY: Rudolf Steiner Press.

Rudd, H. (19840. Infants' manipulative exploration of objects: Effect of age and object characteristics. *Developmental Psychology, 20*, 9–20.

Ruff, H. A. (1986). Components of attention during infants' manipulative exploration. *Child Development, 75*, 105–114.

Ruff, H., Salterelli, L. M., Capozolli, M., & Dubiner, K. (1992). The differentiation of activity in infants' exploration of objects. *Developmental Psychology, 8*, 851–861.

Sergeant, J. A., Geurts, H., & Oosterlaan, J. (2002). How specific is a deficit of executive functioning for attention-deficit/hyperactivity disorder? *Behavioural Brain Research, 130*, 3–38.

Straus, M. A., & Stewart, J. H. (1999). Corporal punishment by American parents: National data on prevalence, chronicity, severity, and duration in relation to child and family characteristics. *Clinical Child and Family Psychology Review, 2*, 55–70.

Swing, E. L., Gentile, D. A., Anderson, C. A., & Walsh, D. A. (2010). Television and video game exposure and the development of attention problems. *Pediatrics, 126*, 214–221.

Thompson, R. A., & Nelson, C. A. (2001). Developmental science and the media. *American Psychologist, 56*, 5–15.

Toga, A. W., & Thompson, P. M. (2005). Genetics of brain structure and intelligence. *Annual Review of Neuroscience, 28*, 1–23.

Troje, N. F., & Westhoff, C. (2006). The inversion effect in biological motion perception: evidence for a "life detector"? *Current Biology, 16*(8), 821–824.

Turiel, E. (2006). The development of morality. In N. Eisenberg (Ed.), *Handbook of child psychology, Vol. 3: Social, emotional, and personality development* (6th ed.), pp. 789–857. Hoboken, NJ: Wiley.

Vuontela V., Carlson S., Troberg A. M., Fontell T., Simola P., Saarinen S., & Aronen E. T. (2012). Working Memory, Attention, Inhibition, and Their Relation to Adaptive Functioning and Behavioral/Emotional Symptoms in School-Aged Children. *Child Psychiatry Hum Dev. 2012 June 4.* (Epub ahead of print.)

Webb, S. J., Monk, C. S., & Nelson, C. A. (2001). Mechanisms of postnatal neurobiological development: Implications for human development. *Developmental Neuropsychology, 19*, 147–171.

Weinberg, R. A. (1989). Intelligence and IQ: Landmark issues and great debates. *American Psychologist, 44*, 98–104.

Willcutt, E. G., Doyle, A. E., Nigg, J. T., Faraone, S. V., & Pennington, B. F. (2005). Validity of the executive function theory of attention-deficit/hyperactivity disorder: A meta-analytic review. *Biological Psychiatry, 57*, 1336–1346.

Winn, M. (1985). *The plug-in drug.* New York: Viking.

Wolff, J. J., Gu, H., Gerig, G., Elison, J. T., Styner, M., Gouttard, S., Botteron, K. N., Dager, S. R., Dawson, G., Estes, A. M., Evans, A. C., Hazlett, H. C., Kostogopoulos, P., McKinstry, R. C., Peterson, S. J., Schultz, R. T., Zwaigenbaum, L., & Piven, J. (2012). Differences in white matter fiber tract development present from 6 to 24 months in infants with autism. *American Journal of Psychiatry, 169*(6), 589–600.

Yamaguchi, M., Kuhlmeier, V. A., Wynn, K., & vanMarie, K. (2009). Continuity in social cognition from infancy to childhood. *Developmental Science, 12*, 746–752.

Young, S., & Myanthi Amarasinghe, J. (2010). Practitioner review: non-pharmacological treatments for ADHD: a lifespan approach. *Journal of Child Psychology and Psychiatry, 51*(2), 116–133.

Zimmerman, F. J., & Christakis, D. A. (2005). Children's television viewing and cognitive outcomes. *Archives of Pediatrics and Adolescent Medicine, 159*, 619–625.

Zimmerman, F. J., Christakis, D. A., & Meltzoff, A. N. (2007). Television and DVD/video viewing in children younger than 2 years. *Archives of Pediatrics and Adolescent Medicine, 161*, 473–479.

Chapter Two

The Psychology of the Child

1. THE CHILD AS A WHOLE PERSON

From birth onward, children normally grow and develop in a relatively coordinated, synchronous, yet dynamically vacillating manner. All children move through development, to varying extents, toward adulthood. Head, heart, and hands develop producing a unique biomental individual. Each child's multitiered developmental progress consists of many disparate biomental components constantly transforming to create more synthesized functioning wholes.

Typically, dimensions of the physical body and mind undergo developmental progressions together, though some features may excel while others proceed more slowly. Growth and developmental progression normally show variations in three major parameters. These may be compared against age-defined norms and include rate, pattern, and ultimate level reached.

Although rigidly fixed developmental sequences absolutely determined by innate maturational tables do not occur, characteristic trends are usual in most children. When variations or interferences occur, the child's behavior may be within normal ranges, reflect unevenness, or reveal developmental lags, delays, atypicalities, or disorders. Slow pace may be transitory after which it may normalize by early adulthood. However, if abilities do not return to normal ranges, professional assessment may be required. The entire field of learning disabilities, for example, has emerged to identify persistently slower or varied cognitive capacities in children in order to offer suitable compensatory remediation.

For example, recognition of atypical development found in persons with *autistic spectrum disorders* is possible when problematic social skills or communicational symptoms become clearly apparent during the second and third years of life. While social and communicational development com-

143

mences at birth and is evident in the first year, atypical, attenuated, or irregular expressions may be subtle. There may be signs of greater vulnerability in areas of social initiation rather than social responsiveness in contexts of "joint attention" between seven to nine months. Infants may also be recognized to be slow feeders and accept solid foods later (well after about six months) than typical infants. At twenty-four months and thereafter, signs become more apparent. These behaviors may include minimal eye contact, absent or minimal language, and/or inability to relate to one's peers. Insistence on sameness and difficulty adapting to change may also emerge. Earlier recognition of such problems, at twelve months for example, may be indicated by an infant's atypical exploratory or object manipulation behaviors: more manual rotation of objects (such as turning or spinning them) and prolonged lateral gazing (which is fixating on a visual target with the pupils turned toward an extreme corner of the eye socket, as in peering).

In order to gain a better understanding of the complexity of child development, some of its more discernable dimensions or developmental sectors are enumerated in table 2.1. While recognizing these dimensions is useful, the child as a whole and complex person should be a primary focus. This also implies valuing the child as an individual with a uniquely integrating set of characteristics that include traits, temperament, attachment pattern, and personality. As mentioned, distilling child development into a few words is an oversimplification of a multifaceted phenomenon. This book does not seek to fully detail all the nuances of development, but to outline them in hopes of stimulating further study. Temperament, attachment patterns, and personality as distinct constructs will be discussed.

The extent to which variations in development are recognized, together with an appreciation of individual differences in temperament and personality, gives immeasurable adaptive flexibility to parents in parenting. Each child is inevitably different from the next. This overarching concept of heterogeneity cannot be overemphasized.

2. THE MEANING OF EGO, SELF, SENSE OF IDENTITY, "I," AND MIND

In individual psychology, terms such as *ego*, *self*, *sense of identity*, and *I* refer to the overall way an individual experiences him or herself to the extent possible at a given age and in relation to social context. Although these terms denote self-reference, they are grounded in an interactive mode—self in relation to another.

Table 2.1. Dimensions of Typical Child Development

The following broad categories describe important biomental sectors of a child's overall development. These psychobiological/biomental dimensions include both the physical body and its psychosocial aptitudes—emotional, cognitive, and social:

Physical growth and CNS maturation

Temperament

Attachment

Psychological and emotional development

Cognitive/intellectual development

Social development

Communication and language

Psychosexual: viewing self in terms of gender

Moral development

The presumption of a *self*—the broadest characterization denoting an individual—always implies some degree of awareness of others. The term *ego* used here derives from its understanding in psychodynamic psychology. This definition describes the structure and functioning of the individual, notably cognitive and emotional information processing. *Ego* connotes an instrument of measurement—the mind constructing boundedness that gives shape to forms such as mental images that correlate with external persons and things. The term *self* used in the present text is virtually synonymous with the term *ego* unless otherwise specified. No pejorative connotations relating to overconfidence or excessive self-pride are implied when using the term *ego*.

A *sense of identity* is intimately related to social awareness and the way a person articulates—explicitly and implicitly—his or her individuality and characteristic style of attitude and behavior. One's sense of identity chiefly denotes a personal awareness or belief about who he or she is, for example, male or female, young or old, happy or unhappy, and so forth.

Self-identity or "I" denotes self-assigned (labeled and named) personality characteristics distinguishing individuals from others; in other words, self-identity is an individual's conscious belief about who they are as separate individuals. By contrast, *sense of self* implies a more, nonconscious self-experience.

Mind usually refers to the subjective awareness of self—how one experiences her- or himself as a person. It is the broad faculty encompassing sensation, perception, conception, and information processing both nonconscious and conscious. In relation to self, the mind forms mental models—knowledge about the perceived self as "self-concepts." In the biomental perspective, the mind is understood to be the interior dimension of the body, and the body is seen as the exterior dimension of mind. From birth onward, the developing ego and self gradually consolidate, notably by developing memory systems and by dreaming processes occurring during sleep.

While primitive, foundational, and unmatured aspects of all these "self" faculties are present at an early age, they each have a time-sensitive developmental trajectory reflected in their expansion and refinement from infancy, through childhood, and into adulthood.

At birth, infants sense—in still primitive ways—themselves as distinct from the environment. By three months, research demonstrates that infants have an implicit sense of self versus other. The more substantive development of intermodal perception supports this ability. The nuances of this skill develop slowly but are evident in the progressively responsive and anticipatory behaviors that indicate an explicit sense of self-other differentiation: "peek-a-boo," waving "bye-bye," "stranger anxiety," and "separation anxiety" seen during the first year, at approximately eight to ten months. During the second year, more explicit self-awareness develops. Toddlers begin pointing to themselves in a mirror, identifying parts of their own body, referring to self by name, and by saying "I" and understanding the concept "mine" typically between twenty-four and thirty to thirty-six months. These abilities connote self-recognition and a clearer sense of separateness from others. The cognitive ability to have a conception of "two" is emerging. This is a basic feature of *adaptive socialization*—the self's sense of possessing and interacting with both other people and inanimate objects. Other indications of self-differentiation and self-categorization include indicating self by using terms such as "baby," "boy," "big," and also by self-selecting play items that imply sexual stereotypes such as dolls and tea sets for girls and trucks for boys.

At about thirty-six months children can label some feelings they experience. That they are able to recognize their own shadow, for example, evidences bodily self-awareness. On the other hand, the presence of *scale errors*—performing actions that actual body size makes impossible, such as putting on doll's clothes—shows the attendant immaturity and unevenness of cognitive development during this time. Between ages four and five, most children sense themselves and many of their emotional and physical characteristics as having a sustained continuity over time. By age six, a relatively more realistic grasp of self, body, and body capabilities becomes evident, though it is still fragile compared to that of an adult.

2.1 Identity and Culture

Viewing the child as a whole person, individual yet part of social structures, takes a wider perspective into account. This view gives deeper insights to both individual and social development. The term *identity* highlights the individual's sense of self while the term *culture* connotes identity as shaped by experiences in groups. Since these two ideas are rooted in the very essence of the human condition, this section addresses them in detail.

As is true for an understanding of the knowledge behind the skills relating to child development and parenting, fully savoring the facts of an individual's life in its dynamic group or social context is crucial. The individual and the social group have both similarities and differences, notably material structure and worldview that distinguish each in complex ways. For each developing person, the task is to rationally modulate his or her identity as an individual with identity as a member of the group. Individuals reference groups for the values, beliefs, and models of conduct the group espouses. Civilized group existence is neither primitive, ruthless self-sufficiency in a survivalist horde nor more cooperative adaptation in a tribal society. In its optimal sense, the civilized group encompasses a sense of enthusiastic self-regard within the cooperative individual-group synergy of human civilization.

My almost twenty years of work with children—individual therapy and participation in group process on a weekly basis—in a large residential school has been witness to the bold interplay between the organization of individual and group identity. Individual and group experience are essential to the survival and development of one another since individuals need groups to carry out functions that the individual alone cannot; the reverse of this need is also true. The synchronies and inevitable clashes of this transactional dynamic are the crucible of identity formation. These longitudinal observations have lent support to ideas in this section. Understanding the individual in the context of group culture indeed highlights characteristics of individuals that might not easily be distinguished if both perspectives are not taken into account.

A significant consideration that will not be elaborated upon in this section is that individuals in groups are typically described using the interpersonal and social paradigm of "the family." The biomental perspective includes this notion, but counts heavily the intrapsychic composition of each individual as being projected outward in order for this externalization to manifest materially as a set of dynamic forces that shape and motivate a group's structure. Individual conflict, therefore, is given a vicarious opportunity via the group for resolution so that a higher level of psychological refinement may occur. With the individual element so enhanced, the group in turn further cultures its identity and civilizes its functions. While individuals comprise groups and communities of groups, attention to the uniqueness of the individual, as such, remains the focus of this book.

Individual psychology is intimately related to *social psychology*. Each type of thinking influences the other. The sociohistorical context of an individual's childhood in society is explicit. In addition, individuals live out socio-prehistorical evolutionary adaptations embedded by genetics in less explicit ways. A society's cultural evolutionary adaptations also impose themselves on an individual at birth and throughout development by their modeling influence.

Basic assumptions having both conscious and nonconscious foundations shape individual (identity) and group identity (culture). The broad platform underlying these assumptions is the asymmetrical exchange between people and individuals and groups. These transactions involve exchanges of resources in a field whose dynamics involve expressions of power, influence, the ability to control, and a dominance-subordination framework. As has been a theme of this book, *envy theory* understands the aforementioned to constitute the impulses that generate social hierarchies and the social stratification reflecting real and perceived differences, often sensed as inequalities. Such social rankings reflect arrangements that denote a continuum from superior to inferior status. Child development theories demonstrate that such an interpersonal and social hierarchical awareness is present early on. The expression of this awareness becomes increasingly acute during middle childhood and adolescence. In adulthood, asymmetry, whether healthy or excessive, between and among people is a regular feature of daily life (family life, educational ranking, occupational position, and so forth).

An individual's *self-concept* is composed of beliefs, mostly conscious self-perceptions, whose elements typically encompass gender, race, and academic status. Conscious thoughts, feelings, and behaviors reflect answers to the internal questions of "Who am I?" and "What is it that I do?" These elements develop from both internal dispositional sources and learning through exposure to social norms. A child's not-yet clearly defined sense of self typically struggles to organize in relation to that child's social group experience. Each has distinct features, yet the influence of the microcosmic world of the individual typically trumps its component status in the group macrocosm. Each exists as separate, yet in a field of dynamic synergy.

As will be seen throughout this book, the universal psychophilosophical construct of *the one and the many* is an underlying theme in human development, though it has both conceptual and practical problems. In this framework, an individual's sense of self-identity as "the one" is nested within a culture of "the many."

A person's sense of identity is the set of self-defined characteristics that the individual assigns to him or herself. While distinctions between individual identity and group identity exist, they remain porous. The individual is typically born into and relates to a "first" group—the family.

Many internal individual challenges result from the "groupishness" or multiple experiential dimensions that compose the individual biomental self. This denotes mental experience developmentally organizing itself as ever-occurring groups of dual units with polar opposites. The extremes between the opposites and the relations between them become crucial nodes of self-orientation. For example, recognizing good and bad, right and wrong, delaying gratification in the face of frustration, and making choices in the face of options are tensions that typically contain elements of conflict. Early in life, dynamic, inner struggles crystallize around selected nodes of difficulty and first emerge as individual concerns.

Group affiliation temporarily mutes this initial individual emphasis. It automatically morphs attention to a larger, group emphasis, which presents collective values, options, and expanded opportunities. Indeed, group experience aptitude—the individual's inner core of readiness to establish and then choose a position among groups of dichotomies—is intrinsic to individual psychology. It remains at the heart of individual functioning when individuals operate in groups. Social roles and situational pressures exert powerful influences on social behavior.

Since the human species exists in family and extended social groupings, dynamic social, cultural, and other collective forces inextricably shape self-identity. These reciprocal interactions comprise the process of socialization. Sex, gender, and mating are basic influences in socialization and the establishment of societies. While these factors are particularly evident in groups of younger individuals, they—as well as a "work function"—appear in every group. This section will not address these matters as they are detailed in chapter 6.

Social influences are situational macro-variables that allow the fundamental wish to conform to mix with persuasion and learning to contour personal identity. Hence, social goals, typically more global and diffuse than individual goals, are acquired as beliefs and values. Social and cultural factors promoting habit development and conditioning significantly contribute to the stability, at times "entrenchment," of one's sense of personal identity over time.

Learning from perceived social roles and their rule expectancies influences self-identity, as do innate dispositional predilections. The seeds and roots of self-identity are watered by exposure to a learning environment. Genetic preparedness interacts with learning to release behaviors that are *flexibly* species-typical.

From a cognitive perspective, learned behaviors and their implementation have been shown to correlate positively with explicit, conscious attitudes and preferences. Dispositional behaviors, by contrast, are more innately endowed, although learning influences their archaic moorings.

Dispositional behaviors, therefore, have species-specific, constitutional biases and result from implicit attitudes—varying clusters of biomental traits—that are not in conscious awareness. While this unconscious component is influential, conscious learning in everyday living and through cultural acquisitions secondarily shapes one's overall adaptation.

One example of a dispositional core reaction is visceral fear of predators, such as snakes and wild animals. Evolutionary psychology correlates such fear-eliciting threat detection with the fear, if not archaic reality, of being "food" for these formidable beasts. Biomental child development further speculates that the links between visceral fear and food have become a prime model for propelling human survival—infant with the feeding mother.

Furthermore, fear, anxiety, and stress are highly correlated. Frustration, conflict, change, and pressure to conform to others' expectations are major types of stress. In addition to the activation of specific brain structures such as the amygdala and others, neurochemicals mediated by the hypothalamic-pituitary-adrenal (HPA) axis arise to manage such distress. When increased cortisol and other substances are thus released, a "smell" of vulnerability arises. Whereas prey sense this vulnerability and attack, in human infant development, the beneficent mother's transactional sensitivity is heightened to her infant's distress and responds with increased protection. Therefore, survival predicated on fear instigates avoidance; survival predicated on "love" elicits intimate affiliation. Discussing the complexities that this hypothesis has for humans is beyond the scope of this section, but is addressed further in chapter 3 and elsewhere in my work on envy theory. Fear nonconsciously evokes aversive emotions that influence automatic, implicit, cognitive assumptions. Attentional bias toward threatening information, if prolonged, may generate and maintain anxiety. While such subliminal biases may not be explicitly understood or articulated, they nevertheless forcefully direct behaviors.

Other well-recognized species-typical behaviors include the universal expressions of emotions such as anger, happiness, sadness, surprise, and disgust. Another behavior is the "eyebrow flash"—momentary raising of eyebrows accompanied by a smile. It is a universal human sign of greeting among friends. The presence of other such dispositional responses, for example, that children born blind and deaf manifest emotions such as joy in the same basic way as sighted children, is described in the psychological literature. Since such behavior does not have to be learned through observation attests to the presence of at least some truly innate human instinctual reactions. This dispositional reactivity does not minimize the crucial role of learning in fostering and shaping the *development* of attitudes and behaviors over time.

Individuals seek approval and a sense of belonging from social bonds because of innate drives for needing to belong. In order to feel accepted and included, individuals rely on other group members for cues about how to behave. In fact, groups typically look to a designated leader for orientation and direction. This guide, whose established authority can be precarious, becomes a group's essential reference point.

Often, however, satisfying the urge to share communal bonds provides a stronger adhesion than agreeing on stated beliefs or common aims. Shared camaraderie in a safe and structured setting is pleasurable and reinforcing. Relying on cues from others is, in fact, a normal developmental milestone termed *social referencing*, which becomes evident as early as ten to fourteen months of age.

Individual psychology (individual identity) and group psychology (social identity) are distinguishable by different behaviors and corresponding motivations. Groups as social cultures behave according to their characteristically learned group customs and established norms. The group as a whole behaves differently from the sum of its constituent members. A sort of homogenization of individuals produces waves of shared group identity. Individuals assimilate and establish a group "mind" or ethos having characteristic goals, aims, and sentiments.

Consistent group trends may develop into "stereotypes" that characterize the group and that the group uses to characterize others. In many ways, examining group processes provides an intelligible field in which to study the individual in his or her intrinsically pair-oriented dispositions. This pair orientation is part of the individual's inner "groupishness" template. This concept denotes that both pair-orientations and groupishness clusters exist both within an individual and in an individual's external relations to others—the group. This conceptualization highlights the "betweenness" or "relations dynamic" that exists as the fundamental unit of all mental experience. When alone, individuals tend to behave more consistently with their individual dispositional preferences than with their group's orientations. My experiences with children seen individually and the same children seen in group settings have illustrated this difference that has appeared reliably over years.

Whatever its size and configuration, a group's external forms and rituals reflect its collectively decided values. A group psychology unfolds in the constructs of culture and civilization. *Culture* is the shared attitudes, values, beliefs, aspirations, and practices of organized groups. These features typically appear exaggerated and so distinguish different groups by their distinctiveness. Culture, its group dynamics, and its traditions are transmitted through a number of mechanisms from generation to generation. No one set of standard biological, psychological, or social parameters defines a given culture since its highly numerous variables change dynamically over time.

The broader term *civilization* emphasizes a culture's complex technology and operations aimed toward protection against nature; furthermore, its complex social hierarchies and institutional governments afford needed regulation of individual and group relations. These work-oriented systems include occupational specializations, trade, financial institutions, legal regulations, political arrangements, religions, and organizations such as city, state, tribe, or nation. Cleanliness, order, and aesthetics characterize civilizations. Art and literature may be considered the jewels of civilization.

Cultures are typically smaller communal groups nested within larger civilizations. Cultures, with their more implicit influence, and civilizations, with their greater material expressions, nonetheless have similar typographic configurations. Such structures as the cultural family or nation civilization are fractal dimensions. In other words, these perspectives may be similar in form and function across diverse geographical groups even though their scale and specific contents may differ. Cultures and civilizations enhance individual and group survival and advancement. Law is an indispensable, although imperfect, requirement to prevent individual and social violence. Laws and their enforcement are representatives of individual conscience externalized to support not only individual but also group survival. *Ethics* is a culture's guiding censor outlining right versus wrong behaviors among individuals. Guilt, whether imposed from outside or derived internally, provides a compass for restraint along lines of legal and moral regulation. Laws and conscience make possible both individual and group survival.

Biomental child development views individual behaviors and group organizations as expressions of *both* genetic and learned influences. Genetics invariably expresses itself in individual behaviors that become demonstrated and observed. This is the context in which learning occurs. Particular cultures as organized groups of individuals then display these innate, learned, and preferred behaviors. Random events, such as individual genetic mutations or qualitative cultural changes in technology, also play a part in influencing both individuals and the collective group. Individuals and groups thus transactionally affect one another.

When one is born into a culture, that culture provides a ready-made identity to internalize. This template reinforces a sense of security and becomes an attitudinal "comfort zone" that is difficult to alter. Often, collective or social identity fosters diffusion of individual boundaries and personal responsibility. This diffusion stimulates feelings of individual anonymity as occurs in crowd and mob phenomena, which typically are driven by unconscious assumptions having irrational aims. When conformity to this group-endowed identity is questioned or challenged, especially by outside forces, problems of anxiety and discontent typically arise.

Group emotion has a collective fervor that passionately organizes its members. This peer pressure is similar to the susceptibility that peer pressure causes in adolescents. The term "groupthink" denotes the group's suspension of critical thinking in a misguided effort to promote a semblance of agreement. Implicit stirrings can quickly overshadow and mesmerize the group's trajectory of actions, which often become directed to a perceived enemy in the form of another group or even an idea. For example, when groups become hyperunified and take on characteristics of mobs, a robust detonation may erupt for no apparent reason, linger, and then fizzle. During these episodes, the will of individuals becomes submerged and deferred to that of a leader. In addition, the group's sense of time vanishes along with any linear flow of logic. Uncritical limbic system neurological processes allow for emotions to prevail over reason. Numerous psychological studies over the years have demonstrated the remarkable unleashing of the darkest of emotions and behaviors—torture and murder—that groups, mobs, and charismatic leaders may trigger. It is undeniable that most people harbor negative inclinations, at least in fantasy. Some, however, may have qualitative differences in brain structure and functioning (for example, variations in amygdala size or circuitry) that predispose them to more easily enact such unrestrained brutality.

While it is true that groups help individuals contain and deal with primitive impulses that individuals alone cannot adequately manage, groups may reverse this function in pathological ways. For example, the self-destructive aspects of envy force individuals—subsets within groups and subgroups who behave as if regressed to tribal values—to construct misperceptions of unfamiliar or strange others as "enemies." Group processes that govern the regulation of power in social systems then structure, externalize, and superimpose such subgroup envy-driven fantasies on the larger group level. The bitter politics of envy, therefore, ultimately becomes enacted on a large scale through aggression and war. It is often said that war is politics carried out through humankind's most primitive devices.

In addition to the outside influences from groups, an individual may also question his or her own cultural values. At this point, both the previous unity that characterized the individual and group as well as the individual's sense of his or her unified group dissociates. When he or she dissents, a social dilemma results. An individual may wish a previous sense of personal self-identity to develop into something more unique than merely reflecting "an acquired collection of ideas learned from others." When this impulse to self-differentiate occurs, it launches the search for a new identity. In many ways, leadership orientation moves from being perceived as an outside authority toward greater internalization. This process is typical, to some extent, in the adolescent years.

By contrast, when an individual's embedded cultural identity remains unassailed by either self-questioning or dissenting challenges from outside, it continues to remain stable. Such consolidation tends to reinforce itself by intragroup polarized opinions that, in turn, highlight intergroup distinctions. Extremes of "in-group" identity approach particularism, which is a dedicated, exclusive positive interest in one's own group. Using superior-inferior framed exaggerations, the "in-group" typically views the "out-group" as foreign, strange, or challenging. In-group favoritism and out-group derogation emerge as both themes and behaviors. Stereotyping, prejudice, and mis-perceiving others as "the enemy" develop. These dichotomies further cement the positive identity between an individual and his group.

Normal consolidation of self-identity, in contrast to rigid or conflictual diffuseness, is conducive to mental health. It correlates with its prosocial tolerance, agreeableness, and cooperation without inordinate biases. Secure self-identity denotes an individual's conscious and intentional engagement with the larger group. Rather than blind and unreflective compliance, normal self-identity consolidates by means of an active consideration and integration of personal and group values, beliefs, and aspirations.

Healthy groups—family, cultures, civilizations, and so forth—have clear yet flexible parameters, reasonable beliefs, adaptable goals, and self-reflective monitoring. The structure and functioning of these groups are beneficial to individual members as well as the group as a whole. One's self-identity in such groups is supported, enhancing both individual and group goals. An effective and mutually satisfying transactional sensitivity, accordingly, is constructively operational.

Rigidity and inflexibility in both individuals and groups, by contrast, may produce feelings of *xenophobia*—disdain, fear, and threat of those perceived as "different." This atmosphere typically results from beliefs that are held with intransient conviction that is inflexible to reason and reality testing. When these feelings are nonconscious, they act as implicit assumptions that subliminally bias attitudes and behaviors. When these xenophobic feelings are more explicit, they may take the form of clear-cut fears and irrational prejudices that elicit destructive hostilities and designations of "the other" as "the enemy." The significance of such polarized attitudes and xenophobic feelings is discussed at length in chapter 6 in sections discussing the family and attitudes of envy, greed, and jealousy in human development and social psychology.

2.2 Self-Other Awareness and the Developmental Trajectory of Social Communication: Psychological and Neuroscience Perspectives

Attention to self-other status and how it becomes differentiated have been major areas of focus in the psychological sciences for almost one hundred years. The psychoanalytic tradition termed an individual's sense of this differentiation as *ego versus object* and described it in ways that highlighted emotion, phenomenological experience, and relationships both perceived and expressed.

Modern cognitive developmentalists emphasize more objectively measurable, empirical aspects of self-other awareness. Such psychological and neuroscience research stresses this awareness's implications for social intelligence, encompassing both cognitive and emotional understanding, communication, and interpersonal skills. Highlights of the self-other and social communication trajectory will be briefly discussed.

The newborn's attention to mother's face, typically the primary caregiver, increases in intensity over the first few weeks. Both the characteristics and the movements of the face are essential. During this period of initial transactional sensitivity, the infant engages in affective reciprocity—recognizing and implicitly deciphering early social signals through attention to facial expression, eye contact, quality and prosody of voice, gesture, and body language. A great deal of nuanced development, some of which will be addressed in later sections, occurs in early and mid-infancy. In this section, however, only major empirical achievements in the last half of infancy into early childhood are surveyed.

Joint attention denotes sharing interest—both attentional and emotional—in an object with another person as well as recognition that both participants acknowledge their shared interest. Joint attention involves two people and a referred-to object. In this attentional process, one person initiates the referencing by eye gazing, pointing, or other verbal sign or gesture such as holding up and showing, while the other participant responds indicating a meaningfully salient understanding. The incipient emergence of joint attention arises at approximately seven to eight months and is well established by about nine to twelve months.

Gestures are characteristic motions of the body, such as facial expression, gaze, and hand movements, that convey meaning. These behaviors demonstrate a clearly social intention of showing another person an object rather than merely performing an instrumental action to obtain something. An infant's gestural attempts at reaching for objects can be seen at three to four months (for example, swiping at dangling objects). A two-handed reach is possible at four months, and reaching with only one hand is good at six months. Pointing is seen at about nine months.

Intentionality defined as the goal-directed, instrumental *behavior* of an infant begins to emerge at about eight months and is clearly present at twelve months. This early progenitor of understanding intentionality probably denotes understanding the goals of an action, rather than imputing the locus of intention to the mind of another person. The preverbal gestures and pointing of the typically developing infant may arise at between nine and twelve months. Such activity connotes the infant's fascination (eyes and mouth wide open with an air of surprise and pleasurable expectancy) with learning more about the world; it is a reflection of the epistemophilic impulse. Caregivers may support this with their transactional sensitivity and the suitable use of supportive language that labels and suggests meaning.

While emerging at about eight months, intentionality develops slowly. Inferring the intentions of others is suggested to occur at twelve months. Later on, between fourteen and eighteen months, toddlers appear to be able to imitate and try to complete actions an adult tries to produce, even if the adult fails to complete the intended act. A more substantive understanding of the intentions of others is empirically measurable between twenty-four and forty-eight months, and refines itself into perspective taking—understanding the intentions of others—between three and six years old.

Intentional agency or understanding the locus of intentions as existing in the mind of another and behind their goal-directed behaviors is probably more substantively established in the second year, perhaps by approximately eighteen months, in consonance with language development and expression.

Social referencing appears later at approximately between ten and fourteen months, notably when the infant and toddler experience significant ambiguity. A child looking at an adult to see if the adult is watching him or her, what he or she is doing, and how the adult labels this by emotional expressions, constitutes social referencing. Social referencing presumes the infant's abilities to recognize, understand, respond, and alter behavior in response to understanding the emotional meanings conveyed by the adult.

Intentionality, joint attention, and social referencing that emerges approximately from seven to twelve months strongly suggest the infant's actualized ability for explicit self-other awareness and differentiation. Significant advances in social-emotional comprehension are also evident in these developments. The phenomenon of intersubjectivity—infant's awareness that their feelings, wishes, desires and intentions can be understood, to some extent, by others, typically caregivers—organizes.

Between twenty-four and forty-eight months, earlier established capacities for intentionality further refine themselves. The toddler and preschooler understand the intentions of others in a crude manner. At this age, children believe that desires are the sole determinants of others' behavior. By four years, this belief—understanding and acceptance of the truth of an idea—becomes more nuanced. A child now understands that both desires (emotional influences) and personal beliefs (cognitive influences) jointly determine the behavior of others.

Perspective taking denotes the ability to gain an explicit knowledge about perspectives in various domains, including perception and knowledge. This comprehension correlates with a greater understanding of the intentions of others. It denotes imagining what others think and feel. Between three and six years, children understand *self* and *other* to have different thoughts and feelings, although the ability for such a distinction is still unstable and variable. By about seven years, the cognitive capacity for mental inference arises and permits degrees of abstract thought to be used in the absence of tangible perceptions. This permits children to begin to "step into another's shoes."

For example, self-reflective perspective taking occurs when a child refrains from expressing comments to a person with an obvious physical handicap (such as being wheelchair bound), as he says to a friend, " I thought he would feel embarrassed if I asked him why he was 'crippled.'" Hence, in the elementary school years between ages six and twelve, children more substantively understand that another may have truly different perspectives from their own.

A great deal of social intelligence, including communication, is based on the identification of emotion in others. Learning to use this knowledge contributes to governing social interactions. While studies demonstrate that the mastering of social communication has at least moderate genetic hereditability and is distributed in a continuous fashion in the general population, environmental factors play an outstanding role. For example, certain risk factors that affect the maternal fetal environment and place the fetus at risk for atypical social-communicational development include parental age and maternal infection during pregnancy. Another nongenetic factor is low birth weight. Moreover, learning from experience and good parenting adds significant shaping to this endowment. Many of the aforementioned nongenetic factors are clearly modifiable and so are outstanding opportunities for providing infants and children with development-facilitating environments.

One particularly important skill in the development of social intelligence is the ability to perceive emotion in facial stimuli. This begins in infancy and is reflected in capacities for joint attention, social referencing, and perspective taking as mentioned.

Biomental child development is keenly aware of the nexus between biology and psychology. The following discussion highlights the neurological aspects of social intelligence. The neural substrates of these social abilities are in the forefront of current child development studies. For example, the medial prefrontal cortex (MPFC) of the brain is significantly engaged when people are asked to perform tasks that require representations of mental states, namely, metacognition, self-reflection, and self-evaluation. Of special interest for the biomental perspective is that several recent fMRI studies show that the MPFC is activated for envy to a greater degree than other social emotions. The dorsal MPFC, in particular, shows increased activation when subjects are asked to assess what they believe others think and feel. The dorsolateral prefrontal cortex, moreover, has been implicated in its role correlated with complex attention, working memory, and top-down cognitive control during emotional processing and anticipation. Other areas of the brain such as the superior temporal sulcus, amygdala, insula, and fusiform gyrus also correlate with social intelligence. The fusiform gyrus is crucial for processing the recognition of faces, bodies, colors, numbers, and words. This brain area located in the temporal lobe allows for recognition and identification of similarity among items within a category, for example, that cats and dogs are both pets with four legs.

In addition, a more precise understanding of the neural basis of awareness of the differentiation between self and others is emerging. *Differentiation* here denotes the general capacity to comprehend the multiplicity, at times polar contrasts, that exists within the overall unity of the perceptual field, for example, seeing individual trees as distinct components of the one forest. To possess a concept of *self*, such a differentiation of this self amidst surrounding others must occur.

The neurological basis for this capacity as it pertains to cognitive and emotional aspects of interpersonal skills is complex, but a great deal of research on the anterior cingulate cortex (ACC) is beginning to elucidate this brain region's role in the process of metacognition. *Metacognition* represents one's ability to think about one's own thoughts and thinking. This skill might be exemplified by the thought, "I can't stop thinking about food," wherein the speaker is aware of the content of his own thoughts and the fact that they are thoughts.

The terms "metacognition" and "theory of mind" are similar. The difference between them lies in emphasis and context. *Metacognition* deals mainly with task-related mental processes. It is a term frequently employed in discussions surrounding, for example, strategies improving cognitive performance, as the term places emphasis on knowledge about one's own thinking states. Metacognition is particularly used when considering the reasoning of elementary school children and young adolescents. *Theory of mind* (*ToM*), on the other hand, refers to basic knowledge about more general mental states such as desires, thoughts, and beliefs, with emphasis on understanding the mental states of other people. This construct encompasses grasping the thoughts and feelings of others, and some realization that they may not be the same as one's own. It also encapsulates some level of self-reflection and self-evaluation. This term is used predominantly to describe the thinking processes of preschoolers between ages three to five years.

The neural basis of interpersonal and social processes has been further described and localized, for example, using specifically designated areas of brain regions termed *Brodmann's areas*. Different researchers, however, use designations with slight terminological variations such as the term "ventromedial prefrontal cortex" or ventral MPFC. Names and numbers that refer to particular subregions are not uniform across species and investigators. For example, this cortex designation may refer to the area above the medial orbitofrontal cortex; at other times, "ventromedial prefrontal cortex" is used to describe a broad area in the lower (ventral) central (medial) region of the prefrontal cortex, of which the medial orbitofrontal cortex constitutes the lowermost part. This latter, broader area corresponds to the area damaged in patients with decision-making impairments as described in the research of Bechara, Damasio, and colleagues. Activation in this area correlates with self-referential thinking. In the general ventral MPFC, emphasis is on self, whereas in the more anterior regions of the ventral MPFC emphasis may be greater in regard to others. When citing proposed correlations between neuroanatomical regions and psychological functions, this book uses the preferred terminology of the specific neuroscience study that reported these findings.

These neuroanantomical locations or Brodmann's areas are distinguished by their specific microcellular cytoarchitecture and have been demonstrated to positively correlate with the expression of different emotional, conceptual, and motor experiences. Salient brain regions encompass the ventromedial prefrontal cortex, the orbitofrontal cortex, and the amygdala. For example, the interrelated role of cognitive awareness (found in Brodmann's dorsal ACC area 32 that connects with the prefrontal cortex and motor areas) and its affective valence (found in Brodmann's ventral ACC areas 24–25 that connects with the amygdala and nucleus accumbens) are crucial to an individual's sense of interpersonal "two-ness." This sense is the awareness of the distinction between self and other.

The medial frontal cortex (MFC) has also been shown to correlate with determining future behavior. fMRI studies have demonstrated that the more caudal region of the MFC associates value with actions, and the more orbital region associates value with outcomes. It has been proposed that these representations become more abstract the more they are measured anteriorly. The most anterior region of the MFC is presumed to be associated with metacognitive representations that enable individuals to reflect on the values linked to both actions and outcomes—thinking about thinking. The latter encompasses social cognition—reflecting on what other people think about us.

These cognitive and emotional skills are also involved in the awareness of discrepancies, such as the cognitive identification of error detection and the emotional experience of conflict. Studies have demonstrated that as the aforementioned ACC matures, it increasingly facilitates effortful control of emotional arousal during periods of conflict. For example, functional magnetic resonance imaging (fMRI) of the ACC shows activation when people self-report social rejection or feelings of envy. From infancy through adulthood, as such brain structures mature, their emotional monitoring ability attains greater precision. Because social intelligence correlates with the awareness and resolution of such conflict, this neural development supports the integration of empathy with problem-solving skills and conflict resolution. Hence, these enhance emotional and social competence.

A last consideration is the role of the orbitofrontal cortex (OFC). Most investigators agree that this area plays a crucial role in impulse control, maintaining mental set, and monitoring ongoing behavior and socially appropriate behavior. The OFC is considered to be the area that represents the value of rewards and punishments. This capacity for experiencing hedonic salience has been correlated with research on substance abuse and addictive behaviors, especially decision making and emotional processing.

In human studies, pleasant touch, painful touch, tastes, smell, and more abstract reinforcers such as winning or losing money activate the OFC. Thus, evidence shows that this area is involved in decoding and representing some primary reinforcers such as taste and touch, and in learning and reversing/ unlearning associations of visual and other stimuli to these primary reinforcers. Controlling and correcting reward-related and punishment/aversion-related behaviors interfaces with emotion and motivation and ultimately impacts social behaviors. While further details about these neural substrates of emotion and behavior are beyond the scope of this text, their developmental salience is unquestionable. The infant meets the world at first through taste and touch. One may infer that the OFC activates in some way at this time and begins to organize its patterning that influences future reward and aversive predilections and associated emotions and motivations.

2.3 Further Considerations of the Developing Ego and Self

Ego is that overarching aspect of an individual that processes experiential information gathered from the internal and external environments *over time*. Simply stated, it is one's characteristic way of perceiving, interpreting, and managing oneself, others, and events in the environment. It begins as a psychophysiological phenomenon and retains that stamp as it becomes more "mentalized" and felt as a psychological or subjective personal experience over time, namely, an aspect of the self.

Ego or "I," moreover, is the principal locus of subjectivity of one's biomental unity as an individual. The terms *ego* and *self* emphasize the psychological side of the whole person. *Ego* and *mind* particularly denote information processing and learning associated with thinking and feeling but also include contributions from the physical body. The mind seeks knowledge, while emotions, thinking, and imagination (forming subjective mental images to test subjective ideas with objective presentations) give understanding and meaning to the mind's data collection. *Self* is broader and typically refers to the whole person. *Sense of identity* describes the content of how the ego processes understanding itself as an individual and as an individual in relation to others.

The ego processes sensory data, forms perceptions, and organizes these observations into mental conceptions that have meaning. Through this process, orientation to the world can be achieved. This point of reference imparts an underlying sense of location, that is, of being positioned in both the inner and outer worlds. Cognitive and emotional components operate simultaneously. Memory and emotions are organized through the ego's functioning.

In addition to its synthetic and integrative capacity to generate meaning, the ego modulates impulse control with varying levels of reasoning strategies. To illustrate this point, consider the following. First, when the risk of danger is sensed or when competing feelings strive for dominance, anxiety is felt. Often, the mind is confronted with ambiguity, which may waver between a sense of confusion and one of ambivalence. This state of conflict prompts choosing among alternative options and becomes a need that causes discomfort.

To manage anxiety and to try to avoid conflict, the ego generates mechanisms that both realistically cope and also are self-defensive in automatic ways, by unconscious and subliminal reactions. Defense mechanisms are spontaneously elicited self-protective constructions that arise when one experiences the anxious sense of risk of impending harm. While the ego typically possesses a natural tendency to experience conflict by eliciting extreme reactions such as denial or overreactivity, ego defense mechanisms that are in the middle range—more realistic and modulated by reason—are more adaptive. They prevent conflict from wielding potentially incapacitating stress. These tempered reactions help contain anxiety by reducing affective dissonance.

With the assistance of conscious thought, constructive coping behaviors that are less reactive and more intentional are figured out to minimize anxiety, manage conflict, and maximize safety and continued adaptation. These ego functions reflect its capacity for *reality testing*—discriminating what is real from what is not—in order to promote successful adaptation and continued self-development. Self-development positively correlates with realistic self-awareness. The ego may have to, for example, test whether a threat—the risk of danger—is real or not in order to effectively manage anxiety. Seeing reality in both its acceptable and, by contrast, "dark" dimensions helps minimize turning to omnipotent fantasy—unrealistic strategies—to manage mental pain and provide solutions that, in effect, are precarious, if not in the end self-undermining.

Perhaps the prime drive of the ego is to seek out others—interpersonal objects of profound emotional and cognitive significance. These *objects,* as they are technically referred to, are those persons with whom the individual becomes deeply involved and to whom intense emotional attachments develop. Contrary to the conventional idea of the term *object* connoting something either inanimate or dispassionately objectified, the psychodynamic term *object* denotes the experience of kindred humans sharing emotional intimacy and subjective affiliation whose aim is survival.

Object here means the perceived experience of the subject's intimate attention to the presented other. The classical, psychodynamic construct indicating a sense of self in relation to others—*object relations*—gains its name from this meaning of object. Object relations is itself a complex term. It denotes that emotional and cognitive changes in sense of self and interpersonal relations are constantly being reconfigured in the face of maintaining an updated *self-signature* and an object relations identity. One's self-signature and identity, therefore, remain current in the real-time moment of experience and behavior. The role of biomental motivations and unconscious fantasies is the undergirding of this and all psychological development.

Object relations emerge in infancy and become prototypes for all later interpersonal relationships. For example, substantive social interaction can be observed empirically when the child exhibits typically normative responses: a social smile at about two months, discrimination of strangers at about six months, anxiety about strangers at about seven months, anxiety about separation from loved ones beginning at about eight months, waving "bye-bye" at ten months, and pointing to indicate a capacity for joint attention at about eleven months.

In a figurative sense, the mind has two perspectives. It has a subjective side that looks at itself; this is the inner, private world of feelings, thinking, imagination, and fantasy. The ability to form mental images in the absence of concrete sensory data also occurs here. But the mind also has an objective side that looks out into the world. As the mind develops over infancy and childhood, it uses both these sides to recognize the difference between the two. The concept *reality testing* denotes the developing, age-appropriate ability to distinguish what is in the mind as one's personal thoughts, feelings, wishes, and fantasies (subjectivity) from what exists independently in the outside environment (objectivity). Reality testing is one of the crucial foundations for developing perspective taking abilities and the experience of empathy.

The ego also coordinates intelligence. Human *intelligence* is a biomental function that denotes the awareness and discrimination of relevant and novel environmental and subjective stimuli. This information is then used in integrated fashion to maintain mental and physiological infrastructure and promote regulatory expansions in adaptive survival and quality of life. From this perspective, the ego may be equated with processes of linear sequencing, even the broader notion of time awareness, itself. Intelligence encompasses more than just cognitive operations. Human intelligence transforms mere information into value-laden understanding. This insight includes emotional, social, practical, and motivational components. Many nonmeasurable factors such as intuition and the aesthetic sense are also crucial aspects of overall intelligence.

In fact, in addition to orchestrating intelligence in general, the ego specifically coordinates social intelligence. This ability allows one to navigate among other sentient selves. This aspect of intelligence has been called *social cognition*. A large proportion—though not all—of the ego's multifaceted processes are understood to be automatic or nonconscious, that is, not experienced in conscious awareness. Typically, the cognitive term *nonconscious* is relatively similar in meaning to the psychological term *unconscious*. The basic processes underlying social intelligence—both conscious and nonconscious—appear to be universal and mostly automatic for all people, although individual differences exert significant effects on the way these processes are activated or constrained. Each individual responds emotionally in unique ways. How this is translated into behavior significantly differs among people.

Basic emotional processing encompasses personal and interpersonal perception, attunement, and the accuracy of understanding emotions. Its foundation rests on an innate capacity for unconscious emotional recognition. Conscious thinking, trial and error, and conscious learning from experience over time further orchestrate these nonconscious elements that compose one's implicit *sense of self* (which is typically experienced unconsciously) and one's *self-identity concept* (which denotes the specific way one intentionally articulates characteristics that compose his or her personality).

As a result of the orchestration of unconscious and conscious emotional processing at the core of the self, social facilitation and basic social grace may result. Both of these abilities include understanding the emotional atmosphere in interpersonal relationships, notably by using empathy, and being able to successfully manage relationships in a tactfully facilitating and graceful manner. Emotional self-management, accordingly, is enhanced. On the basis of the aforementioned, one's ego gradually becomes a locus of control for decision making over the course of development.

One's sense of self-identity then expresses the content of the ego's relationship to itself and others. This self-identity is a precious possession held dearly by most everyone. Endowed traits and temperament, the developmental process, and experience in the family and in society all contribute to the developing sense of self from earliest childhood into adult life.

Having trusting experiences in infancy and early childhood, particularly through nurturing and protective families, supports stable identity. As will be mentioned in chapter 6 in the section on xenophobia, or irrational fear of strangers, a healthy self-identity becomes vulnerable when inordinate feelings of specialness are felt and entertained. Seeing oneself as set apart by privilege or some form of exclusivity draws sharp contrasts between self and others. This delineation is the breeding ground for envy, hate, suspiciousness, and estrangement. By contrast, *a healthy self-identity is one that perceives itself as one member of both a smaller group and a larger community where variation is the norm*, and wherein distinctions and differences are regarded as interesting rather than threatening.

2.4 The Newborn Self

Newborns come into the world with sense organs that are present in a fragile yet robustly developing condition. The infant as a whole can be likened to a living, resonating sense organ who takes in the newness of the world, interfacing in a discordant clash of undecipherable experience. From the first days and weeks of life, the infant is *profoundly* social. The primary object of attention and love is typically the mother—parts of her or her body parts. She becomes the outside container for the infant in contrast to the infant previously being contained within her. The intimacy of this shared reality contributes to the infant's development of mental functioning.

Recognizing this newborn openness and identity, most delicate in the first six to twelve weeks, requires protection so that it is not unduly overwhelmed. Examples of overstimulation may be exposure to extremes of sounds, temperatures, movements, and so forth that may occur in situations like car travel, the supermarket, or movie theaters. The experience of being overwhelmed disrupts the delicately organizing flow of developmental processes. Good parenting in these early months provides a proper atmosphere for sensory and perceptual impressions to organize. Additionally, the developing self is supported so that it may experience its own rhythms for establishing self-regulation in an environment of modulated containment.

3. ATTACHMENT OF INFANT AND CHILD TO CAREGIVER

Attachment is a term commonly used to describe an infant's or child's physical proximity, dependence, and psychological connection to a primary caregiver. Attachments gradually develop in the first year and are typically established by about twelve months. These patterns are likely to persist throughout childhood into adult life. The construct of *attachment* denotes the infant's and child's attachment, not the primary caregiver's tie or attachment to the child. The term *attachment figure* denotes the primary caregiver, who is typically the mother. In the literature on *attachment theory*, the primary caregiver's responsivity through attitude and behavior is understood to be the principal way that an attachment pattern is formed. Emphasis is on actual caregiving events in contrast to the child's perceptions and fantasies about these.

While attachment theory places prominence on mother as the primary attachment figure for a child, fathers and grandmothers may also serve as mother's own attachment figures during the parenting years. This beneficial support is understood to be healthy. By contrast, when mothers use their child as their attachment figure, an unhealthy "inverted" attachment relationship materializes. This process denotes psychopathology since the mother may establish an overbearing relationship suggestive of anxiety and psychological defense. Impaired functioning in both child and mother may result. Attachment theorists suggest a psychodynamic explanation that entails mother's underlying impetus to receive from her child what she perceived she "missed" from her own mother.

The nature and quality of biomental patterns of attachment derive from a combination of the infant's innate temperament and coping responses, as well as maternal sensitivity. The founder of attachment theory, John Bowlby, however, emphasizes the mutual exclusivity of "attachment" and "temperament" constructs. He has suggested that the notion of temperament appears indefinite and inconsistent in contrast to that of attachment, which has received scientific attention and more consistent theoretical modeling.

Maternal sensitivity encompasses overall receptivity and acceptance of a child, attunement to that child's needs, readiness to provide nurturance, as well as recognition of the inherent limitations of these capacities. The quality of parenting, therefore, is thought to significantly affect how attachment patterns and emotional bonds in children organize themselves. Maternal responsivity in attitude and language are understood to help a child identify its feelings. Such identification occurs implicitly in infancy and then also conceptually by the end of the second year and thereafter. This process helps the child manage emotions and thereby regulate attachment patterns.

Attachment patterns, as such, are not inborn. They are not properties of a child. Rather, attachment patterns are developed through the interactions between a specific child and a specific parent. Patterns may be different between a child and each of his or her primary caregivers.

Attachment theory was first formulated in the 1950s and 1960s in England. Derived at first from seminal work performed in child psychoanalysis, studies on attachment shifted focus from inferences attempting to describe the inner life of the child to an exploration of empirical, observable patterns of behaviors. The goal of these behaviors is to achieve safety through maintaining proximity to the primary caregiver. In this theoretical model, the "to-and-fro" physical proximity and real-life interactions between these two people with their attendant emotional quality are termed *attachment*. Attachment patterns are observable modes of how an infant or child clings to, adheres to, and holds tightly to his or her primary caregiver. In an effort to introduce more objectivity to his theories, Bowlby relied heavily on constructs from cognitive psychology and less on psychoanalytic theory. Many modern theorists regard Bowlby's valuable contributions from an ethological perspective, which recognizes the infant's emotional tie to his or her caregiver as an evolved response promoting survival and not merely a correlation to the caregiver's feeding.

A contemporary development of attachment theory has been the construct of *attachment systems*. This idea elaborates the biobehavioral details of interpersonal attachment with an emphasis on the neurocircuitry underlying the child-parent interaction. It is a conception that describes psychosocial attachments in typical cases and also when stress or psychopathology intervene. Special attention is paid to the activation of behavioral and neural-endocrine protective mechanisms that modulate experiences of adversity and trauma.

The attachment systems construct includes a proposed transgenerational, beneficial effect. When the child of responsive parents becomes a parent, she or he in turn will also demonstrate suitable responsivity. In effect, this process may disrupt the transmission of poor parenting and foster responsive parenting.

The evolutionary drives for infants to develop profound emotional and material connections to their caregivers include a need for survival, helplessness in the early years, and states of dependency that require caregiving nurturance comprising food, love, and understanding. Attachment theorists, moreover, denote that the attachment tie to the primary caregiver is a primary phenomenon. It is not merely a secondary consequence of the child's need for food, warmth, or anything other than the attachment relationship itself. Put differently, attachment systems are in place to ensure survival by alerting the infant to the risk of danger by its experience of anxiety when attachment is threatened. Of note, there has not been any demonstrated hereditability of attachment styles, in contrast to some hereditability found in studies of temperament.

While there are many ways to describe the relationship between the need for closeness and the distress of distancing, two broad categories of patterns of attachment behaviors have been designated: secure and insecure (table 2.2). Studies of children in North American families in the middle socioeconomic bracket show *secure attachment* in about 60 to 67 percent of cases. These children form an "internal working model" about the availability and support of their attachment figures between six months and two years of age; as a result of this process, these children do not exhibit inordinate distress when separations from parents occur. Securely attached children sense that they have a secure base in the availability of an attentive and responsive parent, thus enabling them to sufficiently explore the environment. Upon a parent's return, the child appears comfortable. This capacity develops throughout childhood. In adulthood, it correlates with the ability for secure self-exploration and self-reflection.

Insecure attachment is found in about 33 to 40 percent of children. It is ordinarily expressed in three different ways: (1) avoidant or dismissive (15–20 percent of all children), (2) resistant or anxious-ambivalent (10–15 percent of all children), and (3) disorganized-disoriented (5–15 percent of all children).

Insecure-avoidant children are described as avoiding close contact with people and lingering near, but not too close, to parents when a threat is sensed. Insecure-ambivalent or insecure-resistant children are described as clinging to parents and finding it difficult to explore the extended environment outside this proximity. Those with insecure-anxious attachments may develop nonspecific anxiety as children and adults, and have features of obsessive compulsivity manifested by a constant need for repetitive reassurances. This typically is seen at points of transition, such as in later adolescence when transition out of high school and toward a different academic or work context is anticipated. Anxieties in such situations are best managed by giving realistic, clear-cut guidance. Subsequent to this reality-oriented guidance, using the phrase, "I think you know the answer," particularly when excessive reassurances are demanded, helps bolster self-confidence. The triad of empathy, pointing out discrepant ideas, and encouraging self-dependent thinking is an optimal strategy to use. Insecure-disorganized children are understood to be severely disturbed, have behaviors that are seriously atypical, and have parents who are either emotionally absent or abusive. All patterns of interpersonal attachment are thought to persist into adulthood. This continuation appears particularly true for those infants who appear securely attached and for those who appear disorganized in their attachment.

Although it may be difficult to precisely delineate between secure, insecure, and perhaps other styles of attachments, it is generally agreed that at least four ingredients are needed to support security. These include the following: (1) the early availability of a consistent caregiver; (2) the sensitive quality and reflective functioning of the caregiver's responses to the child's needs; (3) the infant's and child's own characteristics, emerging temperamental traits and attachment indicators, especially tolerance of anxiety and frustration; and (4) the family context, which includes parental mental and

Table 2.2. Patterns of Attachment Behavior

Securely attached	
Insecurely attached:	(a) avoidant or dismissive,
	(b) resistant or anxious-ambivalent, or
	(c) disorganized-disoriented

physical health, marital harmony, socioeconomic stability, and the assistance of suitable extraparental caregivers. This last feature emphasizes parents' own "internal working models" of what sensitive parenting must include.

3.1 Biomental Child Development and Attachment Theory

Using the term *attachment*, therefore, cannot substitute for, nor should it distract from, the relation of *basic love* whose overarching emphasis is experiential rather than merely conceptual. Biomental child development emphasizes basic love to encompass nuanced mixtures of intimacy, fascination, affiliative adhesion, nurturance, beneficial connectedness, emotional binding, and desire for pleasurable closeness. Emotions of happiness and enjoyment are basic elements of love. Yet, love is more complex than merely an adhesive attachment; rather it reflects dynamic levels of emotional interrelatedness. Basic love transcends mere clinging, grasping, and adhesion. Love also includes aspects of ambivalence, disappointment, and conflict. Elicitation of love motivates the delicacy and robustness of the child's relation—transactional sensitivity—to its caregivers. Love and its derivatives such as admiration, gratitude, and empathy become mitigating factors that constrain negative attitudes such as hostility in all its expressions.

Attachments become disturbed when fear, anxiety, and the threat of separation and distancing present themselves. Put differently, distress arises in the very attempt to avoid separations. Children react to perceived separations with feelings characterized by perceived hostility in the other and also hostility arising in themselves. Hostility in many of its forms—frustration, oppositional defiant behaviors, tantrums, and negative moods, for example—may be countered by transactional sensitivity, which promotes agreeableness and cooperation.

The raison d'être within human psychology rests on this goal—maintaining relations of love—and helps organize all aspects of biomental processes, especially emotional development and self-management. Biomental child development goes to great lengths, moreover, to emphasize that attachments by children are to mother, father, and the mother-father relationship, as well as to the extended family and social environments.

Biomental child development prefers to view the attachments of infants and children as *styles* that include a variety of individualized dynamic patterns of interpersonal connectedness beyond that which is merely empirical, observable, and measurable. In other words, greater emphasis is placed on the inferred emotional and cognitive aspects of a child's affiliative, active engagement with its caregiver than on categorization within specific classes. This view highlights the child's perceptions, fantasies, and idiosyncratic interpretations. These construals—however unmeasurable—are the psychological core of a child's attachment.

The complement to styles of attachment or "grasping" is styles of detachment or "releasing." Detachment implies separations, losses, and endings. Children develop and retain patterns of experiencing and managing detachments in a variety of ways. These patterns become habitual modes of reaction throughout life. They range from healthy and successful to unhealthy and self-undermining. They may even result in depression or other mental challenges such as chronic pessimism and negative mood.

4. TRAITS, TEMPERAMENT, AND PERSONALITY

4.1 Overview

Traits, temperament, and personality are biomental components that encompass the structure, function, meaning, and expression of variations in attitude and behavior within individuals.

Traits denote durable dispositions to react, respond, and behave in particular ways that are relatively consistent across a variety of situations. In infants and children, definitional emphasis rests more on the individual and his or her physiological responsiveness. Traits may be understood to be endowed, inherent autonomic patterns that result in congenital activity profiles. These elemental building blocks make up both early temperament and later personality development.

Traits include activity level, approach or withdrawal response to novel situations, adaptability to change, level of sensitivity/reactivity, attention span, distractibility, persistence to tasks, mood, and rhythmicity. All these characteristics have a basis in one's genetic endowment. Their quantitative and qualitative distribution ranges from lesser responsivity to greater expression. As is the case with most other psychological phenomena, subgroups of people having attenuated, modest, or "middle of the road" levels of these features are understood to be typical. The functioning of such persons tends to be healthfully adaptive.

Temperament is a larger cluster of traits or dispositions in attitude or readiness to react. One's temperament may be described most broadly as one's characteristic overall cooperativeness or fearfulness/avoidance. Simply put, temperament indicates the general cluster of likes and dislikes of infant or child and how he or she reacts to them. In contrast to attachment patterns that are gradual in their development, temperament is virtually present in the newborn and persists, to a large extent, thereafter. Each child has his or her characteristic temperament; this disposition has its own individual tempo, which influences physical, emotional, and cognitive processes. Recognizing the temperamental disposition of an individual child helps tailor the environment to enhance his or her interests and abilities.

Together, traits and temperament form the base of personality, which is overlaid with learning and shaping from experience. Personality reflects the continuing consolidation of the interrelated ways one has experienced and managed the environment, handled anxiety and conflict, and negotiated the demands of reality. This process occurs in pursuit of a favorable or, at least, workable, level of functioning and quality of life.

Personality may be understood as a qualitatively distinct category that is recognizable as the integration of traits, temperament, and attachment patterns. The expression *emotional attitude* connotes the overall psychological grasp—cognitive and emotional—that the personality experiences in relation to something. Whereas temperament, as part of an open genetic program, has a strong innate endowment, personality is built on traits, temperament, and attachment patterns and is thus more shaped by parental and cultural influences. Susceptibility, to be sure, does not demand inevitability. Put differently, attitudes and personality are dynamically affected by learning and experience and so are open to change. Temperament and, to some degree, attachment style appear more set and consistent, especially by one year of age.

From birth on, constitutional factors inextricably interact with environmental factors to shape biomental processes. Knowledge of both classes of factors, particularly their interaction, is still incomplete. What happens in the womb, the experience of birth, and the earliest situations of being handled and fed all strongly influence infant development. Mother's unconscious attitudes are inferred to directly influence the infant's unconscious processes. Thus, nurturance as feeding, loving, and understanding facilitates development by accentuating positive trends and diminishing distress and anxiety.

In the end, the complex reciprocal interactions between individual and environment dynamically shape and reshape each other over the course of a lifetime.

4.2 Traits

Traits are enduring attitudes. They can be understood to be the elemental building blocks that shape temperamental styles that, in turn, lay the foundation for the continued development of complex personality configurations. The organization of traits, temperament, and personality—the self—includes a developing ego, inner sense of relation to significant others, attachment styles, personality, and character.

Traits in the personality are biomental characteristics, perhaps predispositions, which are relatively stable and predictable. They are descriptive dimensions, as enumerated in the overview, that summarize observable patterns of behavior—a person's attitude and response to experience. They exist on a continuum from less intense or prevalent to more intense or prevalent.

There are numbers of traits that can coalesce to form larger, recognizable categories such as temperaments. Some of these traits correlate with the factors outlined in table 2.4 below.

Resilience, as such, is an overarching process that encompasses a wide range of adaptive strengths and is generally not understood to be a circumscribed trait. Some have described *resiliency* as a trait that reflects the stability of the personality and its resistance to decompensation under adversity. Both *resilience* and *resiliency* imply an underlying plasticity that calls upon both conscious and nonconscious resourcefulness toward achieving new levels of adaptive reorganization.

Genetic endowment sets up neurophysiological sensory and brain pathways—traits—that influence how experience is sensed and interpreted. They influence patterns of thinking and feeling and may automatically move experience and behavior in specific ways. This process, however, is heavily influenced by chronological age, cumulative past experience, and specific context. Specific responses include perceiving and interpreting in a characteristic fashion (for example, seeing the world as basically safe or threatening) and behaving impulsively or in a restrained manner (for example, jumping to action versus observing situations, and considering options).

A trait may be expressed through different behaviors at different chronological and developmental ages. Different situations also influence the way a trait expresses itself. In other words, as long as the theory of a trait describes the contextual way in which the perceived features of situations elicit trait-related behaviors, traits maintain consistency in the same person over time.

The cross-situational consistencies of traits are relatively enduring features that characterize an individual. Although durable, especially in childhood, they are not immutable. Between persons, they are continuously distributed and their level of intensity approximates a normal or bell shaped curve. That is to say, all persons possess a designated trait (for example, novelty seeking and activity level) to greater or lesser degrees.

The biological basis of psychological traits suggests an innate endowment and maturational trajectory that together contribute to personality formation. These factors, largely, are unlearned ways an individual perceives, assesses, relates, learns, and responds to self and environment. This increases the likelihood of experiencing the world in specific, and not other, ways. Specific traits in a child, for example, can be inferred since their presence can be empirically observed and measured by how a child responds and behaves. Some infants and children, for instance, behave in a timid, avoidant, stilted, and retiring way, which might suggest an attentional bias toward perceived threatening information, its distressing fantasy base, and attendant anxiety. Others appear serene and eager for new experiences.

Traits may be at least 50 percent genetically endowed and appear as constitutional features. These underlying dispositions are automatic responses that can be adaptive. If they become too rigid, however, they may become maladaptive. When they cause clinically significant impairment, psychiatrically diagnosable personality disorders may result.

Each child is born with specific traits that together compose temperamental patterns of emotional state and behavioral response; this is the "how" of behavior. The "why" of behavior correlates more with internal motivating forces.

4.3 Temperament

Temperament, with its composite traits, makes up a small group of different genetically endowed psychophysiological predispositions. In 1987, the distinguished classical temperament theorists, Stella Chess and Alexander Thomas, conjectured that mind and behavior are determined 60 percent by genetics and 40 percent by environmental learning. They understood patterns of behavior to be stable throughout childhood, and found in children across all cultures. Their formulation included three functional constellations or patterns and a mixed group.

The three constellations comprised an "easy-difficult" range of a child's overall behavioral style or pattern of temperament. About 65 percent of children fit a distinct behavioral pattern: (1) easy temperament, found in about 40 percent of children; (2) difficult temperament, found in about 10 percent of children; (3) slow-to-warm-up temperament, found in about 15 percent of children. Mixed patterns, a fourth group, are found in about 35 percent of children (table 2.3).

Infants and children with an *easy temperament* show consistency in feeding and sleeping, are normally curious, show positive attitudes, have low to moderate intensity of reactions, and are adaptable to change. *Slow-to-warm-up* children have a low activity level, are reluctant to approach new situations, are slow in adapting to change, and display emotions that appear less

Table 2.3. Three Functional Constellations or Patterns of Temperament Responsiveness and a Mixed Pattern

Chess and Thomas (1987) conjectured that mind and behavior are determined 60% by genetics and 40% by environmental learning. They formulated an "easy–difficult" range of a child's overall behavioral style or pattern:

In 65% of all children: 40% show an easy pattern

10% show a difficult pattern

15% show a slow to warm up pattern

In 35% of all children, a mixed pattern is seen.

positive but just short of being irritable. Those with a *difficult* temperament show intense and negative emotionality, irritability, and fussiness, are easily overwhelmed, are slow to adapt to change, are less predictable, and cry more often.

The child with a difficult temperament needs special attention to help deal with problem behaviors. Recognizing this temperament, caregivers can provide opportunities that may fit the child's needs for greater success at school, home, and with peers. Often, such children can be mislabeled as having clinical behavior disorders when, in fact, the behavior may reflect a biologically given temperamental style that might respond favorably to proper environmental adjustment.

Compound traits in these constellations include activity level, rhythmicity, regularity, approach versus withdrawal to novel situations, adaptability to change and cooperativeness, threshold of responsiveness, level of sensitivity, quality of mood, intensity of reaction, attention and persistence, and distractibility. These traits described by Chess and Thomas are also referred to as the "Nine Factor Model of Temperamental Categories" (table 2.4). In adults, temperament and traits continue to underlie personality and character, acting as either hazardous or protective factors. Such elements increase the likelihood of positive or negative outcomes depending on their intensity, balance, and adaptational use in specific contexts.

A prominent current model of temperament with a different emphasis proposes two basic categories. The first category is *reactivity*, which includes five subcomponents: (1) activity level (40 percent of children manifest increased activity level), (2) attention span despite frustrations, (3) fearful distress (10 percent of all children show consistent fearful distress), (4) overly sensitive, irritable, rigid, fussy distress (10 percent of all children show such irritable fussiness), and (5) positive affect (40 percent of all children appear consistently comfortable). The second category in this model is *self-regula-*

Table 2.4. Nine-Factor Model of Temperamental Categories

Activity level

Rhythmicity/regularity

Approach versus withdrawal/inhibition/fearfulness to novel situations

Adaptability to change and cooperativeness

Threshold of responsiveness/sensitivity

Quality of mood

Intensity of reaction

Attention span and persistence

Distractibility

tion or effortful control. Effortful control helps regulate the intensity of the subcomponents of reactivity; its emphasis is more on self-regulation than merely impulse control (table 2.5).

Although genetic endowment is significant, the external environment and parenting can accentuate or constrain traits and so modify a given temperament. Endowment and experience both interact and shape temperament.

Patterns in the responses and behaviors of infants between six and nine months, supported by the increasingly more complex coordination of perceptive and motor skills, first express a characteristic temperamental style. Temperament, as such, becomes more apparent in the toddler years, from about twelve to thirty-six months.

Temperament, however, may be relatively consistent in childhood but may change expression over time into adulthood. Put differently, overall patterns of temperamental style are not absolutely fixed in early childhood; they are responsive to the organizing and modulating effects of positive parenting, among other influences.

Researchers have found both consistency and change from childhood into adulthood. They attributed apparent alterations to changing environments and other factors. Stability and variability of behavior, therefore, must include assessment of behavior in its situational context. In this way, consistencies that characterize the individual can be ascertained. Thus, constancies as distinctive but stable patterns of "if-then," situation-behavior relations can be discerned. Different temperaments form contextualized and psychologically salient personality signatures. Innate temperamental traits strongly influence behavior and emotional growth until about age seven when environmental influences tend to modify and may override, to some extent, genetically endowed traits.

Good parenting is characterized by a keenness to understand the specific temperaments and personality styles of children. By doing this, children's strengths, areas of resilience, and needs for improvement become clearer. With this understanding and the ensuing realistic expectations, parenting may be successfully custom-tailored to each individual child's temperament and personality.

Goodness of fit is a technical term used to describe the synchronous accommodation between a child's temperamental traits and a parent's own traits. This idea particularly refers to emotional and physiological arousal and

Table 2.5.   Model of Temperament with Two Categories and Six Factors

1. Reactivity: activity level, attention span and persistence, fearful distress, irritable distress, and positive affect; and

2. Self-regulation: effortful control. In this system, effortful control helps regulate the intensity of the subcomponents of reactivity.

how parents customize the child-rearing environment to enhance adaptive outcomes. Parents' expectations become more realistic when they are in consonance with their child's temperament. Of note, children in a family typically have different temperaments. Knowledge of the temperamental characteristics of a particular child provides parents with a realistic and effective background from which to devise management strategies and action plans to facilitate healthy infant and child development.

When parents adequately recognize the temperamental disposition of a child, parental expectations, mode of response, and guidance can become customized to fit that particular child. Hence, parenting is optimized for success. It is also useful for parents to try to understand their own adult temperament, as discussed in chapter 4, since this knowledge facilitates effective management of both self and children.

Poorness of fit connotes discrepancies and dissonances between environmentally provided opportunities or demands and the child's capacities or temperamental characteristics. At times, poorness of fit might be attributable to potentially modifiable factors, such as a parent's unresolved grief, depression, or past trauma. This possibility always needs careful examination so that suitable interventions may be considered.

As mentioned, different researchers using varied models and measurement techniques have elucidated several ways of describing temperament. Some researchers (table 2.6) have used a model with only two broad patterns: *low reactive* and *high reactive*. This conceptualization essentially connotes a spectrum of how one adapts to environmental experience, either easily (low reactive) or with some difficulty (high reactive).

The two-factor model finds the low reactive temperament in about 80 percent of infants and children. Features that include boldness, sociability, outgoingness, calm, exploration, independence, and less-than-average inhibition characterize it. The high reactive group comprises about 20 percent of infants and children. Its features include more shyness, timidity, cautiousness, oversensitivity, higher inferred anxiety, fearfulness, apprehension, rigidity, aversion to risk taking, and a greater degree of avoidance and inhibition. Interestingly, the high reactive group is more sensitive and receptive to parental direction and guidance.

In psychiatric terminology, the high reactive group is also more susceptible to developing "internalizing" disorders in childhood and adolescence, such as anxiety, and less prone to externalizing disorders, such as conduct

Table 2.6. Two-Factor Model of Temperament

HR (high reactive) to LR (low reactive)

problems. Neither low nor high reactive temperaments are understood to be immutable, though they are nonetheless clearly discernable and relatively stable behavioral and emotional trends, at least through the adolescent years.

Among the various characteristics of temperament, attention, mood, and sensitivity are often listed. Some cognitive abilities such as intelligence, processing speed, and memory, however, are not enumerated. Although anxiety, as such, is not specifically listed as a characteristic temperamental trait in current models, some expression of it is typically part of a child's presentation.

Anxiety as an innate response is elicited by sensing a risk of danger. It may have a base in a predispositional bias toward perceived threatening information. It is certainly at the base of the features termed "approach versus withdrawal," "fearfulness," and "inhibition." Anxiety as a state may be inferred when behaviors reflect avoidance, inhibition, fear, rigidity, oversensitivity, uneven mood, or a generalized constriction of thinking, emotion, and behavior. The "shy" child may have mixed elements of avoidance, fearfulness, and anxiety. In such situations, mental space is narrowed in its ability to permit more fluidity in emotional movement. Difficulties such as these typically are exacerbated at times of transition. For example, when older adolescents are preparing to transition out of high school, a great deal of anxiety, ambivalence, uncertainty, and fearfulness emerge. Both procrastination and a repetitive need for reassurance may surface. This is typical and transitory, but may develop into conditions of pervasive anxiety with obsessive-compulsive features that require professional assessment.

Another important dimension of temperament as mentioned earlier in this section is *effortful control*, which is also referred to as *self-control*. It is part of the developing self's capacity to initiate, inhibit, and manage ideas, feelings, plans, and actions. These abilities for effortful self-control underlie the emergence of overall self-regulation. Effortful control correlates, to a large extent, with aspects of the biomental capacity for self-containment. As growth and development proceed in healthy ways, self-regulation substantially contributes to reasoned volition—the bridge between desire and action—and self-efficacy.

Although most children improve greatly in willfully enlisting effortful control across the first five years of life, there are large individual differences. As is true for other aspects of temperament, individual differences in effortful control are understood to be attributable to both biological factors and broader environmental influences.

Another core, basic trait of temperament to emphasize is that of *tolerance to frustration*. This innate capacity to delay response varies among infants and people. It is, however, crucial in setting the stage for the modulation of a great many sensations, emotions, and developing thoughts. Several temperamental traits are particularly related to this: persistence, attention, approach versus withdrawal to novel situations, and effortful control. Parents as guides can help children learn to tolerate frustration in a variety of ways, notably by their own living example.

4.4 Personality

Personality formation is the complex development of the self over a lifetime. It is never fully realized. An individual's personality largely determines stability and variability of behavior under differing contexts and across differently perceived situations.

Personality develops on the framework of temperament and subsumes within itself temperamental characteristics. Whereas temperament may be figuratively understood as a child's "implicit voice," personality is the child's upfront and "explicit voice." *Voice* here connotes the signature of how a personal identity expresses itself. For example, those who typically appear happy, optimistic, and agreeable have underlying "easy" temperaments and personality styles marked by cooperativeness.

The environment, notably parental upbringing and the influence of extended social and cultural context, largely shapes an individual's personality. Whereas temperament is part of an infant's innate infrastructure, personality gradually forms *in response to* the varied inputs experienced during early and later childhood and adolescence. It is a response that the developing self uses to manage and modulate its emotional reactivity, as well as cope with pleasant challenges and defend itself against unpleasant demands, namely conflict.

Personality is the relatively coherent pattern of functionally interrelated processes that encompass cognition, emotion, interpersonal relatedness, behavior, coping, and defensive mechanisms. In psychiatry the terms *personality* and *character* are used in similar ways. *Character*, however, connotes personality characteristics that have been sublimated in adaptive, healthy ways using the defense mechanisms elicited in middle childhood. The nature and significance of the ego's psychological defense mechanisms is further discussed in this chapter and chapter 3.

In some sense, personality, colorful as it may be, is an accretion of habits and conditioning that the child has used to manage him- or herself in a changing and, at times, challenging world. These groups of habits become more rigid with age and their subsequent entrenchment may become almost unchangeable. Normal life experiences—short of trauma and major illness— seem not to alter early personality patterns already established by the end of adolescence. To the extent that personality is inflexible in early and later adulthood, new learning becomes difficult. Novel events that could offer opportunities for personal growth, reconfiguration, and even self-development, therefore, are either ignored or met with resistance. To the extent that a person holds archaic and outmoded attitudes and behaviors in adulthood, personal change is impeded.

Over the last decades, C. Robert Cloninger, a psychiatrist, has developed a unique set of ideas about temperament, expanded them, and introduced them into a larger frame related to adult personality styles (table 2.7) with particular relevance in the field of personality disorders. Psychiatry uses systems of classification termed "nosologies," that is, biomedical classifications of disease. This categorization contrasts with psychological nomenclature systems dealing with normal personality styles wherein classifications are taxonomies based on the natural relationships of an individual's dominant traits. The importance of this distinction is referenced here, but further discussion is beyond the scope of the present text.

4.5 Significance of Temperament and Personality

The practical significance of the aforementioned considerations of temperament and personality is that human behavior has both dispositional/innate determinants and acquired shaping from the world of experience and learning. *While the hardware of personality, to a significant extent, is endowed at birth, the software programs that animate and may transform the whole system of the self (for example, dynamically evolving self-awareness and self-identity) are exquisitely variable and changeable.* Flexibility in self-concept, openness to new options, and cooperativeness remain the hallmarks for successful personal and social adaptation.

The crucial importance of the environment in general and in learning from the environment of parents, caregivers, other persons, and experiences, therefore, cannot be emphasized enough. This is consistent with the underlying theme running throughout this book—the final product at every moment of the life cycle results from the dynamic transactions of genes, environment, and randomness in each, between each, and among their interactions.

Table 2.7. Four-Factor Model of Basic Higher Order Universal Categories of Temperament

Each factor is genetically independent, the same across cultures and ethnicities; all factors are present in each person, but one factor predominates. Each of the four temperaments has component traits or facets that have been statistically validated as being typically grouped together.

Harm Avoidance (behavioral inhibition): fearful, shy

Novelty Seeking (behavioral activation): extroverted, outgoing

Reward Dependence (social attachment): affectionate, open

Persistence (partial reinforcement): determined, industrious, directed

An understanding of these ideas and accompanying insights strengthens the potential for self-development and can enhance parenting skills. All these considerations help optimize emotional and psychological mental health. In addition, they foster intellectual development and guide children to become self-motivated learners and critical thinkers.

5. NOTES ON INTELLIGENCE

Intelligence is a complex development already in nascent operation at birth. Intelligence facilitates learning and learning, in turn, reconfigures the brain and its information processing systems. During the course of development, learning faculties, compatibilities, and strategies vary. Sensation, perception, and bodily movements optimized by human interaction facilitate early learning. Categorizing experience and implicitly learning by associative connections are foremost. From about eighteen months on, the ability to form mental concepts gradually emerges and adds a conscious dimension to thinking that complements previously more implicit acquisitions. Newly developed locomotion and exploration, as well as the unfolding emergence of play activities, enhance learning at this time. From birth through about age seven, children are best able to engage in learning and exploration by interactive, hands-on demonstrations and "doing" rather than direct instruction.

By the elementary school years, learning capacities expand, notably their ability to enlist cognitive faculties such as greater discrimination, conceptualization, and maturing memory systems. At about six to seven years, cognitive capabilities are compatible with and responsive to formal academic teaching. Pedagogy, namely education in the form of direct child instruction, and academic didactics such as the formal teaching of reading, writing, and mathematics can be introduced and have best chances for successful mastery.

Hence, a discussion of intelligence and learning is part of the foundation of the psychology of the child as a whole. Intelligence (or the group of intelligences) is a distinct factor in development. It is neither a temperament nor an attachment pattern. Intelligence, however, clearly is both influenced and influences how temperament and attachment patterns express themselves.

The most recent genome-wide analyses suggest evidence for high hereditability of measurable genetic factors directly correlated with general intelligence. For example, approximately 51 percent of fluid intelligence appears to be inherited. *Fluid intelligence*, also known as *Gf*, is the ability to solve novel problems by using reasoning. It has been inferred to rely heavily on biological and neurological factors. The data thus points to the presence of innate mechanisms both already operational and *in statu nascendi* for further maturation with interaction in a facilitating environment.

Intelligence is the ability to make sense out of experience and practically adapt to changing environments. Intelligence and its mental abilities include the input, coordination, and integration of perceptions, concepts, emotions, and physical sensations. Intelligence is the personal ability to develop the self.

Information processing perspectives view the structural components of intelligence in the following way. The "sensory register" receives and briefly holds incoming stimuli. It then selectively attends to some data in a more prolonged fashion in "working memory" where "central executive" functions coordinate new and old data, control attention, and modulate problem-solving strategies. When information is processed persistently over time, it becomes integrated into "long-term memory," one's permanent knowledge base. While these basic components of the mind's information processing system do not change, biomental development from infancy to adulthood typically increases both the system's capacity and its speed of processing information.

The *development of cognition* is complex and has been delineated traditionally in terms of the growth of thinking processes. From a cognitive science perspective, *thinking* denotes the capacity to form mental representations that can be stored as information influencing later behavior. The structure of these internal units of information is thought to include perceptual schemas, mental images or pictures, and concepts or categories that signify groups of similar items. These classes of depictions may correlate with brain lateralization. Left hemisphere information processing is sequential, analytic, linguistic, logical, and correlated with positive emotional tone; the right hemisphere processes information in a holistic and spatial manner and also regulates negative emotions. After the development of language into spoken (left hemisphere) and gestural/pointing (thought to be located in the right hemisphere) realms around age two, words can be used as labels for mental concepts. Mental symbols thus allow one thing to represent another thing.

Between twenty-four and thirty-six months, a toddler's capacity for *category formation*, namely, understanding and assembling different items with similar characteristics into single groups, occurs. By thirty-six months, the ability for *dual representation* can be measured; this is the comprehension of a symbolic object as both an object in its own right and a symbolic reference to something different. For example, a traffic light that can turn green and then red is understood as both a changing light and as a signal for "stop" and "go." The basic level of category formation as demonstrated by seeing the common, weight-bearing function of items, such as a chair, develops more complexity by forty-eight months as category formation approaches a more general level. This denotes seeing the common characteristics of large groups of different items and their subcategories, such as "furniture" including recognizing chairs, couches, tables, and so forth as different examples of furniture.

From a developmental perspective, sufficient mastery of *concept formation* to permit memory, recall, imitation, and learning is developed between eighteen and twenty-four months. Such observation is attributed to the early work of the Swiss psychologist, Jean Piaget. Recent work in the field of developmental cognitive neuroscience has substantially refined and amplified these early findings.

Concept acquisition, mental representation, and symbolic understanding are now understood to be gradual developments with roots appearing much earlier in infancy than previously believed. The following is a schematic approximation of current hypotheses. At birth and roughly until about six months, perceptual or image schemas use innate elemental biases or "conceptual spatial primitives" to determine the trajectory of concept formation. These biases are thought to summarize information in three broad developing conceptual domains: (1) an awareness of containment, (2) an awareness of rhythmical motion paths, and (3) an awareness of linking between things. From about seven to eleven months, "early global concepts" with no detailed perceptual distinctions arise. Examples include recognition of animals as self-moving objects versus nonanimals that are stationary unless moved by something else, such as furniture, plants, and actual containers. As cognitive development proceeds, by about eighteen months, the aforementioned conceptual primitives and early global concepts are used to organize more complex, "higher level concepts" characterized by detailed differences such as between dog and cat, and also to recognize human-made objects such as cup, bed, and tools. Sections on implicit and explicit learning and memory in this book's introduction and overview and on intelligence and cognition in chapter 1 have also addressed some of these considerations.

Additional laboratory research has also shown that *deferred imitation*, which is reproducing a behavior learned earlier, is present at six weeks of age. Infants observing the facial expressions of unfamiliar adults are able to imitate these looks when re-exposed to that same adult the next day. With the rapidly increasing development of motor abilities over the next months, infants are able to copy actions in more complexly expressive ways.

Infants have shown the ability to generalize previously learned material. Current developmental research suggests that by six months, infants have the demonstrable *capacity to infer an adult's intention* by, for example, distinguishing inability from unwillingness to do something. This skill indicates that babies have some understanding of the cooperativeness, mutuality, and truth of intentions, goals, and motives of different adults.

These findings suggest that infants can form *flexible mental representations* that include linked chains of relevant associations. Some research has also suggested that by ten to twelve months, infants demonstrate measurable problem solving through the use of analogies. Infants' memory for operantly learned responses in a specific context releases them from their previous context dependency. Thus, there appears to be a shift from a greater dependence on concrete learning toward learning that is less concrete and more influenced by abstract, internal associations and generalization. Between twelve and eighteen months, toddlers can retain modeled behavior for at least several months and directly copy the actions of peers as well as adults. These behaviors are exhibited across contexts. All of these skills show the use of deferred imitation (remembered reproduction) in learning, retaining, and reproducing behaviors.

Researchers have attempted to explore deeper levels of infant mental functioning with laboratory experiments that tap inferred imitation. *Inferred imitation* is behavioral enactment that appears to correctly express the infant's inferred understanding of the intentions of others. Infants' observing other persons will adapt their actions based on inferences of the observed model's goals. This ability can be measured by twelve months. An earlier precursor of toddlers' abilities to represent the intentions of others is the early infant's *reaching* at three to four months. Another antecedent is *pointing*, which strongly suggests social understanding, communication, and *joint attention*. Inferring an adult's intention as, for example, distinguishing being unable versus unwilling to do something, is suggested in current developmental research to occur by six months of age as mentioned earlier.

Further understanding of the infant's developing comprehension of symbols has been gleaned by the construct of *displaced reference*. This demonstrable ability is evident at about twelve months. By this time, infants are able to respond to the spoken label of an absent object (that is, hearing its word) by looking at and gesturing toward the spot where the object is usually seen. The ability to use language and learn from hearing the language of others, however, is fragile and develops more robustly between twelve and thirty-six months.

In summary, the complex infant mind has an active cognitive dimension capable of learning and reproducing information. Observing physical gesture and actions and hearing verbal tone, in addition to infants' actions on objects, primarily mediate learning between birth and twenty-four months. Learning by hearing and then using language as a flexible symbolic tool become significant from the end of the second year into the third year of life. This achievement is reflected in the clearer emergence of the ability for *imagination* and its expression in "make-believe" and "pretend" play. Infants and children use these processes to test reality, namely, to become anchored in the real world in an adaptive functional manner. The ability to distinguish what is probable from improbable continues to develop in a gradually more refined way.

Lastly, since infant and child development progresses on multiple levels simultaneously, it is important to realize that cognition is a complex integration of nuanced aspects of consciousness. Consciousness in the biomental perspective is one entity having a wide range characterized by both conscious and nonconscious dimensions. The description of mental representation and symbol formation emphasizes cognitive perspectives more correlated with attention and conscious awareness. The nonconscious underpinnings of cognition probably have stronger roots in emotional development. Their structural units are closer to experiential "presentations" felt with immediacy and sensed in more nonverbal ways. These mental processes are closer to what may be regarded as "mental depictions in fantasy." Their nature makes them exquisitely subjective and thus less able to be measured by laboratory investigations. They are more readily expressed in dreams, imaginative play, and fanciful creations. Their influence remains poignant throughout the life cycle, though it becomes tempered and modulated as conscious awareness develops through language, logic, and reasoning abilities. Aspects of these considerations are discussed in chapter 6 in sections on unconscious phantasy.

5.1 Intelligence: One or Many

Intelligence, the ability to extract, understand, and use information from a complex situation, is broader than isolated cognition (cognitive functions and cognitive abilities).

Intelligence uses arrays of sensory, perceptual, and conceptual information in integrated fashion in several ways: (1) to *eductively* make sense out of complexity through analysis, synthesis, and reproduction of meaning, (2) to maintain mental and physiological infrastructure, and (3) to promote regulatory expansions in adaptive survival. Language as both internal and interpersonal effective communication facilitates executive functions: selecting, planning, organizing, implementing, and refining behavioral responses. Emotions as well as specific and nonspecific motivational urges give dynamic meaning to the way these executive calibrations for forward planning are integrated, experienced, and performed. Vast arrays of disparate information, moreover, become transformed and add meaning to understanding. In effect, *volition*, the intentional path to actionable aims, is successful when it encompasses focused formulation of goals, motivation, and a sense of self-efficacy.

There are multiple subgroups that compose intelligence, not merely one factor or group of numerical designations, such as reflected in IQ scores. Intelligence, a biomental function, is the awareness and discrimination of relevant environmental and subjective events. Intelligence encompasses more than just the cognitive abilities of language, perceptual reasoning, working memory, and processing speed. Intelligence includes emotional, social, practical, and motivational components. Many nonmeasurable factors such as intuition and aesthetic sense are also crucial aspects of overall intelligence.

The following measurable factors are recognized as significant components of intelligence: fluid reasoning, crystallized verbal ability, visual perception, auditory processing, speed and accuracy of processing, reaction speed, rate of correct decision making, short-term or immediate memory, memory storage and retrieval over longer periods of time, reading and writing abilities, and mathematical knowledge. The presence and relative strength of these abilities vary among individuals and groups. They do not simultaneously emerge in all contexts but are stimulated by situational, task-related, contextual, and cultural opportunities. The general consensus by experts is that gender differences are insignificant, if they exist at all. Attention to learning as well as measuring school-based academics such as reading, writing, and mathematics are best addressed toward the end of the preschool era and formally in the school years.

5.2 Intelligence from a Developmental Perspective

While intelligence has many faces—cognitive, emotional, manual, artistic, practical, and so forth—parents are particularly concerned with cognitional mental abilities. IQ is a global indication of intelligence. More in-depth analysis of an individual's profile of abilities rather than reliance on mere numbers may better reflect the multiple dimensions composing a person's intelligence. Every person, even newborns, exists in the context of the personal and inanimate stimuli that call for some level of intelligent responsivity.

In the preschool years, for example, learning and intelligence are greatly enhanced when children become physically and materially engaged, that is, by using the whole body in learning experiences. Children under seven years old learn best when parents participate in activities such as reading to them and providing generous amounts of time for free, relatively unstructured play. Providing simple materials, toys, and dolls offers the child opportunities for imaginative and creative exploration. Low-tech toys are best until adolescence when electronic items become more interesting and are required academically.

Attention and concentration are stimulated when children become engrossed and absorbed in play. This helps expand the development of executive cognitive functions and the operation of intelligence. Many children are able to lose themselves in a creative zone when absorbed in self-directed play. In elementary school from about six to twelve years, learning is greatly enhanced when children are emotionally engaged, for example, through artistic endeavors and imaginative storytelling. In the adolescent years, learning becomes more cognitively inclined and pointedly intellectual.

As mentioned previously, the preverbal period of infancy correlates with implicit learning and knowledge acquisition that is largely nonconscious. In some sense, the preverbal period is a time of covert, implicit communication by facial expression, eye contact, gesture, tone of voice, and physical handling. Acquisition of experience, perhaps in an imperfect manner, is retained in "cellular memory," although this hypothesis may be viewed to be metaphorical since the construct of "memories" formed and retained outside the central nervous system cannot be measured.

Gestures, such as the use of sign language (whether formal or uniquely devised by parents), are another means of paralinguistic communication. With further language development by about eighteen months of age, more explicit forms of learning, knowledge acquisition, and memory come to the forefront of mental processes. Early language and interpersonal dialogue stimulate mental development and strengthen socialization.

The entire physical body, notably the central nervous system, is the biological base for cognitive processes. Proper nutrition and maintaining good health are essential for its proper operation. At all points in development, but more so early on, the senses are exquisitely receptive. Eastern cultures have traditionally recognized this fact and have paid particular attention to the development of sensory experience. For example, baby massage has been a prominent mother-infant activity over generations in India.

Senses require lively input and stimulation. What must be emphasized is that suitable stimulation is best when modulated and moderate. Overstimulation is experienced as negatively intrusive and disruptive. Visual art, music, dance, and so forth can offer the developing child proper color, dynamically modulated variations in form, and harmony—all of which contribute to enrichment of mental activation.

Developmentally appropriate exposure to arts such as painting, drawing, coloring, or experiences with music utilizes many implicit psychological processes. This exposure includes the activation of emotions, unconscious images and thoughts, and imagination. The best exposure is real-life experience incorporating artistic endeavors. Having a child "bang" on a keyboard, for example, is preferable to only listening to recorded music. Children also need to experience the substance of painting—pigments, brushes, and canvas—and not engage solely by visual appreciation. This difference can be likened to seeing oneself in a mirror versus seeing oneself in a photograph. The photograph is a facsimile of a past event; it is static and lacks the real-life dynamisms that are present in the more direct living experience of the "real thing in real time."

In fact, in the elementary and high school years, some school systems use "integrated curriculums," which use art to teach science, writing to teach mathematics, literature to teach history and geography, and so forth. This multimodal input enhances coordination between left and right cerebral hemispheres and results in effective learning that is vivid, enjoyable, and memorable.

A high IQ alone does not guarantee *creativity* (the ability to combine previously unrelated elements into novel and compelling realizations) or *resourcefulness*. Personality traits that promote divergent thinking are more important. *Divergent thinking* is the ability to grasp multiple strategies applicable to problem solving. Such flexible thought transcends restrictively linear thinking, and has been referred to as "thinking outside the box" of conventionality. Personality traits such as nonconformity, curiosity, willingness to take risks, and persistence enhance divergent thinking. Conscious abilities coupled with nonconscious resourcefulness translate into adaptive behaviors.

It has been found, for instance, that musicians are more adept at utilizing their left hemispheres (the location of convergent, logical thinking) in combination with their right hemispheres (housing imaginative and creative divergent thinking). Furthermore, when reading skills are being taught, *phonemic awareness*—the matching of sound with corresponding print letter—is more of a left-brain activity. If reading combines this left-brain activity with a coordinated right brain function such as motorically enhanced visual exposure, the learning of reading is greatly improved. Pointing to printed words and correlating printed words with specific sounds and meaning (reading semantics) strengthens both preliterate and literate reading skills. In other words, multisensory stimulation fosters memorable learning.

5.3 Intelligence: Its Bodily Platform and Influence on Creating Mental Space

Biomental child development emphasizes that intelligence and learning have a dominant sensory platform that requires stimulation, exercise, and practice. Developmental timetables for sensory maturation illustrate this. Not only does development reflect the capacity to sense material, geographical, and dimensional space such as sensing front-back, up-down, yesterday-today-tomorrow, but also a psychological mental space. This *mental space* is at first an as-yet potential dimensionality; it may be considered to be "an empty psychological room within which thoughts and feelings enter and move." The breadth of mind becomes a container holding sensation, perception, emotion, fantasy construals, and developing thoughts. This mental area gradually becomes populated with thoughts, emotions, imaginations, and fantasies that develop complexity and connectedness over time. Healthy mental space is characterized by an elastic quality able to contain and help ideas resonate and expand in flexible ways. The capacity for conceptual and emotional diversification in mental space increases the fidelity of *transactional sensitivity* between people.

Vision is present but not fully developed at birth. More complex visual perception, including binocular and stereoscopic depth perception, gradually develops from three to six months. A baby's capacity to hear is active as early as the sixth month of pregnancy and fully matured by four weeks of age. Hearing especially contributes to the development of a sense of spatial orientation. This developing ability to provide information about one's location in relation to other persons and objects has both a stabilizing function and a role in safety. Impressions from eyes and ears together support the development of three-dimensional awareness and a sense of space. *Crawling* or some variety of *prone procession* such as slithering on the stomach typically begins at seven to eleven months and enhances developing spatial understanding and motor agility. Such locomotion also contributes to the infant's expanding understanding of the interpersonal world. This also widens the scope of mental space. Outside of the relationship between infant and primary caretaker, others become sensed as "third" persons, and a sense of *triadic relationships* emerges.

Encouraging observation and exploration along with guidance through changes and transitions gives children the tools to navigate experience. Tolerating some messiness, frustration, and mistakes without immediate rectification offers children important learning opportunities. A way to learn to tolerate these states is by experiencing them as continuing learning exercises. Nonobtrusive monitoring and close supervision, especially at the early ages, are important skills for adults.

When these many facets of experience are available, learning over time contributes to both crystallized knowledge and fluid reasoning abilities. Attention, concentration, learning, practice, and repetition are facilitated by the brain's executive functions. They also, in turn, contribute to promoting more refined executive functioning. Included in the multifactorial construct of executive functions is the complex faculty of planning that includes cognitive flexibility, mental set or framework shifting, abstract thinking, rule acquisition, initiating and inhibiting action, goal-directed persistence, and relevance selection.

By the end of the high school years, all previous learning has laid the foundations for clear observation, comparative discrimination, analysis of both subtle and essential commonalities, abstraction abilities, and the synthesis of information. These nuanced calibrating abilities contribute to the development of critical thinking, effective communication, individual aptitudes, prosocial and civic awareness, and a greater sense of responsibility.

5.4 Intelligence Quotients and Learning

IQ is not reflected in a single measurement that remains stable over a life-time. Different IQ tests, times, and individual circumstances all may produce different results. Intelligent IQ testing takes this into consideration and its results should reflect relatively valid findings.

Intelligence encompasses the broad range of mental processing and style of solving novel problems together with learned and achieved knowledge and language skills. Contemporary IQ testing aims to measure a profile of multiple different mental abilities and processes. To do this effectively, testing uses a cross-battery, clinically oriented approach that selectively employs relevant tests from all available IQ protocols. IQ profiles for groups remain fairly constant from early childhood through adulthood. Malleability, however, in an individual's IQ profile is possible.

Various psychological testing procedures are available to identify levels of competence in cognitive abilities. IQ tests measure general intelligence and include subscales/subtests that measure a wide range of specific aptitudes. Global IQ in conjunction with subscores of specific cognitive abilities is regarded as a valid indication of ranges of mental abilities measured on a normal bell shaped curve. Complementary assessments that measure academic performance in reading, writing, and mathematics are termed tests of achievement and are separate from cognitive tests of IQ. Neuropsychological assessments are broader psychometric batteries and cross-batteries of tests, as mentioned in the overview, that are complex assessments of cognitive processing with special attention to the delineation of executive functions.

On tests, the number of items answered correctly are referred to as *raw scores*. These are then processed by standardization techniques. Standardized scores are norm-referenced and correlated with age-equivalent scores. Systematic biases are taken into consideration so that socioeconomic, cultural, and other possible disadvantageous variables have less impact on the reliability of the assessment. Clinical assessments of these lists of scores have defined meanings that are derived from comparable populations of specific ages. Margins of expectable error (also known as "standard errors of measurement") are recognized when interpreting scores. This inclusion supports relative levels of confidence in the significance of the numbers.

Other tests called *adaptive functioning tests* measure the degree of competence in performance activities of daily living. This capability is reflected in personal hygiene, self-dependence, communication skills, mobility, and other socially relevant tasks.

It had been thought that IQ scores typically stabilize at about ten years of age and do not appreciably change over time. Recent studies, however, demonstrate that, during adolescence, brain development is actively occurring.

This serves as the basis for an increase or decrease in measurable IQ, particularly verbal performance, depending on educational availability and resources.

Normal intelligence is a definite protective factor for children to successfully master age-salient developmental tasks. Resilient children show competence in age-salient developmental tasks even though they may have experienced risk or adversity that threatens such competence. In most research findings to date, anxiety level, both as an aspect of personality and in specific test-taking situations, negatively correlates with performance on intelligence tests. IQ scores consistently have been shown to correlate with achievement in school and later success in occupations. Current research also shows correlations between parental educational level and an adolescent's intelligence as measured by psychometric testing. The influences of modeling and even socioeconomic status play important roles in this.

5.5 Borderline Intellectual Functioning and ADHD

Borderline intellectual functioning (BIF) may indicate both below-average intelligence and lowered adaptive competence in activities of daily living. Borderline functioning is well below average and describes a condition that has been underrecognized for decades. Borderline intelligence is not a form of mental retardation or serious intellectual disability. Borderline intellectual functioning is distinct from what in psychiatry is termed "borderline personality disorder," which is a primary mood—not cognitive—dysregulation. Borderline intelligence is prevalent in up to 15 percent of the population and often misdiagnosed. It can be thought of as a potential risk factor for successful development.

BIF is important to emphasize in this text since such a cognitive status may be associated with behavioral, learning, and academic difficulties. Children and adults with borderline intelligence have been observed to be *slow learners*. Performance in many areas, though not all, is sporadic, irregular, and uneven. These children have notable difficulties with rates of information processing, learning, and retrieval expected of students in regular classroom settings. Difficulties with understanding average amounts of material also exist. In some cases, their academic and behavioral problems are misinterpreted as reflecting mental disorders.

The primary misdiagnosis of borderline intellectual functioning is attention-deficit/hyperactivity disorder (ADHD). Attentional problems moreover are common to many disorders, and to many nonpsychiatric motivational challenges. Much more psychiatric and psychopharmacological focus has been given to the difficulties characterized by ADHD rather than those of BIF. When attentional difficulties present as academic and behavioral problems, a convergence of expectations and perspectives has resulted in diagnosing ADHD. This has taken precedence over greater attention to the influence of informational processes, that is, assessing significant limitations in cognitive abilities, such as executive functions that require complex academic remediation over time. Moreover, such diagnostic overshadowing unfortunately continues to remain a robust bias in labeling many presenting impairments in children. This incorrect attribution of children's presenting signs and symptoms to a conventionally (over)used AHDH diagnosis also fails to consider the broader current and past psychosocial components that may underlie impairing and disruptive presentations.

ADHD is a disorder of impulsivity in attention, motor activity, and decision making. It is a primary disorder of the inability to delay thought scatter and impulsive action. Some have proposed that executive functioning problems may be central in adult attention deficit disorder, while behavioral impulsivity may be central in child ADHD. Randomized controlled trials of cognitive behavioral therapy (CBT) for adults with ADHD have replicated previous studies and continue to demonstrate CBT to be more effective than medication. Rather than being a primary learning problem as is borderline intelligence, ADHD instead affects learning secondarily. When someone with ADHD has difficulties learning, a significant factor causing this may be attributed to the impulsivity that, in turn, affects executive functioning, notably attention and organizational skills. For children, judicious treatment encompasses a comprehensive management plan that includes child, parents, school personnel, and intensive behavioral interventions as discussed in chapter 1.

Biomental child development proposes careful scrutiny in assessing apparent ADHD presentations because this label is typically lasting and elicits an almost reflexive recommendation by physicians for stimulant medications whose problematic and extensive side effect profile may be underestimated.

If motoric impulsivity is primary, then ADHD may be present. By contrast, if attentional problems and working memory are primary and impairing features, then executive functions deficits—rather than the conventional designation of ADHD—may be primary. This distinction is significant since the nature of each is different and their treatments may vary in considerable ways. An interesting and perhaps useful consideration is medical screening by obtaining blood levels of ferritin (norm: approximately 20 ng/mL (ug/L) to 300 to 400 ng/mL (ug/L)), an intracellular protein that stores and regulates the release of iron. The condition of "restless leg syndrome" (RLS) is associated with a finding of lowered ferritin, and children who exhibit restless legs and hyperactive motor behaviors may have lowered ferritin levels that are remediable to iron supplementation, after careful medical clinical assessment is made. RLS is described as typically occurring in the evening when sitting or lying down. Along these lines, some pediatric neurologists have suggested other pathophysiological dysfunctions related to iron levels and ADHD. They hypothesize that either a deficiency of peripheral iron or a dysfunction of the blood-brain barrier in the presence of normal iron levels may contribute to low brain iron levels, which would increase risk for ADHD in a subgroup of those with this disorder.

Diligence to considerations in this section, moreover, are important since borderline intellectual functioning, as a primary difficulty in learning, does not require nor benefit from any psychotropic medication. It requires careful assessment with intelligence tests that measure mental processing abilities. Achievement tests that measure scholastic performance in academic subjects such as reading and mathematics are also used. Vision problems, hearing impairments, and sleep apnea are medical conditions that must be ruled out. Determination of IQ scores and areas of strengths, weaknesses, and possible cognitive limitations are the assessment goals. Valid and reliable tests need to be employed. Factors such as child motivation, fatigue, and boredom need to be taken into consideration in evaluating results.

When borderline intellectual functioning is found, or learning disabilities are suspected, primary academically oriented remediations are interventions of choice. A high level of suspicion about the presence of this condition in the early elementary school years may provide needed scholastic and social remediation.

6. ADHD OR ADHDS

The biomental perspective suggests that the complex presentations currently recognized by the single diagnostic label "ADHD" may be multiple disorders and require different treatments. This real group of presentations reflects developmental, neurobiological, and neuropsychiatric impairments in psychological self-control and behavioral self-management. When present, it shows clear evidence of clinically significant impairment in social, academic, or occupational functioning. The complexity of this condition needs to be recognized; hence the current conjectures are heuristic propositions that not only serve to inform clinical management but also await further scientific delineation. At the present level of clinical and neuroscientific understanding, at least, two distinct groups or subtypes can be distinguished: (1) executive functions impairment and (2) hyperkinetic/impulsivity impairment. While details of this conceptualization run throughout this book as discussed, for example, in chapter 1, this brief section encapsulates leading propositions. As is the case in many though not all psychiatric disorders currently categorized, that of ADHD requires greater precision in formulation.

Executive functions (EFs) is not a unidimensional construct, but, in fact, is made up of multiple subcomponents. These include a wide range of forward thinking processes ranging from attentional selectivity through volitional implementation. This variety of ADD and ADHD correlates with what is conventionally described as the "attention deficit" component of ADHD. Whereas each child's range of executive functions typically varies in the strength and weakness of each of its subcomponents, in ADHD presentations with dominant EFs impairment, a central weakness is in the cognitive inhibition subcomponent of EFs. Cognitive inhibition is the ability to inhibit competing thoughts and shift mental set in a fluid manner. This cognitive disinhibition results in cognitive inflexibility seen as inability to focus, attend, and maintain concentration. The biomental perspective suggests that this cognitive variation or weakness in psychological processes is a learning disorder that is best managed by educational remediation and cognitive training. Highly targeted interventions are still in their infancy. Such remediation is imperfectly systematized at the present time.

The hyperkinetic/impulsivity dominant type of ADHD presentations, by contrast, is virtually a brain-based neurological impairment. This behavioral inhibition disorder may be the leading and most common ADHD presentation although these children's reactions to situations remain highly variable, inconsistent, and often unique. It is a deficit in inhibitory control of motor behavior and best described as a hyperkinetic impulsivity—an impaired ability to inhibit actions and inhibit responses, especially associated with intentional movements of the opposite side of the body. This glaring involuntary, nonconscious motoric overactivity or drivenness is typically associated with excessive motor overflow or mirror movements—unintentional, often-bilateral hand, foot, and limb movements. Motor overflow is called synkinesis and understood as a soft neurological sign associated with motor cortex inhibitory dysfunction. Fidgeting and foot tapping are typically seen. While the precise neurobiological mechanisms of this neurologically-based motor overflow are yet undeciphered, their clear-cut impairment is certain, especially because they may weaken kinesthetic memory for refining intentional, goal directed behaviors (an important part of learning from experience). The hyperkinetic/impulsivity dominant subtype of ADHD is most responsive to psychotropic medications that downregulate hyperarousability and indiscriminate overreactivity.

7. LEARNING DISABILITIES

Another area of concern related to intelligence and academic problems is the spectrum of *learning disorders* or *learning disabilities* (LDs). They denote unexpected underachievement in academic subjects. These neurocognitive disorders have a significant adverse impact on scholastic achievement as well as cognitive, emotional, and social learning in school. This constellation of scholastic difficulties—found in up to about 15 percent of children—has been a focus of concern for educators, psychologists, and psychiatrists. Unlike other developmental delays that typically become evident by the first eighteen months of life, LDs typically become apparent in early grade school, at about six through eight years of age. It is important to note that prematurity—birth at 29 to 36 weeks' gestation—may cause or correlate with disorders usually first diagnosed in infancy, childhood, or adolescence. These include all learning disorders, motor skills/developmental coordination/dyspraxia disorders (such as "clumsiness" and poor handwriting), and communication disorders.

Individuals with Disabilities Education Act (IDEA) 2004 defines a *specific learning disability* (SLD) as a disorder in one or more of the basic psychological processes involved in understanding or in using language, spoken or written, that may manifest itself in imperfect ability to listen, think, speak, read, write, spell, or do mathematics. Reading disabilities constitute about 75 to 80 percent of all specific learning disabilities. Reading disabilities or disorders are also termed "dyslexias." Theoretical models describe several subtypes. Although different classifications exist, seven subtypes are the following: (1) orthographic, which involves impaired memory and translating the alphabetic, visual symbols code that allows for representation of printed letters and words, (2) phonological, which translates these symbols into speech sounds, (3) fluency, (4) comprehension, (5) semantic or understanding the meaning of what is read, (6) mixed, and (7) global.

SLDs contrast with and are not the generalized intellectual disabilities that characterize what has been traditionally termed "mental retardation." SLDs are intrinsic to the individual and presumably attributable to central nervous system dysfunction. SLDs are found across ethnic, cultural, language, and economic groups and persist across the life span, though manifestations and intensity may vary with developmental age and environmental demands. Excluded as causes of SLD are visual, hearing, and motor disability, mental retardation, emotional disturbance, cultural factors, socioeconomic disadvantage, and limited English proficiency.

Children with learning disabilities may show a significant discrepancy between measured IQ and measured scholastic achievement in one or more academic areas appearing as unexpected underachievement ("the discrepancy model"), but this is not a required defining feature. Average IQ is presumed. Working memory index (WMI), suggesting executive functions involvement, is often low.

These children may have intracognitive discrepancies such as processing difficulties that may manifest as an uneven ability to learn from hearing or seeing information. Such difficulties may cause learning disabled children to have intra-achievement discrepancies among different areas of academics. There may be differences, for example, between *reading decoding* (translating a printed word into a pronounced word or sound) and *reading comprehension.* Or a child may have good achievement in all subjects except perhaps mathematics. SLDs are characterized by low achievement in the face of cognitive integrities.

Nonverbal learning disabilities (NVLD) are neurodevelopmental conditions that share many of the characteristics of Asperger syndrome. Asperger disorder is a psychiatric condition characterized by poor communicational skills (socially meaningful pragmatic language) in the face of adequate expressive and receptive language, significantly impaired reciprocal social interactions, and restricted, repetitive, and stereotyped interests and behaviors. Children with NVLD, however, appear to have milder social skills impairments (dyssemia) and more difficulty with academics such as mathematics. However, NVLD typically may have measurable irregularities in IQ subtests such as found in "block design" scores, which reflect visuospatial functioning. Children with Asperger syndrome, on the other hand, usually have strong visuospatial abilities.

8. THE ROLE OF EXECUTIVE FUNCTIONS IN DEVELOPMENT AND LEARNING

Difficulties with *executive functions* (EF) have been a relatively recent focus of attention in educational, psychological, psychiatric, and neuroscience research. Decades ago, attention to EF was applied to the rehabilitation of neurologically impaired persons, especially with traumatic brain injuries. As discussed in other sections of this book, executive functions include maintaining an adequate problem-solving set for forward planning toward successful goal attainment. Goal management denotes maintaining intentions in goal-directed behaviors. These executive functions bring coherence to behaviors by controlling the activation or inhibition of actions that promote or oppose task completion. To achieve this, many interrelated processes are required: attention, working memory, organization, prioritization, planning, vigilance, response inhibition/impulse control, ability to modulate and remodulate mental set, and cognitive fluency. The role of executive functions—cognitive processes and behavioral competencies—therefore should not be underemphasized but rather should be understood as a fundamental platform of mental operations.

Empirically, executive dysfunction is reflected in the inability to begin and maintain tasks, stay focused amidst distractors, and work independently. Problems such as these typically appear around the onset of puberty (sixth grade, age eleven years, and in the first and second years in high school). These are crucial times for renewed brain maturation. From a neuropsychiatric perspective, the dorsolateral prefrontal cortex (dl-PFC), moreover, has been implicated in its role correlated with complex attention, working memory, and top-down cognitive control during emotional processing and anticipation. Damage to the dl-PFC can result in the "dysexecutive syndrome," which leads to problems with affect, social judgement, executive memory, abstract thinking, and intentionality.

Often, the misdiagnosis of ADD or ADHD is made since there are features of executive dysfunction in many ADHD presentations, though not all. Distinguished researchers emphasizing the clinical heterogeneity in ADHD have suggested that approximately half of individuals with ADHD display distinct EF deficits. Such childhood EF deficits predict poor adolescent outcomes in academic and social functioning. These findings suggest that deficits in EF have wide-ranging impact on later functioning that may extend to activities of daily living, a global measure of functional abilities. Careful assessments are required, especially since psychostimulant medications, which do not help executive functions, are often prescribed.

Biomental child development suggests that greater emphasis be put on identifying strengths and weaknesses in the range of executive functioning rather than a primary emphasis on motoric hyperactivity-impulsivity and diagnoses of attention deficit. This ADHD constellation may be a primary manifestation of impulsivity. The specific form that impulsivity takes should be characterized in detail, as, for example, motor impulsivity—response inhibition as the inability to stop prepotent responses, or cognitive impulsivity—the inability to tolerate long delays. Impulsivity also requires assessing the way a child is able to estimate the passage of time. Such broad assessments require judicious interpretation that discriminates era-appropriate overactivity from pathology. Motoric impulsivity may require a combined management plan that includes behavioral interventions at home and school and psychotropic medication.

Executive functions are complex and are central to all learning. They encompass both "cold" cognition (cognitive functions) and "hot" cognition (cognitive skills shaped by emotion and motivation). Studies on the developmental trajectories of "hot" executive functions are sparse at this time despite the belief that affective skills, which rely more heavily on the orbitofrontal and ventromedial prefrontal cortices, may emerge prior to "cold" executive abilities.

In summary, executive functions denote one's problem-solving set and capacity for forward planning, especially when challenged by novel stimuli. The elements that compose executive functions require careful examination: attention and vigilance control, selection of data for consideration, working memory and multitasking ability, organization, capacity to inhibit distractors, planning to achieve future outcomes such as rewards, error correction, cognitive flexibility, and ultimately attaining a goal, namely, volitional consummation.

This last factor—volitional consummation—is an underdiscussed component of executive functions. Volitional ability or conation is colloquially termed "will power." It denotes materially putting a plan into action. In carefully assessing volition, factors such as emotional resistance whose roots may be lodged in unresolved psychological conflicts expressed as anxiety and avoidant behaviors must be considered. Biomental endowments such as traits and temperament become shaped by environmental influences—parenting and schooling. These manifold components yield in the end an integration of natural inclinations, motivation, and fluid decision-making that contribute to one's individual and social *adaptive intelligence.*

In assessing presentations of inattention and hyperactivity, it is crucial to clearly distinguish the different forms that impulsivity may take: cognitive, motoric, or emotional response inhibition dysregulation, as well as working memory and vigilance modulation/attentional control. Such assessments may separate out primary problems with executive functions from presentations of hyperactive impulsivity currently described using ADHD diagnoses. At this time, the only reasonable diagnostic category in the DSM-IV-TR to indicate a primary disorder of executive functions may be Learning Disorders, NOS, coded as DSM-IV-TR 315.9. When the fifth edition of DSM becomes available approximately in 2013, a reassessment of appropriate classification may be possible. Remediation of weak areas in executive functions may be best achieved by psychosocial and educational interventions rather than by medications.

Executive functions—cognitive abilities and behavioral performance—may be improved in a variety of ways. Since impulsivity and behavioral inhibition may overlap with and constrain EFs, attention to this area is important. However, EFs as such demand compensatory strategies and environmental accommodations. Much research and development to target specific EF subcomponents and their neurological substrates is in process. Currently, some physical and behavioral devices may be employed. For example, disorders of performance or weak volitional consummation require externalizing guidelines materially in real time: visual and written lists of rules, step-by-step sequences for tasks, and providing contiguously available motivational incentives. These must be as *concrete and specific as possible* (charts, diagrams, visual images, and so forth), and *consistently available in the natural settings where performance is required* (classroom, home, car, grocery store, and so forth). As has been reiterated throughout this book, listening to, hearing, and speaking to children in age and developmentally appropriate ways help them internalize such self-directing and eventually self-reflective language.

9. EDUCATIONAL TESTING AND SPECIAL EDUCATION

A number of problems may interfere with a child's learning in an academic setting. When mild or brief difficulties are identified, schools may offer a district service plan that addresses these transient problems in a general manner within a regular classroom. If an academic or emotional disability is found to more substantially limit a student's classroom performance, a 504 plan may be constructed. Typically, regular education staff may make classroom changes that enable a student to complete curriculum expectations. Such a 504 plan is reviewed yearly. When a student's difficulties with learning appear more substantial, a more formal special education process to identify and introduce more intensive remediation is considered.

Psychometric testing, such as intelligence tests and tests of scholastic achievement are part of a wide assessment process needed to validly determine learning disabilities and formulate an Individualized Educational Program (IEP). National special education services have introduced the concept of "increasing capacity," which denotes the attempt to unify special with general education and to help schools build their own capacity to meet the needs of all students. Procedures included in this venture are (1) *response to intervention* (RTI) and (2) *scientifically research-based interventions* (SRBI) used for assessment, diagnosis, and remediation. RTI provides intensive interventions focused on areas of underachievement and carefully measures academic progress over two to five months. SRBI is a current process used to more validly assess intervention responses through scientific research.

Underlying specific learning disabilities in reading, writing, and mathematics often suggest more central processing cognitive deficits. Neuropsychological testing may aid in identifying impairments in memory (visual, auditory, or both), visual-motor integration, visual perception, processing speed, abstract concept formation, sequential processing, or auditory processing. In addition, some experts have suggested that if a child responds to concentrated academic interventions, it may be indicative of a learning disability that is being remediated.

A combined assessment approach to identifying and remediating disorders of learning may be best. Components of this process would include tests of cognitive functions, tests of scholastic achievement, RTI and SRBI, and curriculum-based measurements (CBMs; sometimes called curriculum-based assessment or CMA). CBMs are teacher's short-term or weekly measurements using direct observation and recording, often with visual graphs, of curriculum (reading, writing, mathematics) instruction with students. This direct assessment using tests of academic subjects reflects mastery and includes measures of speed, proficiency, and accuracy. Results of all assessment strategies indicate the degree of response to interventions, and decisions to continue, change, or stop them.

Indeed, along with their primary learning limitations, persons with borderline intellectual functioning (with or without learning disabilities) may exhibit social, emotional, or behavioral disturbances. Intellectual and scholastic strengths, weaknesses, and vulnerabilities need to be delineated in careful fashion by teams of professionals working with families and schools. Hence, comprehensive cognitive, emotional, and behavioral assessments in addition to SRBI and their results are required for proper identification and suitable intervention planning. There are some, perhaps many, children with behavior and learning problems that do not require psychotropic medications. A large number of psychosocial and academic interventions may be preferred choices for effective and long-lasting remediation. Such learning and behavioral interventions may produce sustainable improvements that carry forward into adulthood.

10. A PHILOSOPHY OF EDUCATION

The previous considerations of the development of intelligence in children are inextricably tied to processes of learning. "Early childhood" was a phrase that had covered birth through the preschool years (ages three, four, and five) until recently, when the concept was extended upward to age eight years.

Early childhood education—its practices and techniques—are markedly important considerations. In addition, the elementary and high school years of successful students are reflected in positive learning outcomes—successful achievement. Proficiency standards may be set by states but can also have broader horizons. Quality education facilitates children's understanding and application of knowledge, life skills, and civic-social responsibility. This section aims to minimize "achievement gaps" among children by attention to some effective learning strategies.

The quality and style of the child's exposure to acquiring information is a crucial component of learning. The way learning is presented significantly influences its effectiveness. Put simply, teaching methods follow one of two models: (1) "direct instruction" that includes explicit inculcation, training, memorization, and practice to promote rote recall, and (2) less structured styles that emphasize exploration, discovery, inquiry, and finding meaning through concrete actions and real-life engagements. The latter approach encompasses teaching styles termed *developmentally appropriate practices* (DAP).

Parents and educators typically gravitate toward one or the other in choosing a learning environment or school. In fact, no one model may be universally applicable or even sufficient. A number of variables to consider include the chronological and developmental age of the child, his or her traits, temperament, and attachment pattern, explicit goals in a particular setting, parents' involvement, and socioeconomic factors such as available resources.

Biomental child development endorses awareness of these considerations in an effort to achieve balance and address specific needs. In regard to early childhood education, notably in infancy and the preschool years, choice of approach toward learning requires a personal decision. In the elementary school years, personal preference continues to be important but may be less ambiguous since the six- to twelve-year-old's cognitive faculties are generally more matured and supported by newly emerging reading and writing skills. The elementary and high school years benefit from formal academic instruction, particularly when discovery and real-world learning engagements are encouraged. In fact, *the essential ingredient in suitable educational practices at any age is the approach taken.* Simply put, the way teaching interactions are handled has greater value than the actual content. Children— from the early childhood years through adolescence—perform best when exposed to quality learning environments.

The biomental child development perspective prefers the following childhood learning strategies. In infancy, toddlerhood, and the preschool years, all children deserve a range of available learning opportunities. Caregivers, particularly parents, who take this obligation seriously can actively choose preferred practices and styles, with particular attention to those of high quality. Differences in educational environments are inevitable, especially in how structured a curriculum is designed. One basic difference is a program's emphasis on building social, emotional, and creative skills versus more pointedly academic skills.

The biomental child perspective suggests more emphasis on exposure to opportunities for exploration, discovery, and experiential "learning by doing" in real-life contexts with real-life examples. Techniques employing this style are most consistent with the biomental perspective—developmental integration of body (sensory-motor), emotions (imagination), and thinking (intelligence). This balanced strategy facilitates acquisition of elements for the development of critical thinking skills. An enthusiastic emotional tone should be embedded within such developmentally suitable practices. This approach, characterized by emphasis on discovering novel realizations, may also be interspersed with some developmentally appropriate direct instruction, often termed "seat learning." This subject matter may include reading skills, mathematics, aesthetics, and fundamentals of citizenship.

A personalized approach, especially by significantly involved adults, enhances cognitive skills. In a personal communication with John Raven, a developer of the Raven Progressive Matrices Intelligence Tests, about enhancing intelligence, Raven stated: "The bottom line is that direct training in strategies has little or no effect. Indirect development of cognitive ability by parents, a very few teachers, and involvement in demanding activities at work does produce a significant effect."

In all learning environments, subject matter should match the child's abilities and processing speed. Learning free of stress, pressure, coercion, and "drilling" is best. This overall approach encourages an "allegro" experience, which denotes its being cheerful, lively, and "fun." Such a style increases motivation and instills values of inquiry and discovering meaning on both emotional and cognitive levels. In addition, recent longitudinal studies show that action-oriented rather than "seat learning" in the preschool years lessens the development of childhood overweight later on. These sentiments run throughout this book and are illustrated here in the discussion about reading.

11. NOTES ON LEARNING TO READ

Reading is a fundamental part of the human developmental repertoire. Its integrating pathways have growth, maturation, and developmental emergences that foster overall development, enculturation, and socialization when appreciated. The neuropsychological processes involved in reading include *phonemic awareness*, the *alphabetic principle* (meaning that letters and their combinations are the written symbols used to represent the speech sounds of a language), *rapid automatic naming*, and *reading comprehension*.

Reading contributes to the fuller development of *literacy*, which is the capacity to speak, listen, read, write, and appreciate language. These skills correlate with the ability to form and understand symbols and to use abstract thinking in communicative activities. *Semantics* (or the meaning of words) and *pragmatics* (or the appropriate, applied use of language in social contexts) are both supported by good reading skills.

From birth until the time when most children enter first grade, the foundations for developing reading and writing skills are laid down. During the period from birth to about age seven, children are in the process of becoming skillful readers. This emerging literacy is supported when parents actively engage children in all aspects of oral or spoken language. *Spoken language* is the group of articulated verbalizations used in talking and listening. This collection contrasts with *written language*, or the language used in writing and reading. Informal experiences through exposure to literacy-rich environments stimulate the development of literacy. The act of reading to children is paramount in stimulating overall development. This focus on oral and spoken language does not include formal didactic instruction, which is best introduced in the elementary school years.

Emergent literacy starts from day one and develops through middle childhood. Parents can foster this skill by ample and suitable spoken language interactions. Putting it more simply, one should not wait until a child is eighteen months old to speak with him or her in sentences. Active adult language exposure (and this may include singing) should start with newborns. Studies show that infants from six to twelve months are especially adept at recognizing and responding to complex tunes and rhythms. Singing and rhythmically moving with an infant can provide soothing stimulation for sensory and central nervous system integration, in other words, fostering biomental coordination.

Story time can also serve as a special parent-child interaction. It may begin in the middle of the first year in simple ways, such as using picture books. By age two, "lap reading" may provide the toddler with opportunities for emotional closeness with parents and also stimulation of *phonological awareness* (seeing and hearing syllables in words that make up sentences) and *phonemic awareness* (distinguishing individual sounds). Reading before bedtime is especially pleasant since the child is less active and more receptive to parental physical and emotional attention. Children often find renewed interest in exposure to the same books or stories dozens of times.

Parents can provide continuing opportunities for children to build their spoken language skills. *Phonological awareness* is one such ability that enhances familiarity with the sounds of spoken language. By speaking and listening to children and by reading to them books suitable for given levels of understanding, a familiarity with hearing and manipulating the sounds of spoken language is provided. Reading aloud to children is one of the most important activities that help build the knowledge required for success in reading. The younger the child, the more that singing and rhyming activities should be included. Reading *to* children, rather than teaching children to read before elementary school, is strongly suggested.

It is important to speak and listen to children. Listening provides adults with opportunities to reflect back the sounds, words, and moods that are being communicated. Asking questions and explaining things as completely as may be suitable to the developmental level of the child supports emergent literacy.

By age five, children are not yet typically capable of fluent reading or writing. These activities should not be forced. Children, nonetheless, are in the process of building the *preliteracy* skills that will then make literacy possible starting in the first grade and emerging more fluently by the end of the third grade. By about seven to eight years of age, most late readers have caught up with early ones if there is no developmental or learning disability present.

In the first three years of elementary school, children typically learn to read. By the end of first grade, most children can begin to read simple material. Printing letters is adequate by age six; and by age seven, many children can write complete simple sentences. At six to seven years, children read about six hundred words. By the end of second grade, at about seven to eight years old, children have developed the ability to read one and two syllable words. At that time, children can read up to three thousand words. Children can write in simple, complete sentences and answer such questions as "How?" "Why?" and "What if?" By the end of third grade, at about eight years old, most children are able to read with some fluency. Written work is more mature and sentences are used in writing. Beginning in fourth grade, reading facilitates the learning of other material.

In second and third grade, at about ages seven and eight, parents should continue to speak often with children to continue to build their listening and speaking skills. Reading to and with children should occur frequently. On an emotional level, feelings such as reverence and compassion are stimulated by the images that imaginative stories arouse in the mind. Children still love to be read to in early elementary school, and fairy tales and animal fables are fascinating stimulators of *imagination* and *creativity*. Some curriculums introduce mythologies, such as Norse tales and Native American stories, starting in fourth grade when interest in fairy tales wanes. From sixth grade on, children are reading historical biographies and books about geographical exploration. Encouraging children to read on their own as well as coordinating home with school activities can help children practice what is being learned at school. Good communication with teachers optimizes this.

A reliable website discussing many of the aforementioned ideas is the National Association for the Education of Young Children, www.naeyc.org.

12. KEY POINTS

12.1 The Child as a Whole Person

Biomental child development emphasizes the biomental integrity of individuals. People experience themselves with a sense of immediacy as both psychological selves and material selves—individuals made up of flesh and blood who feel, think, and move.

Recognizing this biomental reality entails an appreciation of the many levels of functioning on which life is experienced. All these domains undergo exquisitely sensitive integration over time. When caregivers see children in this way, increasingly sensitive attention to the different developmental sectors and their interrelationships is sharpened. Each sector strives to mature and develop both individually and as part of the greater whole. Each sphere has its characteristic tempo of unfolding, both alone and in consonance with the whole. Appreciating these facts includes taking into account the physical, emotional, intellectual, social, aesthetic, spiritual, and consciousness-centered perspectives of a child's life. Consciously providing children with opportunities for exercising each area promotes *integration* rather than "lopsidedness."

12.2 Attachment

Attachment is a term commonly used to describe an infant's and child's physical proximity, dependence, and psychological connection to its primary caregiver. The nature and quality of these binding patterns derives from a combination of the infant's innate temperament and biomental coping responses as coordinated with the mother's sensitivity. Attachment patterns reflect children's awareness of risk, fear, and anxiety and how these may be modulated to ensure safety by the protective ministrations of primary caregivers.

12.3 Traits

Traits are enduring biomental attitudes. They can be understood to be elemental building blocks of the biomental individual. As traits coalesce, they form temperamental styles that, in turn, lay the foundation upon which complex personality configurations develop over the course of childhood into adulthood.

12.4 Temperament

Temperament is a large cluster of dispositions in both attitude and readiness to act and react in characteristic ways. It may manifest, for example, as an attitude of overall cooperativeness or fearfulness.

Temperament and its composite traits, to a large extent, are innate, genetically endowed psychophysiological predispositions. They are notably evident in the individual tempo reflected in children's growth, maturation, and development. This vital awareness allows parents to provide children with the time needed to encounter, assimilate, and master childhood developmental events. Trying to speed up development by forceful or pressured attempts counters progress.

Although genetic endowment is significant, the external environment and parenting—when knowledgeable and facilitating—can accentuate or constrain traits and so modify a given temperament.

12.5 Personality

Personality subsumes traits and temperament and forms psychological scaffolding shaped by learning from experience. While traits and temperament may be understood to be a child's "original face" or "first nature," personality is the face that develops through experience. It is structured by learning, conditioning, and acquiring both skills to adapt to reality and psychological defense mechanisms to manage anxiety.

Personality reflects the continuing consolidation of experience, the management of anxiety, and the way demands of reality are negotiated. Favorable or, at least, workable levels of functioning and quality of life are thus achieved. Personality is the composite sense of personal and social awareness that ensures survival by recognizing risks and realistic dangers. Normal personality functioning manages these challenges by using realistic rather than fantasy-based solutions.

12.6 Intelligence

Intelligence is a complex developmental process already in operation at birth. It is the ability to make sense out of experience and to adapt in practical ways to changing environments. Intelligence includes the input, coordination, and integration of sensation and perception. It also includes concept formation, emotional awareness, and the use of the physical body to establish and facilitate adaptive responsiveness. This responsiveness is the interface between an individual's developing sense of self—*identity*—and the outside world—*culture*.

12.7 Developmental Perspective

The *developmental perspective* reflects an understanding of the changing conditions of childhood—growth, maturation, and overall biomental integration—over time. Development affects and is reflected in the physical body, emotions, cognition, and social aptitudes. Major biomental sectors include physical growth and central nervous system maturation, temperament, attachment, psychological and emotional development, cognitive and intellectual development, social development, communication and language, psychosexual gender view, and moral development.

Within each of these sectors, a child's sense of self remains the overarching, organizational focal point. Viewing a child's development from "inside" emphasizes the primacy of mind, self-identity, and ego. Within these major factors motivating behavior are traits, temperament, and personality. Both the inner mind and the outer physical body are platforms for the aforementioned factors to express themselves.

Knowledge of and skill in the details of development provide caregivers with an orientation and knowledge-based scaffolding toward successful parenting. Dynamic transitions—concordant, complementary, and conflictual—span a lifetime's progress from simple to more complex. These transitions organize the *biomental self* and are facilitated and enhanced by the nurturance, discipline, and personal example of caregivers that comes with understanding this developmental perspective.

REFERENCES

Aguiar, A., & Baillargeon, R. (2002). Developments in young infants' reasoning about occluded objects. *Cognitive Psychology, 45*, 267–336.

Allman, J. M., Hakeem, A., Erwin, J. M., Nimchinsky, E., & Hof, P. (2001). The anterior cingulate cortex: The evolution of an interface between emotion and cognition. *Annals of the New York Academy of Science, 935*(1), 107–117.

Amodio, D. M, & Frith, C. D. (2006). Meeting of minds: the medial frontal cortex and social cognition. *Nature Reviews Neuroscience, 7*, 268–277.

Antshel, K. M., Hargrave, T. M., Simonescu, M., Kaul, P., Hendricks, K., & Faraone, S. V. (2011). Advances in understanding and treating ADHD. *BMC Medicine, 9*(72). doi:10.1186/1741-7015-9-72

Aylward, G. P. (1994). *Practitioner's guide to developmental and psychological testing: Critical issues in developmental and behavioral pediatrics.* New York: Springer Publishing.

Baillargeon, R. (2004). Infants reasoning about hidden objects: Evidence for event-general and event-specific expectations. *Developmental Science, 7*, 391–424.

Bale, T. L., Baram, T. Z., Brown, A. S., Goldstein, J. M., Insel, T. R., McCarthy, M. M., Nemeroff, C. B., Reyes, T. M., Simerly, R. B., Susser, E. S., & Nester, E. J. (2010). Early life programming and neurodevelopmental disorders. *Biological Psychiatry, 68*(4), 314–319.

Barkley, R. A. (2012). *Executive Functions: What They Are, How They Work, and Why They Evolved.* New York: Guilford.

Barnard-Brak, L., & Brak, V. (2011). Pharmacotherapy and academic achievement among children with attention-deficit/hyperactivity disorder. *Journal of Child and Adolescent Psychopharmacology, 21*(6), 597–603.

Barr, R., Marrott, H., & Rovee-Collier, C. (2003). The role of sensory preconditioning in memory retrieval by preverbal infants. *Learning and Behavior, 31*, 111–123.

Bauer, P. J. (2009). Learning and memory: Like a horse and carriage. In A. Woodward & A. Needham (Eds.), *Learning and the infant mind*, pp. 3–28. New York: Oxford University Press.

Bechara, A., Damasio, H., Tranel, D., & Anderson, S. W. (1998). Dissociation of working memory from decision making within the human prefrontal cortex. *Journal of Neuroscience, 18*(1), 428–37.

Bellagamba, F., Camaioni, L., & Colonnesi, C. (2006). Change in children's understanding of others' intentional actions. *Developmental Science, 9*(2), 182–188.

Bion, W. R. (1959). *Experiences in groups*. New York: Basic Books.

Bonawitz, E., Shafto, P., Hyowon, G. H., Goodman, N. D., Spelke, E., & Schulz, L. (2011). The double-edged sword of pedagogy. *Cognition, 120*, 322–330.

Bowlby, J. (1969). *Attachment and loss, Vol. 1*. New York: Basic Books.

Braungart-Rieker, J., Courtney, S., & Garwood, M. M. (1999). Mother- and father-infant attachment: Families in context. *Journal of Family Psychology, 13*, 535–553.

Brownell, C. A., & Kopp, C. B. (2007). Transitions in toddler socioeconomic development: Behavior, understanding, relationships. In C. A. Brownell & C. B. Kopp (Eds.), *Socioemotional development in the toddler years: Transitions and transformations*, pp. 1–40. New York: Guilford.

Burkins, J. M., & Croft, M. (2010). *Preventing misguided reading: New strategies for guided reading teachers*. Newark, DE: International Reading Association.

Bush, G., Luu, P., & Posner, M. I. (2000). Cognitive and emotional influences in the anterior cingulate cortex. *Trends in Cognitive Sciences, 4*, 215–222.

Caldera, Y. M. (2004). Paternal involvement and infant-father attachment: a Q-set study. *Fathering: Journal of Theory, Research, and Practice about Men as Fathers, 2*(2), 13–150.

Carpenter, M., Akhtar, N., & Tomasello, M. (1998). Fourteen- through eighteen-month-old infants differentially imitate intentional and accidental actions. *Infant Behavior and Development, 21*, 315–330.

Carpenter, M., Pennington, B. F., & Rogers, S. J. (2002). Interrelationships among social-cognitive skills in young children with autism. *Journal of Autistic Developmental Disorders, 32*, 91–106.

Carter, C. S., Lederhendler, I. I., & Kirkpatrick, B., eds. (1999). *The integrative neurobiology of affiliation*. Cambridge, MA: MIT Press.

Cattell R. (1950). *Personality: A systematic, theoretical, and factual study*. New York: McGraw Hill.

Chan, R. C. K., Shum, D., Toulopou, T., & Chen, E. Y. H. (2008). Assessment of executive functions: Review of instruments and identification of critical issues. *Archives of Clinical Neuropsychology, 23*, 201–216.

Chess, S., & Thomas, A. (1995). *Temperament in clinical practice*. New York: Guilford Press.

Cloninger, C. R. (1987). A systematic method for clinical description and classification of personality variables. *Archives of General Psychiatry, 44*(6), 573–588.

Cloninger, C. R., Svrakic, D. M., & Przybeck, T. R. (1993). A psychobiological model of temperament and character. *Archives of General Psychiatry, 50*(12), 975–990.

Copple, C., & Bredekamp, S. (2010). *Developmentally appropriate practice in early childhood programs serving children from birth through age 8* (3rd ed.) Washington, DC: NAEYC.

Costa, P. T., & McCrae, R. R. (1985). *The NEO Personality Inventory manual*. Odessa, FL: Psychological Assessment Resource.

Davies, G., Tenesa, A., Payton, A., Yang, J., Harris, S. E., Liewald, D., Ke, X., Le Hellard, S., Christoforou, A., Luciano, M., McGhee, K., Lopez, L., Gow, A. J., Corley, J., Redmond, P., Fox, H. C., Haggarty, P., Whalley, L. J., McNeill, G., Goddard, M. E., Espeseth, T., Lundervold, A. J., Reinvang, I., Pickles, A., Steen, V. M., Ollier, W., Porteous, D. J., Horan, M.,

Starr, J. M., Pendleton, N., Visscher, P. M., & Deary, I. J. (2011). Genome-wide association studies establish that human intelligence is highly heritable and polygenic. *Molecular Psychiatry, 16,* 996–1005. doi:10.1038/mp.2011.85

Dawson, M., Soulieres, I., Gernsbacher, M. A., & Mottron, L. (2007). The level and nature of autistic intelligence. *Psychological Science, 18*(8), 657–662.

Deary, I. J., Strand, S., Smith, P., & Fernandes, C. (2007). Intelligence and educational achievement. *Intelligence, 35,* 13–21.

Ebner, N. C., Gluth, S., Johnson, M. R., Raye, C. L., Mitchell, K. J., & Johnson, M. K. (2011). Medial prefrontal cortex activity when thinking about others depends on their age. *Neurocase, 17*(3), 260–269.

Eibl-Ebenfeldt, I. (1975). *Ethology: The biology of behavior* (2nd ed.) New York: Holt, Rinehart & Winston.

———. (2007). *Human ethology.* New York: Aldine Transaction Press.

Elkind, D. (1987). *Miseducation: Preschoolers at risk.* New York: Knopf.

———. (2006). *The hurried child, 25th anniversary edition.* New York: De Capo Press.

Else-Quest, N. M., Hyde, J. S., Goldsmith, H. H., & Van Hull, C. A. (2006). Gender differences in temperament: A meta-analysis. *Psychological Bulletin, 132,* 33–72.

Erickson, E. (1993). *Childhood and society.* New York: W. W. Norton & Co.

Evans, W. N., Morill, W. Z. N., & Parente, S. T. (2010). Measuring inappropriate medical diagnosis and treatment in survey data: The case of ADHD among school-age children. *Journal of Health Economics, 29*(5), 657– 673.

Eysenck, H. J. (1967). *The biological basis of personality.* Springfield, IL: Thomas.

Fair, D. A., Bathula, D., Nikolas, M. A., & Nigg, J. T. (2012). Distinct neuropsychological subgroups in typically developing youth inform heterogeneity in children with ADHD. *Proceedings of the National Academy of sciences USA,* 2012, April 2. Epub ahead of print; doi:10.1073/pnas.1115365109.

Flanagan, D. P., & Harrison, P. L. (Eds.). (2005). *The Cattell-Horn-Carroll theory of cognitive abilities: Past, present, and future. Contemporary intellectual assessment: Theories, tests, and issues.* New York: Guilford Press.

Flanagan, D. P., Ortiz, S. O., & Alfonso, V. (2007). *Essentials of cross-battery assessment: Essentials of psychological assessment* (2nd ed.). New Brunswick, NJ: Wiley.

Fox, N. A., & Bar-Haim, Y. (2001). Conceptual gaps in the lifespan theory of attachment. In A. Goncu & E. Klein (Eds.), *Children in play, story, and school*, pp. 288–308. New York: The Guilford Press.

Fox, N. A., Henderson, H. A., & Marshall, P. J. (2001). The biology of temperament: An integrative approach. In C. A. Nelson & M. Luciana (Eds.), *The handbook of developmental cognitive neuroscience*, pp. 631–645. Cambridge, MA: MIT Press.

Ganea, P. A., & Harris, P. A. (2010). Not doing what you are told: Early perseverative errors in updating mental representations via language. *Child Development, 81,* 457–463.

Gentner, D., Holyoak, K. J., & Kokinov, B. N. (2001). *The analogical mind: Perspectives from cognitive science.* New York: Bradford.

Gerson, S., & Woodward, A. L. (2010). Building intentional action knowledge with one's hands. In S. P. Johnson (Ed.), *Neoconstructivism: The new science of cognitive development,* pp. 295–313. New York: Oxford University Press.

Gilbert, D. L., Isaacs, K. M., Augusta, M., Macneil, L. K., & Mostofsky S. H. (2011). Motor cortex inhibition: a marker of ADHD behavior and motor development in children. *Neurology, 76*(7), 615–621.

Gray, P. (2007). *Psychology* (5th ed.). New York: Worth Publishers.

Gregory, S., Ffytche, D., Simmons, A., Kumari, V., Howard, M., Hodgins, S., & Blackwood, N. (2012). The antisocial brain: Psychopathy matters: A structural MRI investigation of antisocial male violent offenders. *Archives of General Psychiatry, 69* (9), 962–972.

Gweon, H., Dodell-Feder, D., Bedny, M., & Saxe. R. (2012). Theory of Mind performance in children correlates with functional specialization of a brain region for thinking about thoughts. *Child Development.* Article first published online: 31 JUL 2012. DOI: 10.1111/j.1467-8624.2012.01829.x

Hallmayer, J., Cleveland, S., Torres, A., Phillips, J., Cohen, B., Torigoe, T., Miller, J., Fedele, A., Collins, J., Smith, K., Lotspeich, L., Croen, L. A., Ozonoff, S., Lajonchere, C., Grether, J. K., & Risch, N. (2011). Genetic hereditability and shared environmental factors among twin pairs with autism. *Archives of General Psychiatry, 68*(11), 1095–1102.

Harris, L. T., & Fiske, S. T. (2006). Dehumanizing the lowest of the low: Neuroimaging responses to extreme out-groups. *Psychological Science, 17*(10), 847–853.

———. (2007). Social groups that elicit disgust are differentially processed in mPFC. *Social Cognitive and Affective Neuroscience, 2*(1), 45–51.

Hayashi, M., Kato, M., Igarashi, K., & Kashima, H. (2008). Superior fluid intelligence in children with Asperger's disorder. *Brain and Cognition, 66*(3), 306–310.

Hayne, H. (2004). Infant memory development: Implications for childhood amnesia. *Developmental Review, 24*, 33–73.

Henshaw, S. P., Scheffler, R. M., & Fulton, B. D. (2011). International variation in treatment procedures for ADHD: Social context and recent trends. *Psychiatric Series, 62*, 459–464.

Hespos, S. J., Ferry, A. L., Cannistraci, C. J., Gore, J., & Park, S. (2010). Using optical imaging to investigate functional cortical activity in human infants. In A. W. Roe (Ed.), *Imaging the brain with optical methods*, pp.159–176. New York: Springer Science.

Hirsch-Pasek, K., & Golinkoff, R. M. (2003). *Einstein never used flash cards*. New York: Rodale.

Hirsh-Pasek, K., Golinkoff, R. M., Berk, L. E., & Singer, D. G. (2009). *A mandate for playful learning in preschool: Presenting the evidence*. New York: Oxford University Press.

Hodgson, K., Hutchinson, A. D., & Denson, L. (2012). Nonpharmacological treatments for ADHD: A meta-analytic review. *Journal of Attention Disorders*, May 29, 2012. doi:10.1177/1087054712444732

Insel, T. R. (1997). A neurobiological basis of social attachment. *American Journal of Psychiatry, 154*, 726–735.

Joliffe, T., & Baron-Cohen, S. (1997). Are people with autism and Asperger syndrome faster than normal on the embedded figures test? *Journal of Child Psychology and Psychiatry and Allied Disciplines, 38*(5), 527–534.

Kagan, J. (2010). *The temperamental thread: How genes, culture, time and luck make us who we are*. New York: Dana Press.

Kanwisher, N., McDermott, J., & Chun, M. M. (1997). The fusiform face area: A module in human extrastriate cortex specialized for face perception. *Journal of Neuroscience, 17*, 4302–4311.

Kaufman, A. S. (2009). *IQ testing 101*. New York: Springer.

Keating, D. P. (2004). Cognitive and brain development. In R. M. Lerner & L. Steinberg (Eds.), *Handbook of adolescent psychology* (2nd ed.), pp. 45–84. Hoboken, NJ: Wiley.

Klein, P. J., & Meltzoff, A. N. (1999). Long-term memory, forgetting, and deferred imitation in 12-month-old infants. *Developmental Science, 2*, 102–113.

Kuhn, D. (2009). Adolescent thinking. In R. M. Lerner & L. Steinberg (Eds.), *Handbook of adolescent psychology* (3rd ed.), pp. 152–186. Hoboken, NJ: Wiley.

Mandler, J. M. (2004). *The Foundations of mind: Origins of conceptual thought*. New York: Oxford.

———. (2008). On the birth and growth of concepts. *Philosophical Psychology, 21*(2), 207–230.

Macneil, L. K., Xavier, P., Garvey, M. A., Gilbert, D. L., Ranta, M. E., Denckla, M. B., & Mostofsky, S. H. Quantifying excessive mirror overflow in children with attention-deficit/hyperactivity disorder. *Neurology, 76*(7), 622–628.

Meltzoff A. N. (1995). Infants' understanding of people and things: From body imitation to folk psychology. In J. Bermudez, A. Marcel, & N. Eilan (Eds.), *The Body and the Self*, pp. 43–69. Cambridge, MA and London: MIT Press.

Meltzoff, A. N., & Moore, M. K. (1994). Imitation, memory, and the representation of persons. *Infant Behavior and Development, 17*, 83–99.

Miller, M., & Hinshaw, S. P. (2010). Does childhood executive function predict adolescent functional outcomes in girls with ADHD? *Journal of Abnormal Child Psychology, 38* (3), 315–326.

Mink, J. W. (2011). Faulty brakes? Inhibitory processes in attention-deficit hyperactivity disorder. *Neurology, 76*, 592–593.

Moll, H., & Meltzoff, A. N. (2011). Perspective-taking and its foundation in joint attention. In N. Eilan, H. Lerman, & J. Roessler (Eds.), *Perception, causation, and objectivity: Issues in philosophy and psychology*, pp. 286–304. Oxford: Oxford University Press.

Monte, J. E., Xiang, Z., & Schweinhart, L. J. (2006). Preschool experience in 10 countries: Cognitive and language performance at age 7. *Early Childhood Research Quarterly, 21*, 313–331.

Monte, J. E., Xiang, Z., & Schweinhart, L. J. (Eds.). (2007). *Role of preschool experience in children's development in 10 countries*. Ypsilanti, MI: HighScope Press.

Nigg, J. T., Wilcutt. E. G., Doyle, A. E., & Sonuga-Barke, E. J. S. (2005). Causal heterogeneity in attention-deficit/hyperactivity disorder. Do we need neuropsychologically impaired subtypes? *Biological Psychiatry, 57*, 1224–1230.

Ninivaggi, F. J. (1999). Attention-deficit /hyperactivity disorder in children and adolescents: Rethinking diagnosis and treatment implications for complicated cases. *Connecticut Medicine, 63*, 515–521.

———. (2009). Borderline intellectual functioning and academic problems. In B. Sadock, V. Sadock, & P. Ruiz (Eds.), *Kaplan & Sadock's comprehensive textbook of psychiatry* (9th ed.), pp. 2505–2512. Philadelphia: Wolters Kluwer/Lippincott Williams & Wilkins.

Olinek, K. M., & Poulin-Dubois, D. (2009). Infants' understanding of intention from 10 to 14 months: Interrelations among violation of expectancy and imitation tasks. *Infant Behavior and Development, 32*, 404–415.

Oord, S. V., Ponsioen, A. J., Geurts, H. M., Brink, E. L., & Prins, P. J. (2012). A pilot study of the efficacy of a computerized executive functioning remediation training with game elements for children with ADHD in an outpatient setting: outcome on parent- and teacher-rated executive functioning and ADHD behavior. *Journal of Attention Disorders, August 9, 2012*. [Epub ahead of print] PMID: 22879577.

Philips, M. L., Revets, W. C., Rauch, S. L., & Lane, R. (2003). Neurobiology of emotion perception II: Implications for major psychiatric disorders. *Biological Psychiatry, 54*, 515–520.

Piaget, J. (1952). *The origins of intelligence in children*. New York: International Universities Press. (Original work published 1936)

Ramsden, S., Richardson, F. M., Josse, G., Thomas, M. S. C., Ellis, C., Shakeshaft, C., Seghier, M. L., & Price, C. J. (2011). Verbal and non-verbal intelligence changes in the teenage brain. *Nature, 479*, 113–116. doi:10.1038/nature10514

Raven, J. (2000). The Raven's Progressive Matrices: Change and stability over culture and time. *Cognitive Psychology, 41*, 1–48.

———. personal communication, May 17, 2011.

Rochat, P. (2001). *The infant's world*. Cambridge, MA: Harvard University Press.

———. (2003). Five levels of self-awareness as they unfold early in life. *Consciousness and Cognition, 12*, 717–731.

Rogoff, B. (2003). *The cultural nature of human development*. Boston: Cambridge University Press.

Rolls, E. T. (2004). The functions of the orbitofrontal cortex. *Brain and Cognition, 55*, 11–29.

Rothbarth, M. K., Posner, M. I., & Kieras, J. (2006). Temperament, attention, and the development of self-regulation. In K. McCartney & D. Phillips (Eds.), *Blackwell handbook of early childhood development*, pp. 338–357. Malden, MA: Blackwell.

Saylor, M. M. (2004). Twelve- and 16-month-old infants recognize properties of mentioned absent things. *Developmental Science, 7*, 599–611.

Schwier, C., van Maanen, C., & Tomasello, M. (2006). Rational imitation in 12-month-old infants. *Infancy, 10*, 303–311.

Seitz, R. J., Nickel, J., & Azari, N. P. (2006). Functional modularity of the medial prefrontal cortex: Involvement in human empathy. *Neuropsychology, 10*(6), 743–751.

Simpson, J. A. & Rholes, W. S. (1998). *Attachment theory and close relationships*. New York: Guilford Press.

Steinberg-Epstein, R., Book, T., & Wigal, S. B. (2011). Controversies surrounding pediatric psychopharmacology. *Advances in Pediatrics, 58*, 153–179.

Steiner, R. (2004). *A Modern Art of Education: Foundations of Waldorf Education.* Hemdon, MA: Anthroposophic Press. (Originally published 1921)

Stern, D. (2000). *The Interpersonal World of the Infant.* New York: Basic Books.

Suddendorf, T., Simcock, G., & Nielsen, M. (2007). Visual self-recogntion in mirrors and live videos: Evidence for a developmental asynchrony. *Cognitive Development, 22*, 185–196.

Takahashi, H., Motoichiro, K., Matsuura, M., Moobs, D., Suhara, T. & Okubo, Y. (2009). When your pain is my gain: Neural correlates of envy and schadenfreude. *Science, 323*, 937–939.

Thomas, A., & Chess, S. (1986). *Temperament in clinical practice.* New York: Guilford.

Tomasello, M. M., Carpenter, J., Call, T., Behme, T., & Moll, H. (2005). Understanding and sharing intentions: The origins of cultural cognition. *Behavioral and Brain Sciences, 28*(5), 675–735.

Wallin, D. J. (2007). *Attachment in psychotherapy.* New York: Guilford Press.

Wang, S., Baillargeon, R., & Paterson, S. (2005). Detecting continuity violations in infancy: A new account and new evidence from covering and tube effects. *Cognition, 95*, 129–173.

Watson, S. M., R, Richels, C., Michalek, A. P., & Richels, C. (2012).Psychosocial treatments for ADHD: A systematic appraisal of the evidence. Published online before print May 30, 2012. doi:10.1177/1087054712447857. *Journal of Attention Disorders, May 30, 2012.* doi:1087054712447857.

Weiss, M., Murray, C., Wasdell, M., Greenfield, B., Giles, L., & Hechtman, L. (2012). A randomized controlled trial of CBT therapy for adults with ADHD with and without medication. *BMC Psychiatry , 12*(30). doi:10.1186/1471-244X-12-30

Woodward, A. (2009). Infants' grasp of others' intentions. *Current Directions in Psychological Science, 18*, 53–57.

Zimbardo, P. G. (2007). *The Lucifer effect: Understanding how good people turn evil.* New York: Random House.

Zirkel, P. A., & Thomas, L. B. (2010). State laws for RTI: An updated snapshot. *Teaching Exceptional Children, 42*(3), 56–63.

———. (2010). State laws and guidelines for implementing RTI. *Teaching Exceptional Children, 43*(1), 60–73.

Zosuls, K. M., Ruble, D. N., Tamis-LeMonda, C. S., Shrout, P. E., Bornstein, M. H., & Greulich, F.K. (2009). The acquisition of gender labels in infancy: Implications for gender-typed play. *Developmental Psychology, 45*, 688–701.

Chapter Three

Infant and Child Development

1. OVERVIEW OF INFANT AND CHILD DEVELOPMENT

The complexity of infant and child development is enormous. In deference to this fact, this chapter, detailed as it is, highlights material selected for its central importance and typicality. Although lengthy, the chapter only approximates the vastness of biomental child development.

Observable human development begins at birth. In the womb, human development starts when sperm and egg unite. These two cells transform into a vast number of organized tissues and organ systems over the course of about nine months.

The developmental process is characterized by transitional reorienting of parts and whole—both of structure and functioning—over relatively short periods of time. The process is rich in dynamic change, biomental transformation, and the emergence of new abilities that act as precursors for more complex later operations. As part of the entire life cycle, moreover, development continues as biomental changes and transitions occur and reconfigurations of the whole person emerge.

The multiple aspects of normal development appear to seamlessly unfold in a coordinated manner. Variations are common, and expectations for the emergence of competencies span a range of normalcy. For example, recent cross-cultural studies have described diversity in the emergence of motor skills once understood to be invariant. At times, however, developmental lags, deviations, or patent nonprogressions may require careful assessment to determine whether they are transitory or require interventions. The detection of early manifestations of atypical development is now possible, and makes early intervention and prevention strategies possible.

All aspects of the developmental process and its biomental nature are significant. Emerging findings from developmental neuroscience have greatly augmented psychological perspectives. Special mention here, however, is given to brain development with a focus on the prefrontal cortex (PFC) of the central nervous system. This area is uniquely developed in humans, and the last part of the brain to mature. It is the neural basis of thinking and for overall modulation of many biomental operations, notably cognitive control, emotional regulation, and stress management.

In addition to performing multiple levels of information processing, the PFC correlates with consciousness, inhibition of impulses, and the executive functions of attention, working memory, planning, and monitoring of problem solving. This is a foundational human calibrating operation with an extensive developmental trajectory. Active at birth, activity in this region increases from about two months on. Outside of the PFC, auditory and visual neuronal myelination and synapse formation escalate at this time and then decline toward the end of early childhood. Within the PFC, neuronal synapses rapidly increase (synaptogenesis) from about two months until about age two years, when they start to decline. Synaptic pruning (elimination) occurs in early and mid-childhood when synapses are not stimulated; although the synapses are then lost, neurons remain available for later activation in the process of brain plasticity.

Studies suggest a perturbation in grey matter density development that more or less coincides with the onset of puberty. There is a wave of additional frontal gray matter (synaptogenesis) in the brain just before puberty, followed by extensive pruning in the prefrontal cortex after puberty and during adolescence. Adult levels of synaptic connections are formed and functional from mid-adolescence, approximately twelve to fourteen years old, on. Both MRI and fMRI studies demonstrate a relative linear increase in white matter in the frontal and parietal cortexes of adolescents, whereas gray matter shows a nonlinear decrease in density. At puberty, gray matter peaks, followed by a plateau after puberty, and then a decline throughout adolescence. This cortical remodeling is a neurosynaptic fine-tuning understood to be associated with increased abilities to reason, plan, and inhibit ideas and behaviors.

Very recent findings about attention and working memory and its neurological basis in a cortico-cerebellar brain system are emerging. Further elaboration is beyond the scope of this book, but this advance also demonstrates hitherto unrealized biomental interrelatedness.

The following survey will broadly review ordinarily expectable developmental progression of the typical child to give a sense of the complexity and wide-ranging changes that occur. A great deal of nuanced attention is given to infancy. The conclusion, however, that pronounced attention is put on this developmental period might be misleading. While detailed focus amplifies infancy, the crucial importance of development in later childhood, adolescence, and adulthood cannot be overstated.

The newborn, infant, and young child have a variety of developmental tasks to experience, achieve, practice, and stabilize. A lengthy list of possibilities includes: achieving physiological homeostasis; smooth regulation of biomental states, such as wakefulness to sleep and agitation to calm; organizing biomental rhythms, such as the wake-sleep cycle; coordinating sensory and perceptual experiences; skill in sensorimotor schemas, such as grasping and letting go; emotional and cognitive affiliation with caregivers; mood regulation; anxiety modulation; both nonverbal and language-based communication skills; cognitive recognition of cause and effect; and personal intentionality characterized by directed effort.

In addition, another aspect of development is that infants and children have a different sense of time than do adults. From birth to early adolescence, the past, present, and future are conflated into a here-and-now. Time is felt as a primary present. Younger children live more in an immediate moment awareness, which is accompanied by a need for stability, regularity, and consistency. Living in the here and now precludes attention to and conscious learning from past experience and planning for future events. Thus, children's development is facilitated by adult guidance in the creation of structure and rhythmicity. By about mid-adolescence, the sense of time approaches a more adult-like understanding.

Because of this sense of living in the immediate moment, research studies are cumulatively showing that behavioral regularity, structure, and stability in infancy help lower later anxiety. Circadian rhythms that are harmonious rather than irregular are associated with mental health at all ages. Parents serve their children's need for regularity by adopting daily lifestyles with reasonably predictable timing for daily routines. This approach fosters healthy biomental rhythmicity in both individuals and the family as a whole. For example, by about eighteen months, toddlers have a sense of regular routines and rhythms of the day; in the second year of life, weekly rhythms are felt as expectable; and by about four years old, preschoolers sense that there are special events that characterize each year, such as Christmas and Thanksgiving. Expectable rhythmicity with flexible variations imparts a carbonated—rather than flat—quality to routines.

A note particularly relevant to school-aged children is worthwhile here. The period between about 4:30 p.m. and 7:00 p.m., typically the end of the school day, has been referred to as the "witching hour," which means that children (and adults) may be particularly mood irritable and cranky. This observation has been related to the fact that blood sugars may be at a low while fatigue is high. Parents can minimize difficulties at these times by being prepared. Everyone needs time to decompress after getting home. Parents who have not seen children during the day do best by spending some time with them. A snack or an early dinner at times helps prevent potential "meltdowns" characterized by emotional and behavioral decompensations.

Recognizing the endowed temperament of infants and children and then adapting regular routines may lead to better understanding and predictability of infant demands. Infantile anxieties, in turn, may be diminished by the sense of stability that is thus established. This effect, in turn, supports parental confidence as well as child self-regulation.

Typically, the primary caregiver becomes the infant's center of the universe. Infants implicitly sense parental love. Infants prefer their primary caregiver, and by three months can recognize differences between mother and father. Six-month-old infants can perceptually categorize male faces as different from female faces. Emotional reciprocity develops into an experiential sense of being wanted and valued. This matrix of security is the ground that helps generate developing self-esteem.

Mothers are intimately related to their infants as newborns and thereafter. Fathers' engagement is typically slightly slower and grows in childhood and adolescence. As the infant slowly recognizes and interacts with his or her father, father begins to respond to such advances. Fathers' increasingly more explicit recognition of and interactions with their children serve to lower father's anxiety and enhance interest in the novel parenting challenges and pleasures encountered. Of note, fathers' involvement in routine childcare has been shown to correlate positively with children's higher school grades. Studies show that involvement of either parent in the lives of adolescents has long-term effects on the adolescent's successful psychosocial adjustment.

Last, while this chapter details many developmental milestones and achievements, it also offers suggestions aimed at facilitating them. In addition, behaviors that are challenging are addressed and strategies that may effectively manage them are suggested. This is particularly evident in the sections on toddlers.

1.1 Mothers and Anxiety

Anxiety is a nonspecific, global array of sensations, feelings, and ideas that cause distress and discomfort. Cognitive acuity becomes temporarily impoverished. As previously discussed, anxiety is also accompanied by nonconscious fantasies that reflect fear typically involving unresolved aggressive or sexual matters, particularly since they imply risk of danger. Attentional bias is toward perceived threatening information.

Anxiety is a normal psychophysiological experience. Anxiety and stress, elicited by frustration, conflict, change, and pressure to perform, to some extent are daily experiences. Stressors trigger anxiety, which, in moderation, adaptively signals that upcoming challenges require problem-solving and constructive coping skills. Pronounced anxiety, however, typically produces avoidance, inhibition, inflexibility, and generalized biomental constriction.

When a person questions his or her ability to manage life's inevitable challenges, anxiety escalates, becomes a fear of the unknown, and is sensed as a threat that something will go seriously wrong. People tend to use colloquial terms such as "worries" or "troubles" to describe anxiety states that are attached to specific contents of concern. A mother's level of anxiety has appreciable effects not only on her, but also on her infant and the mother-child relationship. The parental couple is also affected. Since pronounced anxiety can incapacitate a mother's ability to remain poised and confident, her capacity for transactional sensitivity becomes diminished. Mother's mental space becomes more restricted in its ability to receive, accept, contain, and dynamically process emotional events. Thus she becomes a less effective mother.

As reiterated throughout this book, *transactional sensitivity* is one of the foundations for successful parenting, positive interactive engagement, and appropriate responsivity. Anxiety, therefore, requires recognition and management to prevent its escalating to the point of impairing mother and other family members.

The father's support of the mother is essential. Mothers may find additional help from other family members. With such support, inordinate anxiety may become attenuated and its energies channeled into day-to-day activities. Professional guidance, counseling, psychotherapy, and pharmacotherapy are also among available options.

1.2 Fathers and Anxiety

Fathers continue to play important roles in family relationships—to wife as partner, expectant mother, and new mother, as well as to the developing child. As discussed throughout this book, a father's role in parenting is vital both to the mother as a person and in her role as parent. This interactive significance clearly extends to father's attentive engagement with his children.

While the role of intermittent anxiety often is addressed with respect to mothers, the way that anxiety affects fathers is frequently underappreciated. Millennia of biological and cultural reinforcements of female gender roles may make emotional closeness more comfortable and natural in mother's caring for an infant. Fathers as males, however, often share the parenting role in different ways. This can be related to a man's mixed feelings about expressing underlying vulnerabilities about perceived inadequacy, self-image, or self-esteem. One could speculate that one underlying cause of this role

difference is the anxiety elicited when a child is born and previously established routines need to be altered. Adapting to the needs of infant and mother
is a challenge. If anxiety is pronounced, avoidance and inhibition take hold.

Fathers can feel unprepared for their new role. A father may greet his new
child as a stranger, much as the seven-month-old may later greet perceived
strangers—that is, with anxiety. Mothers can help the feelings of unprepared-
ness by discussing anticipated changes in family life well in advance of the
birth. Fathers tend to naturally have concerns about finances, and this material perspective also needs advance attention and planning. While mothers are
given maternity leave, fathers in the United States need to anticipate how to
balance occupational responsibilities with home and parenting duties.

The typically more subdued emotional expressivity of fathers may become even more constricted by anxiety. Anxiety's inhibiting effect on emotions, problem solving, and behavior may make it difficult for fathers to
easily adapt to a child's birth. Anxiety causes mental space to flatten and lose
its capacity for emotional elasticity. Fathers may feel vulnerable if they do
not "instinctively" parent, as mothers may seem to do. This sense may be
reflected in a constricted affect or in physical distancing. Most anxiety states
contain elements of retraction, contraction, and constriction. Mental functioning and behaviors are slowed, shortened, and pulled back. Distancing
himself from mother and infant may become a default reaction and emerge as
the appearance of relative insensitivity over time.

If both parents are attentive to the potential effects of anxiety, they can
plan to minimize the chances that withdrawal and its causes will merely
happen, and go unrecognized. Setting a tone of engagement during pregnancy and after birth can reduce anxiety and optimize a father's more whole-
hearted involvement for the future. When deemed necessary, professional
guidance, counseling, or psychotherapy may be useful.

1.3 Infants and Anxiety

Anxiety or states of earliest infantile distress are inferred to accompany the
transition from womb to world. While many developmentalists have questioned attributing the emotional term and construct, *anxiety,* to this earliest
era, Biomental child development does not underestimate or consider early
infantile anxiety as trivial. Rather, anxiety and fear—often difficult to disen-
tangle—are understood to be part of the typical infant's range of first and
formative experiences. Perhaps, in a parallel fashion, the cognitive term and
construct, *attention*, may also be open to discussion of its appropriate applicability when applied to very early infancy. Nonetheless, infants are empirically able to notice, temporarily focus on, and track people and objects even
if in an unsustained fashion, for example, tracking an object moving through

an entire half-circle in front of him by two months. Shortly thereafter motor maturation enables reaching and longer looking at three to four months, and precarious hand grasping at approximately five months.

The newborn is maximally helpless and prey to multiple unanticipated impingements. Many of these unpleasant stimuli evoke implicit experiential states of vulnerability. One wonders to what extent such states may be felt initially as exceedingly so alien that they are sensed as if they were attacks from an amorphous predator. Such "a sense of attack" may be akin to states of terror and its attendant anxiety. Studies have repeatedly shown that the area in the brain called the amygdala, though relatively silent, is active early on. Its central nucleus is understood to be an important output region for the expression of innate emotional responses and associated physiological arousal. When a novel stimulus is presented in association with a significant event, rather than dissipating, responses are potentiated. At this earliest time, anxiety and fear are raw limbic system responses, notably through the amygdala, unable to be modulated by higher cortical functioning since this functioning is virtually unmatured and unavailable. Such a core, however subtle, of visceral terror cannot be underestimated as part of early infantile experience.

Of course, *anxiety typically vacillates with states of comfort and repose. As these states of pleasure become more frequent and consolidated, they substantially embed a core of patience and security to the infant's stability.* Gradually increasing cognitive processes develop and begin to temper— though not eliminate—the earlier and persisting emotional states.

In the first three months of life, however, infants remain virtually helpless. Motoric unmaturity, though developing, is at its peak, thus preventing the infant from taking substantial action other than simple reflexes to guard itself. All experiences with environmental stimuli are new; most may be felt as overwhelming. Normal physiological needs such as hunger and processes such as "gas pains," bowel and urine discharge, or feeling cold may also be foreign sensations and experienced as sharp impingements. Biomental states of anxiety and fear accompany the sense of this unknown, as if it were dangerous and life threatening. Such concrete reactions typically provoke extreme agitation and crying.

In earliest infancy, the ministrations of a nurturing and understanding mother who responds with her beneficent transactional sensitivity both identifies and addresses these infant needs. This indispensable caregiving, however, adds to whatever abilities—potential and developing—the infant may elicit to actively manage its distress. It may not be unreasonable to infer that implicit infantile impulses to flee or aggressively counter such distress may be evoked. For example, the construct of "omnipotence" has been part of descriptions of infantile states of mind in classical psychoanalytic literature. *Omnipotence* denotes the normative modus operandi of all unconscious processes, notably the "primary process." These unconscious mental dynamics make up the endowed primitive information processing present at birth and out of which emerge developmentally more refined processes of linear thinking, reason, and refinement by the continuing considerations of reality that become available. Primitive here denotes foundational and first, and connotes a quality of innateness.

Omnipotence connotes inferred attitudes concomitant with the infantile sense of helplessness and its counterreactions—the consequent defenses used to make tolerable the overwhelming anxieties provoked. The implicit sense of separateness and real dependence for survival and their attendant emotions elicit a natural state of implicit omnipotence. As a primitive defense, it is a narcissistically centered orientation countering a sense of unintegration and disintegration of whatever the nascent self is experienced to contain. Omnipotence may be regarded as a precarious state of mind that obliterates cause-and-effect sequences by ad hoc equations of impulse or wish with completed fact. Put differently, omnipotent fantasies denote an insular sense of unlimited power characterized by what in adult experience is sensed as an availability of grandiose and opulent resources—unbounded by reason.

Such primary states of omnipotence are normal and typical in infancy and early childhood when cognitive processes have not matured and logic, reason, abstraction, memory, and *reality testing* are not sufficiently developed. The well-recognized animism, magical thinking, and omnipotence of thought characteristic of preschool children in what Piaget termed the "preoperational stage" of thinking reflects this normative developmental era. Reason and one's *sense of reality* denote a cognitive operating system consonant with degrees of mathematical fidelity, distinguishing probable from the improbable, and influenced by one's contextual emotional intelligence. While the term "truth" may represent a metaphysical construct whose concrete approximations approach reality, reality, as such, denotes identifying something more or less as it actually exists regardless of its appearances. By middle childhood and into adolescence, typically developing cognitive processes constrain, though not eliminate, unrealistic wishful thinking and temper fantasy with the logic and reason that feedback from reality provides.

The typicality of colic in earliest infancy, as will be discussed, correlates with these ideas of infantile perceived distress, maternal transactional sensitivity, and adequately responding to infants' needs for soothing. For example, managing infant colic with soothing messages encompasses massage with hands, tone of voice, and emotional attitude. When maternal responsivity is not readily available, the infant's elicitation of intermittent states of omnipotence may be inferred to help the infant temporarily self-soothe. Transitory situations such as this are inevitable. Prolonged nonresponsiveness by the primary caregiver, however, may be felt as traumatic. The practical importance of such considerations is to help parents provide the infant with an expectable environment of safety to modulate this normative period of anxiety and fearfulness.

2. FROM WOMB TO WORLD

2.1 Infancy: A Biomental Overview

The gestational period prepares mother physically and psychologically to attune, adapt, and sensitively respond to her new infant at birth. Full-term pregnancies span about nine months, or thirty-nine to forty-one weeks. At birth and thereafter, mother acts to further contain the infant, but in a differing biomental manner. The gestational period prepares the fetus, which has been shown to be capable of learning while in the womb, for entry into the world.

From a biological and empirical perspective, the newborn comes into the world appearing tense. Face and limbs are more contracted than relaxed. Initially, eyes are shut because of puffiness from residual amniotic fluid retention. Fists are clenched, and both arms and legs flexed and held close to the body. Muscular control of hands, limbs, head, and eyes is virtually absent. Facial expressions are present but exceedingly labile, uneven, and spontaneously changeable, at times, appearing distressed and at others relaxed. Quivering lips suggest a biomental unmaturation in the dynamic process of achieving a more organized integration.

While it may be true that infants are motorically helpless, they are far less helpless mentally, as evidenced by sophisticated research findings. The biomental perspective describes this newborn faculty as an *anticipatory readiness* to wholeheartedly experience persons, objects, relationships, and events. While this innate capacity for expectations is biomentally primed, it is nonetheless crude and malleable. It may be more "a sense of," "preferenced bias for," or "an unmatured knowledge of" experiences rather than the fuller comprehension that comes with further development.

"A sense of" connotes the primacy of perceptual sensation awareness. Before eighteen months, this may be a preconceptual perceptual apprehension, while after eighteen months, it may have an additional conceptual dimension. Although the construct of anticipatory readiness is not an explicit part of traditional conceptual models of temperament, it is an important premise in biomental child development.

This anticipatory readiness construct has characteristics of a subjunctive mood, that is, implicit "if, then" expectations and responses. This readiness is the core feature of normal *reality testing*. It involves detecting, however imperfectly developed, the contingencies that govern events. The strength, sensitivity, and breadth of this core of knowledge congenitally differ among individuals. The developing mind scans the environment through senses and perceptual abilities until nuances of recognition occur.

Biomental child development boldly suggests that the infant mind is complex—unmatured early on, while always in a state of maturation and development. For example, the ways that experience is encoded and information is processed have considerable variation and complexity. Meaning, salience, and meaningfulness have both implicit and explicit components. In the preverbal era of infancy, meaning is charged by, and established primarily in, emotionally salient relationships.

Learning and memory are highly complex. Both involve a number of structural and information processing mechanisms. With this consideration, the following is a relatively simplified discussion of information acquisition.

Incorporating, introjecting, and internalizing information is first a structural encoding that emphasizes attention to the schematic and spatial physical structure of the stimuli. While the structure of appearances is primary, preverbal meaning on an emotional level is intense. Further in development, an intermediate process of phonemic encoding that emphasizes what a word sounds like follows this initial level of complexity. The infant's exposure to tone and prosody in specific contexts supports acquisition of memory. Finally, deep processing reflects semantic encoding, which denotes some grasp, mostly implicit, of the meaning of the verbal input. This "grasp" is more akin to "a sense of" rather than a purely cognitive understanding. In the preverbal period of infancy, these memory processes are real but unrefined.

As growth and development in a typically stimulating environment occur, the sculpting of neural circuitry for memories is refined, amplified, and enriched. Deep, semantic processing, especially influencing explicit memory, may come online only in the second year when substantive concept formation and language develop.

Newborn and infant studies, in fact, demonstrate that *amodal sensory perception*—information that is not specific to a single sensory modality but that overlaps two or more sensory systems—suggests that infants are innately primed to expect sight, sound, and touch to go together. This detection of amodal relationships, especially in the first quarter of life, precedes and serves as the basis for the emergence of intermodal perception thereafter. A salient caregiving consideration to emphasize in view of the aforementioned is the following. Until biomental and neurological coordination increases, feelings of helplessness persist through the first quarter of infancy. Feeding, holding, and comforting, especially if rhythmical, are exceptionally soothing, particularly in the first quarter of the first year.

While valid and reliable data to support the construct of *anticipatory readiness* is either lacking or controversial, some studies on infant cognition lend support. Infants do reveal core knowledge of at least some physical principles. Grasping these aspects of reality denotes an incomplete knowledge early on that may advance in complexity in terms of the nuances that are recognized with age and experience.

The "violation-of-expectation method" in infant cognition studies involves measuring an infant's reactions, typically looking time, to seeing both possible and impossible events. Studies involve showing babies an expected event (one consistent with reality) or an unexpected event (a variation of the first event that violates reality). These methods have been performed both with exposure to and also in the absence of previous exposure to the event. Measurably increased attention to, or noticing through prolonged visual gaze, the unexpected event suggests that the infant is surprised by deviation from material reality, namely, longer looking at an impossible event. This method strongly connotes that infants possess some level of innate "rules of reality" that guide mental operations, and that witnessing failures of these rules is measurable.

The classic example of this experiment involves infants two and a half to three and a half months of age viewing carrots before and after they travel behind a completely occluded screen. No protracted looking at the carrots leaving the screen is noted. When, however, the carrots are moved behind a partially occluded screen of a height that should permit the carrot tops to be seen (though they are not because of experimental manipulation), the infants' visual gaze is significantly lengthened. This result suggests that the children experience a violation of expectation. The surprise is not merely a transient perceptual preference for novelty or avoidance of habit. Instead, it is hypothesized to reflect an ability to evaluatively discriminate real consequences from that not in accord with conventional reality. Such research implies that the infant has some capacity to comprehend real-world expectations, namely what is real versus what is false. This apparently innate faculty supports developing *reality-testing* skills. It presumes a native core of knowledge, primitive but substantial and one that undergoes developmental sophistication over time.

In addition, violation-of-expectation studies about normal or real as opposed to the previously mentioned impossible events have also been performed. They show longer looking times when violations of what are normally real sights occur. This suggests awareness that some mental concept, however frail, of "moved out of sight" is present in the infant's "mind" and is being violated.

2.1.1 Anticipatory Readiness to "Grasp" Mother

From earliest infancy, the newborn is profoundly social. During the entire course of early infancy, the development and structuring of the newborn's grasp of mother—its "attentional" capacities—influence both intellectual and social cognition, which remain central throughout life. The roots of patience, moreover, intimately associated with the idea of *anticipatory readiness* discussed in this chapter's section on "Infancy: A Biomental Overview" are entwined with how attentional grasping develops. Attentional processes at all points in development are crucial to survival, learning, and self-development. The biomental perspective understands "attention" to encompass the following: alertness, vigilance modulation, poised watchfulness, explorative witnessing, indeterminate, experimental anticipation, poised open-handedness, readiness to grasp, and impulse to contain. As information becomes contained in the mind, deferred interpretation develops and organizes. In this conception of attention, the infant comes into the world with endowments that are released into activity by the ministrations of the caregiving mother. Mother simultaneously provides a living example of attentional elements with which the infant may identify and internalize.

The infant's grasp of reality, therefore, requires a match with the primary caregiver's responsiveness in order to support healthy development. To the extent that *subject* (or cognitive-emotional expectations) and *object* (or material stimuli) match and synchronize, varying levels of satisfaction and encouragement are felt. Infants and children manifest this attitude by their expressions of exploratory behaviors, curiosity, cooperativeness, agreeableness, enthusiasm, and affectionate attachment. Without such subject-object harmonization, disappointment, negative mood, and avoidant behaviors may be elicited.

Prenatally, the fetus is understood by many to be capable of receiving stimuli not only from the mother's body but also from the external environment. For example, by about twenty to twenty-six weeks of gestation, hearing has developed receptivity to sounds, especially the higher pitch of mother's voice. Such attunement exquisitely prepares the pre-birth infant to engage in infant-mother transactional sensitivity. Hearing is crudely receptive in utero, online at birth, and reaches adult perceptual levels by about twenty-four months. Postnatally, infants can recognize mother's voice, and if father spoke or sang near mother while she was pregnant, the infant can recognize father's voice as well.

Beginning at birth, sensory development occurs rapidly. Vision is present at birth, but its acuity has a more gradual development over the course of the first year. By two months, the ability to focus on objects is similar to that of adults, and by four months, color perception is similar to that of adults. At six months, sight is similar to adult 20/20 vision. Infant vision, especially for high-contrast black and white, is best at about 8–14 inches from face. Touch is also a powerful sensation, and infants are sensitive to stimulation to lips, skin, and body as a whole. Regarding taste, newborns can distinguish sweet from bitter, and prefer sweet. The olfactory sense enables babies even in their first week of life to distinguish the scent of mother from others scents. Studies have also demonstrated that mothers as well can distinguish their own infants by smell alone. In a corresponding fashion, mothers can also identify their own babies' scents.

The infant's *anticipatory readiness* is also demonstrated by remarkable "tuning in" capacities to familiar speech, faces, and even music. Developmental research has found that, for example, newborns to about six-month-olds are sensitive to virtually all speech sounds. During this time, however, they preferentially respond to mother. *Infant-directed speech* enhances babies' understanding of emotional intentions and their own incipient language development. Developmentalists think that all young babies—regardless of geographical location, culture, and exposure—make the same vocalizations. After about six months, imitation and learning shape vocalizations into culture-specific and context-specific variations.

The time before children can verbally communicate is an ultrasensitive period of communicational receptivity. Paralinguistic communications, such as eye contact, facial expression, physical gesture, skin-to-skin body contact, tone of voice, and emotional attitudes dominate the perceptual field. This is a shared reality of infant and mother that helps organize infant mind. In addition, a parent's quiet pauses and careful communications that are colored by intuitions are powerful in promoting both parental understanding and the communication of this restorative and nurturing support to the infant.

In infancy and up to three years of age, children are particularly attracted to nursery rhymes and lullabies. The cadence, sing-song pattern, higher pitch, phonemic or sound awareness, and repetitive words and sequences compel attention and even teach a child to predict what comes next. Not only linguistic learning but also cognitive patterning is supported.

Preference for human faces is evident early on and continues to develop. In the period from birth to about six months, infants attend primarily to the eyes of another, while at six months, looking is equally divided between eyes and mouth. At eight months, attention shifts to longer gaze at the mouth of the speaker until about twelve months when attention shifts back to the eyes. In social interactions, as has been discussed previously, eyes and eye contact provide emotional information as well as social cues.

At birth, there is a particular interest in the top half of the face, the eyes. Newborns, for example, show an increased attraction to faces that make eye contact as well as recognition of mother's face. At two to three months, however the internal features of the face are focused upon. As early as three months, infants find it easier to discriminate female faces, which they prefer to male faces. This may correlate with females typically being primary caregivers.

At six months, the *inversion effect* is noted in typically developing infants; this term denotes being unable to recognize a face that is upside down. Infants appear to focus on the lips of the caregiver to decipher communicational meaning. Gender distinction is also recognized. In addition, infants can distinguish different human faces from one another as well as different monkey faces from one another. By nine months, however, only the ability to distinguish human faces remains, a species-specific effect. Human face recognition continues to undergo changes over time, even through adolescence.

Six month olds can detect distinctions between Western and non-Western musical melodies. Studies demonstrate that infants in English-speaking environments have no preference for native English over nonnative language through about eight months. By twelve months, however, after prolonged exposure to Western music, babies can no longer discriminate amongst foreign musical rhythms. Hence, findings about speech, face, and musical recognition suggest a sensitive period in infancy between six and twelve months in which infants are biomentally equipped to more easily tune in— *anticipatory readiness*—with some precision to socially meaningful, salient perceptual distinctions.

Although individual senses such as hearing and seeing briskly develop, the integrated coordination of all senses—intermodal perception—occurs slowly over the course of the first three or four months. The initial lack of sensory coordination makes the early infant vulnerable to experiencing ordinary forms of stimulation as strong and intrusive, if not potentially traumatic. Early experience mediated by sensation and perception can be viewed as *presentational*, which signifies an unfiltered, concrete immediacy. This idea contrasts with *representational* experience, which crudely buffers sensory information beginning at about the fourth month and progressing thereafter.

By two months, infants can track moving objects up to 180 degrees. Vestibular (inner ear) senses can implicitly perceive changes of bodily position at birth, namely, *proprioception*.

In more than merely a metaphorical sense, one could regard the newborn and very early infant as being "one ultrasensitive sense organ." This concept suggests that vision, hearing, touch, taste, and smell are unguardedly open and receptive to incoming stimuli, particularly in the awake state. This infantile condition denotes nonconscious experiential awareness. Biomental filtering mechanisms are yet unmatured, undeveloped, and unavailable to adequately modulate sensory information.

Recognition of this state of vulnerability and helplessness requires attentive and sensitive caregiving so necessary to successfully negotiating this transition from womb to world. *Proximal care* denotes holding the young infant and keeping him or her close to mother. This proximity provides containment and is soothing. Reducing harsh and abrupt sensory stimuli, especially during the first six weeks, puts less stress on baby. The fact that newborns sleep during much of the twenty-four hour period—roughly eighteen hours—underscores this need for reduced sensory input.

Containing as well as holding an infant is essential. An important distinction exists in the two different constructs: "holding" and "containment." Holding an infant connotes the physical act of supporting the infant in one's arms. Containment, as advanced in this text, goes far beyond this idea to include the psychological intimacy of sensitively accepting and attuning to the infant's physical, emotional, and cognitive condition. This idea of containment is embedded in the construct of *transactional sensitivity*.

Containment is an active engagement of dynamic, transformative exchange. It connotes both a sense and the experience of *actively integrating boundedness*, *delimitedness*, and *safety*. This counters passive, reactive constriction that infantile feelings of being overwhelmed may engender. Sufficient containment fosters *resilience*, or the capacity to be alone in both the presence and absence of others.

As such, both holding and containment are crucial in the newborn period. The baby has just transitioned from "ideal" containment, namely, protection, safety, warmth, and automatic sustenance of intrauterine life to the newborn world of relatively separate existence. Proper awareness of the exquisite sensitivity to actual physical warmth cannot be overemphasized. It is essential to an infant's basic life functions and radiates its crucial impact on emotional levels.

Newborns need to feel "held," "held together," and "contained." The womb had served as a natural, self-containing holding environment. The newborn continues to need containment through all the material means available—arms, blankets, swaddling, and so forth. Swaddling a newborn and early infant may be an underutilized technique that can be comforting to infants. Blankets should not be excessively tight. Legs should be wrapped so that they do not bind together, and room should be left so legs can move and bend. The nurturing caregiver provides all these outer containing trappings and also their inner emotional dimension—*transactional sensitivity*.

Infant stimulation, first and foremost, is accomplished by mother's physically close touch, soft, harmonious, and rhythmic language, eye-to-eye contact, and nurturing caregiving. The rawness of the baby's biomental self requires the modulated containment provided by mother's emotional and material nurturance, as well as father's support.

Some traditions formalize an awareness of the raw and undefended sensitivity of the newborn by covering the crib with a very light, transparent gauze-like material in a pastel color combination, such as rosy blue or rose. Great care to prevent inadvertent mishaps is required when this technique is employed. This chrysalis-like piece softens incoming stimuli during the infant's transition into the world. The pastel gauze contains the infant who was previously contained in the womb. It is also a reminder of an infant's ultrasensitivity and need for containment. By the third month, this delicate, lightweight sheathing is removed since the infant's maturing sensory capacities have greater filtering strength and are more coordinated with motor abilities. In these early months, the baby goes from containment in the womb to containment outside by its skin, mother, clothing, and bedding.

2.1.2 Relevant Practical Information

The American Academy of Pediatrics (AAP; www.healthychildren.org) provides current guidelines on a wide range of practical information. These guidelines are highly recommended and contain updated information that should be consulted regularly to ensure child safety in a variety of contexts.

For the most part, infant cribs should be as simple and uncomplicated as possible. For example, the AAP advises parents to have cribs without drop sides (a crib construction in which one side drops down), but the website supports drop gates (where the top third portion of one side folds down toward you to permit easier access). Legislation in the United States banned drop-gate cribs in June 2011. This action was based on several considerations: hardware was easily breakable, and incorrect assembly at home could lead to infant entrapment and suffocation.

No blankets should be put in a crib. The baby should have almost nothing else in the crib except a tight-fitting sheet on a mattress to avoid suffocation, strangulation, and other possible calamities. The AAP's website also discusses other updated safety measures such as the use of car seats. A wealth of other valuable and practical information, such as having infants sleep on their backs to prevent injury or death, can be found here as well.

The AAP recommends breastfeeding occur for at least the first six months of life. During the fourth and fifth months of gestation, a variety of maternal hormonal changes occur, especially by the stimulation of prolactin in the hypothalamus. This production causes formation of an immature but vitally important form of milk—*colostrum*—rich in immune factors. At birth, when the placenta is removed, a precipitous drop in progesterone occurs. Along with prolactin, this decrease in progesterone gradually transforms colostrum into mature milk over the course of several days to two weeks. This is termed the "coming in" of mother's milk.

It is recommended to facilitate baby's "latch on" to the nipple, including the surrounding areola tissue, during the first thirty minutes after birth. This latching on and sucking process stimulates an increased production of the hormone *oxytocin* from the pituitary. Together, these processes facilitate contractions of the muscles surrounding the milk ducts in the breast so that milk is ejected, which is called the "the let-down process" or "milk ejection reflex." There is now good evidence to show that starting artificial nipples early on is associated with decreased exclusive breastfeeding and decreased duration of breastfeeding. The AAP generally recommends avoiding bottles and pacifiers for the first several weeks after birth until actual breastfeeding is progressing smoothly.

It is also important to note that from birth to about three weeks, some weight loss is normal. Babies lose about 10 percent of their body weight by day three of life. Breastfed babies may lose a little more weight than bottle-fed babies since breast milk does not fully come in until about the third postpartum day. At about three weeks, mature breast milk is plentiful and expectable weight gain should resume.

During this early time, skin rashes may occur and are normal. Examples include *seborrheic dermatitis* (or "cradle cap") and baby "acne" consisting of small pimple-like eruptions and *milia* (tiny white pimples). Spitting up, coughing and sneezing are also common. A child's normal temperature varies with age, activity, and time off day. Infants tend to have higher temperatures than older children. Typically, a rectal reading of 100.4 degrees Fahrenheit (or 38 degrees Celsius) or less, or an oral reading of 99 degrees Fahrenheit (or 37.2 degrees Celsius) or less is understood to be normal, while higher readings indicate fever. Fever may suggest illness and requires medical attention. For example, professional care is indicated in the following circumstances: in newborns to three months, temperature of 100.4° F or greater; three to twelve months, 102.2° F or greater; under two years, fevers lasting longer than 24–48 hours; any fevers at or above 105° F; and any of the aforementioned that are accompanied by other worrisome signs or changes in behavior

Bowel movements are frequent. Breastfed babies have loose, yellow, mustard-like stools with almost every feeding. Bottle-fed babies have two or three stools per day with a more mayonnaise-like or pudding consistency. Consistency of stool rather than frequency reflects health or illness. Hard, very watery, or blood-tinged stool could reflect infection or formula intolerance.

It is also important to protect infants from choking and falls, especially in the first year. Falls off of a changing table or crib may occur if precautions are not taken. Choking can occur if foods are not either liquid, mashed, pureed, or cooked and cut into very small pieces. Since children cannot chew with a grinding motion until about four years old, caution is essential, especially in the first year and through age four. Infants and children may also inadvertently swallow and choke on non-food items. Common offenders include the following: small toys or toy parts, balloons, baby powder, eggshells, pop-tops from soda cans, safety pins, marbles, marker caps, candy, grapes, peanut butter, and popcorn, to name just a few. Drawstrings on infant clothing have also been banned since they may cause suffocation.

2.2 Infant Psychology

The transition from womb to world takes place beyond the senses, as well. The first six weeks of life make up this transition period, which is a highly sensitive time for both the newborn and parents. Mutual parental support makes it easier for everyone involved. Enlisting the assistance of extended family members and outside help, if practical, is wise, especially if planned ahead. Proper nutrition, prenatal vitamins, regular pre- and postnatal medical visits, emotional self-reflection, and a supportive spouse optimize good outcomes for mother during this switch.

Newborns come into the world as active learners. The complex nature of infant psychology, real as it is, is still uncharted in detail. As discussed, studies suggest that the infant enters the world with a detailed representation of the human face that continues to refine over time. This innate module appears to be sensitive to facial orientation and enables the infant to imitate facial gestures. There have been fascinating claims proposing that newborns begin life with some grasp of people and that they have an innate model of their own bodies. These early innate prototype templates may be part of the phylogenetic and evolutionary endowment of all human beings. They aim to detect identification of who the person is and also what the emotions being communicatively expressed are.

The pioneering work of the British psychoanalyst, Melanie Klein, first advanced such considerations in 1947 in her construct *projective identification*. This innate mental mechanism present at birth is understood to have communicative, exploratory, and emotional functions. The preverbal infant, for example, relates to mother by unconsciously projecting feelings and needs into her. This process characterized by its concrete qualities alerts mother to sense and then respond to the baby's requirements.

The biomental processes of "splitting" denote nonintegration and the default condition of the mind's keeping things split apart and relatively unintegrated. The operation of projective identification always positively correlates with splitting. Developmentally, perception starts out with ephemeral attention to featural experience and only gradually begins to become integrated, approximately after the middle of the first year. Processes of projective identification and splitting, however, are the prime characteristics of unconscious information processing and endure throughout life although overlaid by more integrated and conscious cognitions.

In introducing my published conceptualization of envy theory, I extended the cognitive ramifications of Melanie Klein's idea by proposing the construct of projective internalization. As part of a broader theory of knowledge, *projective internalization* describes an individual's scanning of the environment until finding an aspect of it that positively correlates with an implicit knowledge already mentally present, if only *in potentia*. It is an examination of the apparent unknown in the light of the implicit known. The immediacy of this identificatory connectedness denotes an imprint but not necessarily an elaborated comprehension. This fundamental cognitive process involves a bilateral, simultaneous grasping: mind's grasp of stimuli and external stimuli's grasp of concordant mental receptors. Projective internalization reflects the organic unity between self and environment emphasizing both interpenetration and interdependency. It is the foundation for the infant's anticipatory readiness to begin its grasp of the salience of all experience. The mind's innate structure, notably characterized by the immediacy inherent in projective internalization processes, is the ultimate frame of reference for perceiving, knowing, and developing understanding.

The cognitive concept of *projective internalization* correlates with envy theory's psychophilosophical construct, the *epistemophilia* of the self. This construct denotes the innate impulse to explore the environment in an unrelenting and affiliative manner. The underpinning of this impulse is the aim to grasp, to understand, and to be understood. Implicit in this epistemophilia is a search for unity, connectedness, and meaning. Impulses to biomentally develop both drive and are reinforced by this epistemophilia.

The processes of epistemophilia and projective internalization refer to both dissolution of cognitive and emotional dissonance, and the establishment of affiliative links in interpersonal relationships. Processes of abstraction, however rudimentary, rather than concretization characterize this projective internalization. Psychological interest is projected outward and adhesively binds to aspects of some implicitly familiar event, situation or person, and then encoding occurs. Novelty, in part, is internalized. Rather than being a rigidly hardwired biomental module, the two processes are softly assembled and expressed in differing ways in the context of temperament and personality style.

Epistemophilia, projective identification, and projective internalization here include both the cognitive and affective colorings of the search for understanding. All are inextricably interpersonal and advance biomental development starting in infancy. These three processes make up the foundational scaffolding of transactional sensitivity and empathy. This entire conceptualization remains a cornerstone of both envy theory and biomental child development.

2.3 Mother-Infant Synergy

From the start, the infant needs and seeks a mother for nurturance. During the first few days after birth, mother and baby begin to synchronize the arrangement of her "holding" the infant. This configuration represents a transition from baby being inside to baby being outside of mother. Some mothers say babies are "slippery" at first and that it takes a while to find the most comfortable holding positions. This suggests an indirect reference to the fact of reestablishing *biomental containment after birth*.

Mothers have to "learn" both consciously and intuitively how to access the biomental infant. The infant's gestation previously within her is an important preparation for this. Yet, from the newborn period through about the first quarter of the first year, mothers need to tune in to their infant to establish adequate transactional sensitivity. Infants also do this toward mother, and both gradually form a workable resonance.

The nurturing mother both gives and receives in ways complementary to her infant. Eye-to-eye contact is vitally important for babies. It largely provides the basis for communication, recognition, and self-regulation. Feeding at the breast or bottle typifies in a unique way the giving of food, love, and understanding. It reflects active, outgoing nurturance.

Holding a baby more in front of one's body rather than to the side, and bringing a baby to one's breast rather than bending forward, provides optimal positioning for mother and child. Breastfeeding encompasses the baby's sucking and licking activities, but also some biting. This biting is another way a baby makes contact with mother. It is not a sign of intentional hostility, but may be a way the baby experiments with affectionate action and reaction. Mothers can help soften any biting by sensitive redirection—never by harsh actions or reprimands.

As mentioned, an infant's experiential life begins at its lips and mouth. Continuing biomental development radiates and amplifies itself from this nodal focus. The entry of nipple into lips and mouth in nursing is akin to the notion of "plugging a hole." In many ways, this image suggests the scenario of the intrauterine state of relative oneness that was present in the previous nine months. The relationship of infant to mother also represents the need to make sense out of and adapt to a qualitatively different experience of detachment and loss with greater intermittent distress.

The latching, linking into, and attachment of lips to nipple close the area of dimly sensed vulnerability and separateness. The process provides nourishment so that satisfaction and some degree of fortification are felt. The schema of introjection and projection ("in-out") is activated in baby's experiential awareness. The physical contact between mother and infant during holding, clothing, wrapping, and rocking also provides a sense of containment. As the infant experiences this, both sustenance and relief of distress occur simultaneously. In good feedings, infants and mothers relax. Some have referred to this dynamic in hypothesizing a psychological developmental model characterized by the expression "incorporating the good breast."

The unique significance of the mouth in infancy cannot be overemphasized. In addition to permitting nutrition and intimate contact with mother, the mouth also functions as a prehensory organ, or "third hand." In this sense, it participates in grasping, exploration, and releasing activities. Biomental child development highlights the biomental aspect of this and the implicit influence it plays on all further interpersonal relationships. In other words, the experience of the mouth in earliest infancy is one platform, however submerged from conscious awareness, upon which styles of relationships are built.

It is certainly true that mother's hands and voice become almost immediately recognized and hold a special place for the infant. Soon, the mother's face becomes recognized as a destination for prime visual attention. The breast, however, presents itself instantly after birth. The nursing situation thus has primary status for the infant being fed, loved, and understood. It is his or her primary model of reality.

Although mothers typically are primary caregivers in infancy, it is important for fathers to share in this activity. The early bonding between infant and father has been termed *engrossment*. Skin-to-skin contact and eye gaze help to evoke caregiving impulses in fathers and motivate his sustained engagement and active participation.

With her newborn, the nurturing mother normally experiences a state of *reverie*—a biomental entrainment with infant that establishes an open channel of communication. The British psychoanalyst, Wilfred Bion, first introduced this idea in 1962. Biomental child development refers to this resonance and transformative phenomenon as the earliest moment of transactional sensitivity.

The ideas suggested by *reverie* and *transactional sensitivity* require elaboration. The infant is born in anticipation of signaling mother with its unanswered questions. Mother affords the infant the ability to project into herself all the infant's loving and distressing experiences. This consignment, in a sense, represents the infant's projecting parts of him- or herself into mother, who acts as a sensitively receptive container. In this way, she acts as a beneficent containing field, a resource important for survival. This delicately modulating process helps temper the infant's tolerance for frustration—gaps in satisfaction—on every level.

In a manner of speaking, the infant's emotionally toxic feelings, particularly confusion and fear, are drawn into mother via her sensitive and unspoken capacity to lovingly understand. This requires mother's ability to linger with such distress without becoming unduly intolerant. Any blockage of resonance on mother's part, such as her anxiety or failure to properly recognize the infant's temperament and developing attachment styles, impedes the infant's free-flowing stream of need, distress, and concerns into her. When this occurs at times, the infant may experience it as a form of hostility and, in turn, may become more frustrated, angry, and distressed.

Maternal reverie goes beyond any sense of being dutiful, sensible, rational, and conscientious. It transcends intelligence level, socioeconomic status, and cultural tradition. This imaginative receptivity for perceiving, understanding, interpreting, and communicating back mental states reflects mother's openness to and sense of patience with her infant. The immediacy of this experiential relationship encompasses grasping the infant's needs on all levels. These needs especially include what is sensed as intolerable, and the need to internalize this distress through a transformative and meaningfully salient containment.

Maternal resonance fosters a dynamic quality of biomental containment that helps generate healthy infant self-development—as the basis of personality and character formation. This resonance is iterative; it develops in a to-and-fro manner in the interactive and continuing rapport between mother and child. The infant's internalizing such a model of the transformative containing function of understanding is essential for healthy mental development, as well as developing emotional self-management.

2.4 Making the Preverbal Period Intelligible: Details of a Model

Obviously, *it is impossible to relate with precision using adult language the preverbal experiences of the infant.* The first twelve months have traditionally been regarded as a preverbal period where speech and language are undeveloped and thus not a primary means of communicating inner states. Experience is virtually raw and minimally mediated by the infant's inner developed resources; experiences require the mediation of mother in the form of *transactional sensitivity.*

Until approximately a decade or so ago, early infancy had been understood unequivocally to be incomprehensible in scholarly description. Today, hard data, while still inexact, is progressively emerging. These findings are demonstrating that the infant mind is not only truly complex but also, to some degree, measurably understandable.

Descriptions of this earliest period are models, therefore, entailing *approximations* of sensory and emotional events using adult terminology that is *more suggestive than precise.* Constructs such as this are post hoc descriptions using adult language to suggest the infant's preverbal experiences. For example, a mother's use of vowel sounds with infants matches their own earliest development of language. The emergence of infant cooing at three to four months and babbling at six to eight months is the auditory vehicle transmitting information about the infant's developing personality. Mother's responsiveness and the fidelity of her congruence reflect an entrainment that typically includes similar sounds that have soothing and regulating properties.

A developmental model and metaphors permit us to infer that at times of contentment, infants are stable, calm, and relatively secure. Intolerable distress of the preverbal infant may be felt as terror and fears of falling apart. Otherwise stated, without developed conceptual experience or logical reasoning, the infant feels his or her emotional and physical pain as something akin to disorganization and dying.

Both sensory and nonsensory (amorphous, nonconscious) factors are projected and sent to mother. These nameless elements are both loving and fearful. At times, they are felt as dreaded states of biomental pain subsequent to feeling overwhelmed. Mother then has a chance to absorb, linger with, make sense out of, and restore a modicum of soothing and balance by her sensitive ministrations. Through this unique containing process, she may return the infant to a sense of calm.

This containment and understanding is dynamic and continuing. The infant's primal organismic anxieties are characterized by panic, fragmentation, and confusion. In earliest infancy, the influx of stimuli may be sensed as overwhelmingly numerous and intense. Maternal sensitivity acts to contain and modulate these into more meaningful forms. The infant, in turn, senses and takes in these modulated forms that now have become more differentiated, nuanced, and less strident.

The healthy infant begins to identify and internalize *the caregiver's containing and transforming function*. In other words, this model suggests that the infant's avoidant impulses are remodulated so that receptivity and integrative trends are enhanced. He or she can now organize previously raw, disjointed sensation and emotion. A form of unconscious thinking "alphabetizes" inchoate sensation into the elements of an implicit information processing "grammar" that gradually becomes more conscious over time. Inchoate experience is thus given a more coherent form. In a metaphorical sense, the infant receives letters, words, and a language, all of which contribute to a developing sense of meaning. This alphabetizing process supports the concept of *epistemophilia*. That is, the organization of experience as such is propelled by the infant's innate exploratory and integrative impulses.

A mother who can patiently accept, linger with, and reduce the anxiety of an infant's projected distress provides the infant with a model to observe and with which to identify. The infant is permitted to dynamically project anxiety-laden distress into the mother. She then healthily processes this distress by removing or detoxifying the component of unbearable anxiety. Mother and infant then can together hold the experience with de-escalated stress. Raw anxiety transforms into an anxiety that is less fragmenting and more coherent so that it may act as a signal to more effectively manage distress. This process occurs through understanding, love, and transactional sensitivity. As the infant introjects this containing function, his or her ego further develops into a more coherent self.

The degree to which infant and mother are able to reciprocate in this manner reflects a harmonious nurturance of love and understanding. By recognizing and giving suitable responses—silently, verbally, and through sensitive physical management—to a baby's early developmental achievements, adults provide the foundations for security and developing self-confidence. Certainly, no such ideal condition can be maintained uninterruptedly. It is merely intended to provide a direction, an approximation of a good and adaptive mother-infant rapport.

3. THE FIRST TWELVE MONTHS

The first year of life has characteristic month-by-month, empirical developmental achievements. Typically, developmentalists chart motor, adaptive, language, and personal-social fields beginning at birth and progressing at four-week intervals up to fifty-six weeks, or fourteen months. Beginning at fifteen months, development is gauged at longer three-month intervals. Thereafter, the intervals are increasingly protracted. At the six-year-old level, formal developmental testing ends and is supplanted by other forms of psychological, neuropsychological, pediatric, and neurological assessments.

In the following descriptions, the designation of development month by month is used only for schematic purposes. The timings and developmental accomplishments are only approximately valid. These rough estimates, it must be emphasized, *acknowledge the variations in how timing is designated and how typical milestones are expressed*, as has been mentioned previously. Described milestones are generally apparent in about 60 percent to 75 percent of typical children, although wide normal variations are regularly found. The emergence of milestones must be viewed as an "on average" approximation. Developmental schemas presented in this text are consistent with AAP guidelines.

The following empirical overview shows what infants generally look like in the first year. Newborns through four-month-olds remain supine (on their backs) with hands fisted. At five months when placed on the stomach (prone position), infants can roll over to supine. At about six months, infants can roll from supine to prone. From five to seven months, most infants can sit up with support. From about ten months, infants are able to sit up alone. Standing up and beginning to walk alone occurs at approximately twelve months.

3.1 Newborn to First Three Months

3.1.1 Newborn

In the first month, the *newborn* is very sleepy and may sleep around the clock. It is recommended not to have a baby awake for more than two hours at a time. Feeding typically occurs every three hours. Parents should put the infant or neonate to sleep in a supine (on the back) position until about four to seven months of age. By that time, the infant has greater head and neck control and is able to roll from the stomach back to supine, decreasing chance of suffocation. Sudden infant death syndrome (SIDS) decreases markedly at six months and thereafter.

Sleep patterns are variable; there is no universal answer to how many hours of sleep infants require because individual needs vary with individual genetic makeup. The following approximations are broad outlines according to the American Academy of Pediatrics (AAP). Newborns sleep from fifteen to eighteen hours per day divided into three- or four evenly spaced sleep/nap periods of about three to four hours each between feedings. Biological circadian rhythms are not yet established. Ten percent of the day is spent in quiet alertness. From birth to six weeks, half the day is spent in sleep characterized by the following stages: drowsiness, rapid eye movement (REM) during which time active dreaming occurs, followed by light sleep, deep sleep, and very deep sleep. Of interest is that infantile periods of sleep and wakefulness begin by the eighth month of pregnancy and possibly earlier with sleep having both REM and non-REM phases. By about six weeks old, sleep periods of four to six hours occur more regularly in the evening, and the infant's particular sleep-wake cycle begins to become established.

At two to three months, 66 percent of sleep occurs at night and takes up about fifteen hours of the day. At this time, the organization of sleep stages changes and all the non-REM phases occur first before REM, which occurs last. This pattern maintains itself into adulthood. Infants at three to four months now typically sleep consistently for about six to eight hours through the night. At this time, most formula-fed babies, especially when weighing more than twelve pounds, no longer need a middle-of-the-night feeding because they are consuming more during the day and their stomach capacity has increased. From four to six months, regular sleep patterns are becoming internally established, and parents may support and shape this with their preferred schedules. Infants need eleven to fifteen hours of sleep per day with about eight to twelve hours of sleep at night.

The AAP recommends the following nap routines. Newborns sleep or nap about four times per day. From one to three months, three naps are needed: at about nine a.m., at about one p.m., and at about four p.m. From four to six months, two naps may be sufficient: at about nine a.m., and at about one p.m.

Some infants may need a third nap at about four to six p.m. At six months, dropping to two naps, one at nine a.m. for one hour and one at one or two p.m. for one to two hours may suffice because infants are able to sleep through the night for about eight to twelve hours. If a third nap is needed in the late afternoon between three and five p.m., it may be of variable duration. By about nine months, the third nap can be dropped. At one year, one nap per day of from one to three and a half hours in the afternoon is typically sufficient. Fourteen hours of sleep is needed and bedtime may be moved earlier to about seven to nine p.m. One nap per day is typical until the child is about five years old.

In the first few months of life, infant states of consciousness or level of arousal can be segregated into six categories: (1) quiet sleep, (2) active sleep, (3) drowsiness, (4) quiet alertness, (5) active alertness, and (6) crying. Sleep states alternate about every thirty minutes.

The six arousal states have the following time durations: (1) regular or nonrapid eye movement (NREM) quiet sleep of about nine hours; (2) irregular or rapid eye movement (REM) active sleep of about nine hours; (3) drowsy states that vary in duration; (4) quiet alertness of about three hours; and (5) and (6) waking and crying of about three hours during a twenty-four hour period. By about eight to twelve weeks, longer periods of alert awakeness become gradually more frequent.

Babies should be put to sleep on their backs on a firm sleep surface without soft objects, pillows, toys, stuffed animals, blankets, bumpers, or loose bedding. Sleeping on the back is understood to be the safest position until a baby is able to roll over on his or her own. Other recommendations include not smoking around infants, keeping baby's sleep area close to—but separate from—the parents' bed, not letting baby overheat during sleep, and avoiding too much time in car seats, carriers, and bouncers. It is also recommended to provide "tummy time" for a baby to be on his or her stomach when awake and someone is watching. This "tummy time" is very important to permit infants to use vision and arm and leg movements that foster crawling, creeping, and walking. "Tummy time" also fosters cognitive emotional development by facilitating typical explorative impulses. "Tummy time" can start as early as three months.

The use of pacifiers has both pros and cons. While pacifier use continues to be controversial, the following are generally accepted perspectives by both the AAP and the Mayo Clinic. Pacifiers are associated with a decreased risk of sudden infant death syndrome (SIDS) perhaps because it may position the tongue in a way that keeps the airway open, and when in an infant's mouth during sleep, infants are easily aroused if the pacifier falls out of the mouth. The possibility of "nipple confusion," namely, infants rejecting mother's nipple and preferring an artificial bottle nipple or pacifier, needs consideration. The danger is that the pacifier may substitute for human interaction. In addition, the AAP now states that starting artificial nipples early on is associated with decreased exclusive breastfeeding and decreased duration of breastfeeding. The AAP recommends exclusive breastfeeding for the first six months.

If mothers choose to use a pacifier, they may, but it should never be forced and never substitute for the infant's actual feeding needs. Pacifiers, in a limited manner, may satisfy an infant's biomental need for sucking, which is especially strong in the first six months. The AAP, moreover, states that offering a pacifier when baby is going to sleep may reduce the risk for sudden infant death syndrome. Exact reasons explaining this beyond what has been discussed are yet to be elucidated.

For breastfed infants, however, if mothers choose to introduce a pacifier, this should be done after breastfeeding has been well established, at about two to four weeks. Pacifiers should never be attached to a string or cord that may cause strangulation. Both the AAP and Mayo Clinic generally recommend not using pacifiers after the first year, if possible, since they may interfere with language development and cause dental misalignments. The organizations add, however, that in certain circumstances between twelve and forty-eight months, pacifiers may act as "transitional objects" that soothe and comfort children, especially at bedtime.

Having a baby sleep in the parents' room in a crib for at least the first six months is beneficial. This period includes the peak ages for sudden infant death syndrome (SIDS) risk and the period in which the infant's need for breast- or bottle-feeding is highest—roughly between two and four months, since no solid foods are yet being introduced. SIDS declines dramatically after six months. Fewer than 5 percent of SIDS deaths occur after six months.

Empirically, infant's hands remain clasped in fistlike position until about four months when they begin to remain open. Newborn sneezing and hic-coughing are normal, but coughing is not. The head is able to turn from side to side. Gross motor power is yet unmatured and unorganized. Arms and legs move in flailing, jerky ways. When awake, the newborn can respond to sound, attend to environmental stimuli, and visually fix onto and follow a moving object to the midline. Cooing sounds begin.

Crying in the newborn and very early infant can occur for up to three hours per day. The type of crying, termed *colic*, ranges from mild discomfort to distress. The AAP describes colicky babies as appearing to be in pain with legs drawn up, crying hard, and turning red. Babies may act hungry, but then pull back and refuse the breast. Such bouts of inconsolable colic often begin at about two to four weeks, peak at about six weeks, and then decline to one or two hours a day by about three to four months. Colic is quite common, particularly between 6:00 p.m. and midnight. The AAP states that there is no definite explanation for why this happens. They suggest that colicy infants are unusually sensitive to stimulation or cannot "self-console" or regulate their nervous system. It is typically not associated with physical illness and has been understood to be an expectable developmental phase of earliest infancy in at least 20 percent of all infants. Shrill, shrieking, persistent, and inconsolable crying, however, may indicate an illness. Whimpering cries usually suggest fatigue. As long as physical problems, such as baby heartburn, cow's milk sensitivity or allergy, or caffeine in breast milk are not causes, infant crying is typical. In fact, one-fifth of babies develop normative colic. Crying, therefore, is developmentally normal from birth until about three months when it subsides. Typically, at about four months, infants express ostensible relief by becoming able to manifest their first laugh, known as the "belly laugh." Of note is that some recent findings suggest that regulatory problems such as pronounced crying and sleeping or feeding problems may predict later behavioral and attentional problems in childhood.

Although the specific medical origins of colic are unclear, some have suggested that the baby's transition from womb to world is not instantly comfortable. It may elicit strange sensations that evoke vague feelings of vulnerability, as if being assaulted. This discomfort ranging to intense distress requires a variety of biomental interventions both from baby and from mother. While babies are equilibrating themselves by mustering whatever sensory, emotional, and attitudinal changes they can make in themselves, mothers can address this critical transitional period in a variety of ways.

Comforting and soothing a newborn is essential. Although most mothers somewhat instinctively know how to do this, a few ways that are also useful include the following. While holding the infant in a firm yet sensitive manner, gently speaking, humming, or singing soft tones conveys transactional sensitivity. Rhythmic movements, such as gentle swinging or rocking, may help a baby to entrain to these more coherent motions, rather than noting chaotic sensations. It may also be useful to use the swaddling method to gently but firmly wrap the baby in a blanket to simulate the containment that the womb provided for so many months. Last, letting baby suck by nursing, bottle feeds, or pacifier may help him or her to relax. Licking behaviors in infants, moreover, may be underestimated insofar as their affiliative significance is concerned. In addition, some mothers report that if they are nursing, temporarily eliminating dairy products—cow's milk—from their own diets makes a difference. Remembering to enlist the help of one's spouse and family members is also an option.

Baby's cries in the first year have been differentiated into five categories of causes: (1) hunger, (2) sleepiness, (3) discomfort from an external source (such as a need to change the diaper), (4) intestinal gas, and (5) need to burp. Some suggest helping baby to burp after every two ounces of milk. The meaning of these communications is often elucidated by accompanying signals. For example, sleepiness is attended by yawning and rubbing eyes, and gas is accompanied by the infant pulling his or her legs toward the chest.

Picking up and soothing a crying newborn and infant helps modulate the distress that the child and parent feel at these times. Inconsolable crying, however, may require medical evaluation.

Another cause of infant distress may be feeling overwhelmed by overstimulation. Signs include fists in front of face, arched back, and irregular breathing. If this is sensed to be the case, giving the baby time that is quiet and soothing with little unnecessary stimulation helps baby to down-regulate and relax. Overstimulation may occur inadvertently and can be perceived as alarmingly intrusive by the fragile infant. Both parents need to be sensitive to the disruptive impact of overstimulation.

At about *two months* a true or social smile can be observed. Infants appear to intentionally desire connectedness. Motor function is becoming more organized. The head can be held a little more steadily. If a bell is sounded, there is a facial response, and the head turns toward the sound. Visual tracking of objects by using head and eye movements together by is also possible by two months. Objects are able to be briefly retained in the hand.

3.1.2 Three Months

At three months, the distress signaled by crying usually quiets down, and babies may sleep through the night, perhaps from four to eight hours depending on weight. As the infant's stomach grows, hunger is diminished between feedings. Ninety percent of babies sleep through the night without waking, especially if they reach twelve or thirteen pounds. Sleep and nap schedules can first begin at this time because babies are maturationally ready and circadian rhythms are organizing. Parents can superimpose a schedule on the baby's natural sleep window for naps—an aspect of individual circadian preference. Infants three to six months may take three to four naps of about two hours length during the day. Naps should typically not be less than forty-five minutes or more than three hours. This scheduling helps set the baby's internal clock toward regularity in sleeping cycles.

Cooing continues to be heard, and hand-eye coordination improves. Prehension slowly develops first as a reflexive retention (grasp reflex at one month) and very gradually as more active, intentional holding at about five months. The capacity to retain or hold onto material objects first appears at about three months when a baby can hold a rattle more actively. At four months, a baby can hold a large ring slightly more skillfully. At five months a precarious ulnar grasp (holding with finger tips, pinky, and palm closed) is seen. *The capacity to hold onto or grasp develops much earlier than the capacity to let go of or release material objects*, which occurs roughly at about fifty-two weeks or approximately twelve to fourteen months.

There are also changes in perceptible vocal-social responses. By two to three months, infants empirically respond to a caregiver's face and voice. At three months, anticipatory excitement at the approach of caregiver is seen; by five to six months, they respond in measurable ways to a caregiver's words, showing some understanding of language. In addition, by this time, babies can open and close their hands, put hands and fingers into their mouths, watch faces closely, kick their legs when on back or stomach, and raise their heads and chests when on the stomach.

Teething may begin anytime between three and twelve months with an average onset at about seven months. Dental exams should start a little before twelve months. Drooling, crankiness, and nighttime waking may accompany "cutting" through of a baby's teeth. The eruption of the two central incisors in the lower middle gums typically occurs first, though other teeth may emerge sooner. However, the teeth should appear in symmetrical pairs. Toward the end of the first year and by about thirty-six months, all twenty primary deciduous teeth emerge. By three years, most children can adequately chew a variety of solid foods. These "milk teeth" remain until about six years when they begin to loosen and normally fall out. Baby teeth serve several important functions, including chewing food and speech articulation.

The baby teeth are replaced by the thirty-two permanent teeth of adulthood. Although the onset of the emergence of baby teeth and their replacement by adult teeth is variable, there is a six- to seven-year time span that is relatively constant between the onsets of the two events. By age thirteen years, twenty-eight of the thirty-two teeth are in place with the rest to break through by age twenty-one.

3.2 The First Three Months: Unintegration toward Integration

The first three months of life require great parenting sensitivity and responsiveness. This is a period of unorganized but continually organizing biomental processes and awareness. Parental caregiving is best when patience pervades affectionate warmth and involvement. By three months, the child undergoes a dramatic transformation from a dependent newborn to an active, perceptibly responsive and more curious infant.

Infants gradually and steadily are becoming more personalized by three months. Raw biological reflexes alone are less likely to elicit responsivity. Responsiveness is influenced by emotional attachment as evidenced, for example, by observable anticipatory excitement related to persons. Infants begin to enjoy playing with people. When all goes reasonably well, the roots of patience and a sense of safety are laid down.

3.3 After the First Three Months

3.3.1 *Four to Six Months*

In addition to states of tranquility and homeostasis in the first three months, infants experience a variety of developmental challenges that include primitive fears together with impulses to control these. Shortly after this normatively unintegrated state of experiential mistiness, the capacity for *nascent* understanding and the *seeds* of empathy and reparative synthesis of experience begin to arise. In whatever forms the experience of self and others occurs, the early infant's coarse splitting of emotions becomes less overridingly dominant.

At *four months*, an infants' developing personhood is expressed by the belly laugh, in addition to the social smile that began to emerge at about age two months. The belly laugh is an indication of qualitative enjoyment not obvious in the first three months of life. This presence connotes a substantive change in biomental structure and experience. It is akin metaphorically to an infant's first expression of "Hello." Infants become better able to synchronize the structure and timing of face-to-face interactions. By four months, most infants have the strength to hold their heads up, thus affording them greater visual exploration. They strive to engage with a social partner, typically their mothers, and respond to emotional expressions and social interactions. Routines that include feeding, napping, bathing, and sleeping become more established by this time.

Infants begin to reach out using both arms and hands in a manner that is poorly coordinated but directed. Hands are able to engage in the midline. Some infants are beginning to roll from stomach to back. With a primitive grasp, they put almost everything that can be held into the mouth—"mouthing." Drooling is typical. Crying is used as communication to attract adults. Often, colic disappears spontaneously. A form of distractibility is seen, and infants clearly seek out and desire new objects to experience.

From four to eleven months, infants increasingly attend to and use featural information—paralleling still prevailing psychological processes of "splitting"—to identify objects. Such information includes size, shape, pattern, texture, and color in addition to more gestalt, broad-outline, fuzzy-image recognition. Only gradually during the middle of the first year and emerging subsequently does psychological "integration" more substantially prevail in information processing.

Infants are able to sit upright with assistance. They become quiet in anticipation of an expected event, such as the approach of mother for feeding. Between four and six months, infants can turn their heads toward a noise or sound. There is a beginning awareness in discrimination between the known and the strange unknown. When parents are changing diapers, for example, infants may reach down to touch their genitals. This act is typical and reflects the discovery of new and interesting sensations.

At four months infants first display evidence of both significant yet implicit cognitive and emotional awareness of a distinction between themselves and others. This is demonstrated in research showing increased looking and smiling behaviors when viewing real-time video images of others in contrast to images of themselves. Developmental specialists state that babies at four to five months are able to distinguish different emotional expressions such as smiles, frowns, angry faces, and bored appearances. This dramatic change in awareness attests to their transactional sensitivity in grasping the world of persons. Emotional cognition such as this is a real way of infantile knowing and giving meaning to their experiences.

At *five months*, the body weights of babies doubles. Heads can be held erect and relatively steady; vertical baby carriers can now be used since the baby now has relatively more head control and stability. By this age, keen binocular vision with stereopsis, the visual perception of depth, provides the ability for three-dimensional sight, 20/20 vision, adequate accommodation and focusing, and eye muscle coordination for aiming and alignment.

A baby can roll to supine or face-up position from lying on the stomach. Reaching out and using a "one-handed grab" may be possible. Squealing may be heard, as well as some nonarticulate sounds that appear directly communicational toward children's toys. From five months on, babies are able to distinguish positive emotions, such as smiling and surprise (an indication that suggests new experiences are being learned), from negative emotions, such as fear and sadness. Soon thereafter, by six months, infants have the demonstrable capacity to infer the intentions of adults.

After much preliminary twisting and squirming, infants can roll over from the stomach position to the back position by about five months. From this time, consciously supporting the development of movement, particularly gross motor skills, is especially important. *Supporting* here means allowing the infant to initiate movements on his and her own to the greatest extent possible. Of course, adult monitoring and vigilance is always needed and necessary.

At *six months*, rolling from the back to the stomach becomes possible. The typical range of beginning to crawl on belly is from about five to eleven months. At about ten months, creeping on all fours with belly off the floor becomes possible. Pulling the self up and then sitting voluntarily occurs at about twelve months, and walking typically develops between twelve and eighteen months.

Such progression in mobility and also depth perception, particularly sitting up at six months, allows for the infant's expanded ability to explore and manipulate the environment, thus optimizing three-dimensional awareness and learning on all levels. Perceptual depth understanding (or judging distances between objects) at this time precedes eventual conceptual depth awareness. Concrete perceptual abilities allow for the child to distinguish objects as separate yet having a variety of material relations, such as closeness, distance, overlap, collision, and so forth. This skill is the early foundation for the eighteen-month-old's more matured ability to represent people and their varied emotional relationships.

Parents can reinforce healthy development if they do not force the infant to assume any unnatural resting positions, such as being propped up in a chair or seat. Permitting babies to lie on the floor, especially between about five and eighteen months, affords them beneficial opportunities to stretch, bend, squirm, and practice exercising muscles and neuromuscular connections. This practice strengthens the body and also helps the central nervous system to become increasingly integrated on sensory, perceptual, cognitive, and emotional levels. A sense of perseverance in accomplishing motor development tasks provides a template for task persistence, attention, and concentration in other endeavors in later life.

At six to nine months, infants, capable of sitting up independently, are able to first begin to feed themselves small pieces of food that don't require chewing, such as soft bread or banana. These infants sleep about nine hours at night. Day and night sleeping patterns become more established. From six to nine months, nap length can last for three hours instead of two. By nine months, two naps replace three naps. The baby can grasp a foot, put objects into the mouth, roll over, and reach out to his or her mirror image. Babies can reach for a dropped item and tend to bang it on a table. Introducing some solid foods may be considered at about six months. Along with milk, this adds iron to the diet. Infants and children also need adequate amount of iodine for thyroid health, especially since low-iodine diets may cause impaired mental development. Breast milk, formula, cow's milk, and some solid foods eaten by six months are sources of iodine.

Mention should also be made about the issue of "co-sleeping" or "bed-sharing." Whether or not to have one's infant in bed sleeping with parents is a complex issue. While not disregarding cultural and socioeconomic concerns, in the United States, it is professionally understood that co-sleeping is not the best choice for infants because of safety concerns and increased risk of death. It is clear that there are nonetheless many material and emotional aspects to this oftentimes difficult decision. Sleeping in the same room—but not in the same bed—is suggested. Parents are encouraged to fully communicate with professional consultation about any concerns.

Between three and nine months, babies exhibit clear-cut signs of preferring and looking at human faces. This appears most robust and consistent at nine months and then persists. Human faces provide highly relevant information for the kinds of social inferences that infants are beginning to vigorously make during the latter part of the first year. A greater sensitivity to visual-auditory intermodal regularities in seeing lips articulate emotionally meaningful communication facilitates this attraction, as does a maturing capacity to suppress the effects of distracting background information.

Between six and twelve months, babies are natural explorers. They use all their senses to grasp the world and gather information. Sensory exploration is accompanied by crude but developing prehension or hand manipulation of objects. Typical behaviors with objects include banging, mouthing, and fingering. "Reality tasting," that is, putting almost everything into the mouth for examination, is common and needs to be monitored for safety. Of note, babies can differentiate male and female genders at this time.

3.3.2 Seven to Ten Months

By the end of *seven months*, infants can roll over onto their stomachs in addition to their backs. Most children roll first from their stomach to the back, and later in the opposite direction, although doing it in the opposite sequence is normal as well. Rolling both ways—front to back and back to front—is an important milestone. Babies can reach for objects with one or both hands, drag objects toward self, transfer a toy between hands, put feet into the mouth, and actively bounce up and down. At this time, they can sit up unassisted very briefly, often in a "tripod" fashion using arms on the floor for support. They explore objects with hands—"touch hunger"—in addition to using the mouth. Seven-month-old infants can struggle to obtain objects out of reach. They may even be able to respond to their name.

Babies' normative anxiety to a stranger—stranger anxiety—may now become evident, particularly when someone unrecognized approaches the infant. The appearance of this anxiety is one of the infant's first major emotional milestones. It is evidence of infants' ability to discriminate and indicate awareness of the familiar in contrast to the strange. It is absolutely distinct from separation anxiety, which peaks somewhere between ten to eighteen months and wanes through thirty-six months. Distress and crying are normal with both forms of anxiety.

Stranger anxiety is a pervasive biomental pulling away from what is perceived as different and strange. This capacity suggests that cognitive pathways are differentiating and developing, thus furthering the capacity for discrimination. At about this time, the capacity for *joint attention* is demonstrated when the infant initiates a referenced object to another person, typically mother, who responds. It implies an implicit awareness of "two-ness" (mother and stranger) in a context of "three-ness" (infant, mother, and stranger). Perceptual differences are emotionally amplified by the uncertainty of these differences. It may also suggest a glimmer of the mental capacity—both cognitive and emotional—for confusion, ambiguity, and the seeds of ambivalence. This core experience is the nodal point for the development of all later forms of organized envy, greed, and jealousy. The implicit and explicit assumption of "the other" as "a stranger" eventually becomes equivalent to equating "the other" with "the enemy." This implies perceptions of the other as a strange intruder who may pose a risk for potential harm. All these reactions evoke the need for developing both defensive and constructive coping strategies to manage the anxieties so provoked.

Crying, which had subsided around four- to the seven-month-old time period, re-emerges and suggests a response to both internal and external dissonance. All of these are developmental accomplishments and imply that the infant is canalizing its sense of participation in a universe of space, movement, and time. Social awareness and contact with other persons are becoming more apparent. These are significant indicators of healthy development. Close, affectionate, and encouraging parental attitudes are essential at this time.

At *eight months, separation anxiety* becomes clearly evident when the infant is removed from its primary caregiver. Distress and crying are normative. This begins at eight months and peaks at ten to sixteen or eighteen months. Its intensity wanes between twenty-four and thirty six months.

At this time, infants somewhat understand but cannot say in words what "no" indicates. Attention span is about two to three minutes. They can just begin to crawl on their bellies. If typical crawling does not occur, a variation such as "scooting" on the buttocks or "slithering" on the stomach may be seen. With one object in one hand, a baby can now hold a second item in the other hand. Language shows *babbling*, an array of consonant sounds (for example, "da," "ba," "ka"). Infants can point to objects and search for hidden objects. By thirty-two weeks, biting begins to replace mouthing, to some extent, in the infant's explorative interests and in feeding. Using a pacifier, particularly to help the infant sleep at night, may be useful. If it falls out of the mouth, infants are often capable of putting it back.

At *nine months*, a baby continues to crawl on belly or move forward using other parts of the body. This ability enables *prone procession* and should alert parents to monitor the infant to ensure safety. A baby can now pull his or her self to a standing position and can show some preference for right versus left handedness. Most infants can recognize and respond to their own name, which is a significant indicator of healthy development. Infants bang objects together almost reflexively.

Peek-a-boo games such as covering the face with one's hands can be played in which the infant expects continuation of the game. The basic emotions of surprise and joy are expressed and often accompanied by smiling, clapping, and a sense of fascination. By this time, *joint attention* is well established. He or she can feed self a cracker and drink from a "sippy" or trainer cup with two handles. Infants can now bite off, chew, and swallow food. The AAP states that by nine months, infants are able to eat on the same schedule as older children and adults, and supports creating family meal times and making them a family tradition.

3.3.3 Crawling, Creeping, Standing, and Walking

Crawling, creeping, standing, and walking at around this time are monumental achievements permitting the infant to regain lost objects and find new ones. This procession of abilities reflects the developing capacity to deal with nascent feelings of loss and restoration by using these newfound abilities through an effort of will, with its conscious and nonconscious components. The emotional and cognitive implications of these continuing exploratory processes are crucial for psychological health at this time and in the future.

Infants typically creep, crawl, and then stand up and walk. This, however, is not an absolutely necessary progression. What is essential in the second half of the first year is an infant's manifest exploratory behaviors, for example, in rolling or pulling themselves along the floor with their elbows. Children who never crawl still learn to walk at the expectable times in development. Between twelve and twenty-four months, encouraging opportunities for large-muscle motor skill development with arms and legs by, for example, providing large cardboard boxes for children to get into and out of safely, is useful.

3.4 Ten to Twelve Months

At *ten months*, infants need about fourteen hours of sleep. They are now able to creep on hands and knees with their abdomens raised. Ten-month-olds can wave "bye-bye" and play "pat-a-cake" responsively. These activities reflect typically developing social awareness, social comprehension, and some preparatory ability to cooperate in social games. Infants can indicate wants with gestures: eye gaze, head turning, facial expression, pointing, and so forth. They are further becoming able to respond to their own name. They can match two small cubes together, reflecting an ability to put things that had been separate together. Adults can recognize emotions, such as fear, in these infants. At about ten months, *social referencing* becomes clearly observable, in which infants experiencing ambiguous situations look at mothers' emotional expressions as an indicator of what is safe or not. This paralinguistic gesture is equivalent to an exclamation, "Help." This activity typically includes parents labeling and commenting on what is being jointly observed. This running commentary is instrumental in helping children's interrelated development of language, emotion, and social cognition. In addition, many infants, for the first time, are able to respond with laughter and pleasure to being tickled. The above and following listed steps reflect healthy and typical social and emotional development. While self-identity is emerging from innate dispositions and temperamental styles, the influence of the social group—at first, mother—becomes crucial to the gradual development of sense of self and personality. The culture in which the infant and child is raised contributes greatly to the self-identity developmental trajectory.

At *eleven months*, infants can walk with help and can remove a cube from a cup. Typical manipulation and exploration of objects now includes holding, flinging, shaking, swatting, opening, and closing. Infants show definite preferences for one toy over another, can say one word in addition to "mama" and "dada," and can inhibit activity on command, indicating a fuller grasp of the connotations of "no." This understanding of "no" may not be substantial until about eighteen months when saying it out loud may be possible. Many infants are now able to point, which suggests a social interaction and the capacity for joint attention.

At *twelve months*, a baby can pick up a small item with a thumb-finger pincer grasp, release an item into a cup with demonstration, and drop toys purposefully. Attention span can be sustained for as long as fifteen minutes. These children can sit alone when so placed, cruise using a rail or furniture, and walk alone. The AAP strongly recommends parents not use baby walkers since they have been associated with falling and other injuries. Although able to reach out using one arm, bimanual reaching and grabbing is seen more often. Using both arms to aid balance enhances stability when learning to walk. The twelve-month-old can say "uh-oh" to imply surprise and can look correctly at a picture when that image is named. Infants may also point to an object when it is named. Imitating the activities of others becomes apparent. A sense of humor becomes apparent when mildly discrepant events are responded to by laughter. Some have regarded the twelve-month-old infant as being in the "fun stage."

From about twelve to twenty-one months, toddling begins. Play activities now include the exploratory behaviors made possible by this beginning locomotion. Although toddlers may be able to spin and rotate objects and toys, excessive preoccupation with these activities may not be typical and should be discussed with pediatric caregivers. Morning naps can be phased out when only one nap in the day suffices. Toddlers need about ten and a half to eleven and a half hours of sleep each night plus another one or two hours of naptime during the day. This afternoon nap is beneficial until three years of age, when naps are more optional. It is estimated that 92 percent of three-year-olds take afternoon naps. Less than 50 percent of four-year-olds do, and most children stop napping entirely by kindergarten. For example, if the three- to five-year-old cannot fall asleep by 9:30 p.m., it may be time to stop afternoon napping. When naps first stop, moving bedtime earlier by about thirty to sixty minutes is helpful.

3.5 Fifty-two Weeks

At *fifty-two weeks*, babies now can be seen to let go of and release objects purposefully. If given a small cube, for example, baby can grasp it and then purposefully release it into a cup. At about fourteen months, babies can place three or more cubes into a cup, one by one, without demonstration and can hold and release a small ball voluntarily. This developmental progression characterizes a patterning of behavior—grasping and releasing—that influences development, notably social-emotional relationships, going forward.

Infants first merely look at an object at twelve weeks, then approach it precariously at twenty weeks, then grasp it crudely with the whole hand palmar-wise at twenty-four weeks, then grasp more finely with fingers at thirty-six weeks, then with the pincer at forty-eight weeks, then purposefully release it at fifty-two to fifty-six weeks.

Releasing an inanimate object is an important developmental accomplishment that is matched over long periods of time by the capacity to psychologically let go of something cherished. This capacity to acknowledge endings, let go emotionally—if only temporarily—and move on to another situation, task, or interpersonal relationship develops very gradually. It can be behaviorally observed by the end of the preschool years when the material and emotional capacity to let go and move forward makes its typically long, steady, and protracted journey into mature adulthood. The classic example is leaving parents and home for the majority of the day when entering first grade at age six.

As psychological development and experience with affiliation, disappointment, and letting go occur, the psychological templates of how a child emotionally grasps and releases consolidate. At times, releasing implies endings and correlates in nonconscious experience with intimations of dying and final terminations. This becomes a monumental emotional challenge to process, let go of, and from which to move on.

3.6 Infant Social Development

Social and emotional development in the first year can be observed and has measurable parameters. Affiliative attachments (emotionally grasping a significant other) and detachments (somewhat releasing those affiliations) have their roots in infancy, notably in the mother-child relationship. Later emotional self-management has its roots in the quality of achieving these abilities.

Infants who are healthily developing noticeably show evidence of interest in mother and the surrounding world. Actively and sensitively speaking to one's infant should begin in earliest infancy and not merely when the infant can logically understand or speak. In the first three months, parents may notice the infant attending to sounds with some diminishing of motor activity or turning of eyes toward the auditory source. These naturally occurring responses to sound can serve as development-enhancing opportunities when parents narrate what is happening. This process engages the child's focused attentiveness by articulating the infant's visual experience.

For example, as mother's footsteps are heard and the infant is picked up, she can say, "I am picking you up now; we are walking outside to get into the car to drive to see your grandmother." Combining social engagement with verbal dialogue fosters learning. Put differently, in addition to hearing words spoken, the quality of language development is enhanced by social interactions, especially eye contact. Another shared development is the social smile by two months. By three months, infants look around, focus on objects three feet away, look for vanishing items, show anticipatory excitement, and make cooing sounds.

At this time and thereafter, simple interest intensifies; that is to say, *infants should not appear indifferent or apathetic for prolonged periods.* At about four months one may hear a relatively loud belly laugh accompanying a spontaneous social smile. By six months, infants become able to begin discriminating strangers, reflecting facial mimics, and can reach toward their image in a mirror. By seven months, there is some anxiety in the presence of a stranger. The capacity for *joint attention* is emerging. By eight months, there is evidence of beginning separation anxiety when removed from mother. By nine months, infants respond to familiar words, such as their own name, "no-no," "baby," and "mama."

By ten months, infants can wave "bye-bye" and play "pat-a-cake" responsively. Perhaps an underestimated developmental achievement is the ability to clap. Clapping may show itself as early as seven months but is more available at ten months and surely by twelve months. Clapping is a motivated, interpersonal skill that demonstrates more than mere excitatory overflow. *Clapping* expresses and communicates approval, personal pleasure, enthusiasm, and positive feedback. The capacity for *social referencing* is emerging. By one year, walking begins and a few words may emerge. The infant can inhibit its activity when adults say "no." All the aforementioned reflect healthy developmental progress although their timetables typically may vary, as has been emphasized throughout this book.

Just as the first months of infant life require their own special sensitivity, the second half of the first year requires sensitive parental attentiveness and interpersonal responsivity through demonstrable gesture and emotion. All aspects of caregiving nurturance foster the foundation for infant security and trust. As the twelve- to twenty-four-month-old experiences absolutely novel things, the complementary reinforcement of sensory and motor ministrations through affectionate physical contact—kissing, stroking, and affectionate touching—enhances the infant's sense of security and basic trust.

Since "object permanence" (which implies complex memory storage) significantly evolves from about six months on, lasting memories that may shade later conscious awareness are taking root. Research studies strongly suggest that infants, perhaps as early as birth, have a functioning memory system that cannot be reduced to mere habit formation or simply procedural memory. A kernel of some higher-level memory retention appears to be present at birth.

4. LANGUAGE DEVELOPMENT

4.1 Overview

As the speech producers of jaw, lips, tongue, and voice mature, an infant is able to make more controlled sounds. This process begins in the first few months of life. At about three months, "cooing," a soft, pleasant, repetitive vocalization is heard in all typically developing babies across the world. By six to eight months of age, an infant usually "babbles" in repetitive syllables. Infants' previously prolonged attention to eyes and eye contact now is superseded by greater attention to the caregiver's lips and mouth, suggesting the infants' language shaping through modeling. Babbling soon turns into a type of nonsense speech termed "jargon" that often has the tone and cadence of human speech but does not contain real words. By twelve months, infants return their looking to greater eye gaze, which suggests emotional information gathering, especially for social cues.

In regard to walking and language, the period of infancy can be divided into two phases: (1) the first twelve months during which gross motor functioning, such as walking, and linguistic communication have not yet sufficiently emerged; and (2) months twelve to about twenty-four or thirty-six which is the period of toddlerhood where walking, spoken language, refinements in cognition, and attention to bowel and bladder control become prominent.

The biomental child development perspective has stressed the richness of experience starting at birth and progressively increasing in complexity in the first year, second year, and thereafter. Modern cognitive science proposes a rich conceptual life even before language is learned. By the end of the first year, most children have mastered the ability to say a few simple words. Children are most likely unaware of the meaning of their first words but soon learn the power of those words as others respond to them. Developmental specialists believe that infants' understanding of words and language significantly precedes their manifest ability to use them in explicit ways.

As with all other developmental milestones, the expression of word usage varies. The following, however, are general approximations of the emergence of infants' speech expression. By about twelve months, one or two words are expressed; at fourteen months, four to ten words; at eighteen to twenty-one months, eight to ten and perhaps up to fifty words. A "vocabulary spurt" at this age is typical. In the second year, most children are putting perhaps 250 to 350 words—mostly nouns—together in crude sentences such as "more milk."

During this period, basic level concepts are organizing. Developing language and the emergence of larger spans of conscious awareness and attention focus the toddler on specific perceptual details. In turn, words provide labels that support the development of mental categorization. Children rapidly learn that words symbolize or represent objects, actions, and thoughts. Language both expressive and receptive is a mode for communication of information. Language may involve the use of sounds, voice, words, bodily gestures, facial expressions, and so forth used as signs for the transmission of meaning between people. This transmission is an essential core of typical human social interaction.

Language expression encompasses a reflection of both the developing understanding of (1) semantics and meaning, and (2) pragmatics or the socially appropriate applied use of language in different contexts. This significant development represents a synthesis of language, not merely reflexive mimicry or echoing. At this age, children also begin to engage in representational, imaginative, or pretend play. These behaviors directly reflect inner advances in symbolization and language development. At ages three, four, and five, a child's vocabulary rapidly increases such as with the inclusion of prepositions, verbs, and more complex sentences, and he or she begins to master the rules of spoken language.

4.1.1 Typical versus Atypical Development in the First Year

In summary, the above details of development in the first year indicate typical, also referred to as neurotypical, development. Significant or sustained divergence from this course connotes *atypicality*. Red flags, which suggest possible problems of significance, include the following: no cooing or babbling by twelve months, no single words by sixteen months, no spontaneous two-word phrases by twenty-four months, *no use of social gestures*—such as grasping, pointing, eye contact, waving, and so forth—by twelve months, no response to own name by twelve months, and loss of any word ability, language, or social skill at any age. Even if physical language is present, its social communicative quality is its essential correlate of typical develop-

ment. Early identification and interventions can both address existing problems for children with special needs and help prevent the development of
new or worsening difficulties.

5. TODDLERS: YEARS ONE THROUGH THREE

From twelve to twenty-four months, observational and associative learning
are significant. For example, children are most receptive to eating new types
of foods, especially if they see adults doing so. This trend, however, declines
and may be contrasted with the least willingness to try new foods between
ages four and eight years when relatively less exclusive food-based dependency with parents is typical.

At *twelve months*, babies begin attempting to walk alone, or "toddling."
Toddling appears different from mature walking: legs wide apart, toes pointing outward, and lurching from side to side as movement forward occurs.
Also, toddlers can now cooperate in dressing. For language development in
this time period, refer to the discussion above.

At fourteen months toddling is established, and infants can imitate, to a
clearer extent, adults' speech and behaviors. At fifteen to eighteen months,
pointing in general becomes established. This gesture suggests the maturing
infant's developing sense of space, spatial relations, and sharper awareness
of two-ness between two points

In addition, the infant now has the ability to build a tower of two blocks
and indicate wants by pointing or vocalizing. This implies more of a social
directive rather than imperative, demand gesture. At about fourteen months,
infants are able to hold a crayon and make circular, spiral-like scribbling.
They can also run, but not well. By eighteen months, the ability to make a
vertical line emerges and at about thirty months, infants add to this the ability
to form a horizontal stroke. Between fifteen and twenty-four months, children may be able to say "mine" and "no." "Mine" reflects a newly developing concern about possession. It connotes a wish for a permanent grasp.
Saying "no" and using negatives such as "I won't" at three years old typically comes before the ability to say "yes." At sixteen months, infants can turn
the pages of a book, become attached to a soft toy, and display temper
tantrums.

Temper tantrums have been called "meltdowns." For children between
one and two years, these typically occur at points of frustrated needs, such as
being hungry, being overly tired, or needing a diaper change. To some extent, temper tantrums are fits of hurt pride as the toddler implicitly experiences obstruction against what he or she wants to do. In this sense, they are
"restrictive misunderstandings" attributable to unmatured comprehension.

Temper tantrums are emotional and behavioral decompensations that typically are evoked by and reflect inordinate levels of anxiety, unsuccessful coping skills, and disorganized avoidant reactions. Since children at this time do not have the verbal or other skills to articulate their distressing needs, frustration is expressed in the form of tantrums. Toddlers are experimenting with matters of control—testing parental limits and discovering their own. Identifying these needs and addressing them to prevent or minimize such distraught episodes of moodiness and behavioral breakdowns helps toddlers establish behavioral boundaries—limits within which appropriate versus inappropriate is set. Merely telling the child not to do something is ineffective since the cognitive mechanisms needed for this skill are not yet sufficiently developed. For example, the explicit memory required to follow behavioral orders is not developed until approximately eighteen months, and even then it is rudimentary and transient.

Temper tantrums typically last eight to ten minutes. The prevalence of temper tantrums is greatest at two years old, then lessens at three and four, and becomes far less frequent at five and six years. Destructive aggression is most frequent at three years old, and then subsides. At age two, about four tantrums per week occur. At age three, five tantrums may emerge to subside to only one or two at age four. Although each tantrum has its particular antecedents, circumstances, and requirements, a general guideline is to remove and distract the child toward something else when tantrums arise. Parental poise and creativity in the specific handling of each event is part of the art of effective parenting.

Biomental child development offers a unique perspective on the way tantrums may be perceived. In addition to their biological and neuromaturational inevitability as part of typical development, their behavioral and emotional trappings may be considered a form of artistic "happening." Such happenings are unplanned improvisations, a form of theater, composed of alogical and nonlinear elements. These "improvisations," however, are organically related to the personal and inanimate environment in which they occur. The central audience is typically a parent. Once the child begins his or her seemingly disruptive enactment, the boundary between child and parent dissipates. This is a crucial point since the parent now becomes an integral part of this happening. Hence, the way a parent responds determines the course of how this event develops.

Tantrums may be thought of as amazing happenings that signal emotional unrest needing attention and containment. If parents think of these outbursts as "performances," it is a reminder that these inevitable dramas are developmentally typical and best handled by subtle monitoring, ensuring safety, and providing appropriate distraction. Eliminating any negatively reinforcing au-

dience participation that may perpetuate the tantrums' intensity and frequency needs to be considered—especially ahead of time so that "on the spot"
responses become natural and appropriate to the situation.

Some developmentalists have described the period from about ten to
eighteen months as the child's "love affair with the world." This idea is
reflected in the new capacities to walk alone and use the body as a whole that
can be navigated in space. The developing abilities associated with spatial
proprioception help refine gross motor movements. The motors of curiosity,
newfound freedom, and pleasurable excitement in these competencies drive
the infant to explore and move around as much as possible. Much of this
pleasure in functioning is joyful as such and not otherwise goal directed. This
feature of deriving pleasure merely from motor activity may be trait-like, and
perpetuate itself throughout life. Those who are "temperamentally" athletic
and derive joy from such physical activities as running and experiencing "the
runner's high," or the swimmer's love of swimming, and so forth may have
this characteristic. It may be wise to discern this natural love of motor activity from children's presentations that may be incorrectly labeled as "hyperactive."

Toddlers and, for that matter, all children with active temperaments may
be at risk for injuries and hence require careful surveillance. A careful parental eye toward safety is essential during this time without interfering with
appropriate exploration and curiosity.

Since so much is new, the toddler may have subtle fears related to what is
encountered. Many toddlers manage these fears by paradoxically seeking
these feared objects, acting as "dare-devils" and taking potentially unsafe
risks. The technical term for this tendency is a *counterphobic reaction*, indicating its definitional opposition to behavioral avoidance. This reaction is
largely a nonconscious attempt to confront fears by meeting them head on.
Understanding parents accordingly provide environments that minimize potential injury.

In addition, during twelve and twenty-four months, typically developing
children show clear preferences for the social world of people and interpersonal relatedness. In other words, normally developing infants are clearly
more interested and engaged in dynamic social experiences than nonhuman
interactions. Atypical fascinations, by contrast, may include inordinate attention to geometric images, moving mechanical objects (like fans, wheels, and
flags blowing in the wind), and inanimate objects with high contrast and
some motion (such as window blinds). Intense interest in such things may
require professional assessment.

Play activities during this time are more solitary; they occur in the presence of family but often do not involve other people. Toddlers are technically
more "egocentric," only able to see their own points of view. The term
"egocentric" is used here in its formal academic denotation without the im-

plication of the term "intentional selfishness." Such restrictive perspectives make cooperation, sharing, and joint play virtually impossible. At seventeen months, infants feed their dolls in an imitative way that may be more behavioral than empathetic. Later, in the preschool years, empathetic sensitivity begins to emerge when seeing others' perspectives becomes developmentally more possible.

At *eighteen months*, a baby can squat, seat self in a chair, build a tower of three to four cubes, and use ten to fifty words. The time from eighteen to thirty-six months has been referred to as the period of vocabulary, naming, or language explosion. Speech at this time is termed *telegraphic*, since it is communicative but not nuanced. Infants can point to body parts, show some beginning signs of empathy, and begin to demonstrate symbolic thinking. The development of language helps children add detail to perceptual awareness and build concept formation. In this second year of life, infants become increasingly attracted to the very pleasure of their ability to function. This satisfaction in achieving the mastery of advancing skills, in different ways characteristic of each developmental era, persists throughout life.

Parents may notice that the eighteen-month-old appears to have a sense of conclusions. For example, when he or she puts an item into a box, there may be a communicated sense that "the job is done." Words are now beginning to substitute or take some precedence over gestures. Cognitive processes take on increasingly profound perspectives during this landmark period. This, in part, can create conditions where disequilibriums in attitude, demeanor, and behavior first become apparent. Since qualitatively advanced changes are being newly experienced and achieved, children may seem moody and behaviorally labile. This relationship is explained by the fact that the children are adapting to reconciling continuing reliance on parents with newfound abilities for greater independence.

At about this time, children can recognize cognitive discrepancies in the way things look and make comparisons to inner mental standards of "correctness." This can be inferred through observation of children, for example, laughing as if they find a discrepancy entertaining. Exploring the extended environment as well as a fascination with covering and uncovering boxes with lids, examining containers, turning knobs and pages, playing with articulated objects or toys with moving parts, putting round pegs into holes, and scribbling is evident. Specific food fussiness and refusals may begin at this time.

Of note, observable behaviors include being able to feed self as well as others. Whereas the infant may be seen to begin feeding him- or herself by about nine months, by eighteen months, behaviors demonstrating feeding others may suggest not only imitation but perhaps an awareness or concern of needs existing outside the self and in others. By twenty months, the child as an emerging person now focuses on what others—including himself—are *doing*. This vigilant attention to actions highlights the meaningful acuity of social interactions for the socializing child. Such gaze patterns reflect one empirical demonstration of the construct *object relations* discussed at length in the overview.

At *twenty-one months*, 20 to 150 words are used, and two- to three-word sentences emerge. The AAP states that except for minor variations in size, there are very few differences between the sexes at this age. Boys and girls develop skills at about the same rate although boys generally develop language skills more slowly than girls. Toddlers can ask for food and ask, "What's that?" The period around twenty-four months is one where speech and language are escalating. Language is characterized by three word sentences that use the pronouns: I, me, and you. Children feel a newly found sense of power and influence in using words that can elicit responses from others. It is helpful for parents to try to minimize phrasing questions so that they require a "yes" or "no" answer. It is better to offer choices, such as "Would you like to sit on the couch or play on the floor?" This strategy is very useful when it comes to meals, for example, "Would you prefer a banana or some apple?"

The twenty-one month old can walk up stairs with help, and by about thirty-four months, the toddler can alternate feet going up and down stairs. Around twenty-one to twenty-three months, the toddler can feed self with spoon well.

At *twenty-four months*, the child is beginning to graduate from infancy. He or she can run well, requiring careful monitoring of safety. Falling down still occurs, but less frequently. Children can say now up to about three hundred words and can refer to self by name. As mentioned previously, children can understand much more than they can express. They can build a tower of about four to six blocks and kick a ball. By twenty-four months, toddlers are able to differentiate and understand the difference between animate and inanimate objects. This involves being able to evaluatively discriminate and connect nonlinear motions (such as jumping, hopping, and climbing with people and animals), in contrast to the more restricted linear motions of inanimate objects (such as moving vehicles). This ability strongly suggests that conceptual formation and understanding is amplifying the perceptual ability to differentiate qualitatively distinct domains of objects.

5.1 Impulse Control: Biomental Perspectives

5.1.1 Mental Aspects

At this juncture, a discussion about the development of impulse control is useful. Empirical descriptions with reference to neurobiological substrates will be briefly reviewed. Correlations among behaviors, executive functioning, and the prefrontal cortex will be discussed.

Impulsivity denotes a predisposition toward rapid, unplanned reactions to internal or external stimuli. These reactions are characterized by significantly diminished regard to the negative consequences of the reactions for both the subject and others. Impulsivity may involve poor choices when making decisions or general disinhibition.

Impulse control, broadly defined as a personality trait, is one important feature of the more general biomental process termed *inhibitory control*. Put differently, impulsivity is equivalent to deficits in response inhibition. In effect, this denotes an inability to inhibit ideas, emotions, and action. From both a psychological and neurobiological perspective, inhibition is not unitary; it is a heterogeneous construct.

This insufficiency of controlling impulses can be described in a schematic way as follows. Inhibitory control typically includes three areas that require the regulatory processes (prefrontal lobe reasoning) needed to promote delay. These domains are (1) actual behavior: behavioral action and motoric response delay, (2) cognition: cognitive flexibility and inhibition of nonrelevant information, and (3) emotion: inhibition and modulation of emotional responses. The ability for inhibitory control typically precedes more sophisticated volitionally mature choosing—both nonconsciously and consciously—among alternative options. This biomental capacity—intimately related to executive functioning—does not fully mature until approximately age twenty-five years.

When speaking of impulse control, motoric action and behavioral delay as a reaction to the experience of a gap in immediate satisfaction are typically emphasized. Although behavioral, cognitive, and emotional components become involved in producing a final inhibitory result, each piece has its own neurological pathway, though at times they overlap. This dissimilarity in component pathways correlates with the fact that each system develops differently from infancy to adulthood.

Inhibition of action correlates with constructs such as self-control, effortful control, impulse control, and postponement and delay of gratification. Each idea has a different emphasis although the central focus of each is a preliminary biomental pause before the next biomental step in feeling, thought, decision, and action. Biomental child development's focus on the pivotal role of containment, particularly the modulation of the experience of urgency, is uniquely salient in this regard, as has been discussed in chapter 1.

Although self-regulation, in part, has a hereditary basis, it develops rapidly in the first four years of life with marked improvements occurring in the third year. Individual differences in effortful control are also associated with the quality of mother-child interactions. Warm, supportive parenting, rather than cold, authoritarian parenting, predicts higher levels of effortful control and less learned helplessness. Individual differences in effortful control during the first five years of life have been linked to healthier adjustment, social competence, observance of rules, and conscience, concurrently and in later life.

Toddlers from about twelve to eighteen months have some capacity to restrain themselves, especially in ambiguous situations in which they look at mother's face to gauge an "action plan." This *social referencing* is evident at about ten months. Between fourteen and twenty-two months, toddlers use social referencing, especially when mothers show fearful emotional expressions. Hence, toddlers show hesitancy, some capacity to pause, and respond tentatively with their action-oriented behaviors. They are able to comply with being given simple directions, often including the term "no." An illustrative example follows. Since many toddlers feed themselves quickly and are not aware of the hot temperature of some foods, they risk burning their mouths. Such children have to be guided to pause, identify hot foods, and eat them cautiously, which is consistent with their developing inhibitory skill set. However, a two- or three-year-old may not have the capacity to control the impulse to touch things that attract him or her. Hence, it is unrealistic for parents to expect the child not to touch, for example, displays at the grocery store or even a burning candle.

At about twenty-four months and thereafter, the child is *very gradually* becoming aware of a need to inhibit behaviors on a voluntary basis. This requirement competes with the typical impulse of possessiveness and a wish for things to be "mine." Between eighteen and thirty-six months, studies show children to possess varying degrees of the ability to delay desirable action. Increased capability is associated with children who display well-developed attention and language skills. The newfound capacity for walking, as an example, makes starting and stopping locomotion both a necessity and a skill in progress.

5.1.2 Biological Aspects

While impulse control has neuromaturational roots in very early childhood, the strength and modulation of impulse control typically becomes more consolidated well after childhood with the more extensive interfacing of brain regions. This section broadly reviews some key findings.

White matter denotes myelinated axons located more on the surface of the brain and closely related to connectivity and speed between information processing centers and the integration of learned information. Different white matter pathways mature at different rates.

In contrast, *gray matter* denotes more interiorly located cell bodies, dendrites and unmyelinated axons, synapses, glial cells, and capillaries whose function is directly related to more circumscribed, regional information processing centers. Estimates of the volume of the three categories of gray matter are the following: (1) neurons (about 73 percent): dendrites (30 percent), axons (29 percent), cell bodies (7.8 percent), and synapses (6 percent); (2) glia (about 14 percent): astrocytes (6.5 percent), satellite oligodendrites (6.2 percent), and microglia (1.3 percent); and (3) other (about 18 percent): extracellular space (18 percent), and capillaries (0.5 percent). The timing, degree, and rate of cortical and subcortical gray matter is heterochronous, that is, regional development is different at different times.

As discussed in chapter 1, white matter (correlated with myelination) has a definite neurodevelopmental spatiotemporal trajectory that is different from that of gray matter. Neurons myelinate first in the lower brain regions—the brainstem (midbrain, medulla, and pons), and then advance upward to the cerebral cortex. This is followed by myelination of commissural fibers connecting the left and right cerebral hemispheres. After this, association fibers that interconnect cortical regions within the same hemisphere undergo myelination. In addition, myelination occurs from posterior brain regions forward to anterior regions, notably the frontal and prefrontal cortex.

The neuromaturation of the prefrontal cortex is instrumental for *executive functioning*—attention, control and inhibition of ideas and actions, planning, and reconfiguring problem-solving strategies. Response inhibition and execution, cognitive flexibility, mental set modulation and fluidity, planning, and reorganization provide the scaffolding for higher-level thought processes that rely on abstraction and memory. The observable mature behaviors of adults, moreover, have substrata in imagined or thought-out preparation characteristic of executive functioning. While beyond the scope of the present discussion, the interconnectedness of the prefrontal cortex with the basal ganglia and thalamus, for example, also underlie executive functioning.

Synaptogenesis, forming new synaptic connections between neurons, and *synaptic pruning* or elimination of synapses in the prefrontal cortex have different time courses. Proliferations of synapses, and gray matter increases of 13 percent in the brain and prefrontal cortex, occur in early childhood from approximately nineteen to thirty-three months through later childhood at approximately six to nine years. This early synaptogenesis is complemented by a second wave of synaptogenesis at puberty (approximately age eleven in girls and age twelve in boys), a brief plateau, and then subsequent elimination and reorganization of prefrontal synaptic connections after puberty. This is a linear decrease of approximately 5 percent per decade throughout life. Synaptic pruning after puberty creates fine-tuning of the functional networks of brain tissue that correlate with expanded executive functioning, notably a greater capacity for inhibition and impulse control.

For example, sophisticated diffusion tensor imaging (DTI), an indirect measure of the molecular motion of water in brain tissues, was developed about twenty years ago and allows for the analysis of the integrity and orientation of white matter tracts in the brain (myelinization). DTI shows that neural connections involved in behavioral action inhibition incrementally mature between the age of seven and thirty-one years. White matter follows a more or less linear course of increase in childhood and adolescence. It develops in posterior brain areas and gradually advances anteriorly. Gray matter volume, by contrast, is at times progressive and at other times regressive, reflecting its heterochronous or nonlinear path.

White matter volume rapidly increases from birth to about age eight. In contrast, gray matter steadily increases from birth to reach its maximum at about age five years, a plateau, then another wave of increase at puberty, after which time it declines linearly until approximately age thirty. The nonlinear decrease in gray matter is understood to both reflect its relative position with increases of white matter, and also a second wave of synapse proliferation in the frontal cortex at the onset of puberty and then a synaptic pruning that follows after puberty.

White matter increases more slowly from age eight to a relative plateau at approximately mid-adolescence (when attention and working memory are more substantive). This plateau shows small increases from this time until approximately the late twenties when relative plateauing stabilizes. The prefrontal anterior cortex, therefore, may not fully develop until after adolescence and approximately the end of the twenties.

From a neurochemical perspective, moreover, the neurobiological basis of impulsivity as a personality trait has received much attention. Recent studies have elucidated the significant role of the primary inhibitory neurotransmitter, gamma-aminobutyric acid (GABA), in the dorsolateral prefrontal cortex in addition to serotonin and dopamine as they affect emotion, motivation, and response inhibition.

5.2 The Developmental Timetable for Impulse Control Regulation

Intentionally stopping oneself from immediately acting on an impulse, desire, or intention to achieve a goal is a critical biomental skill. It is a refinement of managing the experience of frustration, which denotes tension in the awareness of a gap in satisfaction. Its inestimable importance can be compared to the function of brakes on a car.

As is true of many other developmental abilities, impulse control regulation has a developmental trajectory, which may be described behaviorally. For example, infants of approximately eight months appear to understand a sense of "no" and may be able to temporarily pause their behaviors. At eighteen months, toddlers are able to both understand and articulate the word "no" and act defiantly. Temper tantrums may regularly occur in two and three-year-olds. Whining, a verbal expression of frustration, starts at about age three. Arguing appears at age five. All these typical behavioral demonstrations of frustration and negative mood are regularly occurring and short-lived.

Impulse control regulation signifies a developing capacity to tolerate delay, which contributes to the adaptive regulation of cognition and behavior to secure safety and survival. It is also an important feature of emotional intelligence that encompasses emotional perception, understanding, regulation, and their integration into successful social behaviors. Behavior so modulated is a type of investing in the immediate moment for later payoff. It is profitable psychological management.

Basic needs often call for immediate gratification. With further *mentalization*, here defined as the refinement of physiological needs in the context of their becoming mental faculties, the mind is better equipped to delay gratification. This occurs through new abilities to form abstract conceptual models from concrete situations and grasp alternative choices. The development of this intricate process of abstraction and imagination occurs in emergent biomental phases from infancy through older adulthood and provides a stopgap to consummating thoughts and emotions into actions.

In childhood, development of delay of gratification correlates with children's internalization of their parents' use of the terms "yes" and "no" to identify what is permitted and what is not. In general, it is best to always follow a "no'" with a "yes," since "yes" amplifies the meaning of "no" by providing a wider range of more acceptable options. This judicious use of "no" expands a child's "knowing." Such effective feedback enhances the probabilities for positive outcomes. Future behaviors, accordingly, become increasingly governed by these positive results.

Refining concrete perceptual experience into more abstract conceptual understanding inevitably stimulates anxiety and waves of confusion, ambiguity, and ambivalence because the process is so new and apparently discrepant from past experiences. The greater developments of thinking skills and concomitant emotions, however, have adaptive value. Such feelings slow, constrict, and hinder mental processes, at least temporarily. Ambivalence, for example, has a more conscious role in modulating impulse control during the elementary school years. Its significance in governing thought processes and emotional states increases through adolescence and adulthood.

This maturational and learned process develops very gradually. While it is difficult to pinpoint a specific developmental timetable for the biological and psychosocial ability to inhibit behavioral impulses, the following descriptions may serve as an outline. Some rudimentary inhibition can be seen at about twenty-four months, though a toddler's compliance is precarious and not internally consolidated. While some level of behavioral inhibition is seen in early childhood, more mature self-regulation typically arrives in young adulthood. At this time, future-oriented self-control can utilize a fuller range of memory from the past, present, and anticipated future. The substantive maturation of prefrontal cortical pathways and their interconnectivity with limbic structures makes this possible. Hence, it is crucial for parents to differentiate a child's normative irresistible impulses from those that, in fact, can developmentally be resisted. With considerations of the developmental perspective, for example, viewing behavior as willful, manipulative, and intentionally destructive may not be valid before age four.

By four years of age, some voluntary capacity to inhibit behavior begins to develop. Studies have demonstrated that four-year-olds use the least effective strategies for self-imposed delay, thus making self-control very difficult. By age five, more effective strategies (greater ability to use abstract thinking and imagination) are used, such as trying to avoid temptations and emotionally provocative thoughts about a behavioral goal told to be unacceptable.

When preschoolers are able to reasonably understand contingencies (for example, "if you wait until I tell you, you can have two pieces not just one"), waiting may span from six to seventeen minutes depending on level of impulse control. By age six, inhibitory control is sufficient to permit some level of reasonably sustained attention. This bodes for success in entry into first grade, with its more formal academic requirements. Recent research has shown that sufficiently developed inhibitory skills in attention and behavioral constraint demonstrated between ages three and five predict social maturity and greater success in reading and mathematics in elementary and high school.

Between ages nine and twelve, some children are able to use more expanded levels of abstract in place of concrete thinking, which helps them inhibit immediate gratification for longer periods of time. However, while impulsivity steadily declines from the preschool years through the elementary school years, this waning typically shows what some authoritative sources refer to as "blip" of impulsivity upward, approximately in the preteen and early adolescent period. It is unclear whether this correlates with the neuromaturational wave of synaptogenesis at puberty and subsequent pruning after puberty as mentioned in the previous section.

Of great interest are the studies that show that between ages fourteen and sixteen, adolescents show a heightened sensitivity to rewards and incentives; these both help inhibit impulses and facilitate effective choices, especially if the environment actively provides healthy incentives. This period of mid-adolescence appears unique since this heightened sensitivity declines in intensity afterwards. It is, therefore, an opportune time to address behaviors understood to be risky (for example, illicit drug, alcohol, sexualized behaviors, and antisocial activities) and to offer methods for addressing their inevitable exposure to these in school and with peers.

Substantial biomental capacity to resist temptation, to delay acting rashly, and to choose self-constructive and prosocial behaviors is typically established in early adulthood with maturation of neural connectivity in the central nervous system. Significantly, the amygdala's modulation by connections to the prefrontal cerebral cortices becomes enhanced. The prefrontal cognitive control networks achieve greater fine-tuning toward the end of the twenties attributable to both biological-maturational and learning influences.

Behavioral inhibition has many significant psychological and behavioral implications in the course of development. It is related to attention, concentration, persistence, and task completion. Studies have demonstrated that individual differences in impulse control and temperament, as they relate to behavioral inhibition, persist into adulthood.

The influence of the environment, particularly parental guidance in helping children constrain impulses and behaviors, is decisively important in the development of this biomental asset. An important example of such continuing guidance would be parents' labeling of transitions using the template: "We have to start to stop . . ." This narration serves several functions. It alerts a child to expect a change, reinforces a child's inhibitory mechanisms, and implicitly supports the child's self-containment.

Teaching and providing children with examples of such "pause" is essential to both good parenting and children's personality development. Pause, impulse control, and thought before action are crucial personal and social skills that require continuous reinforcement and refinement.

An important aspect of environmental aids fostering self-regulation and impulse control is recognizing that infants and toddlers may become easily overwhelmed by overstimulation. Both parents, especially fathers, should recognize this possibility for sound, media, and even playful interactions being too intense. Watching children's responses and helping them constrain overactivation helps them to internalize the experience of self-modulation.

5.3 Reasoned Volition versus Avolition and Malignant Inhibition

Reasoned volition denotes competent performance of tasks considered worthwhile to be accomplished. It develops slowly from infancy through adulthood and is the bridge between desire and action. When development is healthy, self-regulation, self-containment, and effortful control—components of reasoned volition—supersede indiscriminate impulsivity.

Some children, however, may be temperamentally avoidant or have dys-regulated impulse control systems. Inhibitory and avoidant impulses may dominate thinking and feeling, and these urges may contribute to slowed implementation of ideas. Put differently, passivity, helplessness, anxiety, or fear may stall and even disable volition. Inaction may express itself at any age as lethargy or seemingly interminable procrastination. By adulthood, avolitional states may become malignantly inhibiting, causing an inability to complete tasks or pursue normative life goals such as occupational advancement.

While there are wide ranges of adequate performance at all ages, significant avolitional states may be apparent by middle childhood. When lack of volition impairs academic, interpersonal, or social competencies, professional assessment is indicated. Such evaluation attempts to distinguish baseline temperamental and personality styles from the possible presence of psychological health challenges in intelligence or emotional stability.

5.4 Language and Cognition

At about twenty-four to thirty-six months, a language explosion occurs when 200 to 450 words can be used. Many inanimate and animate objects are correctly labeled. Pronouns such as *I*, *me*, and *you* are used. *Parallel play* begins in the company of peers and other people. Children can be seen imitating the behavior of others, such as siblings and caregivers. Socialization and learning the form of conversations begin at this time and should be supported. At thirty months, the young child can refer to self by pronoun (for example, "I want . . .") rather than only by name ("John wants . . .").

Speech and language development are decisive in affording the older infant the ability to signal closeness to loved caregivers. These skills also allow one to find new animate and inanimate objects, thus broadening the interactional environment. Speech and language thus parallel the development of crawling, standing, and walking in affording such opportunities. Some children speak later, perhaps well after eighteen months, because of hearing loss, cognitive impairment, speech disorder, language disorder, autistic spectrum disorders, or other considerations. Pediatricians and hearing specialists should be consulted for proper assessments.

A major cognitive shift occurs as the two-year-old, who was relying on empirical or experience-based events (*sensorimotor period*) for the past two years, begins to use preoperational thinking. Before eighteen to twenty-four months, thinking had used an indicative mode such as "a equals b." Concrete perceptions were experienced as if they were literal objects. The explicit rather than nuanced features of objects remained cognitively prominent for the toddler. By contrast, in the *preoperational period* from about two to seven years, the child achieves the *semiotic function*—the ability to mentally represent a signified external object or event by means of a corresponding internal signifier. This new ability is reflected in symbolic play, drawing, and imitating and verbalizing events that have occurred in the past.

This gradually maturing process of symbolization is reflected in a child's understanding of and ability to ask questions. This correlates with the ability to conceptualize ideas and relationships. Between ages two and three, a child is able to understand simple "who," "what," and "where" questions and answers. Between ages three and four, a child understands simple "how" and "why" constructs. Between ages four and five, simple "when" questions are also understood. Thereafter, most questions can be understood if they are not too complex.

Between ages six and eleven, the cognitive stage of *concrete operations* permits even more cognitive flexibility. Hence, in the elementary school years of middle childhood, thinking has the capacities for *conservation* (the understanding that certain physical properties of objects remain the same despite changes in their outward appearance), *classification* (grouping similar items into single categories), and *seriation* (manually ordering items along a quantitative dimension by using one of their similar features). Children at this age also develop *transitive inference* (seriation performed mentally, particularly using three relationships simultaneously in the absence of physically manipulating items) and *spatial reasoning* (forming cognitive maps or mental representations of large scale geographical spaces).

By eleven years old, hypothetical representations emerge during the stage of *formal cognitive operations*. A beginning capacity for critical thinking and realistic causality begins to mature. Such thinking consists of propositions such as, "A causes B. If A occurs, then B or C or D might follow." In contrast to the previous stage of concrete operations, children can now hypothesize the differing effect of four different variables by considering one while holding the other three constant. This skill enables the early adolescent to project into the future ("what might be") and deduce from the past ("what has been"). All of these mental operations can occur in the absence of strictly perceptual evidence and thus makeup *propositional thought*.

The mental capacity to consider the future has great bearing on the development of greater impulse control, choice, and decision making. It reflects a subjunctive and contingent quality of thinking wherein "if-then" thoughts become substantively possible. Significant states of mind that include competing ideas, confusion, ambiguity, and ambivalence are both nonconsciously and consciously at work in all mental processes. Thinking becomes more abstract and capable of hitherto unavailable theoretical possibilities. Impulse control helps direct and redirect thought processes by using pauses and detours. This ability for *qualitative reality testing* is such a fundamental human capacity for adaptation that it develops gradually by maturation and intentional self-training over the course of a lifetime.

5.4.1 A Note on Answering Children's Questions

This note briefly lays out general guidelines for answering children's questions. An attitude of *addressing* questions rather than merely answering them is optimal. It offers greater mental space for open-ended and productive approaches toward facilitating constructive dialogue. Often, questions contain answers that are hidden or undeveloped. Addressing questions is akin to putting out feelers into children's unconscious processes—probes to explore underlying concerns. Questions, in fact, reflect a "quest" for both knowledge on an apparent level and open-ended understanding on a deeper level—the *epistemophilia within the self.*

　　This note addresses techniques for use across the span of childhood but is placed here because of the toddler's developing cognitive abilities that allow him or her to ask a range of questions. For any question, responses need to be tailored to chronological and developmental age as well as to specific context. Preschoolers require simple, brief answers, elementary school children can understand more complexity, and adolescents are able to comprehend more abstract explanations. As will be discussed, responding to adolescents requires tact, sensitivity, and brevity. In many ways, adolescents labor under "restrictive misunderstandings" of the intentions of others, often expecting negative criticism and reacting with dysphoric anxiety. While the use of humor is effective when speaking with younger children, it should be sparingly used with adolescents since their oversensitivity may misperceive it as being critical or condescending.

　　Responses to questions reflect the articulated narrative of transactional sensitivity. Neither questions nor answers should be "quick." Rather, parental responses are most effective when thoughtful and judicious. Answers encompass responses that address both direct and indirect children's concerns. Answering questions is best viewed as a "dialogue in progress." Relatively brief and frugal responses in the immediate moment set the stage for continuing dialogue.

　　The five phases of relevant responses are the following. First, one sets an atmosphere suitable to the situation. This includes the material environment, choice and tone of words, emotional rapport, and the cognitive framework.

Second, one draws attention to and clarifies core elements of questions and parental answers. Third, one answers explicit queries and also articulates inferred emotional concerns and motivating issues. Fourth, one pays careful attention to children's nonverbal and verbal responses and reconfigures responses accordingly. Fifth, one sets the stage for future exploration by leaving some matters open-ended and by suggesting additional possibilities to be considered. This last approach may take the form of addressing questions with the phrase "Let me think about this for a while before we talk about it again." Such approaches demonstrate to children both respect and the expression of "pause" as a useful way to respond and behave.

5.5 The Terrible Twos

Children begin to more fully enjoy their newfound personhood, manifested in the use of the pronoun *I* at age two and a half. This toddler period, roughly spanning *twelve-month-olds to thirty-six-month-olds*, is one in which routines and expectability is essential. These features reinforce the establishment of a more constant sense of self-identity by consistent parental interactions, regimens, and routines. Personhood shows up, for example, in the toddler's emerging food preferences and anticipation of family routines such as around meals and bedtime. Reading to toddlers at bedtime is a routine with multiple benefits, some of which include allaying the normative separation anxieties common at this developmental period. Parents do best when they do not introduce a great deal of variation in routine at this time.

Toddlers are beginning to independently walk and explore their surroundings. Excitement and enthusiasm often drive this impulse for locomotion, at times in a frenetic fashion. Strivings to gain more control of bodily functions—walking, grasping, holding, and even bowel and urine functions—may appear as oppositional and defiant challenges to parental directions aimed at safety and more constrained behaviors.

During the period of approximately twelve to thirty-six months, both male and female toddlers become seemingly more rebellious and defiant. This period has been called "the terrible twos." Children at this developmental juncture appear to be willful, impetuous, and oppositional. This is a natural part of development. This apparent "negativity" and "contrariness" is energized by new developmental abilities, curiosity, and the pleasure of putting them into action. Refraining from viewing such behavior as driven by conscious intention is a realistic adult perspective since the toddler is filled with irresistible, natural impulses, and a "bounded rationality" that is normal during this time. Sensitive removal from distressing situations and redirection are helpful strategies when these situations arise. In addition, when toddlers refuse to comply with a request, asking them to help you accomplish the designated task is a strategy that marshals greater compliance.

Cross-cultural research confirms that by about seventeen months, males are more physically aggressive than females. This sex difference correlates with male sex hormones and temperamental proclivities, such as higher activity level, irritability, and greater impulsivity. When gender role conventions become more explicit in the preschool years, social expectations and learning reinforce male aggression.

Many parents find this time of toddlerhood particularly stressful. Fathers often see that their involvement with children has been and will continue to be different from mothers'. Rather than interpret this difference in attitude and behavior as problematic, it is beneficial for both parents to value father's typical use of fewer words, style of less intervention, degree of unpredictability, and tendency to entertain as useful complements to mother's approach.

At this time, emotions surge and tantrums are frequent, particularly when needs are frustrated. Negativism is frequent as is the child's use of "no." Aggression, especially in the form of biting, is common, as children cannot yet adequately put feelings and wants into words. Redirecting the child, setting limits, and demonstrating physical and psychological boundaries are very important. As such, parents need to "baby-proof" their homes for safety. Parents must use their own "no's" when significant danger is actually a potential. Children intently watch their parents' facial expressions, which are powerful sources of communications. Gestures, such as a finger gently waving "no," also helps redirect behaviors.

5.6 Weaning

Infants receive nourishment through breastfeeding and through bottle-feeding. Nursing and the bottle promote the material, emotional, and psychological sustenance that fosters the intimacy of love, sharing, and understanding between infant and mother. *Weaning* is a broad term that encompasses the gradual process of guiding the infant to change its feeding patterns. Weaning may also be understood to encompass shifts from the use of pacifiers and transitions from crib to beds. The suggestions outlined here are taken from the everyday experience of real mothers, developmental specialists, and lactation consultants. Specific strategies and timeframes are approximate and should be regarded as flexible depending on individual infant, mother, and differing life contexts.

Weaning reduces the time spent sucking on the breast or bottle, introduces more solid foods, and eventually stops feeds from the breast and bottle completely. The completion of weaning typically means that a child is eating solid foods and drinking from some type of cup. The time frame for weaning encompasses a potential range. The start of the weaning process may occur as early as the middle of the first year (around six months), and the completion of weaning may be as late as thirty-six months, if necessary. The AAP, however, recommends beginning the weaning transition at about nine months and removing bottle by twelve months and definitely by eighteen months. Flexibility in timing based on individual circumstances cannot be overemphasized.

During the child's second year, weaning from breast and bottle exclusively toward more solid foods and liquids is best accomplished gradually and sensitively. Lactation experts emphasize the importance of adequate personal preparation and the inevitability of unforeseen "bumps in the road." These consultants emphasize the benefits of going slowly with the weaning process to minimize the possibility of breast engorgement, which can be distressing. Parents should always ask their children's doctors for guidance about this and other childhood processes.

The infant's attitude toward food is intimately connected with its attitude and relation toward mother; therefore, how weaning is undertaken has profound effects on both child and mother. One needs to remember that mother's actual body was the first source of food for baby in the womb. After birth, breastfeeding or the giving of formula by mother (or father) is associated with biomental containment that includes survival, safety, comfort, satiation, holding, touch, and affection. At the time of weaning, all of these intimate associations are highlighted and subject to renegotiation. It is beneficial, therefore, when these transitions are made as pleasant as possible.

Most authorities recommend breastfeeding exclusively for about the first six months. Feedings may range from about every two to three hours and are optimal when in an atmosphere of calm for both baby and mother. At about six months, solid foods may be introduced and the feeding interval slightly increased. Breast milk is digested more quickly than formula, and infants may be come hungry sooner when nursing on the breast alone. Most babies do not need a middle-of-the-night feeding at between four and six months and may be capable of putting themselves back to sleep.

5.6.1 Feeding Practices and Food

Human milk does not contain sufficient vitamin D. The AAP recommends vitamin D supplementation in a combination multivitamin each day for breastfed babies until they are weaned to at least thirty-two ounces of vitamin D-fortified formula and for all non-breastfed infants who consume less than thirty-two ounces per day of vitamin D-fortified formula. For the first four to six months, breastfed babies need no additional iron. The Academy recommends that babies who do not breastfeed or partially breastfeed should receive an iron-fortified formula from birth through twelve months of age.

Recent studies over a seven-year period clearly demonstrate that cognitive functioning may be significantly enhanced when infants are breastfed. These results support World Health Organization (WHO) expert recommendations on exclusive breastfeeding for six months. In addition, it appears that even shorter durations of exclusive breastfeeding in early infancy can have lasting beneficial effects on the cognitive development of children.

The three basic types of FDA-approved infant formulas are (1) cow's milk-based formula (though not plain cow's milk, which is unsuitable because of its high casein and low whey content), (2) soy-based formula, and (3) protein hydrolysate formula (which is hypoallergenic). Since breast milk is best, infant formulas try to simulate it as much as possible. Formulas are chosen based on the infant's medical needs and parents' preferences, such as an allergy to cow's milk or a vegetarian diet.

Many parents have concerns about the presence of pesticides, herbicides, and genetically modified organisms (GMO) in milk and food products. A GMO is the result of a laboratory process in which genes from the cell DNA of one species are extracted and artificially forced into the genes of an unrelated plant or animal. The foreign genes may come from bacteria, viruses, insects, animals or even humans. Because this involves the transfer of genes, GMOs are also known as "transgenic" organisms. This process may be called either genetic engineering (GE) or genetic modification (GM); they are one and the same. Industry's stated purpose is to enhance flavor and food production, but advocates of "organic" food production seriously question both such motives and also negative health-related and ecologically sustainable outcomes. As natural foods retailers addressed the issue of genetically engineered bovine growth hormone (rbGH or rbST) in dairy products, they raised concerns associated with rbGH. At the same time, they made certain that rbGH-free brands were readily available in their stores. "Organic Milk" is an example of this. Open-minded examination of the scientific and anecdotal literature provides perspectives on these concerns about "synthetic biology" and can be found on websites such as www.biodynamics.com.

5.6.2 Weaning toward Solid Foods

In regard to other aspects of bottle-feeding, mixing the appropriate ration of formula and water is important for proper nutrition and weight. In addition, room-temperature bottles or bottles warmed in a bottle warmer or under the tap are usually safe. One should not use a microwave, as it might create hot spots that can burn baby's mouth. Infant formula is recommended until twelve months of age followed by whole milk until age two, when reduced-fat milk may be an option.

Some mothers comment that using bottles and infant formulas permits fathers to have a more active role in feeding and caring for the infant. In addition, this frees mother for leisure or other responsibilities, such as employment, personal time, or household tasks. There is also the possibility of fathers feeling "left out" since breastfeeding is so intimate and absorbing. Mothers can be cognizant of this and help fathers devise ways of sharing in this aspect of infant care.

At about six months or shortly thereafter, some advise introducing bottle feeds with intermittent breast feeds if breastfeeding is primary. Replacing one breast feed with a bottle or sippy cup approximately every seven days may initiate the weaning process. Infants typically are receptive to this transition between seven and nine months.

There is a question of whether the use of a pacifier as a comforting agent is beneficial. Informed opinions vary. Some think that a pacifier may act as a substitute for human interaction. Pacifier use, however, is fairly common, especially since the infant's need to suck is at its height between two and four months. Licking behaviors, however, persist throughout infancy and into childhood. The use of a pacifier in the crib is preferred to a bottle since putting a baby to bed with formula or juice can lead to dental decay and ear infections.

At about six to eight months, cereals with iron, fruits, and vegetables may be added in addition to three to five nursings or twenty-four to thirty-two ounces of formula from a bottle per day. At about this time, the first set of teeth begins to emerge. Some parents introduce solids later in the day when milk supply from nursing is lower.

Introducing a sippy cup between about six and nine months with formula—and not just water or diluted fruit juice—is recommended by the AAP. A baby becomes capable of using a sippy cup when he or she is able to sit unassisted, hold the head up, and open the mouth for spoon feeding.

At about eight to eleven months, adding soft meats and finger foods, such as avocado, tofu, and cooked zucchini, is suggested in addition to continuing three to five nursings or twenty-four to thirty-two ounces of formula from the bottle each day.

At about twelve to twenty-four months, exchanging bottle formula for about two cups of whole cow's milk per day is suggested. Using low fat milk at and after two years old is suggested by the AAP. Up to 3 percent of children may have an allergy to cow's milk. This is a serious allergy to the protein in milk and requires medical diagnosis and nutritional management. Milk protein allergy is different from the milder lactose intolerance. Of note, some Eastern traditions regularly suggest that all cow's milk be gently boiled, sometimes with a very small amount of ginger or turmeric, to decrease its potentially negative effects and increase assimilability. This, however, remains anecdotal although some recent studies show that cooked milk products have been used with success in the management of milk allergies.

If still nursing at twelve months, however, it is recommended that solid foods make up a baby's main source of nutrition. Solids, for example, may include toasted bread, egg, sliced grapes, some banana, noodles, ground beef, and chopped vegetables. All solids should be in very small pieces. Raw foods and vegetables cannot easily dissolve or be chewed and are not recommended. Advice from pediatricians and other expert sources should be sought.

5.6.3 Inanimate Transitional Objects

Some have suggested introducing a stuffed animal, doll, or soft blanket between twelve to eighteen months. These items are sometimes referred to as "loveys." Some babies have already attached to such a comfort object between eight and twelve months. These *transitional objects* help children feel more at ease with their emotional transition from dependence toward greater independence. These security objects are effective because they have idiosyncratic familiarity and meaning.

Such a comfort item is accepted by about 60 percent of babies and suggests normally developing social development. However, not having a comfort object does not necessarily indicate abnormal development. Preferred "attachment objects" are typically soft and very specific. They are not interchangeable and must be, for example, a specific stuffed dog and not just any dog. These usually stay with children until the elementary school years, but that is very flexible. Typically developing infants do not attach to hard or generic objects, such as trains, robots, or rocket ships.

5.6.4 Weaning from Bottles and Pacifiers

Weaning from the bottle may also be tried between twelve and fifteen months when a baby can drink well from a sippy cup with handles. Parents may eliminate one bottle at a time, the first of which should be the mid-day bottle. Keeping the first and last bottle of the day may be best. When a baby is able to drink whole milk after twelve months, mothers must use flexible judgment about eliminating the first and last bottles. After eighteen months, it becomes more difficult to first start weaning from the bottle to which baby has been uninterruptedly accustomed.

Weaning from pacifiers, if they have been used, can begin between eight and twelve months. It may help to replace the pacifier or "binky" with a blanket or stuffed toy. Parents should try to limit pacifier use to nighttime use only by age one and stop use altogether by age two. Later weaning may lead to problems with developing speech, dentition, and ear infections. If the pacifier is still used past two years (though not generally recommended), it is best to withdraw the pacifier gradually. As the child has become accustomed to its presence, abrupt withdrawal would seem harsh and would probably be opposed.

Taking the lead from an infant's preferences provides optimal information to guide the weaning process. Although there are no firm rules, most developmental experts think that weaning should occur slowly over the course of about a year and be completed by about age three, if not earlier.

Thumb and finger sucking should stop by the end of early childhood before the elementary school years.

5.6.5 Weaning from the Crib

Another important transition involves moving the child from a crib to a bed. The exact timing for this is flexible and depends on several factors. Some of these include when the child is able to climb out of the crib, when parents decide to make this change, and family circumstances, such as the birth of a new baby.

The age at which a child can climb out of the crib may ranges from approximately ten to twenty-six months. Typically, the transition from crib to toddler bed or twin bed is made between eighteen and forty-two months, when a child is around thirty-five inches tall. Many parents finish this transition between thirty and thirty-six months. It may be beneficial for this change to occur about two months before or after the birth of a new baby so that potential difficulties involving overstimulating environments are minimized. Parents find that making this transition is easiest when it is does not occur around toilet training, which typically begins between twenty-four and thirty-six months. Weaning should not occur at the same time as other significant life changes such as moving homes, starting daycare, or even learning to walk, if possible. Waiting about two or three months between significant developmental events facilitates smoother transitions.

Using logic, instinct, and adaptable flexibility to orchestrate transitions is best since they involve many variables and can be difficult. Sensitivity to a child's inner and emotional experience of a transition such as weaning requires short-term, active interventions. These strategies are especially useful at bedtime, when a child exquisitely senses the transition of separation from family, and include reading stories, singing, use of a nightlight, and so forth. Participating in these activities is an opportunity for fathers to share in significant caregiving.

5.7 The Crucial Biomental Significance of Weaning

Weaning is a major biomental process and a significant developmental event. For the infant, weaning is the separation or split of lips from nipple and breast. It is the primary observable process in which appearance and disappearance of nipple, breast, and/or bottle correlate with the repetitive cycles of gaining and losing—the biomental experiences of grasping and releasing, holding on and letting go. This series pertains to material items as well as to their underlying emotional perspectives. If on some primitive level, the infant senses that the splitting of lips from nipple is felt as a wound—a "narcissistic wound" in psychoanalytic terminology—the experience may be traumatic, if not managed with the transactional sensitivity and care required. Being able to let go, transition, and move on without spoiling, souring, damaging, or devaluing these events and experiences correlates with mental and emotional health.

Biomental child development cannot overemphasize the positive correlation—almost to the point of identity—of the infant's sense of food with mother. This is a prototypical illustration what *biomental* denotes. In other words, the infant's emotional apprehension of the salience, significance, and meaning of food is virtually identical to the infant's relation to its mother. This is true for the newborn and early infant. This virtually literal identification only gradually becomes less merged around eighteen months, when thinking becomes relatively more abstract and less bound to concrete tangibles. The way weaning is managed on a material level correlates with the infant's internal emotional experience of its relation to its typical primary caregiver, mother. Sensitively weaning an infant through the nuances of this transition will support the way the infant experiences a positive emotional affiliation with mother.

Thus, weaning a child sensitively gives enormous support to the development of its capacity to permit and accept substitutions throughout life. In other words, a good and trusting relation to mother and feeding (between zero and six months) can become a good relation to bottle and solid foods (from six to twenty-four months), and then to solid foods and liquids without a bottle (from three years on).

Patterning of gain and loss, feelings of frustration, deprivation, confusion, upset, love, hate, ambivalence, and depressive feelings of loss are first shaped through these processes. Mental prototypes are created for managing life's later changes and transitions.

Weaning ordinarily connotes moving away from the breast or bottle. In fact, *weaning* also means approaching something new. The medical term *taper* has the same dual connotations. The child's outward adaptation to these transitions gives a broad indication of his or her ability to hold on, let go, and accept new situations. Sensitive parents remain keen to the nonconscious elements of their children's adjustment in order to support total material and emotional development.

The infant's basic capacity to experience and modulate frustration is exercised in weaning. Guiding the infant through the process of these gaps in satisfaction is a real-time demonstration of showing how to "let go" or transition. Sensitive parents try to guide the infant through this repetitive process in a graceful and nontraumatic way. Infants learn the life skill of emotional self-management in the process of moving on and going forward.

The role of father becomes highly significant during weaning and there-after. When the infant is ready to *partially* turn away from mother and all that has been intimately associated with her nurturing transactions, father presents as an "almost ideal" other. It may be true that some fathers struggle with taking a back seat in early infancy. This may involve reasons of person-al confidence, motivation, mother acting as gatekeeper, and so forth. Both parents need to recognize this mother-father dynamic if it occurs and nego-tiate more explicitly what they both consider reasonable for each parent and the child. If father's availability is physical, emotional, and cognitive, he can offer the infant a chance to experience and explore a relatively new person in contrast to the previous relative exclusivity of being with mother. Father can provide new experiences and complement mother's continuing ministrations.

5.8 Toilet Training

What psychodynamic psychology terms the *anal phase* spans twenty-four to about forty-eight months. This is a time when matters involving control, orderliness, and cleanliness are foremost, and toilet training occurs during this time. Since there is a strong biological and neuromaturational underlay to toilet training, it is best to be keenly aware of when a child's body appears ready. Rather than imposing a predetermined intervention, a child's readiness must guide the process. Parents, of course, provide regulation and support. Like weaning from the bottle or breast, toilet training should be gradual with wide and flexible parameters.

The AAP states that most children who start toilet training around age two are completely trained before their third birthday. Most toilet training occurs from two and a half to four years of age. Most children are dry from urine during the day between two and a half and three, and they are dry at night by age four. Studies show that some bedwetting remains until about age six: 40 percent wet at age three, 30 percent at age four, 20 percent at age five, and 10 percent at age six. Bowel training and hygiene occur in stages. While three- and four-year-olds need extra help in cleaning themselves, by age five children have the manual dexterity for adequate hygiene after bowel move-ments.

6. A NOTE ON NORMATIVE DEVELOPMENTAL VACILLATIONS: EQUILIBRIUMS AND DISEQUILIBRIUMS

The pioneering work of distinguished child psychologist and pediatrician Arnold Gesell (1880–1961) demonstrated the developmental perspective in great detail. He highlighted developmental sequences and the normative vac-illations expressed in the early years of childhood. As noted throughout this text, child development may be relatively continuous, but is not absolutely smooth, linear, uninterrupted, or consistent. The development of progressive abilities, skills, and their accompanying moods has organic roots whose blossoms reflect the innumerable contributions of the environment.

Gesell and his adherents have suggested typical trends in growth sequences and the structuralization of behavior. Equilibriums and disequilibriums of all transitions are noticeable. Stability vacillating with instability is typical. It is normal for caregivers to perceive some undesirable behaviors in the broader context of the forward trend of normal development.

A general and very brief overview follows. From birth to eighteen months, development reflects a typical and relatively consistent pattern of physical, emotional, and cognitive growth, maturation, and development. The two-year-old appears as a relatively stable person who is launching the ability to walk and engage in meaningful language. At two and a half years, there is a perceptible disequilibrium characterized by an almost reflexive oppositional-defiant set of behaviors that are expectable and normal, not pathological. Before age three, however, children are explorers and not purposefully manipulative or retaliatory. *Frustration and overly eager attitudes, however, may appear rebellious.* Making use of distraction, a child's capacity for humor, and some spontaneous "silliness" helps to modulate behavior.

By age three, these seemingly oppositional attitudes mitigate themselves and a calmer equilibrium may become more apparent. By age three and a half, disequilibrium appears in the form of demanding attitudes. At this time, parents are able to identify a child's temperament and personality styles. Understanding this trajectory helps plan for more suitable and successful child management strategies.

By age four, demands settle down. Children are typically seen as exuberant, wonderful, and sure of themselves. This "love affair with the world" demeanor is peppered with many questions—"Whys?"—and a heightened concern with matters related to elimination, such as fascination with bathroom "poo-poo" and "pee-pee." By age four and a half, this constellation of smooth enthusiasm fades and a return to appearing disconcerted, at times "sassy," emerges more often.

By five years old, children regain a more stable equilibrium. They seem calm, serene, optimistic, positive, and self-limiting. Affection to mother is positive, and behavior is often described as "delightful" and "good." Ages five and a half to six show a return to the disequilibrium of ambivalence, extremes, wanting to be more independent, appearing brash, and at times explosive. By age six and a half, equilibrium is again achieved, and behavior and cooperativeness even out. In general, those six and a half, eight, and ten years old seem stable. The eight-year-old is expansive, speedy, and evaluative; the ten-year-old is calm, collected, and appreciative. By contrast, those seven, nine, and eleven years of age show signs of disequilibrium in various ways.

The aforementioned description is painted with a broad brush and subject to variation and nuance. It nonetheless suggests that development is a dynamic process in which progression and regression, stability and instability, and normative shifts in mood and interpersonal cooperativeness are typical and to be expected. These considerations provide a broad perspective describing the ebb and flow of development in children, notably expectable eras of instability. Whereas childhood disorders might occur, caregivers must be vigilant not to label what may be a transitory disequilibrium and so formalize it into a diagnosis requiring medication.

7. PRESCHOOL YEARS: AGES THREE, FOUR, AND FIVE

7.1 Overview

The preschool years, ages three, four, and five, are a wonderful time for children. They are able to begin using burgeoning symbolic and abstract thinking, more effective language, as well as move around, explore, and experience the world—a wonderland of new adventures. At these ages, a sense of purpose is beginning to develop. Testing limits and experiencing consequences, to a large extent, drive learning. Within reason, testing limits is developmentally normal and helps children incrementally yet steadily refine impulse control.

A brief discussion of the preschool child's cognitive development is useful here. In the first two years, the infant's intellectual capacities are almost exclusively centered in the sensory and motor strategies used to know the world. Piaget proposed a cognitive framework that includes the following structures and processes beginning in infancy and progressing in complexity with age. Schemas ("mental models") are infant's and children's ways of relating to the world; experiences introduces similar though different examples of existing schemas and these are internalized; accommodation introduces experiences that existing schemas cannot acquire so that the existing schema is changed or a new schema is constructed. Upon this scaffolding, knowledge is built.

In the first two years, the infant's intellectual capacities are almost exclusively centered in the sensory and motor strategies used to know the world. Learning occurs through the silent witnessing of the infant, and the incipient mobility of the toddler. In the context of an emotional and intimately psychological engagement with caregivers, knowledge is gained and processed using these substantial but still unmature sensorimotor cognitive pathways. Parents' active engagement elicits children's dynamic participation and enhances all learning.

Outlines of traditional Piagetian cognitive development sequences are as follows. While the sequential progression is understood to be relatively invariant, the age parameters may vary. It must be reiterated that the seminal work of Piaget is being significantly refined by modern cognitive science techniques and findings.

During the period from ages two to seven years, mental development changes in significant ways. Important features of this *preoperational period* include the emergence of symbolic activity, capacity for make-believe, imaginative play, egocentrism, and magical, prelogical, animistic thinking. The preschool period has been described as "the magic years" since it is dominated by fantasy and vivid imagination.

Symbolic thinking denotes the child's ability to distinguish between actual objects in the environment and the labels or words used to represent them. Concepts denote mental representations that are becoming more substantively organized. While concept formation and symbolization are assumed to establish themselves at about eighteen months in the Piagetian system, recent research has introduced a refinement that describes primitive conceptualization in early infancy and traces its organization in great detail from that time through apparent stages: newborn to six months, seven months to eleven months, and the landmark point of basic-level concept formation at eighteen months.

Concepts as interpretations of objects, relationships, and events are the elements of conscious thinking and information processing. Memory, imagination, and problem-solving skills are becoming established. Particular concrete items are mentally connected even though they may have no intrinsic cause and effect relation. Children of this age (two to seven years old), for example, now more fully understand the denotation and connotation of the number *two*. This awareness of dualities has a polar quality in which reconciliation or synthesis is not necessarily possible. This "black-and-white thinking" requires years before integration, synthesis, and feeling comfortable with ambiguities becomes possible to varying degrees, if at all, during adulthood. It is the basis for later regressive, polarized absolutistic perceptions.

Egocentrism at this age denotes the child's inability to adequately take the perspective of another; he or she sees and understands things only from his or her own point of view. In *magical thinking*, the child believes that he or she can significantly influence objects in the environment, such as the idea that crying causes the rain outside. *Animism* denotes that the environment is sensed as being alive and sentient, rather than being relatively inert. Egocentrism, magical thinking, and animism are major cognitive limitations at this age. They typically result in the child's believing that what happens in the surrounding world is the result of something that he or she has done. As will be discussed in chapter 6 with regard to unconscious omnipotence, primitive thought inimical to reality typically lies just below the surface of mental operations at every age. Magical thinking is a well-accepted, empirically observable phenomenon that is an age-appropriate, transient manifestation of such omnipotent though processes. These are the beginning stages of cognitive maturation similar to the typical developmental motor sequences such as learning to crawl, then walk, then run well that are undergone during their designated timeframes. Cognitive development, the capacity to understand and remember, and intelligence are still forming. Understanding the developmental nature of cognition helps in more fully appreciating the child's operation in the world, including his or her capabilities at a particular point in time.

Preschool children are notably receptive to and nurtured by experiential and sensory faculties—vision, hearing, touch, smell, and taste. The preschool years are the years of learning by example, by imitation, and through movement. Intelligence is more centered in the body and limbs than in the more mental and abstract cognitive faculties. Thus, learning may be best suited to "hands-on" rather than directly instructional or didactic techniques. Moving the body helps children understand words and concepts that are new. For example, if "airplanes" are discussed, the child may spread her arms and simulate flying.

Children "pick up" the sounds, gestures, and attitudes communicated by adults. Exposing children to nature and encouraging observation of the natural world—plant and animal life, as well as geographical formations—strengthens perception and discrimination of types, categories, forms, and qualities of objects. An individual's intimate connection to the natural world needs to be recognized and fostered. Having living plants in the home, for example, provides children with a continuing opportunity to see and even learn to care for these representatives of the natural world. Having pets also presents opportunities to demonstrate caring and a reverence for life.

For these preschool children, interest centers on the objects they can perceive. They are more interested in the color, size, texture, smell, and so forth of a ball than with what they can do with it. Their eyes often reveal an enchantment with the emotional salience and cognitive fascination that an item elicits. From six years old on, interest recenters itself on what can be done with an object and how it can be handled and used, that is, its functionality.

Preschool children are eager to join parents in mutually enacted tasks such as housework, trips to the grocery store, hiking, gardening, and so forth. They especially enjoy repetition since activities and events are still novel and exciting. Jobs and activities adapted to the changing seasons are particularly stimulating and reinforcing. For example, gardening offers children a vivid range of perceptual experiences: the feel of the soil, the smell of the out-doors, the colors of nature, and the varied sounds of the natural world. Even the experience of getting hands and clothes dirty may be fun and enjoyable. Of course, parents need to be aware of children's possible allergies and take reasonable precautions.

While parents remain a child's prime exemplar, older siblings also signif-icantly influence behavior in many ways. Attention to this and possible cor-rective redirection of older siblings can support family development.

7.1.1 Saying "Yes": The Roots of Cooperation and Agreeableness

Typically, between three and four years, children begin to say "Yes" in a cooperative way. An emphasis on developing oral language skills stimulates both cognitive infrastructure and attentive listening skills. During this and other periods of childhood, learning is facilitated when activity precedes understanding. Doing should come before lengthy verbal description and explanation. Helping children modulate their natural inquisitiveness and en-thusiasm tactfully ahead of or during an activity supports their need to under-stand what is required to do the job at hand. Put differently, a brief verbal "heads up" can precede an activity; once the activity is underway, a more elaborate narration can occur.

Although developing social competence begins in the reciprocal interac-tions of infancy, the preschool years are a time for children to further develop social competence in both understanding a personal need to be helped (pas-sive sense of interpersonal need) and also the need to help others (active wish to help others). Saying "yes" reflects developing emotional and social skill know-how in becoming agreeable and learning cooperation.

7.2 Social Development

Social competence is the social, emotional, and cognitive composite of understanding, skills, and behaviors needed for successful social adaptation. This denotes skill in interpersonal relationships. It presumes an underlying capacity for *social intelligence*, which is the ability to understand the emo-tions, communicative cues, intentions, and expectations of others. Although a great deal of social intelligence may be innate and operate nonconsciously, much can be taught and learned. Basic genetic endowments reflected in the neuroanatomy and functional abilities of central nervous system and sensory faculties are already present at birth. These are the infrastructure through which experiences and learning influence emotional and social intelligence. Social intelligence differs among individuals and, to some extent, may be understood to be a unique and signature-like feature.

Adequate social skills, discussed in a later section, provide children with peer relationships that expose them to various forms of negotiation and the mutual benefits of cooperation. Parents can also facilitate this process. When reading a story to a child who seems to be losing attention, for example, it is best to stop and say, "We will do half the job now, and the other half at another time later." This method models sensitivity and adaptation to situations.

Social effectiveness denotes successful social intelligence, skills, and competence. To a large extent, this is the ground for a child to develop good friendships, to be liked, and to avoid fostering negative treatment, rejection, victimization, bullying, and the inclination for dehumanization of others.

Social organization of gender awareness and identity, moreover, take hold at about thirty-six months and further consolidate over the preschool years. Curiosity about differences, especially between boys and girls, men and women, peaks at this time. Gender identity is becoming established as a child comes to sense his- or herself as being either male or female, as will be discussed further on in this chapter.

7.3 Emotional Development

Socialization and emotional development occur simultaneously and reinforce one another. Individual traits, temperament, and personality also contribute to and are shaped by these processes. Although emotions are present from the start of life, these nonconscious biomental sensations become orchestrated over time into more developed forms. Gradually, they become recognized as the more conscious experiences commonly called "feelings." *Feelings* are the consciously experienced aspects of nonconscious emotions.

There are some typical, basic emotions, such as happiness, sadness, fear, anger, disgust, contempt, and surprise. These become amalgamated with one another and with nuanced thought. Hence, these culturally invariant universals become felt in innumerable ways. Put differently, the basic emotions can be understood to be *primary emotions* that stand for families of related inner sensations.

Emotions, moreover, are brief, subjective experiential states that have strong biomental dimensions. When an internal trigger or interpersonal response elicits emotion, it resounds in the physical body and finally becomes experienced in the mind as a feeling that can be described. Emotions are often amalgamated, although one emotion may predominate and become the label for a leading mood or longer-term feeling state at a given time.

As discussed in chapter 2, *traits* are genetically endowed attitudinal features of a person and are reflected in approach-withdrawal responses and activity and reactivity levels. Traits are internal, broad-based dispositions. *Temperament*, by comparison, is a disposition to act in a specific way. Typically, temperament involves a basic cooperativeness or resistance to comply that is elicited interpersonally. *Personality*, on the other hand, is the overall way one's traits and temperament are experienced and used to interact with the environment of parents, culture, and learning opportunities so that these shape how a person sees the self and interacts with others. Emotions are subcomponents of traits, temperament, and personality. All the aforementioned are ingredients in the attachment patterns between people.

In many ways, *envy* goes beyond merely being a single emotion or emotional state. It is an overarching attitude that encompasses both cognitive and emotional components, most of which are automatic and *nonconscious*, as discussed at length in chapter 6. These factors are also necessary for the healthy ability to discern, discriminate, and choose thought processes and behavioral decisions. In other words, it can be regarded as the achievement of being biomentally able to recognize opposites and begin to make evaluative comparisons followed by choice. Perceiving contrasts and differences are part of the cognitive infrastructure of the envy dynamic, which when more fully developed adds a value judgment such as "superior," "inferior," "better" or "worse." If these contrasts are perceived as too sharp, they act as accelerants provoking envy to further organize. A comprehensive discussion of envy is found in chapter 6.

Children gradually develop the ability to note contrast and difference. Developmental testing, for example, typically shows that children of four years can identify a missing part from a picture and understand at least two or more opposites, such as "up and down" or "girl and boy." At four and a half, two missing parts and at least three or more opposites can be identified, as well as concepts such as "yesterday" and "tomorrow." The child of four and a half can count to four. The four-year-old can pretend, conjure up "as-if" scenarios, and engage in imaginative play. By five years old, children can sense that they have a private mind and that others cannot necessarily know what they are thinking unless they tell them. The five-year-old can count to ten. By six years old, children can define differences, such as between bird and dog, wood and glass, and so forth. At ages six and seven, children are now able to change their minds and recall what they chose to do differently. Whereas children of five show a greater sense of stability and relative decisiveness, age six is more mentally tumultuous, when ambivalent states of mind seem more common.

Biomental child development regards the capacity to see contrasts as one of the healthy foundations of the processes that comprise thinking and emotion. The ability to evaluatively discriminate in a realistic and balanced manner is a sign of healthy intelligence. Of course, in the preschool years, this capacity is cognitively fragile and still governed by a great deal of natural egocentricity. Thus, children in the preschool years are incapable of substantive, informed moral intelligence.

Other significant emotional attitudes that are composites of basic emotions include greed, jealousy, and guilt. At about age five, children show strong desires for possessions—grasping tightly and holding on. This correlates with their exposure to peer groups who may have novel and interesting items such as toys and clothing, as well as to commercialism in the media. Problems around human desire in all its forms begin to organize.

Jealousy, the conscious feeling of being deprived of something or of a relationship that is now lost to another person, is different from envy, which is discussed in chapter 6. Jealousy may be prominent particularly between three and six years old toward a parent. Possessiveness and competitiveness typically accompany jealousy, and this can be observed in boys' typically strong attachments to mothers. Shame and embarrassment develop shortly thereafter along with many other varieties of emotional states. These socially colored emotional attitudes help soften impulsivity and, to some extent, modulate oppositionality. This is due, in part, to the fact that the child develops from a more egocentric perspective to one that is more concerned with how others feel. This organizing sense of concern widens the scope of perspective taking, which, in turn, inserts a sense of psychological pause that dampens immediate action. As cognitive and empathetic expansions occur by both maturation and intentional self-development in later life, the default state of narrow-mindedness diminishes.

The preschool years are the prime time for caregivers to nurture an understanding of emotions and feelings. Being sensitive and empathetic to a child's emotionality, giving names and labels to the expressed emotions, and offering strategies to help manage and regulate them should be continuing. Fairy tales and animal fables can convey user-friendly, assimilable information, especially about emotions, interpersonal communications, and socially relevant interactions. For example, the classic children's story *Snow White and the Seven Dwarfs* beautifully illustrates the operation of attitudes of envy, greed, jealousy, anger, and eventual triumph. The stirrings of compassion are elicited as provocative themes and imaginative pictures running through the story line. Reading this story to children not only fascinates them, but also provides adults opportunities for lively and enriching discussions, all of which enhance preliteracy skills, discerning judgment, and empathy.

Strong emotions in the preschool years, however, typically tax the child's capacity to manage and regulate them. Parents also feel the strain of children's strong emotions. During this era in development, stress tends to disorganize the child and make him or her regress to more "babyish" ways. This response is transitory, although its frequency and intensity can be vexing. It requires sensitive yet firm containment and support. Whining and pouting are also common at this period and usually indicate boredom, hunger, fatigue, or a developing ailment, such as a stomachache or headache. Adequate sleep is essential and should be from ten to twelve hours.

The cornerstone of emotional maturation is the development of empathy, the compassionate ability to experience aspects of the emotional and cognitive perspectives of others. Biological factors such as mirror neuron endowment provide the scaffolding for emotional and social experiences. Interpersonal encounters over time enhance the refinement of empathy from its roots in earliest infancy to a fuller blossoming in adulthood. An essential display of empathy is consideration for the other. As an individual matures and develops age-appropriate social skills, the capacity to defer one's own needs in order to attend to those of others may arise. This skill, like so many other emotional achievements, exists on a dimensional spectrum and varies considerably among individuals. Refinements in the development of empathy occur recursively throughout the lifecycle.

7.4 Play

Children's play both reflects and supports healthy emotional and social development. While some have said that play is the work of children, the biomental perspective adds that play is also the art of children. At any age, play reflects the *epistemophilia* within the self—the impulse toward attraction to novelty and avoidance of habit. Novelty, in this sense, aims toward achieving an extended connectedness in the nexus of experience.

Play encompasses imitation, imagination, creative stimulation, and joyful mental exercise. It is an absorptive and integrating biomental experience that naturally coordinates thinking, feeling, and action in attentive and concentrated fashion. It also affords children the ability to use subjective fantasy and imagination to experiment with different aspects of themselves, others, and relationships. The inner world is stirred to form mental images without needing sensory stimuli as its only source of information. Play is also a bridge that coordinates the interior world with attachments to the external world of material forms—color, shape, mass, sound, smell, and so forth. From a psychodynamic perspective, play is the externalization or graphic representation of unconscious emotions and thinking; play becomes the form and shape that primitive fantasy uses when it is enacted in childhood. In play, unconscious phantasy incarnates in fluid forms and indefinite structures.

Play itself has a developmental trajectory. In the second year of life, infants and toddlers engage in *imitative solitary play*. This reality or perceptually based play involves treating toys in a realistic, literal, and concrete fashion. A child playing with a toy car, therefore, treats it like a toy car without adding fanciful elaborations. In other words, the "toy" car is used on the floor like a "real" car and not used to stand for anything else such as an airplane soaring through the air. This early form of solitary play tends to be repetitive and mimics and imitates what the child is exposed to.

At about thirty-six months, *imaginative play* emerges. This persists throughout the preschool years into middle childhood. Imaginative play is *pretend, make-believe play*. It has a distinctive symbolic and representational quality. In other words, one thing can stand for a variety of other, often unrelated things. A cardboard box may become a house, a fort, or a boat, for example. Unlike earlier imitative play, imaginative play is not solitary. It occurs among several children who cooperate together in playful interactions.

Imaginative or pretend play is best when free and unstructured without adults imposing a plan or direction. Free, pretend play provides opportunities to practice taking different points of view and different roles. Such play epitomizes exploratory endeavors that often include running, jumping, hide and seek, feigned fighting, and attempted trials at conflict resolution. The play of three-year-olds brings about a realization at age four years that false beliefs exist, namely, ideas false in reality but true in the mind of the believer. *Novel imaginary elaborations foster the later development of creative, divergent thinking*. Divergent thinking, which may emerge in the adolescent years, is a nonlinear form of brainstorming that can produce multiple possibilities. It opens up many hypotheticals and can lead to creative insights in adolescence and adulthood. Such hypothetical excursions reflect adaptive diversification in problem solving and skill building. This contributes to both a developing sense of empathy and learning to be cooperative with others.

7.4.1 In Defense of Stones, Water, Plants, and Sunlight

When possible, play should include outdoor activities in the natural elements—air, light, water, soil, and so forth. Walking with children in a park, forest, or garden exposes them to natural sights, sounds, colors, and smells. The crackle of a flowing stream, for instance, introduces sounds not ordinarily heard. Time spent outside in the fresh air promotes stress reduction. Even time spent in one's back yard offers opportunities for play and exploration very different from indoor play. Supplying children with a magnifying glass that can enlarge the visual features of rocks, insects, leaves, and so forth helps encourage focus, attention, and an appreciation for the more subtle aspects of the natural world. Going on hikes and visiting conservation centers and bird sanctuaries offer children interesting opportunities to appreciate the natural world outside the home.

In addition to free, unstructured, and spontaneous play, play using toys is typical. In general, toys are best when they are simple, low-tech, and as "natural" and unartificial as possible. One example would be a set of plain wooden blocks. Fewer toys are better than a very large number. Even dolls can be kept to a minimum with one special doll being foremost. Dolls that are as nondescript as possible may be chosen so that children may use them imaginatively. This entails creatively imputing emotions, attitudes, and behaviors to them in the course of play. Household items such as pots and pans can be useful as toys. Natural materials are useful, such as natural fabrics, pieces of wood, seashells, pinecones, and small rocks. Such playthings foster a beneficial closeness to the features of nature during these sensitive and formative early years. Toys, like foods, are most nourishing and least toxic when minimally processed.

A solid distinction between fantasy and reality is still developing, so that preschoolers live in a world that is not governed by clear-cut reason and logic. Faculties used to distinguish a solid sense of reality from fantasy become stronger in the elementary school years. In adolescence, these distinctions become even more definite.

7.5 Empathy

Observing the roots of empathy in infancy, researchers have described a measurable form of empathy termed "egocentric empathy"—distress in response to perceiving another's distress—observable in newborns up to about fifteen months of age. At approximately fifteen months, this sense of unhappiness in the other and the self prompts an outreach in an attempt to comfort the other in distress. By two years of age, these attempts may succeed at their goal of comforting.

The more organized capacity for *empathy* begins to unfold in the preschool years, notably between ages three and four. What had been external impositions and admonitions—"be nice," "play nicely," now begin to arise from within the child's own inner resources. Feelings of unhappiness and diffuse sorrow at another's misfortune expand and more defined expressions of regret for mistakes lay the foundations for conscious feelings of remorse and contrition in middle childhood. The development of empathy is tied in with feelings that encompass sadness, sorrow, regret, remorse, guilt, grief, mourning, bereavement, and depression depending on chronological age, developmental maturation, and specific social situations.

Empathy, the cornerstone of emotional maturation, encompasses cognitive, emotional, and behavioral processes both nonconscious and conscious whose interrelationship makes concerned response to another person possible. This reaction, based on some level of self-aware positioning in relation to another, occurs through a grasp of what the other is inferred to be sensing, feeling, and thinking. In the preschool years, for example, the presence of a developing sense of empathy is seen when children react to perceived minor injuries in others, such as seeing a Band-Aid on another's finger. Observable reactions of distress to broken items, especially toys, also reflect emerging empathy. Focus on something perceived as damaged and a sense of personal concern are significant roots of conscience.

Empathy presumes a compassionate identification whose prosocial aims are helping, sharing, and comforting. This capacity to care is intimately correlated with healthy moral development and recognizing the distinctions of "good and bad" and "acceptable and unacceptable." The proper development of empathy and the capacity to share develop concurrently. Both counter impulses eliciting greed. These also help modulate urges for excessive possessiveness. Otherwise stated, the urge "to hold on" becomes more appropriately modulated.

Greed in many ways reflects a need to have more than others. The intrinsic value of an object is of much less importance than the intricate ways the object is perceived to be related to another person. This correlates greed strongly with jealousy and an inability to let go or share. Empathy thus can be seen to have its counterpoint in possessiveness, greed, and jealousy. These attitudes are discussed at length in chapter 6.

Defects in the capacity for reasonable empathy result in impaired social intelligence, social skills, and social competence, as well as the possibility of developing antisocial behaviors. Two simple yet obvious concrete examples of impaired empathy are inconsiderate behaviors, and the inability to give gifts. Further, the capacity for moral reasoning is weakened when empathy remains underdeveloped.

Learning from a variety of environmental exposures—both positive and negative—can support or thwart the development of empathy. The external environment provides exteroceptive information to the senses that helps shape the gradual development of empathy. The leading sense is that of vision. Exteroceptive information involves the decoding of the differences and perceived meaning of different facial, gestural, and body expressions of others. Auditory information adds to this by contributing dimensions of volume, tone, and prosody to that which is seen. These processes primarily occur through *real-time, actual human interactions*. For example, parents demonstrating—not just telling about—concern, caring, cooperation, and helpfulness provides the grounds for and enhances children's emerging sense of empathy. By extension, this fact suggests that images and sounds experienced on screen media such as television, computers, cell phones, and films do not provide the substantive stimuli necessary for empathy to develop. The effective ingredients for the development of empathy involve *indispensable human interactions* that concretize *real-time experiences* of agreeableness and cooperation.

7.6 Three-year-olds: Details

At age three, children have developing cognitive faculties that permit a more complex level of interpersonal communication and dialogue, notably through language. A child's use of words and language indicates their developing competence in symbolic capacity, also termed the *semiotic function*. This use of *abstraction*—speaking about and indicating an awareness of the common essence among a number of different things—indicates the degree of proficiency attained in these developing cognitive faculties. The ability to abstract develops very gradually, and is not substantial until adolescence, perhaps emerging adulthood. Although previously reserved for children with hearing difficulties, families are beginning to introduce the use of sign language to preschoolers to build vocabulary, letter recognition, and social skills before the development of verbal language. The American Sign Language system is typically employed.

Language development is reflected in the use of nouns; this use is clear at age two to three. Between two and three years old, prepositions are included. As verbal proficiency develops, children demonstrate burgeoning curiosity and may begin to ask questions: "where," "who," "why." "Help me" is a common command. At times, these abilities may appear newly demanding. Children often say, "No, I won't." Especially in the preschool years, as at other developmental periods, it is wise to offer children choices coupled with directives. For example, saying, "How should we go to get ready for bath time—walk slowly or walk quickly?" musters better cooperation.

Complex processes of memory, learning, and generalization are developing and require continual repetition to increase efficiency. Children at age three are found to operate under "false belief" thinking. While belief denotes the acceptance of the truth of an idea, statement, or event, the term "false belief" indicates that three-year-olds exclusively attribute another person's actions to what the child (not the other) infers is that person's desire. The child, therefore, cannot accurately understand the real situation: other's thoughts, knowledge, ignorance, and the possibility of error or deception. This type of thinking suggests the cognitive immaturity—not absence—of the ability to distinguish appearance from reality. By forty-two months, children are asking, "Why?" and "How come?" questions. This ability reflects a significant change in the nature of representational thinking.

At age three, physical aggression toward others is also typical. This may express itself because taking turns is a newfound ability that sometimes meets with frustration as a result of eagerness, impulsivity, and undeveloped impulse control. Children at this stage don't realize their own strength or may find it amusing to experiment with throwing or knocking things over. Since language is just developing and still not adequate for children to express their desires, wants, feelings, and so forth, biting may still occur.

In general, some level of inappropriate biting may be seen up to about four to five years. After this, it should become a focus of parental attention. Helping children learn that angry biting after ages four to five is inappropriate requires firm and consistent explanation, redirection, and suitable consequences. Making eye contact with the child always intensifies the impact of words. Parents can verbalize what is happening and guide children to see the possible negative consequences so that they may gradually, although imperfectly, begin to connect cause and effect. This approach helps to modulate their behaviors.

Parallel play continues in peer groups. By three and a half, however, imaginative and the beginnings of *cooperative play* can be seen. The ability to use scissors begins. Children are able to match colors and just begin to identify their names when asked. About one thousand words are spoken. Three-year-olds can begin to learn to count.

Gender identity is becoming established; in other words, a child is coming to sense his- or herself as being either male or female. *Core gender identity*—gender self-image constancy—consolidates by about age six. The AAP states that a few of the developmental and behavioral differences that typically distinguish boys from girls are biologically determined. For example, the average preschool boy tends to be more aggressive, while girls are more verbal. Other siblings have a real influence on children beginning at this age. Girls, for example, who have older brothers often notice gender differences. This may evoke comparisons and feelings of unconscious envy and conscious jealousy.

Children of three typically whine, which may appear especially pronounced at age three and a half. Whining is a plaintive, high-pitched, protracted sound, as in pain, fear, supplication, complaint, or protest. Often, children whine because they experience overwhelming, unrealistic expectations and desires. Whining is a "mini" form of harassment, almost simulating bullying. Although some whining is expected, whining should be discouraged over long periods because it may become a habitual reaction to frustration and unfulfilled wishes. Parents can respond to whining by simply acknowledging that they hear it. Often, demonstrating to a child how whining sounds helps them recognize that it is an unacceptable, if not "babyish," way of communicating. Whining and oppositional-defiant behaviors reflect the unmatured development of empathy.

Explaining to the child what a parent infers is the reason for whining and then giving reasons why their wishes cannot be satisfied at this time is a good step. Offering alternatives is the next step. Whining not only connotes children's frustrated wishes but their sense of powerlessness. Although exact formulas to remedy whining cannot be given since each event calls for its own examination in terms of causes and context, parental awareness of this perspective helps keep it from becoming a habitual reaction.

At age three, children are more biomentally organized and are relatively more coordinated. Walking, for example, is now characterized by arms at sides swinging rhythmically to the cadence of the legs instead of being outstretched. Children can count to three, build a bridge out of three blocks, and imitate drawing vertical and horizontal strokes to form a cross following demonstration by example. They are also able to take turns, a prerequisite for nursery school readiness. Even at this early age, it is important to communicate to children that taking turns does not mean losing. Demonstrating the necessity of taking turns in a variety of situations plays a decisive role in emphasizing the value of team efforts. Such explicit displays can also highlight the spirit of fun that surrounds playing the game, rather than the competitive aim of merely reaching a winning endpoint. Cooperative behaviors rather than adversarial struggles are fostered in this way.

Activities of daily living and rudimentary hygiene, such as dressing and washing, now begin. Children can put on shoes at three years old and can wash and dry their hands and face at three and a half years. At this age, they can take off loose-fitting clothing, carry lightweight dishes to the sink, and put dirty clothes in the hamper. In the preschool years, children require about ten to twelve hours of sleep with some naps during the daytime. The preschool years give children a great deal of unfettered pleasure in their newfound abilities and the expanded ways in which they are able to function.

7.7 Four-year-olds: Details

At age four, children are becoming more socially competent and engaged. Their personalities become more distinct and expressive, and energy amplifies their presence. Fantasy and imaginary play become prominent. "Why?" questions abound.

Between four and five years, children become capable of expressing language *narratives*, that is, connected sentences to describe sequences or scenes in a logical fashion. This ability may correlate a now stabilizing sense of self with a consistent set of emotional and physical characteristics that will endure over time. Glimmers of what will develop into a child's enduring personality become more obvious. Between three and a half and five years of age, children clearly possess a *sense of self*, exemplified by their ability to describe themselves using adjectives that indicate both physical and emotional characteristics. This *self-concept* articulation correlates with parental and teacher perceptions.

Children appear assertive, expressive, and bursting with newfound motoric activity, such as hopping, jumping, skipping on one foot only, and climbing. They are wonderfully sure of themselves and are in the midst of their love affairs with the world. Since this enthusiasm is concomitant with children's natural egocentricity, safety issues need constant parental surveillance. For example, a self-involved four-year-old may impulsively run to retrieve a ball that rolls into the street.

At four years, 70 percent of children are dry at night. Children's concerns over elimination may normally appear, and children are fond of such remarks as "poo-poo" and "wee-wee." Children can now name three or more colors, understand the meaning of "up," "down," "sideways," and "under." They can now ride tricycles and engage in cooperative play with peers. In terms of dressing, they can distinguish front and back of clothes, and dress and undress self with supervision. They can water a plant with help, climb into a car seat and close the top clip, and pump legs when on a swing. Many new abilities are facilitated by the four-year-old's greater impulse control and developing ability to take turns when dealing with others. Readiness for eventually entering kindergarten, as evidenced by the ability to learn rules and take turns, can be assessed.

Pretend and imaginative play is obvious and "as-if" imaginings are reflected in play scenarios. *Cooperative play* is one manifestation of the beginning development of inner states of empathy, which is critical for healthy social development.

Children are also becoming more consciously aware of the phenomenon of death as an abrupt and frightening event. While the irreversibility of death is not yet realized, death is felt to be an assault. This may manifest itself in play when one preschooler, in the midst of a playful aggressive interaction says to another, "I dead you." Dreams of monsters also involve death and fear. A great deal of these "irrational fears" is developmentally normal and expectable, and their intensity diminishes by the early elementary school years.

Between ages four and five, typical children have sufficiently developed *theory of mind*. This metacognitive ability allows children to differentiate their own thinking and feelings from those of others. Eye contact helps typical children understand and interpret the emotional expressions and gestures of others. This consistent developmental pattern of emotional achievements and their reflection in language and eye contact has been found across various cultures. Children, therefore, are able to use such expressions as "I believe," "I think," "I know," and "I feel." Pretend and imaginary play is a behavioral expression that reflects these mental states. These developmental achievements also connote that the differentiation between self and other is consolidating. Parents need to be vigilant so that children's conceptualizations of "the other" do not become imbued with misperceptions of the other as "the enemy," which all too often inadvertently occurs.

Lies and lying at this age become apparent. These are related to what developmentalists suggest is the four-year-old's new ability to grasp "false beliefs." *False beliefs* are ideas, language, and actions that do not represent reality or conventional commonsense accurately, and so are virtually untrue. By four years old, therefore, the typically developing subject's mind is able to correctly understand that another person's mind may contain and act upon a "false belief," which denotes an erroneous, mistaken idea not in accord with the subject's more accurate contextual understanding or reality-consonant belief of what is true. These are typically not deliberately malicious; rather, they are mistaken beliefs—false in reality but true in the mind of the believer. This is a peak age for very tall tales with little basis in fact and for imaginative verbalization. Lies at this time indicate strong wishes or concerns with self-preservation, for example, not being punished. Rather than dealing with lies in a negative way, it is useful to point out the motive that one infers has produced the lie. If stealing behaviors appear, telling children "This is something that we do not do" may help suppress the urges. Refraining from accusing and instead asking "What happened?" is helpful. Surges in aggression because of frustrated wishes may precipitate nightmares of monsters and, in turn, sleep disruptions. Typically, these are transitory. Regarding lies and stealing, parents can help the child begin to become aware of cultural and social values and the role of truthfulness and cooperation. This early fostering of socialization counters antisocial impulses and trends toward future deceptions such as misrepresentation and adult malingering. These parental strategies combine nurturance with corrective guidance and example so that the child's newly emerging sense of empathy is fostered. All these support helping a child to develop a sense of *moral self-relevance, moral restraint,* and *effortful self-control.*

Normal fear responsiveness to realistically aversive events and to the threat of appropriate reprimands is a good sign of healthy emotional and moral development. In addition, relationships with peers typically involve more give-and-take than relationships with adults. These interpersonal experiences provide an opportunity for the development of social competencies, such as cooperation and negotiation. All of this forms the basis for reciprocal, prosocial behaviors.

Emotional milestones by the end of this period include an awareness of and curiosity about basic sexuality, both personal and that of others. Sex education is a sensitive matter and may begin when a child asks questions in this regard. Responses should be brief and "matter of fact" without embarrassment or strong emotive expressions. Describing anatomical structures should be simple and use suitable terminology. A child's touching, even playing, with his or her own genitals is typical. Erections in boys, for example, often begin in infancy well before puberty, and are more physiological than sexual. Interest in genital organs is healthy and natural. Nudity and sexual play in public, however, is not acceptable.

Although a child's capacity for attention has temperamental roots and some endowed characteristics, helping children learn to filter and modulate how they respond to the objects of their attention can begin at this time. Gradually teaching children that some behaviors exhibited by others are best ignored is a skill with immense returns. A novel method for reinforcing this socially valuable life skill is using the phrase, "Take no notice," when situations such as these arise and are best left unattended.

7.8 Five-year-olds: Details

Unlike the extroverted, exuberant, and seemingly brash qualities of many four-year-olds, the five-year-old is more contained, restrained, deliberate, and composed. The previous rapid pace of development has slowed, though is still significantly robust. Children appear calmer, optimistic, positive, and are self-limiting rather than wildly expansive like at age four. Children can dress and undress without help, except for tying of shoelaces. Playing outdoors now includes facility with swings and the seesaw. Children are now more able to use silverware, such as spoons and forks, pour cereal and milk into a bowl, make a bed with help, and begin to set the table with guidance. Most children can remember four digits in a row. Since it is now relatively easier to follow rules, kindergarten readiness is evident. Curiosity is expanding, and "Why?" questions continue to abound.

In regard to fine motor skills, while children at age three can copy a circle from printed material, a cross at age four, and a square at age four and a half, at age five children can copy a triangle. The need to imitate by demonstrated example beginning at twenty-four months is gradually superseded by self-dependent copying skills by three years old. Most children can ride a bicycle with training wheels by kindergarten. Training wheels may not be needed sometime between five and seven as practice strengthens coordination. At five years old, children sleep at night for ten to twelve hours. Nightmares are expected, especially of terrifying wild animals. Most children are developmentally able to differentiate their thoughts from their actions. Although this ability is still fragile, it contributes to strengthening impulse control.

Preschoolers at home, in nursery, or kindergarten react to the world through their behavior. Through free play and guidance, children are learning and practicing interpersonal and social skills, such as sharing, cooperating, resolving conflicts, and some sense of self-dependence. Typically high at this age, self-esteem is shaping itself; challenges dealing with autonomy, independence, and personal initiative become paramount. Personality styles are forming on top of children's endowment of temperament. *Socialization*—acquiring socially acceptable values and standards—is in process. Sibling rivalry and jealousy are normal expressions of how the child is positioning himself and herself in regard to others. Within the family, children evaluatively discriminate their strengths and weaknesses using the perceived attention of parents. These hierarchical value comparisons also extend to the classroom, as, for example, wanting to be first in line.

Thinking processes from ages two to seven years are termed *preoperational*. At this stage, egocentrism, magical thinking, and transductive (particular to particular) reasoning predominate. Five-year-olds now are able to sense that they have a mind or subjective self that is private but can be shared, if they so choose. Although the capacity for abstraction is in the process of developing, it remains more literal than figurative until its fuller development in later adolescence. Learning, therefore, is not best facilitated by intellectual lessons but rather by physical demonstrations at this age.

Body image is forming and concerns with bodily integrity are reflected in a preoccupation with Band-Aids. These feared violations of the body are understood to be biologically evolved adaptations in the service of survival. Thumb sucking, nose picking, and nail biting may be present, and gentle attempts to dissuade these should be attempted. Earlier licking behaviors, for example, undergo sublimation and are now directed to culturally acceptable substitutes such as lollipops and ice cream cones.

Incipient guilt over aggressive attitudes and behaviors is beginning to become explicit. So too a rudimentary sense of moral values is starting to appear. *Ethnic awareness*—identity, ancestry, and shared beliefs—becomes organized in the context of family values, culture, and faith traditions.

Children five and six years old seem so exuberant at times that this voraciousness for experience may appear to be greediness. Typically, this insistence on "more" is a child's natural wish to repeat activities for the sake of merely enjoying the activity. However, it can also be a form of testing limits and an opportunity used to develop boundaries. For example, preschoolers may want to splash and extend the time for play in the bath since it is so pleasurable. Supervising parents must offer flexible limits.

Parents can moderate children "pushing the limits" by preparing beforehand. Since transitions and endings are points where this asking for more occurs, providing early warnings of time limits is a useful strategy. Once a reasonable explanation and position are taken, parents need to stand their ground. Sometimes, *offering children choices helps to foster their cooperation*. In such situations, it is always better for a distraught parent to avoid expressing frustration and anger, and instead constructively focus on the child's opposition. Communicating with empathy elicits more cooperation than opposition.

Acquisitive or collecting interests and behaviors begin. Examples include pride in certain personal possessions such as a hat or a drawing. Thereafter until about age ten, amassing picture cards, toy cars, small figures of dinosaurs, dolls, and so forth increases in specificity and quantity. Children take pride in certain personal possessions, such as an article of clothing or a drawing. In many ways, this outer behavior reflects the child's inner development of the dialectic between holding on and letting go. The need to share imposed by adults correlates with the child's inner need to make sure that any sharing is "absolutely just." The intrinsic value of an object is less important than its personal significance and relation to a third person. These attitudes and behaviors are normative derivatives of the elements of unconscious envy and its conscious correlates, greed and jealousy, as will be discussed in chapter 6.

After six months of being relatively more composed, children between five and a half and six years again become more restless and seemingly combative. There may be an upsurge of attempts at independence with associated anxiety and explosive, brash, or ambivalent behaviors.

During this time, parents may see extremes of attitude and temper tantrums. Children appear more rigid and less conforming. Preventive guidance that considers these expectable developments gives parents a way to minimize these behavioral upsets. By about six years old, children become noticeably more relaxed.

7.9 The Significance of Play in Childhood

A further note on children's play helps round out this discussion of the life of the child. Children need to play for a variety of reasons such that it should be encouraged and supported. The natural play of children, notably in the preschool years, is a mixture of gross and fine motor activity, exercise, and exploration. Thinking, emotion, and physical abilities are interactively engaged. The outward display of movements, games, and imaginative scenarios reflects the inner life of the child. This inner development becomes the basis for healthy identification with others and supports cooperativeness and emerging socialization. These situations reflect developing levels of cognitive sophistication as links between cause and effect are beginning to be forged. Exuberant emotional expressivity draws from developing feelings and inner imagination and fantasy. Play activities often are related to household and domestic themes rather than the school related ones that will develop after age six.

Learning from play activities is fundamental in early childhood. Learning through unstructured play activities should not be replaced by direct instruction, for example, in reading or mathematics. Literacy skills before the elementary school years are best promoted by mothers, fathers, and teachers using *oral language stimulation*, such as reading or mutual dialogues. This approach denotes demonstrated learning and encourages discussion, imagination, and thinking skills. Oral language stimulation such as reading to children is a form of play for them.

The preschool years are an ideal time to begin introducing children to fairy tales and folklore from around the world. *Grimm's Fairy Tales* and *Aesop's Fables* are good examples. Folklore consists of legends, music, oral history, proverbs, adages, popular beliefs, fairy tales, mythology, and cultural customs. Selections should be suitable to the chronological age and developmental level of a given child. Three-, four-, and five-year-olds savor repetition. Three-year-olds especially enjoy the repetition and repeating phrases that nursery rhymes provide. Four-year-olds likewise enjoy fairy tales told over and over.

Reading to children focuses attention, evokes conscious mental pictures, and conjures a mixture of conscious and unconscious feelings states; these both stimulate creative imagination. Reading also focuses attention of the child. Some educators have suggested that the reading of fairy tales and animal fables to children under seven should emphasize linguistic cadence and melody rather than the reader's strong expressive emotion. This technique allows children's own feelings of identification, empathy, reverence, and compassion to appear. This process is complex and requires the reader to be sensitively attuned to the child's need for any emotional expressivity.

Like play, children's fantasy life is a natural experience. It is partly conscious and mostly nonconscious awareness of developing defensive strategies against anxieties, conflicts, and fears, and trial attempts to manage these. Adaptive coping reflects the dynamic interaction between inner developmental processes and environmental challenges, all of which can be supported by sensitive parental guidance. A gradual yet steady differentiation of the world of fantasy from the outer world of tangible reality constrains fantasy, matures realistic thinking, and supports successful real-life adaptations. A major shift from magical to more realistic thinking occurs at about age seven.

7.10 Socialization Skills in the Preschool Years

Social development is expressed in social skills and interpersonal behaviors. The preschool years are opportune times to begin familiarizing children with socially appropriate conduct. Good manners are an everyday reflection of civilized behavior. They include taking turns, sharing, not interrupting, saying "please" and "thank you," "hello" and "good-bye," and saying "excuse me" when interrupting occurs. Cooperativeness and being considerate are encompassed in many of these positive politeness markers. By age five, encouraging children to make eye contact when speaking, to not interrupt, and to refine table manners builds on what was earlier learned. Explicit demonstrations of good manners that include descriptions of specific ways to exhibit such behaviors produce effective results. Establishing such a tone in the preschool years guides children to continue using respect and courteousness in subsequent civil discourse. This both reflects and enhances perspective taking and empathy in interpersonal dialogues throughout life.

The important skill of sharing is exercised around age five. "Toy envy" is the consciously felt manifestation of a child's desiring and often grabbing the playthings of another. When this occurs, it provides parents with an opportunity to help children identify possessiveness and to learn alternative coping skills that are constructive and effective. Fostering empathy and sharing helps to mitigate greed and possessive urges. Parents who focus on simple pleasures and experiences, especially *surprises*, rather than material possessions set the emotional tone for willingness to share early on in life. This parental focus can become a prime model for children to experience and internalize. Learning new expectations occurs when uncertainty and surprise are encountered. In many ways, this fosters a sense of the very desirability of valuing goodness, thus adding to moral intelligence and character development.

Preschoolers may experience signs and symptoms of guilt, especially when they sense that they have hurt someone. Parents may take these occasions as learning opportunities to support children's understanding of cause-and-effect relationships and the emotional consequences of negative destructive actions. Although the link between cause and effect may be more associative than substantial, it nevertheless is important to demonstrate. This approach enhances a child's experience of constructive, *empathy-based guilt*.

Social proprieties need to be taught in the preschool years, and demonstrations are particularly important. While most children are developmentally ready to learn and enact them, emotional factors may interfere with their smooth acquisition and expression. Close supervision, guidance, and proper discipline minimize ill manners and rudeness.

Although preschoolers may find it difficult to adequately grasp and experience empathy in their limited ability to see another's perspective, it is important to introduce them to making statements about how they—not others—may feel. In other words, a child may be encouraged to say "I am angry that he won't play with me" rather than "You are stupid," or "He is a jerk." This type of situation presents opportunities for parents to discuss components of interpersonal relations, such as feelings, thwarted wishes, frustration, upset, emerging empathy, and negotiation. Preschool children can grasp parents' encouragement of "I statements" because their cognitive capacities are become increasingly less literal and more abstract. As this occurs, perspective-taking abilities are also advancing. An important byproduct of the aforementioned parental coaching of "I statements" is a parent's demonstration of his and her own listening skills with a child as a sign of respect. Such display teaches communication skills and problem solving by living example.

8. ELEMENTARY SCHOOL: AGES SIX TO TWELVE YEARS

The period of middle childhood typically spans first through eighth grades and has been called the primary or elementary school years. The young preschool child has grown, matured, and developed. Language development, for example, shows that the typical six-year-old has a vocabulary of about 10,000 words; the ten-year-old has a vocabulary of about 40,000 words.

Children from six to twelve are now more receptive to the expanded conceptual learning gleaned from images, pictures, artistic endeavors, and imagination. Play is no longer grounded merely on movement and simple imagination but is now enhanced by greater conceptual abilities. Although a focus on the newness and movements of physical body remains, this emphasis becomes much more implicit and superseded by artistic imagination and conceptual abilities.

In other words, the rawness of infancy and the virtually uncritical openness of the preschool years are now superseded by the school-age child's capacity to learn by using, in increasingly applicable ways, his or her own inner psychological resources. The child now more fully participates in mediating developing *self-agency*. This sense of *agency* is synonymous with intentional, goal-directed behaviors. *Self-concept* manifests its developing maturity by the child's descriptions of him- or herself in terms of competencies, skills, and positive and negative personality traits. Self-concept also includes the sense of *moral self-relevance*, one's leading moral and ethical beliefs, and acceptance of the truth of those ideas.

Peer comparisons become increasingly significant in the process of building a sense of self-worth. These may particularly influence self-esteem as it correlates with perceived physical appearance. "Looks" become progressively more important, both personally and socially, in middle childhood and throughout adolescence. *Peer emphasis* takes center stage, which replaces the preschooler's primary focus on family life. This newfound interest in peers reflects a consciousness of social membership in a group. Discrete individual identity is not foremost. The stirrings of introspection begin to enable the six-year-old to recognize emotions as if he or she were an observer of both self and others. This ability further enhances the ability to make interpersonal comparisons.

Self-esteem, or the way a child evaluates him or herself as competent or "good at" versus not competent or "bad at," is now largely influenced by social comparisons and family attitudes. Self-esteem comprises aspects of physical appearance, physical skill and prowess, social competence, and academic performance (success in both academic achievements and school behaviors). Since the beginning of the elementary school years is a time of greater social and academic feedback with its intrinsic peer comparisons, self-esteem typically declines.

By about ten years old, self-esteem typically increases. Some have speculated that the return to a more positive self-image is spurred by a prepubertal reconfiguration of hormones and emotions that feels excitingly strange and becomes a new source of curiosity to children. As these changes initially appear mysterious, children must grapple with displaying or hiding what they feel. Sexual changes in the body and how to make sense of them become problematic; the need for privacy emerges. As a way to manage the confusion and attendant discomfort related to sexual concerns, intentional and deliberate lying may develop as forms of denial and temporary distraction.

From ages seven to eleven, cognitive development is in its *concrete stage of operations*—a radical reconfiguration from its earlier *preoperational* structure. Symbolic activity strengthens while magical thinking, animism, and egocentricity are beginning to fade. Reasoning becomes more matured and reality-oriented. Thinking is less bound to connecting particular items with one another in an isolated fashion and more able to understand *general cause-and-effect* relationships.

As has been discussed previously, children's understanding of cause-and-effect relationships is complex and nuanced. It may range from simple perceptual associations at birth until approximately eighteen months, and then increase in complexity once formal concepts emerge in the preschool years and thereafter. For example, the ability to predict what will happen next, namely, effect resulting from cause—"because"—is apparent in the elementary school years and becomes more abstract and inferential in adolescence. By approximately age seven, children begin to comprehend the fact that things may undergo apparent changes but nevertheless remain the same. An example would be the conceptual understanding that eight ounces of water in a wide cup is equal to the same eight ounces put in a thin, tall glass. Children are now able to more flexibly change their minds and decide to do something differently than what had been done in the past.

Transition from the preschool years to the elementary school years also shows differences in motor behaviors. At age five and a half to six, children become more restless. They use their whole body when trying to write or draw. Movements of the mouth, legs, and posture are all activated when a single, focused activity is attempted. This "hyperkinetic" responsivity is normal and not a sign of disorder. Between six and six and a half years old, there is some settling down of such visible movement. At seven years of age, children may appear even calmer, more subdued, and more self-absorbed.

Alongside cognitive and emotional expansions, explorations in art through working with pencils, crayons, paints, and watercolors are useful to promote aesthetic sensitivities. Fine motor skills are becoming more precise and allow such activities. By age six, children are skilled at printing letters, including their name, and copying more complex shapes, such as a diamond or a rectangle with diagonal lines inside. Six-year-olds are agile at tying shoelaces and being able to distinguish their left from their right hand, foot, and so forth. Musical activities and rhythmic dance are a wonderful way to exercise gross and fine motor skills, engage cooperation, and stimulate healthy imagination and creativity. Movements that are deliberate and harmonious sharpen proprioceptive skills, coordination, and bodily gracefulness. Examples of such movements are those taught in dance, yoga, and karate in that they are produced by conscious efforts to control the body.

During these elementary school years, appealing to children's emotional life enhances and refines their awareness of their innate cognitive and emotional resources, including delicate feelings and a vivid imagination. Storytelling, recounting fairy tales and fables, and encouraging imaginative explorations, especially at age seven, adds energetic color to children's developing cognitive capacities. Children are now equipped to engage in reading and writing activities, as sequential and logical thinking is developing. Direct instruction is now more suitable than it had been in the preschool era. Children can now print letters, their own name, and some simple words. Number concepts are developing and children are able to repeat at least four digits from memory after hearing a series of six to ten.

8.1 Personality in the Process of Becoming

Personality styles are now beginning to crystallize. Reasoning skills are becoming more "realistic." Children's behaviors at this stage are taken more seriously into account by supervising figures who emphasize more explicit notions of *accountability*. Rules of conduct are echoed, such as "the way we are supposed to behave." Reasons for rules are clearly explained. *Rules*, accordingly, not only outline principles of regulation that aim toward a goal but also act to impart the self-discipline needed to successfully accomplish that goal. For example, teachers may require children to line up in front of the classroom before entering so that attendance may be monitored and entry into the classroom may be orderly, thus imparting overall goal achievement and personal self-discipline.

Moral codes and character-building values are hopefully emerging with influence of home and school. These values support the developing capacity for *moral reasoning* and *socialization*. Furthermore, understanding and maintaining adherence to the rules of civilization and cooperative societies becomes a source of conscious conflict. Children are given the responsibility to think about and intentionally chose between alternatives of right and wrong, which elicits anxiety, distress, and emotional dilemmas. Concerns about *fairness* come to the foreground of social and interpersonal situations.

The demands required for social conformation contribute to the process of conscience building and experiencing normative guilt. In turn, unconscious mental defense mechanisms develop to modulate the anxieties often provoked by having to make conscious choices in the face of competing impulses. *Defense mechanisms* are understood to be consciously experienced "cover-ups" (arising and operating nonconsciously) whose function is to use distracting signs and symptoms to cover over nonconscious conflictual urges and wishes. These unconscious conflicts typically relate to aggressive and destructive fantasies and sexual themes that have potentially incapacitating effects. Examples of such defense mechanisms include denial, rationalization, intellectualization, somatization, and so forth. When moderate, reality-oriented, prosocial, and adaptive, they also may provide *an underpinning for the development of healthy coping skills and character traits*.

For purposes of illustration, only a few defense mechanisms will be described here. *Denial* is the automatic and nonconscious mental process of being unaware of significantly unacceptable impulses; *rationalization* means justifying an irrational situation with seemingly rational arguments; *intellectualization* is using logic in a mechanical way devoid of real-life emotional considerations; and *somatization* is displacing anxiety over mental conflicts into physical signs and symptoms.

Ordinary and inordinate stressors may temporarily relax more mature ways of coping with anxiety and replace them with earlier, typically outmoded reactions. More "babyish" language, more explicit concerns with urination and defecation, and silly behaviors may temporarily emerge. Again, parental recognition of this tendency is essential. Sensitive yet firm containment and limit-setting reminders during these events are important child guidance strategies.

Lying becomes more prominent during this time. This is developmentally normal and expectable but an important feature of social intelligence interspersed among the typical truthfulness that children exhibit. Unlike during earlier ages, lying is not merely an expression of wish fulfillment. The behavior may now have elements of *intentional deception*. Lying is a typical developmental occurrence but should be discussed at length when it occurs.

Lies have great communicational value; the child is trying to convey something that is conflictual and difficult to communicate directly. The psychodynamic defense mechanism of "rationalization" denotes the inadvertent elicitation of proposed reasons, some realistic and others "made up." Rationalized explanations are used to justify emotionally conflictual and irrational attitudes and behaviors. These psychological screening devices characteristically omit the actual reasons behind their proposed defensive reasons. Thoughtful investigation, rather than knee-jerk reprimands, helps make sense out of these behaviors, especially if they occur regularly. At ten years of age, however, very few children admit to either stealing or lying because they anticipate detrimental consequences.

Discipline requires collaboration between both parents in determining family rules. Instructions are most effective when expectations of which behaviors are viewed to be "good" versus "inappropriate" are made explicit. Between ages eight and ten, most children have a reasonable sense of what is viewed to be "right" versus "wrong;" hence consequences need to be emphasized. Awareness of "good" versus "bad" gradually is complemented by awareness of "right" versus "wrong." Enforcement in terms of consequences for unacceptable behaviors should be clear and reiterated often. *Consequences* become meaningfully salient and provide beneficial and *corrective feedback* when delivered immediately, firmly, and consistently.

Middle childhood is the era of team-oriented industry and effort. It is the start of peer comparisons, competitiveness, ambitions, concern with "winners" and "losers," as well as potential feelings of self-doubt and inferiority versus competence for completion of tasks. An awareness of power and powerlessness is becoming an orienting perspective used by children of this age to interpret their world. For example, many boys at this developmental era become enthralled with—if not idealize—the caricaturized wrestling personalities popularized in contemporary entertainment venues. This attraction to superheroes continues into adolescence during which time figures such as Superman, Spiderman, and Batman, to name just a few, are identified with, if only vicariously, because of their special qualities exemplifying omnipotence and control over other larger than life villains.

Fostering the value of cooperative rather than adversarial behaviors supports prosocial attitudes. Reasonable and cooperative attitudes and behaviors are characterized by responsive receptivity to acceptable influence rather than by an overwhelming assault of power. Engagement in competitive team sports requires practice, delay of immediate gratification, sublimation of aggressive impulses, and some planning ahead. Issues of fairness and equity become prominent. This period is one in which children observe peers performing "wrongs" that they believe merit "tattling" to adults.

The random collecting behaviors of the later preschooler now begin to take on greater specificity. Attitudes toward property and *possessiveness* are reflected in *collecting behaviors*. This also connotes the subtle organization of underlying feelings such as greed. At six years, children sporadically collect odds and ends, such as bottle caps, pencils, lip gloss, and so forth. At seven years, collecting possessions becomes more specific and purposeful such as collecting only coca-cola bottle caps, red pencils, and pink lip gloss. At eight years, zeal and strong interest in the size of specific collections are prominent. At nine years, collections become more elaborately arranged and classified. By ten years, collections become more formally and intellectually specialized to reflect temperamental proclivities and learned preferences expressed in, for example, foreign stamp or model racecar collections. In the era before the pervasive availability of electronic devices and sports paraphernalia, objects collected were "low-tech." The last decades have changed selection preferences but not these behaviors.

Some child specialists have described a normative "slump" in the ten-year-old's interest in reading. Recognizing this possibility, parents can support a positive view of reading by offering reading materials that match the child's current interests.

During this developmental period, children become *acutely aware of differences in peers and people* in general. Such greater awareness of differences may trigger subtle anxieties relating to perceptions of what is "strange" and what might be potentially unsafe. Seeing differences often results in polarized feelings and extreme attitudes. For example, if a child's family members wear no jewelry, seeing groups of people in a large city wearing large pieces of jewelry might evoke a sense of strangeness and some fearfulness. These are important opportunities for parents to review the interrelatedness of feelings, perceptions of differences, and concepts of accepting the variety of how others may look and behave. A realistic examination of these factors helps children to differentiate "safe" from "unsafe" as they become fearful—a capacity that has innate survival roots and learned adaptive value. Children can also begin to develop an appreciation and acceptance of natural differences in the interpersonal and social world. Exposure to people of differing skin colors, physical size, degrees of handicap or ability, and so forth is an important opportunity to narrate that variations in people are typical and normal. Parents should explain that differences are expectable and pose no threat of harm. Such communication helps to minimize exaggerated perceptions of discrepancies that may lead to polarized thinking, feelings, and perceptions of harm. Parental coaching also helps minimize feelings of envy, unrealistic perceptions of specialness and superiority, and attitudes of alienation, hate, and exclusion.

During middle childhood, children are able to express their abilities in new and explicit ways. They recognize that they can accomplish—however well or shoddily—certain feats, and they take pride in these achievements. Pride in achievement is a hallmark of these middle childhood years.

During this time, parents may notice *exaggerations and bragging* about accomplishments, skills, or possessions. This is normal and expectable. It reflects the growing abilities for greater self-concept and self-definition. When new abilities are formed, they often require initial exaggeration in definition and practice that over time lessens, as they become more rote. For example, a child's claim that he is "an awesome drummer" after just receiving a drum set might motivate further practice and engagement with the instrument. As in all matters, however, moderation is best. Extremes in emotions and ideas underlie a range of negative mental impulses—envy, jealousy, greed, and exclusion.

When overexaggeration borders on being grossly unrealistic, competitive, or mean-spirited, parents can address what they infer to be the child's motivating impulses. If boasting seems to indicate low self-esteem, it needs exploration. A child may perceive him or herself as not as physically attractive or intelligent as peers. Sensitive parents can explore this self-perception to determine whether or not it is remediable by simple discussion or requires more professional assessment. Helping children to modulate statements about themselves and their possessions—how to modulate grasping and holding on—supports the development of social skills, empathy, and social competence. It is important to note that the psychological theme of holding on to and letting go of exaggerated or unrealistic ideas underlies this process.

8.2 A Brief Overview of the Development of Specific Moods, Attitudes, and Capabilities in the Elementary School Years

What follows is a brief overview of the specific moods, attitudes, and capabilities apparent in the elementary school child; it is intended to provide a composite picture of characteristic highlights at each age. While this section is very brief, it may serve to encapsulate some essential features of the elementary school child.

At *age six*, children appear more relaxed than they had been at age five with more restlessness and temper tantrums. The child likes to have a great many possessions, although he or she does not take care of them. Collections are miscellaneous. At this age, there is a more apparent need to be first in all they do. Many six-year-olds cannot bear to lose and will cheat if necessary to win. This characteristic relates to the developmentally appropriate emphasis on being industrious and achieving task completion. These values launch the work ethic of the elementary school era.

At *age seven*, children become calmer and seem more hesitant. They appear more inwardly focused. There is much collecting with an emphasis on large quantity. There is less lying than at age six and more explicit concern with the wrongness of lying and of cheating. Seven-year-olds can be great listeners and can endure at an activity until they get it "just right." In sports, they repeatedly practice throwing a ball or riding a skateboard until they perceive they have achieved what they view as a "perfect performance." They are just beginning to understand spans of time and to tell the time of day, the season, and the month when viewed on a clock or calendar. Time comprehension is still concrete, as, for example, when a seven-year-old is asked, "What is time?" his or her response might be, "Time is to be ready for going to school." Children of seven have an avid interest in listening to fairy tales and fables since imagination is primed with a widening scope of cognitive abilities.

At *age eight*, children are speedy, expansive, and show preference for making evaluations. Possessions and collecting various similar items become prominent interests. Simple hoarding, arranging, and prideful gloating over possessions is common. A specific interest in acquiring money becomes apparent. Prejudicial and biased attitudes may begin to emerge. Seeing distinctions more clearly and coming to appreciate personal preferences, such as liking chocolate versus vanilla, or baseball cards versus legos, becomes apparent. "Best friends" are chosen, and temporary cliques of children with similar interests become apparent. The eight-year-old, however, can become easily disorganized and requires supervision. Reward systems such as with stickers or gold stars help reinforce desired behaviors.

At about *age nine*, children relish greater self-sufficiency. They show a marked increase in wanting to orderly classify and identify events and objects, including their collections. Using their abstract capacity to tell time, the nine-year-old attempts to plan the day and its anticipated sequence of events. Their ability to comprehend durations of time, such as day, week, or even years, is also reflected in a burgeoning interest in history and prehistory. They appear more self-motivated and follow individually generated interests more than needing external direction. A newfound sense of right and wrong replaces concerns about "good" and "bad." This approach reflects a more cognitively enhanced ability to make evaluations. Issues of fairness and justice are more clearly organized by these steadily developing cognitive capacities. The nine-year-old, for example, can sustain attention for longer intervals and is more interested practicing skills, such as dancing, gymnastics, baseball, and reading. The nine-year-old's task persistence now shows more purpose, scope, and depth. There is an earnest engagement in mastering skills in a manner that is less inconsistent and episodic than that seen earlier. A new sense of "realism" is becoming apparent as evidenced, for example, by a disbelief in Santa Claus, the Easter Bunny, and the tooth fairy, though this is variable. Nine-year-olds now dislike fairy tale narrations and may even refuse to attend religious services.

By *age ten*, many children exhibit a somewhat formed personality style that includes long-lasting preferences, attitudes, and ways of behaving. Ten-year-olds appear balanced and poised. They are particularly receptive to social information and discussions about social problems that involve discrepancies and apparent injustices, such as local and global poverty. This tendency somewhat reflects their increasing engagement in the "adult world." Children's expanding universes outside the home environment pique their interest in subjects such as geography and social studies. They are curious about the children and customs of people in foreign lands. Many ten-year-olds prefer activities and work away from home. Talents become apparent and ought to be fostered by parents and teachers. Of note, ten-year-olds in fifth grade may still be prepubertal. The sexes typically do not mingle, and same-sex groups are the social norm. Consolidation of gains made from age five to now are reflected in the ten-year-old's smooth and equilibrated demeanor. At this age, truthfulness outweighs lying, except for an occasional "white lie" as, for example, when a ten-year-old says that he washed his hands but really did not.

8.3 Learning Problems in the Elementary School Years

Attendance at school or home-based academics is an essential part of middle childhood. The elementary school years are an exciting time of learning and newfound socialization. Closer contact with peers over longer periods of the day may uncover a range of hitherto unrecognized achievement problems. For example, with entry into first grade around age six, the greater emphasis on academic tasks may begin to uncover previously unrecognized learning challenges. Psychological and educational testing can rule in or out any significant academic problems that might require remediation. Very preterm children may be developmentally unprepared to perform according to expectation in grade school, especially compared to peers without this disadvantage. Such developmentally disadvantaged children may show social-emotional and behavioral immaturity and so be labeled diagnostically. Children who are delivered preterm (born at twenty-nine to thirty-six weeks' gestation) require periodic developmental screening (Ages and Stages Questionnaire; Bayley Scales of Infant Development) in order to correctly correlate gestational and postbirth age so that misdiagnoses of attentional, hyperkinetic/impulsive, fine and gross motor disorders, and so forth are not made.

Unsubstantiated or casual diagnoses of attentional problems such as attention-deficit/hyperactivity disorder (ADHD) should be avoided. The *Diagnostic and Statistical Manual of Mental Disorders*, fourth edition, text revision (DSM-IV-TR) clearly states that clinical presentations may be complex and multifactorial. In these cases, clinical judgment is required to determine whether or not the impairments are not better accounted for by other diagnoses that may be more appropriate. Comorbidities are common. *Remembering that children are not naturally sedentary and that motor activity is era-appropriate is important.*

Intelligently challenging dogma is rational. It puts emphasis on strengths and potential strengths rather than deficits in children's problematic conditions and stresses a health orientation rather than merely a focus on pathology. This wider scope of assessment prevents one diagnostic condition from blocking recognition of other, perhaps more central, shortcomings requiring consideration. About a decade ago, a group of luminaries in the field of child psychiatry published a detailed and thoughtful paper on what they termed "evolution and revolution in child psychiatry and ADHD as a disorder of adaptation." This comprehensive statement skillfully presented many of the perspectives in this book in regard to child behaviors that appear disordered at first but could be understood in less pathological and more functional ways.

In addition, more recently, a clinical study further considers some of the aforementioned matters and suggests that diagnoses of ADHD may produce confusion and dissonance in those diagnosed and their caregivers. It is proposed that therapeutic attention be given to structuring "a reflective space" that may address these competing concerns and introduce greater clarity into cloudy situations whose obscurity may add to further impairment.

Another often underrecognized problem is that of diversion and misuse of pharmaceutical stimulants used to treat ADHD. To date, little is known about the frequency and chronicity of misuse or the extent of associated harms. Aggressive research priorities are being recommended in populations most likely susceptible, namely, adolescents, young adults, and illicit substance abusers.

All assessments should be multidisciplinary. Diagnoses of problems with attention, motoric overactivity, and impulsivity require precise classification. Problems with the aforementioned signs need to be specifically positioned. For example, such hyperarousability and self-dysregulation may be primary factors of diagnostic categories such as impulse control disorder, oppositional defiant disorder, or ADHD. Furthermore, they may be secondary features of different primary conditions such as mood disorder, anxiety disorder, obsessive-compulsive disorder, conduct disorder, borderline intellectual functioning, learning disorders, disorders of executive functions, and so forth. Children with conduct disorder may impulsively engage in unsafe behaviors, and children with posttraumatic stress disorder may be inattentive because of distracting internal preoccupations with past traumas. Primary conduct disorders in children and adolescents require particular diligence since adolescent substance abuse and diversion of stimulant medications occur, and have long-term legal and developmental consequences. Motoric overactivity and impulsivity with behavioral disruption in children may also reflect overactivation as a side effect of antidepressant medications. Confounding signs and symptoms attributed incorrectly to diagnostic categories requires careful attention and discrimination.

When pediatricians and psychiatrists complete full assessments that include school collaboration, introducing therapies such as psychostimulant medications often follows. Parents need to be informed of the range of effects, side effects, risk-benefit ratios, and alternatives that include no medications. Studies emphasize that families' perspectives toward evidence-based treatments are mixed, and that they express interest in pursuing alternative interventions not delineated in current mainstream treatment guidelines. Informed consent is crucial since the side effect profile of psychotropic and stimulant drugs may produce undesirable "behavioral toxicity." Of note, is the recent introduction of a long acting medication, guanfacine, to treat ADHD. It is considered to be effective without having many troublesome side effects.

Behavioral toxicity includes a range of negative behaviors such as irritability, mood instability, anxiety, temper tantrums, aggression, poor appetite, difficulty falling asleep at night and waking up in the morning, and suppressed growth in weight and height. These medications may also cause facial tics, twitches, and grimaces, as well as skin picking and pulling out of head hair. Small increases in heart rate and blood pressure are typical. When on psychostimulant drugs, *some children report feeling pressured to work without the natural ability to modulate its intensity and periodically relax.* Although not specifically articulated, this driven quality appears to simulate feeling stressed and may also negatively affect the HPA axis that modulates the immune response.

The behavioral toxicity of psychotropic medications is termed an "iatrogenic" or treatment-induced negative effect. This possibility needs to be identified so that the drug-induced behavioral toxicity is not mistaken for other behavioral or psychiatrically diagnosable disorders in children on medications. Recent studies, moreover, have demonstrated that one in seven adolescents who are prescribed stimulant medications illegally diverts them to other adolescents who seek the activating effect. Moreover, recent European studies have demonstrated that the cigarette smoking prevalence of methylphenidate-treated ADHD patients is twice as high as typical norms. This suggests that methylphenidate use may correlate with tobacco consumption and nicotine craving in later life.

Hence, when the use of psychotropic medications, particularly psychostimulant drugs, is being considered, all the aforementioned factors require diligent deliberation. If medication as *one part* of a comprehensive treatment plan is needed, as may be the case in many situations, careful monitoring and reassessment over time are judicious and rational management strategies. The available range of psychotherapies such as cognitive behavioral and child and family guidance are essential components to guide families (and school personnel) through effective therapeutic interventions.

8.4 Preteens: Middle and Junior High School

Some educational systems recognize a transitional period and overlap between the elementary and high school years. This has been called "middle school" or "junior high school." Its timing varies considerably, but typically may encompass ages as early as nine through fourteen and span fifth or sixth grade through seventh, eighth, or ninth grade. Transitions from elementary school to middle or junior high school can be vulnerable periods, just as the transition from these times to formal high school.

In terms of cognitive capabilities, neurological evidence demonstrates that the ages of eleven to twelve are especially crucial for the start of developmental refinement of the prefrontal cortex, its synaptic anatomy or hardware. Accelerated synaptic pruning at the offset of puberty (around thirteen to fourteen years old for both sexes) follows previously accelerated synapse formation at the onset of puberty. The prefrontal cortex is closely associated with the "executive functions" (EF) that encompass preparing for and implementing complex tasks. With such neurobiological development, the major mental abilities that begin to more rapidly mature include working memory, attention, discrimination, decision making, and complex problem solving. This crucial cognitive juncture places previously absent demands on the preteen. The burgeoning ability for greater organizational skills that require more independent initiation and perseverance on tasks may reveal primary executive functions weaknesses.

Cognizance of these neuromaturational aspects and outer environmental demands is important, especially since EF difficulties along with the expectable spike in impulsivity at this preteen time and into early adolescence may be misdiagnosed as ADD or ADHD. While clearly acknowledging the evolving state of research into the complexity of underlying mechanisms of ADHD presentations, the biomental perspective tends to correlate the attentional dimension of ADHD with EFs, notably difficulties with the ability to inhibit nonrelevant information, cognitive flexibility, and fluidly shifting mental set. If this domain is found to be truly impaired, the so-called ADHD presentation may be understood with more precision as an EF or learning disorder. This then is best treated with intensive, individualized educational interventions and more precisely targeted EF training. Executive functions disorders, while not yet a DSM-IV-TR classification, require careful assessment and educational remediation. In addition to direct instruction about organizational strategies, other supports include cuing from the environment, visual organizational aids, written directions, checklists, breaking long assignments into smaller chunks, organizing workspace, and explicit feedback from parents and teachers. When adequately learned, these strategies act as internal software programs that the child may access in a self-dependent manner. Psychotropic medication is not part of this treatment plan.

This preadolescent and early adolescent period, which may span the onset of puberty, is often a highly sensitive emotional period. Often, but certainly not uniformly, the preteen and early adolescent years show emotional perturbations quite different from those seen before. This period of restlessness and change should not be underestimated. Puberty-specific maturational changes, in force during this period, will be discussed in the next section on adolescence.

From a cognitive perspective, previous cultural beliefs such as in Santa Claus or Easter Bunny dramatically fade due to developmental maturation and a more realistic appreciation of material evidence. It is at this time that new sequences of hormonal upsurges start to change the function and anatomy of the body. Children may become quietly startled by the uncanny genital sensations that suddenly appear. In addition, gender differences begin to consolidate. *Gender* typicality connotes the expression of male and female characteristics. Gender contentedness reflects the degree of comfort versus distress that accompanies gender assignment by self and others. Gender typing conventionally associates the observable behaviors characterized by emotional closeness with females in contrast to behaviors that reflect shared activities and accomplishments with males. Sensitively timed and phrased parental discussions about peer relationships, aggression, sexuality, and tolerance of differences help prepare a child for this transition into sexuality.

Children at this developmental age are sometimes called "'tweens" to indicate that they are be*tween* middle childhood and full adolescence. Emotional development becomes increasingly sensitive to peer and media influences. Today's accelerated cultural demands can be confusing for them. Preteen dramas—intense excitement, tension, and emotional involvement—are typical. Girls may feel anxiety about their weight and breast development. The range of eating disorders might be detected in susceptible children at this time. These and other concerns around this preteen transitional era may cause such an intense level of emotional volatility that adults may describe their previously "sweet" girl as one who is behaving like a "witch." Boys may be concerned about their height and muscular status, and accordingly, exhibit an aggressive bravado absent previously. Dramatic scenarios that may expand into sensationalized, unrealistically exaggerated and unnuanced melodramas—"boy drama" and "girl drama"—begin now, unfold in adolescence, and gradually decline toward the approach of emerging adulthood.

Another concern involves recent findings that have shown an accelerated interest at this preteen age in tanning activities, particularly without the use of sunscreens, thus creating vulnerability to medical problems in the future. The messages from screen media often fuel these dilemmas and, as has been reiterated in this book, require continuing parental monitoring.

Sex education during the school-age years is the continuing dialogue launched in the pre-school era. At that earlier time, discussions were simple and related to anatomy, terminology, and basic differences between the sexes. From six to twelve years, children require more specificity. Questions about erections in boys, "periods" in girls, why people have "sex," masturbation, and hetero- and homosexuality begin to emerge. Using children's books with illustrations or diagrams is useful. Preteens often are concerned about whether they are "normal" or not. Sensitive and direct discussions reiterating that children of the same age mature and develop at different rates help allay these typical concerns. A parent's receptivity and willingness to address questions about sexuality assures children of the affective bonds inherent in secure transactional sensitivity.

Since children at this age are still receptive to parental direction, providing children clear-cut messages that discourage fighting, teasing, and bullying is effective. Parents need to continue to be actively engaged in children's daily activities and to provide direct instruction about nonviolent methods of resolution when peer conflicts surface. Child specialists emphasize that children of this age need relatively more age-appropriate attention, supervision, and parental availability than those before eleven and after fifteen years of age. Parental psychological input—discrete monitoring and tactful discussion—may even be more influential than behavioral control, which entails reprimands such as behavioral restrictions and "grounding." At this time of early adolescence, children are especially sensitive to parents' implicit and explicit levels of anxiety.

This is a crucial time for parents to support prosocial attitudes and behaviors and foster developing social coping skills. Appropriate social scaffolding entails an optimal balance of interest and monitoring from all caregivers to provide and support the development of skills for self-control, self-discipline, and meaningful social engagement. Coaching is essential insofar as it addresses the emotional dimension of attitudes, choices, decisions, and behaviors. Modeling appropriate responses to challenging dilemmas is also effective, especially if anxieties are contained and modulated.

8.4.1 A Note about Homework

An important role that homework plays is that of reviewing and reinforcing lessons covered in class during the day. Homework should also instill a sense of healthy curiosity and help refine study skills, such as organizing tasks and problems, allotting time for each, and testing for understanding and retention. In other words, homework helps children to become lifelong learners.

Parents can support the aforementioned skill development by providing a suitable area, a routine time frame, avoiding distracting screen media, and sensitive monitoring. Mothers and fathers need to provide positive guidance without giving direct answers, avoid punishments, and let children face potential consequences of temporary failure, embarrassment, and the need to redo assignments for not getting them done on time. Parents may also serve as models by demonstrating the accomplishment of their own parental "homework," such as paying bills or reading.

Most educational specialists suggest the "ten-minute rule." This means ten minutes allotted to homework each school day evening beginning in the first grade, which increases by ten minutes for each additional grade: thirty minutes of homework in third grade and sixty minutes in sixth grade. In high school, a maximum of about two hours is suggested. Some studies have shown that academic performance improves among sixth- to ninth-graders who limit homework to ninety minutes a night, and among high schoolers who stop after two hours. Parents, however, often report that the first hour devoted to homework is the most productive, with diminishing returns after that. Support and encouragement with homework needs to be consistent. At times, however, real-world consequences for missed assignments provide a reality check.

9. ADOLESCENCE

Adolescence is the psychological term denoting the transitional developmental period between formal childhood and early adulthood. It is a developmental period of strength and resilience along with difficulties in the management of emotion and behavior. It is the period when children become teenagers and attend high school, which is sometimes called "secondary school." Adolescence may be considered an awkward period between sexual maturation and the attainment of adult roles and accompanying social responsibilities.

Puberty is the physiological term denoting reproductive ability that marks the start of adolescence. Precise chronological timing is flexible depending on frame of reference and markers (for example, hormonal, brain maturation, or anatomical). For girls, puberty may begin at about age nine or ten; for boys, puberty may begin at age ten to twelve. Contemporary conceptualizations of puberty describe it as a suite of changes on multiple biomental levels that occur in relative synchrony. The technical "offset" of puberty for both sexes may occur at thirteen to fourteen years old. The transitional period (roughly ages nine or ten through twelve) between middle childhood and formal adolescence is considered the *preadolescent* or *preteen era*.

Puberty-specific maturational changes in specific developmental domains have been demonstrated. These include romantic motivation, sexual interest, emotional intensity, changes in sleep/arousal regulation, appetite, risk for affective disorders in females, and increase in risk taking, novelty seeking, and sensation/reward seeking. These are believed to be related to physiological pubescent changes rather than merely age, and most correlate with emotion and motivation.

Adolescence or the "period of youth" comprises three phases: *early,* from age ten to thirteen; middle, from age fourteen to sixteen; and late, from age seventeen to twenty-one. Some theorists have termed the period from eighteen to twenty-five as that of "emerging adulthood."

Although this section primarily addresses the psychological dimensions of adolescence, a brief discussion about the neurological maturation of the adolescent brain helps to illustrate the biological basis of some typical behaviors.

9.1 Neurological Maturation of the Adolescent Brain

Recent and remarkable studies demonstrate that brain development continues after childhood as mentioned in the overview to this chapter. In terms of neuroanatomy and neurophysiology, overall brain volume does not change at this time. There are, however, significant decreases in gray matter as a result of normal synaptic pruning; this diminishes less active neural net connections. Synaptic density in the frontal cortex decreases by approximately 40 percent between ages seven and fifteen. This synaptic reorganization is a positive refinement of redundant or unused synapses and is believed to underlie the surge in higher cognitive and social functioning in adolescence. Such an extensive reconfiguration enhances integration of brain function across regions rather than improvements in the computational capacities of local brain function.

White matter, correlated with myelination and connectivity, particularly of the prefrontal lobes, increases linearly in adolescence but does not reach full maturity until approximately the mid-twenties. During the entire course of adolescence, therefore, synaptic pruning and reduced gray matter allow for more efficient local computations, enhancing the ability of discrete brain regions to support high-level cognitive control of behavior including working memory and other executive functions. The most dramatic increase in white matter—myelination—occurs in the dorsolateral prefrontal cortex (DLPC) between ages five and seventeen years. Attention regulation by the frontal lobe increases with larger areas of the anterior cingulate cortex (ACC) over development and correlates with increased myelination.

This region of the prefrontal cortex, the ACC, has also been implicated in cognitive control. This region is active during the target phase of a task when competing responses induce conflict. It is suggested that activity in the ACC might interact with the DLPFC to adjust cognitive control based on the amount of response conflict induced by the task. Models of a dorsolateral prefrontal-anterior cingulate cortical loop suggest that when response conflict occurs, the ACC monitors response output and signals the DLPFC for increased allocation of attentional resources. This model hypothesizes that the monitoring and signaling function of the ACC allows for modification of attention that is based on task demands. While this DLPFC-ACC system has been implicated in tasks requiring that a prepotent response tendency be overcome (impulse control), its role in task switching has not been established. Myelination in conjunction with synaptic pruning, therefore, increases the speed of neuronal transmission supporting the collaboration of widely distributed circuitry that integrates regions supporting top-down cognitive control of behavior such as response inhibition.

The significance of these findings is as follows. The prefrontal areas are the neural bases for executive functioning—judgment, planning, impulse control, postponement of action, execution of action, and self-correction. Different aspects of executive functions may have different developmental trajectories and are linked to synaptic pruning and myelination processes occurring during adolescence in the frontal cortex. The perturbation of gray matter linked with the onset and offset of puberty has been shown to correlate with a dip in cognitive performance that then shows postpubescent improvement.

Since these areas for calibrating behavior are not yet fully matured until approximately age twenty-five, adolescents, in fact, do not have the biological faculties for "mature" decision making and consistent delay of gratification. Adolescents do not have the ability to inhibit responses consistently. In contrast, subcortical areas of the ventral striatum and nucleus accumbens—associated with pleasure seeking and reward—mature earlier and evoke a strong motivation or desire to obtain stimulation. Since synaptic pruning is regionally specific, the phylogenetically older regions such as the striatum and motor cortex prune earlier than higher-level frontal regions associated with cognition. While it true that impulsivity steadily wanes from the preschool years to adulthood, there is a spike of increased impulsivity during the preteen and early adolescent period. The earlier maturation of the ventral striatum (nucleus accumbens) correlates with this peaking of perceived salience and strong motivation.

Recent studies strongly suggest that activation of the ventral striatum is decreased bilaterally in reward anticipation tasks, and greater risk taking is associated with lower gray matter density. Put differently, in individuals found to have high levels of risk seeking, the reward system of the brain does not respond as well to natural rewards. Instead, these individuals are drawn to seeking higher payoff rewards—stimuli that elicit more intense reactions—such as those produced by illicit substances. It has also been suggested that, in adolescence, there is a dramatic decrease in dopamine in the nucleus accumbens, which in turn elicits a need to restore this deficit, resulting in an increase in craving and gratification of the need for experiencing increased pleasurable stimulation. The release of dopamine may not be restricted merely to a few brain sites, but rather may involve a distributed system of complex neural circuits both subcortical and cortical. The looping neurocircuitry of motivational substrates is complex. A primary motivation circuitry involves the prefrontal cortex and ventral striatum; a secondary motivation circuitry involves the hippocampus (memory) and amygdala (affective information).

Hence, the more developed "pleasure" centers of the striatum and nucleus accumbens remain unmodulated by the inhibitory influence of the prefrontal lobes in the forebrain. This condition results in the typical adolescent attraction toward activities that induce excitement. Such behaviors usually involve unsafe risk taking, which includes, for example, involvements with illicit drugs, alcohol, and sexual promiscuity. While these biological considerations expand a broader understanding of adolescence, they remain one part—"the bio"—of the total biomental configuration. Intelligent emphasis on the integrated biomental perspective is the basis for effective caregiving and successful action planning.

Evolutionary psychology has also speculated about reasons underlying the tendency of adolescents, especially males, to exhibit risky, unsafe behaviors. It is suggested that this "young male syndrome" has roots in the ancestral attempts of males to demonstrate strength and valor, in essence high status, in front of peers in order to attract females with an aim toward ensuring reproduction. Status and physical resources associated with males are viewed, therefore, as factors valued by women. Modern-day males who choose safer paths to high status, such as attaining advanced education and secure occupations, have less need to exhibit the risks for prestige that may have been necessary in earlier times.

A last developmental fact of importance for adults to consider is that children's attention, working memory, and processing speed—all crucial for substantive learning, remembering, and altering behavior—do not reach adult levels until approximately fifteen years old. However, adolescent brain function is still not fully mature since it could and often does fail under "hot" or emotionally charged demanding situations. As further development proceeds into young adulthood, qualitative changes in existing capacities become more functionally integrated in a coherent way. This encompasses synchronized activity across brain regions rather than mere hierarchical inhibition by prefrontal processes alone. This fact may help orient caregivers and educators to children's and adolescents' natural abilities and, therefore, to what is reasonable to expect.

9.2 Adolescence: Ending Childhood

Adolescence, in many ways, can be regarded as the process that both ends childhood and ushers in emerging adulthood with its challenges of greater social complexity. How this ending is viewed and negotiated by both adolescent and family is crucial to personal success and family harmony. A deeper level of individuation from the family occurs, which is always accompanied by some difficulty for both adolescents and parents. Disengaging from childhood caregivers, peers, and toys is often accompanied by a show of shadowy force. The shadows of the past push from behind while the imaginations, aspirations, and adumbrations about the future are shadows pulling forward. Rebellion over parental control takes many forms. Nuclear interpersonal relationships are challenged in this separation from the family that had been the major social group. Often, this process is less than graceful. Both adolescents and their parents experience similar transitional crises of ambivalence, fear, anxiety, and loss. A balance of autonomy, mutuality, and interdependence is optimal in this transitional period. A great deal of patience, as had been previously needed in the toddler years, is required now.

In late adolescence, advancing conceptual abilities permit a greater— though limited—understanding of concepts of the future. This limited comprehension of long-term consequences coupled with typical adolescent idealism adds to the older adolescent's cognitive and motivational confusion about goal setting and planning for the future. This period of emerging adulthood often becomes stressful and requires increased parental guidance.

The adolescent years appear qualitatively different from the preceding period of childhood. The capacity for more independent thinking emerges. There is an adolescent quest for new intellectual understanding and discovering the "truth" of things. Ideals and sometimes exaggerated aspirations come to the forefront of consideration.

Role models, often in the form of perceived heroes and heroines, are selected for emulation and direction. It is common for adolescent boys and girls to become fascinated with the perceived glamour and success of their idealized persons. For boys, sports figures and hero figures hold high value. For girls, highly talented movie stars and performers function similarly.

Adolescence is a developmental era exceedingly sensitive not only to the interpersonal environment but also to the actual material environment, namely the high school milieu. This connotes the actual physical setting, architectural design, space allocations, aesthetics, and overall emotional ambience of the educational surroundings. When possible, parents should take these variables into consideration when choosing a suitable learning context for the adolescent. Greater options are becoming increasingly available.

The prolonged transition from the protection, close supervision, and controlled guidance needed in childhood transforms itself toward a greater desire for and achievement of self-reliance. While children under twelve should not be left alone at home for any period of time, early adolescence is the time to consider permitting greater relative autonomy as long as safety issues are adequately taken into account. *Coregulation* is a form of supervision that supports such guided individuation and greater self-reliance. It respects the adolescent's capacity for self-determination in the context of collaborative rather than unilateral decision making. For example, the requirement for sleep changes from the elementary school child's need for ten to eleven hours to the adolescent's need for eight to nine hours. It is common for adolescents to stay up late and need to awaken early on school mornings, which results in a lack of proper sleep. Parental coregulation of sleep patterns with adolescents requires continuing collaboration.

Adolescents become consciously aware of explicit developmental changes, such as burgeoning sexual interests and appearance as well as a need for more privacy. They have to use more intentionality and directed effort to cope with and navigate these real-life transitions felt as intense. For this, adolescents will style their clothing and alter their vocabulary in ways that both mask yet reveal underlying feelings. Limit-setting interventions by parents, however, are decisive in helping adolescents develop appropriate self-management skills. The wonder years of adolescence finally emerge into adulthood, wherein age affords the young adult greater legal and social accountability, obligations, and rights, as well as less need for coregulation.

9.3 Cognitive and Moral Reconfigurations

Significant cognitive abilities also emerge at this time and are accompanied by emotional upheavals and reconfigurations. In childhood, thinking was characterized by greater concreteness and instance-specific awareness. In adolescence, the emergence of *formal mental operations* permits hypothetical and deductive abstract reasoning. In other words, in addition to indicative thinking in which "A equals A or B or C, etc.," a subjunctive capacity is added. This allows adolescents to formulate hypotheses such as "if A is present, then X might occur as a possibility."

Moral capacities—moral reasoning and ethical options for behavior— also come to the forefront of relevant concerns. This change results from both a greater capacity for personal introspection and the greater challenges posed by increasing social complexity. Some theoreticians have described these advances in terms of gender with the moral logic of rules, justice, and fairness being notably prominent for males and the moral logic of caring and compassion more characteristic of females. Certainly, these two moral orientations overlap in both teenage boys and girls.

Adolescence brings many new demands and challenges to the developmentally transitioning child. Many of these specific tasks have been described. Some of them involve body image organization and self-identity formation. Forming a *self-identity* is a gradual process in the adolescent years. Identity correlates with a stabilizing set of preferences that become organized and remembered as a *self-signature*. The author's work on envy theory has discussed in detail the mechanisms of *self-signature updating*. When themes of "freedom" emerge during this time, they typically connote the wish for opportunities and options for expanded experiences. The adolescent's typically solipsistic self-absorption—only sure that his or her mind and its understanding is reliable—adds a dynamic element to adolescent-adult relations. This facet is further enhanced by skepticism of authority figures in family and outside agencies, such as school and political institutions. *Ego identity* is the phrase that psychoanalytic psychology has used to describe the adolescent's dynamically organizing sense of self.

9.4 Socialization and Peer Relationships

In adolescence, there is a more complex reorientation to peer group affiliations. Adolescent self-esteem is enhanced by the need to belong, to be accepted, and to be recognized as valuable by peers. There is a reconfiguration of earlier peer group membership. Individuals seek small peer group affiliation with those who are similar or idealized. In the teenage years, each member of smaller peer group attempts to appear unique in some way. He or she tries to signal individuality while simultaneously being recognized in a common group affiliation. For example, subcultures become prominent in later adolescence wherein an individual may identify as a "punk" or "geek," setting himself apart from the mainstream while also affirming characteristics and desire for inclusion in those groups.

In early adolescence, peer groups become organized around same-sex cliques—small groups of about five to eight members with striking similarities. Mixed-sex cliques, by contrast, become prominent in mid-adolescence. In late adolescence, cliques become less prominent, and the structure of group affiliations at this time is more variable, often including both sexes. Previously held rigidity in gender distinctions and the physical separation prominent in the elementary school years become lessened. Larger groupings or crowds of adolescents and early adults with designations such as "jocks," "nerds," "brains," and so forth may appear.

In addition to these varieties of group affiliations, adolescents in their mid- and later years, measure self-worth by the interpersonal metric of their desirability. A prime interpersonal value is seeking acknowledgment of being attractive, wanted, loved, or singled out by a peer who is perceived as validating desirability, typically in a romantic fashion. While a great deal of time is spent dwelling on these aspirations, little of substance is ever implemented. The immense anxieties attendant on forming relationships, especially intimate ones, makes approach and closeness a challenge. Remaining in and retreat to the safe haven of unrequited personal fantasy is the typical path taken.

9.5 Preparing for Adulthood: Personality Consolidation

Because adolescents typically find it difficult to reconcile their inner life of ideals, aspirations, and fantasy with the more concrete demands of school and preparing for emerging adulthood, a frenetic appearance may vacillate with behaviors that seem indolent or lazy. From a psychodynamic point of view, this intermittent standstill reflects the adolescent taking a "personal time-out" to ponder or merely relax from the overwhelming barrage of new and competing challenges being faced. Parents being aware of this moratorium can be supportive with patience and tact instead of instant negative reactivity.

By the end of adolescence, individuals have virtually consolidated a personality structure that becomes increasingly resistant to change. In many ways, an adolescent's underlying temperamental attitude establishes itself as a relatively enduring social style. For example, a person may be more gregarious or independent.

With the many biomental changes of this age, an adolescent is confronted with a need to incorporate new ways of self-understanding. When this process succeeds, self-esteem is strengthened. Peer group feedback can contribute both positively and negatively. Peer influence and pressure are especially strong in early adolescence. Developmental neuroscience research has recently emphasized the role of the hormone oxytocin on adolescent brain functioning. Such literature notes the hormone's role in heightening emotional sensitivity, receptiveness to peer influence, and risk-taking behaviors of adolescence. In psychology, this susceptibility to being influenced is related to *cue vulnerability*. This term indicates that adolescents are strongly influenced by the cues or stimuli they are exposed to in electronic media. These ideas are related to adolescent brain development as discussed previously.

Self-concept and how an adolescent defines her- or himself have a strong contribution from physical appearance or "looks." Adolescents who are overweight or underweight or have significant acne become self-conscious and require the tactful help of parents in addressing proper well-being. Many adolescent specialists, for example, strongly recommend at least one hour of moderate outdoor exercise at least five times per week to maintain health and set a proper trajectory into adulthood. Parental examples of healthy nutrition, exercise, and weight maintenance are essential. Adolescents who are already overweight find it difficult to sustain both the motivational and physical endurance needed to exercise regularly.

Of interest with regard to exercise and sports at this age are recent studies about nonfatal traumatic brain injuries associated with emergency department visits that show approximate rates of high school athletes who sustain concussions: 15 percent of female soccer players, 11 percent of female basketball players, 10 percent of male football players, 9 percent of male soccer players, and 3 percent of male baseball players. Parents also note that cheer-leading activities positively correlates with sprains and orthopedic injuries. Proper surveillance and injury prevention are encouraged. This is an important consideration since physical injuries or traumatic brain injuries can significantly alter an adolescent's trajectory into adulthood.

9.6 Emotional Development

Two chief features related to emotions and emotional development in adolescence are the intensity of emotion aroused during pubertal maturation, and a greater inclination to actively seek out experiences that create high-intensity feelings such as arousal and excitement.

In regard to emotional health, it has been recognized that depression is prominent in adolescence. Component causes include biological predisposition, less-sensitive parenting, learned helplessness as an attributional perspective, and negative life events. Male adolescent suicide is the third leading cause of death in this group. Suicide is the sixth leading cause of death in children ages five to fourteen. Self-esteem and a supportive family play important roles here.

As has been emphasized throughout this book, emotional development remains important but differs over time. In adolescents, emotions play a major role in influencing attitudes, choices, and behaviors. The phenomenon termed *alexithymia* may have an underestimated prevalence. *Alexithymia* denotes the state of mind in which emotions and feelings are experienced but not identified or labeled. This state may be typical of adolescents in general. Parents can help by tactfully and sensitively using the names of commonly experienced feelings. Adolescents may thus observe and learn how to label feelings through this vicarious method of identification. To be sure, such intervention should begin in childhood as a typical part of parenting.

Another task of adolescence involves the psychological and emotional shift from greater dependence on the family to arenas outside the home. Peer groups and school environments are instrumental in promoting a newfound socialization. In addition, involvement in sports, band, or other group activities provides a context for socialization and development of a social self.

In adolescence, burgeoning sexuality in terms of bodily changes, emotional interests, and vivid fantasy life are major preoccupations that need to be managed by the developing teenager. The previously felt intermittent genital sensations of preadolescence now become an almost unending barrage of thunderous feelings and anatomical, physiological events. Adolescents typically struggle with these changes in nonarticulate ways, that is, through impulsive behaviors that may include sexual activity and illicit substance use. Discussions among small groups of adolescents are usually more confusing than clarifying and add not only to the challenge but also the excitement of managing sexuality at this time. Factors influencing sexual behavior include temperament, personality traits, gender, culture, religion, ethnicity, family dynamics, and values.

Gender identity in terms of masculinity and femininity is also addressed at this time. *Gender intensification* is most evident in early adolescence and declines in mid-adolescence and thereafter. An adolescent's *ethnic awareness* of identity, ancestry, and shared beliefs becomes set in the context of family values, culture, faith traditions, customs, and rites of passage. Adolescents often struggle with their humanity and the perceived enormity of the extended human condition.

Parent's sensitivity to and patience with the expectable awkwardness of adolescence can provide guidance that is empathetic but firm. A great deal of negotiating, redefining, and reorienting can become stressful to the adolescent and family. Adolescents are typically oversensitive to what they perceive as adult redundancies and repetitiveness, particularly admonitions by parents. Ordinary things such as household chores, schoolwork, curfew times, and a right to reasonable privacy become concerns that need to be negotiated.

Sensitivity when asking questions of adolescents is crucial. Tone and wording of questions should be tactful. Asking questions such as "How did your day go?" may be perceived as too intrusive. It may be better to phrase initial inquiries with content that is relatively neutral as, for example, "What was the funniest thing that happened to you today?" Beginning conversations with nonsensitive subjects and then slowly progressing to potentially more important areas of concern requires tact, skill, and patience. Sometimes asking, for example, "What's your impression of . . . ?" is both neutral and engaging.

9.7 Emerging Self-Dependence

An important task for the older adolescent is preparing for the immediate future. *Self-determination* enables the adolescent to influence the course of his or her future. This may mean further educational pursuits or transitioning into work activities. Guidance from school counselors, parents, and potential role models is important and often helpful. Often, adolescents need the advice and guidance of someone outside the family with whom they have less emotional baggage.

Until recently *self-advocacy* was a concept used in contexts with adults with disabilities; increasingly, it is recognized as a skill that teens, especially those with disabilities, need to develop. *Self-advocacy* refers to an individual's ability to effectively communicate, negotiate or assert his or her own interests, desires, needs, and rights. It involves making informed decisions and taking responsibility for those decisions. Self-advocacy includes understanding one's strengths and needs, identifying personal goals, knowing legal rights and responsibilities, and communicating these to others. Self-advocacy is speaking up for oneself.

Premature choosing of values, beliefs, and goal trajectories without exploring alternative possibilities stifles self-development at this time and in adulthood. Adolescence is a period of new exploration and a search for expanded opportunities. Reasonable experimentation that is low risk provides opportunities to search for new experiences and broaden personal and social horizons. This is an aspect of the normative "identity crisis" that is typical in adolescence.

Adolescence is a crucial time for developing a more solid "reality sense"—the capacity to differentiate reality from fantasy and manage challenges safely. Reality denotes ideas and behaviors based on adaptive operations characterized by mathematical fidelity tempered with flexible human compassion; these developments span a lifetime. Often, the adolescent's mental pain around self-identity, sexual identity, and approaching educational and career choices makes it easy to turn to omnipotent fantasy as a solution. Using such unrealistic strategies typically is precarious and in the end destructive, if not eventually recognized and managed more in accord with reality-based constructive coping skills and choices.

As is true of emotional development at the toddler stage, adolescents may attempt to manage fears and challenges of the unknown by confronting them head on. Parents need to be prepared for these counterphobic occasions where such "daredevil" behavior is acted out. Even if met with opposition, it is necessary to take precautions by discussing the real-world riskiness of potentially harmful behaviors in clear, salient, and emotionally meaningful terms.

Adolescents may either inadvertently or deliberately engage in high-risk behaviors for their short-term positive effects. This has a significant biological basis in the as yet unmatured adolescent brain, as discussed previously. Peer pressure is often instrumental in influencing adolescent choices. Areas of concern for parents include unsafe driving, cigarettes, illicit drugs, alcohol, sexual activity, and violence. Studies show, for example, that illicit drug use reaches a peak between ages nineteen and twenty-two.

As mentioned in the discussion on impulse control in chapter 3, mid-adolescence has been found to be a highly sensitive time for behavioral inhibition or impulse control to become effective, if rewards are made appropriately salient and appealing. This fact has implications for the management of behaviors by sensitive parents. In addition, peer pressure is an opportunity for parents to remind children that tactful and sensitive ignoring is a useful social skill.

Recent studies have suggested that close emotional attachment between an involved father and an adolescent significantly decreases the odds of adolescent alcohol use. A father's genuine concern and persuasive counseling, therefore, can be an effective protective factor in this regard. Father-child involvement that is established early provides a foundation for parental effectiveness in adolescence. Overall, protective factors against adolescent substance abuse include resilient temperament, intelligence, prosocial orientation, intact family, and a value on religion. All these can contribute to and support healthy emotional self-management.

Nonetheless, as an adolescent traverses the threshold into adulthood, both eagerness to explore new vistas and anxiety eliciting avoidance interact. A myriad of new challenges such as managing intensely felt, often volatile, emotional states, striving to become more self-dependent, taking on the responsibilities of biological, social, and preferred gender roles, and struggles with matters of control in the context of "the one and the many"—the need to defer and constrain personal wishes in cultural contexts such as occupation, civil law requirements, and so forth can and often do elicit stress, anxiety, procrastination, and avoidance. Many young adults, for example, ambivalently choose to remain living with their families, especially in current times of economic instability and social unrest. Such paths assuage a sharp self-family individuation. Extending educational curriculums (a fifth year of high school) and remaining at home with parents are becoming more frequently chosen, if not practical, courses of action, at least for a time.

9.8 Sex Education in Adolescence

Sex education, to a large extent, is a parent's responsibility. Although many aspects of the anatomy, physiology, and social perspectives of sex and sexuality may be addressed in schools, parents retain primary responsibility. As part of a continuing dialogue, discussions about sex have now advanced from simpler explanations to an emphasis on the emotional aspects of intimacy. This encompasses matters of love, affection, the need to feel loved, and mutual respect. Adolescents typically feel overwhelmed by peer pressure, the media, pervasive curiosity, and also loneliness. Basic ideas are essential to convey. These include the fact that sex is an adult behavior and that any form of forced or violent sexual behavior is wrong.

Sensitivity to an adolescent's curiosity and concerns denotes seizing the moment for discussion whether prompted by overt questions or events that randomly emerge such as occasioned by those portrayed in the media. Honest and direct responses help clarify and articulate an adolescent's perspective and pressing concerns. Listening attentively without projecting adult perspectives helps foster communication.

Although relative brevity and conciseness is best, moving beyond mere facts and highlighting salient issues related to beliefs, values, ethics, and personal responsibility is fruitful. Creating an agreeable common ground by delineating both adolescent and parental perspectives enhances dialogue, transactional sensitivity, and guidance.

9.9 A Note on Bullying

Another concern of adolescence is bullying. Although recent examination has shown bullying to begin as early as the preschool years, it becomes more dangerous in adolescence. *Bullying* is intentional and habitual peer violence and exploitation. It reflects egocentric, antisocial, and dehumanizing interpersonal attitudes.

Typically, the bully is a person with little or no empathy whose aim is to establish prominence by dominating vulnerable others. In addition to more obvious causes that may include negative temperament and adverse life events, conflicts associated with envy, jealousy, and greed may underlie such aggressive behaviors.

Bullying is a form of negative attention seeking. Some have correlated bullying with conduct disorders and antisocial personality traits. While bullies comprise up to 20 percent of children, 30 percent of children may be victims of their peers. The recent introduction and overuse of "energy drinks" that contain high concentrations of caffeine and other over-the-counter stimulants has been proposed to contribute to the rise of the mood irritability and aggressiveness associated with bullying.

Bullying may take several forms: the act of willfully causing harm to others through verbal harassment, such as teasing, name calling, racial slurs, rumors, or malicious gossip; physical assaults, such as hitting, kicking, biting, or destroying property; social exclusion, such as deliberately rejecting a child from a peer group; and cyberbullying that includes harassing emails, instant messages, text messages, blogs, and Internet postings.

Teasing is a form of bullying typically present in the elementary and early high school years. Prevalence rates range from 10 to 20 percent for all students who report being teased at school at least several times per week. Overt teasing may subside in the high school years, but cyberbullying may be taking its place. Special-needs students, minorities, and those with atypical physical appearances show a disproportionately high selection. Children and adolescents with Asperger disorder may be particularly susceptible to being teased and bullied. Vulnerable children may appear more passive, suggestible, and gullible. They appear to be "easy targets" to aggressors who seek to exert power and control to dominate and manipulate others in cruel and antisocial ways. Further perspectives on matters of interpersonal control and manipulation are found in chapters 1 and 6.

Preschool bullying is not uncommon but estimates are yet unavailable. Warning signs at any age may include a child's reluctance to attend school, unexplained stomachaches or headaches, damaged or missing clothing or possessions, unexplained bruises, isolative and withdrawn behaviors, disturbed appetite or sleep, and poor school performance. Parents need to actively address concerns immediately with the child, teenager, parents, and school, whether they feel their child is a perpetrator or victim. Early intervention is best since bullying and peer victimization are being increasingly correlated with depression and possible suicidality.

Parents, the main line of defense against bullying, should maintain a calm and composed demeanor, encourage children to share their concerns, find out as much as possible about the situation, and not encourage retaliation. Sensitively helping children discuss these matters is important since they may be reluctant for fear that exposure may make things worse. Remaining involved, affirming the child's distress, responding with comforting words and plans, and empowering children are essential positions to take. Stressing safety is also important.

Teaching children to avoid situations when possible is best. Avoiding isolation and staying with a group of trusted friends is a very positive strategy. Strengthening positive and active socialization skills deters children from the status of perceived victims. If bullying occurs, children should be advised to try to make eye contact, stand tall, stay calm, tell bullies to stop, and then walk away and seek out teachers or other adults for help and protection. It is also helpful for children, parents, and teachers to designate specific friends that a child can go to during times of need.

Bullies crave attention in negative and dangerous ways. They behave as if they are compelled to dominate and achieve submission. Their need to forcefully control and aggressively manipulate others is apparent. Any safe measures, therefore, that can be taken to circumvent these goals is useful. Helping children to be safe also includes instructing them not to give the bully unnecessary attention to the greatest extent possible.

Parents can show children that the use of laughter, agreeing in a subtly ironic way, and even indifference can confuse the bully whose goal is to elicit a strong negative reaction, especially distress. Contacting school officials immediately and formulating safe and acceptable management strategies are effective plans of action. School antibullying programs, especially enlisting the efforts of observing bystanders, need to be implemented. Clear-cut consequences for perpetrators need to be communicated and enacted. Follow-up and reviews of the entire situation are needed.

Boosting children's self-confidence by thoughtful discussions, encouragement, and involvement in activities like sports, outdoors trips, music, and art is useful. Such positive interventions build personal courage, confidence, and the ability to persevere in the face of adversity. Counseling and professional guidance may be useful. Both perpetrators and victims need interventions. Both perpetrators and victims who are involved in frequent or intense bullying may require screening for psychiatric disorders.

9.10 Adolescents and Mental Health

In addition to correlations with bullying, parents and caregivers need to monitor children's and adolescent's behavior to rule out possible mental disorders. Keeping a finger on an adolescent's "nonverbal pulse"—changing emotional attitudes, facial expressions, behaviors, and gestures—provides valuable information even in the absence of words. Maladjustment is believed to occur in up to 20 percent of children and may include the following mental disorders: depression, anxiety, Asperger disorder, autistic spectrum disorders, bipolar, schizophrenia, obsessive-compulsive disorder, anorexia, bulimia, Tourette's syndrome, substance abuse, and antisocial behaviors.

Protective factors that offer an adolescent mental, emotional, and behavioral resilience include relatively stable temperament, healthy personality formation, supportive family, sound intelligence, and good health status. Exposure to values, morals, and ethical guidance beginning in the preschool years helps foster empathy, a sense of moral relevance, and prosocial cooperativeness in the adolescent years. All these factors interact to facilitate larger-scale adaptational processes encompassing the individual, family, and extended social resource group. The plasticity of human nature can modulate a variety of assaults and support wide-ranging health-oriented reconfigurations.

REFERENCES

Adolph, K. E., Karasik, L. B., & Tamis-LeMonda, C. S. (2010). Motor skill. In M. H. Bornstein (Ed.), *Handbook of cultural developmental science*, pp. 61–88. New York: Psychology Press.

Ages and Stages Questionnaires website:www.agesandstages.com.

American Academy of Child and Adolescent Psychiatry website:www.aacap.org.

American Academy of Pediatrics website:www.healthychildren.org.

American Academy of Pediatrics (2009). *Caring for your baby and young child* (5th ed.). S. P. Shelov (Ed.). New York: Bantam.

American Academy of Pediatrics. (2010). *Your Baby's First Year* (3rd ed.). S. P. Shelov (Ed.). New York: Bantam.

American Academy of Pediatrics (2011). *Preventing childhood obesity in early care and education programs*. Elk Grove, IL: Author.

American Academy of Pediatrics and American College of Obstetricians (2005). *Breastfeeding handbook for physicians*. Elk Grove, IL: Author.

American Psychiatric Association (2000). *Diagnostic and statistical manual of mental disorders, 4th edition, text revision (DSM-IV-TR)*. Washington, DC: American Psychiatric Press.

Anderson, V., Jacobs, R., & Anderson, P. (2008). *Executive functions and the frontal lobes: A lifespan perspective* (*Studies on neuropsychology, neurology and cognition*). London: Psychology Press.

Apfel, N. H., & Provence, S. (2001). *Infant-toddler and family instrument manual (Itfi)*. New York: Brookes Publishing.

Arnett, J. (1999). Adolescent storm and stress, reconsidered. *The American Psychologist, 54*, 317–326.

Aylward, G. P. (1999). *Bayley Infant Neurodevelopmental Screener (BINS)*. San Antonio, Texas: Psychological Corporation.

Baillargeon, R. (1987). Object permanence in 3½-and 4½-month-old-infants. *Developmental Psychology, 23*, 655–664.

Baillargeon, R. H. (2002). The acquisition of physical knowledge in infancy: A summary in eight lessons. In U. Goswami (Ed.), *Blackwell handbook of childhood cognitive development*. Oxford: Blackwell.

Baillargeon, R., & DeVos, J. (1991). Object permanence in young infants: Further evidence. *Child Development, 62*, 1230.

Baillargeon, R., Spelke, E. S., & Wasserman, S. (1985). Object permanence in five-month-old infants. *Cognition, 20*, 191–208.

Baillargeon, R. H., Zoccolillo, M., Keenan, K., Cote, S., Perusse, D., Wu, H. X., & Boivin, M. (2007). Gender differences in physical aggression: A prospective population-based survety of children before and after 2 years of age. *Developmental Psychology, 43*, 13–26.

Baldwin Dancy, R. 2000. *You are your child's first teacher*. Berkeley, CA: Celestial Arts.

Bahrick, L. E., Hernandez-Reif, M., & Flom, R. (2005). The development of infant learning about specific face-voice relations. *Developmental Psychology, 41*, 541–552.

Barber, A. D., & Carter, C. S. (2005). Cognitive control involved in overcoming prepotent response tendencies and switching between tasks. *Cerebral Cortex, 15*(7), 899–912.

Barnea-Goraly, N., Menon, V., Eckert, M., Tamm, L., Bammer, R., Karchemskiy, A., Dant, C. C., & Reiss, A. (2005). White matter development during childhood and adolescence: A cross-sectional diffusion tensor imaging study. *Cerebral Cortex, 15* (12), 1848–1854.

Bartrip, J., Morton, J., & de Schonen, S. (2001) responses to mother's face in 3-week to 3-month-old infants. *British Journal of Developmental Psychology, 19*, 219–232.

Batki, A., Baron-Cohen, S., Wheelwright, S., Connellan, J., & Ahluwalia, J. (2000). Is there an innate gaze module? Evidence from human neonates. *Infant Behavior and Development, 23*, 223–229.

Bava, S., Thayer, R., Jacobus, J., Ward, M., Jernigan, T. L., & Tapert, S. F. (2010). Longitudinal characterization of white matter maturation during adolescence. *Brain Research, 1327*, 38–46.

Berk, L. (2011). *Infants, children, and adolescents* (7th ed.). Boston: Allyn & Bacon.

Bierman, K. L., & Powers, C. J. (2009). Social skills training to improve peer relations. In K. H. Rubin, W. M. Bukowski, & B. Laursen (Eds.), *Handbook of peer interactions, relationships, and groups*, pp. 603–621. New York: Guilford.

Blair, C., & Razza, R. P. (2007). Relating effortful control, executive function, and false belief understanding to emerging math and literacy ability in kindergarten. *Developmental Psychology, 78*, 647–663.

Blakemore, S., & Choudhury, S. (2006). Development of the adolescent brain: implications for executive function and social cognition. *Journal of Child Psychology and Psychiatry, 47*(3–4), 296–312.

Bornstein, M. H., & Arterberry, M. E. (2003). Recognition, discrimination, and categorization of smiling by 5-month-old infants. *Developmental Science, 6*, 585–599.

Boy, F., Evans C. J. , Edden, R. A., Lawrence, A. D., Singh, K. D., Husain, M., & Sumner, P. (2011). Dorsolateral prefrontal ã-aminobutyric acid in men predicts individual differences in rash impulsivity. *Biological Psychiatry, 70*(9), 866–872.

Braungart-Rieker, J., Courtney, S., & Garwood, M. M. (1999). Mother- and father-infant attachment: Families in context. *Journal of Family Psychology, 13*, 535–553.

Brazelton, T. B. (1992). *Touchpoints: The essential references*. Cambridge, MA: Perseus Books.

Brazelton, T. B., & Sparrow, J. D. (2002). *Touchpoints 3 to 6.* New York: De Capo Press.

———. (2006). *Touchpoints: Birth to three.* New York: De Capo Press.

Breastfeeding.com website:www.breastfeeding.com.

Bridges, W. (2004). *Transitions: Making sense of life's changes.* New York: De Capo Press.

Bron, T. I., Bijlenga, D., Kasander, M. V., Spuijbroek, A. T., Beekman, A. T., & Kooij, J. J. (2012). Long-term relationship between methylphenidate and tobacco consumption and nicotine craving in adults with ADHD in a prospective cohort study. *European Journal of Neuropsychopharmacology,* July 17. (Epub ahead of print)

Bushnell, I. W. R., Sai, F., & Mullin, J. T. (1989). Neonatal recognition of the mother's face. *British Journal of Developmental Psychology, 7,* 3–15.

Caldera, Y. M. (2004). Paternal involvement and infant-father attachment: a Q-set study. *Fathering: Journal of Theory, Research, and Practice about Men as Fathers, 2*(2), 13–150.

Card, N. A., Stucky, B. D., Sawalani, G. M., & Little, T. D. (2008). Direct and indirect aggression during childhood and adolescence: A meta-analytic review of gender differences, intercorrelations, and relations to maladjustment. *Child Development, 79,* 1185–1229.

Carter, C. S., Lederhendler, I. I., & Kirkpatrick, B. (Eds.). (1999). *The integrative neurobiology of affiliation.* Cambridge, MA: MIT Press.

Casey, B. J., Tottenham, M., Liston, C., & Durston, S. (2005). Imaging the developing brain: What have we learned about cognitive development? *Trends in Cognitive Sciences, 9,* 104–110.

Centers for Disease Control and Prevention (2011). Nonfatal traumatic brain injuries related to sports and recreation activities among persons aged ≤ 19 years: United States, 2001–2009. *Morbidity and Mortality Weekly Report, 60*(39), 1337–1342.

Chambers, R. A., Taylor, J. R., & Potenza, M. (2003). Developmental neurocircuitry in adolescence: A critical period of addiction vulnerability. *American Journal of Psychiatry, 160,* 1041–1052.

Chawarska, K., Klin, A., Volkmar, F. R., & Powers, M. D. (2010). *Autism spectrum disorders in infants and toddlers: Diagnosis, assessment, and treatment.* New York: Guilford.

Courchesne, E. Chism, H. J., Townsend, J., Cowles, A., & Covington, J. (2000). Normal brain development and aging: Quantitative analysis at in vivo MR imaging in healthy volunteers. *Radiology, 266,* 672–695.

Dahl, R. E. (2004). Adolescent brain development: A period of vulnerabilities and opportunities. Keynote address. *Annals of the New York Academy of Sciences, 1021,* 1–22.

Daniels, M. (2000). *Dancing with words: Signing for hearing children's literacy.* New York: Bergin & Garvey.

Davis, C. C., Claudius, M., Palinkas, L. A., & Leslie, L. K. (2011). Putting families in the center: Family perspectives on decision making and ADHD and implications for ADHD care. *Journal of Attention Disorders,* October 5. doi:10.1177/1087054711413077

Denham, S. A. (2006). Emotional competence: Implications for social functioning. In J. L. Luby (Ed.), *Handbook of preschool mental health: Development, disorders, and treatment,* pp. 23–44. New York: Guilford

Deoni, S. C. L., Mercure, E., Blasi, A., Gasston, D., Thomson, A., Johnson, Steven S. M., Williams, C. R., & Murphy, D. G. M. (2011). Mapping infant brain myelination with magnetic resonance imaging. *The Journal of Neuroscience, 31*(2), 784–791. doi:10.1523/JNEUROSCI.2106-10.2011

Dillon, D. G., & Pizzagalli, D. A. (2007). Inhibition of action, thought, and emotion: A selective neurobiological review. *Applied and Preventive Psychology, 12,* 99–114.

Dunstan, P. (2006). *Dunstan Baby Language.* [DVD]. ASIN: B000PDZ9SU.

Eisenberg, N., Eggum, N. D., & Edwards, A. (2010). Empathy-related responding and moral development. In W. F. Arsenio & E. A. Lemerise (Eds.), *Emotions, aggression, and morality in children: Bridging development and psychopathology,* pp. 115–135. Washington, DC: American Psychological Association.

Elias, C. L., & Berk, L. E. (2002). Self-regulation in young children: Is there a role for sociodramatic play? *Early Childhood Research Quarterly, 17,* 216–238.

Eliot, L. (2000). *What's going on in there?* New York: Bantam.

———. (2010). *Pink brain, blue brain.* New York: Mariner.

Evans, W. N., Morill, W. Z. N., & Parente, S. T. (2010). Measuring inappropriate medical diagnosis and treatment in survey data: The case of ADHD among school-age children. *Journal of Health Economics, 29*(5), 657– 673.

Fagan, J. F., & Singer, L. T. (1979). The role of simple feature differences in infant recognition of faces. *Infant Behavior and Development, 2*, 39–46.

Farroni, T., Csibra, G., Simion, F., & Johnson, M. H. (2002). Eye contact detection in humans from birth. *Proceedings of the National Academy of Science USA, 99*, 9602–9605.

Farroni, T., Menon, E., Rigato, S., & Johnson, M. H. (2007). The perception of facial expressions in newborns. *European Journal of Developmental Psychology, 4*, 2–13.

Farroni, T., Pividori, D., Simion, F., Massaccesi, S., & Johnson, M. H. (2004). Gaze following in newborns. *Infancy, 5*, 39–60.

Fox, N., Kimmerly, N. L., & Schafer, W. D. (1991). Attachment to mother/attachment to father: A meta-analysis. *Child Development, 62*, 210–225.

Frankenburg, W. K., Dodds, J., Archer, P., Bresnick, P. et al. (1990). *Denver II screening manual*. Denver: Denver Developmental Materials.

Freeman, H., & Newland, L. A. (2010). New directions in father attachment. *Early child development and care, 180*, 1–8.

Gao, Y., Raine, A., Venables, P. H., Dawson, M. E., & Mednick, S. A. (2010). Association of poor childhood fear conditioning and adult crime. *American Journal of Psychiatry, 167*, 56–60.

Garcia, J., & Rusinak, K. W. (1980). What the nose learns from the mouth. In D. Muller Schwarze & R. M. Silverstein (Eds.), *Chemical signals in vertebrates*. New York: Plenum.

Gesell, A., & Ilg, F. (1946). *The child from five to ten*. New York: Harper & Brothers.

Gessel, L. M., Fields, S. K., Collins, C. L., Dick, R. W., & Comstock, D. (2007). Concussions among United States high school and collegiate athletes. *Journal of Athletic Training, 42*(4), 495–503.

Gibson, E. J. (2000). Perceptual learning in development: Some basic concepts. *Ecological Psychology, 12*, 295–302.

Giedd, J. N. (2008). The teen brain: Insights from neuroimaging. *Journal of Adolescent Health, 42*, 335–343.

Giedd, J. N., Blumenthal, J., Jeffries, N. O., Castellanos, F. X., Liu, H., Zijdenbos, A., Paus, T., Evans, A. C., & Rapoport, J. L. (1999). Brain development during childhood and adolescence: A longitudinal MRI study. *Nature Neuroscience, 2*, 861–863.

Giedd, J. N., Snell, J. W., Lange, N., Rajapakse, J. C., Kaysen, D., Vaituzis, A. C., Vauss, Y. C., Hamburger, S. D., Kozuch, P. L., & Rapoport, J. L. (1996). Quantitative magnetic resonance imaging of human brain development: Ages 4–18. *Cerebral Cortex, 6*, 551– 560.

Gilligan, C. (1982). *In a different voice*. Boston: Harvard University Press.

Giorgio, A., Watkins, K. E., Douaud, G., James, A. C., James, S., DeStefano, N., Matthews, P. M., Smith, S. M., & Johansen-Berg, H. (2008). Changes in white matter microstructure during adolescence. *NeuroImage, 39*, 52–61.

Gogtay, N., Giedd, J. N., Lusk, L., Hayashi, K. M., Greenstein, D., Vaituzid, A. C., Nugent, T. F., Herman, D. H., Clasen., L. H., Toga, A. W., Rapoport, J. L., & Thompson, P. M. (2004). Dynamic mapping of human cortical development during childhood through early adulthood. *Proceedings of the National Academy of Sciences of the United States of America, 101*(21), 8174–8179.

Gopnik, A., Meltzoff, A. N., & Kuhl, P. K. (2000). *The scientist in the crib*. New York: Harper.

———. (2010). *The philosophical baby*. New York: Picador.

Hadjikhani, N., Kveraga, K., Naik, P., & Ahlfors, S. (2009). Early (N170) activation of face-specific cortex by face-like objects. *Neuroreport, 20*(4), 403–407.

Hannon, E. E., & Trehub, S. E. (2005). Tuning in to musical rhythms: Infants learn more readily than adults. *Proceedings of the National Academy of Sciences, 102*, 12639–12643.

Hayter, A. L. (2007). Cerebellar contributions to working memory. *NeuroImage, 36*(3), 943–954.

Healy, J. (1988). *Failure to connect*. New York: Simon & Schuster.

———. (1990). *Endangered minds*. New York: Simon & Schuster.

———. (1994). *Your child's growing mind*. New York: Doubleday.

Hemmi, H. M., Wolke, D., & Schneider, S. (2011). Associations between problems with crying, sleeping and/or feeding in infancy and long-term behavioural outcomes in childhood: a meta-analysis. *Archives of Disease in Childhood*, published online. doi:10.1136/adc.2010.191312

Henderson, A., & Pehoski, C. (2005). *Hand function in children*. New York: Mosby.

Henshaw, S. P., Scheffler, R. M., Fulton, B. D., et al. (2011). International variation in treatment procedures for ADHD: Social context and recent trends. *Psychiatric Series, 62*, 459–464.

Hoffman, M. L. (2000). *Empathy and moral development: Implications for caring and justice*. Cambridge: Cambridge University Press.

Holt, K., Wooldridge, N., & Story, M. (2011). *Bright futures: Nutrition*. Elk Grove, IL: American Academy of Pediatrics.

Huttenlocher, P. R. (1979). Synaptic density in human frontal cortex: Developmental changes and effects of aging. *Brain Research, 163*, 195–205.

Illingworth, R. S. (1987). *The development of the infant and young child* (9th ed.). London: Churchill Livingstone.

————. (1991). *The normal child*. London: Churchill Livingstone.

Insel, T. R. (1997). A neurobiological basis of social attachment. *American Journal of Psychiatry, 154*, 726–735.

Jedrychowski, W., Perera, F., Jankowski J, Butscher M, Mroz E, Flak E, Kaim I, Lisowska-Miszczyk, I., Skarupa A., & Sowa, A. (2011). Effect of exclusive breastfeeding on the development of children's cognitive function in the Krakow prospective birth cohort study. *European Journal of Pediatrics, 171*(2), 405.

Jensen, P. S., Mrazek, D., Knapp, P. K., Steinberg, L., Pfeffer, C., Schowalter, J., & Shapiro, T. (1997). Evolution and revolution in child psychiatry: ADHD as a disorder of adaptation. *Journal of the American Academy of Child and Adolescent Psychiatry, 36*(12), 1672–1681.

Johnson, M. H. (2001). The development and neural basis of face recognition: Comment and speculation. *Infant and Child Development, 10*, 31–33.

Johnson, M. H. (2005). Developmental neuroscience, psychophysiology, and genetics. In M. H. Bornstein & M.E. Lamb (Eds.), *Developmental science: An advanced textbook* (5th ed.), pp. 187–222. Mahwah, NJ: Erlbaum.

Johnson, S. B., Blum, R. W., & Giedd, J. N. 2009. Adolescent maturity and the brain: The promise and pitfalls of neuroscience research in adolescent health policy. *Journal of Adolescent Health, 45*(3), 216–221.

Kaye, S., & Darke, S. (2012). The diversion and misuse of pharmaceutical stimulants: What do we know and why should we care? *Addiction, 107*(3), 467–477.

Kildea, S. (2011). Making sense of ADHD in practice: A stakeholder review. *Clinical Child Psychology, 16*(4), 599–619.

Kim, J. S., Nowak-Wegrzyn, A., Sicherer, S. H., Noone, S., Moshier, E. L., & Sampson, H. A. (2011). Dietary baked milk accelerates the resolution of milk allergy in children. *Journal of Allergy and Clinical Immunology, 128*(1), 125–131.

Klein, M. (1952). On observing the behaviour of young infants. In M. Klein, P. Heiman, S. Isaacs, & J. Riviere (Eds.), *Developments in psychoanalysis*, pp. 237–270. London: Hogarth Press.

Knobloch, H., Stevens, F., & Malone, A. E. (1980). *Manual of developmental diagnosis*. New York: Harper & Row.

Kochanska, G., & Knaack, A. (2003). Effortful control as a personality characteristic of young children: Antecedents, correlates, and consequences. *Journal of Personality, 71*, 1087–1112.

Kochanska, G., Murray, K. T., & Harlan, E. T. (2000). Effortful control in early childhood: Continuity and change, antecedents, and implications for social development. *Developmental Psychology, 36*, 220–232.

Kuhn, D. (2009). Adolescent thinking. In R. M. Lerner & L. Steinberg (Eds.), *Handbook of adolescent psychology* (3rd ed.), pp. 152–186. Hoboken, NJ: Wiley.

La Leche League websites:www.llli.org;www.lalecheleague.org;www.lllusa.org.

LeDoux, J. (2007). The amygdala. *Current Biology, 17*(20), 868–874.

Lemos, G. C., Almeida, L. S., & Colom, R. (2011). Intelligence of adolescents is related to their parents' educational level but not to family income. *Personality and Individual Differences, 50*(7), 1062–1067.

Lewkowicz, D. J., & Hansen-Tift, A. M. (2012). Infants deploy selective attention to the mouth of a talking face when learning speech. *Proceedings of the National Academy of Science, 109*, 1431.

Light, K. C., Smith, T. E., Johns, J. M., Brownley, K. A., Hofheimer, J. A., & Amico, J. A. (2000). Oxytocin responsivity in mothers of infants: A preliminary study of relationships with blood pressure during laboratory stress and normal ambulatory activity. *Health Psychology, 19*, 560–567.

Liston, C., Watts, R., Tottenham, M., Davidson, M. C., Niogi, S., Ulug, A. M., & Casey, B. J. (2006). Frontostrialtal microstructure modulates efficient recruitment of cognitive control. *Cerebral Cortex, 16*, 553–560.

Luna, B., & Sweeney, J. A. (2004). The emergence of collaborative brain function: fMRI studies of the development of response inhibition. *Annals of the New York Academy of Sciences, 1021*, 296–309.

Luo, Y., & Baillargeon, R. (2005). When the ordinary seems unexpected: Evidence for incremental physical knowledge in young infants. *Cognition, 95*, 297–328.

Luxford, M. (1994). *Children with special needs.* Hudson, NY: Anthroposophic Press.

Mandler, J. M. (2004). *The foundations of mind: Origins of conceptual thought.* New York: Oxford.

———. (2008). On the birth and growth of concepts. *Philosophical Psychology, 21*(2), 207–230.

Marsh, H. L., Legerstee, M., Stavropolous, J., & Nienhuis, T. (2010). Six- and nine-month-old infants discriminate between goals despite similar action patterns. *Infancy, 15*, 94–106.

Martin, A., & Volkmar, F. (Eds.). (2007). *Lewis's child and adolescent psychiatry: A comprehensive textbook* (4th ed.). Philadelphia: Lippincott Williams &Wilkins.

McArney, E. R. (2008). Adolescent brain development: Forging new links? *Journal of Adolescent Health, 42*(4), 321–323.

McCabe, S. E., West, B. T., Teter, C. T., Ross-Durow, P., Young, A., & Boyd, C. J. (2011). Characteristics associated with the diversion of controlled medications among adolescents. *Drug and Alcohol Dependence, 118* (2), 452–458.

McCarthy, M. M. (1995). Estrogen modulation of oxytocin and its relation to behavior. In R. Ivell and J. Russell (Eds.), *Oxytocin: Cellular and molecular approaches in medicine and research.* New York: Plenum Press.

Melby, J. N., Conger, R. D., Fang, S., Wichrama, K. A. S., & Conger, K. J.(2008). Adolescent family experiences and educational attainment during early adulthood. *Developmental Psychology, 44*, 1519–1536.

Meltzoff, A. N. (1990). Towards a developmental cognitive science: The implications of cross-modal matching and imitation for the development of representation and memory in infancy. *Annals of the New York Academy of Science, 608*, 1–31.

———. (1995). Infants' understanding of people and things: From body imitation to folk psychology. In J. L. Bermudez, A. Marcel, & N. Eilan (Eds.), *The Body and the Self*, pp. 43–69. Cambridge, MA and London: MIT Press.

Merikangas, K., Avenevoli, S., Costello, J., Koretz, D., & Kessler, R. C. (2009). National comorbidity survey replication adolescent supplement (NCS-A): I. Background and measures. *Journal of the American Academy of Child and Adolescent Psychiatry , 48*, 367–369.

Merikangas, K. R., He, J., Burstein, M., Swanson, S. A., Avenevoli, S., Cui, L., Benjet, C., Georgiades, K., & Swendsen J. (2010). Lifetime prevalence of mental disorders in U.S. adolescents : Results from the National Comorbidity Survey Replication—Adolescent Supplement (NCS-A). *Journal of the American Academy of Child and Adolescent Psychiatry , 49*, 980–989.

Miller, C. F., Lurye, L. E., Zosuls, K. M., & Ruble, D. N. (2009). Accessibility of gender stereotype domains: Development and gender differences in children. *Sex Roles, 60*, 870–881.

Mischell, W., Shoda, Y., & Rodriquez, M. L. (1989). Delay of gratification in children. *Science, 244*(4907), 933–938.

Moeller, F. G., Barratt, E. S., Douugherty, D. M., Schmitz, J. M., & Swann, A.C. (2001). Psychiatric aspects of impulsivity. *American Journal of Psychiatry, 158*, 1783–1793.

Montessori, M. (2009). *The absorbent mind*. New York: BN Publishing.

Mullen, E. M. (1995). *Mullen Scales of Early Learning*. Sydney, Australia: Pearson/Psych-Corp.

Nagy, E. (2008). Innate intersubjectivity: Newborns' sensitivity to communication disturbance. *Developmental Psychology, 44*, 1779–1784.

National Association for Education of Young Children website:www.naeyc.org.

National Institute for early education website:www.nieer.org.

Nelson, C. A., & Luciana, M. (2008). *Handbook of developmental cognitive neuroscience* (2nd ed.). Boston: MIT Press.

Nelson, C. A., Thomas, K. M., & de Haan, M. (2006). Neural bases of cognitive development. In D. Kuhn & R. Siegler (Eds.), *Handbook of child psychology, Vol. 2: Cognition, perception, and language* (6th ed.), pp. 3–57. Hoboken, NJ: Wiley.

Newborg, J., Stock, J. R., Wnek, L., Guidubaldi, J., Svinicki, J., Dickson, J., & Markley, A. (2005). *Battelle Developmental Inventory (BDI-2)*. Rolling Meadows, IL: Riverside Publishing.

New York Academy of Sciences. (2004). Adolescent brain development: Vulnerabilities and opportunities. *Annals of the New York Academy of Sciences, 1021*, entire issue.

Ninivaggi, F. J. (1999). Attention-deficit/hyperactivity disorder in children and adolescents: Rethinking diagnosis and treatment implications for complicated cases. *Connecticut Medicine, 63*, 515–521.

———. 2008. *Ayurveda: A comprehensive guide to traditional Indian medicine for the West*. Lanham, MD: Rowman & Littlefield.

———. (2009). Borderline intellectual functioning and academic problems. In B. Sadock, V. Sadock & P. Ruiz (Eds.), *Kaplan & Sadock's comprehensive textbook of psychiatry* (9th ed.), pp. 2505–2512. Philadelphia: Wolters Kluwer/Lippincott Williams & Wilkins.

———. (2009). Malingering. In B. Sadock, V. Sadock, & P. Ruiz (Eds.), *Kaplan & Sadock's comprehensive textbook of psychiatry* (9th ed.), pp. 2479–2489. Philadelphia: Wolters Kluwer/Lippincott Williams & Wilkins.

Parents' Evaluation of Developmental Status (PEDS). PEDSTest.com, LLC.

Pascalis, O., de Haan, M., & Nelson, C. A. (2002). Is face-processing species-specific during the first year of life? *Science, 296*, 1321–1323.

PEDS: Developmental Milestones (PEDS:DM). PEDSTest.com, LLC.

Pelham, W. E., & Fabiano, G. A. (2008). Evidence-based psychosocial treatments for attention-deficit/hyperactivity disorder. *Journal of Clinical Child and Adolescent Psychology, 37*(1), 184–214.

Petrash, J. (2002). *Understanding Waldorf education: Teaching from the inside out*. New York: Gryphon House.

Porter, R. C. (1991). Human reproduction and the mother-infant relationship: The role of odors. In T. V. Getchell, R. I. Doty, L. M. Bartoshuk, & J. B. Snow (Eds.), *Smell and taste in health and disease*, pp. 429–442. New York: Raven Press.

Pruitt, D. (1999). *Your adolescent: Emotional, behavioral, and cognitive development from early adolescence through the teen years*. New York: William Morrow.

———. (2000). *Your child: Emotional, behavioral, and cognitive development from birth through preadolescence*. New York: Harper.

Quinn, P. C., Yahr, J., Kuhn, A., Slater, A. M., & Pascalis, O. (2002). Representation of the gender of human faces by infants: A preference for female. *Perception, 31*, 1109–1121.

Reeb, B. T., & Congers, K. J. (2011). Mental health services utilization in a community sample of rural adolescents: The role of father-offspring relations. *Journal of Pediatric Psychology, 36*(4), 661–668.

Rhoades, B. L., Greenberg, M. T., & Domitrovich, C. E. (2009). The contribution of inhibitory control to preschoolers' social-emotional competence. *Journal of Applied Developmental Psychology, 30*, 310–320.

Rochat, P., & Striano, T. (2002). Who's in the mirror? Self-other discrimination in specular images by four- and nine-month-old infants. *Child Development, 73*, 35–46.

Rogers, C. E., Anderson, P. J., Thompson, D. K., Kidokoro, H., Wallendorf, M., Treyvaud, K., Roberts, G., Doyle, L. W., Neil, J. J., & Inder, T. E. (2012). Regional cerebral development at term relates to school-age social-emotional development in very preterm children. *Journal of the American Academy of Child & Adolescent Psychiatry, 51*(2), 181–191.

Ruble, D. N., Martin, C. L., & Berenbaum, S. A. (2006). Gender development. In N. Eisenberg (Ed.), *Handbook of child psychology: Vol. 3. Social, emotional, and personality development* (6th ed.), pp. 858–932. Hoboken, NJ: Wiley.

Ruble, D. N., Taylor, L. J., Cyphers, L., Greulich, F. K., Lurye, L. E., & Shrout, P. E. (2007). The role of gender constancy in early gender development. *Child Development, 78*, 1121–1136.

Schilthuis, W. (1994). *Biodynamic agriculture*. Hudson, NY: Anthroposophic Press.

Schneider, S., Peters, J., Bromberg, U., Brassen, S., Miedl, S., Banaschewski, T., Barker, J., Conrod, P., Flor, H., Garavan, H., Heinz, A., Ittermann, B., Lathrop, M., Loth, E., Mann, K., Martinot, J., Nees, F., Paus, T., Rietschel, M., Robbins, T., Smolka, M., Spanagel, R., Ströhle, A., Struve, M., Schumann, G., & Büchel, C. (2012). Risk taking and the adolescent reward system: A potential common link to substance abuse. *American Journal of Psychiatry, 169*, 39–46.

Schultz, R. T., Grelotti, D. J., Klin, A., Kleinman, J., der Gaag, C., Marois, R., & Skudlarski, P. (2003). The role of the fusiform area in social cognition: Implications for the pathobiology of autism. *Philosophical Transactions of the Royal Society, Series B, 358*, 415–427.

Shure, M. B., Digeronimo, T. F., & Aher, J. (2000). *Raising a thinking child workbook: Teaching young children how to resolve everyday conflicts and get along with others*. New York: Research Press.

Simion, F., Cassia, V. M., Turati, C., & Valenza, E. (2001). The origins of face perception: Specific versus non-specific mechanisms. *Infant and Child Development, 10*, 59–65.

Simion, F., Valenza, E., Umitta, C., & Barba, B. D. (1998). Preferential orienting to faces in newborns: A temporal-nasal asymmetry. *Journal of Experimental Psychology: Human Perception and Performance, 24*, 1399–1405.

Simpson, J. A., & Rholes, W. S. (1998). *Attachment theory and close relationships*. New York: Guilford Press.

Simard, M., Luu ,T. M., & Gosselin, J. (2012). Concurrent validity of ages and stages questionnaires in preterm infants. *Pediatrics*, 2012 Jun 11 [e-pub ahead of print].(http://dx.doi.org/ 10.1542/peds.2011-3532).

Slater, A., & Quinn, P. C. (2001). Face recognition in the newborn infant. *Infant and Child Development, 10*, 21–24.

Somer, L., & Caset, B. J. (2010). Developmental neurobiology of cognitive control and motivational systems. *Current Opinion in Neurobiology, 20*(2), 236–241.

Spelke, E. S. (2000). Core knowledge. *American Psychologist, 55*, 1233–1243.

Spelke, E. S., & Kinzler, K. D. (2007). Core knowledge. *Developmental Science, 10*, 89–96.

Steinberg, L. (2008). A social neuroscience perspective on adolescent risk-taking. *Developmental Review, 28*, 78–106.

Steiner, R. (2004). *A Modern Art of Education: Foundations of Waldorf Education*. Hemdon, MA: Anthroposophic Press.

Stern, D. (2000). *The Interpersonal World of the Infant*. New York: Basic Books.

Turati, C., Cassia, V. M., Simion, F., & Leo, I. (2006). Newborns' face recognition: Role of inner and outer facial features. *Child Development, 77*, 297–311.

Valenza, E., Simion, F., Cassia, V. M., & Umitta, C. (1996). Face preference at birth. *Journal of Experimental Psychology: Human Perception and Performance, 22*, 892–903.

Volkmar, F., & Martin, A. (2011). *Essentials of Lewis's child and adolescent psychiatry*. Philadelphia: Lippincott Williams & Wilkins.

Vouloumanos, A., & Werker, J. F. (2004). Tuned to the signal: The privileged status of speech for young infants. *Developmental Science, 7*, 270–276.

Vuontela V., Carlson S., Troberg A. M., Fontell T., Simola P., Saarinen S., & Aronen E. T. (2012). Working memory, attention, inhibition, and their relation to adaptive functioning and behavioral/emotional symptoms in school-aged children. *Child Psychiatry Hum. Dev.* June 4 2012. [Epub ahead of print]

Vygotsky, L. S. (1934, 1986). *Thought and language.* A. Kozulin (Trans.). Cambridge, MA: MIT Press.

Wallin, D. J. 2007. *Attachment in psychotherapy.* New York: Guilford Press.

Wellman, H. M. (2002). Understanding the psychological world: Developing a theory of mind. In U. Goswami (Ed.), *Blackwell handbook of child cognitive development*, pp.167–187. Malden, MA: Blackwell.

Wellman, H. M., Cross, D., & Watson, J. (2001). Meta-analysis of theory-of- mind development: The truth about false belief. *Child Development, 72*, 655–684.

White, B. L. (1986). *The first three years of life.* New York: Prentice Hall.

———. (1988). *Educating the infant and toddler.* Lexington, MA: D.C. Health & Co.

Wilcox, T., & Woods, R. (2009). Experience primes infants to individuate objects. In A. Woodward & A. Needham (Eds.), *Learning and the infant mind*, pp.117–143. New York: Oxford University Press.

Wild, R. (2000). *Raising curious, creative, confident kids: The Pestalozzi experiment in child-based education.* Boston: Shambhala Press.

Wolraich, M. L., Drotar, D. D., Dworkin, P. H., & Perrin, E. C. (2008). *Developmental-behavioral pediatrics: Evidence and practice.* Philadelphia: Elsevier Mosby.

Wynn, K. (2008). Some innate foundations of social and moral cognition. In P. Carruthers, S. Laurence, & S. Stich (Eds.), *The innate mind: Foundations and the future.* New York and Oxford: Oxford University Press.

Yeates, K. O., Kaizar, E., Rusin, J., Bangert, B., Dietrich, A., Nuss, K., Wright, M., & Taylor, H. (2011). Reliable change in postconcussive symptoms and its functional consequences among children with mild traumatic brain injury. *Archives of Pediatrics and Adolescent Medicine.* Published online March 5, 2012. doi:10.1001/archpediatrics.2011.1082.

Yudofsky, S. C., & Hales, R. E. (Eds.). (2012). *Clinical manual of neuropsychiatry.* Washington, DC: American Psychiatric Press.

Zero to Three: National Center for Infants, Toddlers and Families website:www.zerotothree.org.

Chapter Four

The Psychology of Parents as Adults

1. OVERVIEW

Parenting is a complex reality that entails caring for and supporting the life of a child to maturity. The broad range of parental functions encompasses nurturance, discipline, and living example. Embedded in all these roles are the tasks of modeling and teaching children to learn, recognize, and optimize opportunities for problem solving and constructively coping with stress. With these skills, a child is prepared to successfully interact with others in a mutually satisfying manner. In other words, parenting is demonstrating to young, inexperienced children how to live successfully. The aims of parenting are directed toward comprehensive care of the whole child who will eventually be able to make deliberate, self-directed choices.

Adult personality has its own childhood archived in biomental memory. While some material is easily accessible, most remains inaccessible, just underneath the surface of awareness. Parents as adults, unlike their children, bring a great deal of past experience—unresolved emotional clutter or "baggage"—to their parenting. This consideration becomes even more meaningful when parents fully realize that being a child with a parent and in a family is a "first" for children. Parents as adults have already been children and gone through childhood, which is for many a distant, if not obscure, memory.

In the early childhood development literature, this phenomenon of past experience being in the present moment had been referred to as "ghosts in the nursery." Theories explaining attachment patterns correlate with these transgenerational ideas of past family experiences influencing the present. Past experiences, notably with one's own parents, strongly color adult personality and how interpersonal relationships are negotiated. Past experiences introduce a mix of positive and negative features. The positive aspects include

335

fond memories and a history of rich experiences. Matters that are often incompletely resolved remain conflictual, yet they accompany affirmative assets. The negative aspects include unresolved problems, whether clearly remembered or not. These implicit memories indirectly affect one's attitude and customary style of relating to others—both adults and children.

Two fundamental areas of "unfinished business" or continuing unresolved challenges from the past make up the basis of all interpersonal relationships in the present moment: attachments and detachments. Attachments are the affiliative bonds of love, involvement, and dependency associated with significant people, notably mothers, fathers, family members, and significant others. Detachments encompass losses, separations, endings, and terminations of relations with these significant others. Detachments and the plethora of nuances accrued around this aspect of relationships pose greater difficulties than do attachments. The roots of such difficulties stem from incomplete or unsuccessful disengagements as far back as earliest childhood. Both attachments and detachments remain "unfinished" in the sense that they are natural, continuing processes that continually emerge in everyday experience. These reappearances, in fact, are challenges that offer new opportunities for further reconfiguration and refinement, namely, finishing what was only incompletely brought to a satisfactory close.

Ending some relationships can be less finite, such as moving out of a parents' home, finishing school, or moving to a new city, when compared to other acts of letting go. When other endings, such as the death of a loved one, are permanent, they are often never accomplished in a way that is emotionally sufficient. *Sufficient* here means complete enough to permit one to move on to new beginnings, possibly sadder but wiser, *so that repetitions of old conflict-producing scenarios are minimized.*

Adults aware of the aforementioned can work toward resolving less-than-optimal modes of relating to others by several means. These include personal self-reflection and discussions with others, such as coaches, counselors, or psychotherapists. In any event, being aware of how the past becomes known in the present can be a sobering revelation. Further, such cognizance can be the beginning of an adventure of insight.

Children compared to adults do not have this experiential clutter. Far from being innocent or mindless, however, they come equipped with a rich repertoire of abilities and emotional complexities. This collection includes undeveloped, partly developed, and developing components. Children have a fertile emotional life that is sensitive and full of wondrous fantasy and imagination. Children's fantasy life is normal and enormous. Keeping this in mind helps parents to maintain mindful and open-minded attitudes, a dynamic *transactional sensitivity.*

1.1 Parenting Problems

Three commonly encountered problems that may thwart effective parenting are impaired communication, overprotection, and inadequate discipline. Another area of concern involves the common occurrence of the "double standard." While this discrepancy may emerge between adults and children, it is more troublesome when prominent in a parental relationship. The term *double standard* refers to any set of principles containing different provisions for different but similar persons or groups. Valid and sufficient reasons to support the different provisions are absent. Such standards may take the forms of expectations of conduct, rules, rights, obligations, or restrictions. These are perceived and labeled as "acceptable" for some and "unacceptable," often taboo, for others. A double standard connotes a biased, morally unfair exclusion implying a significant limitation of freedom. Typically, matters of control, dominance, power, and irrational manipulation underlie conflicts around "double-standard" issues in relationships of relatively equal status.

Some people have raised concerns about whether the notion of a double standard implicitly and unwittingly surrounds perceptions of female and male gender freedoms and restrictions. A plethora of biological, legal, moral, philosophical, and psychological concerns surrounds this sensitive question. No definitive answer can be given. The recurring theme of mutual negotiation and renegotiation of roles between parents that directly addresses matters of interpersonal power, control, and interdependence best addresses the pragmatic implications of this question. This process facilitates successful couples relationships, parenting, and family life. Well thought out, conscious, and intentional sharing of matters dealing with power and control is essential in any emotionally meaningful adult relationship.

1.2 Adult Psychology

To better appreciate the psychology of parenting, a brief discussion of adult psychology is useful. *Personality*, the technical term applicable to adults over eighteen years, describes unique and relatively enduring patterns of attitudes and behaviors. These patterns are learned and developed primarily from familial, cultural, and social influences. At about age four, glimmers of a child's sense of self and self-acknowledged personality traits are observable.

As mentioned in previous chapters, personality is composed of layers of biomentally endowed traits. In turn, these traits lie beneath infant and childhood temperamental profiles. Traits and temperament then interact with caregiving to emerge as attachment patterns. Throughout childhood, all these coalesce to form relatively structured and enduring configurations of feelings, thoughts, and behaviors—personality.

Personality covers an individual's characteristic and relatively consistent patterns of emotional expression, self-regulation, motivation, cognition about self, choices, interactions with others, and behaviors in general. These established and long-lasting patterns have influential roots in adolescence and early adulthood. Healthy personality styles are flexible, adaptive, cooperative, and open to learning from experience.

Biomental child development reviews constructs such as personality and personality cluster types with the overriding proviso that any simple classification system sorely underestimates the almost infinite variety, complexity, and nuance of each individual's personality. Although insufficient, the concept of personality styles helps organize self-reflection and enhances appreciation for individual differences.

2. ADULT TEMPERAMENT

The work of C. Robert Cloninger greatly expanded the construct of *temperament* as expressed in adulthood. Using sophisticated studies from a broad range of fields, he has distilled the idea into four categories. These complex and multifaceted categories also contain a great deal of useful information about the nature of adult personality as a whole. They describe normal configurations, not psychopathology. Cloninger states that these dimensions have been repeatedly shown to be universal across different cultures, ethnic groups, and political systems. Each of the four categories is composed of an item with a polar spectrum; these wide ranges permit dimensional assessment by means of referencing extreme variants. *As is true of other ranges of psychological attitudes and behaviors, when extremes are present in attenuated and modest degrees, they are adaptive and useful in everyday functioning.*

For Cloninger, temperament forms personality's hereditable biases of emotional, motivational, and adaptive makeup. While four temperamental dimensions are differentiated, they are understood to occur in all possible combinations within an individual, rather than being mutually exclusive categories. An individual, however, may demonstrate a higher loading of specific categories and thus seem to be dominated by that single temperament or combination.

The four categories of adult temperament are (1) harm avoidance, (2) novelty seeking, (3) reward dependence, and (4) persistence (table 4.1).

Harm-avoidant temperaments reflect several component traits or facets. These include qualities such as fearful, shy, reticent, and anxious versus more risk taking, impulsive, outgoing, daring, aggressive, and optimistic. The primary emotion associated with harm avoidance is fear. Fear as an

Table 4.1. Four Categories of Adult Temperament

1. Harm Avoidance
2. Novelty Seeking
3. Reward Dependence
4. Persistence

emotional component of adult temperament and personality cannot be under-estimated. Fear and anxiety are often felt together as avoidant impulses and steer an individual toward different interpersonal, social, and occupational consequences. Adults who appear "high-strung," "ill-tempered," or "mean" may have aspects of this temperament. Harm avoidance correlates with the term *melancholic* as it was used thousands of years ago to mean "rigid" and "inflexible." This idea was also carried through psychological systems in India, Greece, and Rome to designate one type of a range of normative constitutional profiles.

Novelty-seeking temperaments reflect exploratory, interest-seeking, open to new experiences, excitement-oriented, impulsive, extravagant, and irritable components versus reserved, complacent, deliberate, and thrifty styles. Novelty-seeking temperaments go to great lengths to avoid habit; rather, they seek adventure and excitement. The primary emotional experiences associated with novelty seeking are frustration and anger. This action-oriented and stimulus-seeking temperamental dimension correlates with the ancient constitutional type termed *choleric*.

Reward-dependent temperaments reflect affectionate, engagingly extroverted, warm qualities versus independent, lone, detached, and aloof styles. The primary emotional experience associated with reward dependence is affiliative attachment. This profile was termed *sanguine* in ancient writings.

Persistence reflects determined, industrious, enthusiastic, and perfectionistic styles versus underachieving and unmotivated temperaments. The primary emotional experience associated with persistence is ambition. It was termed *phlegmatic* in older writings when its more stable, constrained, impassive, and uncolorful qualities were emphasized.

Cloninger's delineations derive from technical, academic, and tested temperamental categories. Other less-scholarly systems delineate temperamental types into less complex categorization. For example, such commonly used divisions include (1) extrovert, (2) introvert, (3) "thinker," and (4) "feeler."

3. ADULT PERSONALITY

Personality refers to the relatively stable pattern of functionally interrelated processes that include cognition, emotion, interpersonal relatedness, behavior, coping, and defenses. Both genders share, at times in different ways, the basic qualities that comprise personality.

About five decades ago, English psychologist H. J. Eysenck proposed the first modern Western psychological model of personality. It had only two dimensions, each with polar opposites: *extroversion-introversion* and *stable-unstable*. This act led the way for other psychologists to research and attempt to capture the essence of basic personality characteristics. This was an effort to describe individuals both as they experience themselves and as they are seen and described by outside observers. It has been a growing field of both researching and distilling detailed categories of personality styles, aimed at describing all people. The emphasis was on mentally healthy persons but contained explicit descriptors of atypical or less-than-optimal mental stability.

The "Big Five adult general personality factors or dimensions" is a widely used technical phrase describing a model of fundamental adult personality characteristics or traits. It is a comprehensive descriptive personality system, a taxonomy that classifies the relationships among common traits, theoretical concepts, and personality scales. The pioneering work of psychologist Raymond Cattell using factor analysis in mid-twentieth-century America led to development of a detailed personality trait theory. In this system, adult traits denote durable dispositions to behave in particular ways across varieties of situations. Emphasis rests on descriptions of psychological clusters describing interpersonal interactions.

The "Big Five," as it is often referred to, developed by other psychologists later on is a much briefer derivative of Cattell's work, and is recognized by many psychologists (though not all) as a standard way to view personality profiles, which are lists of descriptive attributes with an emphasis on typicality and normality. The "Big Five" may be similar across cultures since they usually show consistencies that emerge in cross-cultural studies.

Current estimates place the average genetic component of personality in the range of .40 to .60. Rather than serving to infer motivations, this classification system is a taxonomy whose descriptive categories are derived from empirical, not merely theoretical, observations. This *five-factor model*, or, more informally, the "Big Five," are large groupings of traits that describe prominent features of normal adult personalities. The five dimensions include (1) openness, (2) conscientiousness, (3) extroversion, (4) agreeableness, and (5) neuroticism, or negative emotions. The acronym is OCEAN, or CANOE, if rearranged (table 4.2).

Each of these five factors is on a continuum or spectrum ranging from low to high expression; that is, they are described by dimensional ratings. The intensity level of these continuous dimensions is understood to be optimal when moderate and avoiding extremes in either direction. Each of these five higher-order factors consists of clusters of more specific traits, subtraits, and subfactors that validly correlate in statistical analyses. The "Big Five" personality factors are as follows.

Openness to new experiences includes traits such as being creative, intellectual, open-minded, inventive, problem-solving, and curious. Flexibility rather than rigidity in thinking, feeling, and ease of suitably altering mental set characterize this openness. Encompassed here are appreciation for art, emotional expression, adventure, unusual ideas, curiosity, and interest in new experiences. At the other end of the spectrum are traits such as being cautious, conservative, and conventional. The psychological literature also includes terms such as "simple," "shallow," and "unintelligent" at the negative end.

Conscientiousness includes traits characterized as being organized, responsible, reliable, watchful, and efficient. Tendencies to show self-discipline, act dutifully, demonstrate ethical behaviors, aim for achievement, and demonstrate pre-planned behavior are present. High levels of conscientiousness reflect the cognitive restraints that characterize effortful self-control. Such self-restraint allows one to fulfill interpersonal obligations in the context of a reasoned sense of caring for others. Conscientiousness is one of two factors regarded as a best predictor of mental health. The opposite end of the conscientiousness spectrum includes carelessness, frivolousness, irresponsibility, and noncaring behaviors.

Extroversion includes being talkative, energetic, assertive, and outgoing. Energy, positive emotions, surgency, ambition, assertiveness, self-direction, the tendency to seek stimulation in the company of others and to pair bond are its features. These contrast with attitudes characterized by seeking quietude, being reserved, shyness, and demonstrating loner or isolative behaviors.

Agreeableness includes features of personalities that are sympathetic, kind, affectionate, helpful, empathetic, cooperative, able to share, friendly, kind, and compassionate. In contrast to conscientiousness, agreeableness em-

Table 4.2.   The "Big Five" Personality Factors

1. Openness to New Experiences

2. Conscientiousness

3. Extroversion

4. Agreeableness

5. Neuroticism or Negative Emotions

phasizes caring in more emotional than cognitive terms. Agreeableness is nonetheless the other factor regarded as a best predictor of mental health. Opposite traits include being competitive, oppositional, suspicious, antagonistic, and obstinate toward others. Adults who are "difficult" are those who do not demonstrate an open capacity for cooperating, negotiating, and agreeing. In some cases, however, extreme agreeableness may imply the anxiety of not feeling confident enough to disagree, which might also suggest an interpersonal passivity and avoidance.

Neuroticism or negative emotions reflects negative moods including being stressed, nervous, anxious, worried, unstable, hostile, and vulnerable, as well as being lonely, helpless, and mood-labile. High neuroticism denotes poor stress management. Research suggests that hostility may be the most toxic element of the Type A syndrome (stressed personality) and subsequent vulnerability to disease, notably compromised immune function. The other end of the spectrum includes positive moods of being secure, confident, emotionally stable, calm, and content. Low neuroticism denotes the ability to manage stress well. People feel negative emotions as "bad," while positive emotions are felt as "good." As with other personality features, neuroticism is understood to be moderately heritable and a relatively unchanging personality trait. Of interest is the fact that research involving large groups in some European countries has shown that persons with high neuroticism have a negative financial impact on their country's economy.

Abnormal personality profiles as defined in conventional psychological systems have been characterized as having combinations of the above five factors with a predominance of negative emotions or neuroticism. People like this appear habitually distraught. Such abnormal personality profiles include negative emotionality, introversion or social isolation, antagonism, disinhibition or impulsivity, compulsivity or rigidity, and bizarre beliefs. Cognitive processes, for example, show executive functioning to be less flexible and so unable to easily reassess situations and develop alternative problem-solving strategies. Persons with abnormal personality profiles are vulnerable to anxiety, depression, eating disorders, and psychiatric personality disorders. There is also a positive correlation of abnormal profiles with medical illnesses such as asthma, irritable bowel syndrome, and cardiovascular disease.

In general, the aforementioned studies of personality have been more "psychological" than "psychiatric" in orientation. This denotes that normality and measurement, not psychopathology and treatment, are their primary reference points. By contrast, in psychiatry there is a developed repertoire of personality or character profiles that are deemed to be a problematic source of adaptive difficulty. These psychiatrically defined "personality disorders" include paranoid, schizoid, schizotypal, antisocial, borderline, histrionic, narcissistic, avoidant, dependent, and obsessive-compulsive personality styles.

These inflexible attitudes and behaviors definitionally cause functional impairments. As psychiatric conditions, personality disorders may cause subjective distress in the person possessing them.

Cloninger's comprehensive work over the last two decades has also advanced a comprehensive theory of personality. It posits that personality is made up of three subgroups: (1) temperament, or the basic emotional core of personality responsible for how we respond; (2) character, or rational concepts about self and interpersonal relations that give meaning to what we notice; and (3) psyche, or intuitive self-awareness and symbolic invention. The term *psyche* indicates adaptive problem-solving ability that utilizes fantasy, wisdom, generativity, and creativity (table 4.3).

The subgroup termed *temperament* includes novelty seeking, harm avoidance, reward dependence, and persistence. The *character* subgroup includes self-directedness, cooperativeness, and self-transcendence. The *psyche* subgroup transcends these dimensions and includes intuitive self-awareness and adaptive problem-solving metafunctions. These qualities of psyche are understood to be speculations about consciousness.

Some correlations exist between Cloninger's personality dimensions and the "Big Five" factor model. Novelty seeking correlates with openness to experience and extroversion, and harm avoidance correlates with extroversion. One finds that reward dependence correlates with extroversion, while persistence correlates with conscientiousness. In addition, self-directedness correlates with conscientiousness, and cooperativeness correlates with agreeableness. The two "Big Five" factors, conscientiousness and agreeableness, have been shown to be the best predictors of mental health and correlate with Cloninger's self-directness and cooperativeness.

Table 4.3. Seven-Dimensional Model of Personality with Psyche Added

(a. Temperamental Subgroup)

Novelty Seeking

Harm Avoidance

Reward Dependence

Persistence

(b. Character Subgroup)

Self-Directedness

Cooperativeness

Self-Transcendence

(c. Psyche Subgroup)

Intuitive Self-Awareness

Symbolic Invention

The prolific work of Cloninger has produced a final systematization that takes into account what he calls "five planes of being" (table 4.4). These planes of being have a philosophical orientation and address personality and its subgroups: temperament, character, psyche, and how they fit into the larger perspective of being and existence. The five layers begin with what is dense, most obvious, and material, and then graduate upward toward to what is least material, that is, consciousness or the spiritual. In this system, Cloninger takes into account abstract psychophilosophical notions such as consciousness of being, freedom of will, truth, beauty, and goodness.

4. ADULT ATTACHMENT STYLES

An additional way of looking at adult personality is from the perspective of relational or attachment styles. The underlying feelings driving these attachment styles are conscious and nonconscious perceptions of being interpersonally connected or disconnected. To be sure, the number of ways of relating to others is virtually infinite. Four basic styles seem to capture the general trends observable in relationships. Each describes an individual's style of relating to another. These styles include: (1) self-assured, (2) distant, (3) needy, and (4) anxious and frightened (table 4.5).

People who are *self-assured* show low fears of abandonment and little avoidance of being close. They are confident and do not need to seek inordinate approval from their mate. Since they are basically trustful, they allow others a reasonable amount of space. In other words, they are comfortable giving their partners the freedom to act without explicit consent or chaperoning.

Those who are *needy*, by contrast, have high fears of abandonment and strong needs for closeness, both affectionately and materially. They seem to always see their partners as not close or attentive enough. Such clingy, needy persons fear rejection and seem to use nagging as a way to exert control and

---

Table 4.4.   Cloninger's Five Planes or Layers of Being

1. Sexual-corporeal regulated by Harm Avoidance

2. Material-power and possessions regulated by Novelty Seeking

3. Interpersonal attachments regulated by Reward Dependency

4. Intellectual-communication, knowledge, and culture regulated by Persistence

5. Spiritual—what is beyond the ordinary—regulated by character traits of foresight, judgment, insight leading to behaviors that are peaceful, patient, charitable, respectful, and hopeful

Table 4.5. Adult Attachment Styles

1. Self-assured
2. Distant
3. Needy
4. Anxious and frightened

influence. Spouses who are nagged often feel childish and resentful. Those who are needy may say that they have more regard for the relationship than their partner does and thus feel an underlying disappointment.

A third attachment style is reflected in those who appear *distant* and relatively uninvolved. These people have a low fear of abandonment and have a high avoidance of interpersonal closeness. They may have been "loners" since childhood and may have inadvertently become involved in relationships because of ambivalence or outside pressure. Their apparent indifference is difficult to understand and relate to.

People who are *anxious and frightened* characterize the last and fourth attachment style. They have a high fear of abandonment and a high avoidance of becoming close. They fear rejection, are distrustful, are suspicious, and may be prone to jealousy.

5. THE PRACTICAL IMPLICATIONS OF PERSONALITY THEORY

Hypotheses and conceptual models of personality have practical applications in explaining one's sense of self and interpersonal relationships. Adults may seek self-understanding by self-reflection and examining enduring attitudes and behaviors or personality. Basic life goals, therefore, aimed at achieving a better quality of life can be formulated when a person scrutinizes his or her own personality features. Features noted to be nonadaptive can, in turn, be remodulated. Once recognized, life goals, values, and beliefs can be made explicit and serve to guide success and satisfaction. In this way, lifestyles and relationships can be improved.

Some explicit themes and many underlying currents correlating with a better life run through personality theory. Two of the "Big Five" factors—conscientiousness and agreeableness—have been demonstrated to be the best predictors of mental health. These correlate with Cloninger's character subgroups, self-directness and cooperativeness.

Conscientiousness connotes self-reflection, acting responsibly, maintaining overall diligence, and a locus of personal control. Fostering a continuing sense of attentiveness to the details and overall course of life supports this. Implicit in this factor is a sense of caring that is informed by both reason and effortful self-control. A normalized locus of personal control counters tendencies toward unhealthy interpersonal control issues characterized by manipulation, force, and hostility. Both conscientiousness and self-directedness presume personal responsibility for recognizing task demands and expediting their outcomes.

Agreeableness is an attitude of openness, receptivity, and cooperativeness. It is a nondefensive stance that makes sharing and helpfulness easily accessible. Agreeable people are typically pleasant and comfortable working in groups that are goal directed; in other words, they are usually emotionally motivated and congenial team players. Highly competitive and adversarial attitudes are virtually absent. Agreeableness and cooperativeness have a great deal in common. Conscientiousness, self-directedness, agreeableness, and cooperativeness as basic values set a positive tone to everyday living.

Biomental child development heartily endorses the above values as having vital, life-promoting psychological qualities. This text also supports incorporating three additional "Big Five" factors into one's repertoire. They are extroversion, openness, and low neuroticism.

Openness implies receptivity to new experience. Comfort with chance situations may prove beneficial if more thoroughly explored for the newfound opportunities they may surprisingly offer. *Extroversion* implies the impulse to extend oneself beyond the confines of one's comfort zone, especially in meeting new people. This trend is healthy if moderate and contained. Random or driven socialization, on the other hand, is indiscriminate, and may be motivated by an underlying sense of loneliness.

Last, *neuroticism* that is low translates to states of low anxiety and fewer negative moods. In its positive dimension, it denotes a relaxed frame of mind and a calm demeanor. Such people are more agreeable, cooperative, openminded, and socially engaging. The construct of neuroticism denotes states of "ill-being." These contrast with states of well-being that encompass positive feelings, such as happiness, contentment, and peace of mind. Also implicated in well-being are positive engagement, positive relationships, self-acceptance, and strivings toward personal growth and self-development.

The attachment style termed "self-assured" is ideal. Of course, this ideal is, in fact, only a guideline. The other attachment styles, especially the needy variety, have not proven successful. They breed conflict, distress, malcontent, jealousy, insecurity, and interpersonal tensions.

Typically, men and women communicate differently for a variety of reasons, some of which are alluded to in this chapter and in chapter 6. Women tend to be more adept at communication and adapting their communicational styles to meet the needs of those with whom they interact. Recent cross-cultural studies continue to demonstrate that, on average, females score slightly higher on tests of verbal ability than do males. Men, many times, find such sensitive flexibility in communication more difficult.

Women, for example, can often communicate needs to other women by subtle hints. Men tend to prefer direct and specific communications about topics characterized by both clear and logistical solutions. Typically, men do not feel comfortable with and avoid discussions about feelings and relationship matters.

Since genders are not uniform, it is useful to remember that each person—man and woman—has characteristics making that person virtually unique. Gender communicates something about the self and therefore elicits reactions from others. These gender-elicited reactions, in turn, may be general or specific to the person perceiving these communications. That is, they may be filtered through temperament, attachment style, and personality, but also through cultural lenses and the precedents of tradition.

Some relationship and marital specialists have suggested guidelines to enhance relational success. It is suggested that men follow through on promises, share inner thoughts and concerns at times, make time to listen carefully, provide evidence of their commitment, and establish reasonable boundaries that include emotional and material degrees of acceptable closeness. Wives tend to want their husbands to care about and discuss matters that go beyond merely practical or material concerns. Women are advised to maintain self-respect and respect for the adult status of their partners, not need to seek approval, not overanalyze their partner's behaviors or the motivations, not unreasonably demand discussions of feelings or the relationship, and not require unreasonable proximity or closeness.

Each partner can maximize chances of relational success when he or she steps out of the "stubborn zone," pauses, listens attentively, and reasonably adapts to the stated needs of the other. Such cooperativeness, negotiation, and reorientations may go far to dispel stereotypes of the "needy" wife and the husband "who just doesn't listen."

The above personality guidelines create a state of psychological readiness and sensitivity to perceiving experience in positive, growth-promoting ways. They allow one to recognize opportunities that may be personally and interpersonally beneficial. The past becomes the matrix or platform propelling one into a potential positive future. This future is "in potentia," meaning able to be created, to some extent, by one who has workable goals and enduring intentions.

Such positive and motivated attitudes provide problem-solving strategies. Successful problem solvers recognize challenges, take control of situations, list options, test proposed solutions, modify strategies, and move forward as the changing future unfolds. Transitions demand recursive adaptations that naturally occur and inevitably recur.

6. MOTHERING AND FATHERING

As discussed thus far, the commonalities across the psychology of adults are numerous. Many measurable traits, for example, largely transcend gender, although positive correlations of some features are associated more with either females or males. There are, however, distinguishable differences between how mothers and fathers behave in parenting situations. It cannot be denied that traditional stereotypes, which in the past may have correlated to some degree with actual behaviors, still persist to some extent. Women's roles as wives had included not working outside the home, shopping for clothing and food, cooking, cleaning, washing clothes, and raising children. Men's roles as husbands included the primary function of leaving the home to work and secure an income, take care of the family automobile, and attend to household mechanical chores.

Whatever the actual tasks that wives and husbands perform in today's world, neither role can rightfully be over- or undervalued. Seeing marital and parenting roles in a balanced though nuanced fashion is useful for everyone in a family. The extent to which current parental roles have been "handed down" from the cultural mores of sixteenth- and seventeenth-century Euro-American traditions is unclear. There is, however, some definite degree of cultural inheritance. Common roles of fathers include family problem solver, children's playmate, children's disciplinarian, major financial provider, and liaison to the social and "real" world outside the family. These blatant stereotypes, to a large extent, have been self-fulfilling prophecies. The research literature on mothering is extensive and goes back decades. Studies on fathering are still in their early stages and cover the last twenty-five to thirty-five years. In view of this, this section addresses fathering in much greater detail.

Parenting includes mothering and fathering, but also the parental couple as a living model, hopefully within a cohesive family. Respecting parental style differences, mothers and fathers do best when they trust each other's care for their children. Each parent offers the child a unique perspective on understanding, problem solving, and navigating in the world. Knowledge of basic child development and good child-rearing skills are optimized when each parent applies them in an enthusiastic manner commensurate with his or her particular style and individual preferences.

6.1 Mothering

Maternal involvement tends to be natural, spontaneous, and all-embracing. Mothering is synonymous with essential caregiving. Its core includes all the characteristics of nurturance, the indispensable essence of good parenting. Effective mothers are intimately attuned and attached to their children from

birth onward and even before. Good mothers recognize a child's uniqueness—his or her individual strengths, weaknesses, vulnerabilities, preferences, and temperaments.

Mothering is an interactive dialogue of emotions, meaning, and caregiving occurring on a daily basis. This sensitivity encompasses attention to a
child's needs for material resources, affection, comfort, and mental stimulation. Mothers are quintessential provocateurs of emotional development.
"Mother love," notably when not inappropriately overinvolved, directly elicits emotions of love and affiliation and helps modulate negative emotions. In
fact, appropriate displays of love by both mothers and fathers attenuate negative emotions in reciprocal ways that affect all involved.

Mothers tend to be more verbal, proactive, predictable, soothing, and
concerned with safety than fathers are. This sensitive attunement and long-
term commitment operates nonconsciously and automatically. It makes up
the silent bond of affiliation between mother and child.

Mothers typically engage in intimate, shared experiences with their children beginning in earliest infancy. They are devoted to the dedicated attention and care of their children. To a large extent, this is natural and spontaneous. On many occasions, mother-child interactions are without words. Communication has a proximal quality of frequent touching and physical contact.
Mothers appear to instinctively perceive their children's needs and intentions
in the absence of direct language. This silent rapport may have its origins in
earliest infancy when language is absent. It is at this time that patience,
understanding, and consistency are foremost features in maternal caregiving.

Mothers report that they assume the bulk (about 60 percent) of direct
physical ("hands-on") childcare responsibilities and that fathers share in
about 38 percent of this direct care. Fathers, by contrast, state that mothers
assume about 34 percent of all childcare responsibilities and that their share
is about 60 percent. Indirect childcare by fathers involves activities undertak-
en for the child, such as supplying money for food and material goods,
childcare arrangements, and promoting a child's community connections.
Some research shows that in 77 percent of cultures that have been studied,
fathers typically provide more of the provisions for young children than do
mothers. Fathers are primary caregivers for one in four preschoolers. Studies
estimate that fathers spend about twenty-three hours a week on housework
compared to forty-two hours for wives. These statistics have pragmatic salience since clinical work in marital therapy demonstrates that when fathers
take initiative with children, mothers typically feel cared for and supported.

6.2 Fathering

Fathering counts. The position of fathers toward children is complex. Fathering can be understood to pivot around matters of personal and interpersonal involvement. Fatherhood includes the physical, cognitive, and emotional presence that make up active nurturance.

Fathers' involvement has been fraught with a variety of real and sociocultural barriers. Compared to mothers, fathers may use fewer words, intervene less, let frustrations build in ambiguous situations, seem more unpredictable, and tolerate marginally more risky and novel exploration and behaviors. At the same time, fathers have been stereotyped as unemotional, disinterested, ineffectual, and even absent. They have been pigeonholed at times into being only financial providers. Divorce typically emphasizes these economic perspectives. The idea of being a parent is all too often unequally associated with mothering. Mothers unwittingly may reinforce this framework. In addition, fathers claim that they have not been "socialized" to become caregiving male adults, let alone parents. However, these facts cannot excuse men from being good fathers. They can instead become motivated to learn caregiving action plans.

Many fathers from all walks of life, in fact, are motivated self-learners who fashion themselves to be better caregivers. In other words, it is suitable for fathers to self-direct parenting towards grasping and satisfying the needs of their children.

Fathers, on average, spend less total time with children than mothers. The actual time spent, however, may be qualitatively and uniquely valuable. Attempting to broadly understand fathering avoids narrow, restrictive, and possibly incorrect assessments. Fathering plays an important role in caregiving and influencing child well-being.

Involvement of fathers is best when it includes degrees of engaged, direct interaction. These levels of care do not merely involve dispensing a commodity but should be a bidirectional engagement. This role includes active listening to both wives and children. This requires men to develop a greater modicum of patience and pause. It also connotes deferring problem-solving attempts until adequate deliberation has occurred. Developing and reinforcing a family climate of listening is valuable to everyone in the family. In contrast to mother's caregiving, involvement for fathers may be less spontaneous and require more intentional effort and directed focus.

Also, in contrast to mothers who may be accused of overinvolvement and gatekeeping with their children, fathers have been seen as relatively underinvolved. Many attribute this to the traditional roles of father working outside the home and mother staying at home with children. It has been estimated that 70 to 75 percent of mothers with children now work outside the home. As family arrangements have changed over the last decades, the details of caregiving by fathers are also changing.

Some theorists discuss paternal involvement in terms of three subcomponents: accessibility, engagement, and responsibility. Others add factors of biological relatedness, protection, providing material and economic support, and socialization. Protection evokes feelings of safety in dependent children. Direct care by a father indicates direct interaction with the child, whereas indirect care might include arranging services for the child, supplying material goods, managing the child's social and community involvements, and supporting mother's direct role.

Fathers also have a characteristic style of direct language interaction that includes more directives, questions, requests for clarification, and references to the past. Although sparse in quantity, fathers' use of language is qualitatively strong and unambiguous. This communicational style is described as distal (more interpersonally distant) rather than proximal (more intimate). Such "left brain" interaction is characterized by attention to detail, linear reasoning, and strategizing. In children, hearing such speech evokes greater verbal expressivity and a pressure to be explicit. The direct effect on children is a fostering of expanded socialization and experience with the outside world. Such language usage contrasts with other more intimate and less question-laden experiences within the family.

Moreover, fathers indirectly influence the family through their economic and emotional support. Fathers can serve as role models who teach children how to be parents and teach boys how to be fathers. *The way fathers treat and behave with their spouses provides a compelling model that children observe and incorporate over time.* This internalization then affects the way children treat others in a variety of relationships. A father's material and affective supportive relationship with mother determines family harmony or discord. Father's living example, therefore, is instrumental in inculcating children with emotional self-management models and strategies that optimize success.

Effective fathering crucially requires active, participant caregiving. Such caregiving adds a psychological dimension to biological endowment and relatedness. Quantity of time spent with children, quality of the direct father-child interaction, and responsibility for taking charge and making decisions are all important. Effective fathers set the tone for appropriate discipline by setting fair and firm limits; they do not rely on force but on suitable consequences. Fathers and mothers are most effective when enforcement of family rules is agreed upon and support between parents is mutual and relatively unambivalent.

A child's attachment to father, as to mother, is grounded on a developing sense of trust. Trust requires sufficient interaction with a person over time. Experiences in a variety of different interactions (for example, feeding, toileting, playing, and displays of affection) builds trust. This process is complemented by regular and expectable interactions. In other words, continuity in caregiving and support over time build trust.

Proper fathering goes beyond merely playing with a child. Fathers have been "accused" of acting more as children's play companions than as adult nurturers. This interactional style contrasts with that of mothers, who are described as more "containing," less playful, and less likely to overly stimulate children with robust, rough-and-tumble activities.

Since mothers tend to spend more time with their children, fathers are thought to "pack in" more stimulating, exciting, and entertaining activity. One might speculate that because of such increased intensity, fathers may have a more difficult time listening, validating, and exploring rather than reacting to problematic behaviors. Instead, they engage their children in play activities that require less long-term deliberation. Play is more immediate than activities involving less physical action; problems encountered in play situations offer more rapid, often simpler, and more obvious solutions.

A great deal of the research literature demonstrates that sensitive fathering has effects on children that are similar to those produced by sensitive mothering. Such parenting involves responding to children, communicating, teaching and demonstrating, and encouraging them to learn. All of these acts—performed by either parent—predict children's positive socioeconomic, intellectual, and language achievements.

Fathers have a role in the emotional development of both male and female children. Although it may be more difficult for men in contrast to women to be in touch with emotional states of love, tenderness, sensitivity, compassion, or empathy, such insight is nonetheless a necessity for personal and interpersonal success. Successful and effective men require an awareness of their own emotional states, particularly those related to sensitivity and affection. Once such self-awareness is established in the adult, it is more spontaneously communicated in all caregiving activities.

A central matter of significance in biomental child development is for fathers to adequately recognize, identify, and manage internal anxiety states. Anxiety acts to constrict, contract, retract, and diminish emotional experience; it motivates avoidance. Although both mothers and fathers may feel anxious at times, anxiety in fathers tends to further constrict access to an already lower baseline of emotional fluidity.

The emotional development of infants, children, and adolescents is supported and nurtured by the modulated emotional expressivity of fathers. Father's facial expressions communicate emotional information that provides needed feedback and emotional stimulation to children. Male children may particularly benefit from identification with healthy, gendered, emotional awareness of emotions. This transactional emotional modulation and flexibility supports emotional development. It is a powerful model for emotional self-management that may become internalized by the child and thus personally experienced.

Studies suggest that the results of involved fathering on children have multiple benefits. Some of these include fewer legal problems, fewer teen pregnancies, reduced divorce rates, reduced substance abuse, greater literacy in both girls and boys, greater mathematics competence of girls, less emphasis on gender stereotyping, and less aggressivity, or a child's tendency to react violently. A father's influence on a son is vitally important for many reasons, one of which is serving as a healthy role model. A father's relationship with his daughter is also of prime importance since he is usually the first man she knows and from whom she learns strategies of interacting with males. Her future expectations can be shaped by this first emotionally close relationship. By contrast, the withdrawal or absence of a father's nurturance may play a large role in children's personality and psychological maladjustment, proneness toward delinquent behaviors, and substance abuse.

In the Western hemisphere, twenty-first-century culture demands that fathers be more involved. Common parental roles such as caregiving, guiding, playing, and material care transcend gender. Although it cannot be denied that mothers and fathers act in important ways as gender models, the scientific literature puts higher value on the broader characteristics of parents' nurturance and holistic care of children. A male gendered parent can demonstrate to children that they are both needed and loved. Such expression may be instrumental, for example, in defusing the aggressivity typically associated with males.

Although conventional descriptions of fathering are commonly observed or perhaps presumed true, a great deal of their objectivity and consistency across cultures is far from having scientifically measured validation. Mothering and fathering, however, may be different enough to require different assessment criteria. Put more simply, promoting child well-being may require different strategies by each parent. It has been suggested that when two parents are involved in caregiving, each somewhat observes the other and reacts to do what is perceived as missing or incomplete. In this respect, different gender-based strategies may be complementary, supportive, and mutually enhancing.

As reiterated throughout this book, in a child's eyes, the parental relationship is a central focus of attention. When this relationship is complementary, there is less chance for a "win-lose" competition to occur between parents. Adversarial positions are best when they are virtually absent. An essential perspective to be fostered is avoiding both parental and child misperceptions of "the other" as "the enemy." In other words, all members of the family team share in the reward of a cooperative family life.

7. KEY POINTS

7.1 Adult Temperaments

Four types of adult temperament are recognized. They are: (1) novelty seeking, (2) harm avoidance, (3) reward dependence, and (4) persistence.

7.2 Adult Personality

Adult personality is made up of the "Big Five" factors and includes the seven-dimensional model.

Big Five Factors of Adult Personality: The "Big Five" factors are sub-components that characterize personality structure and functioning. They include: (1) openness to new experience, (2) conscientiousness, (3) extroversion, (4) agreeableness, and (5) negative emotions.

Seven-Dimensional Model of Personality: The seven-dimensional model is complementary to the "Big Five" factor model of personality and includes: (1) novelty seeking, (2) harm avoidance, (3) reward dependence, (4) persistence, (5) self-directedness, (6) cooperativeness, and (7) self-transcendence.

Five Planes of Being: The five planes of being comprise a psychological and philosophical model of personality. They include: (1) sexual-corporeal, (2) material-power and possessions, (3) interpersonal attachments, (4) intellectual, and (5) spiritual.

7.3 Adult Attachment Styles

Four types of adult attachment styles are (1) self-assured, (2) distant, (3) needy, and (4) anxious/frightened.

7.4 Mothering

Maternal involvement tends to be naturally long-term, spontaneous, and all-embracing. Mothering is synonymous with essential caregiving. Its core includes all the characteristics of nurturance, which is the indispensable essence of good parenting. The concept of transactional sensitivity discussed throughout this book epitomizes this. Effective mothers are intimately attuned and attached to their children from birth onward and even before. Good mothers recognize a child's uniqueness—his or her individual strengths, weaknesses, vulnerabilities, preferences, and temperaments.

Mothering is an interactive dialogue of emotions, meaning, and caregiving occurring on a daily basis with attention to a child's needs for material resources, affection, comfort, and mental stimulation. Mothers are quintessential provocateurs of emotional development.

7.5 Fathering

Fathering encompasses engagement, involvement, accessibility, protection, providing material and economic support, socialization of children, and responsibility. Involvement of fathers should include degrees and levels of engaged, direct interaction. It is not merely dispensing a commodity, but a bidirectional transactional sensitivity.

Active engagement elicits active child participation and reinforces learning and development. Engagement includes active listening to both wives and children. Fathers' characteristic style of language interaction directly influences the socialization of their children. The indirect effects of fathers operate through their economic and emotional support of the family, especially of mother. The way fathers treat and behave with their spouses is a compelling model that children observe and incorporate over time.

Effective fathering requires active, participant caregiving. Such parenting adds a psychological dimension to biological endowment and relatedness. Effective fathers set the tone for suitable discipline by setting fair and firm limits, which provide a powerful model for emotional self-management.

A child's attachment to father is grounded on a developing sense of trust. Trust requires sufficient interaction, both dependable and satisfying, with a person over time. Experiences in a variety of different interactions, namely feeding, toileting, playing, and displays of affection, for example, build trust. This process is complemented by regular and expectable interactions. In other words, continuity in caregiving and support over time conveys genuine availability and builds trust.

REFERENCES

Cath, S. Z. H., Gurwitt, A., & Gunsburg (Eds.). (1989). *Fathers and their families*. Hillsdale, NJ: Erlbaum.

Cattell, R. (1950). *Personality: A systematic theoretical, and factual study*. New York: McGraw-Hill.

Costa, P. T., Jr., & McCrae, R. R. (1992). *Revised NEO Personality Inventory manual (NEO-PI-R) and NEO Five-factor Inventory (NEO-FFI) professional manual*. Odessa, FL: Psychological Assessment Resources.

Eysenck, H. J. (1967). *The biological basis of personality*. Springfield, IL: Thomas.

Feldman, R. (2003). Infant-mother and infant-father synchrony: The coregulation of positive arousal. *Infant Mental Health Journal, 24*, 1–23.

Flouri, E. (2005). *Fathering and child outcomes*. New York: Wiley.

Goncy, E. A., & van Dulmen, M. H. M. (2010). Fathers do make a difference: Paternal involvement and adolescent alcohol use. *Fathering: A Journal of Theory, Research, and Practice about Men as Fathers, 8*(1), 93–108.

Griswold, R. (1993). *Fatherhood in America: A history.* New York: Basic Books.

Grossmann, K., Grossmann, K. E., Fremmer-Bombik, E., Kindler, H., Scheuerer-Englisch, H., & Zimmermann, P. (Eds.). (2002). The uniqueness of the child-father attachment relationship: Father's sensitive and challenging play as a pivotal variable in a 16-year longitudinal study. *Social Development, 11*, 307–331.

Habib, C., Santoro, J., Kremer, P., Toumbourou, J., Leslie, E., & Williams, J. (2010). The importance of family management, closeness with father and family structure in early adolescent alcohol use. *Addiction, 105*(10), 1750–1758.

Lamb, M. E. (Ed.). (2010). *The role of the father in child development* (5th ed.). Hoboken, NJ: Wiley.

Lamb, M. E., Pleck, J. H., Charnov, E. L., & Levine, J. A. (1985). Paternal behavior in humans. *American Zoologist, 25*(2), 883–894.

Marlowe, F. (2000). Parental investment and the human mating system. *Behavioural Processes, 52*, 45–61.

Marsiglio, W. (1995). *Fatherhood: Contemporary theory, research, and social policy.* Thousand Oaks, CA: Sage.

Marsiglio, W., Amato, P., Day, R. D., & Lamb, M. E. (2000). Scholarship on fatherhood in the 1990s and beyond. *Journal of Marriage and the Family, 62*, 1173–1191.

McCrae, R. R. (2005). Personality structure. In A. Derlega, B. A. Winstead, & W. H. Jones (Eds.), *Personality: Contemporary theory and research.* Belmont, CA: Wadsworth.

McCrae, R. R., & Costa, P. T. (2003). *Personality in adulthood: A five factor theory perspective.* New York: Guilford.

Nelson, D. A., & Coyne, S. M. (2009). Children's intent attributions and feelings of distress: Associations with maternal and paternal parenting practices. *Journal of Abnormal Child Psychology, 37*, 223–237.

Popenoe, D. (1999). *Life without father: Compelling new evidence that fatherhood and marriage are indispensable for the good of children and society.* Cambridge, MA: Harvard University Press.

Rohner, R. P., & Veneziano, R. A. (2001). The importance of father love: History and contemporary evidence. *Review of General Psychology, 5*, 382–405.

Tamis-LeMonda, C. S., & Cabrera, N. (2002). *Handbook of father involvement: Multidisciplinary perspectives.* Mahwah, NJ: Earlbaum.

Veneziano, R. A. (2003). The importance of paternal warmth. *Cross-Cultural Research, 37*, 265–281.

Wai, J., Cacchio, M., Putallaz, M., & Makel, M. C. (2010). Sex differences in the right tail of cognitive abilities: A 30-year examination. *Intelligence, 38*, 412–423.

Wall, G., & Arnold, S. (2007). How involved is involved fathering? An exploration of the contemporary culture of fatherhood. *Gender & Society, 21*, 508–527.

Williams, D. R. (2003). The health of men: Structured inequalities and opportunities. *American Journal of Public Health, 93*, 724–731.

Yogman, M. (1982). Development of the father-infant relationship. In G. Fitzgerald, F. Lester, & M. Yogman (Eds.), *Theory and research in behavioral pediatrics* (Vol. 1), pp. 221–297. New York: Plenum.

Chapter Five

Parenting Styles

1. PARENTAL PERFORMANCE COMBINES SKILL AND STYLE

Nurturance, discipline, and example are three significant pillars of good parenting. Each has a major role, and no component is singularly sufficient. When heartfelt, genuine, and informed by basic developmental understanding, parenting skills may be implemented by a diverse range of individual styles. A developmental and positive parenting perspective has been the basis of this book. Knowledge behind the skills enables one to see past short-term challenges so that the necessary motivation, optimism, and enthusiasm that fuel continued forward developmental progress can be successfully engaged. With thoughtful consideration and self-reflection, it is translatable into parenting action plans.

Understanding child development may be viewed to be the fundamental infrastructure of parenting. Developmental details are ever-expanding and reorganizing platforms that inform parental behaviors. While such knowledge is important, practical application thereof makes up skillful parenting and competent performance.

Since each parent is an individual with evolving past, present, and future, the application of skills is not uniform. There may be as many styles of parenting as there are parents. Effective parenting has both decisive and authoritative components that communicate a sense of purpose and direction. Parenting encompasses numerous skill dimensions that draw from evolutionary necessity, biological impulse, cognition and emotion, psychological intuition, and acquired knowledge and competencies, all of which operate in specific sociohistorical contexts.

1.1 Parental Coaching

Parenting, to a large extent, involves coaching children toward experiencing themselves and the world in healthy and adaptive ways. Successful parents are credible communicators that present plausible reasoning along with authoritative guidance. Children, like all adults, feel an almost "desperate" need to be understood. Listening carefully and then speaking effectively to communicate this understanding are essential parental strategies. This axiom reflects an continuing dialogue from earliest childhood through the adult years.

Parents are the team leaders of a family and responsible for providing, monitoring, and maintaining their authoritative leadership roles. When established as a foundation of the family system, this strategy makes discipline a continuing learning experience mutually acceptable and effective. Team-oriented leadership respects the transactional nature of the family system and enhances healthy generational boundaries. It minimizes members acting in opposition to one another, namely, as "opposers."

A core component of parental coaching is suitably implementing effective feedback. Feedback can promote learning and improve future performance. Put simply, effective feedback works and produces intended results. *Coaching, feedback, and practice with a focus on the specifics of desired behaviors are decisive elements for success.*

Feedback can provide validation for achieved competencies. Properly timed feedback is also corrective and can introduce new and better ways for children to manage behaviors. To be effective, feedback is best delivered as a motivational message ("Try your best") and should occur immediately following a set of behaviors, as discussed in chapter 1.

To enable learning, feedback must describe specific behaviors in clear and simple language. Effective feedback also provides a practical plan for improvement. The most effective feedback is delivered in a positive, enthusiastic tone that connotes mutuality in aspirations. Biomental child development prefers this sort of positive attitude in contrast to one of "praising." Put simply, specifically articulating successful aspects of behavior is usually more effective than merely saying "Good job" routinely.

Focusing on both the positive and specific aspects of desired behaviors is essential. For example, it is more effective to say, "The way you straightened up your room by putting those toys and clothes away was good," than "Good job." Rephrasing problem behaviors in the form of expectations and anticipations for positive outcomes is more powerful than negative feedback. In addition, permitting a child to practice the improved version several times offers real-time opportunities for internalizing the new behavior. While responding with "Good job" reinforcement is appropriate at times, varying such a comment is best. Preschoolers delight when parents say "Hurray," and adolescents respond to enthusiastic comments such as "Bravo," if not too routine and repetitious.

Several other factors increase the efficiency of coaching. Parental coaching that focuses on parental responsivity and sensitivity to child cues is important. Parents should also regard infancy and early childhood as highly teachable developmental eras. Individualization of strategies geared to each child's particular strengths, competencies, weaknesses, vulnerabilities, and unmatured or potential abilities is also essential. Focusing on a broad range of target areas to support and refine is also important. It is best to begin as early as possible with sustained and consistent effort. Encouraging specific aspects of good behavior supports the likelihood of such actions continuing into the future.

Emphasizing the emotional dimensions of coaching is a fundamental part of teaching and modeling effective coping skills. Fathers benefit from taking emotional aspects seriously, particularly in interactions with their sons. Integrating a positive, enthusiastic, and encouraging emotional tone to behavioral directives increases their effectiveness. Such coaching and encouraging delivery styles contribute to the building of character. Character is reflected in a sense of admiration, gratitude, thankfulness, and the ability to admit mistakes. Hearing a child say, "I'm sorry" implies positive learning from experience.

1.2 Positive and Negative Parenting

Parental performance combines skill and styles. Skills first require knowledge, and subsequent application of this knowledge. *Skills* are abilities to do something well and perform effectively in a relatively sustained way over time. Skill is the more objective and technical aspect of enduring performance; it can be learned and measured. *Styles*, by contrast, include form, appearance, shape, mode, method, and the implementation of how something is carried out and expressed. Styles are more personalized applications of skills. Skill and style are reflected in the way parents respond to children's behavior.

Parenting skills and styles are, in part, based on parents' beliefs about why a child behaves, including attention to the particular motivations unique to each child. Self-reflection, as will be discussed in chapter 6, supports adults' self-knowledge and insight into children's motivations. An understanding of the principles of child development together with self-reflection enhances effective parenting, especially building good behaviors.

Both parents' and children's skills are important. *The value of understanding the developmentally age-appropriate skill sets of children cannot be emphasized enough.* In addition, it is important to always remember that a young child's behavior will not always be consistent or absolutely predictable. It is inevitable that parents feel intermittently disappointed with the behavior of children. In addition, parents may feel dissatisfied with their own effectiveness in helping children achieve good results, for example, academically or in decision making. Parents do best at such times by pausing and reassessing the situation at hand, especially the psychological component of blame. Maintaining a positive and realistically optimistic attitude opens the way for new and alternative considerations. This strategy minimizes feelings of learned helplessness for both parents and children.

How individual parents perform is varied. Good parenting, however, is creative and stays fresh in attitude, ideas, and how they can be implemented. Mixtures of predictability and novelty are essential.

To reiterate a major theme of biomental child development: *Parenting children is co-parenting—a team effort encompassing shared care.* Sharing never means absolutely equal distribution, but each partner must earnestly attempt to actively contribute. Parenting involves listening, respecting, committing, negotiating, appreciating, acknowledging, and valuing the other parent's contributions. This overarching theme needs constant reflection, renewal, and reiteration, both individually and between parents.

"Triangulations," in which one parent excessively allies with a particular child in opposition to the other parent, are signs of family difficulty. Clearly maintaining parental, marital, and generational boundaries is important. It is true that organic coalitions will form and change in any flexible system. Yet consistent triangulations, especially those that are subtle or covert, are inevitably disruptive. They counter the forward progress of a family system.

Boundaries should be healthy, flexible, and semi-permeable. They exist where an individual begins and ends psychologically and materially with regard to where others begin and end their roles and age-appropriate behaviors. Ideally, proper boundaries should develop on three levels: (1) at the level of the individual, (2) between the generations, and (3) between a family and its extended community.

Parents with "high neuroticism" are those who become easily discouraged, anxious, angry, and pessimistic. Stress management strategies are poorly developed. Such negative reactions may particularly occur in response to children who are challenging, have difficult temperaments, or are slow to warm up. Mothers and fathers with negative outlooks may view parenting as futile—instead of as frustrating yet feasible. In some cases, parents may intermittently give up on trying. This behavior can be perceived by children as abandonment and provoke extreme reactions of hopelessness or aggressive defiance.

Positive and negative emotional energies stirred within families may stimulate stress. When parents feel out of control and at a loss for effective management, fear is typically evoked in these adults. This fear can cause more negative moods and behaviors. At such times, pausing for self-reflection is needed to examine the situation and plan for correctively reconfiguring parenting strategies and skills.

1.3 Stress and Stress Management

Stress and the stress response are fundamental in interpersonal relationships of all sorts, especially parenting. Although complex in its detailed operation, stress activates when people feel a sense of urgency and emotional pressure. Temporary cognitive confusion typically accompanies stress. The phrase "hurried lives" aptly applies to this feeling in daily routines on a regular basis.

Recognizing overt and subtle triggers for stress is essential for planning ahead, minimizing stressful situations, and ameliorating negative reactions. If stressful event patterns become apparent, such as children not punctually waking up in the morning for school, one should examine holistic details. For example, one should consider aspects of not only the morning but also the night before in order to change existing patterns. Effective parents might consider creative inducements rather than bribes. Such strategies may involve a variety of parent-child collaborations to examine and arrive at workable strategies. Thinking of this partnership as a fun engagement, rather than one of drudgery, optimizes chances of success.

Unexpected and unanticipated demands are potent stress triggers. Expecting unforeseen events to occur on an intermittent basis can minimize the extent to which stress impairs one's functioning. Procrastination is also one of the chief causes of unhealthy stress. Parental and family stress, moreover, puts undue burdens on children.

Parents should strive to correctly identify and appreciate a child's innate aptitudes while not expecting "too much." In other words, expectancies of effort and performance need to be founded in reality. Denying a child's limitations or learning disorders, for example, is harmful. Unrealistic over- or underestimation of capabilities prevents identification of remediable difficulties. Unrealistic estimation may instead reinforce either unrealistically defeatist or narcissistic attitudes.

In addition, stress-provoking situations often arise when parents have to say "no" to a child. Saying "no" in a way that minimizes stress on everyone is possible. A useful technique is to empathize and validate a child's request by saying something like, "I know you want to . . ." A parent should follow this statement by saying "Not now," or "Instead, let's . . ." Offering a wise and available alternative can manage the stress of having to deny a child.

When the child says "no" to a parent's directions, one must consider the child's developmental level in order to understand probable reasons behind this "no." Such consideration greatly facilitates disciplinary directions becoming positive inducements. "Win-win" reactions may thus supplant adversarial relations. For example, between two and six years, a child's apparent refusal may reflect normal inability for adequate empathy—understanding a parent's perspective. Additionally, refusals often communicate the child's normal struggle toward personal mastery and self-dependence. Reframing defiance in terms of a child's budding strengths helps parents respond more constructively and effectively.

Guided discipline consists of context-specific learning interventions. After considering what is inferred to be behind a stated "no," parental responses should first be based on safety matters. Next, it is important to try to empathetically validate a child's inferred feelings and motivations. Such empathic support does not, however, entail validating displays of unacceptable behaviors.

Empathetic sensitivity is a large part of good parenting, as it conveys to children that they are, in fact, valued and nurtured. This approach entails listening first before communicating. In order to ensure accurate exchange, a parent might ask, "Did you say . . . ?"

It is never redundant to affirm and validate the value of a child's communication. The content of one's response should communicate understood feelings and frustrations. Also beneficial are comments about the normativity of having such feelings, especially of frustration, and their relation to behaviors. Attempting to communicate a best course of action while permitting the child some freedom is effective, as is offering a range of alternatives.

Another stressful situation may occur when one child hits another. One may flag such situations by labeling them "learning moments" for discussion. The best technique is to remain calm and stop the hitting while saying something along the lines of: "We do not hit; we don't touch anybody else without asking." It is important to also model such behavior in concrete and detailed ways. When the context permits, brief "learning moment" discussions are better than automatically using "time-outs." When deemed necessary, however, brief time-outs to facilitate settling down for a few minutes may be helpful, especially for children between the years of preschool and early adolescence. This intervention also gives a parent time to regain composure and reflect on the best course of action.

Another fundamental antistress guideline is being diligent about commitments. Broken promises, procrastinating, and habitual lateness maximize an unhealthy stress response. Planning ahead to try to promptly start and end tasks on time is an effective antistress maxim. This approach helps a child gain relative precision in anticipating time frames and planning transitions. Such time management strategies provide children with concrete examples of how successful forward planning and effective executive functioning operates.

Both explicit and implicit disregard of verbal promises and time allotments can have negative effects. Breaking a promise is often subliminally felt as a spoiling and traumatic act. Disappointments spoil and sour anticipated pleasures. Likewise, chronic difficulty in ending on time and detaching from events reflect impairments in "letting go" and fostering healthy relationships. Parental modeling of reliability and responsibility helps children establish antistress behavioral styles inside and out of the home.

A last consideration is that the "mass effect" or pressure of family problems often manifests as a focal deficit in only one family member. For example, a materially absent father may trigger depression in the mother. Another example would be chronic marital stress reflected in a child's academic or behavioral problems in school. In all these cases, family functioning as a whole is impaired.

1.3.1 Positive Parenting: Summary

Parent-child attachments are optimized when parents feel secure and are sensitively responsive to children's needs for structure, support, and reasonable autonomy. *Preparation, warning, and "heads up" before transitions, changes, separations, and absences are critical strategies in effective parenting.* Transitions are primary examples of essential mediating functions having both an experiential process and requiring adult supervision, that is, mediation to smoothly guide the process toward suitable, if not progressively successful, completion. Each transitional experience may be considered to provide a dynamic structure in which expectations and standards are clearly defined and during which concrete, constructive feedback is given to refine success. These techniques greatly facilitate the rewarding navigation of transitions; they assist children through the developmental process and also the adolescent process of psychological individuation and later management of challenges in adulthood.

This book offers a professional attitude toward children and parents. In the past, studies on parenting have sometimes insensitively described parenting as ineffective, uncaring, and harsh. Mothers, for instance, have been stereotyped, at times, with almost inhumane labels, such as rejecting, cold, overpossessive, overprotective, smothering, and so forth. Names such as "helicopter mother," "refrigerator mother," and "drill sergeant" have even been applied. In contrast, the following descriptions illustrate parenting styles that have proven to be more effective.

Formal research over the last thirty years has supported the effectiveness of two combined dimensions of parenting, (1) realistic parental expectations and (2) affectionate and timely parental responsiveness. Of course, the number of successful parenting styles may be virtually infinite, but these two components ensure effectiveness. An implicit third factor is the manner in

which a parent coregulates decisions and modulates the granting of autonomy in relation to a child's age and developmental status. A ban on "bad
behavior," moreover, is typically ineffective. Along with direction and guidance, helping children to devise solutions stimulates thinking skills, adaptivity, and self-empowerment. Suitably explaining parenting decisions is also
important in promoting an atmosphere of teamwork rather than opposition in
the parent-child relationship.

2. BASIC PARENTING STYLES

Studies have typically described four basic types of parenting styles with
different characteristics and results. These are (1) authoritative, (2) permissive, (3) authoritarian, and (4) neglectful (table 5.1).

2.1 Authoritative Parenting

Authoritative parenting has two major components: (1) high responsiveness
and (2) high demandingness. Its high responsiveness component is characterized by warmth, acceptance, and involvement. Its high demandingness component is characterized by firm behavioral control, close supervision, and
demands for age-appropriate maturity. Biomental child development understands the term "demands" to be a communicative style characterized by
developmentally realistic expectations, concrete guidance, and constructive
feedback. The term "induction" correlates with this method of verbal reasoning. These demands are neither manipulative nor authoritarian; rather, they
are firm and decisive.

Authoritative parenting is understood to be optimal since it is most effective for helping children successfully learn socially responsible and cooperative behaviors. The optimally involved parent uses prudence and balances his
or her involvement with the child's real needs, harm reduction, and ability to
gradually explore the environment and become more self-dependent.

"High responsiveness" parents are physically present, emotionally responsive, and not overly involved. They communicate explicit demonstrations of love, affection, warmth, and genuine involvement. Such authoritative

Table 5.1.   Four Basic Parenting Styles

Authoritative
Permissive
Authoritarian
Neglectful

parents monitor and judge behaviors, set and enforce firm and realistic rules, and use level-headed, fair, and nonpunitive discipline. Reasons for rules are intermittently explained in a way that a given child may understand. This continuing process takes into account developmental age and changing circumstances.

An expectation for reasonable obedience is the goal behind "high demandingness." In fact, such "demanded" expectations are best considered to be *preferences*—requests rather than commands or questions that optimize successful behavioral outcomes. For example, saying to a child "I prefer that you clean your room" usually meets with less resistance than saying "You must clean your room" or "Will you please clean your room?"

Unrealistically high expectations bring disappointment to parents as well as frustration and lowered self-esteem to children unable to meet goals beyond their capabilities. Expectations and directions create conditions for children to develop self-regulation, self-directedness, and relatively independent thinking. By observing how children respond both spontaneously and after having been given directions, parents may recognize unique emotional and motoric rhythms of temperament and personality. Expectations and directions may then be refined accordingly. Parental limits become internal models for children to assimilate. Reliable expectations also add to internal comfort, stability, and safety that, in turn, foster receptivity to other environmental challenges.

A more subtle point involves children's needs for limits and boundaries—containment—required for healthy psychological development. Children need to see and believe that parents are reasonably able, confident, and competent to exert mild, positive control. This "control" denotes affectionate and safe guidance that is clearly in the best interests of the child. If children are permitted to "get away with too much," they often feel a confused sense of guilt because of unconsequenced behaviors perceived by them to be bad or destructive. When children are not effectively monitored and given constructive feedback, their own ability to discriminate right from wrong and see consequences becomes ambiguous. In authoritative parenting, mutual dialogues that are *age and developmentally appropriate* are empathetic, validating of feelings, and respectful of differing points of view. Reasonable negotiation and dialogue that clarifies both children's and parents' perspectives adds clarity and plausibility to parental recommendations. This helps build a child's social skills—social perception and communication—both inside and outside the family.

Biomental child development is fully allied with the authoritative parenting style. When successfully implemented, it is neither overly attentive nor unrealistically controlling. Rather, this parenting approach is affectionate, empathetic, reasonable, flexible, and transactionally sensitive.

2.2 Permissive Parenting

Permissive parenting is characterized by high responsiveness and low demandingness. Such parenting is indulgent, excessively lenient, and appeasing. Overly permissive parenting is characterized by minimal discipline and caregiving intemperance. In nonprofessional terms, the colloquial expression—"spoiled child"—is used to describe such children whose behaviors are often impaired in the sense of their lacking adequate self-discipline because of temperamental unruliness or overindulgence, for example.

Some have referred to this parenting style as "democratic." Other theorists have questioned the extent to which pronounced parental guilt makes it difficult for them to assert suitable authority. Guilt, in this sense, may foster a passive parenting style. Permissive parents tend to use inconsistent disciplinary strategies as they yield to the demands of children, who may whine, be defiant, or otherwise provoke parental guilt.

Motivations for inordinate permissiveness range widely. In some instances, parents perceive that their child is limited, disabled, or vulnerable in some way. They may thus believe that a lower level of demandingness is appropriate. In situations where a disability may be present, parents need to remain realistic and seek evaluative corroboration from specialists to ascertain the actual strengths and possible limits of the child.

In addition, parents may be overly involved with their children because of their own unmet needs and insecurities. If this unhealthy merger and confusion of parent-child boundaries is pronounced and long-standing, it may present formidable challenges to outside providers such as teachers, behavioral consultants, and mental health providers who suggest remedial changes in parenting strategies. After consultation, parents may have to adjust their caregiving approaches to be more flexible.

Parents, however, must be aware of the possibility of feeling some guilt. Feeling guilt may entail feeling badly, distressed, or fearful that one's limit setting is too harsh, unreasonable, or unacceptable. Parents may fear not being liked—or even being "hated"—by their children. On the other hand, in some cases when children feel that they have gotten away with too much, they may feel implicit guilt, which evokes parental guilt. Parental self-reflection is useful in discerning the source of mixed feelings that include ambivalence, guilt, fear, and anxiety.

2.3 Authoritarian Parenting

Authoritarian parenting is characterized by high demandingness but low responsiveness. Such parents appear strict and overbearing and seem to be micromanaging their children. This apparently well-intentioned behavior has been called "overparenting." Such parenting seems overly controlling and these parents may see their children as willfully manipulative. This parenting style may reflect a broader personality style characterized by impairments in the development of the sense of a healthy locus of personal control, agreeableness, and cooperativeness. As such, authoritarian parenting may entail extremist, selective indoctrination. Such a dogmatic style tends to inculcate principles, values, and ideologies that have an uncritically restrictive and biased focus, typically illustrated using superior-inferior dichotomies.

Authoritarian parents have been referred to colloquially as "drill sergeants." The style is also characterized by children's perceptions of its unrelenting "preaching" quality. In many ways, authoritarian parenting demands "blind faith" and unquestioned compliance. Some studies have shown that parents with less education and lower occupational status employ authoritarian parenting styles. Children in these families tended to have relatively lower IQs.

Authoritarian parenting becomes coercive when it includes yelling, shouting, or some hitting. Such psychological aggression may escalate to harsher discipline, corporal punishment, or blatant physical assault, including slapping, intense hitting, or beating. Beating is clear-cut physical abuse. It can never be condoned. When these harmful extremes are reached, children learn to use aggression (fighting and threats of fighting); in some cases, depressive problems develop.

Typically, authoritarian expectations are excessive and unrealistic. Little or no explanations accompany parental directives. Such an autocratic style may evoke disappointment, upset, and anger in parents. Children feel dominated, subjugated, and unwillingly controlled. Arrogantly domineering parenting may evoke rebelliousness on the one hand, or passivity and submissiveness on the other.

Many studies have demonstrated that authoritarian parents may have had these personality traits in childhood and adolescence. They may have had parents who themselves were authoritarian. In adulthood, parents, especially fathers, bring such attitudes to the marriage and family. Authoritarian, coercive parenting may result in the disciplinary use of corporal punishment in stepfamilies. This possibility requires careful attention and scrutiny. Such adults may require counseling to examine and modify their parenting towards greater efficacy without resorting to aggressive techniques.

Although often a subcategory of authoritarian parenting, unrealistically overinvolved parenting practices affect both children and outside caregivers such as physicians and school personnel. Such overinvolvement, however well-intentioned, acts as interference to collaborators whose aim is to help. This thwarts the smooth implementation of caregiving services, especially outside the home. Unreasonable noncooperativeness may be particularly detrimental to children when parents do not sufficiently trust professionals such as teachers, school psychiatrists, and social workers whose aim is to remediate educational difficulties by enhancing and supporting intellectual achievement and emotional health *simultaneously*. Often, parents who focus exclusively on academic success may give short shrift to emotional development.

The authoritarian style, as such, may be dark, often intense, in mood and focus on single issues characterized by a need to maintain unilateral control. Openness to the inevitability of developmental change and concomitant treatment plan changes is blocked. Such parents fail to realize how emotional and social development may enhance or stall intellectual achievement. Hence, successful collaboration requires all members of the team—parents, caregivers, and child—to maintain an atmosphere of open-minded, cooperative agreeableness with regard to a child's total range of performance—academic, emotional, social, and behavioral. However well-intentioned parents may be, if they fail to adhere to constructive collaboration with regard to mutually agreed-upon interventions and treatments with other caregivers, good-will relations may become spoiled and, in turn, the resulting stress and disharmony makes effective care less than optimal. A school psychiatrist, for example, goes to great lengths to foster such beneficial mutuality in an actively continuing manner that is empathetic, flexible, and adaptive, especially when recommending a judicious balance of educational, psychosocial, and psychopharmacological interventions that are in proportion to a child's changing needs.

Mothers who appear overly involved may have anxieties stemming from dual sources: unmet needs from parents in her own childhood, and unmet needs from spouse or father of the child at this moment. These compensatory behaviors may employ a variety of defense mechanisms that primarily act to contain, however precariously, parental anxiety. Their long-term ineffectiveness contributes to chronic states of feeling anxious and insecure, both of which cause confusion, ambivalence, and unstable decision making.

Moreover, mothers who appear particularly controlling have been found to respond not only to their own higher anxiety and insecurity needs, but also to increased anxiety in their children. Such children, who may be temperamentally avoidant, may also have one of a range of anxiety disorders such as generalized anxiety, social phobia, or incipient panic disorders. Such children may otherwise have aspects of *selective mutism*, which is failure to speak in selective situations, such as outside the home, in school, or in public places. A prominent group of children may have serious social-skills impairments such as those occurring on the autistic spectrum, and so be anxious and needy. Overly involved parents often are driven to rescue their children, whether the children are atypical or neurotypical, from real or perceived harm. The problematic aspect of this is overinvolvement rather than realistic, balanced and rational guidance.

Avoidant difficulties of children may be recognized by parents and elicit protective responses. At times, parents may overly compensate for the perceived limitations of their children by authoritarian control that vacillates with unreasonable permissiveness. A term referring to this tendency is "helicopter parenting," wherein anxiety drives constant, frenetic surveillance and excessive intrusiveness. Inordinate and irrational overinvolvement is often an attempt to avoid feared outcomes, such as academic and social failure or low self-esteem. For example, teachers may encounter parents who micromanage educational curriculums, often in inappropriate and conflict-eliciting ways. Such parents may also try to control psychiatric recommendations in a manner that is defensive and unreasonable rather than cooperative. One of the primary tasks of professionals is to provide and encourage clear and collaborative communication, and foster agreed-upon interventions between families and themselves. Continuing informed consent strategies are essential.

Social fearfulness in children, moreover, naturally provokes parental concern and frustration. These feelings may lead to vicarious attempts to provide direction, guidance, and structure thought to be lacking. Anxious mothers tend to grant their children less autonomy. Parental beliefs and attitudes, as well as the specific anxiety status of parents and children, often need consideration in professional evaluation.

Often, healthy parental styles change as children develop. If authoritarian and excessively controlling behaviors remain static and impair the healthy transactional family system over the course of time, outside interventions and remediation may be needed.

2.4 Neglectful Parenting

Neglectful parenting is characterized by low demandingness and low responsiveness. Negligent attitudes, remiss behaviors, disengagement, and detachment are outstanding features of such "absentee" parents. Some have referred to this style of parenting as "dismissive." Dismissive parents may see their children as "spoiled" or overly manipulative. This perception makes the job of parenting more difficult. Dismissive parents themselves may be so emotionally immature or needy or suffer from a mental or physical condition that centers attention exclusively on themselves leaving little consideration for the needs of children.

Neglect may take many forms, including supervisory, environmental, care-related, educational, and medical. Supervisory neglect is understood to be the most common form. Any form of neglect, however, is child maltreatment. Recent studies show that child neglect may be one of the most under-recognized conditions, especially prevalent in socioeconomically strained cultures and countries. Child neglect in childhood is positively correlated with later development of shame and even clinical depression in childhood and thereafter.

2.4.1 Parent Inadequate Discipline

Parent inadequate discipline is a parental style understood to be poor parenting from a psychiatric perspective. This construct was proposed in 1996 for inclusion in the *Diagnostic and Statistical Manual of Mental Disorders* (DSM-IV), but was not formally accepted. Such discipline has the following characteristics: irritable, explosive, mood-dependent, erratic, inflexible, rigid, and inconsistent. There may be low parental supervision or involvement. Alternatively, there may be pronounced and unreasonable overprotection attributable to anxiety in parent or child. Lapses in rational empathy and lack of balanced understanding of children's needs contribute to such poor parenting. Any cold or hostile parental attitude, moreover, elicits oppositional defiance in children and reinforces the cycle of poor parenting from generation to generation. The predictive validity of parent inadequate discipline and disruptive behaviors in childhood with later antisocial and psychiatric disorders has been suggested.

While this construct is not included in the latest DSM-IV text revision of 2000, the condition termed *parent-child relational problem* is included. In contrast to the more psychological, interpersonal, and social perspectives that led Baumrind to formulate her four basic parenting styles in 1971, parent-child relational problem is a psychiatric construct. In this way, it broadly denotes impaired parent-child communication, overprotection, inadequate discipline, and associated impairment in the functioning of individuals or families that becomes clinically significant.

2.5 Parental Expectations and Developmental Capabilities

Parents may experience frustration and disappointment when their expectations are not met. At these times, it may be necessary to pause and reevaluate the quantity and quality of expectations, especially in relation to the developmental status of the child. With preschool children, for example, demands should be relatively fewer and less complex. The need for repetition and redundancy at this age is natural and typical.

As the elementary school years begin around age six, expectations should become greater. Abiding by established rules at home and at school is generally expected. At this age, memory systems are more developed, and children have a greater capacity to pause and think before acting, even though impulsivity may supersede delay. Nonetheless, parents should expect a reasonable level of alignment and compliance with their directives. When agreeable behavior does not occur, although frustrating and disappointing, it is best for

parents to maintain composure and rethink new and better strategies. This "plan, do, act, and revise" protocol is, in fact, an effective strategy for successful living applicable in all life's activities.

2.6 Crucial Aspects of Successful Parenting

To the extent that parents develop a sense of personal security and empowerment, they enhance their ability to effectively guide. Children experience this parental attitude as genuine, credible, and attractive. Humor, playfulness, sharing, and helpfulness with little insecurity provide optimal family climates. As children grow and develop, rules and guidelines for behavior need to be reassessed and perhaps renegotiated.

3. SKILL SETS: ACTION PLANS FOR IMPLEMENTING INTELLIGENT DISCIPLINE

Biomental child development offers a compendium of fundamental principles that outline a philosophy of parenting, the psychology of children and adults, and an overview of parenting styles and practices. These resources provide *understanding* of the knowledge behind the skills.

It must be emphasized that the information described in this book up to now has been aimed at informing parents about the overriding impact of growth, maturational unfolding, and experiential development in children. With an understanding of these areas, great sensitivity to the inner life of the child may remain foremost. Knowledge, understanding, insight, and intuition are core values to this approach.

Emotions, feelings, thinking, and the animate and inanimate environment all dynamically interact in a child's experiential world and in the formation of a sense of self-identity. To the extent that this self-configuration or *self-signature* remains flexible—rather than rigid or prematurely foreclosed—openness and cooperation are options for altering behavior.

Motivation and self-directed change, however nascent and fragile, are presumed to be underlying impulses in every child. Professionals and parents may draw from the wellspring of understanding these psychodynamic perspectives in order to better inform effective parenting. The essence of producing intended results is nurturance and caregiving, communicated in day-to-day family living and interactions.

The next section will briefly outline actual performance strategies—tangible behavioral interventions—that underlie part of biomental child development's framework for effective discipline. These broad guidelines are action-oriented and directive. As *one part* of good parenting, these parenting practices can serve to inform reasoned judgment in implementing intelligent child guidance.

The primary aim of biomental child development has been to create, elicit, and foster a mindset of nurturance, empathy, and helpfulness. A supporting aim is to provide some concrete guidelines for compassionate correction and sound discipline. These strategies, useful as tools to assist good parental decision making, are geared toward typical children. In other words, these strategies are not exclusively based on psychotherapeutic techniques and are not intended to serve as treatment for children with significant mental disorders. The general principles in this book, however, may be helpful in all parenting contexts.

Consistent with the tone and presumptions of this parenting philosophy, individual parents are respected for their intrinsic sense of how to parent their own children. Guidelines merely provide suggestions for parents to consider. Hence, the following section is succinct. It enthusiastically defers to parents' creative impulses in the actual implementation of the suggested dos and don'ts.

4. COMPASSIONATE DISCIPLINE

Compassionate discipline is composed of transactionally sensitive techniques aimed toward building good, healthy behaviors. Such discipline also seeks to eliminate, redirect, and diminish bad, inappropriate, and maladaptive behaviors. In this sense, the observable performance of actual behavior is targeted, along with parental expectations.

Effective parenting always combines nurturance, discipline, and example in an effort to promote cooperative compliance—change in behavior according to directions given. To effect change, parents need to articulate plausible arguments that are clear and reasonable. Emphasizing that the requested change will make a positive difference to better the child and the family as a whole enhances effectiveness. When parents appeal in a reasonable way, they highlight the child's natural wish to be good and his or her need to merit the respect deserved. Using this strategy obviates blind-faith acceptance and encourages reasonable dialogue. Of course, the younger a child is, the simpler the explanations. Older children require more complex dialogue.

This section focuses on behaviorally based interventions. These techniques apply to both parental and child action, including attitude, language, and all other behaviors. Targeted undesirable behaviors may take the form of active wrongdoings or refusal to fulfill expected obligations.

As is true of many other aspects of life, seeing an isolated event as it exists on a time continuum with a past, a current presentation, and an expected future course is useful and practical. Behaviors that occur earlier in life, such as in the preschool years, are less entrenched and habitual than those that occur later. A developmental perspective understands that the automatic and inescapable conditioning that occurs through everyday experience causes increasingly more crystallized personality configurations. This increasingly deep consolidation typically is accompanied by automaticity in behavior—habit—that correlates with a trenchant inability for introspection, self-reflection, and behavioral change. In early childhood, personality is still in formation; in adolescence, it is beginning to consolidate; in early adulthood, it becomes much more routine; and in later life, personality and behaviors may become so fixed that only minor changes are possible.

Behavioral strategies for change must therefore take age into consideration. The older a child or adolescent, the more he or she has been exposed to environmental cues and stimuli that repeatedly activate established behavioral patterns. Doing the same thing repeatedly reinforces a given behavior. This conditioning process is the basis for the effectiveness of practicing skills one seeks to acquire. Hence, parents need to consider *consistent implementation* of their own interventions as well as regular practice by children when devising behavioral change strategies. Put differently, removing cues that have previously stimulated undesirable behaviors significantly helps to diminish their future occurrence.

Another aspect of the influence of cues on behavior is related to group participation. This includes both identifying with the beliefs and values of a group and actually being present in a group. Physical presence in a group typically overrides individual preference even if different from what the group is actually doing at that moment. Considering this strategy, parents find it useful to remove children and adolescents from groups when such group affiliation supplies overwhelming cues that provoke individually undesirable behaviors.

By refining behavior toward becoming less coarse and unadaptive, children may begin to build an inner world where pause, self-reflection, self-regulation, and self-discipline take root. Over time, this internalization of values and strategies for adaptive behaviors becomes a significant inner locus of self-control.

4.1 Preparing ahead of Time for "On the Spot" Discipline

Advance preparation is important; it lays a foundation of crystallized intelligence from which to draw, especially when quick thinking is needed. Understanding oneself, one's child, and parenting in general is the base for such preparation.

Calm, slow breathing, and mental, emotional, and behavioral poise foster presence of mind for "on the spot," fluid decision making and implementation. A useful mnemonic is the "RICE" acronym adapted here as a reminder for such preparation. "R" stands for *responsivity* that is sensitively engaged; "I" stands for *icing* hot reactivity and knee-jerk reactions, in other words, allowing ample time for all to cool down; "C" stands for remaining *cool, calm*, and *collected*; and "E" stands for *effective* problem solving suitable to the context and developmental level of the child.

4.2 Behavioral Redirection and Discipline Must Be Age Appropriate

Communication with children is optimized when parents consider the current age and developmental capacities of their child. With these facts clearly in mind, parents can tailor their language and behavior to permit the child reasonable understanding. Using "I statements" in a tactful and sensitive manner is helpful when dealing with children, especially adolescents. Such phrasing first addresses personal feelings and responses to children's behaviors. A clear follow-up statement should next outline a corrective action plan; a good example might be, "Now we need to work together to clean up the dinner dishes and take out the trash."

The efficacy of this strategy especially applies to discipline and reprimands. Children between one and two benefit from mild corrective and protective guidance about safety and basic instruction. An example might be, "Don't touch the hot stove." Firmer redirection is needed with preschoolers ages three, four, and five. At this stage, gentle and clear language works best. Direction phrased as appealing inducements is always more persuasive than blunt commands. *Redundancy and a great deal of repetition are needed to be effective.* This requirement is normal and typical during the preschool years, but may not be as necessary for children of elementary school age. *Inducements for preferred behaviors should always be concrete, clear, succinct, and relatively brief. Preaching in a commanding tone and nagging in a mindless repetitive fashion are ineffective and best avoided.*

Each direction used with preschoolers may be brief but nonetheless repeatedly occur many times in a day or week about similar behavioral matters. Elementary school children require more intense and circumscribed learning sessions, for example, once or twice over the periods of a day or week. These guidelines, however, are only broad approximations. Rational discipline must always remain flexible and sensitive in addition to being beneficent.

4.3 Building Good Behavior

Building good behavior entails reinforcing existing behaviors that are desirable. The process also includes introducing new ways of initiating actions, as well as guiding constructive responses to events. As in most parent-child interactions, tone of voice, facial expression, physical posture, eye contact, and gesture are essential in producing desired outcomes. To encourage good behavior, tone should be clear, confident, and calm, yet it should also be enthusiastic and anticipatory.

This all-encompassing strategy for reinforcing good behaviors has been referred to as "motivational messaging." The positive psychology movement and virtually all self-improvement techniques call attention to this driving force in helping oneself and others. *Motivation* is the energetic desire or willingness to take action toward a goal. The emotional side of motivation is arousal toward or away from something. Its cognitive side entails persistence despite challenges toward these ends. In motivational messaging, parents identify children's needs, connect them to a specific context and its challenges, and then motivate children to take the proposed action. Parents who demonstrate their own motivation in an enthusiastic and positive manner provide an example for children to emulate. This beneficent persuasion helps to stir interest and the desire to achieve a targeted goal. Implicit in this strategy is eliciting a determination to regard change as valuable, since motivational messaging provides plausible reasons and incentives for preferred action.

A fundamental strategy for fostering the perpetuation of desired behaviors is to call attention to them as they occur—contingent positive reinforcement. Timely acknowledgement of what is positive has been a repetitive theme throughout this book. Essential tasks of effective parenting, therefore, are to recognize, identify, and approve behaviors that are deemed good, desirable, and healthy. This process should occur daily. It is most effective when communicated in explicit ways using language and gestures that are energized by positive emotions. False praise, however, is inauthentic, and children can see through such disingenuous exercises.

Efforts to help children improve performance and learn adaptive behaviors are best reinforced by authentic positive encouragement. Helping children to recognize their current personal best is a very effective strategy, as it allows them to measure themselves against a realistic yardstick in order to make further gains.

Using adjectives such as "good," "very good," and "exceptional" to describe a child's work helps to solidify highlighted behaviors. This emphasis on good behaviors must be regular and consistent. Other effective techniques include adding clear and specific details of what was accomplished and, at times, pairing behaviors with desired tangible rewards. The immediacy of such positive reinforcement that quickly follows a child's behavior is more effective than that provided after a delay. Positive reinforcement actively spotlights actions that are conducive to personal growth and development. Supporting behaviors that are socially adaptive promotes mutuality between people and within group situations, such as family and school.

Positive reinforcement is not to be confused with bribery, which is a form of disingenuous, counterfeit encouragement. Its inauthenticity is obvious, and its possible short-term results are short-lived. In fact, parental directives do not need to be rewarded in expectable or formal ways all the time. Intermittent, unexpected surprises add a characteristic freshness to parent-child interactions. In general, this intermittent use of surprise can encourage a family atmosphere of pleasant astonishment and general good will. In addition, the brain systems indexing uncertainty, surprise, and learning are strengthened.

Although occasional surprises are beneficial, the consistent use of a "heads-up" approach regularly optimizes desired outcomes. Informing children of expectations, rules, reasons for rules, desirable behaviors, unacceptable behaviors, and positive and negative consequences sets up a clear contract for success. Having written guidelines for preferred behaviors prominently placed in children's rooms and other frequented areas in the home are effective visual reminders. In addition to explicit verbal directions, parents can utilize the efficacy of implicit cues. *Cues* are subtle signals or target-specific stimuli that produce the probability of an expected reaction. They are powerful communications that prompt consequent behavior, particularly behaviors that previously have been imperfectly learned. Daily reminders and cues before misbehavior or poor choices take place are helpful. A typical example is looking at a child's hands before and after he or she uses the toilet; this simple action cues the need to wash one's hands. A conscious de-emphasis—though not denial—of negative behaviors is essential for good outcomes. The magnanimity and fair-mindedness of the aforementioned strategies cannot be emphasized enough.

One of the best ways to build good behavior is to model it through example and demonstration. This process encompasses facial expression, gesture, physical posture, and tone of voice, as well as actions and behaviors. Such living example may be the primary way that children learn the fundamentals of behavior.

Remembering the vital importance of the developmental perspective empowers one to use customized, developmentally appropriate strategies in attempting to produce desired outcomes. Parents can use combinations of intuitive resourcefulness, subrational logic, and explicit knowledge to adapt their modeling to the temperament and personality style of the child. As proposed throughout this book, conscious abilities coupled with nonconscious, instinctive, and intuitive resourcefulness translate into adaptive behaviors.

The most influential models for infants and children to observe are adults themselves. Adolescents, however, tend to emulate their peers. These living examples act as compasses implicitly and explicitly guiding toward specific behaviors. Adolescents seek social peer approval and look to peers for reinforcement. This fact implies that the positive or negative complexion of teenage groups significantly influences each individual's choice of behaviors. Early adolescence is a time when influence by and modeling from peers especially occurs. Parental monitoring of adolescent peer groups is essential since adolescent behaviors are erratic and at times undesirable.

Whereas children may benefit from discipline applied both individually and in groups, adolescents profit most from correction by adults on a one-to-one basis. Within a group of adolescents, an adult's interactions require finesse and discretion in demeanor, tone, and use of language. There are several reasons for this. Singling out an individual adolescent in a group gives strong positive attention and reinforcement to him or her. If negative behaviors (for example, power plays or control issues) are involved, then these negative behaviors will also be reinforced and perpetuated. Additionally, such focused attention on an oppositional individual may provide an exciting model for other group members, who may try to join in and emulate opposition.

Children and adolescents require instruction to learn new ways of behaving and responding, particularly to negatively provocative situations. Instruction should begin early in life, for infants can sense intent from facial expression, eye contact, gesture, and tone of voice. Toddlers begin to more fully understand the spoken word, and they try to express themselves with their own newly developing language. Instruction progresses from describing desired behaviors in words, to modeling it, and then to rehearsing desired scenarios.

Any finally successful learning starts with simple exposures that progress toward more complexity. In other words, one first clearly describes a desired behavior beforehand and then proceeds to break it into steps. Each component step is explained, demonstrated by the adult, and then enacted by the child. Demonstration entails concrete and practical exhibition of "how to" skills. Incrementally breaking down and practicing behaviors provides opportunities for small accomplishments quickly and early in the learning sequence. Formulating and practicing intermediary subgoals orients children, adds structure, and enhances odds of successful implementation. Such concrete techniques for putting ideas into action is engaging and facilitates learning. Incremental learning is more easily accepted and assimilated than learning that is presented in large, complicated chunks.

The preschool and elementary school years are prime times for introducing an understanding and modeling of socially appropriate behaviors. Good manners help establish proper interpersonal boundaries and an awareness of respecting other people's personal space. Some examples of building good behaviors in childhood include trying to maintain a quiet voice, not interrupting others except in emergencies, asking permission, knocking on closed doors before entering, and saying "thank you" for gifts. Other important examples of good manners and socially appropriate behaviors include refraining from name calling and teasing, covering one's nose when sneezing, holding a door open for others, eating slowly, and not reaching for food across the table.

Building good behavior is an essential part of the parenting skill set. The process can be explicit at times, but should always be an implicit part of all interactions. Explicit reminders and implicit cues prompting desired behaviors are very helpful. Reminders and directions need to also be given before any misbehavior begins.

4.4 Diminishing Misbehavior

Diminishing bad behaviors aims to reduce, redirect, and possibly eliminate behavior that is undesirable and maladaptive. One can incrementally modify the frequency and intensity of misbehavior—its two core dimensions—until they are no longer problematic. Standardized strategies for managing misbehavior should remain flexible, since each event is relatively unique. In addition to frequency and intensity, duration of misbehavior, its threshold—the level of frustration or disappointment that typically triggers a reaction, and its context need consideration.

Corrective disciplinary strategies are not to be misconstrued as "punishments." Aversive stimuli such as harsh language, severe scolding, and corporal punishment are not useful. They can often be damaging and are not recommended.

Misbehavior is typically disruptive, troublesome, and uncooperative. It is oppositional and thwarts teamwork, goal achievement, and practice of health-promoting behaviors. As had been discussed in chapter 3 in the section on temper tantrums in toddlers, viewing disruptive behavioral events as "happenings" that are determined by both context and audience is partly though not entirely useful. While the misbehaviors of younger children are typically inadvertent and nonmalicious, those of older children and adolescents include more willfulness and elements of greater intentionality. In any event, parental responses are best when some degree of emotional distancing from the event is maintained. Reactive and unconsidered emotional overinvolvement adds to and may reinforce children's own negativity.

Negative behavior may be viewed on a continuum from low to high intensity and frequency. *Low-level undesirable behaviors* may be demanding, annoying, irritating, or inappropriately attention seeking. In colloquial terms, their persistence is "aggravating," "pesky," and a "nuisance." Some children are peevish or hard to please and fretful by temperament; other children become irritable when tired or hungry. Other examples of such low-intensity misbehaviors include excessive speaking or singing, interrupting, nagging, whining, speaking too loudly, excessively noisy behaviors, and so forth. *Medium-intensity behaviors* may be ill-tempered, cantankerous, overly demanding, oppositional, or defiant. They may include talking back, arguments, petulant hyperirritability, and temper tantrums. *High-intensity misbehaviors* are typically destructive to self, others, or property. They pose risks to health and may merge into violations of moral or civil laws. Physical fighting, punching holes in walls, damaging other's electronic media devices, running away, setting fires, and significant stealing of valuable items are some examples. These high-intensity behaviors substantially interfere with biopsychosocial functioning.

Disciplinary interventions need to match the level of the misbehavior, whether it is low, medium, or high intensity. Feedback and consequences for misbehavior must be more concrete and tangible, immediate, frequent, and child-salient. All corrective strategies, however, are most effective when they are delivered consistently and in a neutral tone of voice. Tone of voice should not be acerbic, harsh, or mean. Facial expression, physical posture, and gesture should indicate a lack of hostility. A quiet, firm, and decisive attitude is best. This has been described as a "business-like" approach. Discipline is one of the few parenting situations in which austere and frugal expression is recommended. Extreme emotional expressivity tends to have detrimental short- and long-term effects. Intense emotional tones, especially of hostility, have negative effects that are not useful in disciplinary interventions.

Troublesome behaviors are typically habits that have been learned over time and are durable. While this is true, misbehaviors are amenable to both unlearning and change toward preferred, adaptive behaviors. An effective parenting perspective is providing a framework for children to incrementally become aware of the consequences of behavior and hence to learn to recognize their ability to make choices that produce positive outcomes. Parents can do this by consistently providing concrete preferences, setting consistently enforced limits, offering reasonable choices, and minimizing power struggles. Clarifying behavioral expectations, verbal and written agreements demonstrating "if-then" behaviors and consequences, and framing desirable behaviors and their reinforcements as privileges help consolidate building good behavior and diminishing misbehavior.

Low-intensity misbehaviors often seek attention in inappropriate ways. Ignoring is one of the best behavioral interventions to diminish such behaviors. A parent may withdraw attention and not respond in any way other than by discrete, nonintrusive observation. This subtle intervention—"take no notice"—can be quite effective in the right circumstances. Often, ignoring a negative behavior is followed by a temporary increase in that undesired behavior. This paradoxical effect is termed the "extinction burst." Although such temporary exacerbation of negative behavior may be distressing, it is very important to continue to ignore. Attention may reinforce the exaggerated behavior with the unintended consequence of strengthening and perpetuating it.

Initial verbal warnings should address escalating misbehaviors. Clear and succinct communication should redirect the child toward more desirable behaviors. These "soft reprimands" interfere with the escalation of developing bad behavior. Along with a calm and firm tone, a positive orientation helps to mobilize cooperation. Such warnings may take the form of statements such as, "Let's start behaving like this, not that."

Use of consequences may be effective for frequent or *medium-intensity behaviors*, for they help children understand the demarcation between acceptable and nonacceptable behaviors. Prearranged statements should indicate which behaviors are not appropriate and, if enacted, will merit end results that the child does not desire. This level of discipline requires discussions of acceptable behavior well in advance of the need to invoke such measures. Such discussions about behaviors are most effective when relatively frequent and attentive to age-appropriate revisions and updates.

Consequences for negative behaviors ordinarily denote the removal of desired privileges, objects, or activities. Although parents' choice of such consequences can involve just about anything, they should not remove activities of daily living (for example, food, eating, or hygiene) or significant contact with important people (for example, not being able to visit a parent or grandparent). In other words, consequences are reasonable and fair when they involve the removal of discretionary pleasures.

High-intensity misbehaviors that are frequent, intense, or pose a real threat to the health of a child, others, or property require interventions that are more reasonably forceful and restrictive. If a child becomes unduly disruptive and cannot settle down after a reasonable period of time, for example, then "time-out" in a quiet, less stimulating and distracting area is appropriate. Effective time-outs place a child in a less stimulating location—a place with less noise, media availability, and interaction with others. Time-outs provide opportunities for the child's behavior and mood to settle down. Harsh isolation in locations such as closets, basements, or garages is too extreme. The area should also allow periodic observation and monitoring of one's child. For toddlers and preschool children, the length of time can range from two to five minutes. Older children may need ten to fifteen minutes. The American Academy of Pediatrics states that a good rule of thumb is one minute of time-out for each year of the child's age. This guideline applies until adolescence, when other measures may be more suitable.

Particularly intense or high-frequency misbehaviors may require professional evaluation. Categories of such behaviors include, but are not restricted to, the following: placing self or others at risk of serious harm, bizarre behaviors that appear extraordinarily atypical, and major violations of moral and civil law. Specific examples might be property damage, explosive aggressivity, illicit drug abuse, and illegal gang affiliation.

5. GUIDELINES FOR COMPASSIONATE CORRECTION: THE BEST DISCIPLINE

This book provides intelligent parents and professionals with a compendium of child development facts, psychological perspectives, and tangible strategies for successful parenting. Though not comprehensive and exhaustive, this text highlights a number of central matters relevant to caregiving and the well-being of children.

Compassionate correction is one part of a range of strategies for raising healthy, well-developed children with good character and suitable self-regulatory skills. Compassionate correction is the best discipline, for it incorporates intelligence, empathy, informed decision making, and contextual fairness in childcare and efforts toward the refinement of behavior. Tables 5.2, 5.3, 5.4, and 5.5 summarize many of the principles of effective caregiving that have been discussed throughout this text.

Table 5.2. Guidelines for Compassionate Correction/Discipline 1

Attitude of nurturance

Family cohesion: no or minimal splitting between mother and father

Optimistic and creative attitudes fostering motivation

Modeling positive attitudes and behaviors

Modeling concrete examples of helpfulness

Always encouraging effort

Being firm but flexible

Modeling respect and listening

Developing a family climate of listening

Using "save face" strategies

Avoiding any implications of dehumanization in attitude, language and behavior

Table 5.3.   Guidelines for Compassionate Correction/Discipline 2

Developing family routines and clear schedules

Establishing rules that are clear and straightforward

Clearly teaching behaviors by saying, "In our home, we do . . . ; in our home, we do not . . ."

Being consistent and predictable

Giving ample warning, a "heads up," before significant transitions

Table 5.4.   Guidelines for Compassionate Correction/Discipline 3

Indicating that significant misbehavior has consequences

First approach: "This is a learning moment, let's do it over a better way"

Pointing out unacceptable behavior

Offering several possible alternatives

Providing redundancy in the preschool years, less thereafter

Table 5.5.   Guidelines for Compassionate Correction/Discipline 4

Second approach: Natural consequences are logical learning moments

Consequences should be delivered immediately with merciful resolve

Consequences should be appropriate, brief, and emphasize the positive

Consequences and reprimands must be suited to the child's age and developmental level

Reprimands should be swift, brief, and limited in intensity

Avoiding harsh physical punishment

Targeting behaviors, never the child's character

Following through, and being consistent

Moving on positively and enthusiastically

Forgiving, learning, remembering, and improving

6. KEY POINTS

6.1 Parental Performance: Skill and Style

Caregivers effectively parent through the combined actions of nurturance, discipline, and living example. While these techniques emerge and evolve in the day-to-day transactions of family life, a thoughtful understanding of the principles of child development can refine them.

Skills are abilities to do something well and perform effectively in a relatively sustained way over time. Skill is the more technical aspect of enduring performance; it can be learned and measured. Understanding a child's level of development allows a caregiver to more effectively parent, exercising both parental and developmentally informed skill sets.

Styles include form, appearance, shape, mode, method, and the implementation of how something is carried out and expressed. Styles are personalized applications of skills. Parenting styles are, in part, based on parents' beliefs about why a child may behave or misbehave. Typically, four broad categories of parenting styles are recognized: (1) authoritative, (2) permissive, (3) authoritarian, and (4) neglectful.

Authoritative Style: The authoritative parenting style is most effective in producing good outcomes. Its two components are (1) high responsiveness and (2) high demandingness. High responsiveness includes warmth, acceptance, and involvement. Firm behavioral control, close supervision, clear expectations, and consistent directives characterize its high demandingness component or preference for age-appropriate maturity.

Permissive Style: The permissive parenting style includes high responsiveness and low expectations. Permissive parenting is typically variable and unpredictable. It lacks clear boundaries and consistent directives.

Authoritarian Style: The authoritarian parenting style includes low responsiveness and high expectations. It maintains a sense of purpose and beneficent direction, although its style tends to be harsh. Anxiety, whether explicit or implicit, elicits rigidity in interactions and underlies a subtle sense of ambivalence rather than trust.

Neglectful Style: The neglectful parenting style includes both low responsiveness and low expectations. It is ineffective and to be avoided.

6.1.1 Intelligent Discipline

Understanding the developmental philosophy of parenting, the psychology of children and adults, and an overview of parenting styles and practices provides the knowledge behind parenting skills. These components add up to intelligent discipline—teaching, guiding, and helping children learn self-containment, self-discipline, and cooperative dialogue. Living example, corrective redirection, and shared dialogue are effective strategies.

6.1.2 Compassionate Discipline

Compassionate discipline is intelligent discipline with an emphasis on transactional sensitivity. *Transactional sensitivity* is the conscious and nonconscious receptivity toward grasping and being influenced by the emotional, cognitional, and motivational state of mind of a child. It is both active and receptive. This resonance of receptivity, of being influenced, and in turn, of influencing through a synchronous responsiveness is its main element. This mutuality fostered by transactional sensitivity includes giving, receiving, and relationship adaptation. It encompasses both the emotional and cognitive dimensions of empathy and understanding, though action oriented in its disciplinary strategies.

Building Good Behavior: Building good behavior includes two main activities: (1) reinforcing existing, desirable behaviors by using timely, effective feedback and (2) introducing new ways of improving attitudes, initiating actions, and promoting constructive responses to events.

Diminishing Misbehavior: Diminishing bad behaviors aims to reduce, redirect, and possibly eliminate behavior that is undesirable and maladaptive. Strategies to alter troublesome behaviors take into account frequency, intensity, duration, threshold, and context with regard to the undesirable event. Notifying children of expectations, rules, desirable behaviors, undesirable behaviors, and potential consequences sets up a clear contract for success. Both long-term consistency in the aforementioned and providing an enduring learning environment with regard to acquiring and remembering strategies for making choices and appreciating consequences support success. Cues and reminders from parents before misbehavior develops, or when poor choices seem imminent, are helpful to children on a day-to-day basis. These signals—at times, concrete, tangible, immediate, frequent, meaningfully salient, and prominent—are instrumental in consistently orienting children toward positive choices. An emphasis on reinforcing positive behaviors helps to diminish negative behaviors.

REFERENCES

American Academy of Child and Adolescent Psychiatry website:www.aacap.org.
American Academy of Pediatrics website:www.healthychildren.org.
American Academy of Pediatrics (2009). *Caring for your baby and young child* (5th ed.). S. P. Shelov (Ed.). New York: Bantam.

Baldwin Dancy, R. (2000). *You are your child's first teacher*. Berkeley, CA: Celestial Arts.

Baumrind, D. (1967). Child care practices anteceding three patterns of preschool behavior. *Genetic Psychology Monographs, 75*(1), 43–88.

———. (1971). Current patterns of parental authority. *Developmental Psychology, 4*(1, pt. 2), 1–103.

———. (1978). Parental disciplinary patterns and social competence in children. *Youth and Society, 9*, 238–276.

———. (1991). Parenting styles and adolescent development. In R. Lerner, A. C. Peterson, & J. Brooks Gunn (Eds.), *The encyclopedia of adolescent development*, pp. 746–758. New York: Garland.

Chess, S., & Thomas, A. (1995). *Temperament in clinical practice*. New York: Guilford Press.

Cline, F., & Fay, J. (2006). *Parenting with love and logic*. New York: NavPress Publishing.

Goncy, E. A., & van Dulmen, M. H. M. (2010). Fathers do make a difference: Paternal involvement and adolescent alcohol use. *Fathering: A Journal of Theory, Research, and Practice about Men as Fathers, 8*(1), 93–108.

Green, R. (2010). *The explosive child*. New York: Harper.

Grusec, J. E. (1988). *Social development: History, theory, and research*. New York: Springer-Verlag.

———. (2006). The development of moral behavior and conscience from a socialization perspective. In M. Killen & J. Smetana (Eds.), *Handbook of moral development*, pp. 243–265. Philadelphia: Erlbaum.

Habib, C., Santoro, J., Kremer, P., Toumbourou, J., Leslie, E., & Williams, J. (2010). The importance of family management, closeness with father and family structure in early adolescent alcohol use. *Addiction, 105*(10), 1750–1758.

Isaacs, S. (1968). *Children and Parents*. London: Routledge & Kegan Paul.

Kazdin, A. (2009). *The Kazdin method for parenting the defiant child*. Boston: Mariner Books.

Lamb, M. E. (Ed.). (2010). *The role of the father in child development* (5th ed.). Hoboken, NJ: John Wiley & Sons.

Mayes, L. C., & Cohen, D. J. (2002). *The Yale Child Study Center guide to understanding your child*. Boston: Little Brown & Co.

Meins, E., Fernyhough, C., Wainright, R., Gupta, M. D., Fradley, E., & Tuckey, M. (2003). Maternal mind-mindedness and attachment security as predictors of theory of mind understanding. *Child Development, 73*, 1715–1726.

Ninivaggi, F. J. (2010). *Envy theory: Perspectives on the psychology of envy*. Lanham, MD: Rowman & Littlefield.

Patterson, B., & Bradley, P. (2000). *Beyond the rainbow bridge*. Amesbury, MA: Michaelmas Press.

Payne, K. J., & Ross, L. M. (2010). *Simplicity parenting*. New York: Ballantine Books.

Pelcovitz, R., & Pelcovitz, D. (2005). *Balanced parenting*. New York: Shaar Press.

Peterson, C., & Seligman, M. E. P. (2004). Character strengths and virtues. Oxford: Oxford University Press.

Peterson, C. C., & Slaughter, V. P. (2003). Opening windows into the mind: Mother's preferences for mental state explanations and children's theory of mind. *Cognitive Development, 18*, 399–429.

Ross, R. (2010). *Adventures in parenting*. Spring Valley, NY: Rudolf Steiner Press.

Seligman, M. E. P. (1975, reprinted 1992). *Helplessness: On depression, development, and death*. San Francisco: W. H. Freeman.

———. (1991). *Learned Optimism: how to change your mind and your life*. New York: Knopf. (Paperback reprint edition, Penguin Books, 1998; reissue edition, Free Press, 1998).

———. (1993). *What you can change and what you can't: The complete guide to successful self-improvement*. New York: Knopf. (Paperback reprint edition, Ballantine Books, 1995).

———. (1996). *The optimistic child: Proven program to safeguard children from depression and build lifelong resilience*. New York: Houghton Mifflin.

———. (2002). *Authentic happiness: Using the new positive psychology to realize your potential for lasting fulfillment*. New York: Free Press.

———. (2004). Can happiness be taught? *Daedalus, 133*(2), 80–87.

————. (2011). *Flourish: A visionary new understanding of happiness and well-being*. New York: Free Press.

Shure, M. B., Digeronimo, T. F., & Aher, J. (2000). *Raising a thinking child workbook: Teaching young children how to resolve everyday conflicts and get along with others*. New York: Research Press.

Taylor, S. E. (2002). *The tending instinct: How nurturing is essential to who we are and how we live*. New York: Holt.

Wood, J. J. (2006). Parental intrusiveness and children's anxiety in a clinical sample. *Child Psychiatry and Human Development, 37*, 73–87.

Chapter Six

More Worth Noting on Psychology and Parenting

The previous chapters have presented an orientation to parenting, the particulars of child development, and general child and adult psychology. Specific guidelines made the philosophy of parenting concrete. The chapters outlined observable developmental tasks and achievements. Measurable adult personality configurations were also reviewed, as were specific features of parenting styles and interventions.

This chapter, by contrast, outlines more theoretical, biomental perspectives. Abstract dimensions of parenting and general psychological development are discussed. These nontrivial core considerations include family, gender, envy, greed, jealousy, competitiveness, self-reflection, aesthetics, resilience, and protective factors.

This book considers these perspectives significant, if not central, to general human psychology, including the act of parenting. *Although the text elaborates on envy, greed, jealousy, and competitiveness, it places greater emphasis on love and empathy in its model of human development.* Examining the multifaceted aspects of both positive and more troublesome emotions helps develop a richer understanding of human development and the skills of parenting.

Indeed, it is the *interplay of positive and negative attitudes* that motivates and propels biomental development. As a particular example, *the healthy maturation of negative envy* into positive admiration, gratitude, empathy, helpfulness, and generosity reflects the essence of wholesome human development. As will be discussed, this process is a means of enabling forgiveness of self and others.

387

1. THE FAMILY

1.1 Defining "Family"

A *family* is a unit of several people with a shared history and future. While such a definition may appear simple, the family remains a complex and vital system that provides children with a culture of safety and quality.

More than merely collections of individuals, families are organizational structures. Familial operations are optimized when interactions are team oriented and aim for relative coherence. Parents as team leaders establish values, goals, and beliefs, and ways to achieve these. Reasonable and flexible familial directions are maintained and refreshed by almost uninterrupted reflection and refinement, often implicit. Refining family strategies is essential since change is ineluctable. Both individual and family needs undergo maturation and adaptive requirements. When family atmosphere is mission driven, an air of enthusiasm optimizes win-win objectives making a forward trajectory continuing and productive.

Parents provide nurturance, discipline, and living example to their children. In addition, parental roles include protecting children from aggression, traumatic force, hostile attack, and violence both inside the family and from influences outside. Family functioning maintains the biomental well-being of its members, and protects them from serious harm. The family is the first group of which the child becomes a member.

The term *family* can no longer be understood as it had been traditionally perceived. Until the last few decades, this term referred to the basic cultural group of a woman (wife and mother) married to a man (husband and father) residing with their biological children in the same home. Sociological landscapes, especially in Western countries, have changed significantly in recent years. Such changes warrant greater flexibility in and expansion of such previously understood sets of meanings.

The term *family* within this text indicates a dedicated group of individuals with mutually shared responsibilities. The overarching aims of this delineated social group include providing continuity of care, fostering secure and mutually beneficial relationships, and demonstrating genuine caregiving. These aims positively correlate with a child's need to be genuinely wanted in an atmosphere of family love and cohesion. *A child's deep need to be and feel wanted, loved, and intimately connected to his or her family cannot be overemphasized.* Relatively uninterrupted care, notably through lasting relationships in infancy and childhood, is essential to a child's healthy development and well-being. Healthy families—whether traditional or nontraditional—promote growth and differentiation of all of their members, especially though continuity of care.

Although this book has focused on mother, father, and child in the course of child development and parenting, the roles of siblings are also important. The number, gender, order, and biological relation of siblings affect all family members. Such relationships are, however, complex and beyond the scope of this discussion. An interesting consideration, however, that illustrates the roles that temperament and attachment play in families may be seen in the behavior of twins both identical and nonidentical. Each child, particularly those with identical genetic makeup, can be distinguished by his or her temperamental and attachment styles. This demonstrates how environmental experience and the role of random events along the line of development may influence different outcomes.

Family systems are hierarchies within which asymmetrical relationships are typical. The uneven power dynamic between a parent and a child is one example of such asymmetry. Another interaction occurs as a *mass effect*, in which overall familial configurations are affected by one member's behavior. In most families, when one member does not conform to established rules, other members attempt to restore the family's predesignated homeostasis. *Error activation* is such automatic recognition. The family as a whole is influenced by a family member's behavioral deviations. In this system, the members of the "mass," or family, detect focal "error" and attempt to enact resultant change on the family as a whole. This attempt can retain the previous pattern if errors are "soft" or transient; it may also introduce a new functional operating configuration if errors are "hard" or persistent. For example, if a mother becomes significantly depressed, there might be a detrimental mass effect on the functioning of the whole family if she is unable to cook or otherwise care for her children. Error-activation may then take place, establishing a new system in which the father temporary compensates by taking on greater childcare responsibilities.

The family, as a complex adaptive system, experiences the inputs and outputs of each member. The family continuously processes these communicational signals and correspondingly equilibrates each member and the system as a whole. The family also participates both directly and indirectly in a wide net of larger systems that include nonbiological housemates, nonresident parents and children, and extended family members. The nested nature of the unit within a larger unit is manifested as the parental dyad within the family and the family within the extended society and culture.

Family alliances often act as teams to afford members access to what they need to survive. Survival depends, in part, on an ability to understand others and establish and participate in relationships. The periods of infancy and childhood are particular times of helplessness, wherein family systems activate and foster necessary social intelligence management strategies.

1.2 Families as Partnerships of Parents

Families form relatively unified teams of interdependent partnerships. These units may come about through marriage and biological reproduction in addition to remarriage, adoption, and other alliances that may or may not be socially and legally supported. Common law marriage is an example of a partnership agreement that is recognized socially but not legally. Traditionally defined nuclear families are composed of a mother, a father, and their children. The extended family, as such, is made up of kinship relatives, such as grandparents, uncles, aunts, and cousins.

In contemporary times, families may also be composed of a single parent, two parents of the same sex, transient members, or various other nontraditional arrangements. For example, fathers may be biological fathers, stepfathers, resident or nonresident biological fathers, adoptive fathers, gay fathers, bisexual fathers, or transgendered fathers. These varied systems of caregivers may each be understood to be a *family* when the term is generally defined as "adults raising children."

Each member of a family, however made up, has designated roles. Specific roles include their own sets of rights, obligations, duties, and expected behavior patterns. The responsibilities of each family member require accountability for designated performance.

In terms of the parental couple, each spouse typically chooses the other based on an implicit recognition of the other's complementary nature. Each member of the relationship may perform best at a delimited number of things, though not at others. Partners choose one another, to some extent, with only vague recognition of this partly conscious and partly nonconscious compatibility. Relationships involve the allocation of expected roles with their own authority, control, and decision-making characteristics.

The division of labor in a family and between couples is typically unequal. Each parent has a unique temperament, personality, and set of preferences, strengths, and limitations. These variations influence the way that a family manages itself. As long as each parent acts in the best interests of the family and also supports the other parent, a given family system has a good chance of running smoothly.

Each parent's unique perspective on understanding and adapting to real-world situations can positively impact children's intellectual and social development. Different parental perspectives should be complementary rather than oppositional; in this sense, the two styles should foster conciliation rather than antagonism. Thoughtful parenting creates an atmosphere of "win-win" rather than "win-lose" scenarios between family members.

In traditional arrangements, women typically shop for and prepare meals and take major responsibility for caring for children. Men, by contrast, take care of mechanical needs, mow the lawn, and choose automobiles. Although this conventional delegation may appear stereotypical, many families feel comfortable accepting such role assignments. In such families, this tacit division of labor is understood as the way a typical family culture is and should be.

When two people decide to start a family, many choices have to be made. Career choices encompass the career of motherhood, fatherhood, careers in addition to these that are outside the home, and other permutations. Today, families are often described as either "dual income" or "single parent." The economic downturn of the early part of the twenty-first century has taken part in altering some aspects of traditional family systems. For example, since both women and men are actively engaged in the workforce, some fathers have become "stay-at-home dads" (SAHDs). Motivations behind this change include some parents being reluctant to place children in daycare and wives having the opportunity to make more money than their husbands. A new phenomenon colloquially called the "new neither father" has emerged. This term refers to men who neither stay at home nor are primary breadwinners—that is, men who are employed and also spend time at home. An essential characteristic of the "new neither fathers" described by this term is that such men worry about this familial arrangement that they perceive to be awkward. These men often miss their traditionally defined work identity, though it is also important to point out that other men may be comfortable with this arrangement. Overall, modern dads can no longer be judged by "old-time" or traditional expectations. For instance, "maternal gatekeeping," which denotes a mother choosing and directing a father's interactions with children, is becoming more flexible and less rigidly stereotyped. Mothers are encouraging more spontaneous paternal involvement, for example.

As each partner grows, develops, and changes, he or she may begin to question his or her "jobs" in the family situation. Such individuals may feel dismay or discomfort. At these times the couple needs to examine, discuss, and potentially renegotiate each person's roles. Marriage counseling may provide a forum for these matters, for it offers partners an opportunity to restructure roles in more mutually acceptable terms. Renegotiation of roles, however, typically occurs numerous times and is often processed unconsciously over the lifetime of a relationship.

1.3 Roles of Fathers and Mothers in the Family

Roles of fathers, mothers, and children have established traditions in different human societies. Role responsibilities emerge from mixtures of biological, psychological, and cultural factors. The expectations and actions of each parent come from both biological and learned resources. Any statements about roles need to be understood and interpreted in the specific historical and geographical contexts in which they occur. Needless to say, contexts are infinitely varied and changeable.

The role of fathers, for example, in preindustrial times emphasized the father as a moral model at the head of household in contrast to the mother, who was seen as its heart. After the Industrial Revolution (circa the early 1800s), a father was seen as the parent who provided primary economic support, that is, he was the "breadwinner." Since the 1980s, the role of fathers has expanded to include emotional and social involvement.

When the parental couple is composed of a mother and father, gendered parenting may operate. The wide scope and meaning of *gender* will later be discussed. Suffice it to say here that gendered parenting does exist, and resulting differences need to be recognized, valued, and optimized. Mothers and fathers typically prefer and choose different activities within the family, and these activities may or may not fall along typically designated gender lines. In broad terms, while *both parents have the capacity to nurture successfully*, fathers as men do not "mother," and mothers as women do not "father." Some—though not all—differences are based in biology; other differences presume an elusive and perhaps qualitative distinctness that characterizes "mother" as such, and "father" as such, especially in the infant's eyes. For example, only mothers breastfeed, though fathers may also feed infants using bottles. In each circumstance, gender partly influences style and delivery. Understanding gendered behavioral differences minimizes artificially forced or blurred roles and expectations, although natural overlapping of roles occurs. The section on gender in this chapter further clarifies nuances of these distinctions.

Nuanced variation exists among different families and within the same family over time. A major characteristic of contemporary families is *contingency*—dynamic change and adaptive transitions that rapidly occur over short periods of time. Significant psychological reorientations are necessary to negotiate such life changes, particularly in the era of electronic media and almost instantaneous communication. In this environment, rapidly changing communication influences informational needs—both satisfying old ones and introducing new ones. Given the quick introduction of so much new data, family roles and planning must promote efficiency while also attempting to hold onto other important values.

1.4 Family Atmosphere

The general family climate is also important. It is an atmosphere created and sustained by parents that largely reflects how partners interact with one another on a spectrum of agreeableness and cooperativeness. For example, how a mother behaves toward her husband significantly affects the family environment.

Relatedly, the integrity and emotional harmony between the parental couple set the family emotional tone of affection versus hostility. Splitting of the parental couple's integrity undermines each parent and the family as a cohesive and effective whole. Parents need to protect against such possible division. For example, when mothers value their spouses' abilities to effectively parent, men tend to feel especially confident, secure, and supported in their role as caregiving fathers to children. Within nontraditional families, possible parental couples can also be vital in maintaining overall family integrity.

Adequate and frequent discussions about household roles and chores are necessary. A shared approach is balanced by the unilateral skills and styles of each parent. Each parent should make clear and explicit statements about his or her obligations. In addition, it is wise for each parent to be explicit about suggestions and preferences for his or her partner's role. Parents also need to create a blueprint for discipline in which neither parent is the sole "disciplinarian" or "fun one." Roles should remain flexible and receptive to change. Discussions about expectations need constant vigilance and periodic renegotiation.

Familiarity with the basic principles of child development helps parents to organize their family around a roadmap of what a child is capable of and interested in at particular ages. Each adult parent and the family as a whole simultaneously undergo their own developmental trajectories. Seeing family life as dynamic helps to make its naturally occurring changes and transitions more expectable and manageable. Remembering that change and transitions are the norm, not the exception, is valuable.

The parental relationship is of essential importance in influencing, if not determining, the harmony versus dysfunction of the entire family system. A positive parental relationship occurs with mutual support between mother and father. Studies repeatedly find that such relationships, in turn, predict the level of involvement of the father in the family and with children. Additionally, socioeconomic circumstances such as parental employment status help to determine a father's role and level of involvement in the family.

When family life remains stable, turbulence and anxiety are low. No matter how planned one's day is, activities of daily living meet inevitable obstacles and unforeseen impediments. Dynamically changing states of mind, feelings, and levels of physical health may stir turmoil within an established routine. The potential impact of such disruptions needs to be understood before they even occur.

Within families, the intense expression of emotion needs to be monitored. Emotional expressivity should be modulated so that extreme highs and lows are not regularly demonstrated. The markedly malignant effect of negative emotional expressivity cannot be overemphasized. Longitudinal studies in psychiatry have demonstrated that consistently strong displays of anger and hostility by parents have been found to be traumatic and pathogenic to both children and families. Anxiety in all family members is increased, for example.

Typically, parents' perception of child misbehavior triggers intense emotional expression in these adults. After reasonably assessing and managing safety issues, attention to such emotions is essential. Resultant behaviors may unfortunately include retaliation, retribution, revenge, and avenging misdeeds by inflicting punishment. If left unchecked, hostile emotional states may take on gigantic proportions. Level-headedness and a calm demeanor are essential at these times. Rational evaluation and a cool assessment of reasonable consequences can then be determined. A healthy emotional model then becomes a template for children to internalize and apply in family and social situations.

1.5 Perception of Strangeness

The perception of strangeness is understood to be a typical developmental milestone that is first seen in the infant at seven months. This normative event reflects both the cognitive and emotional ability to discriminate unfamiliar from familiar persons. Hence, family members are sensed as familiar and safe, while others are sensed as unfamiliar and potentially dangerous. This development sets the stage for parental influence in introducing realistic balance in these interpretations through ongoing parental attitudes and ministrations.

An important consideration is the inculcation of values and potential tension between the family as a unit and society at large. The interface between family and society is a pivotal, bidirectional transaction node between individual and culture. Children become enculturated within families. They explicitly and implicitly learn the values and mores of their families, namely a family social identity. In a manner of speaking, children are clothed in the fabric of upbringing and social context.

Xenophobia is an unfortunately common, irrational, and deep-rooted fear of or antipathy toward those perceived as strangers or foreigners. The term comes from the Greek (*xenos*), meaning "stranger" or "foreigner" and from (*phobos*), meaning, "fear." Embedded in the word "stranger" is the word "anger," which is an intimately related emotional response. Fear evokes feelings of vulnerability, being controlled, and being at the mercy of unknown and uncontrollable forces. Perception of a "stranger" elicits anxiety about a potential risk of personal harm, thus activating the "fight-or-flight" response. The fight behavior emphasizes anger (thus relating perception of a "stranger" to the feeling of anger), whereas the act of flight emphasizes fear. Such anger and fear typically dehumanize faceless strangers into perceived enemies and arouse irrational and often destructive hostilities.

The perception of strangeness has roots in concepts from evolutionary psychology. Even recent research has demonstrated that people generally can distinguish between the odors of two strangers. Historically, while humans originally banded in hordes and groups, their later introduction of a nongroup *self-concept*, an awareness of self-identity, was probably coincident with the development of language—to ability to say "I." Humans began to sense themselves as differentiated members, as "individuals" rather than merely a collective. With this more isolated state of mind, their greatest personal threat was of being prey to "monstrous" animals, which ingrained great fear and terror into an organized threat-detection mental module. Trial, error, intention, and serendipity were strategies used to increase chances of survival. This led to individuals increasingly rebanding into groups for protection.

We may speculate that ancient predators gave little to no perceived warning. Attack and fear emerged in an atmosphere of faceless silence. This may be related to such events being "new" to ordinary experience, at least until time passed and experience provided some association between attack and its antecedents. Thus, human primates had to develop both instantaneous warning reactions such as anxiety as well as more developed means. The aim was to ensure increased chances for survival. The development of language may have afforded a survival vehicle for rapprochement with one another and communicating warning of predators.

After millennia, this cultural strategy of fearing dangerous others and enlisting defense by means of group cohesion became internalized in group structures and in individuals' minds. While speculation about the prehistoric emergence of human language abounds, perhaps at the dawn of language development about 200,000 years ago, the adaptive fear of the "life-threatening unknown" became a typical xenophobic reaction of individuals. This may have generalized and become displaced and linked to other humans perceived as unfamiliar and strange. An implicit dehumanization of others into monstrous threats—amorphous and faceless unknowns—became an underpinning of survival strategies that persist to modern times.

Xenophobic feelings are rooted in implicit perceptions of the stranger as a threat: "monster," "beast," "dragon," "bogyman," and predator. These implicit perceptions arise in a milieu of menacing silence, for actual features of the stranger typically remain unknown. Since action is typically an automatic

reaction to crisis, these fearful misrepresentations had practical consequences, which were defensive, aggressive, and destructive in nature. Such
aggressive defense and offense often leads to the setting up of a "straw man"
with motivations aimed toward slaying this sham misrepresentation of a
perceived opponent.

These ideas are expounded in evolutionary psychology as "kin versus
non-kin awareness" found across cultures and aimed toward survival. Setting
up distinctions, fearful emotions, and defenses to contain these exaggerated
fears are part of the universal tendency for social categorization, which entails categorizing oneself and others into contrasting groups. Xenophobic
attitudes draw from implicit assumptions that remain outside conscious
awareness yet heavily bias perception, as well as form explicit prejudices.
When such attitudes are both intolerant and extremist, they become irrational
and destructive largely because intolerable levels of fear and feeling perse-
cuted dominate one's perspective.

1.6 Xenophobia and Families

During the course of development, children may be exposed to the xenophobic beliefs of their family members. Fear, anger, and hostility implicit in
xenophobic attitudes may develop into paranoid ideation, which serves as a
defensive way to interpret and manage what is perceived to be unknown and
possibly threatening. In paranoid thinking, one's sensory perceptions are
correct, but one's cognitive and emotional interpretation and judgment of
these perceptions are erroneous. The "enemy" in xenophobic constructs is
clothed in a uniform not of the enemy's design, but styled by xenophobic
perceptions. Significantly rigid thinking correlates with this serious distor-
tion of reality, which may develop early in life.

While rooted in evolutionary-based kin selection dispositions, xenophobia—an extreme, unmodulated bias—can manifest itself in many uncon-
structive ways. This is especially true because xenophobia is deeply rooted in
primitive, developmentally typical, early paranoid-like fears that ordinarily
and normally resolve throughout childhood. Feeling estranged from the larger group is a feeling of alienation that compels one to adhere closely to
persons nearest to oneself and avoid those deemed distant or strange. In
individual development, attachment to those nearest oneself, for example,
mother, father, siblings, and other family members strengthens throughout
early childhood and persists as a model for establishing relations with others
outside the family group. The paranoia and fear behind xenophobia by
contrast have never been sufficiently mitigated, resolved, or superseded.
Thus the ruthless and irrational elements of these fears (alienation from the
larger group) remain, extend at times to include humanity at large, and act as
an implicit platform orienting experience toward misperception and false

belief. This irrational fear utilizes the innate mental ability to compare and contrast in an unmodulated, untempered manner. Put simply, the one and perhaps a few select others feel and so remain pitted against the many.

Xenophobic feelings and thoughts typically involve the relations and perceptions of an "in-group" towards an "out-group." For example, a person might compare the "in" family to the outer society at large. Xenophobics may fear loss of their identities, which includes a sense of power, control, and superiority. Implicit in this wish to protect identity is a striving to preserve a perceived self-purity and defend against contamination. They may perceive activities of the "other" to be suspicious or hostile and believe the other has a desire to eliminate their own group's existence.

Whereas xenophobia has dimensional characteristics (high-low level, intense-mild quality) as do most psychological traits, attitudes, and their enacted behaviors, the balance of reason, passion, fantasy, moral relevance and constraint, and context influences its consonance with reality and justness or injustice. The material expressions of xenophobia notably accompanied by some form of destructive action, for example, may manifest on a spectrum of behaviors prompted by retaliation, revenge, or retribution. Retaliation is a reflexive striking back with hostile actions to a perceived assault; such "payback" usually reflects an automatic self-defensive event. Revenge or vengeance, however, is extreme and may be the boldest and most malignant material expression of envy and paranoia. Revenge is characterized by intentional action motivated by hatred and resulting from a perceived wrong or injury. Revenge is typically ruthless and almost insatiable in its aim to avenge a perceived injustice. The dynamics of power and control fuel the ferocity behind the brutality associated with revenge. Retribution, by contrast, connotes a more or less planned punishing consequence aimed at correcting an act believed unjust, and typically unjust in fact. Retribution is characterized by more overall containment, proportion, informed moral review, and attempts toward impartiality.

Cultural groups, for example, tribes, states, and nations with armies, as well as ethnic peoples that have experienced real trauma by other groups retain, to varying degrees, memories of these assaults. If such trauma is not resolved, at least to some extent, at its roots, this source maintains an underlying sense of doubt with regard to trusting. It may evolve into pathological doubt—the inability to distinguish between what is possible, probable, and unlikely to occur in interpersonal and group relationships, not historical but in the moment. From a behavioral perspective, this highly ambivalent distrust may reflect itself in overly assertive control, which functions as a self-defense strategy. Conscious and nonconscious ideas become transmitted from generation to generation and propagate skepticism and mistrust of the "out-group," namely, out-group derogation. Often, these biases are so culturally ingrained that they act as organically shared axiomatic beliefs. The traumas that have forged these beliefs remain as ultrasensitive, scathing wounds. These virtually indelible imprints propagate automatic, continuing "memories" of colossal proportion that circumvent self-reflection that in turn reinforces, if not defies, modification by reason. As alluded to throughout this book, especially in this chapter's section on "The Healthy Maturation of Envy," the triad of empathy, compassion, and forgiveness—however sparked into action—is an antidote to be hoped for. This triad is the scaffolding for addressing and reframing presuppositions, and then constructively messaging and reinforcing the bigger triadic truths.

For example, nations having a dual political party system demonstrate subtle features of xenophobia. Each party, suspicious of the other's ideas and activities, aims to downregulate the other's power, dominance, and membership. The fragility of regularly occurring civilized discourse reflects precarious relations. The term "oligarchy," for example, denotes a governing power structure whose members hold superior, elite, and privileged status in sharp contrast to those they govern. A deeper appreciation of xenophobia experienced early on in childhood may give insight to the bitter politics of envy and its acerbic struggles around power plays between governing groups within countries and between nations.

Xenophobia can also take the form of uncritical exaltation of one's own idealized culture to which is ascribed an unreal, stereotyped, and exotic quality. For example, an ethnic group sharing common identity, ancestry, beliefs, and history typically idealizes its status in normative ways by exhibiting ethnic pride. In-group cohesion may increase chances of in-group favoritism or preference for helping those similar to oneself. Across political, financial, and religious domains, cross-cultural research shows that "nepotism"—favoritism granted to relatives regardless of merit—has been and is a common part of experiences in groups. When this pride becomes pronounced and irrational, other ethnic groups are stereotyped as being inferior, not preferred and helped, and so left unsupported.

Additionally, many religious groups attribute a divine origin to their founding, which is idealized in the form of "faith" beliefs, typically arising out of a profound sense of the sacred and awe in relation to and for explaining the complexity of the human condition. While this inclination may be understandably reasonable in faith-based cultures, if it becomes irrational, hostile, or intolerant, xenophobic trends emerge. In addition, xenophobic prejudice may be masked by attitudes of apparently benign disregard. Such seeming neutrality toward a perceived out-group may imply an underlying sense of superiority hidden behind a veneer of smug indifference. Attention to these nuanced emotional attitudes provides insight into human relations and actively promotes prosocial direction. Families that instill fundamental human values and vigilance about xenophobic attitudes employ good parenting.

1.7 Approaches to Modifying Xenophobia

An interesting approach to the aforementioned problems associated with xenophobia can be drawn from the almost six-thousand-year-old Ayurvedic medical tradition of India. In that system, two fundamental principles guide all medical theory and treatment: "like attracts like," and "opposites balance and so cure each other." The "like attracts like" component supports the idea that people both attract and are attracted to one another based on their similarities, whether explicit or implicit. My proposed construct of *projective internalization* addresses the basic framework of processes of knowing. This conceptualization argues that when an object presented in reality is encountered, the object is perceived or recognized based on the identity of both its subjective and objective common reference points; namely, a bilateral grasping takes place.

Put simply, "finding" is, in fact, "re-finding" with a contextually novel coloring. This tendency, however, may be seen to exist in dynamic balance with the companion model of the Ayurvedic principle of "opposites balance and so cure each other." This complementary idea puts emphasis on *the realistic nature of typical human cognition to grasp events, to some extent, as they are, and so exercise reason and proportion rather than exaggeration of seemingly irrevocable differences in processes of understanding.*

From a psychological and interpersonal perspective in the context of xenophobia, these medical principles strongly suggest that perception of difference or strangeness emerges from a naturally assumed commonality. The overriding principle, however, is the *perception* of "opposites" and the resulting modulation of like and opposites.

For "healing" of pathological states of alienation or paranoia, rather than intensifying the alienation, a rapprochement can be brought about. When a mutually beneficent engagement is sought and fostered, differences and similarities are no longer sensed as extremes that provoke fear and avoidance. In contrast, variation is felt as an interesting source of exploration and learning. Parents can indeed apply such wise contributions from the East to modern family life.

The family is the crucible of socialization. It can instill prosocial values and a working awareness of biases and prejudices. Prosocial values counter the politics of exclusion on many levels. A conscious attempt to minimize irrational biases in the upbringing of children is a large part of good parenting. Another important role of the family is to establish a healthy group cohesiveness, which serves as a safe and protective field within which to raise children. Part of establishing a coherent familial society includes instilling the value of group cooperativeness and recognition of the rights of others to coexist.

Viewing nonthreatening strangers as valuable and worthwhile is a value to pursue. Realistic perceptions preclude inculcating implicit biases of inferiority or the envy-based template of superiority versus inferiority. If adequately supported, the typical developmental progression from "black-and-white"—a position of polarized absolutism—thinking toward more nuanced attitudes can lessen unrealistic fear, mistrust, and hateful feelings toward others. Positive parenting demonstrates considered moderation in word and action. Tendencies toward extremist attitudes and behaviors are constrained. Successful parenting monitors and addresses both irrational prejudices and the politics of irrational exclusion.

Teaching peaceful coexistence—respect, pause, understanding, and cooperativeness—helps children within the family to see each person as having intrinsic value. While unconscious envy, conscious jealousy, and rivalry cannot be eliminated, they can become tempered both in the family and in relationships outside the family.

2. GENDER AND PSYCHOLOGICAL-BEHAVIORAL STYLES

Typically, boys and girls show discernible differences in appearance and behavior, as do men and women. Gender denotes features that typically distinguish one sex from the other. This generalization is an approximation that may be typical in various cultures, but is highly variable in both the same culture and across cultures. This section, moreover, must be prefaced with the statement that it attempts to present a generalized orientation while noting that variations constitute the "rule" rather than the exception. Gender as a construct, accordingly, is discussed using descriptions and classifications. This is distinct from the real facts that may be attributable ideographically to people as real, individual persons.

The precise reasons for gender-lateralized human behaviors have been the subject of speculation for decades; no definitive consensus has yet been reached. Numerous hypotheses, theories, and conjectures have been proposed. The construct of *stereotypes* has received a great deal of attention, and its value and limitations are apparent.

Stereotypes are common, generalized, and self-perpetuating sets of beliefs about particular groups of people to which the same characteristics are assigned in absolutist fashion. Many stereotypes are based on implicit assumptions; some of these suppositions may be valid, while others are merely prejudicial. Attitude strength in these situations is very strong. Stereotypes as implicit mental images become labels used to automatically classify individuals as having similar or identical characteristics. In psychology, these irrational biases are termed "ultimate attribution errors." When such pronounced emphasis is placed on the perceived genetic basis of dispositions to the exclusion of significant situational variables and qualifying contexts, fundamental cognitive attribution errors arise. Such stereotypes apply principally to group cultures and may not be consistently found in individuals, whose behavior may result more from preferences and rational choice.

Formulating distinctions about contrasting groups, including gender-lateralized assessments, have both individual and group-based influences. Evolutionary-based innate biases in learning underlie this inclination for mental distinctions and contrasts. Not only identifying but also magnifying small differences both cognitively and emotionally is intrinsic to perception. Arriving at these differentiating characteristics is based on fundamental cognitive mechanisms that encompass sensation, perception, and evaluation. Vision, for example, grasps "objects" principally by identifying their contours, namely the edges, borders, and boundaries that create a sense of "in-betweenness" and hence result in operations that formulate definitions.

A universal inclination eliciting cognitive dualisms, contrasts, exaggerations, and polarizations typically organizes perceptions and thus assigns quick interpretations. On a social level, this predilection for stereotyping is an example of such dualistically structured thinking. Stereotyping and "splitting," as has and will be discussed, also have an emotional foundation in the biomental dynamics of fear, namely sensing the self as a vulnerable, fear-filled opposite to a perceived threatening other.

Stereotyping applies to a number of broad categorizations. Its ultimate aim is to support a sense of self-identity. Individuals use such inclinations to support their personal identities by affiliating with what are perceived to be superior "in-groups" in contrast to "out-groups." While distinctions related to gender appraisals may not be overly explicit, they are nevertheless deeply rooted.

"In-groups" connote power and high rank; "out-groups" connote inferiority and diminished worth. Studies demonstrate that "in-group" bias denotes favoritism toward those people who are members of their own group. There is typically a sense of neutrality toward the "out-group," although this is often tinged with suspiciousness and avoidance. When "in-group" bias is excessive, attitudes toward the "out-group" become negatively prejudicial and fearful. In such cases, negative beliefs and stereotyping are constructed to justify these attitudes and are accompanied by either strict avoidance or tendencies to control, dominate, or eliminate the object of prejudice. Various expressions of sexism and bias toward the value of one sex or gender in contrast to the other has been and continues to be evident in most cultures. As will be discussed later, this template of superiority versus inferiority is part of the infrastructure of the envy dynamic and may lead to personal and interpersonal impairment.

However imprecise and imperfect, stereotypes do play a role in the construction of gender, its variations, and its differences. Rational cultural norms learned within families and societies also contribute to the expression of gender. Children's own gender stereotyping, performed in an absolute and unnuanced manner, is most adamant from about age five to eight. Over time, this normative, developmentally expectable rigidity becomes softened and nuanced by experience and reason.

Sexual dimorphism, or qualitative sex and gender differences, of brain anatomy and development is scientifically factual. Oversimplified polarizations, however, about definitions of masculinity and femininity must remain open to continuing examination. Scientists state that a large number of physical and psychological traits including gender, height, and intelligence are under at least partial genetic control. The present discussion, however, will focus more on the phenomenological or everyday expressions of gender.

People tend to recognize generally defined *masculine* and *feminine* attitudes and behaviors. In reality, individuals exhibit behaviors that are heterogeneous; there are no objective or universally agreed-upon standards for exclusively male or female behavior and attitude. Distinctions indeed are complex. Physical anatomy, however, does play a substantial role in self-identification and perceived gender by others.

While masculine behaviors are associated with men, and feminine behaviors linked with women, it is true that each person also has some of the opposite sex's typical qualities. Each individual has both masculine and feminine characteristics, with one dimension typically taking the lead. Emotional development, expression, and management, for example, are strongly related to one's given biomental temperament, though also have the influence of gender.

Biomental child development concentrates attention on principles of good parenting. These principles presume ideas about mothering and fathering that also take into consideration constructs of gender, masculinity, and femininity. The significance of fathering on child well-being is a current topic of research, parenting education, and social policy. The contemporary idea of fathering encompasses a *father* as a caregiving person who is "merely" a parent with a male gender. While acknowledging real distinctions, emphasis is now on emotional sensitivity and caregiving behaviors rather than gender. Many interesting questions stem from this concept of fathering. For example, can the infant distinguish father from mother? Is, or how is, a father's influence on his child linked to his level of masculinity?

Additionally, some researchers question the extent of a father's unique position in terms of whether it is "replaceable," "indispensable," or "substitutable." The relative lack of clear-cut societal supports for fathers as parents in part has contributed to such questions and ambiguities about the potential role of fathers in the lives of children and families.

Biomental child development offers general ways of thinking about these concerns rather than giving definitive answers. These questions are viewed as open areas needing further exploration, examination, and study. Clear-cut agreement among experts does not yet exist. Certainly, divorce is correlated with father absence or relative absence in contrast to mother who typically remains the custodial parent. Absent parenting—whether material or emotional—by either parent clearly correlates with negative effects on children. It can be said, however, that when any parent is genuinely and enthusiastically motivated to care for children, the results are essentially positive for children, spouses, and families.

2.1 Sex and Gender

In scholarly research, defining *sex* refers to assessing the XY chromosomal genotype as well as the primary sexual organ morphology. This morphology in turn consists of internal reproductive structures, such as female ovaries, fallopian tubes, and uterus, and external reproductive structures in males, such as the penis and testes.

Sex may also describe the external phenotype, or observable appearance, of secondary sexual characteristics, such as female breasts and male beards and larger musculature. Typically, secondary sexual characteristics distinguish one sex from the other, as well as not being essential for reproduction. All of these considerations suggest that some of the behavioral differences that set men and women apart may have biological roots.

Culture interacts with biology-based sex differences to create *gender* as the degree of socially recognized masculine or feminine expression a person has internalized and displays. Biology in isolation, therefore, does not determine gender. Complex and nuanced gender may reflect psychological extensions of one's biological givens, as for example, with female interests in nurturing and caring, and male interests in strength and force.

Gender makes up the array of psychological and behavioral characteristics associated with boys and men and with girls and women. Two broad categories—*masculine gender* and *feminine gender*—are typically recognized, yet there are overlapping states that blur such clear distinctions. Within each category, moreover, variations are common.

Although gender expectations and behaviors are not absolutely identical within or across cultures, male and female gender expression have consistencies that are ordinarily recognized by most children and adults. In his classic text of 1950, *Childhood and Society*, Erik Erikson described distinct and typical gender behaviors characteristic of the early childhood years. Most of his findings have been consistently observed throughout succeeding years.

There has been a great deal of controversy about the extent to which "gender-typical" male and female attitudes and behaviors have endowed genetic and hormonal dimensions. While not all behavior is reducible to biological determinants, evolutionary psychology has advanced many significant considerations about survival-enhancing psychological mechanisms as "detection modules" originating in the Pleistocene epoch about 2.5 million to twelve thousand years ago. For example, a proposed "cheat detection" module warns against unequal or unfair distribution, a "snake fear" module increases avoidance toward reptiles, and a "waist-hip ratio" module predisposes males to choose female mates having a 0.7 ratio. Some psychological trait adaptations were ancestrally needed as problem-solving strategies for survival, while other archaic adaptations still present today may not be essential for survival in the present age.

Human studies, for example, have demonstrated that a female's reproductive status during her ovulatory cycle has predictable effects on her interest in selected aspects of men's presentations. The short-term and long-term effects of these mating behaviors, however, differ. Interestingly, just before and during ovulation, women are highly attracted to males that show robust secondary sexual characteristics, especially those suggesting physical health and later reproductive success. For example, larger musculature and increased body hair imply high testosterone levels and ability to protect. Females' selections of mates for the long-term, however, place greater implicit and conscious emphasis on status, ability to provide resources for family survival, and capacity for long-term commitment.

Extrapolating these considerations about gender-lateralized styles, one wonders whether a female's incubatory experiences with infant gestation underlies containment mental models, notably an ability to be comfortable with processes that require more prolonged waiting and lingering. By contrast, male's relatively greater physical prowess may underlie action-oriented mental models, notably concern over seeking results in the form of more immediate, concrete outcomes. A female's anxiety over her (and her child's) need to be protected may be matched by a male's reactivity to fear-eliciting stimuli that require protective measures. These typical styles, to some degree shared by both genders, have satisfying and pleasurable qualities and are reinforcing. Both approaches—long-term and short-term perspectives, in fact, have value and complement one another.

There is no universally accepted consensus on the origins of many typically observed gender differences. Some brain-based work has suggested that female brains have relatively more white matter that connotes greater interconnectivity between brain regions and thus greater overall grasps of situations. Males with less white matter and greater gray matter, by contrast, are hypothesized to be able to grasp circumscribed situations with a more problem-solving predilection. For example, one of the most studied and reliably replicated cognitive differences between the sexes is a male advantage in the ability to rotate three-dimensional images in his head; other spatial skills that tend to show a male advantage are aiming and predicting a projectile's trajectory. The fact that males engage in more throwing activities, such as baseball, football, and golf, may have some of its impetus in differential male genetics. On the other hand, such behaviors may be thought of as requiring "manly" physical prowess by society and thus expected for sons to develop.

Sets of personal hobbies and interests appear dominant for each gender. These characteristic gender preferences are *gender-typical* in that they are elastic though not absolutely fixed or homogenous. Male-identified interests, however, such as with action figures, mechanical objects, cars, tools, repairing broken items, large machinery, scientific instruments, and competitive sports seem to be somewhat common across cultures. Aesthetic endeavors for men are typically large-scale creations. Competitive sports require strength, power, skill, physical prowess, force, brisk movements such as running, and cleverness. Such robust behavioral expressions are also culturally more associated with male gender. Until a few decades ago, war and armed services had been a domain inhabited by only males. While these examples show commonalities, there are also differences. For example, diversity in male attitude about conscription was apparent in the 1970s as some men accepted recruitment while others consciously objected to this conventional norm and chose less hostile alternatives.

In general, though, male gender appears stylistically direct, outwardly oriented, and concerned with short-term problems and solutions managed in overt, practical ways. Data transfers that deemphasize emotion characterize male communicational styles. Males are also typically less flexible in their repertoires of parenting and seem to find even the challenges of caregiving to be more "boring" and repetitive than do females. Recent studies have demonstrated fetal testosterone levels to inversely correlate with measurable empathy quotients. Social reward and neural activity during emotional perception using fMRI studies have lent support to this testosterone exposure. Female-identified behaviors are associated, on the other hand, with child rearing, nurturing, repairing in the form of mending, and aesthetics such as personal adornment. Women are typically more flexible and offer a wider range of options when dealing with children.

Between men and women, similarities in information processing, attitudes, emotional and cognitive abilities, responses to stress, strategies for problem solving, and behaviors are undeniable. There are, however, obvious and important differences that even newborns and infants recognize. By six and eight weeks, for example, infants respond differently to maternal versus paternal interactive styles. While the capacity to discriminate gender differences has significant innate roots, it is not uncommon for adult men to state that they perceive women as inscrutable and enigmatic. Women, accordingly, typically state that they perceive men to be emotionally insensitive, and that they find this inexplicable.

Such gender-identified distinctions are commonly, though not necessarily, held as expectations. Noting gender differences has descriptive and heuristic value. Such perception, if seriously considered, may provide women with more realistic expectations of men's interests, capabilities, and enthusiasm for caregiving. Considering these matters, on the other hand, may help men to understand themselves better and to anticipate the needs of wives as both women and mothers. Nonetheless, it is important for both genders to recognize that these are complex issues and to avoid simple stereotyping.

Gender stereotypes about the international equivalents of "femininity" and "masculinity" exist in all societies and cultures. Complex debates and questions about what is "objectively real," however, cannot be addressed easily. People may see themselves and behave in masculine, feminine, or mixed ways. Hence, the immense complexity of sex identity and gender cannot be disentangled definitively. In fact, a new field dealing with gender-specific research is emerging: the *neurobiology of parenting*. Findings have scientifically demonstrated that mothers show higher levels of amygdala activation responsiveness along with oxytocin increases than fathers who, by contrast, show greater activation in social-cognitive circuitry correlated with increases in vasopressin during child care and mother-father synchrony. This book's perspective is clinical and empirical in that it relies on typical and common manifestations of behaviors that are described and understood, to some extent, in conventionally interpreted ways, yet the book also remains open and flexible to individual variations in these gender patterns. Examining gender and gender differences cannot be simplistically construed as mere sexism or gender stereotyping. This book, in fact, eschews notions of superior versus inferior among persons and, in particular, between men and women.

2.2 Gender and the Neurophysiology of the Stress Response

Gender has an influence on the way that stress—frustration, conflict, change, and pressure to perform—is perceived and managed.

What follows is a brief discussion of the neuroscientific aspects of sex and gender as they relate to *biomentalism*. Qualitatively distinct genetic endowments, hormones, and neurophysiological pathways are undeniable. For example, human population research studies suggest that female subjects respond with greater hypothalamic-pituitary axis (HPA) activation to interpersonal stressors, such as social rejection; male subjects, on the other hand, respond more appreciably to stressors related to achievement and competition. The open biogenetic programs of all humans receive modulating influences from environmental experiences.

Male and female observable responses to stressors also differ in various ways. In general, men's behavior correlates with intellectual or 'material activity-based' maneuvers such as building, solving, and repairing. Women's reactions include nurturing, comforting, and caregiving—all of which are mood and interpersonally oriented. Whereas men tend to build and destroy, women tend to preserve and maintain.

Hostility may be the most toxic element in the entire program of perceiving and reacting to stress. Men typically show "fight or flight" reactions to stress. Some researchers add "freeze" behaviors to "fight" and "flight" as another possible reaction to acute, unexpected stressors in men. The male hormone testosterone correlates positively with the feelings of dominance and aggression of the fight reaction. Aggression here typically expresses itself as fighting and threats of fighting.

For males and females, any stress activates the norepinephrine system of the locus coeruleus. The locus coeruleus, found in the pons area of the brainstem, principally operates to regulate psychological arousal and activation. Stressors cause this structure to release norepinephrine, which activates stress-induced fear circuitry and initiates biomental "general alarm" reactions to minimize risk of harm and ensure survival. The action of the locus coeruleus on the prefrontal cortex and cognition is complex. While a moderate amount of norepinephrine agonizes (activates) a-2 receptors to increase working memory and attention, an excess amount may decrease working memory and attention by binding to lower-affinity a-1 receptors. In conjunction with brainstem norepinephrine, epinephrine from the adrenal medulla also contributes to stress responsivity, especially its physiological dimensions. All these operations are adaptive for short-term survival in the face of stress, whether the organism fights or flees.

During acute stress, the HPA axes of both sexes release cortisol, epinephrine, and other neurochemicals. More enduring states of stress, such those experienced by elite soldiers, increase men's hypothalamic corticotrophin-releasing factor and lower their testosterone levels. Decreased testosterone measured in the cerebrospinal fluid is part of the profile seen in depression and posttraumatic stress disorder (PTSD).

Women have been found to behave somewhat differently in response to stressors. They have heightened mood reactivity to daily interpersonal stressors. Women also respond with the classic fight-flight response, but this reaction is typically superseded by a more interpersonally affiliative set of behaviors. Researchers have termed this typical female response "tend and befriend." Protection of offspring by "tending" and seeking mutual social support by "befriending" characterize this response to most stressors.

When the HPA axis is activated in women, there is an increased release of the neuropeptides oxytocin and vasopressin that enhances the "tend and befriend" effects of estrogen. Oxytocin, in particular, has been found to be associated with increased approach and bonding responses. The brief increase in estrogenic effects by oxytocin dampens HPA axis activity and thus behavioral reactivity to psychological stressors. Long-term increases in stress and estrogen exposure in premenopausal women, by contrast, significantly alter the beneficial changes evoked by brief exposure and may increase risk for depression and anxiety.

It is important to acknowledge that scientific understanding of how male and female hormones and physiological stress systems operate is still largely elusive. It is reasonable, however, to infer that these measureable differences have some impact on the experience and behavior of gender.

With the recent recognition of sex-based differences in disease development, there is a burgeoning literature addressing sex-associated differences in normal physiological and hormonal function. Indeed, there are prominent differences between the cardiovascular, musculoskeletal, and immune systems of men and women. Many of these sex-based differences are mediated by the actions of estrogens and androgens.

2.3 Perception of Gender in Self and Others

Short of some essential biological differences and capacities, men and women share manifold capabilities. Applied to gender distinctions, careful discrimination merits differentiating illusion and deception from actual differences. Indeed, the intrinsic mental tendency toward dichotomous thinking is common. The degree to which such polarizations in thought are valid or helpful always requires critical review and careful examination.

At the risk of oversimplifying the complexity of gender, it may be reasonable to say that male and female psychologies tend to show different styles and preferences, as gendered biologies have different functions. These differences are neither better nor worse than one another, merely different.

A foundation of one's *self-concept* is the way he or she understands personal gender. While nonconscious themes abound, consciously ascribed attributions make up a large part of the gendered dimension of *self-concept*. Gender typing and categorization are one dimension of cognition's proclivity toward making distinctions, often trending toward polar dualisms. This splitting and naming process occurs in order to makes sense out of the multiplicity of features perceived in the world. Comparing, contrasting, and categorizing help organize the infinite amount of information in the world. Young children tend to conceive of groups in standard and simplified ways that allow for stereotypes. As thinking becomes more complex in middle childhood, adolescence, and adulthood, attention to the specific characteristics of individuals may lessen the developmentally earlier propensity to magnify differences and so automatically think in terms of polar opposites.

For example, by eighteen months, toddlers appear to distinguish "maleness" (with rough, sharp features) from "femaleness" (with soft, round features) in their perceptions of persons. Twenty-four-month-olds can use words such as "boy," "girl," "man," and "woman." By thirty-six months, children self-identify as boys or girls. Preschool children segregate themselves into same gender playgroups. This segregation, to varying degrees, persists throughout childhood. By the end of the preschool years, gender behavioral roles become established. These gender schemas become mental filters that act to make male or female characteristics more salient in perceptual processes. Cross-cultural research demonstrates that stereotyping of many personality traits becomes like that of adults by eleven years of age. For example, both boys and girls attribute being tough, aggressive, and dominant to males and associate being gentle, affectionate, and dependent with females. Whether gender role constancy is primarily established from observed modeling and reinforcement, from innate sources, or from both remains an open question. What is known is that some degree of successful gender expression and perception as they relate to underlying sex is required on a group level to facilitate reproduction.

Obvious at birth, biological and morphological sex identity is determined by chromosome assortment and by exposure and responsiveness of target tissues to endogenous and exogenous sex steroids. Gender can be understood as a psychological and behavioral expression of *gender identity* (or self-image as male or female) and *gender role* (male or female behavioral style).

While gender determination has biological roots in genetic makeup and hormonal influence, it is also developed by expectations and behavioral patterns learned in early childhood. Parental, familial, peer, and social models all have an effect. Developmental theorists suggest that male, female, or mixed-gender identity is established and perhaps fixed by about three years of age. Gender role for most children becomes fixed by about five years and is largely irreversible thereafter. Gender labeling of children by families, beginning as early as twelve to thirty months, especially reinforces a child's sense of being either male or female when it is concordant with the child's own sense of him or herself. In boys, gender role may appear as early as age two, even before gender identity. Gender stability for both boys and girls in identity and role is typically achieved by the early school years.

During the adolescent years, there is organization of *sexual orientation*, which is a person's relative responsiveness to sexual stimuli and erotic gender preference. By early young adulthood, there typically occurs the establishment of *sexual identity,* which is the self-labeling of one's psychological sexual orientation.

Studies indicate that the social environment amplifies modest, innate differences between the brains of boys and girls. The brain's neuroplasticity responds by inducing additional anatomical changes. Such alterations then give rise to the greater differences apparent in the attitudes and behaviors of these brains as they reach adulthood.

Gender preferences in attitude, choice, communication style, ideation, emotion, and behavioral repertoire progressively consolidate over early and middle childhood and during adolescence. Of note, the usage of the words "established" and "fixed" do not imply that changes cannot occur. Essentially nothing in the mind or in behavior is truly immutable, for development occurs over a lifetime.

Psychological gender and biological sex identity are not necessarily synchronous. Each person interprets cultural expectations differently and so incorporates a variety of idiosyncratic construals. For this reason, any discussion of different gender styles is a discussion of approximations and context-specific typical behaviors.

2.4 Parenting and Gender

Biomental child development recognizes that men as fathers and women as mothers do, in fact, take on the universal role of "parent" to children. This biparental executive care is found to a reasonably large extent in many animals, and humans also participate in this phenomenon. The emotions of romantic love and sexual jealousy in particular elicit and support both mating and parenting. Each parent is obliged to recognize children's needs and initiate caregiving in a self-directed manner. One parent advising another, if not excessive, is not only acceptable but highly desirable. Mutual discussion and cooperation between parents is optimal.

While cooperation and agreement between parents may be the most effective approach to successful parenting, differences between men and women, as well as individual differences among persons, are important to consider. Evolutionary psychology, for example, has explored sex and gender differences and suggested findings that appear cross-culturally consistent. Taking these variations in style into account helps understand—rather than mandate—parental guidelines. The aim of this understanding is to promote parenting that is contextually suitable yet flexible and nuanced according to parental preferences, whether disposition or intentionally chosen.

Evolutionary psychology proposes the theory of "parental investment." This theoretical perspective presumes the sex-shared universal goal of reproductive success, and describes the different way this is experienced and expressed by men and women. Differences encompass the variations in aims that each sex invests in terms of time, energy, survival risk, and closing off future opportunities for goals other than parenting in order to produce and nurture offspring. The amount of parental investment between females and males is usually not equal.

According to this theory, females invest substantial time, energy, and risk to maximize reproductive success by seeking partners who can supply material resources to facilitate offspring well-being. Females, therefore, have less interest in uncommitted sexual activity, have a smaller number of sex partners over a lifetime, and value status, income, and ambition in desirable male partners. Males, by contrast, invest minimal time, energy, and risk in parenting pursuits. They maximize the universal goal of reproductive success by seeking more sexual partners who have greater reproductive potential. In "parental investment theory," therefore, males are understood to exhibit more interest in uncommitted sex, seek a greater number of partners over a lifetime, and seek youthfulness and physical attractiveness in desirable partners.

While evolutionary psychology and its valuable contributions provide important insights, Biomental child development reiterates that biology does not absolutely determine behavior, nor should it. A judicious understanding of a range of speculations and theoretical considerations, however, is reasonable and the basis for informed decision making. With this in mind, the following discussions review a range of perspectives on the ingredients of mothering and fathering and their relationship to gendered parenting.

2.5 Gender Intelligence and Psychological Style

Gender intelligence denotes the differential understanding and coping skills of each gender. Standard personality tests, for example, do demonstrate relatively consistent differences between men and women, small to moderate in size, in average scores on many personality traits. In regard to caregiving, each parent adds a fresh perspective, complementary repertoire of behaviors, and unique expression of gender intelligence. These gendered differences provide the child with real-life diversity and a capacity for "social binocular vision," that is, seeing the world from these varying perspectives.

Female psychological styles often highlight language, dialogue, affectionate relationships, receptivity, sensitivity, empathy, intuition (decoding emotional messages), soft touch, long-term maintenance and stability, ethics, caring, and compassion. Women score higher than men on the personality traits of agreeableness and conscientiousness. This overall style is depicted in traditional images of a mother holding an infant close to her left side, near to her breast and heart. Mothers tend to grasp and snuggle babies very close to their bodies. In contrast, men typically hold infants and children with two hands in front of themselves with some perceptible space in between.

Women may tend to be less short-term-oriented in their decision-making styles. Recent studies strongly suggest that women have a greater capacity for empathy, namely consideration for others. This implies deferring their own needs to attend to those of others. Women form strong same-sex alliances whose aim is cooperation and mutual helping rather than aggression whether spontaneous or for entertainment. Mothers ordinarily use greater language interactions, and they tend to enlist cooperation, care, nurturance, and a long-term orientation in relating to children. The predictable and regulatory style of maternal nurturance has soothing qualities. Females also tend to use coping skills that have more internalizing qualities based on feelings.

Male psychological styles reflect an orientation toward action, stimulation, overtly robust activity, tangible achievements, details, team and work partnerships, and ethics of rules, laws, rights, and justice. Identification of problems needing repair elicits short-term, direct solutions. Strong concerns with work, occupation, and making a living are foremost in Western cultures. Many men view jobs as tasks or problems that pose challenges. Whatever the biological and culturally determined components may be, men tend to avoid expressing vulnerability.

Otherwise stated, men become excited when they are faced with problems to be solved or tasks to be accomplished, particularly when requiring action. Challenges ranging from simply digging a hole to the more complex building of a house tend to spark male interest. Implicit motivations behind such problem-solving tasks include protection, safety, and minimizing vulnerability. The capacity to protect presumes prowess, power, and physical and psychological control.

In interpersonal transactions, fathers use a brisk, robust style in approaching and interacting with children. For example, it is more common to see a young father holding his infant with both hands and raising the infant above his head as he stares into baby's eyes. Fathers are also fond of carrying older infants and younger preschool children on their shoulders.

In general, men tend to use more externalizing coping skills that may range from a constructive action orientation to blatant aggression. Contemporary fathers spend 30–35 percent less time than mothers in direct childcare but spend more time engaged in robust play activities. Researches have suggested that these play performances increase fathers' salience to children; in other words, fathers become novel sources of interest. In addition, studies show that school-age children demonstrate significant gains in intellectual development when their fathers are involved with them as infants. Factors that affect the degree of paternal involvement include personal motivation, skill confidence, and support from spouse and society.

Most researchers agree that children with involved fathers have fewer problems; they have better language skills and fewer behavioral difficulties. When fathers take the time to ask about their children's academic and social activities, it enhances their perceived credibility. The involved male figure can be a biological father, adoptive father, stepfather, or other adult male such as an uncle, grandfather, or mentor. Male involvement can encompass, among other things, reading to a child, taking a child on outings, and taking a role similar to that of mothers in the actual management tasks of direct childcare.

Research has also shown that sons with involved fathers are less likely to have negative interactions with law enforcement over time. Daughters of involved fathers are less likely to have mental health problems later in life and tend to develop greater personal autonomy and self-confidence.

A father's effectiveness is enhanced when he pauses, listens, and communicates genuine caring, concern, and empathy. Fathers may take these steps using their own succinct communicational styles. This conciseness, however, must be sensitive to continuing spouse-to-spouse dialogue because fathers often think they are "giving a lot," only to later realize that they were not doing what their wives wanted. Female spouses often admire husbands that demonstrate caring, both short-term and long-term, in ways that reflect romance and generosity. Mothers also need to be flexible. Male spouses value a wife's continuing efforts to maintain an attractive appearance, demonstrate a sense of humor, minimize emotional overreactions, and convey a sense of wanting rather than needing affection in ways that appear demanding. Men typically believe they communicate their intentions at "face value" and wonder why females add what men perceive as "drama" or overly emotional content to relatively insignificant matters. In addition to demonstrating nurturant support, women can also limit unnecessary discussion, pose more direct requests, and offer concrete, action-oriented strategies. Couples therapy has suggested the value of the aforementioned approaches in optimizing successful relationships between men and women.

In summary, biomental child development recognizes variance in gender and gender styles in themselves and in their influence on children. Although gender and matters of masculinity and femininity are important, *what overrides all considerations is the quality of the interpersonal relationship between parent and child.* An intentional, thoughtful, effortful relationship characterized by sensitivity, responsiveness, affectionate mutuality, emotional meaningfulness, and compassionate discipline—not gender—has the greatest positive influence on a child's development and well-being.

3. ENVY, GREED, AND JEALOUSY

3.1 Overview

In an attempt to give ample emphasis to understanding and promoting healthy emotional development, this book includes discussions about envy, greed, and jealousy. While deeply rooted in emotions, envy, greed, and jealousy have outstanding cognitive components that make them and discussions about them more akin to understanding them as intricate states of mind. These "passions" are complex, having both positively inspiring and darker, more ominous dimensions. These foundational human experiences are both developmental and transcendental; they are integral to the life span. In fact, appreciating the cultural significance of negative emotions such as envy having cascading disruptor effects has been thematic throughout history.

For example, Mediterranean and Middle Eastern traditions have correlated core elements of envy—superior-inferior dichotomies, hostility, spoiling, and destructive intent—with the functions of gaze, the "evil eye." In ritualistic charms, the arts, and throughout literature, moreover, envious hostility has been correlated with the manner in which eyes communicate a range of emotional and cognitive salience from empathy to envy. In biblical Genesis, chapter 3, Eve was told that if she ate from the tree of the *knowledge* of *good* and *evil* situated in the center of the garden of Eden, "your eyes will be opened and you will be like God, knowing good and evil." After she and Adam ate, "the eyes of both of them were opened and they realized that they were naked . . ." From a psychological perspective, this event reflects a first or at least millennia old instance of human cognition's ability to grasp the starkness of polar opposites—the capacity for both dualistic thinking and feeling at the root of envy. Appreciating the complex influences of how positive and negative emotions interact and impact human behavior illuminates this understanding. Elements intrinsic to the development of moral self-relevance, moral restraint, and effortful self-control weigh heavily in such an understanding.

For example, one might automatically think that envy is absolutely "bad," egregious, malignant, and pathological. This idea is incorrect. Unconscious envy is merely a given predisposition to becoming aware of distinctions and to assign value—usually polar extremes—to these differences. Such value judgments then motivate behaviors. Envy is the tendency toward noticing the privation as a lesser good, if not an extremely spoiled goodness. Envy theory goes to great lengths to emphasize in repeated fashion that an indispensable and powerful component of envy is love in the form of attraction, often idealization

Unsuitable, inappropriate, and negative outcomes correlate with the destructive material comportments—personal and social acts—that might result from multiply determined choices—not merely inclinations preferenced by envy. Revenge, for example, as discussed in this chapter's sections on xenophobia, is a clear-cut example of one of the negative and destructive material actions prompted by core envy yet nuanced by life experiences and situational context.

My 2010 book, *Envy Theory*, is a conceptual model detailing the primacy of love in all its dynamisms and syllogisms with its negative companions, and will not be addressed further in this section. The pivotal importance of empathy, as has and will be discussed, denotes in concrete and empirical fashion the primacy of love, affiliation, agreeableness, cooperation, and pro-social perspective taking. This positive emphasis cannot be underestimated, and needs to be viewed in the context of discussions about envy. The synergy between love and envy in envy theory's model of the mind holds titanic strength in its foundational effect on emotional, cognitive, and social human functioning.

A critically important emphasis must be given to the fact that the envy referred to in this text is *unconscious envy*. This unconscious envy is distinct from conscious experiences that are labeled by terms casually suggesting "envy," especially in everyday discourse. Unconscious envy, therefore, is technically and academically understood to be a *construct*, that is, a subsurface proposition inferred to be the implicit source of empirical and measurable expressions. Constructs denote the conceptual underpinnings characterized by focus, simplicity, and resilience that influence key research and its application in a designated field. Although the consciously identified derivatives of an unconscious construct may appear unrelated, they instantiate or make concrete their source.

Unconscious envy is composed of primitive love as idealization and of reactive, raw hate. Primitive and raw denote first and foundational innate biomental biases whose driving force is need.

Idealization connotes implicit attitudes imbued with unrealistic, fanciful, and aspirational ideals. Raw hate is characterized by an almost absolute intolerance of any perceived biomental need, for example, for food or warmth. Both idealization and intolerance of neediness presuppose a foundational propinquity of "like attracts like." The constructs of epistemological *projective internalization* and neurophysiological mirror neuron activity initiate an automatic attraction to something outside the self that matches something already present in the mind, if only *in potentia*. This trajectory of implicitly sensed identity is colored by unconscious envy. It implies that one feels one either has an insufficient amount of or is deprived of a previously possessed resource.

Special mention must be made of the significance of the concept "re-source" in envy theory. In its elemental sense, resource denotes food, notably mother's milk. For the infant, milk is a unique resource. Unlike air, milk requires some degree of intentional expectation, acquisition, loss, and refind-ing. The infant's perception of milk is multisensorial—taste, smell, vision, and touch. All these considerations make milk—or "the breast"—the primal object of desire. Thus, at their primitive roots, idealization and hate—the core of unconscious envy—crystallize around the infantile experience of relations with this primal resource.

Need implies sensing incompleteness, helplessness, and a desire to over-come it. Infancy is the prototypical state of proximity and kinship closeness. In the earliest stages of infancy, pronounced idealization may become ade-quately tempered in the process of maternal transactional sensitivity. This process then constrains disorganizing hostility and frustration. When exces-sive idealization is dominant, however, it may center on inflating the devel-oping sense of self. This then contributes to unhealthy egoism, which is a narcissistic sense of self characterized by rigid self-centeredness, lack of empathy, omnipotent self-attributions, and a fixedness with regard to matters of control. When unorganized love and hate become normatively modulated, however, primitive envy progressively morphs into more consciously felt states of social satisfaction. Preverbal attitudes of feeling safe and secure are concomitant with a sense of admiration for the other. As this deepens, emerg-ing gratitude, albeit in its amorphous, infantile manner, is experienced as the urge to return kindness felt for the perceived beneficence given by the other. These earliest of nonverbal experiences become templates for all later emo-tional attitudes.

The essence of unconscious envy is the reactive need to spoil and devalue other people's enjoyment. This need to spoil extends to destructively devalu-ing both the perceived possessor of valued resources and, in the end, nega-tively impacts the envier. Those struggling with unconscious envy appear to others as unhappy, miserable, mean, and withholding. The envier cannot satisfy himself nor be satisfied by others; the mental pain of unconscious envy, if excessive, is gnawing and inconsolable. Implicit biases and overt prejudices reflect the more accessible derivatives of unconscious envy. Un-conscious envy accordingly may be compared to psychological bedrock—foundational, adamant, intransient—*but not altogether unapproachable and unalterable*. This is an exceedingly important point to dispel any notion that unconscious envy is an irrevocable given. Modifications and modulations as will be discussed in the section on envy management skills address this in detail.

The roots of unconscious envy arise developmentally in the infant's rela-tion to the primary caregiver, typically mother. Envy theory describes this as the *infant's dilemma*. In this model, at birth, the prototypical state of utter dependency gives the infant no other recourse than to simultaneously experience need and mother's ministrations that temporarily quell these discomforts. The infant mind can only sense the poles of this recurring situation as extreme. The precarious infantile mechanism of idealization as raw love vacillates with almost intolerable pain felt as raw hate in relation to unmet infantile needs. Since the typical infant-mother interaction is one of transactional sensitivity, typical nurturance brings moderation to these primitive, unconscious feelings during the earliest months of infancy. It is important to reiterate that *nurturance and loving transactions ordinarily take precedence and make up the ordinary, typical mother-infant relationship.*

By about the middle of the first year, polar extremes become modulated. This adjustment spurs a reconciliation of love with hate. Raw love transforms itself toward emerging states of admiration, wonder, emulation, mutuality, and gratitude. This reconciliation and its emerging states lay the foundation for the development of perspective taking and gradually unfolding states of empathy. Hence, the raw, primitive qualities of early inchoate sensations and affective states refine themselves into an array of more nuanced emotions. These feelings become further refined as cognition tempers passion toward the end of the second year and beyond. In other words, as more cortically based cognition matures, it constrains primitive, limbic system-based emotional reactivity.

My work on envy theory asserts that *unconscious* envy is an innate part of human nature and cannot be avoided. Since envy has its potent origins at birth, this legacy endows it with a primitive quality that endures. Its malignant forms always remain unconscious. Throughout life, the primitive quality of envy makes it insular and deeply "impersonal" in contrast to substantively interpersonal. It remains a *reflexive reaction* that typically spoils one's attraction to and grasp of goodness. This implicit spoiling denotes psychological processes that turn sour, acidify, and make stingingly disagreeable what previously had been sensed as ideal. Deletion follows in various forms such as ejection, repulsion, expulsion, or dismissal.

Spoiling and soiling phenomena are closely related and the sense of both terms harkens back to typical activities in infancy and toddlerhood. Spoiling is based on the envier's idiosyncratic "unconscious phantasy" construals, as will be discussed.

Unconscious envy, therefore, remains a core feature of all subsequent emotional and cognitive positions although perception and its interpretation may and can mitigate, to varying extents, envy's primitive coloring in subsequent psychological processes. *Normal perception is capable of distinguishing reality from phantasy, to some degree, even as early as infancy.* Typical infants possess a remarkable ability to distinguish what is probable from improbable in realistic ways. The fact that human cognition can agree, at least partially, on "objective" findings reflects a consensual validation attesting to typically functioning normal perception in most persons.

Special attention must be given to the envy theory construct of envy as an innate disposition present at birth in a primal way. The experiences that envy produces in an infant are sensed and felt but not understood or known other than in amorphous, primitive ways. This point is crucial to understand, particularly as it pertains to infancy, when cognitive maturation and development are rudimentary.

This book lays strong emphasis on the construct of *transactional sensitivity*, notably maternal sensitivity and containment of the infant. Gratification and nongratification of the infant's biomental needs partly determine the strength of primitive infantile destructive impulses. These drives then affect the subsequent pathogenicity of unconscious envy or the capacity for love to promote admiration and gratitude.

Envy has an amorphous, ephemeral quality that makes it exceedingly difficult to grasp. It is more indirect and seemingly intangible than greed and jealousy. By contrast, greed and jealousy are more well-defined realities. Adequate attention to these three potent mental dynamics has preventive value, since they constitute the matrix out of which unrealistic fear, hate, and hostile interpersonal biases emerge.

Further readings are suggested in the references, and a full exposition of the nature of envy can be found in *Envy Theory*. Envy's unique role is therein described to have its genesis in the innate roots of mental information processing. The inextricable ties among envy, jealousy, and greed are also discussed in that text.

In summary, therefore, as described in chapter 3 of this book, the newborn enters the world with an intrinsically established cognitive and emotional template of dispositions. Findings from evolutionary psychology lend support to this perspective. A primitive, native core of knowledge exists, which becomes more sophisticated over time. This *anticipatory readiness* seeks out and identifies with objects, events, and relationships in the real environment that have some commonality with the infant's already established psychological proclivities. The biomental perspective terms this process *projective internalization*.

In relationship with his or her mother, an infant alphabetizes primitive sensation into more organized experiential units, which may be understood to be rudiments of unconscious thinking. The infant's projective internalization, in conjunction with mother's transactional sensitivity, is the core of the mind-building interaction between mother and infant. Essential elements that influence the development of the gradually developing process of abstraction are set in motion through these interactive synchronies. The infant's innate sense of incompleteness requires mother's ministrative additions to further the progressive resolutions of its ever-emerging questions.

All the aforementioned connotes that at birth, little if any aligned biomental stability is present. During infancy and childhood, caregivers—as well as children themselves—operate under a preliminary yet normative illusion of biomental unity. Biomental structure forms itself and becomes recognized, for example, as physical posture, characteristic behaviors, emotional reactivity, and cognitional attitudes. Structure, which implies relationships among parts, guides function, movement, and behavior. In fact, a contradictory condition of random disunity is the norm. The natural biomental default condition, therefore, is characterized by greater randomness and less self-reflection. These patterns of relative coherence consolidate over time and tend to perpetuate themselves in more rigid rather than malleable ways. Love in interaction with envy crucially influences how one's identity and *self-concept* organize and interact with others.

The goal of achieving and maintaining biomental health is to intentionally promote orderliness in unconsidered randomness. This denotes intelligent attention—alertness to and developing understanding of the physical body and psychological functioning. Proper alignment in all sectors of biopsychosocial experience optimally results in a good to high quality of life. Orderliness and alignment encompass understanding the details of development, self-reflection, and modulating experiential dichotomies, notably attitudes of envy with attitudes of love.

3.2 Unconscious Phantasy as Nonconscious Information Processing

The psychoanalytic work of both Melanie Klein and her London school has referred to the psychological modules that make up the *unconscious system of the mind* and termed its units *unconscious phantasies*. This spelling of "phantasy" deliberately differentiates these unconscious units of information processing from more conscious "fantasy" that is characterized by imagination, daydreaming, and conscious wishful thinking.

Special emphasis is given to the proposition advanced here that *unconscious phantasies and envy, for example, are innate proceedings that determine how information processing operates*. This innate psychological bias in mental infrastructure denotes that innate concepts as formed and conscious entities are not present either as such or in toto at birth. Concepts, technically defined, denote declarative knowledge constructed and developed throughout infancy and adulthood.

Envy operates principally as unconscious phantasy models—primitive thought activity—throughout life. It is the voice of the unconscious in a form that resembles metaphor. Unconscious phantasy is the implicit underpinning for the gradual development of all conscious thought. In infancy, the typical baby tests its preverbal phantasies—corporeally mentalized maps—against encounters with real perceptions, both gratifying and distressing. Normal development presumes an adaptive correlation characterized by a realistic fidelity that promotes biomental development. This process is termed *reality testing*.

As growth and development proceed throughout life, all psychological processes always rely on the primacy of perception in making and maintaining contact with reality. The interplay of phantasy as primitive, unconscious thought activity and conscious thinking always influences perception. This fact is reflected in the métier of scientific methodology. For example, contemporary psychological theory posits the construct of "confirmatory bias," by which a person searches for and recognizes data that confirms already held beliefs while rejecting or ignoring information that may contradict those beliefs. Unconscious phantasy and confirmatory bias are similar constructs in that both begin with an established attitude that seeks actual or imagined realization through experience in the world.

Partly innate and partly shaped by experience, unconscious phantasy is the form that sensation, emotion, and primitive experience take in the mind throughout life, beginning at birth. It is how the self "as information" experiences itself in terms of a "lived processing": embryonic, oscillating, organic motifs. Unconscious phantasy is always implicitly rooted in concrete, presentational icons reflecting dynamic aspects of the infant's interpersonal relationships with primary caregivers. Since it is active at birth, the very nature of infancy—its virtually utter helplessness—elicits implicit states of omnipotence to counter the pervasive experience of powerlessness. Ironically, a principal characteristic of unconscious phantasy is its obstreperousness—unruliness and inability to be controlled. Whereas this is how it exists in the unconscious as a system, its expression in both subliminal and conscious awareness is marked by the need to control. This operational configuration is discussed in a following section "Omnipotence and Control."

Unconscious phantasy as a process is unconscious thought activity. As a structure, unconscious phantasy is the mental model(s) or pictures housing these informational units of "object relations"—the unconscious construals of perceived relations with others. The construct of "object relations" is the psychodynamic description of physical and psychological propinquity—the unique encoding of intimate kinship proximity.

Through the vehicles of unconscious phantasy, emotionally meaningful interpersonal action scenarios are encapsulated as nonconscious or implicit primitive memories. As development proceeds, meaningful survival reinforces its salience in this way through a person's beliefs, values, and motivations. As components of unconscious phantasy, they are the implicit and automatic assumptions that guide attitudes. Unconscious phantasy in the end governs emotional and cognitive information processing and so biases perception, interpretation, and memory throughout the life cycle.

While unconscious phantasies are a typical part of infancy and early childhood*, reason, logic, and reality testing eventually emerge and modulate these profoundly nonconscious motivators in middle childhood into adulthood.* Throughout development, however, the primitive, nonverbal, and nonrational nature of unconscious phantasy remains intact. These unconscious phantasies cluster as encampments that are relatively coherent and enduring, yet dynamically influential. As basic assumptions, they subliminally influence emotions, thinking, attitudes, and behavior. Unconscious phantasy correlates with the implicit assumptions that underlie all biases—rational and irrational. Unconscious phantasy, moreover, expresses itself symbolically in many ways, only one of which is through aesthetic productions—painting, sculpture, music, and so forth.

Omnipotence, left unmodulated by reason, is a principal feature of unconscious phantasy. The development of emerging logic and reality testing may modulate these primitive levels of phantasy as they interfuse into preconscious, subliminal thinking and also into fully conscious awareness. In its pure state in the unconscious, however, nonreality, all-powerful grandiosity, opulence, strength, and an imperious authority attend the feelings and thinking unbounded by reason that characterize unconscious phantasy.

Indeed, omnipotent phantasy is inimical to reality. Unconscious phantasies are automatically erected defensive obfuscations evading the pain and suffering that attends many reality challenges. Although part of unconscious information processing, such phantasy may be glimpsed in memories of dreams, which are its closest conscious reflections. Unstructured children's free play also reflects the externalization of unconscious phantasy. Unconscious phantasy in general, however, is a ubiquitous component of all unconscious thinking and so is not pathological as such. For example, unconscious phantasy may express itself when an individual expresses a deep aspiration by using the phrase "This is my dream."

All mental and behavioral change, at its root, results from *subtle* alterations in the structure, functioning, and dynamic organization of unconscious phantasy. It is not static, although it always retains its omnipotent characteristics. These units of psychic life naturally grow, mature, and develop through experiences of all kinds. Unconscious phantasy becomes attenuated at different levels of consciousness such as in preconscious, subliminal thinking (implicit or basic assumptions) and in fully aware consciousness in which reason and logic have a more prevailing influence (conscious preferences).

Freedom of thought and thinking is required for the forward progression and expansion of personality maturation. This presumes valuing the fact that no thought—whether pleasant, neutral, or distressing—can be unthinkable, but must be examined. This capacity for uncensored examination expands as information processing and reasoning mature throughout life. In this way, thinking constrains and modulates unconscious phantasy toward reality rather than permitting it to remain fueled by omnipotent aspirations, notably emotional impulses.

Accelerated, intentionally sought personality change resulting in alterations in unconscious phantasy may also occur through self-development strategies and the psychotherapeutic process. The verbal dialogues that make up psychotherapy, for example, are major routes toward bringing the more silent mental dialogues of unconscious phantasy to light. In envy theory, the *conscious discovery* of aspects of unconscious phantasy is referred to as *insight*. Insight produces and reflects a vital reduction in the omnipotent nature of unconscious phantasy and personal confusion, such as the uncomfortable dichotomies that are usually at the base of conflict and anxiety. Insight, indeed, is a state of cognitive and emotional awareness characterized by immediacy. These roots of sudden awareness only later become cultivated by efforts powered by an enduring wish for intentional understanding—a search for one's personal truth. This understanding comprises both subjectivity and objectivity in the form of progressively realizing one's unique share of the universally shared experience of being human.

3.3 Emotional States: Positive and Negative

In general, emotions and emotional attitudes can be understood as falling into positive or negative categories. Positive emotions are pleasurable and constructive; negative emotions are aversive and usually destructive. Envy is a negative emotion that operates through unconscious phantasy.

Envy, greed, and jealousy are forms of craving that are naturally occurring and typical states of mind for all people. Envy itself can be understood to be a master regulator in human psychological development. These three variations of craving may be detrimental when they are pronounced and unmodified. Envy, greed, and jealousy are nonetheless expectable emotional reactions that can be understood and managed so that positive results may trump negativity.

These three negative states of mind generate conflict, distress, and behavioral problems. Conflict occurs when envy, greed, and jealousy naturally collide with more positive inclinations such as love, empathy, and cooperativeness. When children and adults appear unempathetic, ungrateful, or unable to share, underlying envy, greed, and jealousy are usually present. The same relationship is true for problems with matters of fairness and justice.

Envy, greed, and jealousy have an overriding tendency to be self-destructive and insular. The provocateurs and emotional consequences of a conscious sense of *guilt*, by contrast, are typically more interpersonally motivated than for the other listed psychological experiences. Guilt is understood to be a more self-conscious emotion related to damage done to another with whom there is some level of affection and respect. Conscious guilt, such as that accompanied by feelings of remorse and realistic wishes to make amends, is typically experienced more obviously and "out in the open" than are the three negative emotions. Thus guilt has a higher chance of having positive psychological outcomes than do envy, greed, or jealousy. This fact suggests that such guilt can be managed in a relatively more direct manner.

A less accessible and more unconscious variety of guilt, however, may be more malignant. An example of this type is found in persons with obsessive-compulsive disorder (OCD) in which doubt, ambivalence, ruminations, inhibitions, and a harsh conscience dominate experience. Such people are often described as "conscience-stricken." They may feel so compelled by an unrealistic fear of contracting germs or being contaminated that they wash their hands repetitively to the point of abrasion. In the face of the implausibility of such a conscious OCD belief, psychodynamic theorists infer that there is an underlying, unconscious feeling of risk of being contaminated or damaged by some nebulous threat that is inside and part of the self. The unconsciously perceived threat of self-damage and damage done to others denotes the anxiety component of "unconscious guilt" in psychodynamic models.

Potentially maleficent properties of human nature, in fact, play parts in the dynamics of affection, empathy, sharing, and helping, for each contains mixtures of love, envy, greed, and jealousy. Unreconciled psychological contrasts between maleficent and beneficent attitudes underlie conflict, a struggle which is felt as anxiety. All people experience conflict, for it is intrinsic to human mental functioning. When utilized adaptively, it can ratchet up self-refinement, expand conscious awareness, and foster empowerment. At times, the provocative and clashing nature of contrasting emotional climates may energize a person's sense of power, control, and *surgency* (a term that indicates the decisive ability to actively accomplish something effectively). That is, when the opposites of a dynamic psychological clash are not pronounced, they may be perceived as pleasant, interesting, and motivating.

How these contrasting attitudes—egocentric dysphoric states and prosocial altruistic engagements—are experienced and negotiated is instrumental in affecting one's quality of life and vulnerability to stress. Vulnerability can potentially lead to psychopathology and impaired psychosocial functioning. Since stress is inevitable, the goal of health promotion and wellness is to identify, understand, and modulate positive and negative attitudes and behaviors. This stress management strategy reflects a positive psychology that appreciates biomental plasticity toward healthier levels of conflict resolution. The aim of such a perspective is to encourage and support personal and social competence.

3.4 Conscience and Empathy

The development of conscience and empathy—real-time compassionate care for another—is an important consideration to review. The healthy functioning of conscience and empathy substantively mitigates the inevitability of self-defeating trends characterized by envy, greed, and jealousy. Current findings in neuroscience are beginning to provide data that suggest that both conscience and empathy, like other psychological processes, have measurable genetic and constitutional components—"endowed givens." These natural qualities, however, are accessible to the significant influences of infantile and childhood environments, which may act to enrich them.

In psychodynamic psychology, the nonconscious development and functioning of conscience is subsumed in the term *superego*. This term encompass one's values, morals, aspirations, and critical judgment, which motivate and also constrain behaviors. *Conscience has innate roots, and becomes shaped by environmental learning, notably parental modeling.* Beginning in the preschool years, media exposure, school, and everyday family and societal directives shape burgeoning conscience. Laws and police who enforce them may also be viewed as external representatives of conscience, to some degree.

Conscience orients a person's life direction and choices. Along with constructive, empathy-based guilt, conscience enables conflict's ability to simultaneously provide both distress and opportunities for choice. Such occasion for choice is a normal "self-righting" mechanism for correcting imbalances and providing opportunities for dynamic change, growth, and self-development.

The experience and management of envy, greed, and jealousy heavily contribute to moral development and the functioning of conscience. Such emotional management refines moral reasoning by mitigating the central dynamic of envy—extreme exclusionary and competing mental contrasts that indicate faulty assessments of fairness and justice. While children naturally perceive and evaluate experience using "black and white" perspectives, the nuanced emergence of empathy developed by adulthood should obviate the more primitive, linear, and ruthless qualities of conscience's earlier beginnings. Put simply, attitudes that only gravitate toward perceived ideals or perceived devaluations become substantively mitigated toward more qualified and realistic composite assessments.

One aspect of both conscience and the envy dynamic is the natural tendency to make idealizations in mental comparisons. *Idealization* is a cognitive and emotional strategy used to exaggerate features of an object to make it more distinctive. Although this process of overimprovement is typically precarious and unrealistic, it establishes a needed, relatively short-lived reference point around which other feelings and ideas may organize and develop.

Idealizations may take the form of aspirations. They positively correlate with extreme perceptions of status and represent extreme polarization. What is good becomes ideal goodness and what is bad becomes ideal badness. The tensions produced by this split fuel a continuing need for reconciliation, especially prompted by feelings such as anxiety and guilt. Person perception is heavily influenced by attraction to "good-looking" or perceived "powerful" others. These diverse assessments are usually made between others perceived to be glamorous and the lacking self—between "the haves" and "have nots." This adversarial dichotomy, if left unchecked by outside clarifications, develops into misguided, demonized perceptions of the others who "have" as "the enemies."

Another example of dichotomous thinking that may promote envy in a developing conscience is parents' use of phrases such as "our own kind" to highlight and promote perceived differences and attribute "specialness" to groups. Conscience's values are established early during childhood and are easily swayed by environmental influences that promote "superior-inferior" dichotomous templates.

Biomental child development regards empathy as crucial for developmental success and social competence. It is a prime characteristic of a healthy superego and conscience. *Empathy* encompasses cognitive, emotional, and behavioral processes whose interrelationships make it possible to respond to another person through a grasp of what the other is inferred to be sensing, feeling, and thinking. These processes, having both unconscious and conscious components, mitigate the perceiver's sense of sharp demarcation from the other and provide him or her with a beneficent state of transitory identification. Empathy as an understanding of the mental states of others draws on profound intuitive capacities that enable the richness of experience to be grasped. Empathy may be regarded as the ultimate development of refined emotional grasping.

While empathy has its roots in the preverbal period of infancy and is characterized by a preponderance of nonconscious information processing operations, it becomes the cornerstone for the development of intuition in later life. *Intuition* denotes an empathetically based cognitive grasp of persons and events that supersedes mere reason. While difficult to pinpoint with precision, the functional capacity for intuition may arise in adolescence and become more organized in adulthood.

The observable capacity for empathy begins its long development in the preschool years, especially between ages three and four. Learning from life experiences, notably the reality of inevitable losses and transitions, enhances this early biological maturation of empathy. Adequately working through these events and processes over time requires integrated cognitive and emotional efforts. This entails properly mourning losses and the recursive psychological enrichments that ensue. The refinement of empathy facilitates its developed *healthy maturation* and counters deleterious effects, as will be discussed in later sections.

Empathic perceptions of "the other" synthesize positive, negative, and ambivalent perspectives. A realistic anticipation of beneficence becomes the norm for understanding others—in contrast to paranoid-like suspiciousness toward "the enemy." Empathy presumes a compassionate identification of one's own needs with those of others and reinforces the prosocial aims of helping, sharing, and comforting. This capacity to care is intimately correlated with healthy moral development, moral reasoning, and recognizing balanced distinctions between attitudes of good and bad or acceptable and unacceptable in one's thinking about self and ideological systems.

Defective empathy results in impaired social intelligence, social skills, and social competence; it also allows for the possibility of conduct disorders and antisocial behaviors. Cutting-edge studies using advanced techniques such as fMRI have correlated variations in amygdala anatomy and functioning with empathy and psychopathy in young adulthood. Some studies on the development of psychopathy—excessive use of instrumental aggression in association with violence and criminal activity—posit a stronger genetic as opposed to social "ultimate cause." A substantial impairment in the capacity for empathy and appropriate social learning from experience are considered rooted in central nervous system defects in amygdala and orbito/ventrolateral frontal cortex systems.

3.5 The Innate Roots of Envy

Envy, greed, and jealousy go beyond merely being simple emotional reactions. These impulses—at root the dissonant perception of opposites—are variously described as forms of need, wish, and desire; they are embedded in the phylogenetic, evolutionary past of the *human* race. My envy theory model advances the proposition that while visceral fear is a universal feature of all animals, envy, greed, and jealousy rooted in visceral fear are characteristically and uniquely human experiences. This correlates with the fact that only humans typically develop into sentient organisms with personalities that participate almost inextricably in a tapestry with both cascading subjective and cultural dimensions.

Envy as discussed here and in envy theory denotes *unconscious* envy in contrast to the typically experienced conscious feelings of greed, jealousy, and competitiveness. As emphasized previously, biomental child development denotes that unconscious envy is not an innate concept. Rather, it is an innate information processing operation that determines how perception, attitude, emotion, nonconscious thinking, and eventually conscious thoughts are structured (i.e., given form, content, and function). This innate psychological bias is the hallmark of the unconscious information processing system.

Visceral fear—the hardwired memory of predators—provides the neuro-psychological platform for the development of emotions that detect threat toward the self and its resources. A primitive and nonconscious sense of being prey connotes that the individual, him- or herself, is food. Put differently, resources may nonconsciously be equated not only with one's assets such as food and valuables, but also with oneself as a foundational asset—prey for a predator. Awareness of resources includes awareness of their limitedness and importance. Fear may be the "rawest" of emotions in that it is unprocessed by the containing functions of higher cortical modulators. Fear connotes a sense of entrapment, hopelessness, and a dire lack of options. Raw fear is faceless; it is a primitive dehumanized experience of impending extinction.

Fear as the "rawest" emotion is etched by evolution as a foundational, preverbal, and prehistoric mental module. Likewise, envy, greed, and jeal-ousy—ultimately rooted in fear—may be genetically endowed, species-typical emotions similar to fear in order to ensure preparedness for survival. They do tend to be more biomentally processed, however, and structured as unconscious phantasy with interpersonal content. Together, these emotions provide the basis for a perpetual sense of incompleteness and need alongside unrelenting attempts to satisfy these requirements for survival.

Unconscious envy is the principal root of greed and jealousy, both of which are typically conscious experiences. These inheritances are, in part, evolved adaptations that have become conserved in attempts to foster fitness, adaptive diversity, safety, and survival of ancestral populations on a group level. These complex emotions drive behavior in both subtle and palpable ways. Their negative effects become prominent when they remain unma-tured, pronounced, and unconstrained by the positive opportunities they may offer. Envy is the potential basis for emulation and admiration; greed, when identified, offers opportunities for greater self-regulation and realistic moder-ation; jealousy, when mild, may foster robust competiveness and apprecia-tion of resources attained.

The innate roots of envy, greed, and jealousy in no way imply that human nature or one's disposition is fixed. *Babies are not born "bad," "poison-ous," or "evil."* The endowed dispositions in various ways permitting im-pulses of envy, greed, and jealousy—it must be emphasized—provide end-less opportunities for adaptive diversifications in conflict resolution and problem solving across the life cycle.

The innate roots of envy predispose toward splitting and dualisms in cognitive and affective experience. The normative development of conscience fosters perspective taking and empathy. Both of these provide constraining and containing functions that help integrate disparate experiences.

The experience and expression of envy and conscience, as well as those of social and antisocial behavior, are endlessly variable. These attitudes and behaviors have appeared in some form in all human cultures for thousands of years. In Eastern cultures (for example, the *Vedas*, circa 4000 BC) and philosophical systems, the Western philosophical problem of "the one and the many" has been addressed through considerations of unity versus diversity. The axiomatic reality of Eastern ideas of "nonduality," which philosophically connotes unity behind apparent diversity, is also the foundation of Western nondual constructs such as ontological monism and Gestalt theories of perception.

I have discussed these considerations at length in several texts on Ayurveda, the traditional medical system of India. In that medico-philosophical system, the very foundation of "mind," termed *Manas*, is principally composed of what in Sanskrit is called *Akasha*. Akasha in this sense suggests etherous mental space, and is roughly akin to Western conceptions of the Higg's field—a silent, directionless vacuum of "formless potential." This unifying matrix is in some way transitional between energy and matter within which primary individual particles may arise and move.

In addition, the importance of this consideration of "one versus many" also has roots in the innovation attributable to the Mesopotamian born Abraham's biblical proposition of the oneness of God, ancient Greek philosophy (Heraclitus and Parmenides, circa 450 BC), and was reiterated in the works of Thomas Aquinas in Europe in the thirteenth century. Eastern and Western epistemological systems that ascribe to constructs of nonduality as being foundational understand all "knowing" to have a cognitive platform of unity, on top of which is a phenomenological veneer of perceptual flux and apparent change.

Dichotomous thinking and psychological "splitting" lead to superior versus inferior polarizations in attitudes; these splits themselves and their consequences elicit visceral fear and trigger the envy dynamic. Recognizing "nonduality" can reconcile trends toward polarizations and quell the dynamics of envy such that greater mental equanimity is achieved. The capacity for nuanced cognition enhances balanced appraisals and supports the *healthy maturation of envy*. This even-handed symmetry in judging and planning processes allows for self-gratifying and prosocial behaviors to become typical. The innate roots of unconscious envy, however, block easy access and, in turn, attenuation of envy, though such attenuation is possible when high levels of motivation, intentionality, and persistence drive such change.

3.6 Envy, Greed, Jealousy, and Their Relation to Loss

Loss is experienced as a sense of absence, detachment, and oftentimes finality. Loss aversion denotes the emotional intensity of psychological processes toward forcefully avoiding and averting loss. This encompasses the release or letting go of anything, whether on material or psychological levels. Envy, greed, and jealousy all deal with loss in different ways. Different individuals at different chronological ages also deal with loss in characteristic ways.

Such differences define themselves in the way an individual experiences the release or letting go of what he or she is losing. This relinquishment process is significantly shaped by a person's sense of finality in the experience of loss. Indeed, one's earliest experiences with becoming accustomed to holding on and the needing to let go in relation to both the material grasp of inanimate objects and the emotional grasp of significant caregivers serves as the earliest template guiding how future losses are managed. Often, people have unrealistic beliefs that stem from being unable to let go, mourn a loss, and move on. Imagination, fantasy, exaggeration, and distortions in thinking often color how loss is felt. Such misconstrued interpretations may then lead to emotional conflict.

Different innate levels of intensity and manners of expression characterize the experiences of envy, greed, and jealousy for a given person. The experience of loss also differs with the changing experiential contexts in which they arise. In envy, loss is typically a "virtual" loss in that what is envied is something that was never possessed and has no hope of attainment. Envy commonly spoils the value of what is envied. This spoiling reactively sours and makes bitter what had been sensed as ideal. Its accompanying ill will is a quintessential characteristic of unconscious envy. In greed, loss is based on the hopeful though feverish expectation of gaining more in the future based on previous acquisition, notably its not being enough; idealizing the value of what is desired is common. In jealousy, loss is felt as an excruciating deprivation of what was once passionately enjoyed and is now ambivalently sought again; damaging the lost object may be an attempt to dampen the intensity of jealousy. In jealousy, reuniting with a "restored" other is the goal. Feelings of guilt more closely attend jealousy than they do with greed and envy.

In envy, loss is accompanied by implicit finality and resentment; in greed, loss is sensed as temporary yet reversible; in jealousy, loss may be regarded as temporary although its ultimate finality is wistfully realized as a plaintive yet emerging despair.

Social psychology proposes a "social comparison theory" that states that people evaluate their own abilities and assets by comparing them to others. Such comparison is a conscious endeavor that implies perceived deficit or loss. The sense of loss may also occur on an unconscious level when a person feels that what she or he has is not sufficient. Loss elicits mixtures of anxiety and depressive feelings. These in turn provoke *defense mechanisms*, which are self-protective psychological constructions activated because of a sense of impending harm. Defense mechanisms by definition are unconscious reactions triggered by anxiety and aimed at reducing affective dissonance.

Feelings of loss associated with endings are more powerful than feelings of gain. People tend to have difficulty with suitably letting go of and moving on from almost anything. It is common to deal with loss and disappointment by spoiling, devaluing, and damaging that which one can no longer have. The expression "sour grapes" conveys the sense of this reactive spoiling. Loss is understood to be empty, vain, useless, and meaningless. Varieties of disappointment and frustration accompany experiences of loss. The following sections briefly review ways to recognize and manage envy, greed, jealousy, and the implicit sense of loss in each. Recognizing and mourning losses successfully over the course of a lifetime sparks creative efforts to attain deeper values and a higher quality of life.

3.7 Envy

Envy can be thought of as a "primitive dimension of mind" dominated by fear, a sense of incompleteness, absence, and neediness. *Primitive* here connotes deeply unconscious perspectives unmodulated by reason that only indirectly filter into preconscious and conscious awareness. In Eastern traditions, envy is understood as "the problem of desire." In these traditions and in *envy theory*, the desires of envy exert a tectonic impact on the mind.

3.7.1 Envy: Sense of Gap and Missing Parts

Envy's primitive quality denotes its profoundly unconscious nature. This quality makes it virtually, though not absolutely, impermeable to reason. Envious states of mind characterized by deeply unconscious feelings of a "gap" or "lack" elicit the intolerable pain of envy, even when environments appear rich and full of opportunities. Such anxiety provokes impatience that centers on awareness of absence. This psychological dissonance, a perpetual state of sensing that something is missing, finds consistent activation in all experience in life's target-rich environments. For example, many standard children's tests of mental ability such as the Wechsler subscales, picture completion and matrix reasoning, specifically assess the capacity to recognize when something appears absent or missing and "needs to be filled in for completion." Awareness of missing parts and needing to complete what is sensed as empty is typical and clearly apparent at ages four and four and a half.

In everyday life experiences, moreover, intolerance of the experience of "not having" elicits ill will and defensive reactions that seek to obliterate feelings of implicit emptiness. In the process, envy attempts to negate the unconsciously perceived high-value target and even the very mechanisms that produce envy. What is felt to be ideal is thus debased. As apparent objects of envy are devalued with such immense force, a self-undermining blowback triggers itself and so in the end corrupts the envier.

In everyday experience, perhaps, the most revealing demonstration of unconscious envy is seen in those who can neither give nor accept help. Persons such as these are frozen in the grip of unconscious envy. Emotional as well as intellectual communication is stifled. Unconscious envy expresses itself as a conscious sense of arrogant self-righteousness. Such people appear smugly independent and insular. They have great difficulty believing that others may have something valuable to offer. Rigidity and brittle, easily disrupted moods are typical. Furthermore, those laboring under strong envy are help-rejecting and reactively contradictory; attempts at constructive dialogues are met with nonagreeable, noncooperative attitudes. A core of irrational fear underlies this impasse in emotional development and makes advances in understanding and accomplishing work tasks seemingly intractable. The age-old and current exacerbations of bitter sectarianism within the same religion, moreover, across the West, Near East, Middle East, and East attests to such polarizations.

3.7.2 Omnipotence and Control

Unconscious envy goes hand-in-hand with "the psychological control dynamic." This dynamic is central to all interpersonal relationships and its externalization is empirically demonstrable in a number of interpersonal control phenomena. Omnipotence denotes "all powerful," and power denotes different levels of crucial influence analogous to what commodities such as electricity or crude oil connote.

Envy theory expands in detail the psychodynamics of envy and *interpersonal control*. A brief synopsis is useful here. The need to control is based on three powerful pillars: (1) the phantasy of omnipotence—strivings toward exerting power and superiority, and reversing one's sense of passivity into activity; (2) the underlying sense of powerlessness; and (3) the envy dynamic.

The unconscious sense of omnipotence is a presumed core feature of unconscious processes at their root, since they remain unmodulated by reason and flexible linear thinking. Omnipotence presumes that all control is within the self and nonexistent outside. Omnipotence, in effect, maintains an insularity that prevents dialogue with reality and subsequent learning. Only as development proceeds over time, does contact with reality—*reality test-*

ing, which assumes developed cognition and mature self-reflection—partly override narcissistic entrenchment in phantasy's influence. The triad of unconscious phantasy, omnipotence, and envy counter the *epistemophilia within the self* and truncate healthy exploration, learning, understanding, and expanded development.

Omnipotence has a core of aggressivity that propels the subject to strive toward forcefully controlling or possessing an overvalued object in the end to fuse and identify with it. This engulfment reduces urges to control by eliminating, at least temporarily, the imagined, dissonant phantasies of superiority-inferiority provoking it. In addition, aggressive omnipotence also seeks to control the overvalued object by domination, subjugation, manipulation, and torture.

Since the core of the envy dynamic is the experience of intolerable dissonance and anxiety resulting from perceived superiority in others and inferiority in the self, the aim of unconscious envy is to spoil and devalue these perceptions to delete unbearable mental pain. Envy uses aggressive control and manipulation both nonconsciously and through empirically observable forceful behaviors to achieve its goal of eradication, however unstable this eradication may be.

Envy arouses implicit questions about fairness and unequal distribution of resources for the person experiencing it. Unconscious feelings of omnipotence and striving to control resources drive envious behaviors. Some everyday examples may illustrate this sense of perceived injustice. Since people typically feel that they need more than they already have, it is not uncommon for them to scavenge for hidden treasures. "Treasure hunting," for example at tag sales, is rooted in implicit envy, although this activity is typically not pathological. The underlying assumption is that the "hunter" does not have the idealized items the privileged purveyor is offering. The implicit feeling of this being unfair and needing remediation remains a subliminal attitude that drives the excitement of the hunt. Another example is seen in those who engage in "white-collar crime," such as hoarding office supplies from the workplace. Such exploitation is justified as the acquisition of what is perceived to be without cost, although it is at the expense of the more privileged. Such tendencies reside on a dimensional spectrum of typical to morally questionable and imply underlying unconscious envy and more consciously felt greed.

Envy can be destructive to psychological processes. As part of human nature, however, envy is not as bleak and unsparing as it may first appear. Recognized and intelligently managed, envy transforms its primitive roots and may spur admiration, emulation, aspiration, empathy, and developmental advantages.

The unconscious experience of envy is natural and inevitable from birth onward. Its wide-ranging influence persists throughout life. Envy is innately restricted to develop only a limited range of positive or negative outcomes, as, for example, the capacity for empathy or its absence and all that this implies. The complexity of these outcomes, however, is virtually infinite.

Unconscious envy is peculiarly insular. Although the dynamics of envy are principally intrapsychic and cause autodestructive anxiety, bitter feelings, and chronic unhappiness, some behavioral correlates are outwardly observable. For example, studies demonstrate that explicit displays of aggression in males are elicited when their status is threatened or insulted, thus calling upon the superior-inferior envy appraisal. While envy as such is silent and internal, aggression is overt and typically displayed as fighting and threats of fighting, which manifest in several ways: material, ritualized, or symbolic. Female primates, by contrast, are not unaggressive but will display aggression in two specific situations: (1) when needing to obtain resources and (2) defending their young.

The dichotomy underlying envy and aggression often appears in the form of perceived contrasts between power and powerlessness. In both sexes, this superior versus inferior evaluation presupposes the mind or ego as a "container" with an underlying experiential sense of "full versus empty." This sense correlates "full" with desirable and "empty" with undesirable. Such contrasts are rooted in models of unconscious envy whose cores involve unbridled omnipotence. Omnipotence and power in its various forms—impulse, wish, sense, feeling, thought, and phantasy—have been recognized as significant in both philosophy and psychology. For example, Plato in his discourse the "Sophist" equated being with power. Freud in his 1913 work, "Totem and Taboo," devoted a large section to a detailed discussion of animism, magical thinking, and the omnipotence of thought.

By prosocial contrast to the more negative interpretations of dichotomies marked by omnipotence, a person might regard another as having superior talent and then try to emulate this. Advantageous adaptation by developing an implicit reference point of relational symmetry rather than polarizations in appraisals is possible and may result from the *healthy maturation of envy*. One should thus broadly consider the nature and role of envy as having potential advantages for motivating positive self-development.

In summary, the concepts of omnipotence and control—foundational to the human condition—materially imbue everyday life. While a ballast in all unconscious operations, these diverse processes are interfused with many other unconscious and conscious motivations. All components significantly influence the differing ways they interact with one another and how this complex web of interactions contributes to behavioral outcomes. Whereas omnipotence is considered to be an inferred psychodynamic construct, control denotes its proxy in the operationalized form of more consciously sensed attitudes and behaviors.

Omnipotent impulses are typically inimical to reality; such impulses for example prompt the formation of psychological defense mechanisms, which may be normatively adaptive or if excessive impairing. Controlling attitudes and behaviors are manifested derivatives of unconscious phantasies of omnipotence characterized by some degree of envy, narcissism, self-absorption, and grandiosity. Such attitudes and behaviors are typically seen as "manipulative"—subtly or forcefully influencing others for one's own purposes rather than primarily for the welfare of the other. Both omnipotence and matters of control are developmentally typical and, to some extent, normative; both range from being subtle and nonpathological to coarse and excessive. When excessive, both omnipotence and control suggest unmatured development or psychopathology.

To illustrate this, some examples though inexact and highly simplified are the following. Excessive omnipotence and control are reflected in a political dictator who orders the death of innocent people, or in a bank robber who attempts to steal the opulent wealth he desires. Normative examples of control by contrast would be a parent who "makes" a child wear a coat in the winter, and someone who relishes owning an unaffordable luxury car but instead chooses to buy a modest automobile. In everyday transactions, those who "must have" the last word are reacting to control impulses that feel urgent; those who say "Why didn't I think of that first?" reveal an implicit sense of feeling powerful and also disclose an envious reaction. As discussed in a previous section, experiences of "loss" or the threat of loss activate unconscious omnipotent phantasies and influence manifest behaviors. In all examples given, the essential message pivots around the manner in which one distinguishes self from other and has developed a capacity for perspective taking. Reacting, responding, and choosing to exert self-control, moreover, both personally and in the way these influence social relations reflects the manner in which unconscious omnipotence is modulated in one's innerworld.

3.7.3 Projective Internalization and the Epistemophilia of the Self

According to my envy theory, knowledge and self-understanding arise from projective internalization. *Projective internalization* describes an individual's biomental capacity, in the awake state, for scanning the environment to find something that positively correlates with and, in turn, grasps an already present implicit knowledge. The cognitive concept of projective internalization correlates with envy theory's psychophilosophical construct, the *epistemophilia of the self*. These ideas imply the axiomatic notion of *contain-*

ment, in which internal expectations identify with external perceptions and result in understanding. Psychological interest is projected outward and adhesively binds to aspects of some implicitly familiar event, situation, or person, and is then encoded. Novelty, in part, is internalized. Biomental development and the capacity for abstraction are advanced. Both projective internalization and the epistemophilia of the self are prime motivators that drive human development.

This construct of an impulse of coherence and integration indicates the innate drive one has to unrelentingly explore the environment in an affiliative manner. This exploratory impulse denotes the aim to grasp, to be understood, and to understand. Implicit in this epistemophilia is a search for unity, connectedness, and meaning. This construct of an exploratory impulse has three major components: (1) the dissolution of cognitive and emotional dissonance, (2) the establishment of interpersonal relationships, and (3) the advancement of biomental development. The target-rich environment of experience explicitly expands the implicit identity sensed between self and other. Rather than being a rigidly hardwired biomental module, epistemophilia is softly assembled and expressed in differing ranges of temperamental and personality styles.

The roots of envy lie in the mind's automatic capacity to sense differences and contrasts, typically polar opposites that imply superior or inferior and ideal or devalued. This capacity for differentiation is based on a more fundamental sense of connectedness characterized by the phrase "like attracts like." The field of evolutionary psychology, for example, has demonstrated universally consistent preferences for one's own in-group, over the other out-groups among humans and other biological species.

Strong preference for native language is universally measurable in infants, children, and adults. Inferences speculate that this is a phylogenetic endowment embedded to biomentally ensure safety in what is familiar versus foreign, and so obviate potential threats. The roots of social unrest, when examined closely, are traceable to underlying unconscious and conscious forms of envy and may correlate with the alerting and fear reactions triggered by such innate discrepancy recognition.

The field of *epistemic cognition* within the cognitive sciences is devoted to studying how thinking arrives at facts, ideas, and beliefs. This field has demonstrated that the process of discovering perceived truth has a broad developmental sequence that consolidates by early adulthood. Three phases are described: (1) dualistic thinking from birth until about the end of adolescence, (2) relativistic thinking that views all knowledge as embedded in contextual diversity of thought and opinion, and (3) commitment within relativistic thinking wherein apparent contradictions are analyzed, synthesized, and integrated. Most persons by adulthood only arrive at the second phase of thinking but continue to trend toward reasoning in terms of the third phase's reconciliation of wide-ranging opposites. This progression, it is suggested here, reflects the cognitive base of the envy dynamic by highlighting typical polarizations potentially followed by incremental reconciliations.

3.7.4 Envy Load: Level of Dispositional Envy

Envy as defined in *envy theory* is an inherent part of human nature. One's "envy load"—his or her level of dispositional envy resulting from innate factors and constitutionally learned experience—can be understood as softly assembled, not absolutely hardwired. In some ways, envy load is akin to the medical ideas of biomarker and endophenotype. For example, as an endophenotype, envy load may suggest an individual trait predisposing to risk for experiencing nonadaptive envy. As a biomental marker, one's envy load reflects the manifestation of one's envious expression. In all these senses, envy load is both a construct and an empirical probe into mental functioning. Envy load's neuromental signature may either cause envy or reflect its effects.

Envy is a readiness to perceive differences, missing parts, and to assign emotional salience to these; this envy load exists on a spectrum from intense to mild. The extremes of this spectrum are experienced as the sense of superior, ideal, or powerful, in contrast to inferior, valueless, or impotent. At the devalued end, surface derivatives of envy may manifest when things and persons are taken for granted or when opinions are sensed as without meaning. Emotionally, envy is felt on a gradient from an insidiously aching malaise to a sharp, biting, and destructive impulse to spoil. When the unconscious roots of envy eventually reach some semblance of conscious awareness, destructive behavioral actions may arise from attitudes of spite and urges for revenge. Unconscious envy at its root is self-undermining, namely, its inevitable "blowback" is characterized by unintended, destructive consequence to oneself.

Envy is the phenomenon of a single person making intrapsychic comparisons to others. In envy, the innate ability to compare and contrast takes on extreme, unmodulated proportions that may become cognitive and emotional distortions if left unchecked.

When not pronounced, however, the dynamics of envy help organize emotions and thinking. In its rudimentary form, envy dynamics set up the perception of contrasts that help one to differentiate and attribute distinguishing meaning to events, attributes, and relations. In the broadest sense, extremes of idealization versus devaluation or superior versus inferior models always remain the mind's default reference points.

The complex array of envy dynamics is a major organizing principle of mental functioning. In other words, the basic roots of envy are not only needed but are necessary for the normal development of the mind; only when envy becomes excessive does its extreme consequences take on disturbing outcomes.

Envy has several core elements. It is almost exclusively subjectively generated and is essentially a nonconscious psychological experience. Envy is exquisitely irrational, intolerably agonizing, eerily silent, resistant to straightforward change, and self-undermining. Such self-damaging effects predominantly pertain to those with inordinately high dispositional envy, but also tend to be features of unconscious envy at any level. When envy's consequences extend beyond the envier's own undermining of self, envious spoiling associated with this occurs. This spoiling negatively transforms attitudes toward others, relationships, and situations that might have been pleasurable into marred and devalued perceptions. In a figurative sense, envy sours the once beneficent milk that fed it.

Lastly, while *envy theory* adheres to assertions of envy as innate and dispositional, it also clearly acknowledges and describes envy's environmental triggers. It is beyond the scope of this book to delineate the plethora of these, but, for example, both personally experienced and group traumas such as life threatening assaults, wars, and genocides may be so devastating as to elicit and reinforce lasting fear and an almost irrevocable mistrust of perpetrators. Subsequently, these may become culturally perpetuated and crystallized in xenophobic dispositions that resist realistic reconciliation.

3.7.5 Envy: Privation Singularly Felt

In attempting to describe unconscious envy, only analogous descriptive approximations can be used since envy is unconscious and "nonverbal." What appears to be a "two-person scenario" only inadequately approximates a provisional working model of envy's self-other dynamics. Envy and polarizations always go hand in hand. Thus the self-other situation is one in which the envier perceives the envied one to be superior. Otherwise stated, the envied one is felt to possess a highly desirable trait, faculty, or experience—all of which are sensed as inferior or absent in the envier. If this contrast is too sharp, it stimulates further growth of envy. Since envy focuses only on *partial aspects* of whole situations, small differences may trigger envious reactions.

Intolerable unhappiness, not mere sadness or depression, may stem from the perceived assets of others. This experience is one of the most outstanding effects of envy. An old adage suggests that envy is the uncanny and ill feeling stimulated by "seeing your neighbor get rich."

Although it is easier to describe envy as a "two-person" phenomenon, envy is *exquisitely singular*. It happens *intrapsychically*, within the privacy of an individual's mind, whether or not another actual person is present. In other words, unlike situations of greed and jealousy that require real material goods and people, scenarios of envy are "virtual"—*unconscious phantasy* productions. Envied others are essentially fantasy creations, and the evoked impulses, feelings, and actions take place in unconscious imagination. This constellation of processes describes *true envy*. Of course, envy's typical manifested development into greed and jealousy takes on more consciously recognized tangibles in the real world of people and things.

Envy does not have to be provoked by frustration, deprivation, withholding, or a sense of injustice, although it typically is. Vitally important to understanding the profound nature of envy is recognizing that, at its experiential core, nuclear envy is the agonizing sense of lacking a quality or power, notably influence. *At its deepest root, envy is energized by a desperate need to control, which counters underlying feelings of helplessness and utter dependency.*

Envy is the experience of true privation, the painful ache and silent suffering that stem from feeling a primordial gap, absence, and hole in the very fabric of one's being. The feeling of loss in envy transcends the idea of having and then not having. Rather, envy is an empty state of proto-detachment—being unattached in a primitive way, as if never having been attached. The envier feels an inner sense of devitalization, primarily experienced through unconscious processes. This privation is a subliminal and silent brooding and loneliness. It is a sense of existential gap or chasm. The varying experiential forms of this sense of privation depend on chronological and developmental age. Boys, girls, men, and women are all subject to envious experience to varying degrees.

Envy is feeling the absence of a highly desirable thing that cannot be possessed—even if a feeble expectation may be present. It is important to restate, however, that the kernel of truth that ignites envy is the actual possession of the desired feature—however nondeveloped—in the envier. Put differently, *epistemophilia* searches the interpersonal environment in an effort to detect even a trace of what is present yet undeveloped in the self. The cognitive mode of *projective internalization* illustrates this.

From an interpersonal perspective, envy is instigated when one compares and contrasts personal results, values, merits, or outcomes with those of another. Objects of such comparisons may be payoff, compensation, reward, recognition, and so forth. Since envy uses its own fantasy standard of comparison to evaluate outcomes, an individual with an excessive quota of dispositional envy will feel resentment when personal outcome is perceived to be less than "ideal." This resentment occurs despite actual merits of the differing efforts of the two, highlighting envy's irrational and illogical base.

However irrational and illogical, such imbalances are felt by the envier to be unjustified and unfair. If they are also perceived to be unrectifiable, resentment and hostility emerge. Consequently, the envier overwhelmingly wishes to rob and deprive the perceived "enemy" of assets and to destroy and spoil them so no enjoyment can be had by anyone. Although such situations are often characterized as *jealousy*, they are more accurately incisive descriptions of individual-to-individual envy. Jealousy is always a three-person situation with clear-cut conscious expression. Envy is far more subtle and unconscious. Although envy is the root of jealousy, envy-based emotions are often simply identified as if they were merely expressions of jealousy.

The envious feeling of personally being "not good enough" may become unbearable. A simple yet direct example of this is the sense of feeling "distressed" by the beauty (woman to woman) or prowess (man to man) of another. In a less obvious way, envy manifests itself in mindless graffiti that spoils the appearance of buildings or vehicles whose value is recognized as disturbingly provocative to the point of needing to deface it. This sort of graffiti typically results from the "artist" protesting a perceived injustice rather than intending to create a work of art.

Envy seeks to spoil and nullify what provokes it. In contrast to the acquisitive and appropriative nature of greed and jealousy, envy in the end aims toward negation through destructive impulses. The very existence of perceived goodness and value threatens the envier. Only by attempts to ruin the perceived source of envy and transform good into bad can the intolerable distress of envy be precariously eliminated.

Unconscious envy, therefore, is a fantasy-generated sequence of pronounced idealization, subjective emptiness of privation, and consequent urges to spoil what is perceived as ideal existing outside the self. Conscious feelings of spitefulness, indignation, and hating what appears "good" are empirical attributes of unconscious envy.

Not all envy is unconscious or destructive. "Simple envy" may be conscious. For example, a mother might say, "I envy my infant's long eyelashes" or "I envy my child's endless supply of energy." In fact, such conventional uses of the term "envy" may be misleading. This imprecise use and its confusion with consciously perceived benign emotions (for example, admiration) are embedded into vernacular conversations and even literature. These colloquial uses of the term *envy* imply consciously experienced emotions of attraction to what is perceived to be an ideal possession of another. The typical mother, for example, experiences these feelings as wonder, admiration, approval, appreciation, and pleasurable without destructive intent. The roots of such admiration are based on love and benign forms of idealization. Unconscious envy, by contrast, is always characterized by hostility and destructive intent.

3.7.6 Envy and Disgust

Envy theory has also proposed that the primary emotion of *disgust* is a conscious indicator of unconscious envy. Envy and disgust are intimately linked. Disgust connotes repulsion in relation to something perceived as spoiled. Research has demonstrated that taste aversions, for example, are virtually unique in their almost instantaneous connectedness; they appear impossible to prevent. Evolutionary programming is suggested as the basis for this finding of what it suggests is an evolved module to enhance adaptation. It is not uncommon to see infants "spitting up," which suggests they sense a food as not agreeable and so automatically eject it. In fact, taste and smell are understood to be more dominant than visual inspection in eliciting automatic states of attraction and aversion in food choices and also related to interpersonal pheromone chemistry.

Envy theory suggests the following in regard to envy and disgust. The envier idealizes something desirable, realizes it is unattainable, and so devalues it. Exaggerations pervade appraisals on the entire polarized spectrum. This devaluation then elicits a need to eject what is sensed as spoiled and hence implicitly sensed as persecuting; thus, the emotion of disgust is elicited. By analogy, spoiling of what had been desirable is akin to encountering milk that is spoiled. A first approach is made to obtain what is understood to be good and palatable. When contact is made, recognition of its being spoiled elicits aversion and disgust. If inadvertently consumed, it is quickly expelled. Studies demonstrate that in addition to happiness, the emotion of disgust is universally recognized through its facial expression across cultures.

Findings that have been replicated across different age groups, professions, genders, and cultures show that disgust appears to be unique. When compared to anger, fear, sadness, happiness, and surprise, it consistently produces a slower heart rate and lower body temperature. These findings suggest a negative reaction in contrast to forms of excitement, and correlate with envy's qualities of privation, gap, and absence.

This discussion has focused on the basics of unmodulated, unconscious envy. Since envy is a natural part of the mind's normal composition, the positive aspects of the *healthy maturation of envy* will be addressed later and also in the section on *envy management skills*.

3.8 Greed

Greed denotes the mental state wherein one voraciously desires and aggressively attempts to take in more than one actually requires or more than the giver is willing to supply. Such acquisitiveness is not directly influenced by the material prosperity actually possessed since one's idiosyncratic construals of value—essentially subjective assessments—motivate greed.

In greed, one's grasp of an object or event is not easily dissociable, namely separable; rather it is adhesively trenchant. An implicit underlying fear is that of not having enough. Contemporary concern, for example, with a perceived concentration of wealth in the 1 percent versus the 99 percent who believe they pay a hard price for this inequality illustrates the pain of such emotional fears, at least on an implicit level.

Greed is based on underlying unconscious envy, but its motives and operation differ significantly in that greed is *more consciously felt* than envy. Greed tends to focus directly on valued inanimate things, whereas jealousy typically involves a direct wish to possess a valued person. Jealousy expresses itself in an actual three-person context, whereas greed only indirectly involves others.

Greed and craving are intimately correlated. These aspects of desire, like envy, are powered by a motivation for expansion. In an important sense, greed is motivation gone wrong; it is pathologically contractured grasping. Greed is the impulse prompting a person to acquire more resources, usually of material goods, so that others have less. Signs and symptoms of inordinate greed are reflected in ungratefulness, an inability to share, exploitation, and excessive accumulation. Feelings of greed and the ways they are enacted are typically in conscious awareness. It is an empirical phenomenon that is directly observable since it is accompanied by explicitly measurable behaviors. Greed may act like a feverish, all-consuming preoccupation that drives actions. Greed's mindset is driven by the compelling mandate, "What's in it for me?"

Greed is an unquenchable hunger whose primitive goal is ruthless extraction to the point of damaging the valued resource. In many ways, greed reflects an impairment in normal impulse control. Greed is the inability to modulate "stopping." The quality of this capacity originates in both the traits and temperament endowed in infancy and in parent's imparting containment skills—how to start and how to stop—in childhood.

Greed is typically associated with matters of money and wealth. These matters are, in essence, resources viewed differently by males who place great value of accumulation of financial assets in contrast to women who prize having a companion who can supply adequate resources for her and her offspring. Ambitions toward these ends in both men and women are normal when not excessive or inimical to the possibilities that reality offers.

Realistic anxieties about economic uncertainties and financial matters are common, but greed and its anxieties may also be experienced in subtle and insidious ways. This area of acquisitive impulses is evident in psychiatric disorders such as kleptomania, compulsive buying, and pathological gambling. The intrinsic value of objects of greed may be secondary to their perceived significance in relation to a third person. Put differently, greed may seek material items perceived to be valued by others. On the deepest level, greed is the irrational impulse to rob and drain resources.

The clearest example of the destructive role of greed on a large scale in everyday life is the contemporary deterioration of financial markets. Groups and institutions may share and enact complex greedy impulses through excess profiteering. Children needing to be first in line or to have more toys are examples of simple greed. Adults and children who are "collectors" and "hobbyists," however, may have socially appropriate acquisitive impulses that are not forms of irrational greed.

The extent to which greed may be a component of stealing and other antisocial, sometimes criminal, behaviors is an interesting and unsettled question. The neurobiological basis of such callous and unemotional behaviors of both children and adults is just beginning to be uncovered.

Although it is beyond the scope of this book to examine these matters in detail, abnormalities in parts of the limbic system have been correlated with abnormal fear conditioning and the perception of threatening stimuli. One example of a correlated biomarker is hyporesponsiveness of the amygdala detected by fMRI studies in early childhood. Researchers have proposed that such information may help identify subgroups with a biological predisposition to criminal behavior, often marked by greed. In addition, studies measuring impulse control and choice show strong correlations between the functioning of the amygdala and the prefrontal cortex, an area that directs reason, learning, and selection. Increased grey matter in the medial orbitofrontal and anterior cingulate cortices also correlate with aspects of psychopathy. The anterior cingulate has been shown to correlate with a diverse range of experiences such as social comparison, unfairness, high provocation, aggression, and empathy. The medial prefrontal cortex and the anterior cingulate cortices, moreover, are both implicated in the core features of envy. This research is mentioned to reiterate the biomental nature of personality and behavior.

Objects of greed may include actual material items such as food, money, and assets, as well as nonmaterial items such as knowledge or superior rank. Neuroimaging studies have demonstrated that part of the evolutionarily older reptilian brain of humans called the "nucleus accumbens" is strongly activated by stimuli perceived to be pleasurable and rewarding. Activators may include food, sex, and money. This positive brain correlation is part of the biomental basis of the desire dimension of greed.

Empirically, greed involving food can have purely subjective significance. Most greed, however, involves conscious, premeditated, excessive acquisitions of material having socially regarded objective value. Greed may be so ingrained, however, that actual conscious awareness becomes submerged in an automatic, nonconscious activity.

Greed and exploitation have strong positive correlations. For example, some people take pleasure in cleverly exploiting and hoarding resources that appear to be accessible to everyone. This may even include materials labeled "free." Greedy people typically scan local and remote resources in order to target what seems to be free or lawfully abundant. They then make concerted efforts to take full or greater advantage of these perceived opportunities. Greed's exploitative course is typically preceded by strategies that increase fear in others. Fear elicits inhibition and weakens others' resistance to the exploitation. When acquisition becomes excessive, it is predicated on the impulse of ruthless exploitation. A serious lack of empathy and capacity to share underlies such potentially destructive depletion. Greedy acquisitiveness is often hidden beneath a façade of seemingly lawful entitlements or rationalizations emphasizing arguably justified deservingness.

Although destructiveness is an incidental though not insignificant by-product of greed, it is not a primary goal as it is in envy. The destructive quality of greed, however, may be intense; often, a hateful, rapacious demeanor accompanies greed. Greed and exploitation act to deplete resources over time, leading to upsets in social and financial markets.

Greed is based on the underlying feeling of always being "hungry" for additional supplies and resources. This subliminal feeling frequently becomes conscious. The emphasis in greed is on hungriness rather than unhappiness, as is the case with envy. Greed's irrational sense of being insatiable originates from the unconscious notion that possessed resources are somehow damaged and not sufficiently complete enough to provide adequate satisfaction. Pronounced idealization may make objects of greed appear more valuable than they are. This exaggeration drives greed's relentless need to consume.

The greedy person is cognizant of his or her desires in contrast to their underlying base of unconscious envy. Greed is often a defense against envy since greed is consciously felt, less emotionally intense, and seemingly more manageable. The anxiety of envy is implicit and amorphous, whereas the anxiety that accompanies greed is explicitly disturbing. Greed and indiscriminate identifications with desperately needed objects are positively correlated. Greedy people typically have action plans to obtain what they desire.

Greed results in two related phenomena. One is a trend toward the feverish hoarding of inanimate objects. The other is instability in maintaining interpersonal relationships over time. Greed is a clear-cut feature of obsessional disorders in which irrational collecting and pronounced, repetitive ruminations are prominent. This excessive need also reflects mental defense mechanisms evoked by the perception of damage or spoiling since "perfect specimens" are often sought.

In greed, the defense mechanism of "doing and undoing" is prominent. It is a precarious attempt to reduce the anxiety provoked by unrelenting greedy impulses. "Doing" is evident in repetitive thinking and behaving. "Undoing" is motivated by an underlying feeling of perceived damage or imbalance, often attributed to personal shortcomings. Greed has features similar to obsessive-compulsive constellations, such as ruminations, doubt, ambivalence, and a harsh conscience or superego. "Doing" seeks to restore and undo the implied damage. Pathological hoarding ("doing") results in the collection of such quantities of goods that they are often damaged (impetus eliciting the need to "undo") by virtue of sheer quantity, mass, and deterioration over time.

The psychodynamics of these activities have a base in greed and envy. In envy, emphasis is on active spoiling; in greed, emphasis is on robbing, accumulating, and inadvertently damaging. The psychodynamics of greed can be observed in interpersonal relationships when a greedy person feels he or she has damaged or harmed the previously valued other and then tries to deny this by some form of emotional distancing such as separation or divorce.

In contrast to greed, normal ambition is the adaptive striving for improvement of self and significant others. When not excessive or destructive, healthy rivalry and competition accompany ambition.

3.9 Jealousy

Jealousy is related to, though distinct from, greed and envy. Jealousy involves a three-person situation in which the jealous one feels deprived of positive attention of the loved other, which has been given to a third person judged to be a rival. Jealousy is a more social phenomenon than greed or envy, for it has exteriorized, discernible interpersonal behavioral accompaniments. In contrast to the intrapsychic and singular nature of envy, jealousy is always an actual interpersonal phenomenon. The aim of the jealous person is to become reunited with a restored love object even though these attempts are thwarted by the obfuscating interference of another. Greed, by contrast, is more often a relationship to inanimate materials.

Typically, the jealous man or woman feels more comfortable near the desired partner and far from the perceived rival. A gender difference, however, is clearly displayed in the phenomenon of jealousy, in which both parties act in ways designed to prevent the other from involvement with a third person. Men try to separate their lost love object from the rival; women try to separate their former loved object from their current love interest. In men, emphasis is on sexual infidelity; in women, it is on emotional infidelity. For example, men report stronger negative feelings than women when suspecting sexual infidelity, while women report stronger negative feelings than men when suspecting emotional infidelity that threatens long-term relational stability. While these suspicions and their consequent behaviors are observable, they typically arise from intense, implicit reactions. Sexual and emotional aspects of jealousy directly correlate with pair bonding, and reproduction. It has been suggested that romantic love creates affiliative bonds, whereas sexual jealousy—when moderate and normative—tends to preserve such bonds.

In jealousy, there is a conscious sense of being dismissed. The nonconscious root sense of "deletion" is characteristic of jealousy's base in unconscious envy. Feelings of loss, dismissal, and deletion in jealousy having a basis in unconscious envy, therefore, may be inferred. Jealous behaviors are reflected in explicitly personal and interpersonal dramas. Shakespeare's play *Othello* beautifully demonstrates how jealousy operates in various ways in the lives of the players.

Jealousy is the feeling of conscious deprivation, of being deprived of something desirable that once was clearly believed possessed and enjoyed with sufficient satisfaction. It can also be the result of feeling the loss of what might have been had. In other words, the object of jealousy may either be real or an aspirational fantasy. Both the actual and imagined loss are clear and conscious experiences. Jealousy is the acutely poignant and conscious feeling of being excluded, being left out, and losing something. Fear, uncertainty, and ambivalence accompany these feelings. The conscious cognitive quality of jealousy is reflected in the frequency of conscious ruminations, obsessions at times, involving the lost object and the rival.

Jealousy feverishly seeks to maintain its dependent social bonds. Ambivalence in these interpersonal relationships characterizes the clash between feelings of love and protection with feelings of hate, protest against loss or its threat, and a wish to delete the rival to undo such feelings of unrequited love. Attempting to hold on to what is ambivalently loved and at risk of being lost constitutes jealousy-based possessiveness. Jealous loss, or the threat of loss, may be felt as sorrow, grief, sadness, bereavement, mourning, or even clinical depression. In all these reactions, a sense of loss of control, passivity, and deep hopelessness is dominant. The sense of loss is principally experienced as feeling left out and excluded. If these feelings are directly related to the inability to let go and are not directly confronted and worked through, a nonconscious retreat to feelings of persecution—characteristic of envy—may result. Envy so uncovered is expressed as a brutal hatred of the rival with accompanying devaluing, even destructive, attacks, whether ideational or enacted.

When defense mechanisms are elicited to deny and mask jealousy's depressive feelings, they may precariously shore up one's sense of stability. Jealousy itself has defensive features that vacillate from manic excitement characterized by rage, control, manipulation, and domination to sheepish plaintiveness. Jealousy, however, often serves as a more ego-syntonic defense (felt as acceptable to the person experiencing it) than ego-dystonic envy (felt as deeply distressing and conflictual). The mental anguish of consciously experienced jealousy, however tormenting, is more accessible to conscious attempts at management than unconscious envy's gnawing resentment, which can only be handled instinctually by some sort of an ultimate deletion.

Jealousy always has an unconscious core of strong envy. This can be seen clearly in the jealous person's attitude toward the rival, notably in love triangles. The rival is the object of envy-based hate in that the competitor is seen as superior to the inferior, excluded envier. The envier feels an overwhelming deficiency of a vital personal resource—a sense of impotence and valuelessness. In addition, jealousy is based on an envious wish to spoil the relationship between the other two lovers who also are seen as a combined unit—"a couple." In contrast to jealousy's core of envy and hate, its more refined expression is reflected in the guilt experienced when one senses that he or she has damaged an ambivalently loved object.

Jealousy is powerfully driven by "love gone wrong." Although the jealous person aims to destroy or eliminate the rival, this is only secondary to his or her primary affectionate wish to regain the ambivalently loved person. Jealousy fears to lose what it has or had; envy feels pain at seeing the rival have something desirable. *A jealous person is threatened by the loss of something good; an envious person is threatened by the very existence of something good.*

Whereas envy is an intensely private, brooding, and silent intrapsychic experience with relatively little "acting out," jealousy manifests itself as intensely passionate. Jealousy expresses itself on interpersonal levels where motoric and behavioral action and reaction are prominent and glaring, as in the phenomenon of protests seen in a variety of different situations. Sexual jealousy, for example, is among the leading motives for murder among men in every culture.

Envy is cold, bitter, seemingly dispassionate, and humorless. Jealousy behaviorally expresses itself in a frenetic, passionate, hyperactive, and frenzied interpersonal drama. As mentioned, clinically significant depressive and manic-like features accompany jealousy, though not envy. Jealousy's emphasis is on exclusive possession—not destruction—of what is perceived as the desirable.

3.10 Dynamics of Frustration in Envy, Greed, and Jealousy

Envy, greed, and jealousy usually operate together in varying combinations after infancy. When one predominates, its own characteristic sense of frustration overshadows the mind.

Frustration is a strong negative emotional reaction to an aim or goal that is not achieved because of some obstruction, obstacle, opposition, blockage, or personal deficiency. While frustration is an angry, automatic reaction that taps into fantasy expectations, its correlate *disappointment* is a more consciously sad feeling of distress and upset when an expectation is not realized. Feelings of disappointment may range from very mild to seriously traumatic depending on the realistic versus idealized characteristics of the anticipated result.

Envy contains an intolerable feeling of elemental frustration and virtual emptiness. It is sensed as an aching privation, attributable to the perceived absence of a highly desirable trait or tenuous possession never fully owned. It is a loss of something never even possessed. Feeling envy and behaving in a withholding manner (for example, unhelpful, stingy, or miserly) are almost synonymous since the envier psychologically "freezes his assets." That is, he or she makes unavailable anything believed to be personally valuable for fear of even greater losses. In jealousy, frustration follows feeling strong passivity from being dismissed; in envy, frustration is an ache of emptiness that further seeks to delete.

Frustration's relation to greed is in the feeling of partial but disturbingly incomplete satisfaction. It is the feverish pursuit of attempting to acquire, but never achieving, a satisfactory procurement of what is felt to be needed. The greedy person can never feel satiated.

Jealousy is the feeling of depressive frustration. This frustration, often accompanied by protest, nonacceptance, and fighting, is clearly reactive to perception of a real or threatened loss of what one once possessed but now feels deprived of. Feelings of disappointment and sadness run through jealousy.

The jealous person believes that he or she fundamentally needs what might be lost or could have been had. Jealousy is feeling disappointingly excluded from being permitted to adequately love. The jealous person feels a strong sense of responsibility for loss of a damaged relationship. Unlike in envy, feelings of guilt are prominent in jealousy. When the jealous person cannot let go of what is or will become lost, he or she becomes "stuck" and experiences difficulties with thinking clearly and carrying out activities of daily living.

Jealousy awkwardly seeks to repair and restore damage, unlike envy's attempts to spoil. In envy, this amounts to a paradox of autodeprivation. In jealousy, deprivation is determined in different ways by the roles of each of the three players—the jealous person who feels deprived, the person he or she wants to regain, and the hated rival believed to be the cause of the deprivation.

The jealous one suffers because he believes he has deprived himself of what he wants. She suffers because of her damaging actions to the heart of the loved one, her destructively damaging intent to the rival, and her wish to spoil the new connection between the rival and the lost love object. Though jealousy's intent is not to further ruin the interpersonal relationship with the loved one, it may nonetheless cause this outcome through its feverish, outward behaviors.

3.11 Competitiveness

The roots of competitiveness can often be traced to envy, greed, jealousy, and their permutations. A nonconscious underpinning is fear originating in a predatory defense system of dominance-submission to avoid and escape predators. The biological drive to obtain energy in the form of food morphs into a drive to achieve superiority in the competition for resources such as mates, safe dwellings, money, and so forth. Issues of power, control, and dominance underlie competitiveness. In this sense, competition is a trigger for aggression. Attitudes and behaviors characterized by exploitation have competitive elements that may morph into contemptuous victimization of others.

Ritualized strategies such as competitive sports, for example, reflect competition between rivals with an underlying tone of passion and jealousy. A "win-lose" scenario is the context within which competitiveness plays itself out. The awareness of distinctions, differences, and strengths drives competition. These themes are expressed when others are viewed as adversaries, contenders, and "opposers."

The mind naturally categorizes events using a superior-inferior template, placing loss at the negative pole. Losing assumes that a person is a "loser," which implies failure and inadequacy. Often, unrealistic extremes are established as "winner or loser," "first, second, or third place," and so forth. While these distinctions may have relative meaning, they are often overgeneralized and implicitly imbue a person's everyday values with subtle and not-so-subtle distortions. When ambition is grounded in normal competitiveness, extreme underlying conflicts involving envy, greed, and jealousy are absent.

Competition aims to possess a desired, limited resource, often at some expense to another. Competition is typically an observable and overtly complex behavior. When competitiveness is hostile, aggressive, and destructive (for example, in ruthless business deals or war), unmodulated negative emotions drive its ferocity. When competitiveness is more cooperative (for example, with team effort and community solidarity), its roots have undergone a more benign maturation.

4. THE HEALTHY MATURATION OF ENVY

The healthy maturation of envy correlates with a greater development of the capacity for empathy. The roots of unconscious envy are attenuated by the development of empathy. This mitigates envy's undesirable influence on attitudes and behaviors. This diffusion also modulates the intensity of greed, jealousy, and competitiveness. These beneficial changes add balance to emotional life and subsequently shift implicit thinking from polarized thought toward more modest assumptions.

The early childhood roots of beginning to feel separate in the sense of being parallel and becoming aware of an explicit wish to acquire materials and objects, along with saying "mine" in the toddler years, sets a persisting mental template of experiential and perceptual "two-ness," which typically implies opposites. The ability to go beyond strong impulses to acquire and maintain sole proprietorship, that is, the ability to share, needs to be learned and developed over time. It occurs in consonance with recognizing that two individuals, though separate, can develop the ability to partake equitably of similar resources. Perhaps, one could say that the developmental onset of the capacity for cooperative play and perspective taking that emerges between ages three and four sets the stage for this lifetime endeavor. As this realization takes hold, ease in giving in addition to taking is developed. Giving over time may refine itself into attitudes of generosity and so enhance nobility of character.

The attenuation of unconscious envy and the expansion of empathy create conditions for an inner experience characterized by greater freedom of choice; that is, one is not necessarily enslaved by emotion—thought bridled by fear. Instead, cognitively flexible freedom of thought enables one to ask questions, ponder diverse ideas, and select intentional choices. These reallocations in information processing alter the experience of the self and others in ways that are felt to be restorative. Self-development is *constructive personal activism* predicated on a sense of adequate self-agency and self-efficacy. Self-volition—the power to change—both drives self-change and helps consolidate it.

The *healthy maturation of envy* occurs naturally, to varying degrees, in infancy and childhood. In an elemental way, this healthy maturation is propelled by an individual's innate "instinctive resourcefulness." This is ordinarily a latent capacity consisting of implicitly based understanding and procedural reaction patterns. It emerges out of the silent assessment of the meaning of a situation and the preconscious, almost automatic deployment of actions to reinstate—correctively—equilibriums after stressors have caused disruptions.

Raw love as idealization becomes modulated into states of admiration characterized by awe, wonder, pleasure, and approval. As these further develop, appreciation and incipient gratitude further enrich personal feelings. As perspective taking expands, both admiration and gratitude as personal feelings transcend merely egocentric concerns and subsequently are displayed in the complex capacity for lived empathy. Gratitude manifests itself as a form of ultimate cooperation and reciprocity—responsively returning help given with help either in kind or raised to a higher level. Empathy is a personal sense of caring, understanding, and intuiting the mental states of another, but includes the potential for action in the form of helping behaviors.

Empirically, the healthy maturation of envy denotes both internal and behavioral attitudinal shifts. There is a diminution of anxious feelings, and an increased capacity to experience and express consideration for others. The capacity for and implementation of concern denote greater increases in agreeableness and cooperativeness. Carefully taking the feelings, ideas, and needs of others into account parallels deferring one's own exclusively self-oriented concerns. Such *consideration for the other*—a crucial component of helpfulness—may be one of the most striking features of matured empathy. The grasp of another's needs and an accommodating responsiveness reflect this.

The above descriptions reflect mechanisms that correlate with the healthy maturation of envy. Lasting psychological change, however, always has an indolent quality, and remains resistant to "easy" change. Change, slow and lengthy as it is, is possible. Yet, the transformations toward developing empathy require continuing vigilance, intentionality, effort, reflection, and strategic remodulation over time. The typical, initial, natural beginning maturation of *agency* or goal-directed behaviors at approximately ten months of age requires further nuanced sophistication, namely, one shaped by intentionality that only the refinement of empathy provides. Ordinary processes of growth, maturation, and development, when normal and typical, suggest a naturally occurring emergence of empathy. This initially natural occurrence requires intentional efforts over time for greater development and subsequent pragmatic expansion. This essential dimension of consolidating the healthy maturation of envy, therefore, must be *actively earned*.

The ability to experience patience in the face of ambiguity is crucial to furthering this development. The underlying modulation of automatic cognitive and emotional splitting mechanisms (the sense of "two-ness" as opposites) that underlie such uncertainty requires experience over time. These attitudinal shifts from educing polarized dualisms toward grasping multiple perspectives—a meeting of opposites—require practice to consolidate. This development exemplifies the indispensible significance of situational learning from experience to secure emotional conviction over time. To effectively modulate primitive dispositional endowments such as fear and envy, learning from experience must include nuanced and repetitive challenges seen from different angles and managed in novel ways over time.

Indeed, advances in the capacity for empathy occur recursively over a lifetime. Experiences of loss, the way losses are faced, and how one manages their "letting go" can help consolidate empathy.

Self-reflection emerges from self-development strategies such as practicing *envy management skills*, psychotherapies, and self-help endeavors. Such reflection promotes the refinement of envy and the expansion of empathy. Merely supplying the facilitators that may lead to the development of empathy is not enough to produce change. A core factor underlying change is an individual's motivated ability to accept and use these resources effectively over time. Both personal motivation and help from others is essential. Finding the "right" mentor, coach, guide, therapist, and so forth creates a productive interpersonal field in which emotions creatively resonate and support the clarification and emergence of ideas consolidated with conviction.

Significant psychological change entails the integration of thought, feeling, and attitude reinforced in diverse situations over a lifetime. This maturational development denotes the experience of effective *creativeness*, namely, sensing innovations in both short-term problem solving and ushering in longer-term visions that integrate and use new technologies in realizing and implementing more effective life skill strategies.

Empathy denotes identifying and sharing in a "common experience" compassionately perceived to be in another person. This capacity arises from continuous biomental maturation, developmental progression, and learning from experience. As empathy develops, primitive cognitive dissonance, polar attitudes, featural perception, and mutually exclusive categorization become more integrated. Psychological splitting, therefore, is lessened.

More unmatured perception views experience in "parts" with emphasis on distinction and separateness. The purview of empathetic experience by contrast is characterized by an awareness of all aspects of an experience as interactive participants of a synergistically operating whole. The development of empathy is inversely related to the mitigation of envy.

The emotional aspects of "perspective taking" include the capacity for recognizing porous though substantive boundaries between self and others, as well as taking increased responsibility for thoughts, actions, and obligations. This entails developing a healthy locus of personal control and self-regulation. Self-other distinctions, perspective taking, and personal responsibility lead to an emerging sense of caring about the effects of one's behavior on others. In many ways, empathy embodies identifying with another's thinking and feeling. The empathic person then experiences a sense of concern—compassion and the impulse to help.

Guilt has a fundamental role in the development of empathy. A healthy sense of guilt emerges from a base in the capacity for empathy. Healthy guilt denotes impulses of remorse and regret for perceived damage done to a loved or ambivalently loved other. Reparative strivings to repair the damage done are, in fact, creative acts. In the broadest sense, the resolution of psychological splitting—perceived in unconscious phantasy as damaging—and of tendencies toward envy are achieved by the active integration of love and hate. The damage done to a loved one, at first elicited by hateful feelings, is now felt as healthy guilt—beneficent remorse. Healthy responses to guilt evoke reparative urges. Thus, constructively managed guilt signals that envious processes are in a state of maturation.

Another aspect of guilt is identifying with the problems, faults, or guilty feelings of others. This often-overlooked dimension of both empathy and guilt may be nuanced and expressed in the experience of compassion. It calls for mercifully acknowledging damages done, whether by the self to the self or from others to others.

Isolated events involving guilt, remorse, and reparation are significant but not sufficient to consolidate empathy. The emergence of the experience of guilt and the progressive development of empathy are recurring developmental processes that refine themselves over the course of development. Guilt, reparative endeavors, and expansions of empathy are iterative and novel sequences rather than cyclic repetitions.

The healthy maturation of envy is reflected in a person's level of empathy, and empirically in attitudes and demonstrations of gratitude—the impulse to return kindness with kindness. The quality of a person's empathy may differ as it expresses itself in differing relationships of intimacy—family, community, and society. Social anthropology has referred to these "self-other relations" as differentially existing in family, village, clan, tribe, and nation.

The development of empathy, moreover, softens the competitive edge of the overt manifestations of envy, greed, and jealousy. When modulated, these emotions contribute to gratifying drives toward ambitious achievements. The healthy maturation of envy and the development of empathy connote that the emphasis in "losing" shifts from resentment and failure toward satisfaction in having tried to achieve success and sensing a more optimistic need for continued improvement. In social and financial commerce, moreover, empathy promotes cooperativeness and demonstrates the long-term survival strategy afforded by trade rather than plunder.

The healthy maturation of envy lessens inner persecutory and tyrannical attitudes and so permits greater freedom for ranges of positive, creative thinking to occur. This offers rather than constricts opportunities for choice. Accepting the fact of having inclinations for destructive and damaging attitudes and acts is followed by a healthy acknowledgment rather than denial of guilt. Such responsibly acknowledged guilt is constructive. A sense of wholeness, not brokenness, imbues these perspectives. In a practical way, personal inclinations for revenge become sublimated by being transferred to group, cultural efforts toward just, less violent resolutions. On a material level, moreover, inhumane aggression in the form of truly irreversible destructiveness, for example, murder and nuclear war, may be qualitatively modulated, if not significantly diminished.

Parents can foster healthy cooperativeness by reminding children that play, learning, and teamwork may entail enjoyment and fun in the process itself, rather than in needing to win at all costs. Developmentally, a healthy cooperative striving can be seen in the industriousness of the elementary school child. Team sports may begin to interest the six- to twelve-year-old and function as healthy expressions of competitiveness that promote social competence and personal developmental mastery.

The healthy maturation of envy mitigates the harshness of greedy and jealous impulses by softening their stridency as described above. Biomental child development and envy theory advance the proposition that mental health and creativity emerge from the challenges that the dynamic interplay between love and destructiveness provides. The adhesive and affiliative forces of love, together with the inevitable human trends toward destructiveness, provide endless opportunities for personal and social advancement.

Indeed, it is through such *adaptive diversification* in identifying and meeting these challenges across the life cycle that resilience is activated and reinforced. This adaptive diversification denotes a healthy *reality sense* by which the positive and negative experiences of life's challenges are met. When rational thinking is not obliterated and supplanted by omnipotent fantasies used to evade reality, empathy and compassion are nurtured.

Two strategies for facilitating the healthy maturation of envy, for example, are the conscious use of envy management skills and the conscious and unconscious biomental reparation elicited by aesthetic endeavors. fMRI studies demonstrate that emotional conflict can be resolved through top-down inhibition of fear. This pathway includes activation of the rostral anterior cingulate cortex to inhibit the amygdala. Cognition—error detection, aspects of empathy, and decision making—can thus constrain visceral reactivity.

While a more complete elaboration of forces driving the healthy maturation of envy is beyond the scope of this schematic discussion, the healthy maturation of envy to proceed in substantial and enduring ways requires *unconscious consent*. This complex psychodynamic process entails motivation, intentionality, self-development techniques, and randomness. Random events connote indeterminate, apparently unintentional, and nonconscious operations that may or may not be discoverable. This consideration correlates with the primary nature of unconscious envy's persistent mental template over the lifespan.

During the healthy maturation of envy over a lifetime, one's self-schemas and unconscious phantasies refine themselves. Self-identity and self-concept organize more coherently. Impulsivity and fear are mitigated as the sense of patience and impulse control strengthens. Ambivalence and guilt stimulate reparative trends that foster greater security and trust in the self. Three dimensions of one's basic identity become enhanced: emotional self-confidence fosters a stronger sense of belief in oneself; cognitive self-efficacy promotes greater surgency in the belief that one has a real ability to take action; and active self-competence increases effective action based on beliefs and goals.

On an empirical, interpersonal level, the normalization of dispositional envy is seen in a lessening of unhealthy interpersonal control and manipulation. Possessiveness diminishes. One's grasp on people and situations is less adhesive and more flexibly dissociable. Attachments and separations, therefore, occur within normative ranges. Mental dynamics undergo a paradigm shift. Envy, with its egocentric emphasis on control, intrusion, and aggressive manipulation, attenuates. Empathy supersedes modulation of cognitive and affective processes through greater self-integration, self-regulation, and the capacity and willingness to help others in an agreeable, cooperative, and mutually beneficial manner.

In summary, the healthy maturation of envy reflects a high-end integration. Both a passive and an active dimension characterize such integration. The reflective self must, to some extent, surrender to its impersonal, reactive, primitive biomental givens, notably those neural substrates endowed through biological transmission. This occurs naturally only to a limited degree. Integration, to be effective, requires active work on the self—motivation to search for one's own psychological truth. This self-reflective work is an active receptivity to grasping one's own mental contents over the course of a lifetime.

Such motivation may arise intentionally or merely appear; its provocateurs have a real-time but implicit history. Herein is the element of unconscious consent discussed above. Moreover, whatever primitive emotional impulses a person has must be acknowledged and superseded by survival wishes whose grasp denotes and embraces self in the company of others. This necessitates rational perspective taking and the refinement of empathetic concern that encompasses self with others—whether kin or those perceived as being more distant. This refined quality of mind denotes higher-level self-containment. It adds a humane, transcendental quality of inclusiveness to the way a person experiences him- or herself, and others.

Psychological integration, moreover, results in coalescence of cognitive executive functions with balanced feeling states. This in turn brings about a sense of greater self-efficacy. The capacity for volition—intentionality and decisive action—strengthens and is brought into production, that is, real-time productivity becomes enhanced.

3.1 Envy Management Skills

The development of the envy theory model has sought to contribute a great deal to an understanding of the theoretical foundations of mental and emotional psychodynamics. One beneficial yield has been the development of *envy management skills* to practically recognize and manage envy toward positive ends. This group of skills adds pragmatic traction to envy theory.

The construct and practical application of *envy management skills* are useful extensions of the elegant work of Melanie Klein's theoretical contribution—the normally occurring *depressive position,* which is the psychological reconfiguration that both attenuates and supersedes the earlier normative *paranoid schizoid position* characterized by unconscious envy (newborn to approximately three to four months of age). Both "positions" denote the infant's psychological relation ("ego") to the primary caregiver ("object"), thus establishing the configuration of the first developmental "object relations" as template for all further personal relationships throughout life. Empirically, the paranoid-schizoid position in earliest infancy correlates with the observable period of infant "colic" characterized by crying, inconsolable discomfort, and appearing to be hungry but refusing the breast. Whereas the *normal* developmental configuration characterized by the paranoid-schizoid position is more "impersonal," its later reconfiguration into the *normal* depressive position becomes "personal," namely, characterized by the emerging capacity to perceive the other as another person and to care for that other.

With three main papers in 1935, 1940, and 1945, Klein described the infant's substantive ego integration of loving and hateful attitudes toward the same primary caregiving parent, which occurs around six months of age. This dynamic unification vacillates in healthy ways from enduring feelings of affection to intermittent feelings of ambivalence and anger. The coherent integration of love and hate enhances a sense of paused concern. Subsequent feelings of consideration support the incipient development of empathy.

Envy management, in essence, creates conditions whereby the inevitable experience of intolerable ambiguity often at the base of envy is not felt as a compelling need to jump to a conclusion or resolve the pressure of the accompanying desires. By contrast, envy management quells the need for immediate reaction wherein impulse control is strengthened. A person gradually begins the lifelong process of learning to pause, step back, and wait in ambiguity. Such conscious envy management, as described here, denotes engagement in a learning program that entails a series of cumulative lessons, practice, and incrementally refining performance.

Envy management skills may be regarded as prerequisites to "conflict resolution training." This training encompasses recognizing emotions, extremes in attitudes, interpersonal aims, options for reconciliation, potential decisions, and the ability for self-correction. The use of "I statements" such as "I am feeling upset about the way things are going" reflects assertiveness and constructive criticism. Such professional training has found a vital place in interpersonal and social conflicts, such as marital discord, intraorganizational strife, and even war. The envy theory model sees the primitive roots of these social predicaments to be in the *infant's dilemma—the clash between needing to love and hating to need.*

Like all basic psychological attitudes and states, envy cannot be eliminated. The aim of envy management skills is to employ conscious techniques to modulate the waxing and waning of naturally occurring envy and its adverse effects on the personality and behavior.

Various strategies to recognize and strengthen envy management skills follow. It is important to reiterate that besides nurturance and discipline, effective parenting includes a third superfactor for success: example. Exposing infants, preschoolers, school-age children, and adolescents to positive behaviors, such as sharing and helping, enriches biomental input and activates innate resources for furthering positive behavior. These are the intermediary subgoals leading to refinements in perspective taking and empathy.

Helping children recognize inaccurate foundations and unjustifiable consequences of extreme emotions and attitudes should be a continuing practice. In some sense, this exposure is a form of learning that constitutes an essential part of the developing capacity for resilience to counter stress and life's inevitable adversities. To the extent that a child already has some natural capacity for developing empathy, envy management skills may enlist the range of an individual's biomental plasticity to facilitate further empathy's emergence. Envy management skill training also can become a part of larger life skills programs in academic settings, or can be part of social skills training in a variety of educational and counseling contexts.

Envy management skills are a form of psychoeducation, which is a therapeutic educational strategy that directly informs people about a variety of matters relevant to mental health and quality of life. Providing an understanding of mental challenges and emotional attitudes, psychoeducation can uncover mental strengths and constructive coping strategies while offering a range of further management resources. In psychiatry, such education may include information about mental disorders, their signs and symptoms, and the extensive interventions (psychosocial, psychopharmacological, self-help, dietary, hygiene, legal, and so forth) used to prevent, treat, and manage them.

In academic settings, envy management skills can become a part of larger life skills programs, or they can be part of social skills training in counseling contexts.

The goal of psychoeducation is to provide people with a practical approach to understanding and constructively coping with distressing psychological challenges, especially their prevention and consequences. Psychoeducation employs a format of reason, logic, and common sense. It incorporates accepted principles of social propriety and compliance.

Psychoeducational envy management skills are derived from envy theory. Psychoeducation, though often understood to be an important part of interventions within psychiatry, is not formal psychotherapy. It uses conscious cognitive processes to convey and teach the logic and reasons related to psychological problems and treatments. Psychoeducation addresses the circumference of personality and learning with the hope of creating conditions that permit the individual to actively seek out more intensive strategies that may reach nonconscious processes at the center of the self. Put differently, psychoeducational skills are a peripheral, though important, route in the approach toward attitudinal change.

Psychoeducational and didactic formats cannot address the unconscious dynamics of envy. Psychodynamic psychotherapies and other professionally guided techniques aimed at motivated, intentional, self-introspection over time are more directly suitable for such an endeavor. In contrast, more consciously based learning and explorative techniques can be useful preliminary tools for recognizing envy and providing strategic skill sets to help regulate envious experience. For example, direct work on conscious greed and conscious jealousy, which are derivatives of unconscious envy, may be useful in engaging, if only to a limited extent, access to unconscious envy. Such motivated, conscious approaches may provide incentives that support the healthy maturation of envy. The acquisition of envy management skills can also complement formal psychotherapies when needed, even though these therapeutic approaches are distinct in aim and technique.

Unmodulated envy is a matrix for the experience of continuing, low-grade stress. This stress results in both subjective and interpersonal difficulties. Recognizing and managing stress and envious attitudes are skills that can be taught. Emotional intelligence and skills in social communication are supported. Exposure to empathetic states of mind is thus initiated.

3.1.1 Fundamentals of Envy Management Skills

Three fundamental principles are at the core of envy recognition and stress management. First, a person learns that change characterizes all real-life experience at every moment. His or her needs continuously change. Thus individuals are alerted to prepare perceptions to anticipate and grasp change as real, inevitable, possible, and desirable; this helps restructure negative expectations that may be chronic. Recognition of such inevitable life changes implies preparation for transitions. Second, an individual's personal best level of performance is used as the primary measure for comparison with his or her future goals for improvement. Third, a person explores alternative choices, such as cooperation, reciprocation, and sharing, in various contexts where disruptive envy is apt to emerge.

Envy management skills are best kept simple in explanation and application with children. Avoiding overload in either maintains more sustained focus and encoding. Gradual elaboration—identifying principles, setting goals and planning, and initiating, executing, and regulating these—complemented by visual imagery introduced gradually over time—is beneficial. It is essential, furthermore, to explicitly review how to proceed when something goes wrong.

"Functional fixedness" or perceiving things limitedly and rigidly in terms of their common use and associations, and "mental set" or using strategies that have worked in the past but may no longer be viable in the present, are addressed in great detail. Thus, psychological conditions are created that may induce a new fluidity in both of these limiting attitudes to readapt to newly recognized, current life situations. These strategies (expecting transitions, identifying one's own personal best, and fluidity of perception) minimize comparisons between people and center attention on the individual primarily in comparison to him- or herself. They foster a renewed impetus to regard change as possible, valuable, and workable.

Respect and citizenship perspectives underlie emerging abilities for alternative choices, and both of these are identified. Pause and attention to developing self-reflection are reinforced. Implicit attitudes that foster dehumanization are countered by making explicit each individual's basic human rights, such as for food, clothing, shelter, freedom to choose, the need to be respected and not harmed, and to be treated justly.

Feelings for valuing the trait and expression of "likeability" are stimulated. *Respect* is both an attitude and a behavior that includes recognizing boundaries between persons, paused reflection in the face of interpersonal differences, and empathetic listening. *Citizenship* connotes behaviors that reflect an individual's respectful and helpful participation in small and large group situations, from the family, peer group, and classroom to the neighborhood, community, and society at large. These principles, and their social-ecological implications, emphasize that sustainable successes always require "win-win" motivation and shared outcomes. The value of equitable justice between people and within groups, as denoted by envy management's emphasis on developing agreeableness and cooperativeness, is addressed in this way and counters the hostility engendered by "us versus them" dichotomies. Perspectives encouraging a meeting of opposites are encouraged. A likeable face with agreeable names is put on perceptions of others.

Since unconscious envy is reflected in conscious attitudes of prejudice and hostility, fostering cooperation between individuals and groups may be a tangible aim of intervention. Engaging all members of a group is essential to minimize the "bystander effect" of passivity and diffusion of responsibility. The central strategy is to identify common issues, struggles, problems, and challenges among all involved. Once this is achieved, an action plan that targets goals is formulated. The last step is proposing that solutions may only be achieved through cooperative action and shared problem solving. Conveying envy management skills in this way taps into the innate need to belong and feel approval in group interactions. Cooperative action and shared problem solving also enhance feelings of safety and security in group affiliations. Belonging, approval, and feeling safe reinforce adherence. These in turn reinforce taking cues from others for prosocial behaviors. This overall guideline is the basis for consciously approaching aspects of envy through coaching and guidance.

Envy management skills help people reorient motivation from its primitive ground in a reflexive need for unconsidered acquisition to a more temperate attitude of self-expansion, self-development, cooperativeness, and sharing. Allied emotions and attitudes shift from subliminal pessimism and stagnation based on resentment, negativity, and destructive behaviors toward more enthusiastic, flexible, option-focused thinking. A more sustainable development of these pragmatic skills is achieved by techniques that emphasize the linguistic identification, clarification, and recognition of envy in everyday life. Since envy and its expressions may be subtle and provoke delicate feelings, tact and great sensitivity in applying these techniques are important. Periodically redefining problems helps recognize change and maximize fresh perspectives.

The healthy maturation of envy correlates with diminished greed and jealousy. To the extent that envy is modulated, healthy and adaptive pro-self and prosocial feelings and attitudes come to the fore: empathy, sharing, helpfulness, gratitude, and cooperation. Emotional intelligence and its skill set of competencies enhance a person's ability to relate positively to others. Those who have achieved degrees of these skills tend to be flexible, self-motivated, confident, cooperative, helpful, and efficient adults.

Psychoeducation has a protective effect on many levels. As primary prevention or exposure preparedness, it may decrease the incidence of envy-related problems. Secondary prevention using cognitive envy management skills may help lower the rate of malignant envy-related problems through early detection and intervention. The tertiary level of illness intervention directly treats established envy and so decreases the complications that may arise. This level may require psychotherapeutic intervention. Each of these approaches has important temporal aspects of corrective action—before, when, and after difficulties arise.

Ingredients promoting resilience, therefore, encompass wide ranges of abilities and strengths. Some of these techniques build personal and social competence, self-confidence, social connectedness, character, values, self-regulation, effortful control, self-efficacy, and adaptive coping skills.

It behooves the astute parent, physician, or teacher to recognize that, even in cases of apparent school difficulties or borderline intellectual functioning, the presence of important derivative aspects of unconscious envy may be among the primary reasons for a child's difficulties. I have elaborated many of the details of these ideas and techniques in other work, found in the references.

5. AESTHETICS: EVOCATIVE AND REPARATIVE DYNAMICS OF ART

Biomental child development offers parents a unique, if unusual, approach to raising and nurturing children. Besides its foundation on the principles of child development, this text also highlights considerations of envy, greed, and jealousy. Sections on envy management skills and also aesthetics are included for their development-enhancing, preventive, and reparative value. Understanding envy management skills is a conscious endeavor with strong cognitive requirements. Adding complexity to this idea, the biomental perspective understands *aesthetics* to be a grasp of unconscious processes that empowers their materialization through sensually conscious awareness.

Attention to envy management and aesthetics are not superfluous or unrelated considerations. Both are vital to well-being and mental health. An appreciation of emotions and their relations to the arts deepens understanding of growth, maturation, and development. It also fosters prevention, restoration, resolution, and creativity. Understanding child development in the light of potentially health-promoting perspectives on envy, greed, and jealousy makes the biomental child development perspective life-positive.

Recognizing the dark side of human nature reflected in these emotions requires a capacity to pause, step back, and temporarily tolerate such typically disturbing experiences. Pause and self-reflection permit an individual to become in touch with often avoided, yet compelling attitudes and feelings. If not faced, these feelings tend to impede successful emotional development. When identified and managed properly (for example, through effective parental guidance, psychoeducation, psychotherapies, or aesthetic endeavors), development becomes transformative. In other words, what had been a hidden impediment may become a source of insight and inspiration.

Envy management skills are preventive and partly remedial approaches that use conscious awareness of the more obvious and relatively tangible derivatives of envy—pronounced idealizations, superior-inferior polarizations, disdain, and xenophobic attitudes. Further, the broad area encompassed by aesthetic considerations—art appreciation and artistic endeavors—shares similar goals yet employs a significantly different format.

Aesthetics—the empathetic appreciation of and involvement with a range of artistic pursuits—is a prime avenue toward accessing and creatively managing latent conflict and untapped personal potential. To accomplish such resolution and creativity, aesthetic productions evoke idealization in its many forms. As alluded to in an earlier section, art forms are symbolic representations of unconscious phantasy that are lucidly, at times enigmatically, displayed. This process of regarding something as "art" denotes that the artist or person viewing or hearing the "art" projects his or her own unconscious phantasy construal into the considered object of art.

According to the theory of aesthetics proposed here, the salient aesthetic experience requires the participant to actively defer his or her psychological position to a state of biomental receptivity. This includes, at least in the beginning, suppressing awareness of aims, intentions and a preconceived plan along with consideration of technical rules of composition. Placing oneself in this relative state of openness both reduces the ego's approach of logic and reason and also stimulates the nonconscious processes wherein the wellspring of creativity resides. Such unconscious processes so provoked are given an entry point into conscious awareness. The participant, therefore, allows art to happen, that is, to creatively emerge so that it then may be handled by the more technical abilities that the conscious mind may apply toward managing it through appreciation or actual implementation. What is unconsciously sensed as incomplete or lacking in the self is projected into the art object and undergoes a partial transformation. Together with this base of subjective privation, an unconscious sense of damage done to an ambivalently loved other launches the aesthetic impulse. These unconscious motivations are rooted in what envy theory terms *the infant's dilemma* and its provocation of early unconscious guilt. This primitive infantile template seeks repeated reconciliation over the life cycle. Aesthetics provides a major modality—however vicarious—toward this end. Impulses so stirred aim at transforming this experiential subjective gap into something more complete, powerful, and superior through reconciliation—the maturation of unconscious envy via compassionate repair. Guilt is the motor that drives more complex impulses aimed at repairing damage done. Such iterative transformations induce incremental remodeling of psychic structure and function over a lifetime.

While envy spoils inner creativity, external creations of art are attempts to restore this damage. Aesthetic operations on levels that address—yet transcend and so refine—the primitive clash of feelings of love and destructiveness seek to accomplish this. These transformative actions operate on nonconscious information processing as a "poetry" attempting to give significance to one's grasp of meaning. In this sense, anything natural or artist-made can be appreciated as artful and used to accomplish repair. For example, a landscape, sunset, painting, symphony, literature, and so forth may provide the outer trappings used to impute aesthetic meaning. Both one's projection into the object as well as contextual variations contribute to definitions of aesthetics. The intentions and work of the artist make what might have been ordinary into something extraordinary, just as is true of the intentions of one appreciating the artful beauty of a natural rainforest.

Aesthetic meaning is driven by the epistemophilia within the self; it is in the end the search for salient relatedness to other persons. Envy theory advances the proposition that the healthy maturation of envy is, in fact, a self-vivification. The healthy maturation of envy and the capacity for empathy make up the essence of self-integration and the creativity from which meaningful personal enhancement and successful interpersonal transactions emerge.

The outer structure taken by artistic impulses—its formal aspects—may be visual (in drawing, painting, sculpture, and so forth), auditory (in music and spoken word), movement-based (in dance, yoga, tai chi, and so forth), written (in literature and poetry), architectural, or any combination of these forms. The written word, as an example, has survival-enhancing properties. The form, proportion, rhythm, balance, and harmony within language are felt as attractive and even pleasurable. In this sense, language reinforces its continued experience. Both the communicational value and aesthetic beneficence of language motivate and propel adaptive explorations.

Aesthetics implies sensitivity to an appreciation of stimuli primarily supplied by the senses—seeing, hearing, touching, smelling, and tasting. Conventional Western art forms typically employ mostly seeing and hearing. Other traditions use these but expand them by including the use of other sensory modalities. Touching may be subsumed within the kinesthetic and proprioceptive processes that accompany movements of dance and exercise. The olfactory sensation of experiencing aromas may be stimulated by a renewed appreciation of the natural scents of flowers, greenery, soil, and running water. Aromatherapy with fragrant essential oils, such as lavender, rose, lemon, and so forth, can be creatively used to heighten perception and induce tranquility. Taste is most available during the process of eating, wherein one can renew appreciation of the complexities of spices and herbs. Such sensitizing awareness of sensory faculties helps focus attention and can promote periods of pause and appreciation that help regulate impulse control. These strategies emphasize the eco-corporeal nature of persons.

Well-done art is inspired more by unconscious and subliminal urges than by reason and logic. Fantasy, imagination, and even dream images play a large part in facilitating the skillful transition from inner emotional experience to outer material manifestation. Artistic endeavors reach beyond mere sublimation of sexual wishes; they become procreative. To produce a work of art, however, conscious skill, intentional planning, and directed effort contribute heavily to art's platform of basic intuitive impulses. The interplay of unconscious phantasy and actual reality, therefore, influences perception. Subsequent implementation into material representations is based on such perceptions. Works of art, accordingly, may be regarded as concrete symbols. The power of these symbols derives from their bridging the inner and outer worlds. To the extent that this succeeds, an emotional detonation erupts. Both the artist and the one viewing or hearing the work of art experience this "in-touchness" with nonconscious processes, principally felt and difficult to articulate. Perhaps badly done art may be the wild and chaotic manifestations of unresolved unconscious phantasy whose translation is awkward, fragmented, and garbled.

The composition of a work of art includes features of balance, space, geometry, focal emphasis, movement, time, contrast, proportion, unity, variety, and repetition. Elements of design may include line, color, melody, shape, form, mass, harmony, light, and texture. The skillful blending of all these components makes up the artist's technique.

Art appreciation encompasses interpretation of the meaning of a work as well as evaluation of its form, artist, and the context in which it was created. Judgment about a work results from an informed opinion. All forms of art reflect underlying unconscious phantasies of the artist as they resonate with and evoke those of the viewer. The observer identifies, to varying degrees, with the art experienced. Art appreciation is the product of the implicit (unconscious) and explicit (conscious) feelings and ideas that a work of art stirs. All these considerations differentiate art from mere cognitive action. Art, however, may complement consciously applied envy management skills as well as other psychological techniques aimed at self-improvement.

Not only art appreciation but also the very act of producing a work of art requires a state of mind that the author has previously described in chapter 3 in the section, "Anticipatory Readiness to 'Grasp' Mother." This state of mind entails attentional processes that resemble the infant's attention. Elements of this include alertness, vigilant modulation, poised watchfulness, explorative witnessing, indeterminate, experimental anticipation, poised open-handedness, readiness to grasp, and the impulse to contain. Such a mental set is bidirectional; it simultaneously looks within and without. It is receptive to grasping ephemeral unconscious phantasy, and it is receptive to forming or expressing images that are reparative constructions of this experience of simultaneity. Moreover, in other domains where self-development is valued, such experience is termed "meditative awareness."

A more detailed discussion of aesthetics is worthwhile at this juncture. While envy management skills use and work on the conscious aspects of envy, greed, and jealousy, aesthetic pursuits address unconscious processes, especially implicit aspects of values, morals, and aspirations that underlie conflict. In many ways, the influence of conscience and the experience of guilt so crucial to the healthy maturation of envy also spur the creative process. Specifically, it is the nonconscious collision between goodness, beauty, and benevolence against destructiveness, ugliness, and cruelty that fuels the drive to repair the subliminally felt damage caused by such recurring clashes. Otherwise stated, at all stages of life both children and adults struggle with resolving and repairing specific instances of damage to perceived goodness. Depressive anxieties over damage press for resolution. This complex process of identification, engagement, and reparation is, in essence, rooted in an underlying wish for personal expiation and self-forgiveness.

The artist struggles to reconcile unconsciously felt exaggerations and distortions in the experience of the self by reworking them into more consciously experienced harmonies. Aesthetic sensitivity, in fact, may be the acknowledgment of both beauty and benevolence alongside an inescapable but hoped-for management of ugliness and cruelty.

Creativity, therefore, is an integration of disparate elements to produce a result characterized by novelty, originality, elaboration, flexibility, and some sort of value and usefulness. Put differently, creativity is the dialectical interplay of beauty as harmony and wholeness and ugliness as fragmented asymmetry. Artistic production is more a re-creation of unmatured, tenuous, and damaged ideals than a production *ex nihilo*. In this sense, art is a restoration of underlying conflict and reparative attempts at resolution. All great works of art, however, typically manifest "flaws" that suggest their underlying source in unresolved unconscious conflicts between typically enduring polar opposites existing within the self. These "fault lines" are a sense of gap and guilt that may be understood to be nodes out of which creativity is spurred.

Art, whether by observation or actual production, provides new opportunities for recognizing and positively enabling the healthy maturation of envy. This enhancement, in part, results from the fact that art demands some level of psychological (emotional and cognitive) work rather than merely being passively entertaining. Art offers generative propositions and permits cognitive processes to draw from an enhanced ability for divergent thinking, namely more fluid mental operations that transcend the restrictions imposed by linear thought. For example, the evocative aspects of art stir admiration and emulation and so lessen the envy, greed, and jealousy that constrain freer thought. Empathy, in fact, is reinforced by renewed feelings of admiration that are enhanced by the sense of awe that art fosters. Although a work of art may be a completed act, each time it is newly perceived, fresh perceptual, emotional, and conceptual reconfigurations are aroused in the viewer.

Although formal works of art embody the aforementioned principles in more sophisticated ways, family art projects can serve as valuable parenting tools. Such projects may be mutual activities that involve children in shared attention to, reflection on, and decision making about what materials to choose and how to arrange them. Art made and exhibited in the home may be exemplified by a table display specially arranged to reflect the season of the year. For example, in autumn, a yellow or orange colored cloth plus items such as pumpkins, colored leaves, and apples can be artistically arranged. In summer, a range of bright colors can provide the background for seashells, sand, and seasonal flowers. This decorative table can also provide a sense of unity between nature and indoor life. It can be a reminder of what I have termed the *eco-corporeality*—the biomental self as an integral part of extended nature—of humankind. The construct of eco-corporeality suggests an organic unity between self and environment highlighting both interpenetration and interdependency. I have also been impressed with visual art that emphasizes not spatial but color-perspective, because dynamic colors often evoke a range of subliminal feelings that piques the imagination and stimulates a fresh sense of wonder. Mental space is both excited and expanded hence providing greater potential and room for creativeness.

Artistic endeavors offer parents opportunities to palatably address a range of negative developments that had been previously shunned or ignored, even if inadvertently. Such negativity includes irritable mood, fearful temperament, and aggressive behaviors. In effect, possibilities of evoking creativeness may stir enthusiasm and renewed hopefulness.

In envy theory, *creativeness* is a conceptualization that is foundational. It includes but transcends the idea of creativity. Creativeness encompasses both cognitive and emotional expressions aimed toward the continuing achievement of empathy. As discussed in the overview, nonconscious, experiential ingredients transacted in infancy are coded nonverbally and sensed as memories within feelings. These biomental "petroglyphs" are embedded impressions in unconscious memory. Again, in a metaphorical sense, an individual's infancy is preserved as his or her own ancient culture. Self-reflection and creative impulses excavate this seemingly lost personal "cradle of civilization." Access may also occur through "recognition memory," which is noticing when a stimulus is similar to one previously experienced even though there may not be cognitional thought representing that stimulus. The entire

range of aesthetic experience from viewing to doing trigger these nonconscious elements that, in turn, are cues around which creativeness is spurred
and creative ideas and actions crystallize.

Creativeness underlies the vivifying quality of motivation, enthusiasm,
and perseverance. It reflects the *epistemophilia within the self*. Such a love
for understanding introduces new ideas, forges continuing innovations, and
resourcefully invents biomental designs for living. The ability to grasp and
then let go of both unconscious phantasy and its materialized expressions
over time may be a core feature of the aesthetic experience.

Creativeness both elicits and helps consolidate processes that engender
novel ideas. Their creative use supports the implementation of a number of
quality-of-life skills. Cognitive and emotional shifts, as described previously,
reconfigure personal experience. The disconcerting discrepancies and anxieties provoked by envy, greed, and jealousy are thus downregulated. Aesthetics therefore constrains, if not disempowers, this ultimate psychological default state of dissonance.

6. SELF-REFLECTION

Self-reflection is the periodic turning of attention inward toward oneself in
order to make sense out of one's attitudes and behaviors. It is a process of
becoming aware of subtle as well as more explicit feelings and attitudes.
Interactions with other people typically evoke a variety of implicit emotional
reactions; self-reflection helps bring these previously unrecognized feelings
to awareness.

Self-reflection is a consciously understood and intentional effort to direct
attention to the integration of new information with that stored from past
experience. Self-reflection helps select, apply, and monitor the effectiveness
of attitudinal and behavioral strategies.

Everyday living often is replete with demands, obligations, and schedules
that force people, particularly parents, to set agendas and routines that become rote and automatic. This process has provisional utility but can blind a
person to being present in the immediate moment, especially how children
are feeling and the difficulties they may be experiencing. Rigid routines
diminish the harmonious rhythmicity of planned yet dynamically flexible
sequences of activities of daily living.

Self-reflection serves many purposes. Self-reflection, which includes self-
exploration and self-discovery, offers periods of pause during which incipient knowledge may organize. Previously considered ideas are afforded a
chance to consolidate, latent possibilities are given opportunities to germi-
nate, and novel aspirations may emerge in these apparently quiet times. Pre-

viously experienced extremes of emotion can be examined, become attenuated, and then be re-experienced at more modest levels. Thus, learning from experience has a chance to formulate itself, and the energy of activation for new beginnings can be set in motion.

Although this section is brief, self-reflection remains fundamental to good parenting. It is a skill that can be developed and refined. Consciously remembering to examine one's reactions and responses, especially when intense, helps develop self-reflection skills. Times of self-reflection yield intermittent glimpses of hitherto unrecognized insight.

Self-reflection may occur "on the spot" or may occur in retrospect, after the heat of the moment subsides. Self-reflection after moments of intense emotion can provide a period of pause, thus defusing, discovering, and deepening understanding of self, child, and parenting. In any event, it is a necessary parental skill that offers insight into oneself and fosters a greater empathy toward children.

7. RESILIENCE AND PROTECTIVE FACTORS IN CHILDREN, ADULTS, AND FAMILIES

Psychological resilience to adversity expresses itself as the positive adaptive resonance that emerges when risk of harm collides with protective factors against harm. Resilience safeguards psychologically valuable, adaptive coping skills and minimizes undesirable outcomes. It drives one's capacity to negotiate successful outcomes under stressful and adverse conditions. Each child and adult has arrays of explicit strengths and untapped innate potentials that stressors, conflict, and trauma call into action. Rather than an "all or none" phenomenon, resilience provides individuals with a plasticity of potential fail-safe mechanisms for survival.

Resilience is *adaptive resourcefulness*. It is not a circumscribed trait but rather a dynamic process encompassing cognitive, emotional, and physiological strengths. Resilience stems from *adaptive intelligence, instinctive resourcefulness*, and *biomental plasticity*. Resilience, by definition, comes forward in response to significant distress. Risk factors may result in future potential harm, damage, and loss; hazards are severe risks that have a relative certainty of resulting in serious harm. Both risks and hazards and the stressful anxieties they provoke can be avoided or ameliorated by preventive measures.

Resilience is dynamic stability that prevents or modulates major biomental decompensation. Resilience results from active learning from experience. This multilevel process encompasses and coordinates the individual, family, and extended social resource groups into alliances that are collaborative and mutually beneficial. Hence, the resilient individual withstands regression and decompensation, thus becoming psychologically more competent in an enduring and sustainable fashion.

An individual's resilience has both endowed and learned components. Resilience helps individuals not only seek help but also actively negotiate what the facilitating environment has to offer. Intelligently managing trauma denotes short-term adversity that is successfully overcome and may result in what is termed "posttraumatic growth." Such growth further strengthens the personality, leading to greater protection against subsequent stressful events.

An array of potential child risk factors for negative psychological and social outcomes includes poverty, low socioeconomic status, inadequate parenting, parents with mental illness, low birth weight, trauma, and child abuse, to name just a few. These factors may increase the likelihood of adversity, although they are not absolutely causative. The personal qualities of the child under stress may powerfully mitigate potentially negative outcomes.

Recent research findings substantially suggest that harsh discipline is a strong, consistent predictor of *externalizing* symptoms such as aggressive and conduct-disordered behaviors in children up to age nine. By contrast, in children from birth to age five, multiple factors consistently predict *internalizing* symptoms such as anxiety and depression. Some of these factors include poor physical health of the child, maternal emotional distress, harsh discipline, and overinvolved, overprotective parenting. A plethora of evidence-based research is now strongly suggesting that early-life adversity induces epigenetic alterations in multiple gene regulatory regions on a molecular level.

Risk factors for adults may result in increased vulnerability to the negative effects of stress and to the development of psychological disturbances such as anxiety and depression. Behaviors may also become impaired depending on temperament and situational stressors. Major risk factors include unresolved adversity from childhood, poor intellectual functioning, negative bias in information processing, and negative attitudes. Pessimism, learned self-helplessness, unhelpfulness to others, uncooperativeness, social disconnectedness, incapacity to manage high levels of fear, avoidance of teamwork, and failure to seek needed help are all associated with poor outcomes. Protective factors for adults are the reverse of their risk factors, with particular emphasis on a capacity for cooperative teamwork, a high value placed on altruism and helpfulness, and the capacity to tolerate high levels of fear and still perform effectively.

Stressful life events trigger the stress response of the body's hypothalamic-pituitary-adrenal axis (HPA axis). Cortisol, released from the adrenal cortex, is called the "stress hormone" since it is crucial in modulating the stress response. Research has demonstrated that chronic traumas, particularly early in life, may lead to enduring abnormalities in the HPA axis and associated neurotransmitters (serotonin, dopamine, and so forth). These neurophysiological changes, in turn, may underlie the development of psychopathological states. In other words, profound early adversity can cause biological changes that are difficult to reverse. In later life, stressful life events can trigger pathophysiological changes associated with medical conditions such as cardiovascular disease.

Protective factors for children include nurturing parents, intelligence, positive self-perceptions, reasonable self-regulation in temperament, mood, and impulse control, strong motivation, self-efficacy, and controlled exposure to risk. The development of constructive coping skills, responsibility, self-confidence, and social competence allows for successful management of stress and adversity.

Protective factors related to resilience particularly include strong family relationships that are caring, encouraging, and supportive. Effective parenting helps children develop self-confidence, high motivation, positive self-image, emotional self-regulation, intelligence, flexible problem-solving skills, effective communicational skills, proclivities toward strong social engagement, and appropriate support seeking.

Protective factors may be more important than risk factors in determining outcomes. Protective factors that strengthen families include parents' continuing efforts to build their own resilience. This process entails recognizing stress and its effects, developing and refining constructive coping skills, developing creative problem-solving strategies, using strong and succinct communicational skills, maintaining a positive attitude, and seeking help when outside assistance is needed. Developing networks of support and social connectedness as potential resources for parenting information, problem solving, and emotional support are protective strategies. Such networks are especially useful when concrete support (such as food, clothing, and shelter) is required.

Protective factors also are built from adequate knowledge of parenting skills and child development—among the goals of biomental child development. The awareness and refinement of transactional sensitivity over the life cycle engenders protective factors. And last, the social and emotional competence of children and their ability to interact positively with others, to self-regulate emotions and impulsivity, and to effectively communicate enhance the parent-child relationship and strengthen a family's ability to become more resilient in overcoming adversity.

Most experts in the field of resilience and stress research agree that, while stress and risk factors are unavoidable, controlled exposure accompanied by successful coping is instrumental in promoting resilience. Experts in this field state that the strongest predictor of resilience is, in fact, exposure to childhood trauma that has been handled successfully. The proven neuroplasticity of the brain provides the biological foundation for the development of substantive resilience along the entire life cycle.

Resilient children demonstrate reasonable competence in successfully mastering age-salient, culturally expected developmental tasks. The entire process of development and its natural challenges are made up of positive and negative features, easy and hard tasks, and successes both easily achieved and acquired through more effort. Resilient children resonate in positive, adaptive ways with the to-and-fro rhythms of the interactions among physical growth, maturational unfolding, and developmental experience.

REFERENCES

Allison, C., Baron-Cohen, S., Wheelwright, S. J., Stone, M. H., & Muncer, S. J. (2011). Psychometric analysis of Empathy Quotient (EQ). *Personality and Individual Differences, 51*, 829–835.

Baron-Cohen, S. (2004). *The Essential Difference: Male and Female Brains and the Truth about Autism.* New York: Basic Books.

Baron-Cohen, S., Lombardo, M. V., Auyeung, B., Ashwin, E., Chakrabarti, B., & Knickmeyer, R. (2011). Why are autism spectrum conditions more prevalent in males? *PLoS Biology, 9*(6), 1–10.

Bayer, J. K., Ukoumunne, O. C., Lucas, N., Wake, M., Scalzo, K., & Nicholson, J. M. (2011). Risk factors for childhood mental health symptoms: National longitudinal study of Australian children. *Pediatrics, 128*(4), 865–879.

Bayers, K. (1994). *Living Architecture.* Hudson, NY: Anthroposophic Press.

Bion, W. (1962). A theory of thinking. *International Journal of Psychoanalysis, 43*, 306–310.

———. (1962). *Learning from experience.* London: Heinemann.

Bjorklund, D. F., & Hernandez-Blasi, C. (2005). Evolutionary developmental psychology. In D. Buss (Ed.), *The Handbook of Evolutionary Psychology*, pp. 828–850. Hoboken, NJ: Wiley.

Blair, M. L. (2007). Sex-based differences in physiology: What should we teach in the medical curriculum? *Advances in Physiological Education, 31*, 23–25.

Blair, R. J. R., Peschardt, K. S., Budhani, S., Mitchell, D. G. V., & Pine, D. S. (2006). The development of psychopathy. *Journal of Child Psychology and Psychiatry, 47*(3/4), 262–275.

Brown, T. A., Osterman, L. L., & Barnes, C. D. (2009). School violence and the culture of honor. *Psychological Science, 20*(11), 1400–1405.

Buss, D. (2005). *The handbook of evolutionary psychology.* Hoboken, NJ: Wiley.

———. (2007). *Evolutionary psychology: The new science of the mind.* Boston: Allyn and Bacon.

Charney, D. S. (2004). Psychobiological mechanisms of resilience and vulnerability: implications for successful adaptation to extreme stress. *American Journal of Psychiatry, 161*(2), 195–216.

Cohen, S., & Wills, T. A. (1985). Stress, social support, and the buffering hypothesis. *Psychological Bulletin, 98*, 310–357.

Costa, P. T., Terracciano, A., & McCrae, R. R. (2001). Gender differences in personality traits across cultures: Robust and surprising findings. *Journal of Personality and Social Psychology, 81*, 322–331.

Craik, F. I. M. (2002). Levels of processing: Past, present . . . and future? *Memory, 10*(5–6), 305–318.

Damasio, A. (2000). *The Feeling of what happens: Body and emotion in the making of consciousness.* New York: Mariner Books.

De Brito, S. A., Mechelli, A., Wilke, M., Laurens, K. R., Jones, A. P., Barker, G. J., Hodgins, S., & Viding, E. (2009). Size matters: Increased grey matter in boys with conduct problems and callous-unemotional traits. *Brain, 132*, 843–852.

Drury, S. S., Theall, K., Gleason, M. M., Smyke, A. T., De Vivo, I., Wong, J. Y. Y., Fox, N. A., Zeanah, C. H., &Nelson, C. A. (2011). Teleomere length and early severe social deprivation: Linking early adversity and cellular aging. *Molecular Psychiatry*, May 17. doi:10.1038/mp.2011.53

Dumas, J. A., Albert, K. M., Naylor, M. R, Sites, C. K, Benkelfat, C., & Newhouse, P. A. (2012). The effects of age and estrogen on stress responsivity in older women. *American Journal of Geriatric Psychiatry, 20* (9), 734–743.

Eliot, L. (2000). *What's going on in there? How the brain and mind develop in the first five years of life.* New York: Bantam.

———. (2010). *Pink brain, blue brain.* New York: Mariner.

Erikson, E. (1993). *Childhood and society.* New York: W. W. Norton. (Originally published 1950)

Etkin, A., Egner, T., Peraza, D. M., Kandel, E., & Hirsch, J. (2006). Resolving emotional conflict: A role for the rostral anterior cingulate cortex in modulating activity in the amygdala. *Neuron, 51*(6), 871–882.

Fagan, T. F., & Faustman, D. L. (2004). Sex differences in autoimmunity. *Advanced Molecular Cell Biology, 34*, 295–306.

Feldman, R. (2003). Infant-mother and infant-father synchrony: The coregulation of positive arousal. *Infant Mental Health, 24*(1), 1–23.

Freud, S. (1974). [1913]. "Totem and taboo." In: *Standard edition of the complete psychological works* (Vols. 13). James Strachey (Ed.). London: Hogarth Press.

Gao, Y., Raine, A., Venables, P. H., Dawson, M. E., & Mednick, S. A. (2010). Association of poor childhood fear conditioning and adult crime. *American Journal of Psychiatry, 167*, 56–60.

Garcia, J., Brett, L. P., & Rusiniak, K. W. (1989). Limits of Darwinian conditioning. In S. B. Klein & R. R. Mowrer (Eds.), *Contemporary learning theories: Instrumental conditioning theory and the impact of biological constraints on learning.* Hillsdale, NJ: Erlbaum.

Gerritsen, L., Tendolkar, I., Franke, B., Vasquez, A. A., Kooijman, S., Buitelaar, J., Fernández, G., & Rijpkema, M. (2011). BDNF Val66Met genotype modulates the effect of childhood adversity on subgenual anterior cingulated cortex volume in healthy subjects. *Molecular Psychiatry*, May 17. DOI: 10.1038/mp.2011.51

Hetman, G. D., & Legare, C. H. (2004). Children's beliefs about gender differences in the academic and social domains. *Sex Roles, 50*, 227–239.

Huxley, V. (2007). Sex and the cardiovascular system: The intriguing tale of how women and men regulate cardiovascular function differently. *Advances in Physiology Education, 31*, 31–40.

Inagaki, T. K., & Eisenberger, N. I. (2012). Neural correlates of giving support to a loved one. *Psychosomatic Medicine, 74*(1), 3–7.

Isaacs, S. (1948). On the nature and function of phantasy. *International Journal of Psychoanalysis, 29*, 73–97.

Klein, M. (1930). The importance of symbol formation in the development of the ego. *International Journal of Psychoanalysis, 11*, 24–39.

———. (1931). A contribution to the theory of intellectual development. *International Journal of Psychoanalysis, 12*, 206–218.

———. (1935). A contribution to the psychogenesis of manic-depressive states. *International Journal of Psychoanalysis, 16*, 145–174.

———. (1940). Mourning and its relation to manic-depressive states. *International Journal of Psychoanalysis, 21*, 125–153.

————. (1945). The Oedipus complex in the light of early anxieties. *International Journal of Psychoanalysis, 26*, 11–33.

————.(1957). *Envy and gratitude*. London: Tavistock.

Labonte, B., Suderman, M, Maussion, G., Navaro, L., Yerko, V., Mahar, I., Bureau, A., Mechawar, N., Szyf, M, Meany, M.J., & Turecki, G. (2012). Genome-wide epigenetic regulation by early life trauma. *Archives of General Psychiatry, 69* (7), 722-731.

LeDoux, J. (2007). The amygdala. *Current Biology, 17*(20), R868–874.

Legato, M. J. (Ed.). (2004). *Principles of gender-specific medicine*. London: Elsevier.

Legato, M. J., & Legha, J. K. (2004). Gender and the heart: Sex-specific differences in normal myocardial anatomy and physiology and in the experiences of some diseases of the cardiovascular system. In M. J. Legato (Ed.), *Principles of gender-specific medicine*, pp. 185–192. London: Elsevier.

Levenson, R. W., Ekman, P., & Friesen, W. V. (1990). Voluntary facial action generates emotion-specific autonomic nervous system activity. *Psychophysiology, 27*, 363–384.

Maccoby, E. E., and Martin, J. A. (1983). Socialization in the context of the family: Parent-child interaction. In P. Mussen and E. M. Hetherington (Eds.), *Handbook of child psychology, volume IV: Socialization, personality, and social development*, pp. 1–101. New York: Wiley.

Masten, A. S. (2001). Ordinary magic: resilience processes in development. *American Psychologist, 56*(3), 227–238.

McCarthy, M. M. (1995). Estrogen modulation of oxytocin and its relation to behavior. In eds. R. Ivell and J. Russell (Eds.), *Oxytocin: Cellular and molecular approaches in medicine and research*. New York: Plenum Press.

McCrae, R. R., & Terraciano, A. (2005). Universal features of personality traits from the observer's perspective: Data from 50 cultures. *Journal of Personality and Social Psychology, 88*, 547–561.

Mendelsohn, M. E., & Karas, R. H. (2005). Molecular and cellular basis of cardiovascular gender differences. *Science, 308*, 1583–1587.

Miller, V., & Hay, M. (Eds.). (2004). *Principles of sex-based differences in physiology: advances in molecular and cell biology* (Vol. 34). London: Elsevier.

Neigh, G. N., Ritschel, L. A., & Nemeroff, B. (2010). Biological consequences and transgenerational impact of violence and abuse. *Psychiatric Times, 27*(11).

Ninivaggi, F. J. (2008). *Ayurveda: A comprehensive guide to traditional Indian medicine for the West*. Lanham, MD: Rowman & Littlefield.

————. (2010). *Envy theory: Perspectives on the psychology of envy*. Lanham, MD: Rowman & Littlefield.

Nisbett, R. E., & Cohen, D. (1996).*Culture of honor: The psychology of violence in the south*. Boulder, CO: Westview Press.

Peterson, C., & Seligman, M. E. P. (2004). *Character strengths and virtues*. Oxford: Oxford University Press.

Pruett, K. (2009). *Partnership parenting: How men and women parent differently—why it helps your kids and can strengthen your marriage*. New York: De Capo Lifelong Books.

Rutter, M. (2007). Resilience, competence, and coping. *Child Abuse and Neglect, 31*(3), 205–209.

Sax, L. (2006). Why *gender matters: What parents and teachers need to know about the emerging science of sex differences*. New York: Broadway.

Schmitt, D. P. (2005). Fundamentals of human mating strategies. In D. M. Buss (Ed.), The handbook of evolutionary psychology. New York: Wiley.

Schutzwohl, A., Morjaria, S., & Alvis, S. (2011). Spatial distance regulates sex-specific feelings to suspected sexual and emotional infidelity. *Evolutionary Psychology, 9*(3), 417–429.

Segal, H. (1955). A psycho-analytic approach to aesthetics. *International Journal of Psychoanalysis, 33*, 196–207.

————. (1973). *Introduction to the work of Melanie Klein*. New York: Basic Books.

————. (1991). *Dream, phantasy, and art*. London: Routledge.

————. (2007). *Yesterday, today, and tomorrow*. London: Routledge.

Seligman, M. E. P. (1996). *The optimistic child: Proven program to safeguard children from depression and build lifelong resilience.* New York: Houghton Mifflin.

Serbin, L. A., Powlishta, K. K., & Gulko, J. (1993). The development of sex typing in middle childhood. *Monographs of the Society for Research in Child Development, 58* (2, serial no. 232).

Shir, S., Hendler, T., & Feldman, R. (2011). Specifying the neurobiological basis of human attachment: brain, hormones, and behavior in synchronous and intrusive mothers. *Neuropsychopharmacology, 36*(13), 2603–2615.

Shir, A., Hendler, T., Zagoory-Sharon, O, Winetraub, Y., & Feldman, R. (2012). Synchrony and specificity in the maternal and the paternal brain: Relations to oxytocin and vasopressin. *Journal of the American Academy of Child and Adolescent Psychiatry, 51*(8), 798–811.

Stroud, L. R., Salovey, P., & Epel, E. S. (2002). Sex differences in stress responses: social rejection versus achievement stress. *Biological Psychiatry, 52,* 318–327.

Tamres, L., Janicki, D., & Helgeson, V. S. (2002). Sex differences in coping behavior: A meta-analytic review. *Personality and Social Psychology Review, 6,* 2–30.

Taylor, S. E. (2002). *The tending instinct: How nurturing is essential to who we are and how we live.* New York: Holt.

Taylor, S. E., Klein, L. C., Lewis, B. P., Gruenewald, T. L., Gurung, R. A. R., & Updegraff, J. A. (2000). Biobehavioral responses to stress in females: Tend-and-befriend, not fight-or-flight. *Psychological Review, 107,* 411–429.

Thevenin, T. (1993). *Mothering and fathering: The gender differences in childrearing.* Garden City Park, NY: Avery Publishing.

Trivers, R. I. (1972). Parental investment and sexual selection. In B. Campbell (Ed.), *Sexual selection and the descent of man.* Chicago: Aldine.

University of California, Irvine (2005, January 21). Intelligence in men and women is a gray and white matter. Science Daily. Retrieved March 5, 2012, from www.sciencedaily.com/releases/2005/01/050121100142.htm

Verbrugge, L. M. (1985). Gender and health: An update on hypotheses and evidence. *Journal of Health and Social Behavior, 26,* 156–182.

Wechsler, D. (2002). *Wechsler Preschool and Primary Scale of Intelligencence, 3rd edition (WPPSI-III).* San Antonio, TX: The Psychological Corporation/Pearson.

White, N. P. (1993) *Plato: Sophist.* Indianapolis, IN: Hackett.

Wizemann, T. M., & Pardue, M. L. (Eds.). (2001). Exploring the biological contributions to human health: Does sex matter? *Institute of Medicine Committee on Understanding the Biology of Sex and Gender Differences.* Washington, DC: National Academy.

Acknowledgments

The author is appreciative for the insightful feedback and unflagging support of Fred R. Volkmar, M.D., director of the Yale Child Study Center in New Haven, as well as the sensitive and diligent comments of Linda Mayes, professor of pediatrics and child psychiatry also at the Yale Child Study Center. Cheryl Tedesco, LCSW, a gifted mother and talented psychotherapist, also read preliminary drafts and offered useful comments, for which I am thankful. The continuous support and encouragement of Hanna Segal, M.D., child psychoanalyst in London, over the years has been inestimable.

A special note of appreciation is due to Michelle Joy for her editorial assistance. Her erudition in literary matters is outstanding; in addition, her intellectual acuity has provided valuable impetus in suggesting higher levels of precision and clarity. As a medical student at the Yale University School of Medicine, she has been able to devote precious time to editing and has brought her developing theoretical skills to bear upon forging the structure of this text. I both admire her and am grateful for her help.

Additional References

Ages and Stages Questionnaires website: www.agesandstages.com .

American Academy of Child and Adolescent Psychiatry website: www.aacap.org .

American Academy of Pediatrics (2009). *Caring for your baby and young child* (5th ed.). S. P. Shelov (Ed.). New York: Bantam.

American Academy of Pediatrics website: www.healthychildren.org .

Antshel, K. M., Hargrave, T. M., Simonescu, M., Kaul, P., Hendricks, K., & Faraone, S. V. (2011). Advances in understanding and treating ADHD. *BMC Medicine, 9*(72). doi:10.1186/1741-7015-9-72

Aylward, G. P. (1994). *Practitioner's guide to developmental and psychological testing: Critical issues in developmental and behavioral pediatrics*. New York: Springer Publishing.

———. (1994). Bayley Infant Neurodevelopmental Screener (BINS). San Antonio, TX: Psychological Corporation.

Baldwin Dancy, R. (2012). *You are your child's first teacher: Encouraging your child's natural development from birth to age six* (3rd ed.). New York: Ten Speed Press.

Barkley, R. A. (2000). *Taking charge of ADHD*. New York: Guilford.

Baumrind, D. (1967). Child care practices anteceding three patterns of preschool behavior. *Genetic Psychology Monographs, 75*(1), 43–88.

———. (1971). Current patterns of parental authority. *Developmental Psychology, 4*(1, pt. 2), 1–103.

———. (1978). Parental disciplinary patterns and social competence in children. *Youth and Society , 9*, 238–276.

———. (1991). Parenting styles and adolescent development. In R. Lerner, A. C. Peterson, & J. Brooks Gunn (Eds.), *The encyclopedia of adolescent development*, pp. 746–758. New York: Garland.

Berk, L. (2011). *Infants, children, and adolescents* (7th ed.). Boston: Allyn & Bacon.

Berlin, L. J., Ipsa, J. M., Fine, M. A., Malone, P. S., Brooks-Gunn, J., Brady-Smith, C. & Bai, Y. (2009). Correlates and consequences of spanking and verbal punishment for low-income White, African American, and Mexican American toddlers. *Child Development, 80*(5), 1403–1420.

Bion, W. R. (1977). *Seven servants*. New York: Jason Aronson.

Blair, M. L. (2007). Sex-based differences in physiology: What should we teach in the medical curriculum? *Advances in Physiology Education, 31*, 23–25.

Bloomquist, M. L. (2006). *Skills training for children with behavior problems: a parent and practitioner guidebook* (Revised edition). New York: Guilford Press.

Bowlby, J. (1969). *Attachment and loss* (Vol. 1). New York: Basic Books.

Braungart-Rieker, J., Courtney, S., & Garwood, M. M. (1999). Mother- and father-infant attachment: Families in context. *Journal of Family Psychology, 13*, 535–553.

Brazelton, T. B. (1992). *Touchpoints: The essential references*. Cambridge, MA: Perseus Books.

Brazelton, T. B., & Sparrow, J. D. (2002). *Touchpoints 3 to 6*. New York: De Capo Press.

———. (2006). *Touchpoints: Birth to Three*. New York: De Capo Press.

Bridges, W. (2004). *Transitions: Making sense of life's changes*. New York: De Capo Press.

Brown, K. D., & Hamilton-Giachritsis, C. (2005). The influence of violent media on children and adolescents: a public health approach. *Lancet, 365*, 702–710.

Bulkeley, K. (2001). *Dreams: A reader on religious, cultural and psychological dimensions of dreaming*. New York: Palgrave Macmillan.

Burke, M. G. (2010). The impact of screen media on children: an environmental health perspective. *Psychiatric Times, 27* (10). www.psychiatrictimes.com/child-adolescent-psych/content/article/10168/1696463?GUID=EECFB175-AE44-4D0E-83D2-5E8647829E94&rememberme=1

Buss, D. M. (1989). Sex differences in human mate preferences: Evolutionary hypotheses tested in 37 cultures. *Behavioral and Brain Sciences, 42*, 459–491.

———. (1994). *The evolution of desire: strategies of human mating*. New York: Basic Books.

———. (1995). Evolutionary psychology: A new paradigm for psychological science. *Psychological Inquiry, 6*, 1–30.

———. (1999). *Evolutionary psychology: The new science of the mind*. Boston: Allyn & Bacon.

Caldera, Y. M. (2004). Paternal involvement and infant-father attachment: a Q-set study. *Fathering: Journal of Theory, Research, and Practice about Men as Fathers, 2*(2), 13–150.

Carter, C. S., Lederhendler, I. I., & Kirkpatrick, B. (Eds.). (1999). *The integrative neurobiology of affiliation*. Cambridge, MA: MIT Press.

Cath, S. H., Gurwitt, A., & Gunsburg. L. (Eds.). (1989). *Fathers and their families*. Hillsdale, NJ: Erlbaum.

Charney, D. S. (2004). Psychobiological mechanisms of resilience and vulnerability: Implications for successful adaptation to extreme stress. *American Journal of Psychiatry, 161*(2), 195–216.

Chess, S., & Thomas, A. (1995). *Temperament in clinical practice*. New York: Guilford Press.

Cline, F., & Fay, J. (2006). *Parenting with love and logic*. Colorado Springs, CO: NavPress.

Cloninger, C. R. (1987). A systematic method for clinical description and classification of personality variables. *Archives of General Psychiatry, 44*(6), 573–588.

Cloninger, C. R., Svrakic, D. M., & Przybeck, T. R. (1993). A psychobiological model of temperament and character. *Archives of General Psychiatry, 50*(12), 975–990.

Cohen, S., & Wills, T. A. (1985). Stress, social support, and the buffering hypothesis. *Psychological Bulletin, 98*, 310–357.

Costa, P. T., & McCrae, R. R. (1985). *The NEO Personality Inventory manual*. Odessa, FL: Psychological Assessment Resource.

Crawley, S. B., & Sherrod, R. B. (1984). Parent-infant play during the first year of life. *Infant Behavior and Development, 7*, 65–75.

Dalcroze, E. (2009). *Rhythm, music, and education*. Ithaca, NY: Cornell University Press.

Dillon, D. G., & Pizzagalli, D. A. (2007). Inhibition of action, thought, and emotion: A selective neurobiological review. *Applied and Preventive Psychology, 12*, 99–114.

Donate-Bartfield, D., & Passman, R. H. (1985). Attentiveness of mothers and fathers to their babies' cries. *Child Development, 59*, 506–511.

Dunstan, P. (2006). *Dunstan baby language*. [DVD]. ASIN: B000PDZ9SU.

Eliot, L. (2000). *What's going on in there? How the brain and mind develop in the first five years of life*. New York: Bantam.

———. (2010). *Pink brain, blue brain*. New York: Mariner.

Elkind, D. (1987). *Miseducation: Preschoolers at risk*. New York: Knopf.

———. (2006). *The hurried child, 25th anniversary edition*. New York: De Capo Press.

Erickson, E. (1993). *Childhood and society*. New York: W. W. Norton & Co.

Evans, W. N., Morill, W. Z. N., & Parente, S. T. (2010). Measuring inappropriate medical diagnosis and treatment in survey data: The case of ADHD among school-age children. *Journal of Health Economics, 29*(5), 657–673.

Eysenck, H. J. (1967). *The biological basis of personality*. Springfield, IL: Thomas.

Fagan, T. F., & Faustman, D. L. (2004). Sex differences in autoimmunity. *Advanced Molecular Cell Biology, 34*, 295–306.

Feldman, R. (2003). Infant-mother and infant-father synchrony: The coregulation of positive arousal. *Infant Mental Health, 24*(1), 1–23.

Festinger, L. (1949). The analysis of sociograms using matrix algebra, *Human Relations, 10*, 153–158.

———. (1950). Informal social communication. *Psychological Review, 57*, 271–282.

———. (1954). A theory of social comparison processes. *Human Relations, 7*, 117–140.

———. (1957). *A theory of cognitive dissonance*. Evanston, IL: Row, Peterson.

Festinger, L., Schachter, S., & Back, K. (1948). *Social pressures in informal groups*. Cambridge, MA: MIT Press.

———. (1950). *Social Pressures in informal groups; A study of human factors in housing*. Palo Alto, CA: Stanford University Press.

Flanagan, D. P., & Harrison, P. L. (Eds.). (2005). *The Cattell-Horn-Carroll theory of cognitive abilities: Past, present, and future. Contemporary intellectual assessment: Theories, tests, and issues*. New York: Guilford Press.

Flanagan, D. P., Ortiz, S. O., & Alfonso, V. (2007). *Essentials of cross-battery assessment: Essentials of psychological assessment* (2nd ed.). New Brunswick, NJ: Wiley.

Floet, A.M., Scheiner, C., & Grossman, L. (2010). Attention-deficit/hyperactivity disorder. *Pediatrics in Review, 31* (2), 56-69.

Flouri, E. (2005). *Fathering and child outcomes*. New York: Wiley.

Fonagy, P. (2001). *Attachment theory and psychoanalysis*. New York: Other Press.

Fox, N., Kimmerly, N. L., & Schafer, W. D. (1991). Attachment to mother/attachment to father: A meta-analysis. *Child Development, 62*, 210–225.

Frankenburg, W. K., Dodds, J., Archer, P., Bresnick, P., et al. (1990). *Denver II Screening Manual*. Denver: Denver Developmental Materials.

Freeman, L. C. (1992). The sociological concept of "group": An empirical test of two models, *American Journal of Sociology, 98*, 152–166.

Freud, S. (1974). *Standard edition of the complete psychological works* (Vols. 1–24). James Strachey (Ed.). London: Hogarth Press.

Gao, Y., Raine, A., Venables, P. H., Dawson, M. E., & Mednick, S. A. (2010). Association of poor childhood fear conditioning and adult crime. *American Journal of Psychiatry, 167*, 56–60.

Gentile, D. A., Choo, H., Liau, A., Sim, T., Li, D., Fung, D., & Khoo, A. (2011). Pathological video game use among youths: a two-year longitudinal study. *Pediatrics, 127*(2), 319–329.

Gershoff, E. T. (2008). *Report on physical punishment in the United States: What research tells us about its effects on children*. Columbus, OH: Center for Effective Discipline.

Gerritsen, L., Tendolkar, I., Franke, B., Vasquez, A. A., Kooijman, S., Buitelaar, J., Fernández, G., & Rijpkema, M. (2011). BDNF Val66Met genotype modulates the effect of childhood adversity on subgenual anterior cingulated cortex volume in healthy subjects. *Molecular Psychiatry*, May. doi:10.1038/mp.2011.51.

Gesell, A., & Ilg, F. (1946). *The child from five to ten*. New York: Harper & Brothers.

Gessel, L. M., Fields, S. K., Collins, C. L., Dick, R. W., & Comstock, D. (2007). Concussions among United States high school and collegiate athletes. *Journal of Athletic Training, 42*(4), 495–503.

Gilligan, C. (1982). *In a different voice*. Boston: Harvard University Press.

Goncy, E. A., & van Dulmen, M. H. M. (2010). Fathers do make a difference: Paternal involvement and adolescent alcohol use. *Fathering: A Journal of Theory, Research, and Practice about Men as Fathers, 8*(1), 93–108.

Gopnik, A., & Meltzoff, A. N. (1997). *Words, thoughts, and theories*. Cambridge, MA: MIT Press.

Gopnik, A., Meltzoff, A. N., & Kuhl, P. K. (2000). *The scientist in the crib*. New York: Harper.

————. (2010). *The philosophical baby*. New York: Picador.

Goswami, U. (2010). *The Wiley-Blackwell handbook of childhood cognitive development (Blackwell handbooks of developmental psychology)* (2nd ed.). London: Wiley-Blackwell.

Granovetter, M. (2005). The impact of social structure on economic outcomes. *Journal of Economic Perspectives, 19*, 33–50.

Green, J. A., Torney-Purta, J., & Azevedo, R. (2010). Empirical evidence regarding relations among a model of epistemic and ontological cognition, academic performance, and educational level. *Journal of Educational Psychology, 102*, 234–255.

Green, R. (2010). *The explosive child*. New York: Harper.

Griswold, R. (1993). *Fatherhood in America: A history*. New York: Basic Books.

Grossmann, K., Grossmann, K. E., Fremmer-Bombik, E., Kindler, H., Scheuerer-Englisch, H., & Zimmermann, P. (2002). The uniqueness of the child-father attachment relationship: Father's sensitive and challenging play as a pivotal variable in a 16-year longitudinal study. *Social Development, 11*, 307–331.

Habib, C., Santoro, J., Kremer, P., Toumbourou, J., Leslie, E., & Williams, J. (2010). The importance of family management, closeness with father and family structure in early adolescent alcohol use. *Addiction, 105*(10), 1750–1758.

Hadjikhani, N., Kveraga, K., Naik, P., & Ahlfors, S. (2009). Early (N170) activation of face-specific cortex by face-like objects. *Neuroreport, 20*(4), 403–407.

Harris, M. (1975). *Thinking about infants and young children*. London: Clunie Press.

Healy, J. (1988). *Failure to connect*. New York: Simon & Schuster.

————. (1990). *Endangered minds*. New York: Simon & Schuster.

————. (1994). *Your child's growing mind*. New York: Doubleday.

Hemmi, H. M., Wolke, D., & Schneider, S. (2011). Associations between problems with crying, sleeping and/or feeding in infancy and long-term behavioural outcomes in childhood: a meta-analysis. *Archives of Disease in Childhood*, published online. doi:10.1136/adc.2010.191312.

Henshaw, S. P., Scheffler, R. M., & Fulton, B. D. (2011). International variation in treatment procedures for ADHD: Social context and recent trends. *Psychiatric Series, 62*, 459–464.

Huxley, V. (2007). Sex and the cardiovascular system: The intriguing tale of how women and men regulate cardiovascular function differently. *Advances in Physiology Education, 31*, 31–40.

Illingworth, R. S. (1987). *The development of the infant and young child* (9th ed.). London: Churchill Livingstone.

————. (1991). *The normal child*. London: Churchill Livingstone.

Insel, T. R. (1997). A neurobiological basis of social attachment. *American Journal of Psychiatry, 154*, 726–735.

Isaacs, S. (1968) [1948]. *Children and parents*. London: Routledge & Kegan Paul.

Isaacs, S. (1970) [1948]. *Childhood and after*. New York: Agathon Press.

Isaacs, S., Klein, M., Middlemore, M. P., Searl, N., & Sharpe, E. F. 1952. *On the Bringing Up of Children*. New York: Robert Brunner Publishers.

Jaspers, K. (1997; [1913]). *General Psychopathology*. Baltimore, MD: Johns Hopkins Press.

Jedrychowski, W., Perera, F., Jankowski J, Butscher M, Mroz E, Flak E, Kaim I, Lisowska-Miszczyk, I., Skarupa A., & Sowa, A. (2011). Effect of exclusive breastfeeding on the development of children's cognitive function in the Krakow prospective birth cohort study. *European Journal of Pediatrics, 171*(2), 405.

Johnson, S. B., Blum, R. W., & Giedd, J. N. 2009. Adolescent maturity and the brain: The promise and pitfalls of neuroscience research in adolescent health policy. *Journal of Adolescent Health , 45*(3), 216–221.

Kagan, J. (2010). *The temperamental thread: How genes, culture, time and luck make us who we are*. New York: Dana Press.

Kaufman, A. S. (2009). *IQ testing 101*. New York: Springer.

KidsLife website: www.kidslife.com.au.

Klein, M. (1952). On observing the behaviour of young infants. In M. Klein, P. Heiman, S. Isaacs, & J. Riviere (Eds.), *Developments in psychoanalysis*, pp. 237–270. London: Hogarth Press.

————. (1975). *Love, Guilt, and Reparation*. London: Hogarth Press.

————. (1975). *The Psychoanalysis of Children*. London: Hogarth Press.

————. (1975). *Envy and Gratitude and Other Works*. London: Hogarth Press.

————. (1975). *Narrative of a Child Analysis*. London: Hogarth Press.

Klingberg, T., Fernell, E., Olesen, P. J., et al. (2005). Computerized training of working memory in children with ADHD—a randomized, controlled trial. *Journal of the American Academy of Child and Adolescent Psychiatry , 44*, 177–186.

Knobloch, H., Stevens, F., & Malone, A.E. (1980). *Manual of developmental diagnosis*. New York: Harper and Row.

Kunda, M., McGreggor, K., & Goel, A. (2009). Addressing the Raven's Progressive Matrices test of "general intelligence." Fall AAAI Symposium on Multimodal Representations, November 2009, Arlington, VA.

Lamb, M. E. (Ed.). (2010). *The role of the father in child development* (5th ed.). Hoboken, NJ: John Wiley & Sons.

Lamb, M. E., Pleck, J. H., Charnov, E. L., & Levine, J. A. (1985). Paternal behavior in humans. *American Zoologist, 25*(2), 883–894.

Leboyer, F. (2009). *Birth without violence*. Rochester, VT: Healing Arts Press.

LeDoux, J. (1996). *The emotional brain: The mysterious underpinnings of emotional life*. New York: Simon & Schuster.

Legato, M. J. (Ed.). (2004). *Principles of gender-specific medicine*. London: Elsevier.

Legato, M. J., & Legha, J. K. (2004). Gender and the heart: Sex-specific differences in normal myocardial anatomy and physiology and in the experiences of some diseases of the cardiovascular system. In M. J. Legato (Ed.), *Principles of gender-specific medicine*, pp. 185–192. London: Elsevier.

Lemos, G. C., Almeida, L. S., & Colom, R. (2011). Intelligence of adolescents is related to their parents' educational level but not to family income. *Personality and Individual Differences, 50*(7), 1062–1067.

Light, K. C., Smith, T. E., Johns, J. M., Brownley, K. A., Hofheimer, J. A., & Amico, J. A. (2000). Oxytocin responsivity in mothers of infants: A preliminary study of relationships with blood pressure during laboratory stress and normal ambulatory activity. *Health Psychology, 19*, 560–567.

Liston, C., Watts, R., Tottenham, M., Davidson, M. C., Niogi, S., Ulug, A. M., & Casey, B. J. (2006). Frontostriatal microstructure modulates efficient recruitment of cognitive control. *Cerebral Cortex, 16*, 553–560.

Loewald, H.W. (1980). *Papers on psychoanalysis*. New Haven, CT: Yale University Press.

Maccoby, E. E., & Martin, J. A. (1983). Socialization in the context of the family: Parent-child interaction. In P. Mussen & E. M. Hetherington (Eds.), *Handbook of child psychology, volume IV: Socialization, personality, and social development*, pp. 1–101. New York: Wiley.

Malloch, S. T., & Trevarthen, C. V. (2010). *Communicative musicality: Exploring the basis of human companionship*. New York: Oxford University Press.

Mandler, J. M. (2004). *The foundations of mind: Origins of conceptual thought*. New York: Oxford.

Marsiglio, W. (1995). *Fatherhood: Contemporary theory, research, and social policy*. Thousand Oaks, CA: Sage.

Marsiglio, W., Amato, P., Day, R. D., & Lamb, M. E. (2000). Scholarship on fatherhood in the 1990s and beyond. *Journal of Marriage and the Family, 62*, 1173–1191.

Masten, A. S. (2001). Ordinary magic: Resilience processes in development. *American Psychologist, 56*(3), 227–238.

Mayes, L. C., & Cohen, D. J. (2002). *The Yale Child Study Center guide to understanding your child*. Boston: Little Brown & Co.

McCarthy, M. M. (1995). Estrogen modulation of oxytocin and its relation to behavior. In R. Ivell and J. Russell (Eds.), *Oxytocin: Cellular and molecular approaches in medicine and research*. New York: Plenum Press.

Meltzoff, A. N. (1990). Towards a developmental cognitive science: The implications of cross-modal matching and imitation for the development of representation and memory in infancy. *Annals New York Academy of Science, 608,* 1–31.

———. (1995). Infants' understanding of people and things: From body imitation to folk psychology. In J. Bermudez, A. Marcel, & N. Eilan (Eds.), *The body and the self,* pp. 43–69. Cambridge, MA and London: MIT Press.

Meltzoff, A. N., & Prinz, W. (2002). *The imitative mind: Development, evolution, and brain bases.* Cambridge: Cambridge University Press.

Mendelsohn, M. E., & Karas, R. H. (2005). Molecular and cellular basis of cardiovascular gender differences. *Science, 308,* 1583–1587.

Miller, V., & Hay, M. (Eds.). (2004). *Principles of sex-based differences in physiology: advances in molecular and cell biology* (Vol. 34). London: Elsevier.

Mischell, W., Shoda, Y., & Rodriquez, M. L. (1989). Delay of gratification in children. *Science, 244,* 933–938.

Mitrofan, O., Paul, M., & Spenser, N. (2009). Is aggression in children with behavioral and emotional difficulties associated with television viewing and video game playing? A systematic review. *Child Care Health Development, 35,* 5–15.

Montessori, M. (2009). *The absorbent mind.* New York: BN Publishing.

Montoya, A., Colom, F., & Ferrin, M. (2011). Is psychoeducation for parents and teachers of children and adolescents with ADHD efficacious? A systematic literature review. *European Psychiatry, 26*(3), 166–175.

Mullen, E. M. (1995). *Mullen Scales of Early Learning.* Sydney, Australia: Pearson/PsychCorp.

Murray, J. P., Liotti, M., Ingmundson, P. T., Mayberg, H. S., Pu, Y., Zamarripa, F., Liu, Y., Woldorff, M. G., Gao, J. H., & Fox, P. T. (2006). Children's brain activations while viewing televised violence revealed by fMRI. *Media Psychology, 8*(1), 25–37.

Musso, M. W., & Gouvier, W. D. (2012). "Why is it so hard?" A review of detection of malingered ADHD in college students. *Journal of Attention Disorders ,* May 11, 2012, doi: 10.1177/1087054712441970.

Neigh, G. N., Ritschel, L. A., & Nemeroff, B. (2010). Biological consequences and transgenerational impact of violence and abuse. *Psychiatric Times, 27*(11). www.psychiatrictimes.com/ptsd/content/article/10168/172775.

Newborg, J., Stock, J. R., Wnek, L., Guidubaldi, J., Svinicki, J., Dickson, J., & Markley, A. (2005). *Battelle Developmental Inventory (BDI-2).* Rolling Meadows, IL: Riverside Publishing.

Nicholson, J. S., Howard, K. S., & Borowski, J. G. (2008). Mental models for parenting: correlates of metaparenting among fathers of young children. *Fathering: A Journal of Theory, Research, and Practice, 6,* 39–61.

Ninivaggi, F. J. (1999). Attention-deficit /hyperactivity disorder in children and adolescents: Rethinking diagnosis and treatment implications for complicated cases. *Connecticut Medicine, 63,* 515–521.

———. (2009). Borderline intellectual functioning and academic problems. In B. Sadock, V. Sadock, & P. Ruiz (Eds.), *Kaplan & Sadock's comprehensive textbook of psychiatry* (9th ed.), pp. 2505–2512. Philadelphia: Wolters Kluwer/Lippincott Williams & Wilkins.

———. (2010). *Ayurveda: A comprehensive guide to traditional Indian medicine for the West.* Lanham, MD: Rowman & Littlefield.

———. 2010. *Envy theory: Perspectives on the psychology of envy.* Lanham, MD: Rowman & Littlefield.

Ohman, A. (1986). Face the beast and fear the face: Animal and social fears as prototypes for evolutionary analyses of emotion. *Psychophysiology, 23*(2), 123–145.

Olesen, P. J., Westerberg, H., & Klingberg, T. (2004). Increased prefrontal and parietal activity after training of working memory. *Nature Neuroscience, 7,* 75–79.

Parents' Evaluation of Developmental Status (PEDS). PEDSTest.com, LLC.

PEDS: Developmental Milestones (PEDS:DM), PEDSTest.com, LLC.

Pelham, W. E., & Fabiano, G. A. (2008). Evidence-based psychosocial treatments for attention-deficit/hyperactivity disorder. *Journal of Clinical Child and Adolescent Psychology, 37*(1), 184–214.

Perry, W. G. (1998). *Forms of intellectual and ethical development in the college years: A scheme.* San Franscisco: Jossey-Bass. (Originally published 1970)

Pestalozzi, H. (1951). *The education of man.* New York: Philosophical Library.

Petrash, J. (2002). *Understanding Waldorf education: Teaching from the inside out.* New York: Gryphon House.

Popenoe, D. (1999). *Life without father: Compelling new evidence that fatherhood and marriage are indispensable for the good of children and society.* Cambridge, MA: Harvard University Press.

Porter, R. C. (1991). Human reproduction and the mother-infant relationship: The role of odors. In T. V. Getchell, R. I. Doty, L. M. Bartoshuk, & J. B. Snow (Eds.), *Smell and taste in health and disease,* pp. 429–442. New York: Raven Press.

Pruett, K. (2009). *Partnership parenting: How men and women parent differently—why it helps your kids and can strengthen your marriage.* New York: De Capo Lifelong Books.

Pruitt, D. (1999). *Your adolescent: Emotional, behavioral, and cognitive development from early adolescence through the teen years.* New York: William Morrow.

———. (2000). *Your child: Emotional, behavioral, and cognitive development from birth through preadolescence.* New York: Harper.

Ramos, B. P., & Arnsten, A. F. (2007). Adrenergic pharmacology and cognition: focus on the prefrontal cortex. *Pharmacological Therapy, 113,* 523–536.

Raven, J. (2000). The Raven's Progressive Matrices: Change and stability over culture and time. *Cognitive Psychology, 41,* 1–48.

Reeb, B. T., & Congers, K. J. (2011). Mental health services utilization in a community sample of rural adolescents: The role of father-offspring relations. *Journal of Pediatric Psychology, 36*(4), 661–668.

Riviere, J. (1991). *The inner world and Joan Riviere.* London: Karnac Books.

Roberts, A. L., Gilman, S. E., Fitzmaurice, G., Decker, M. R., & Koenen, K. C. (2010). Witness of intimate partner violence in childhood and perpetration of intimate partner violence in adulthood. *Epidemiology, 21* (6), 809–818.

Rojas, N.L., & Chan, E. (2005). Old and new controversies in the alternative treatment of attention-deficit/hyperactivity disorder. *Mental Retardation and Developmental Disabilities Research Reviews, 11,* 116–130.

Ross, R. (2010). *Adventures in parenting.* Spring Valley, NY: Rudolf Steiner Press.

Rueda, M. R., Rothbart, M. K., McCandliss, B. D., Saccomanno, L., & Posner, M. I. (2005). Training, maturation, and genetic influences on the development of executive attention. *Proceedings of the National Academy of Sciences USA, 102,* 14931–14936.

Rutter, M. (2007). Resilience, competence, and coping. *Child Abuse and Neglect, 31*(3), 205–209.

Sadock, B. J., & Sadock, V. A. (2008). *Kaplan and Sadock's concise textbook of child and adolescent psychiatry.* Philadelphia: Lippincott Williams & Wilkins.

Sax, L. (2006). Why *gender matters: What parents and teachers need to know about the emerging science of sex differences.* New York: Broadway.

Schoppe-Sullivan, S. J., Brown, G. L., Cannon, E. A., Mangelsdorf, E. A., Sokolowski, S., & Margaret, S. (2008). Maternal gatekeeping, coparenting quality, and fathering behavior in families with infants. *Journal of Family Psychology, 22*(3), 389–398.

Segal, H. (1977). Psychoanalysis and freedom of thought. Freud Memorial Lecture delivered at University College London, October 17.

Shure, M. B., Digeronimo, T. F., & Aher, J. (2000). *Raising a thinking child workbook: Teaching young children how to resolve everyday conflicts and get along with others.* New York: Research Press.

Simpson, J. A., & Rholes, W. S. (1998). *Attachment theory and close relationships.* New York: Guilford Press.

Somer, L., & Caset, B. J. (2010). Developmental neurobiology of cognitive control and motivational systems. *Current Opinion in Neurobiology, 20*(2), 236–241.

Spelke, E. S. (2004). Core knowledge. In N. Kanwisher & J. Duncan (Eds.), *Attention and performance* (Vol. 20), pp. 29–56. Oxford: Oxford University Press.

Spelke, E. S., & Kinzler, K. D. (2007). Core knowledge. *Developmental Science, 10*, 89–96.

Steiner, R. (2004). *A modern art of education: Foundations of Waldorf education.* Hemdon, MA: Anthroposophic Press. (Originally published 1921)

Stern, D. (2000). *The Interpersonal world of the infant.* New York: Basic Books.

Stroud, L. R., Salovey, P., & Epel, E. S. (2002). Sex differences in stress responses: Social rejection versus achievement stress. *Biological Psychiatry, 52*, 318–327.

Swing, E. L., Gentile, D. A., Anderson, C. A., & Walsh, D. A. (2010). Television and video game exposure and the development of attention problems. *Pediatrics, 126*, 214–221.

Tamis-LeMonda, C. S., & Cabrera, N. (2002). *Handbook of father involvement: Multidisciplinary perspectives.* Mahwah, NJ: Lawrence Earlbum Associates.

Tamres, L., Janicki, D., & Helgeson, V. S. (2002). Sex differences in coping behavior: A meta-analytic review. *Personality and Social Psychology Review, 6*, 2–30.

Taylor, S. E. (2002). *The tending instinct: How nurturing is essential to who we are and how we live.* New York: Holt.

Taylor, S. E., Klein, L. C., Lewis, B. P., Gruenewald, T. L., Gurung, R. A. R., & Updegraff, J. A. (2000). Biobehavioral responses to stress in females: Tend-and-befriend, not fight-or-flight. *Psychological Review, 107*, 411–429.

Taylor, C. A., Lee, S. J., Guterman, N. B., & Rice, J. C. (2010). Use of spanking for 3-year-old children and associated intimate partner aggression or violence. *Pediatrics, 126*, 415–424.

Thevenin, T. (1993). *Mothering and fathering: The gender differences in childrearing.* Garden City Park, NY: Avery Publishing.

Trout, P. (2011). *Deadly powers: Animal predators and the mythic imagination.* New York: Prometheus.

Verbrugge, L. M. (1985). Gender and health: An update on hypotheses and evidence. *Journal of Health and Social Behavior, 26*, 156–182.

Volkmar, F., & Martin, A. (2011). *Essentials of Lewis's child and adolescent psychiatry.* Philadelphia, PA: Lippincott Williams & Wilkins.

Wall, G., & Arnold, S. (2007). How involved is involved fathering? An exploration of the contemporary culture of fatherhood. *Gender & Society, 21*, 508–527.

Weiten, W. (2011). *Psychology: Themes and variations* (8th ed.). Belmont, CA: Wadsworth.

Wenning, K. (1996). *Winning cooperation from your child.* Northvale, NJ: Aronson.

Westerberg H., Hirvikoski T., Forssberg H., Klingberg T. (2004).Visuo-spatial working memory span: a sensitive measure of cognitive deficits in children with ADHD. *Child Neuropsychology, 10*, 155–161.

White, B. L. (1986). *The first three years of life.* New York: Prentice Hall.

———. (1988). *Educating the infant and toddler.* Lexington, MA: D.C. Health & Co.

Wild, R. (2000). *Raising curious, creative, confident kids: The Pestalozzi experiment in child-based education.* Boston: Shambhala Press.

Williams, D. R. (2003). The health of men: Structured inequalities and opportunities. *American Journal of Public Health, 93*, 724–731.

Winn, M. (1985). *The plug-in drug.* New York: Viking.

Wizemann, T. M., & Pardue, M. L. (Eds.). (2001). Exploring the biological contributions to human health: Does sex matter? In *Institute of medicine committee on understanding the biology of sex and gender differences.* Washington, DC: National Academy.

Wolff, J. J., Gu, H., Gerig, G., Elison, J. T., Styner, M., Gouttard, S., Botteron, K. N., Dager, S. R., Dawson, G., Estes, A. M., Evans, A. C., Hazlett, H. C., Kostogopoulos, P., McKinstry, R. C., Peterson, S. J., Schultz, R. T., Zwaigenbaum, L., & Piven, J. (2012). Differences in white matter fiber tract development present from 6 to 24 months in infants with autism. *American Journal of Psychiatry, 169*(6), 589–600.

Wolraich, M. L., Drotar, D. D., Dworkin, P. H., & Perrin, E. C. (2008). *Developmental-behavioral pediatrics: Evidence and practice.* Philadelphia: Elsevier Mosby.

Wynn, K. (2008). Some innate foundations of social and moral cognition. In P. Carruthers, S. Laurence, & S. Stich (Eds.), *The innate mind: Foundations and the future.* New York and Oxford: Oxford University Press.

Yogman, M. (1982). Development of the father-infant relationship. In G. Fitzgerald, F. Lester, & M. Yogman (Eds.), *Theory and research in behavioral pediatrics* (Vol. 1), pp. 221–297. New York: Plenum

Yue, J. J., Guyer, R. D., Johnson, J. P, Khoo, L. T., & Hochschuler, S. H. (2011). *The Comprehensive Treatment of the Aging Spine: Minimally Invasive and Advanced Techniques*. Philadelphia: Elsevier Saunders.

Index

About the Author

Dr. Frank John Ninivaggi is an associate attending physician at Yale–New Haven Hospital, an assistant clinical professor of child psychiatry at the Yale University School of Medicine's Child Study Center in New Haven, Connecticut, a member of the Yale–New Haven Community Medical Group, and the medical director of Devereux, Connecticut—the Glenholme School in Washington, Connecticut.

Dr. Ninivaggi received his adult psychiatric training at Johns Hopkins University School of Medicine in Baltimore, Maryland. He received fellowship specialty training in child and adolescent psychiatry at the Yale Child Study Center, where he continues to hold academic and hospital appointments. He also is in private practice, performs school consultations, and teaches at Yale.

He is board certified in psychiatry and neurology. In 2004, he received the distinction of certification as fellow of the American Psychiatric Association.

Dr. Ninivaggi's fundamental orientation is rooted in the clinical encounter—an exploration into and understanding of an individual's inner-world and behaviors. His clinical emphasis has been on integrated, collaborative, patient-centered care that encompasses the biopsychosocial perspective within an integrated "systems of care" approach. Having spent the last thirty-five years treating children, adolescents, and adults, Dr. Ninivaggi has observed well over thousands of children with a variety of temperaments, personality styles, strengths, limitations, and potentials for improvement. His clinical care in this longitudinal data field has included well-child guidance as well as diagnosis and interventions for psychiatric and behavior problems.

In his capacity as medical director of the Devereux-Glenholme School for almost twenty years, he has held this position as the psychiatric member of a team of psychologists, social workers, educators, and nurses. This position has privileged him to oversee the mental, emotional, and behavioral health of up to one hundred children each year. The average number of residents at this boarding school is about one hundred at a given time and changes yearly. He has observed and cared for such youngsters from childhood through adolescence. For example, systematic psychiatric and behavioral observation occurs weekly over the course of the children's three to six years in this residential school setting. Students also participate in individual psychotherapy with Dr. Ninivaggi every three to four weeks for their entire stay. This intensive, longitudinal involvement has deepened his understanding of these children's emotional life and the variety of ways to manage their developmental trajectories. In collaboration with psychologists, social workers, and teachers, he has helped parents deal with normative and problematic child presentations, regular and special academic needs, and family dynamics.

This experience in large numbers and varieties of problems encountered over long durations has contributed to an empathetic and clinically effective style that is integrated, user-friendly, and practical for children, parents, and their educational situations.

His long-standing research on intelligence has been published in Sadock, Sadock, & Ruiz (Eds.), *Kaplan and Sadock's Comprehensive Textbook of Psychiatry*, eighth edition (2005), and updated in the current ninth edition (2009). Also included in the ninth edition is his new chapter, "Malingering." Dr. Ninivaggi's recent publications include the textbook, *Envy Theory: Perspectives on the Psychology of Envy* (2010), and a chapter, "The Psychology of Aging," in Yue et al. (Eds.), *The Comprehensive Treatment of the Aging Spine: Minimally Invasive and Advanced Techniques* (2011).